USEFUL REFERENCE SERIES NO. 28

INDEX TO FAIRY TALES MYTHS AND LEGENDS

Once on a Time

"Once on a time" was a magical phrase,
Thrilling with promise of marvelous stories,
Tales of the pixies and nixies and fays,
Princes and fairyland kings in their glories;
I was a boy, and these chronicles, all of them
Bore me away in a mythical clime
Ruled by strange wizards, and I was in thrall of them
Once on a time!

Once on a time I was slender and young,
Love was enchantment and life was a dance,
Youth was but coin to be squandered and flung,
Days were all sunshine and nights were romance.
Now when I think of those days and the fun of them,
When I see youngsters still flush in their prime,
I can sigh, "Well, at the least I was one of them
Once on a time!"

Once on a time I had wonderful dreams,
Made up of rainbows that glowed in the distance;
Once I sought life, but today, so it seems,
All I have won to is merely existence.
This is the fruit of the blithe and the merry tales—
Middle-aged plodding through workaday grime—
Still, thank the Lord, I believed in the fairy tales
Once on a time!

Berton Braley, in Saturday Evening Post.

INDEX TO FAIRY TALES, MYTHS AND LEGENDS

BY

MARY HUSE EASTMAN
Wilmington (Del.) Institute Free Library

SECOND EDITION
Revised and Enlarged

BOSTON
THE F. W. FAXON COMPANY

Published, April, 1926

Printed in the United States

CONTENTS

PAGE

Preface vii

Index to Fairy Tales, Myths and Legends . . 1

List of Books Analyzed 563

Lists for Story Tellers 593
Geographical and Racial

Helps for Story Tellers 604

Directory of Publishers 607

PREFACE

INDEX TO FAIRY TALES, MYTHS AND LEGENDS

The increased use of the story hour in work with children and the ever-widening use of fables and myths in school work have shown the need of an index which would save time by indicating at a glance the source of an asked-for story. When eight out of ten versions of a myth are given in their respective books under different titles bearing little or no resemblance to the one sought for, when each new translator or compiler may give an entire set of new titles to old favorites, mechanical aid is necessary to save reason as well as time.

This index includes, besides fairy tales and fables, the stories from Greek and Norse mythology which seemed most likely to be called for, also hero stories and some modern stories like the "Leak in the dyke," which are not strictly fairy tale or legend but which are constantly asked for by teachers and story tellers. The mythology entries have been considerably extended for the second edition, and a special effort has been made to include folk stories of as many nationalities as possible; but, the variants of well known tales have been noted from the viewpoint of the story teller rather than of the student of folk lore.

Since inquiries for stories are mainly by title this is first of all a title index. When the same story appears under various titles, it is indexed under the best known or under the one that seemed most descriptive of the story, and references are made from all the other titles. The title as contained in each particular book, when differing from the one under which it is indexed, is given in parenthesis at the end of the entry. In the case of mythology and hero stories the titles have been inverted, or invented if necessary, in order to bring the entry under the name of the character. When a book contains a number of stories about the same person but bearing different titles, a general reference to the book is given; when two only, but not in direct sequence, the titles are given in parenthesis at the end of the entry.

The cross references from one story to another are intended to aid story tellers by suggesting similar stories in case the one wished for is not obtainable. The cross references from subjects—holidays, stars, flowers, etc.—are intended to aid in identifying stories when the inquirer has forgotten the title and asks for the story by subject or contents. During the years the index was in use in card form at the Wilmington Institute Free Library, there were many calls for stories to illustrate some point of ethics, geography or history. As this demand for stories by subject seems to be increasing and comes from many sources—speakers, community workers, teachers, and volunteer story tellers—an effort has been made to meet it in some degree by extension of the cross references; by the inclusion of some material not fairy tale or myth but adapted for special occasions; and by including a list of story tellers' books which contain classified stories and subject lists.

Since the different editions of Grimm, Andersen and Æsop vary so much, not only in the stories included but also in the titles given them, a number of editions were indexed giving as complete a collection as possible of the author's work in editions suitable for libraries. The edition as well as the variation of title, if there be any, is given in parenthesis at the end of the entry.

Where two editions of the same work, not exactly alike as to contents, are indexed, no note of the edition is made in the entry of titles which are in both editions; note of the edition is made only in the entry of those which are contained in one of the editions and not in the other. To distinguish editions the name of the editor, compiler, translator or publisher is used in parenthesis after the entry and preceding the variant title, if there be one; a publisher's name is followed by ed. for edition, as Burt ed., Warne ed.

Paging is not given, as editions differ in paging even when the contents are exactly the same. The use of the exact title which the story bears in any particular book, either as the main entry or in parenthesis at the end of the entry, makes it easier to locate the title in the table of contents of the book indexed; but it is unfortunate that so many otherwise up-to-date collections of children's stories still have the cumbersome unalphabeted table of contents instead of an index.

Authors' initials are not used in the second edition even when there are several of the same surname since full imprint is given in the list of books indexed.

Roman numerals are used for two purposes,—to distinguish different stories having the same titles, and to bring together stories on the same theme instead of referring from one to the other; for instance, Why the sea is salt. I, II, III, and IV instead of Why the sea is salt. *See also* Magic coffee mill; Quern at the bottom of the sea.

The star (*) is used to mark versions suitable for small children.

Prices have been given in the list of books indexed as an aid in estimating cost; but, it has not been possible in many cases to bring them up to date. Neither has it been possible to locate and examine new editions of all the books indexed in the first edition. Editions vary disconcertingly by leaving out old material and also by including new, so it has been thought well to leave the old imprint while adding a later one when known.

Grateful acknowledgment is made to members of the staff of The Wilmington Institute Free Library and friends who helped in the work of compiling and preparing for publication. Indeed without the help of the library it would have been as impossible to complete this index as the previous one.

The generosity of the various publishers in loaning books has done much to make this index possible and thanks are due them for their courtesy and kindness in response to requests.

M. H. E.

Wilmington, Del.
November, 1925.

A

Abbot of Innisfalen (poem).
Graves. Irish fairy tales.
See also Monk and the bird's song.
Abdallah. Cross and Statler. Story-telling. (Jew's tale.)
Field. Quest of the four-leaf clover.
Laboulaye. Fairy book.
Abdallah of the land and Abdallah of the sea. Arabian nights, More tales (Olcott).
Abi Fressah's feast. Landa. Aunt Naomi's Jewish fairy tales and legends.
See also Barmecide feast.
Aboo Mohammed the lazy. *See* Abou Mahomed the lazy.
Abou Hassan; or, The sleeper awakened.
Gibbon. Reign of King Cole. (Abu-l-Hasan the wag.)
Arabian nights (Dodge ed.).
Marshall. Fairy tales of all nations. (Caliph for one day.)
Olcott and Pendleton. Jolly book. (Abul Hassan the wag.)
Scudder. Children's book.
See also Death of Abu Nowas and his wife.
Abou Mahomed the lazy. Arabian nights (Colum. Abu Mohammad the lazy.)
Arabian nights, More tales (Olcott).
Gibbon. Reign of King Cole. (Aboo Mohammed the lazy.)
About angels. Richards. Golden windows.
About Leviathan, king of the fish. Friedlander. Jewish fairy book.
About the real and unreal devils. Wenig. Beyond the giant mountains.
Abraham. Landa. Aunt Naomi's Jewish fariy tales and legends. (Star child; Higgledy, piggledy palace.)
Abraham and the old man. Scudder. Book of legends.
Abraham's tree. Friedlander. Jewish fairy book.
Abu-l-Hasan the wag.
See Abou Hassan; or, The sleeper awakened.
Abu-Mohammad the lazy. *See* Abou Mahomed the lazy.
Abudah and the search for the talisman of Oromanes, History of. Olcott. Tales of the Persian genii.
Abused boy. *See* Hong Kil Tong.
Accommodating circumstance. Stockton. Queen's museum.
Accomplished and lucky tea kettle. Griffis. Japanese fairy tales. (Wonderful tea-kettle.)
Hearn. Japanese fairy tales. (Tea-kettle.)
James. Green willow. (Tea-kettle.)
Lang. Crimson fairy book. (Magic kettle.)

Accomplished and lucky tea kettle—*continued.*
Lang. Snow-queen and other stories. (Magic kettle.)
Patten. Junior classics. v. 1.
Peck. Stories for good children. (Magic tea kettle.)
Tappan. Folk stories and fables.
Wiggin and Smith. Tales of laughter. (Wonderful teakettle.)
Williston. Japanese fairy tales. 1st series. (Wonderful teakettle.)
According to how the drop falls. Harris. Uncle Remus and his friends.
Accursed lake. Lummis. Pueblo Indian folk stories.
Achieving of the Quest. *See* Holy Grail.
Achilles. Baldwin. Story of the golden age. (*In* Heroes in strange garb.)
Evans. Heroes of Troy.
Guerber. Myths of Greece and Rome. (*In* Trojan war.)
Haaren and Poland. Famous men of Greece.
Achusetts's ride to Philadelphia. Aspinwall. Short stories for short people.
Acis and Galatea. Carpenter. Long ago in Greece. (Polyphemus, Acis and Galatea.)
Guerber. Myths of Greece and Rome. (*In* Adventures of Ulysses.)
Kupfer. Stories of long ago. (Giant who loved a sea nymph.)
Acorn. Boston collection of kindergarten stories. (Story of an acorn.)
Acorn and the pumpkin. Dyer and Brady. Merrill readers. 3d reader. (Pumpkin and the acorn.)
(poem). Wiggin and Smith. Talking beasts.
Acrobatic steamer. Henderson. Sea yarns for boys.
Actæon. *See* Diana and Actæon.
Actor and the pig. Æsop. Fables. (Burt. Merry-Andrew and the countryman).
Æsop. Fables (Jacobs. Buffoon and the countryman.)
Bryce. Fables from afar. (Mimic and the countryman.)
Olcott and Pendleton. Jolly book.
Wiggin and Smith. Talking beasts. (Buffoon and the countryman.)
See also Critics silenced; Owl critic.
Adalantado of the seven cities. Smith. Mystery tales.
Adam Bell, Clynn of the Clough, and William of Cloudesly. *See* Three gallant outlaws.
Adder Queen. Baumbach. Tales from wonderland.
Adder that did not hear. Cowles. Art of story telling.
Admetus and Alcestis. Adams. Myths of old Greece. (Alcestis.)
*Bailey. Wonder stories. (When Apollo was herdsman.)
Baldwin. Old Greek stories.
Buckley. Children of the dawn. (Sacrifice of Alcestis.)
Cox. Tales of ancient Greece.

Admetus and Alcestis—*continued.*
Guerber. Myths of Greece and Rome. (*In* Apollo.)
Mabie. Heroines every child should know.
McFee. Treasury of myths. (King Admetus.)
Peabody. Old Greek folk stories. (Admetus and the shepherd.)
Peabody. Old Greek folk stories. (Alcestis.)
Shaw. Stories of the ancient Greeks. (How death was conquered.)
Adonis. Guerber. Myths of Greece and Rome. (*In* Venus.)
Hyde. Famous Greek myths.
Judd. Classic myths. (Legend of the anemone.)
*Klingensmith. Just stories. (Wind flower.)
McFee. Treasury of flower stories. (Anemone.)
Olcott. Wonder garden. (Legend of the anemone and the rose.)
Adventure in the big bog. Thomas. Welsh fairy book.
Adventures. Ketchum and Jorgensen. Kindergarten gems.
Adventures of, etc. *See* the first important word of the title.
Adyevich. *See* Where love is, there God is also.
Ægir's feast. *See* Thor: Thor's fishing.
Ægis of the Gods. Bacon. True philosopher.
Æneas. Guerber. Myths of Greece and Rome. (Adventures of Æneas.)
Patten. Junior classics. v. 3. (Wanderings of Æneas.)
Storr. Half a hundred hero tales.
Tappan. Stories from the classics.
Æneas in Hades. Patten. Junior classics. v. 3. (Dwellings of the dead.)
Æolus. *See* Ulysses and the bag of winds.
Æsculapius. Baldwin. Old Greek stories. (*In* Lord of the silver bow.)
Æsop and the impertinent fellow. Æsop. Fables (Black ed.).
Æsop and his fellow servants. Æsop. Fables (Burt ed.).
Baldwin. Fifty famous people. (Clever slave.)
Welsh. Stories children love.
Wiggin and Smith. Talking beasts.
Æsop and the poultry. Æsop. Fables (Burt ed.).
Æsop at play. Æsop. Fables (Black ed.).
Æsop. Fables (Burt ed.).
Æsop the fable maker, Story of. Storytellers' magazine. March and April. 1915, p. 74, 114.
Afang the monster. Griffis. Welsh fairy tales. (Mighty monster Afang.)
Thomas. Welsh fairy book. (Hu Gadarn.)
African Jack. Harris. Nights wih Uncle Remus.
After-Christmas reindeer. Potter. Pinafore pocket story book.
Agamemnon. *See* Trojan war.
Aged lion. Success library. v. 3.

Agnar. *See* Geirrod and Odin.
Aicha's stratagem. Gask. Folk tales from many lands.
Gask. Treasury of folk tales.
Noyes. Twilight tales. (Trick of old Aicha.)
Storytellers' magazine. Nov. 1915, p. 381.
Aida. McSpadden. Stories from great operas.
Pleasanton. Fairyland of opera.
Aiken-Drum. *See* Brownie of Blednock.
Ainsel. *See* My own self.
Al Borak. *See* Mohammed.
Ala-ed-Din, Story of. *See* Aladdin.
Aladdin. Arabian nights (Colum. Story of Ala-ed-Din; or, The wonderful lamp.)
Arabian nights (Dodge).
Arabian nights (Lang).
Arabian nights (Olcott).
Arabian nights (Wiggin and Smith).
Arnold and Gilbert. Stepping stones to literature. v. 4.
Aunt Louisa's book of fairy tales.
Blaisdell. Child life. 4th reader. (Lamp of Aladdin.)
Chisholm. In fairyland.
Coe and Christie. Story hour readers. 3d book. (Aladdin and the magic lamp.)
Coussens. Child's book of stories.
Dyer and Brady. Merrill readers. 3d reader. (Aladdin and the wonderful lamp.)
Favorite fairy tales.
Jerrold. Big book of fairy tales.
Ketcham. Oriental fairy tales.
*Lang. Aladdin and other stories.
Lang. Blue fairy book.
*Lang. Dick Whittington and other stories.
Mabie. Fairy tales every child should know.
Mabie. Heroes and fairies. (Story of Aladdin.)
Norton. Heart of oak books. v. 3.
Pyle. Mother's nursery tales.
Scudder. Children's book. (Story of Aladdin.)
Sly. World stories retold.
Success library. v. 3.
Tappan. Stories from seven old favorites.
Welsh. Fairy tales children love.
Alaka's eyes. Johnston. Little colonel in Arizona.
Alarm clock that was alive. *See* Little rooster.
Alba, Story of. *See* Horatii and Curiatii.
Alcestis. *See* Admetus and Alcestis.
Alchemist. I. Darton. Tales of the Canterbury pilgrims. (Canon's Yeoman's tale: The alchemist.)
Alchemist. II. Guerber. Legends of the Rhine.
Ale of the trolls. Stroebe and Martens. Danish fairy book.
Alectryon. Guerber. Myths of Greece and Rome. (*In* Venus.)

Alenoushka and her brother. Chisholm and Steedman. Staircase of stories.

Alexander Jones. Campbell. Beyond the border.
Douglas. Scottish fairy tales.
Johnson. Fir-tree fairy book.

Alexander the Great. Bailey. In the animal world. (Bucephalus.)
Baldwin. Fifty famous stories. (Alexander and Bucephalus.)
Baldwin. Horse fair. (Bucephalus.)
Baldwin. Thirty more famous stories. (Gordian knot; Why Alexander wept.)
Landa. Aunt Naomi's Jewish fairy tales and legends. (King Alexander's adventures.)
Magnus. Russian folk-tales. (Tale of Alexander of Macedon.)

Alfred, King. *See* King Alfred.

Ali Baba and the forty thieves. Arabian nights (Colum).
Arabian nights (Dodge).
Arabian nights (Housman).
Arabian nights (Olcott).
Arabian nights (Wiggin and Smith).
Chisholm. In fairyland.
Coussens. Child's book of stories.
*Crane. Red Riding Hood's picture book. (Forty thieves.)
Favorite fairy tales.
Johnson. Birch-tree fairy book.
Ketcham. Oriental fairy tales.
Lang. Blue fairy book. (Forty thieves.)
*Lang. Dick Whittington and other stories. (Forty thieves.)
Lang. Forty thieves and other stories. (Forty thieves.)
Mabie. Fairy tales every child should know. (History of Ali Baba.)
Mabie. Heroes and fairies. (History of Ali Baba.)
Marshall. Fairy tales of all nations.
Norton. Heart of oak books. v. 3.
Scudder. Children's book. (History of Ali Baba.)
Tappan. Stories from seven old favorites.
Welsh. Stories children love.
See also Simeli Mountain; Forty-nine dragons.

Ali Cogia, a merchant of Bagdad. Arabian nights (Dodge ed.).
Arabian nights (Lang. Story of Ali Cogia.)
Arabian nights (Townsend).
Favorite fairy tales.
Ketcham. Oriental fairy tales.
Pyle. Tales of folks and fairies. (History of Ali Cogia.)
(play). Stevenson. Plays for the home. (Story of Ali Cogia.)

Ali Hafed's quest. Hartwell. Story hour readings. 7th year.

Ali Mahmoud finds treasure. Pearson. Laughing lion.
Ali of Cairo. Arabian nights, More tales (Olcott).
See also Heir of Linne; Merchant.
Alice and Patty. Dillingham and Emerson. Tell it again stories.
Alice and the white knight. Hodgkins. Atlantic treasury of childhood stories.
Alice in Wonderland. Patten. Junior classics. v. 6 (Abridged).
Alison visits Mrs. Owl. Bouvé. Lamp-light fairy tales.
All change. Jacobs. Europa's fairy book.
See also Monkey's bargains; Rat's wedding; Travels of a fox.
All-gone. *See* Cat and the mouse in partnership.
"All I possess!" Djurklo. Fairy tales from the Swedish.
All the wild waves of the sea. Nyblom. Jolly Calle.
All things are as fate wills. Pyle. Twilight land.
All think their own offspring the best. Thorpe. Yule-tide stories.
All women are alike. Asbjörnsen. Fairy tales from the far north.
Dasent. Norse fairy tales. (Not a pin to choose between them.)
Dasent. Popular tales from the Norse. (Not a pin to choose between.)
Tappan. Folk stories and fables. (Not a pin to choose between them.)
Thorpe. Yule-tide stories. (Such women are; or, The man from Ringerige and three women.)
See also Clever folks.
Allan-a-Dale's wedding. Stebbins. 3d reader.
See also Robin Hood.
Allerleirauh. *See* Many-furred creature.
Alligator and the jackal. *See* Little jackal and the alligator.
Alligator and the moorhen. Stafford. Animal fables.
Alligator war. Quiroga. South American jungle tales.
Allwise the dwarf. Jerrold. Reign of King Oberon.
Almeah, the rose flower. Olcott. Red Indian fairy book.
Almond blossom Fyleman. Rainbow cat.
Almond-tree. *See* Juniper-tree.
Alnaschar. *See* Barber's fifth brother.
Along the way. Richards. Silver crown.
Alphege; or, The green monkey. Lang. Invisible prince and other stories.
Lang. Yellow fairy book.
Wiggin and Smith. Magic casements.
Alphege the archbishop. Wilmot-Buxton. Stories of early England.
Alpine hunter and his fairy guardian. Griffis. Swiss fairy tales.
Alvis. *See* Thor.

Alwin and the blue water children. Eliot. House on the edge of things.
Storytellers' magazine. Nov. 1915, p. 393. (House on the edge of things: Alwin and the blue water children.)
Alyásha Popóvich. Magnus. Russian folk-tales.
Amadan Mor and the Gruagach of the castle of gold. Curtin. Hero tales from Ireland.
Amadan of the Dough. MacManus. Donegal fairy stories.
Wiggin and Smith. Tales of wonder.
Amadis of Gaul. Patten. Junior classics. v. 4. (How the child of the sea was made knight.)
Amasis. Brooksbank. Legends of ancient Egypt. (Shadow of the end.)
Ambassadors of Siam. *See* How the Siamese ambassadors reached the Cape.
Amber-seeker. Thorpe. Yule-tide stories.
Ambitious carp. Griffis. Japanese fairy tales.
Ambitious cattail. Storytellers' magazine. Sept. 1916. p. 482.
Ambitious hunter and skilful fisher. Baker and Carpenter. Language readers. 3d year. (Princes Fire-flash and Fire-fade.)
Ballard. Fairy tales from far Japan. (Lucky hunter and skilful fisher.)
Griffis. Japanese fairy tales. (Fire Glow and Fire Gloom.)
James. Green willow. (Sea god and the magic tide jewel.)
Johnson. Elm-tree fairy book. (Lucky hunter and the skilful fisherman.)
Olcott. Wonder garden. (Prince Fireshine and Prince Firefade.)
Ozaki. Japanese fairy book. (Happy hunter and the cheerful fisher.)
Stebbins. 3d reader. (Matchless hunter.)
Storytellers' magazine. Feb. 1914, p. 417. (Happy hunter and the lucky fisherman; or, The two brothers.)
Tappan. Myths from many lands. (Palace of the ocean-bed.)
Wiggin and Smith. Tales of wonder. (Princes Fire-flash and Fire-fade.)
Ambitious laborer. Success library. v. 3.
Ambitious rocking-horse. Richards. Joyous story of Toto.
Ambitious tailor. *See* Sham prince.
Ambitious thrush. *See* Talking thrush.
Amelia and the spider (poem). Wiggin and Smith. Talking beasts.
(poem). Æsop. Fables (Burt ed.).
Amelings. Guerber. Legends of the middle ages.
Amys and Amyli. Lang. Red romance book.
Anansi the spider-man. Olcott. Wonder garden.
See also Spider-man.
Ananzi and baboon. Dasent. Popular tales from the Norse.

Ananzi and Quanqua. Dasent. Popular tales from the Norse.
Ananzi and the lion. Dasent. Popular tales from the Norse.
Mabie. Folk tales every child should know.
Ancient ballad of Chevy Chace. *See* Chevy Chase.
Ancient Man. Martens. Chinese fairy book.
Ancients of the world. Griffis. Welsh fairy tales. (Welshery and the Normans.)
Thomas. Welsh fairy book.
Ander's new cap. Bailey. For the story-teller. (Cap that mother made.)
Coe. Second book of stories.
(play). *Field second reader. (Cap that mother made.)
My Bookhouse. v. 2. (Cap that mother made.)
O'Grady and Throop. Teachers' story teller's book.
Storytellers' magazine. Nov. 1914, p. 715.
Wickes. Happy holidays. (Wonderful cap that mother made.)
Andras Baive. Lang. Orange fairy book.
Andrew Coffey. Jacobs. Celtic fairy tales.
See also Teig O'Kane and the corpse.
Androcles. *See* Androclus and the lion.
Androclus and the lion. Æsop. Fables (Jacobs. Androcles.)
Baker and Carpenter. Language readers. 3d year. (Androcles.)
Baldwin. Fifty famous stories.
Curry. Little classics. (Androcles and the lion.)
*Dyer and Brady. Merrill readers. 2d reader. (Story of a lion.)
Jacobs. Europa's fairy book. (Androcles and the lion.)
Lang. Animal story book.
Patten. Junior classics. v. 1. (Androcles.)
Sly. World stories retold. (Androcles and the lion.)
Andromeda. *See* Perseus.
Andvare's golden ring. Guerber. Legends of the Rhine. (Story of Siegfried.)
Klingensmith. Old Norse wonder tales. (Andvare's golden ring; Stories of the Nibelungen; Mimi's story.)
See also Ring: Rhine gold; Sigurd the Volsung.
Anemone. I. *See* Adonis.
Anemone. II. Olcott. Wonder garden. (Legend of the frail windflower.)
Anemone and the rose. *See* Adonis.
Anent the giant who did not have his heart about him. *See* Giant who had no heart.
Angel. *Andersen. Best fairy tales (Henderson tr.).
Andersen. Fairy tales (Dodge ed.).
Andersen. Fairy tales (Lucas tr.).
Andersen. Fairy tales (Paull tr.).
Andersen. Wonder stories (Author's ed.).
Tappan. Folk stories and fables.

Angel and the flowers. Field. Second book of tales.
Angel of the flowers. I. *See* Dandelion, Legend of. I.
Angel of the flowers. II. Bryce. That's why stories. (Flower legend.)
Angel page. Guerber. Legends of the Rhine.
Stebbins. Sunken city.
Angels in the churchyard (poem). Alexander. Hidden servants.
Angel's robe. I. *See* Robe of feathers.
Angel's robe. II. Chisholm and Steedman. Staircase of stories. (Angels' robe.)
Anger-eating ogre. Burlingame. Grateful elephant.
Anger of Tirawa. Nixon-Roulet. Indian folk tales.
Angler and the little fish. *See* Fisher and the little fish.
Angler and the salmon. Æsop. Fables (Burt ed.).
Animal fairies. Kennedy. New world fairy book.
Animal picnic. Vân Sickle and Seegmiller. Riverside readers. 3d reader.
Animals' ball game. *See* Birds' ball game.
Animals' Christmas tree. I. Skinner. Pearl story book.
Animals' Christmas tree. II. Sawyer. This way to Christmas. (Uncle Joab and a new Santa Claus.)
Animals in the pit. Magnus. Russian folk-tales.
Animals in the sky. Farmer. Nature myths.
Skinner. Topaz story book. (Why the autumn leaves are red.)
Stanley. Animal folk tales. (Deer and the rainbow.)
Animals' peace party. Davis and Chow-Leung. Chinese fables and folk stories.
Wiggin and Smith. Talking beasts.
Animals sick of the plague (poem). Wiggin and Smith. Talking beasts.
Animals take a bite. *See* Fox and his five hungry comrades.
Animals that found a home. *See* Ram and the pig.
Animals' winter quarters. Magnus. Russian folk-tales.
Anna and the fairies. Boys' and girls' fairy book.
Anna and the prince. Chisholm and Steedman. Staircase of stories.
Anne Lisbeth. Andersen. Fairy tales (Paull tr.).
Andersen. Stories and tales (Author's ed.).
Annette; or, The magic coffee mill. Harrison. Old-fashioned fairy book.
Annie's dream. *Hall and Gilman. Story land. 2d reader.
Annungitee and the bad boy. Young. Algonquin Indian tales. (*In* Ch. 7.)
Another changeling. Thomas. Welsh fairy book.
Another haunted mill. *See* Mill.
Another little red hen. *See* Little red hen. II.
Another story of the rainbow. *See* Rainbow snake.
Anselmo. Blaisdell. Child life. 5th reader.
Ingelow. Stories told to a child. v. 2.
Smith. Good old stories.

Ant and the chrysalis. Æsop. Fables (Burt ed.).
Ant and the cricket. Baldwin. Fairy tales and fables.
(poem). Lansing. Dramatic readings.
(poem). Van Sickle and Seegmiller. Riverside readers. 4th reader.
Ant and the dove. Æsop. Fables (Black ed. Dove and the ant.)
Æsop. Fables (Burt ed. Dove and the ant.)
Æsop. Fables (Stickney ed.).
*Alderman. Classics old and new. 1st reader. (Dove and the ant.)
Bailey. Folk stories and fables.
Bailey and Lewis. For the children's hour.
Boston collection of kindergarten stories.
*Elson and Runkel. Elson readers. Book 1.
*Jones. 2d reader.
Sly. World stories retold. (Dove and the ant.)
(poem). Wiggin and Smith. Talking beasts. (Dove and the ant.)
Young and Field. Literary readers. Book 2.
See also Mrs. Thrifty-Ant's fall.
Ant and the fly. Æsop. Fables (Black ed.).
Æsop. Fables (Burt ed.).
Wiggin and Smith. Talking beasts.
See also Ant and the grasshopper.
Ant and the glowworm. Bryce. Fables from afar.
Ant and the grasshopper. Æsop. Fables (Black ed.).
Æsop. Fables (Burt ed. Ants and the grasshopper.)
Æsop. Fables (Jacobs).
Æsop. Fables (Stickney. Ants and the grasshopper.)
Arnold and Gilbert. Stepping stones to literature. v. 2.
Bailey. Folk stories and fables.
Bailey and Lewis. For the children's hour.
*Bowen. Second story reader.
*Elson and Runkel. Elson readers. Book 2.
*Jones. 2d reader.
Keyes. Stories and story-telling.
Patten. Junior classics. v. 1.
Scudder. Children's book.
Scudder. Fables and folk stories.
Sly. World stories retold.
(poem). Wiggin and Smith. Talking beasts. (Grasshopper and the ant.)
Wilson. Nature study reader.
See also Ant and the fly; Mrs. Grasshopper Gay; Nightingale and the rose.
Ant and the mouse. *Spaulding and Bryce. Aldine readers. 2d reader.
Ant and the snow. Chandler. In the reign of coyote.
Ant that hurt his leg. *Field first reader.
Antæus. *See* Hercules and his labors: Pygmies.

Antelope boy. Lummis. Pueblo Indian folk tales.
Antelope, woodpecker, tortoise, and hunter. *See* True friendship.
Antillia, the island of the seven cities. Higginson. Tales of the enchanted islands of the Atlantic.
Anting-Anting of Manuelito. Miller. Philippine folklore stories.
Anton's errand. Poulsson. Top of the world stories.
Ant's adventures. Bailey. Friendly tales. (Adventures of the herd.)
Ants and the grasshopper. *See* Ant and the grasshopper.
Ants, Origin of. Fielde. Chinese fairy tales.
See also First ants.
Ants that pushed on the sky. Lummis. Pueblo Indian folk stories.
Wiggin and Smith. Tales of wonder.
Anxious leaf. *Bailey. Folk stories and fables.
Bailey and Lewis. For the children's hour.
Skinner. Topaz story book.
*Wiltse. Kindergarten stories.
Anybody. Richards. Golden windows.
Ape and her two young ones. Æsop. Fables (Burt ed.).
Æsop. Fables (Black ed.).
Ape and the bee. Æsop. Fables (Burt ed.).
Ape and the boar. Bidpai. Tortoise and the geese.
Ape and the carpenter. Æsop. Fables (Burt ed.).
Ape and the crab. *See* Crab and the monkey.
Ape and the dolphin. Æsop. Fables (Burt ed.).
Æsop. Fables (Black ed.).
Ape and the firefly. *See* Battle of the firefly and the apes.
Ape and the fox. Æsop. Fables (Black ed.).
Ape Sun Wu Kung. Martens. Chinese fairy book.
Ape, the glow-worm, and the popinjay. Bidpai. Tortoise and the geese.
Ape, the snake, and the lion. Bateman. Zanzibar tales.
Apelles. Haaren and Poland. Famous men of Greece. (*In* Aristotle.)
Apes and the two travelers. Æsop. Fables (Burt ed.).
Ape's head (poem). Success library. v. 3.
Apollo. Baldwin. Hero tales told in school. (How Apollo came to Parnassus.)
Baldwin. Old Greek stories. (Lord of the silver bow.)
Baldwin. Story of the golden age. (*In* Silver-bowed Apollo.)
Firth. Stories of old Greece. (Apollo, the beautiful.)
See also Admetus and Alcestis; Daphne; Vengeance of Apollo.
Apollo: Apollo and the python. Baldwin. Story of the golden age. (*In* Silver-bowed Apollo.)
Firth. Stories of old Greece.
Wilson. Nature study reader. (Killing of the python.)

Apollo: Birth of Apollo. Francillon. Gods and heroes. (Latona and Niobe.)
Hutchinson. Orpheus with his lute. (How Apollo came to Delphi.)
Pratt. Greek myths, v. 1. (Leto and Apollo.)
Apollo and Daphne. *See* Daphne.
Apollo and Hermes. *See* Hermes and Apollo.
Apollo and Hyacinthus. *See* Hyacinthus.
Apollo and the crow. *See* Why the crow is black.
Apollo's cows. *See* Hermes and Apollo.
Apollo's mother. *See* Latona and the frogs.
Apollo's sister. *See* Diana.
Apple dumpling. Lindsay. Story-teller.
Apple of contentment. Pyle. Pepper and salt.
Apple of discord. *See* Paris: Apple of discord.
Apple-seed John. *See* Johnny Appleseed.
Apples of glory. Bailey. Little man with one shoe.
Apples of Hesperides. *See* Hercules and his labors.
Apples of Idun. *See* Iduna's apples.
Apples of life. *See* Iduna's apples.
Apples of youth. *See* Iduna's apples.
Apprentice thief. MacManus. In chimney corners.
April Fools' Day. *See* Bruin and Reynard partners; Believing husbands; Diccon, the foot-boy; Good bargain; Heyo house; Little farmer; Wise men of Gotham.
Apron-string. Richards. Golden windows.
Apuleius. *See* How the ass became a man again.
Aqua; or, The water baby. Wiggin and Smith. Story hour.
Arab and his camel. Æsop. Fables (Stickney).
Baldwin. Another fairy reader. (Camel and his master.)
*Hall and Gilman. Story land. 2d reader.
Scudder. Children's book.
Scudder. Fables and folk stories.
Sly. World stories retold. (Camel in the tent.)
Van Sickle and Seegmiller. Riverside readers. 4th reader.
Wiggin and Smith. Talking beasts. (Camel and his master.)
See also Snake and the hedgehog.
Arab and his horse. *See* Hassan the Arab and his horse.
Arabian pipe, Story of the. Harrison. Bric-a-brac stories.
Arachne. *Bailey. Wonder stories. (Picture Minerva wove.)
Bailey and Lewis. For the children's hour.
Beckwith. In mythland. v. 1. (Little weaver.)
Baldwin. Old Greek stories. (Wonderful weaver.)
Cooke. Nature myths and stories.
Craigie. Once upon a time.
Dyer and Brady. Merrill readers. 3d reader.
Firth. Stories of old Greece. (Arachne, the little spinner.)
Guerber. Myths of Greece and Rome. (*In* Minerva.)
Holbrook. Round the year in myth and song. (Minerva and Arachne.)
Hyde. Favorite Greek myths.

Arachne—*continued.*
Johonnot. Stories of the olden time.
Kupfer. Stories of long ago. (A web and a spider.)
McFee. Treasury of myths.
Olcott. Good stories for great holidays.
Peabody. Old Greek folk stories.
Pratt. Greek myths. v. 2.
Skinner. Turquoise story book.
Tappan. Myths from many lands.
Arbor Day. *See* Boy who hated trees; Gifts the trees gave; How the cliff was clad; How the oak tree came to have notches; Maple seed; Plucky prince.
Arbutus. *See* Old Winter Man and the Spring. I.
Arbutus and violet. Stebbins. 3d reader.
Archer and the eagle. *See* Eagle and the arrow.
Archer and the trumpeter. *Burchill. Progressive road to reading. Book 3.
Are you hopping along behind? Potter. Pinafore pocket story book.
Are you not satisfied? or, The tale of the noses. Gask. Folk tales from many lands. (Farmer and the noses.)
Laboulaye. Fairy tales.
Laboulaye. Fairy book. (Story of the noses.)
See also Hans Humdrum; Keep Cool.
Arethusa. Baldwin. Hero tales told in school. (Alpheus and Arethusa.)
Baldwin. Story of the golden age. (*In* Bow of Eurytus.)
Buckley. Children of the dawn. (Flight of Arethusa.)
Cox. Tales of ancient Greece.
Guerber. Myths of Greece and Rome. (*In* Ceres and Proserpine.)
Olcott. Wonder garden.
Storr. Half a hundred hero tales.
Argo. *See* Argonauts.
Argonauts. *Almost true tales. (Golden fleece.)
*Beckwith. In mythland. v. 2. (Jason and the golden fleece.)
*Bailey. Wonder stories. (Winning of the golden fleece.)
Baker and Carpenter. Language readers. 5th year. (Jason and the golden fleece.)
Baldwin. Fifty famous rides. (Flight of the golden ram.)
Burt and Ragozin. Herakles and other heroes. (Jason, the hero of Thessaly.)
Canton. Reign of King Herla.
Church. Greek story and song. (Voyage of the Argo.)
Cole. Heroes of the olden time. (Golden fleece.)
Cox. Tales of ancient Greece. (Golden fleece.)
Field third reader. (How Jason brought home the golden fleece.)
Francillon. Gods and heroes. (Golden fleece.)
Guerber. Myths of Greece and Rome. (Jason.)

Argonauts—*continued.*
Haaren and Poland. Famous men of Greece. (Jason and the golden fleece.)
Hawthorne. Tanglewood tales. (Golden fleece.)
Hutchinson. Golden porch. (Lad with one sandal.)
Hyde. Favorite Greek myths. (Jason and the golden fleece.)
Jacobs. Book of wonder voyages.
Judson and Bender. Graded literature readers. v. 4. (Golden fleece.)
Kingsley. Heroes (Everyman's ed.).
Kupfer. Stories of long ago. (Golden fleece.)
Lowell. Jason's quest. (Golden fleece.)
Mabie. Myths every child should know.
Norton. Heart of oak books. v. 3.
*Olcott. Wonder garden. (Ram with the golden fleece.)
Patten. Junior classics. v. 3.
Pratt. Myths of Old Greece. v. 3. (Golden fleece.)
Scudder. Children's book. (Expedition of the Argonauts.)
Shaw. Stories of the ancient Greeks.
Stories of classic myths. (Story of the golden fleece.)
Storr. Half a hundred hero tales. (Quest of the golden fleece.)
Tappan. Myths from many lands. (Golden fleece.)
Tappan. Stories from the classics.

Argus. *See* Io.

Ariadne. *See* Theseus.

Arion and the dolphin. Baldwin. Fifty famous people. (Saved by a dolphin.)
Hyde. Favorite Greek myths.
Johonnot. Stories of the olden time. (Arion.)
Olcott. Wonder garden.
Patten. Junior classics. v. 2. (Story of Arion.)
Shaw. Stories of the ancient Greeks. (Singer and the dolphin.)

Aristaeus. *See* Bee-man of Arcadia.

Aristides the Just. Haaren and Poland. Famous men of Greece.

Ark of Deucalion. *See* Deucalion and Pyrrha.

Armistice Day. *See* Birds go to war; Fairy of the poppies; How Mars lost a battle; Invisible wall; Seven kingdoms and the hidden spring; Ways of giving advice.

Arndt's night underground. Wiggin and Smith. Tales of wonder.

Arrow and the swing. Colum. At the gateways of the day.

Artful lad. Djurklo. Fairy tales from the Swedish.

Arthur, King. *See* King Arthur.

Artisan's wonderful wings. *See* Dædalus and Icarus.

Aruman, a hero of Java. My Bookhouse. v. 3.

Arundel the swallow. *See* Sir Bevis.

As-ai-yahal. Judson. Myths and legends of the Pacific Northwest.

As rich as Crœsus. *See* Crœsus.
As the crow flies. Ingelow. Stories told to a child. v. 2.
Aschenputtel. *See* Cinderella.
Ash maid. Baring-Gould. Crock of gold.
Ash tree. *See* Mountain Ash; Rowan tree.
Ashenputtel. *See* Cinderella.
Ashes of deceit. Pitman. Chinese fairy stories.
Ashes that made trees to bloom. *See* Old man who made withered trees to flower.
Ashiepattle and his goodly crew. Asbjörnsen. Fairy tales from the far north.
Asbjörnsen. Tales from the fjeld. (Boots and his crew.)
Patten. Junior classics. v. 1.
See also Ship that could sail over land and sea.
Ashiepattle and the king's hares. Asbjörnsen. Folk and fairy tales.
Asbjörnsen. Tales from the fjeld. (Osborn's pipe.)
Stroebe and Martens. Norwegian fairy book. (King's hares.)
See also Enchanted whistle; Jesper who herded the hares.
Ashiepattle and the stoorworm. Douglas. Scottish fairy tales. (Assipattle and the Meester Stoorworm.)
Grierson. Scottish fairy book. (Assipattle and the Meester Stoorworm.)
Pyle. Tales of folk and fairies. (Meester Stoorworm.)
Wiggin and Smith. Tales of wonder. (Stoorworm.)
Williams. Fairy tales from folklore. (Stoorworm.)
Ashiepattle who ate with the troll for a wager. Asbjörnsen. Fairy tales from the far north.
Dasent. Norse fairy tales. (Jack and the troll have an eating match.)
Dasent. Popular tales from the Norse. (Boots who ate a match with the troll.)
Tappan. Folk stories and fables. (Boots who ate a match with the troll.)
See also Boy who contended with the giant in eating.
Ashiepattle who made the princess tell the truth at last. Asbjörnsen. Folk and fairy tales.
Dasent. Norse fairy tales. (Lad who made the princess say, "That's a story.")
Dasent. Popular tales from the Norse. (Boots who made the princess say, "That's a story.")
Patten. Junior classics. v. 1. (Boots who made the princess say, "That's a story.")
See also Princess who said:—
Ashik-Kerib. Jokai and others. Golden fairy book.
Ashish, Story of. Judson. Myths and legends of the Pacific Northwest.
"Ask the robin." Molesworth. Fairies afield.
Aslaug and Ragnar. Baring-Gould. Old English fairy tales. (King Edmund.)
Edmison. Stories from Norseland.

Aslaug and Ragnar—*continued.*
Storytellers' magazine. Jan. 1917, p. 10. (Fostering of Aslaug.)
See also Sigurd the Volsung. II.
Asmund and Signy. Lang. Brown fairy book
See also Three robes
Aspenclog. Stroebe and Martens. Norwegian fairy book.
Asphurtzela. Wardrop. Georgian folk tales.
Ass and his master. Æsop. Fables (Burt ed.).
Wiggin and Smith. Talking beasts.
Ass and his purchaser. Wiggin and Smith. Talking beasts.
Ass and his shadow. Æsop. Fables (Burt ed. Ass's shadow.)
Æsop. Fables (Stickney).
Wiggin and Smith. Talking beasts.
Ass and the bullock. Æsop. Fables (Burt ed.).
Ass and the dog. *See* Ass, the dog and the wolf.
Ass and the fly. Wiggin and Smith. Talking beasts.
Ass and the frogs. Æsop. Fables (Stickney).
Success library. v. 3.
Ass and the gardener. Æsop. Fables (Burt ed.).
Ass and the grasshopper. Æsop. Fables (Stickney).
Arnold and Gilbert. Stepping stones to literature. v. 2. (Donkey and the grasshopper.)
Ass and the lap-dog. Æsop. Fables (Black ed. Ass and the little dog.)
Æsop. Fables (Jacobs).
Æsop. Fables (Stickney).
My Bookhouse. v. 1. (Donkey and the lap-dog.)
Patten. Junior classics. v. 1.
(poem). Wiggin and Smith. Talking beasts.
Ass and the lion hunting. Æsop. Fables (Black ed.).
Æsop. Fables (Burt ed.).
Ass and the little dog. *See* Ass and the lap-dog.
Ass and the nightingale. Success library. v. 3.
Ass and the wolf. Success library. v. 3.
Ass carrying an idol. Æsop. Fables (Burt ed.).
Ass carrying relics (poem). Wiggin and Smith. Talking beasts.
Ass eating thistles. Æsop. Fables (Black ed.).
Æsop. Fables (Burt ed.).
Æsop. Fables (Stickney).
Ass in the lion's skin. Æsop. Fables (Black ed. Fox and the ass.)
Æsop. Fables (Burt ed. Fox and the ass.)
Æsop. Fables (Jacobs).
Æsop. Fables (Stickney).
Baker and Carpenter. Language readers. 3d year.
*Hall and Gilman. Story land. 2d reader. (Donkey in the lion's skin.)
Jacobs. Indian fairy tales.
My Bookhouse. v. 1.

Ass in the lion's skin—*continued.*
Scudder. Children's book.
Scudder. Fables and folk stories.
Tappan. Folk stories and fables.
Wiggin and Smith. Talking beasts.
Ass laden with salt and with sponges. *See* Donkey and the salt.
Ass that saw the angel. Griffis. Swiss fairy tales.
Ass, the ape, and the mole. Æsop. Fables (Burt ed.).
Ass, the dog, and the wolf. Æsop. Fables (Burt ed.).
(poem). Wiggin and Smith. Talking beasts. (Ass and the dog.)
Ass, the lion, and the cock. Æsop. Fables (Black ed.).
Æsop. Fables (Burt ed.).
Ass, the lion, and the fox. Bidpai. Tortoise and the geese.
Ass, the ox, and the labourer. Arabian nights (Townsend. Fable of the ass, the ox, and the labourer.)
Arabian nights (Dodge ed.).
Ass, the table, and the stick. *See* Table, the ass, and the stick.
Assassin priest. Guerber. Legends of the Rhine.
Assipattle. *See* Ashiepattle.
Ass's brains. Æsop. Fables (Jacobs).
Ass's shadow. *See* Ass and his shadow.
Aster and the goldenrod. *See* Goldenrod and aster.
Astounding voyage of Daniel O'Rourke. *See* Daniel O'Rourke.
Astrologer. Scudder. Children's book.
Astrologer's niece. Fairy tales retold from St. Nicholas.
At long last. Richards. Silver crown.
At the behest of the pike. Magnus. Russian folk-tales.
At the doll's hospital. Bouvé. Lamp-light tales.
At the edge of the polar sea. Pyle. Counterpane fairy.
At the foot of the rainbow. Stewart. Once upon a time.
At the owl's school (play). Lansing. Quaint old stories.
Atalanta and Meleager. *See* Calydonian hunt.
Atalanta's race. *Bailey. Wonder stories. (Wonders Venus wrought.)
Baldwin. Old Greek stories. (Race for a wife.)
Baldwin. Story of the golden age. (*In* Race for a wife.)
Buckley. Children of the dawn. (Winning of Atalanta.)
Carpenter. Long ago in Greece. (Atalanta's foot race.)
Guerber. Myths of Greece and Rome. (*In* Calydonian hunt.)
Patten. Junior classics. v. 3. (Winning of Atalanta.)
Peabody. Old Greek folk stories.
Pratt. Greek myths. v. 3. (Race of Atalanta.)
Shaw. Stories of the ancient Greeks. (Race of Atalanta.)
Tappan. Myths from many lands.
See also How the princess was beaten in a race; Rosamund the swift of foot.
Athena. *See* Minerva.

Athens. *Bailey. Wonder stories. (How Minerva built a city.)
Baldwin. Horse fair. (Ship of the plains.)
Baldwin. Old Greek stories. (Horse and the olive.)
Dyer and Brady. Merrill readers. 3d reader. (Naming of a great city.)
Guerber. Myths of Greece and Rome. (*In* Minerva.)
Hartley. Stories from the Greek legends. (Story of Athene and Poseidon; or, The quarrel over naming a city.)
Judd. Classic myths. (Gift of the olive tree.)
Patten. Junior classics. v. 2. (Gift of Athene.)
Atlantis, Story of. Higginson. Tales of the enchanted islands of the Atlantic.
Atlas. Brown. When the world was young. (Atlas, the burden bearer.)
Attila. Evans. Old time tales. (Scourge of God.)
Haaren and Poland. Famous men of the middle ages.
Au-ke-le the seeker. Colum. At the gateways of the day.
Aucassin and Nicolette, Story of. Wilmot-Buxton. Stories from old French romance.
Auld Robin Gray. Greenwood. Stories from famous ballads.
Aunt Tempy's story. Harris. Nights with Uncle Remus.
Aunt's tale. *See* Two companions.
Aunty. Andersèn. Stories and tales (Author's ed.).
Aurora and Tithonus. Beckwith. In mythland. v. 2. (Old man of the meadow.)
Cooke. Nature myths and stories.
Farmer. Nature myths. (Old man of the meadow.)
Francillon. Gods and heroes. (Man who never died.)
Holbrook. Book of nature myths. (Story of the first grasshopper.)
Hyde. Favorite Greek myths.
Judd. Classic myths. (Old grasshopper gray.)
Olcott. Wonder garden. (Tithonus the grasshopper.)
Skinner. Turquoise story book.
Wilson. Nature study reader.
Aurora, the white arch, and the great bear. Pratt. Legends of the red children.
Aurora's steeds. Stories of classic myths. (*In* Mythological horses.)
Austrian paper-knife's story. Harrison. Bric-a-brac stories.
Autolycus. *See* Sisyphus and Autolycus.
Autumn and spring. James. Green willow. (Spring lover and autumn lover.)
Tappan. Myths of many lands.
Avalanche that was a peace maker. Griffis. Swiss fairy tales.
Avaricious and envious. Æsop. Fables (Black ed. Envious man and the covetous.)

Avaricious and envious—*continued.*
Æsop. Fables (Burt ed. Envious man and the covetous.)
Æsop. Fables (Jacobs).
Awakening. Cabot. Ethics for children.
Gatty. Parables from nature. (*In* Earth's many voices.)
See also Snowdrop.
Awful fate of Mr. Wolf. Harris. Uncle Remus, his songs and his sayings.
Axe and the trees. Æsop. Fables (Stickney).
Axe of Ranier. English. Fairy stories and wonder tales.
St. Nicholas. Sept. 1878, p. 709.
Aydevich. *See* Where love is, there God is also.

B

Baa, baa, black sheep. *Grover. Folk lore readers. v. 1.
Baba Abdalla, Story of. Arabian nights (Dodge ed.).
Arabian nights (Lang. Story of the blind Baba Abdalla.)
Arabian nights (Townsend).
Ketcham. Oriental fairy tales.
Scudder. Children's book.
Baba Yaga. Pyle. Wonder tales retold.
Baba Yaga and the little girl with the kind heart. *See* Vasalisa the beauty.
Bába Yagá and Zamoryshek. Magnus. Russian folk-tales.
Babe in the manger. Stein. When fairies were friendly.
Babes in the wood. Chaplin. Treasury of fairy tales.
Chisholm. In fairyland. (Children in the wood.)
(poem). *Coe and Christie. Story hour readers. Book 2.
Coussens. Child's book of stories.
Jacobs. More English fairy tales. (Children in the wood.)
Johnson. Fir-tree fairy book.
(poem). Keyes. Five senses.
(poem). Lansing. Tales of old England. (Children in the wood.)
Macleod. Book of ballad stories. (Children in the wood.)
(poem). Mother Goose rhymes, jingles and fairy tales (Altemus ed.).
(poem). Norton. Heart of oak books. v. 3.
(poem). Scudder. Children's book. (Children in the wood.)
Success library. v. 3. (Children in the wood.)
Tappan. Old-fashioned stories. (Children in the wood.)
Tweed. Fairy tales everyone should know.
Welsh. Stories children love. (Children in the wood.)
Babieca, the booby. Baldwin. Horse fair.
Babiola. Valentine. Old, old fairy tales.
Aulnoy. Fairy tales. (Babiole.)
Babiole. *See* Babiola.

Baboon-skins. Bourhill and Drake. Fairy tales from South Africa.

Babouscka. Bailey and Lewis. For the children's hour.
Curtiss. Christmas stories and legends.
Dickinson and Skinner. Children's book of Christmas stories. (Legend of Babouscka.)
Storytellers' magazine. Dec. 1914, p. 760. (Legend of Babouscka.)

Baby. Richards. Golden windows.

Baby Bess's ribbon. *Dillingham and Emerson. Tell it again stories.

Bacchus and Pentheus. Guerber. Myths of Greece and Rome. (*In* Bacchus.)
Hutchinson. Orpheus with his lute. (God of the ivy crown.)

Bacchus and the sailors. Guerber. Myths of Greece and Rome. (*In* Bacchus.)
Farrar. Old Greek nature stories.

Bacon, Roger. *See* Friar Bacon and the brazen head.

Bacon pie. Rhys. Fairy gold.

Bad boy and the Leprachaun. Olcott. Book of elves and fairies.

Bad boy, Story of the. Bellamy. Wonder children.

Bad little goblin's New Year. Skinner. Pearl story book.

Bad poppy-seeds. Olcott. Wonder garden.

Bad Wild Cat. *See* Rabbit and the wild cat.

Bad wishers. Finger. Tales from silver lands.

Badger. Storytellers' magazine. Oct. 1915, p. 367.

Badger and the bear. Eastman. Wigwam evenings.
(play). * Field first reader. (Bear and the badger.)
Zitkala-Sa. Old Indian legends.

Badger and the birds. Partridge. Glooscap the great chief.

Badger and the rock magician. Partridge. Glooscap the great chief.

Badger and the star wives. *See* Star wives.

Badger in the bag. Baring-Gould. Old English fairy tales.
Brooks. Wonder stories from the Mabinogion. (Pwyll and Rhiannon.)
Griffis. Welsh fairy tales. (Powell, Prince of Dyfed; Powell and his bride.)
Jacobs. More Celtic fairy tales. (Powel, Prince of Dyfed.)
Lanier. Knightly legends of Wales. (Pwyll, Prince of Dyved.)
Patten. Junior classics. v. 4. (How Pwyll outwitted Gawl.)
Tappan. Stories of legendary heroes. (Pwyll and the game of badger in the bag.)

Badger's money. Mabie. Folk tales every child should know.
Success library. v. 3.
Wiggin and Smith. Tales of wonder.
See also Farmer and the badger.

Bag of flour. Hartland. English folk and fairy tales.
Bag of marbles. Bailey. Friendly tales.
Bag of minutes. Rhys. Fairy gold.
Bag of sand (poem). Alexander. Hidden servants.
Bag of smiles. Alden. Why the chimes rang.
Bag of winds. *See* Ulysses and the bag of winds.
Baker boys of Andernach. Guerber. Legends of the Rhine. (Prophecy; Baker boys.)
Noyes. Twilight stories.
Stebbins. Sunken city. (Two baker boys.)
Baker's daughter. Johnson. Birch-tree fairy book.
See also Why the woodpecker's head is red.
Baker's three daughters. *See* Three sisters. I.
Bala lake. Thomas. Welsh fairy book.
Balboa. Baldwin. Thirty more famous stories. (Upon a peak in Darien.)
Bald-head. Byrne. Modern Greek fairy tales.
Bald knight. Æsop. Fables (Black ed.).
Æsop. Fables (Burt ed.).
Bald man and the fly. Æsop. Fables (Burt ed.).
Æsop. Fables (Jacobs).
Balder. *See* Baldur.
Balder forgives. *See* Frithiof.
Baldur and the mistletoe. Arnold and Gilbert. Stepping stones to literature. v. 5.
Baker and Carpenter. Language readers. 5th year. (Death of Balder.)
Brown. In the days of giants. (Balder and the mistletoe.)
Brown. Stories of childhood and nature.
Chisholm and Steedman. Staircase of stories. (Balder the beautiful.)
Cooke. Nature myths and stories. (Balder.)
Edmison. Stories from Norseland. (Death of Baldur.)
Foster and Cummings. Asgard stories. (Baldur.)
Guerber. Myths of northern lands. (*In* Balder.)
Judd. Classic myths. (Mistletoe.)
Klingensmith. Old Norse wonder tales. (Balder.)
Litchfield. Nine worlds.
Mabie. Myths every child should know. (Death of Baldur.)
Mabie. Norse stories. (Death of Baldur.)
McFee. Treasury of myths. (Balder the beautiful.)
Partridge. Story telling in home and school. (Death of Baldur.)
Patten. Junior classics. v. 2. (Story of Balder the beautiful.)
Pratt. Legends of Norseland. (Dying Baldur.)
Tappan. Myths from many lands. (Balder and the mistletoe.)
Wickes. Beyond the rainbow bridge. (Balder the beautiful.)
Wilmot-Buxton. Stories of Norse heroes. (Story of Balder; How Hermod made a journey to the underworld.)

Baldur and the mistletoe—*continued.*
See also Horse that brought the spring.
Balin. *See* Sir Balin.
Baling with a sieve. Fielde. Chinese fairy tales.
Ball-Carrier and the Bad One. Lang. Aladdin and other stories.
Lang. Brown fairy book.
Ball game. *See* Birds' ball game.
Ball of thread. Gregory. Kiltartan wonder book.
Balloon boy. Brown. Star jewels.
Balloons. Brown. Star jewels.
Balten and the wolf. Bosschère. Christmas tales of Flanders.
Bambino. Bailey. Stories for Sunday telling.
See also Stone baby.
Bamboo and the turtle. Pitman. Chinese wonder book.
Bamboo-cutter and the moon-child. Coussens. Jade story book. (Princess Moonlight.)
Griffis. Japanese fairy tales. (Lady from the silver moon.)
James. Green willow. (Moon maiden. Abridged.)
Ozaki. Japanese fairy book.
Williston. Japanese fairy tales. 2d series. (Bamboo-cutter's daughter.)
See also Princess Moonbeam.
Bamboo-cutter's daughter. *See* Bamboo-cutter and the moon-child.
Band, the bob-wig, and the feather. (poem). Æsop. Fables (Burt ed.).
Banished king. Stockton. Bee-man of Orn.
Bank swallows, Origin of. Hall and Gilman. Story land. 2d reader. (A story that Eskimos tell their children.)
Banshee of the MacCarthys. Yeats. Irish fairy tales.
Bantugan, Story of. Coussens. Jade story book.
Banyan deer. *See* Banyan deer king.
Banyan deer king. Babbitt. Jataka tales. (Banyan deer.)
Cabot. Ethics for children. (Banyan deer.)
Partridge. Story telling in home and school.
Shedlock. Eastern stories and legends. (Banyan deer.)
Stanley. Animal folk tales. (Banyan deer.)
Bar of gold. Gask. Folk tales from many lands.
Noyes. Twilight stories. (Lump of gold.)
Patten. Junior classics. v. 6.
See also Wishing ring.
Barak Hagel and his wives. Jokai and others. Golden fairy book.
Barbara Allen (poem). Lanier. Boy's Percy. (Sir John Grehme and Barbara Allen.)
Barbarossa. *See* Emperor's sleep.
Barbarossa's beard. Guerber. Legends of the Rhine.
Barber. Arabian nights, More tales (Olcott. Story told by the barber: The beheaded ten.)
Arabian nights (Townsend. Story of the barber.)

Barber—*continued.*
Olcott and Pendleton. Jolly book. (Story told by the barber: The beheaded ten.)
See also Little hunchback; Tailor.
Barber of Seville. Pleasanton. Fairyland of opera.
Barber's clever wife. Steel. Tales of the Punjab.
Barber's eldest brother. Arabian nights (Townsend).
See also Milkmaid and her pail.
Barber's second brother. Arabian nights (Townsend).
Barber's third brother. Arabian nights (Townsend).
Barber's fourth brother. Arabian nights (Townsend).
Barber's fifth brother. Arabian nights (Colum. Story of Alnaschar.)
Arabian nights (Lang).
Arabian nights, More tales. (Olcott. Story told by the barber: Tray of glass.)
Arabian nights (Townsend).
Jacobs. Europa's fairy book. (Day-dreaming.)
Olcott and Pendleton. Jolly book. (Tray of glass.)
See also Broken pot; Milkmaid and her pail of milk.
Barber's sixth brother. *See* Barmecide feast.
Barefoot on ice and snow. Curtis. Indian days of long ago.
Storytellers' magazine. Nov. 1916, p. 575. (Tales of an Indian grandfather.)
Barmecide feast. Arabian nights (Lang. Story of the barber's sixth brother.)
Arabian nights, More tales (Olcott. Story told by the barber: The Barmecide feast.)
Arabian nights (Townsend. Story of the barber's sixth brother.)
Baldwin. Fifty famous stories.
(play). Lansing. Quaint old stories.
Olcott and Pendleton. Jolly book.
Scudder. Children's book. (Story of the Barmecide feast.)
Barnaby's goose. Lindsay and Poulsson. Joyous travelers. (Second tale told by the chapman.)
Barney Noonan's fairy haymakers. Esenwein and Stockard. Children's stories.
Storytellers' magazine. Oct. 1913, p. 239.
Barnyard mystery. Storytellers' magazine. July. 1917, p. 332.
Barring of the door (poem). Lansing. Tales of old England. (Get up and bar the door.)
Tappan. Book of humor.
Tappan. Old ballads in prose.
Barza the boastful. Wilmot-Buxton. Stories of Persian heroes.
Basil-plant. Houghton. Russian grandmother's wonder tales.
Basket of flowers. Gask. Folk tales from many lands.
Basket woman. Austin. Basket woman.

Bat and his partners. Cather. Educating by story telling.
Bat and the two weasels. Æsop. Fables (Burt ed.).
Æsop. Fables (Stickney. Bat and weasels.)
Wiggin and Smith. Talking beasts.
Bat, birds and beasts. Æsop. Fables (Black ed. Birds, the beasts and the bat.)
Æsop. Fables (Burt ed. Birds, the beasts and the bat.)
Æsop. Fables (Jacobs).
Æsop. Fables (Stickney. Birds, the beasts and the bat.)
Dyer and Brady. Merrill readers. 3d reader. (Cowardly bat.)
Patten. Junior classics. v. 1.
Bata, the Egyptian boy, Story of. Storytellers' magazine. Oct. 1915, p. 319.
Jewett. Egyptian tales of magic. (Two brothers.)
Batcha and the dragon. Fillmore. Shoemaker's apron.
Bath-boy's daughter. Byrne. Modern Greek fairy tales.
Bats, Origin of. *See* Children with one eye; Birds' ball game; When Old Mr. Bat got his wings; Little guards of the night.
Battle of Leipsic. Guerber. Legends of the Rhine.
Battle of Roncesvalles. *See* Roland. II.
Battle of the beasts. See War of the wolf and the fox.
Battle of the birds. Grierson. Children's book of Celtic stories.
Douglas. Scottish fairy tales.
Jacobs. Celtic fairy tales.
Jacobs. Europa's fairy book. (Master maid.)
Lang. Lilac fairy book.
Lang. Little King Loc.
See also Nix Nought Nothing.
Battle of the birds and beasts. Bosschère. Fairy tales of Flanders.
Battle of the firefly and the apes. My Bookhouse. v. 2.
Stanley. Animal folk tales. (Ape and the firefly.)
Battle of the frogs and mice. Carpenter. Long ago in Greece.
Darton. Wonder book of beasts.
Patten. Junior classics. v. 2.
Battle of the kegs (poem). Tappan. Old-fashioned stories.
Battle of the monkey and the crab. *See* Crab and the monkey.
Battle of the sheep. Tappan. Stories from seven old favorites.
Battle of the swans and the peacocks. Storytellers' magazine. May 1916, p. 280.
Battle of the third cousins. Stockton. Bee-man of Orn.
Battle that never was fought. Kennedy. New world fairy book.
See also First strawberry.
Baucis and Philemon. *Bailey. Wonder stories. (How Jupiter granted a wish.)

Baucis and Philemon—*continued.*
Bailey and Lewis. For the children's hour.
Beckwith. In mythland. v. 1.
Blaisdell. Child life. 5th reader. (Miraculous pitcher.)
Chisholm and Steedman. Staircase of stories. (Strange visitors.)
Cooke. Nature myths and stories. (Philemon and Baucis.)
Firth. Stories of old Greece.
Guerber. Myths of Greece and Rome. (*In* Jupiter.)
Hartwell. Story hour readings. 6th year. (Hospitality rewarded.)
Hawthorne. Wonder book. (Miraculous pitcher.)
Hodgkins. Atlantic treasury of childhood stories. (Miraculous pitcher.)
Hyde. Favorite Greek myths. (Philemon and Baucis.)
Johonnot. Stories of heroic deeds.
Judd. Classic myths. (Linden and the oak.)
Kupfer. Stories of long ago. (How a wicked city was destroyed.)
Olcott. Good stories for great holidays.
Patten Junior classics. v. 2. (Baucis and Philemon who were changed into two trees.)
Pratt. Greek myths. v. 2.
Storr. Half a hundred hero tales.
Tappan. Stories from the classics. (Miraculous pitcher.)
Wilson. Nature study reader.

Bauernkrieg. Mendel. Our little Austrian cousin.

Bayard I. Evans. Old time tales. (Bayard, the knight without fear and without reproach.)
Lansing. Page, esquire and knight. (Chevalier Bayard.)
Storytellers' magazine. Jan. 1914, p. 381. (Chevalier Bayard.)

Bayard II. *See* Sons of Aymon.

Bear. Lang. Grey fairy book.
Lang. Invisible prince and other stories.

Bear and skrattel. Bailey. In the animal world. (White bear's Christmas. Adapted.)
Baker and Carpenter. Language readers. 3d year. (Bear and the troll.)
Dasent. Norse fairy tales. (Cat on the Doverfell.)
Dasent. Popular tales from the Norse. (Cat on the Dovrefell.)
*Grimm. Fairy tales (Wiltse. Bear and the skrattel.) v. 1.
Grimm. Household tales (Everyman's ed. Bear and the skrattel.)
Jerrold. Reign of King Oberon.
Johnson. Book of fairy-tale bears. (Bear and the skrattel.)
Pyle. Wonder tales retold. (Great white bear and the trolls.)

Bear and skrattel—*continued.*
*Stanley. Animal folk tales. (Hans and his white pussy cat.)
Wiggin and Smith. Fairy ring.
Bear and the badger. *See* Badger and the bear.
Bear and the bee-hives. Æsop. Fables (Black ed.).
Æsop. Fables (Burt ed.).
Bear and the fowls. Æsop. Fables (Burt ed.).
Wiggin and Smith. Talking beasts.
Bear and the fox. I. Æsop. Fables (Burt ed.).
Bear and the fox. II. Patten. Junior classics, v. 1.
This includes: Slip root, catch Reynard's foot; Bear and the fox make a wager; Bruin and Reynard partners; Reynard wants to taste horseflesh.
Bear and the fox. III. *See* Why the bear has a stumpy tail.
Bear and the fox bet on pork and a bee's nest. *See* Bear and the fox make a wager.
Bear and the fox go into partnership. *See* Bruin and Reynard partners.
Bear and the fox make a wager. Asbjörnsen. Fairy tales from the far north.
Asbjörnsen. Tales from the fjeld. (Pork and honey.)
Dasent. Norse fairy tales. (Pork and honey.)
Gade. Norwegian fairy tales. (Bear and the fox bet on pork and a bee's nest.)
Johnson. Book of fairy-tale bears. (Grandsire bear and Reynard the fox.)
Patten. Junior classics. v. 1. (Bear and the fox.)
Wiggin and Smith. Tales of laughter. (Pork and honey.)
Bear and the little old woman. Bailey. Once upon a time animal stories. (Bear who lost his supper.)
Bailey. Stories children need. (Bear who lost his supper.)
Houghton. Russian grandmother's wonder tales. (Disappointed bear.)
Johnson. Book of fairy-tale bears.
Wiggin and Smith. Tales of laughter. (Disappointed bear.)
Bear and the mouse. Fillmore. Mighty Mikko.
See also Lion and the mouse.
Bear and the skrattel. *See* Bear and skrattel.
Bear and the tailor. *See* Clever tailor.
Bear and the troll. *See* Bear and skrattel.
Bear and the two huntsmen. *Bowen. Second story reader. (Bearskin.)
Johnson. Book of fairy-tale bears.
Noyes. Twilight stories. (Bearskin.)
See also Travelers and the bear.
Bear and the two travelers. *See* Travelers and the bear.
Bear and the wrens. *See* Wren and the bear.
Bear as partner. Fillmore. Mighty Mikko. (Osmo's share.)
See also Bruin and Reynard partners.
Bear hunt. Johnson. Elm-tree fairy book.

Bear in a forest pitfall. *See* Father Bruin in the corner.
Bear in the forest hut. Glinski. Polish fairy tales.
Bear in the woods. *See* Travelers and the bear.
Bear man. I. Grinnell. Pawnee hero stories.
Bear man. II. Eastman. Indian legends retold.
Bear says, North. Fillmore. Mighty Mikko.
Bear story. I. Johnson. Book of fairy-tale bears.
Johnson. Oak-tree fairy book.
Bear story. II. Coolidge. New Year's bargain.
Bear that played at soldiers. *See* What the moon saw: 31st evening.
Bear, the boar, and the fox. Houghton. Russian grandmother's wonder tales.
See also Bruin and Reynard partners.
Bear, the dog and the cat. Magnus. Russian folk-tales.
Bear, the eagle and the fish. Baudis. Czech folk tales.
Bear, the monkey and the pig (poem). Wiggin and Smith. Talking beasts.
Bear, the moose and the walrus. Roberts. Flying plover.
Bear who lost his supper. *See* Bear and the little old woman.
Bear who played soldier. *See* What the moon saw: 31st evening.
Bear who was an enchanted king. *See* King Valemon, the white bear.
Bearman. *See* Bear man.
Bears. *See* Old man and the bear magicians.
Bears and the magician. Johnson. Book of fairy-tale bears.
See also Manabozho and the lake magicians; Manabozho and the wolf pack.
Bear's bad bargain. Baldwin. Another fairy reader. (Pears and the pudding.)
Johnson. Book of fairy-tale bears.
Patten. Junior classics. v. 1.
Steel. Tales of the Punjab
Bear's daughter. Brown. Kisington town.
Bear's short tail. *See* Why the bear has a stumpy tail.
Bearskin. I. Grimm. Household tales (Everyman's ed.).
Bearskin. II. Pyle. Wonder clock.
Bearskin. III. *See* Bear and the two huntsmen.
Beast slayer. Eells. Tales of giants from Brazil.
Beato Torello da Poppi, Life of the. Mabie. Legends every child should know.
Beau Disconus. *See* Fair unknown.
Beaumains, the knight of the kitchen. *See* Sir Gareth.
Beautiful blanket. *See* Raven's dancing blanket.
Beautiful bride. I. *See* Maiden with the wooden helmet.
Beautiful bride. II. Cornyn. When the camp fire burns. (Six-in-one.)
Partridge. Glooscap the great chief.
See also How six men travelled through the wide world.
Beautiful dancer of Yedo. James. Green willow.

Beautiful helwa maiden. Kunos. Forty-four Turkish fairy tales.
Beautiful herd-girl. Thorpe. Yule-tide stories.
Beautiful land of flowers and trees. Storytellers' magazine. April 1917, p. 245.
Beautiful Maria di Legno. Pyle. Fairy tales from many lands.
Beautiful Melissa. Pyle. Tales of wonder and magic.
Beautiful palace east of the sun and north of the earth. Thorpe. Yule-tide stories.
See also East o' the sun and west o' the moon.
Beauty and Brownie. Babbitt. More Jataka tales.
Beauty and the beast. Adams. Folk-story and verse.
Aunt Louisa's book of fairy tales.
Baker and Carpenter. Language readers. 3d year.
Bates. Once upon a time.
Bay. Danish fairy and folk tales. (Beauty and the horse.)
Bourhill and Drake. Fairy tales from South Africa.
Boys' and girls' fairy stories.
Chisholm. In fairyland.
Coussens. Child's book of stories.
Douglas. Favourite French fairy tales.
Favorite fairy tales.
Forty famous fairy tales.
Harris. Favorites from fairyland.
Howard. Dick Whittington and other stories.
Jacobs. Europa's fairy book.
Jerrold. Big book of fairy tales.
Johnson. Oak-tree fairy book.
*Klingensmith. Just stories.
Lang. Beauty and the beast, and other stories.
Lang. Blue fairy book.
Lang. History of Jack the giant killer, and other stories.
Lansing. Fairy tales. v. 1.
Mabie. Fairy tales every child should know.
Mabie. Heroes and fairies.
Mother Goose rhymes, jingles and fairy tales (Altemus ed.).
Mulock. Fairy book.
Nursery tales.
Patten. Junior classics. v. 1.
Perkins. Twenty best fairy tales.
Perrault. Old-time stories.
Perrault. Tales of passed times.
Pyle. Mother's nursery tales.
Quiller-Couch. Sleeping beauty.
Scudder. Book of folk stories.
Scudder. Children's book.
Scudder. Fables and folk stories.
Success library. v. 3.
Tappan. Folk stories and fables.
Tweed. Fairy tales everyone should know.
Valentine. Old, old fairy tales (Warne ed.).

Beauty and the beast—*continued.*
Van Sickle and Seegmiller. Riverside readers. v. 3.
Welsh. Fairy tales children love.
Winnington. Outlook fairy book.
See also Chinese beauty and the beast; Lily and the bear; Three roses.
Beauty and the horns. Fillmore. Laughing prince.
See also Little soldier; Nose tree.
Beauty and the horse. *See* Beauty and the beast.
Beauty of form and beauty of mind. Andersen. Fairy tales (Paull tr.).
Andersen. Stories and tales. (Charming.)
Beauty of the lily. Olcott. Wonder garden.
Beaver and Porcupine. Allen. Indian fairy tales.
Eastman. Indian legends retold.
Judson. Myths and legends of Alaska.
Lang. Strange story book.
Beaver crest, Origin of. Judson. Myths and legends of Alaska.
Beaver stick. Grinnell. Punishment of the stingy.
Pyle. Tales of wonder and magic.
Beaver story. Bakewell. True fairy stories.
Beaver's lodge. Coe and Christie. Story hour readers. Book 3
"Becos! becos! becos!" Baldwin. Fifty famous people.
Bedr-Basim and Jawharah, the daughter of the king of the sea, Story of. *See* Gulnare of the sea, Story of.
Bee and the beetle. Bryce. Fables from afar.
Bee and the cuckoo. Æsop. Fables (Burt ed.).
(poem). Wiggin and Smith. Talking beasts.
Bee and the fly. Æsop. Fables (Burt ed.).
Bee and the orange tree. Aulnoy. Fairy tales.
Bee and the spider. Æsop. Fables (Burt ed.).
Bee-man of Arcadia. Bailey. Wonder stories.
Bee-man of Orn. Stockton. Bee-man of Orn.
Stockton. Fanciful tales.
Stockton. Queen's museum.
Bee, the harp, the mouse, and the bum-clock. MacManus. Donegal fairy stories.
Pyle. Fairy tales from many lands. (Three cows.)
Skinner. Merry tales. (How Timothy won the princess.)
Wiggin and Smith. Fairy ring.
Beer and Bread. Magnus. Russian folk-tales.
Bees. Bryce. Fables from afar.
Bees and the bears. Johnson. Book of fairy-tale bears.
Bees and the flies, Story of the. Holbrook. Book of nature myths.
Bees and the sugar. *Bryant. New stories to tell to children.
Bees, the drones, and the wasp. Æsop. Fables (Black ed.).
Æsop. Fables (Burt ed.).
Bryce. That's why stories. (Drones and the workers.)

Beethoven's Moonlight Sonata. *See* Moonlight Sonata.
Beetle. *See* Beetle who went on his travels.
Beetle who went on his travels. Andersen. Fairy tales (Paull tr.).
Andersen. Fairy tales (Turpin. Beetle.)
Andersen. Stories (Riverside ed. Beetle.)
Andersen. Wonder stories. (Beetle.)
Nordau. Dwarf's spectacles. (Golden beetle that went on his travels.)
Beg and the fox. Houghton. Russian grandmother's wonder tales.
Johnson. Book of fairy-tale foxes. (Fox and his friends.)
Stanley. Animal folk tales. (Faithful friends.)
See also Fox and the king's son.
Beggar and his dog. Æsop. Fables (Burt ed.).
Beggar and the princess. Johnson. Oak-tree fairy book.
Beggar at the wedding. Friedlander. Jewish fairy tales.
Beggar king. Landa. Aunt Naomi's Jewish fairy tales and legends.
See also Robert of Sicily.
Beggar princess. Brady. Green forest fairy tales.
Beggar's Christmas feast. Meigs. Kingdom of the winding road.
Beggar's curse. Guerber. Legends of the Rhine.
See also Woman with three hundred and sixty-six children.
Beggar's daughter of Bethnal Green. Greenwood. Stories from famous ballads. (Beggar's daughter of Bednall Green.)
Lansing. Dramatic readings.
Macleod. Book of ballad stories.
Beginning (The). *See* Creation of the world (Norse).
Beginning of birds. *See* How the birds came.
Beginning of medicine. *See* Beloved warrior.
Beginning of poetry. *See* Odin and the mead.
Beginning of the armadillos. Kipling. Just so stories.
See also Three tails.
Beginning of things. I. *See* Creation of the world (Norse).
Beginning of things. II. Nixon-Roulet. Indian folk tales.
Beheaded ten. *See* Barber.
Beleaguered city. Mabie. Legends every child should know.
Belgian bunny. *See* Moon's message.
Believing husbands. Lang. Lilac fairy book.
Lang. Magic book.
See also Three sillies.
Believing voyage. *See* Davy and the goblin.
Bell. I. Andersen. Fairy tales (Lucas tr.).
Andersen. Fairy tales (Paull tr.).
Andersen. Wonder stories.
Scudder. Children's book.
Bell. II. Bakewell. True fairy stories.
Bell-deep. Andersen. Fairy tales (Paull tr.).
Bell of Atri. Bailey. Stories children need.

Bell of Atri—*continued.*
Baldwin. Fifty famous stories.
*Bowen. Second story reader. (King's bell.)
*Burchill. Progressive road to reading. Book 3.
Crommelin. Famous legends.
*Dillingham and Emerson. Tell it again stories.
Dyer and Brady. Merrill readers. 3d reader.
*Elson and Runkel. Elson readers. Book 2.
Gask. Folk tales from many lands.
Guerber. Legends of the Rhine. (Dumb plaintiff.)
Sly. World stories retold. (Bell of justice.)
Stebbins. Sunken city.
Storytellers' magazine. March 1915, p. 94.
Noyes. Twilight stories.
Bell of Dojoji. Griffis. Japanese fairy tales. (Power of love. Adapted.)
James. Green willow.
Bell of justice. I. Bryce. That's why stories. (Stone of gratitude.)
(play). Lansing. Quaint stories. (Stone of gratitude.)
Scudder. Book of legends.
See also Bell of Atri.
Bell of justice. II. *See* Bell of Atri.
Bella del Mondo. Macdonell. Italian fairy tales.
Belle-Belle; or, The Chevalier Fortuné. Aulnoy. Fairy tales.
Valentine. Old, old fairy tales. (Fortunio.)
Belle dame sans merci (poem). Rhys. Fairy gold.
Bellerophon. *See* Pegasus.
Belling the cat. Æsop. Fables (Black ed. Mice in council.)
Æsop. Fables (Burt ed. Mice in council.)
Æsop. Fables (Jacobs).
Æsop. Fables (Stickney. Mice in council.)
(poem). Æsop. Fables (Stickney. Supplement. Council held by rats.)
*Alderman. Classics old and new. 1st reader. (Mice and the cat.)
Arnold and Gilbert. Stepping stones to literature. v. 2. (Mice in council.)
Baldwin. Fairy tales and fables. (Mice and the cat.)
Baldwin. Fifty famous people. (*In* Clever slave.)
*Bowen. Second story reader. (Rats and the cat.)
*Elson and Runkel. Elson readers. Book 1. (Fine plan.)
Hall and Gilman. Story land. 2d reader. (Who will bell the cat?)
(play). Lansing. Quaint old stories.
My Bookhouse. v. 1.
Patten. Junior classics. v. 1.
Scudder. Children's book.
Scudder. Fables and folk stories.
*Spaulding and Bryce. Aldine readers. 2d reader.
Tappan. Folk stories and fables.
Wiggin and Smith. Talking beasts.

Belling the cat—*continued.*
Wiggin and Smith. Tales of laughter.
See also Rat meetings.
Bell's hollow. Andersen. Wonder stories.
Bells of the Solomon's seal. Seton. Woodland tales.
Belly and the members. Æsop. Fables (Burt ed.).
Æsop. Fables (Jacobs).
Patten. Junior classics. v. 1.
Scudder. Children's book.
Beloved of the sun.
Eastman. Wigwam evenings.
Beloved warrior. Donaldson. Little papoose listens.
Tanner. Legends from the red man's forest. (Beginning of medicine.)
Ben Flicker's mistake. *Bryant. New stories to tell to children.
Bend the bough in time. *See* Most obedient wife.
Bended rocks. Cather. Educating by story telling. (God of the thundering water.)
Compton. American Indian fairy tales.
Judd. Wigwam stories. (Legend of Niagara Falls.)
Tanner. Legends from the red man's forest. (Legend of the Horse Shoe Falls.)
Beneficent frog. *See* Benevolent frog.
Benevolent frog. Aulnoy. Fairy tales. (Beneficent frog.)
*Aulnoy. Children's fairyland. (Hood of roses.)
Jerrold. Reign of King Oberon.
Lang. Blue parrot. (Frog and the lion fairy.)
Lang. Orange fairy book. (Frog and the lion fairy.)
Perrault. Old-time stories. (Friendly frog.)
Perrault. Tales of passed times.
Valentine. Old, old fairy tales.
Wiggin and Smith. Magic casements.
Benevolent goblin. *See* Fairy horn.
Benibaire. Caballero. Spanish fairy tales.
Benjy in Beastland. *Klingensmith. Just stories.
Wiggin and Smith. Story hour.
Benkéi and the bell. Griffis. Japanese fairy tales.
Bennie's sunshine. *See* Grandmother's sunshine.
Bensurdatu. Lang. Grey fairy book.
Lang. Trusty John and other stories.
Beowulf. Baker and Carpenter. Language readers. 5th year. (Beowulf and the dragon.)
Bryant. Treasury of hero tales. (Beowulf and Grendel.)
Church. Heroes of chivalry and romance.
Guerber. Legends of the middle ages.
Holbrook. Northland heroes.
Mabie. Legends every child should know.
My Bookhouse. v. 5. (How Beowulf delivered Heorot.)
Tappan. Stories of legendary heroes.
Wilmot-Buxton. Stories of early England.
Bergamot. Bailey Seven peas in the pod.

Bertha with the big foot. *See* Queen Bertha.
Beryn. Darton. Tales of the Canterbury pilgrims. (Merchant's second tale: Beryn.)
Best defense. Guerber. Legends of the Rhine.
Best fairy of all. Bigham. Overheard in fairyland.
Best of the bargain. Olcott and Pendleton. Jolly book.
Best that life has to give. Pyle. Wonder clock.
Best wish. I. Dasent. Norse fairy tales.
Dasent. Popular tales from the Norse.
Thorpe. Yule-tide stories. (There is no fear for those with whom all women are in love.)
Best wish. II. Fillmore. Laughing prince.
Beswarragal. Gregory. Kiltartan wonder book.
Beth Gellert. Forty famous fairy tales.
Jacobs. Celtic fairy tales.
Scudder. Book of legends. (Dog Gellert.)
(poem). Scudder. Children's book. (Llewellyn and his dog.)
(poem). Tappan. Old fashioned stories. (Llewellyn and his dog.)
Thomas. Welsh fairy book. (Martyred hound.)
See also King and his hawk.
Bethlehem's children. Lagerlöf. Christ legends.
Betrothal gifts. Fillmore. Czechoslovak fairy tales.
See also Three feathers.
"Better than that!" Gask. Folk tales from many lands.
Betty Chidley, the witch. Hartland. English folk and fairy tales.
Bevis. *See* Sir Bevis.
Beware of bad company. Rouse. Talking thrush and other tales from India.
Bewitched bottles. *See* Magic bottles.
Bewitched butter. I. Yeats. Irish fairy and folk tales.
Bewitched butter. II. Yeats. Irish fairy and folk tales.
Bewitched donkey. Keyes. Stories and story-telling.
Bewitched huntsman; or, Three ivory bobbins. Harris. Little Mr. Thimblefinger.
Bewitched lady. Guerber. Legends of the Rhine.
Bewitched mine. Guerber. Legends of the Rhine.
Beyond the fire island. Judd. Classic myths.
Biancabella. Macdonell. Italian fairy book.
Bibi, Baba and Bobo. Macé. Home fairy tales.
Big bear. Donaldson. Little papoose listens.
Big Bird Dan. Dasent. Popular tales from the Norse.
Dasent. Norse fairy tales.
Big brother's valentine. Wickes. Happy holidays.
Big Eye Buzzard. Cocke. Bypaths in Dixie.
Big Ferré. Evans. Old time tales.
Big frog and the little frogs. Chandler. In the reign of coyote.
Big Klaus and Little Klaus. *See* Little Claus and Big Claus.
Big Peter and Little Peter. *See* Little Claus and Big Claus.

Big spider and the little spider. Wiltse. Folklore stories.
Big quar'l. Young. Plantation bird legends. (De big quar'l.)
See also One's own children are always the prettiest.
Bikku Matti. Hodgkins. Atlantic treasury of childhood stories. (Pikku Matti.)
My Bookhouse. v. 2.
Thorne-Thomsen. Birch and the star.
Billy B——'s adventure. Hartland. English folk and fairy tales.
Billy Beg and the bull. Bryant. How to tell stories.
Bryant. Best stories to tell to children. (Billy Beg and his bull.)
*Klingensmith. Just stories. (Billy Beg and his bull. Adapted.)
MacManus. In chimney corners.
Wiggin and Smith. Tales of wonder.
Billy Bent and the echo people. Linderman. Indian Old-man stories.
Billy Binks. *Spaulding and Bryce. Aldine readers. 2d reader.
Billy Coon braves the fire. Bailey. Friendly tales.
Billy goat and the king. Lang. Olive fairy book.
Billy Goat and the wolf. *Coe and Christie. Story hour readers. Book I.
See also Wolf and the kid. II.
Billy goats gruff. *See* Three billy goats gruff.
Billy's wildcat. Bailey. Friendly tales.
Bimini and the fountain of youth. Higginson. Tales of the enchanted islands of the Atlantic.
Binding of Fenris. *See* Binding of the Fenris wolf.
Binding of the Fenris wolf. Arnold and Gilbert. Stepping stones to literature. v. 5. (Loki and his children.)
Baker and Carpenter. Language readers. 5th year. (Binding of Fenris.)
Bradish. Old Norse stories. (Fenris wolf.)
Brown. In the days of giants. (Loki's children.)
*Burchill. Progressive road to reading. Book 3. (Chaining of the wolf.)
Edmison. Stories from the Norseland. (How the Fenris wolf was tied.)
Foster and Cummings. Asgard stories. (Tyr and the wolf.)
Guerber. Myths of northern lands. (*In* Tyr.)
Keary. Heroes of Asgard. (Binding of Fenris.)
Klingensmith. Old Norse wonder tales. (Fenris-wolf.)
Litchfield. Nine worlds. (Binding of the wolf.)
Mabie. Norse stories. (Binding of the wolf.)
Patten. Junior classics. v. 2. (How the Fenris wolf was chained.)
Pratt. Legends of Norseland. (Loki's wolf; The Fenris wolf.)

Binding of the Fenris wolf—*continued.*
Tappan. Myths from many lands. (How the wolf Fenris was chained.)
Wickes. Beyond the rainbow bridge.
Wilmot-Buxton. Stories of Norse heroes. (How the Fenris wolf was chained.)
Binding of the wolf. *See* Binding of the Fenris wolf.
Binnorie. Jacobs. English fairy tales.
Richards. Little Master. (Bonny mill dams of Binnorie.)
See also Singing bone.
Bird. Farmer. Nature myths.
Bird and the bee. *Bowen. Second story reader.
Bird-boy. Beston. Firelight fairy book.
Bird cage maker. Noyes. Twilight stories. (Blue bird. Adapted.)
Silver fairy book.
Wiggin and Smith. Fairy ring.
Bird catcher and the thrush. Success library. v. 3.
Bird chief. Judson. Myths and legends of the Pacific Northwest.
Judson. Old Crow and his friends.
Bird Dauntless. Asbjornsen. Fairy tales from the far north.
Bird Day. *See* Broken wing; Magpie's nest; Scare crow.
Bird Grip. Lang. Pink fairy book.
Lang. Satin surgeon.
Success library. v. 3.
Bird in the linden tree. Pyle. Pepper and salt.
Bird lover. Patten. Junior classics. v. 2.
Schoolcraft. Indian fairy book.
Bird of paradise. I. My Bookhouse. v. 2.
Bird of paradise. II. *See* Monk and the bird's song.
Bird of popular song. Andersen. Stories and tales (Author's ed.).
Bird of prey. Messer. Next time stories.
Bird of sorrow. Kunos. Forty-four Turkish fairy tales.
Bird of truth. Baldwin. Another fairy reader.
Caballero. Spanish fairy tales.
Lang. Fairy nurse.
Lang. Orange fairy book.
Wiggin and Smith. Tales of wonder.
See also Three sisters. I.
Bird songs. Young. Plantation bird legends.
Bird, the fox and the dog. Houghton. Russian grandmother's wonder tales.
Johnson. Book of fairy-tale foxes. (Reynard and the little birds.)
Bird wife. Bayliss. Treasury of Eskimo tales.
Bird which laid diamonds. Eells. Tales of enchantment from Spain.
Bird with breast of fire. *See* Why the robin has a red breast. IV.
Bird with nine heads. Martens. Chinese fairy book.

Bird with the golden gizzard. Fillmore. Czechoslovak fairy tales.
Bird with the sweet wing song. *See* Humming bird's colors.
Bird wounded by an arrow. *See* Eagle and the arrow.
Birdhouse. Potter. Pinafore pocket story book.
Birdie and her friend. *See* Fundevogel.
Birdie and Lena. See Fundevogel.
Birds. I. Burlingame. Grateful elephant.
Birds. II. *See* Christ-child and the clay birds.
Birds and the lime. Tappan. Folk stories and fables.
Birds and the monkeys. Wiggin and Smith. Talking beasts.
Birds and their nests. Ketchum and Jorgensen. Kindergarten gems.
See also Magpie's nest. II.
Birds' ball game. Judson. Old Crow and his friends. (Ball game.)
Olcott. Red Indian fairy book.
Stanley. Animal folk tales. (Animals' ball game.)
Birds, beasts and bat. *See* Bat, birds and beasts.
Birds' buildings. *See* Magpie's nest. I.
Birds' Christmas. Dickinson and Skinner. Children's book of Christmas stories.
Poulsson. In the child's world.
Birds go to war. Storytellers' magazine Oct. 1917, p. 399.
Birds of Killingworth. * Dillingham and Emerson. Tell it again stories.
Birds, the beasts and the bat. *See* Bat, birds and beasts.
Birds who befriended a king. Armfield. Wonder tales of the world.
Birds with arrow feathers. Judd. Classic myths.
Birth of the arbutus. *See* Old Winter Man and the Spring. II.
Birth of the violet. Skinner. Emerald story book.
Birthday of the Infanta. Wilde. Fairy tales.
Birthday present. Lindsay. More mother stories.
Birthdays. Grierson. Scottish fairy book.
Bisclaveret. Harrison. Old-fashioned fairy book.
Bishop of Bingen. *See* Mouse tower.
Bishop of Börglum and his kindred. Andersen. Stories and tales (Author's ed.).
Bishop Troilus (poem). Alexander. Hidden servants.
Bishop's ghost. Hartland. English folk and fairy tales.
Bishop's treachery. Guerber. Legends of the Rhine.
Bishop's valentine. Wickes. Happy holidays.
Bit of candy. Sologub. Sweet-scented name.
Biter bit. Lang. Green fairy book.
Lang. Forty thieves and other stories.
Bittern and the hoopoe. Grimm. Fairy tales (Paull tr.).
Black Agnace of Dunbar. Grierson. Children's tales from Scottish ballads.
Black Agnes. Johonnot. Stories of heroic deeds.

Black arts. Martens. Chinese fairy book.
Black bowl. *See* Maiden with the wooden helmet.
Black box and the red. *See* Black box and the red box.
Black box and the red box. Tappan. Golden goose. (Black box and the red box.)
See also Mother Holle.
Black brothers. *See* King of the Golden River.
Black, Brown and Gray. Curtin. Myths and folklore of Ireland.
See also Finn MacCool.
Black bull of Norroway. Bone. Children's stories.
Grierson. Scottish fairy book.
Jacobs. More English fairy tales.
Lang. Blue fairy book.
Rhys. Fairy gold.
See also Red bull of Norroway.
Black bull of the Castle of Blood. MacManus. In chimney corners.
See also Blue Beard.
Black cat. I. English. Fairy stories and wonder tales.
Black cat. II. Johnson. Oak-tree fairy book. (Tale of a black cat.)
My Bookhouse. v. 1. (Tale of a black cat.)
Black cat. III. Faulkner. Story lady's book.
Black cat's journey. Storytellers' magazine. March 1917, p. 131.
Black Douglas. Baldwin. Fifty famous stories.
Black dragon and the red dragon. Kunos. Forty-four Turkish fairy tales.
Black flies, Origin of. Partridge. Glooscap the great chief. (Badger and the rock magician.)
Black horse. Jacobs. More Celtic fairy tales.
Wiggin and Smith. Tales of wonder.
Yeats. Irish fairy and folk tales.
Black lamb. Yeats. Irish fairy and folk tales.
Black Margaret. Thorpe. Yule-tide stories.
Black Prince. Evans. Old time tales. (Edward, the Black Prince.)
Blaisdell. English history story book. (Edward the Black Prince.)
Black robin. Thomas. Welsh fairy book.
Black Thief and King Conab's three horses. *See* Black Thief and Knight of the Glen.
Black Thief and Knight of the Glen. Curtin. Hero tales from Ireland. (Black Thief and King Conab's three horses.)
Lang. Red fairy book.
Black thing. *See* Tom Tit Tot.
Black tower; or, The silver house. Storytellers' magazine. Oct. 1913, p. 210.
Blackamoor. Æsop. Fables (Black ed.).
Æsop. Fables (Burt ed.).

Blackamoor—*continued.*
Wiggin and Smith. Talking beasts.
Blackbird and the doves. Hall and Gilman. Story land. 2d reader.
See also Two foolish birds.
Blackbird and the swallows. Pitrè. Swallow book.
Blackey moves her home. Faulkner. Story lady's book.
Blackie and Madison Square. Bigham. Merry animal tales.
Blackie and Mr. Bullfrog. Bigham. Merry animal tales.
See also Mouse, the frog and the hawk.
Blackie in the trap. Bigham. Merry animal tales.
Blackie's country home. Bigham. Merry animal tales.
Blackie's egg. Bigham. Merry animal tales.
See also Rats, the fox and the egg.
Blackie's fright. Bigham. Merry animal tales.
See also Mouse, cat and cock.
Blackie's picnic. Bigham. Merry animal tales.
Klingensmith. Just stories.
See also Mouse and the weasel.
Blackskin. Lang. Strange story book.
Blacksmith's sons (poem). Fairy stories from St. Nicholas.
Blacksmith's stool. Fillmore. Shoemaker's apron.
See also Smith and the devil.
Blacksmith's wife of Yarrowfoot. Douglas. Scottish fairy tales.
See also Witch and the horseshoes.
Blanch and Rosalinda. *See* Blanche and Rosalind.
Blanche and Rosalind. Jerrold. Big book of fairy tales. (Blanch and Rosalinda.)
Olcott. Book of elves and fairies. (Blanche and Rose.)
Valentine. Old, old fairy tales. (Blanch and Rosalinda.)
Welsh. Fairy tales children love. (Blanch and Rosalinda.)
Wiggin and Smith. Fairy ring. (Blanche and Vermilion.)
Blanche and Rose. *See* Blanche and Rosalind.
Blanche and Vermilion *See* Blanche and Rosalind.
Blankets, Indian. Judson. Myths and legends of Alaska. (Origin of the Chilkat blanket.)
Bleacher, the crane and the hawk. Bidpai. Tortoise and the geese.
Bleeding hearts, Legend of the. *See* Enchanted necklace.
Blind Baba-Abdalla. *See* Baba Abdalla.
Blind Bartimaeus. Cross and Statler. Story-telling.
Storytellers' magazine. Dec. 1913, p. 313.
Blind boy's fall. Fielde. Chinese fairy tales.
Hall and Gilman. Story land. 2d reader. (Story of a Japanese boy.)
Blind child. Richards. Silver crown.
Blind doe. Quiroga. South American jungle tales.
Blind Hercules (poem). Æsop. Fables (Burt ed.).
Blind Major. *Bryant. New stories to tell to children.
Blind man and the lame man. Æsop. Fables (Burt ed.).
Æsop. Fables (Stickney).

Blind man and the lame man—*continued.*
Arnold and Gilbert. Stepping stones to literature. v. 2.
(play). Cabot. Ethics for children. (Lame man and the blind man.)
*Haaren. Songs and stories. 2d reader.
Scudder. Book of legends. (How the lame man and the blind man helped each other.)
Blind man and the snake. Bidpai. Tortoise and the geese.
Blind man and whelp. Æsop. Fables (Stickney).
Blind man, the deaf man and the donkey. Frere. Old Deccan days.
Wiggin and Smith. Tales of laughter.
Blind men and the elephant (poem). Baker and Carpenter. Language readers. 5th year.
Baldwin. Fifty famous stories.
Burlingame. Grateful elephant.
(poem). Hartwell. Story hour readings. 5th year.
Sly. World stories retold.
See also Red-bud tree; Two sides to every question.
Blind mole. *See* Sun a prisoner. I.
Blind mother. Richards. Golden windows.
Blind sheep. Æsop. Fables (Burt ed.).
Blind singer. *See* Saint Hervé.
Blinded giant. Hartland. English folk and fairy tales.
Jacobs. More English fairy tales.
Blindness of Pi-wap-ok. Grinnell. Punishment of the stingy.
Blockhead Hans. *See* Hans Clodhopper.
Blockheads. Marshall. Fairy tales of all nations.
B'Loggerhead and B'Conch. *See* Brother Loggerhead and Brother Conch.
Blondina; or, The turkey-queen. Harrison. Old-fashioned fairy book.
See also Caliph Stork.
Blondine, Bonne-biche and Beau-minon. Segur. French fairy tales.
Segur. Old French fairy tales.
Blue beard. *See* Bluebeard.
Blue belt. Dasent. Popular tales from the Norse.
Dasent. Norse fairy tales.
Pyle. Fairy tales from far and near.
Blue bird. I. Aulnoy. Fairy tales.
Lang. Green fairy book.
Lang. Magician's gifts.
Mulock. Fairy book.
Perkins. Twenty best fairy tales.
Valentine. Old, old fairy tales (Warne ed.).
Blue bird. II. Bailey. Stories children need.
Storytellers' magazine. March 1915, p. 83.
Blue bird. III. *See* Bird-cage maker.
Blue calico witch. Potter. Pinafore pocket story book.
Blue cat. Jokai and others. Golden fairy book.

Blue flower. I. *See* How flax was given to men.
Blue flower. II. Patterson. Enchanted bird.
Blue glove, Tale of. Sholl. Faery tales of Weir.
Blue heron and the wolf. Judd. Wigwam stories.
Blue jackal. Coussens. Jade story book. (Dyed jackal.)
Stanley. Animal folk tales. (Jackal king.)
Wiggin and Smith. Talking beasts.
Blue jay. Young. Algonquin Indian tales. (Legend of the whiskey jack.)
Blue Jay, the imitator. Grinnell. Punishment of the stingy.
See also How Master Rabbit went fishing; "I know what I have learned"; Rabbit and the woodpecker girls.
Blue Jay visits the ghosts. Grinnell. Punishment of the stingy.
Judson. Myths and legends of the Pacific Northwest. (Chinook ghosts.)
See also Ghost land; In the land of souls.
Blue jay's story. Stewart. Once upon a time.
Blue lake. Segovia. Spanish fairy book.
Blue light. Grimm. Household tales (Everyman's ed.).
Grimm. Fairy tales (Lucas tr.; Paull tr.).
Norton. Heart of oak books. v. 3.
Welsh. Fairy tales children love.
See also Tinder box.
Blue lily. Caballero. Spanish fairy tales.
See also Singing bone.
Blue lotus and red lotus. Bradley-Birt. Bengal fairy tales.
Blue Mountains. Lang. Blue parrot and other stories.
Lang. Yellow fairy book.
Blue parrot. Lang. Blue parrot and other stories.
Lang. Olive fairy book.
Blue riband. Dasent. Popular tales from the Norse.
Thorpe. Yule-tide stories.
Blue robin. Bailey. For the story teller.
Blue rose. Baring. Blue rose fairy book.
Shedlock. Art of the storyteller.
Bluebeard. Chisholm. In fairyland.
Coussens. Child's book of stories.
Forty famous fairy tales.
Jerrold. Big book of fairy tales.
Johnson. Fir-tree fairy book.
Lang. Blue fairy book.
*Lang. Princess on the glass hill.
Lansing. Fairy tales. v. 2.
Mabie. Fairy tales every child should know.
Mabie. Heroes and fairies.
Mother Goose rhymes, jingles and fairy tales (Altemus ed.).
Nursery tales.
Patten. Junior classics. v. 1.
Perrault. Fairy tales.
Perrault. Old-time stories. (Blue Beard.)

Bluebeard—*continued.*
Perrault. Tales of Mother Goose.
Perrault. Tales of passed times.
Quiller-Couch. Fairy tales far and near.
Quiller-Couch. Sleeping beauty.
Scudder. Children's book.
Tappan. Folk stories and fables.
Tweed. Fairy tales everyone should know.
Valentine. Old, old fairy tales.
Welsh. Stories children love.
See also Black bull of the Castle of Blood; Evil one who married two sisters; Pueblo Bluebeard; Wine-crust.
Bluebell. McFee. Treasury of flower stories.
Bluebells. *See* Little nymph who rang the bells.
Bluebird. I. *See* Blue bird.
Bluebird. II. *See* How the bluebird got its color.
Bluebird and coyote. Eastman. Indian legends retold.
Judson. Old Crow stories. (When coyote was blue.)
Olcott. Red Indian fairy book. (Coyote the proud.)
Bluebird, Origin of. *See* How the bluebird came.
Bluebottle who went courting. Wiggin and Smith. Tales of laughter.
Bluejay. *See* Blue jay.
Bleuette's butterfly. Olcott. Whirling king.
Blunder. Keyes. Stories and story-telling.
My Bookhouse. v. 2.
O'Grady and Throop. Teachers' story teller's book.
Whittier. Child life in prose.
See also Pretending woodchuck.
Blunderhead. Underhill. Dwarfs' tailor and other stories.
Blush-rose and the sun. Olcott. Wonder garden.
Boar and lion. Burlingame. Grateful elephant.
Boar and the ass. Æsop. Fables (Black ed.).
Æsop. Fables (Burt ed.).
Boar challenges an ass. Æsop. Fables (Black ed.).
Æsop. Fables (Burt ed.).
Boaster. Noyes. Twilight stories.
Boastful bamboo. Lyman. Story telling.
Nixon-Roulet. Japanese folk stories and fairy tales.
Boastful field wren. Young. Behind the dark pines.
Boasting traveler. Æsop. Fables (Black ed.).
Æsop. Fables (Burt ed.).
Wiggin and Smith. Talking beasts.
Boasting wolf. *See* Wolf and the man.
Bobby and the keyhole. Eggleston. Queer stories for boys and girls.
Bobby Balloon-foot. Potter. Pinafore pocket story book.
Bobby Bluebird's adventure. * Bryant. New stories to tell to children.
Bobby's dream. Skinner. A very little child's book of stories.
Bobino. Lang. Grey fairy book.

Bobino—*continued.*
Lang. Trusty John and other stories.
Bobolink and the owl. Eggleston. Queer stories for boys and girls.
Body. Richards. Silver crown.
Body that deserted the stomach. Davis and Chow-Leung. Chinese fables and folk stories.
Boggart. Hartland. English folk and fairy tales.
Johnson. Elm-tree fairy book. (Farmer and the boggart.)
Olcott. Book of elves and fairies.
Rhys. Fairy gold.
Tyler. Twenty-four unusual stories.
See also Farmer Grigg's boggart; Goblin workman.
Bohemian girl. McSpadden. Stories from great operas.
Boiled eggs. Bay. Danish fairy and folk tales.
Bokwewa, the humpback. Schoolcraft. Indian fairy book.
Bold bad bicycle. Aspinwall. Short stories for short people.
Boliawns. *See* Field of Boliauns.
Bomere pool. Hartland. English folk and fairy tales.
Bona and Nello, Adventures of. Macdonell. Italian fairy book.
Bond of friendship. Andersen. Fairy tales (Paull tr.).
Bones of Djuling. Coe and Christie. Story hour readers. Book 3. (Fairy tree.)
Lang. Lilac fairy book.
Lang. White doe.
Bonfire in the sea. Coe and Christie. Story hour readers. Book 3.
Bonny Earl of Murray (poem). Lanier. Boy's Percy.
Bonny little drummer boy. Gibbon. Reign of King Cole.
Bonny milldams of Binnorie. *See* Binnorie.
Booby. Wiggin and Smith. Tales of laughter.
See also How six travelled through the world.
Booby Hans. *See* Hans Clodhopper.
Boots and his brothers. Bailey and Lewis. For the children's hour. (Peter, Paul and Espen.)
*Baldwin. Second fairy reader. (Wondering Jack.)
Coe. Second book of stories. (Wondering Jack.)
Dasent. Norse fairy tales. (Jack and his brothers.)
Dasent. Popular tales from the Norse.
Hodgkins. Atlantic treasury of childhood stories. (Peter and Paul and Espen the cinder-lad.
Laboulaye. Fairy tales. (Thumbkin.)
Laboulaye. Last fairy tales. (Poucinet.)
Lansing. Dramatic readings. (Boy who wondered.)
My Bookhouse. v. 2.
Rolfe. Fairy tales. (Poucinet.)
Storytellers' magazine. July 1914, p. 619. (Jack and his brothers.)
Sly. World stories retold.
Tappan. Folk stories and fables.
Thorne-Thomsen. East o' the sun and west o' the moon.

Boots and his brothers—*continued.*
Van Sickle and Seegmiller. Riverside readers. 2d reader.
Wiggin and Smith. Tales of wonder. (I wonder.)
Boots and his crew. *See* Ashiepattle and his goodly crew.
Boots and the beasts. Asbjörnsen. Tales from the fjeld.
Wiltse. Folk stories and proverbs.
Boots and the Princess. *See* Ashiepattle who made the princess tell the truth at last.
Boots and the troll. Dasent. Popular tales from the Norse.
Dasent. Norse fairy tales.
See also Esben and the witch.
Boots, cloak and ring. Baudis. Czech folk tales.
Boots made of buffalo leather. Grimm. Fairy tales (Wiltse). v. 2.
Boots who ate a match with the troll. *See* Ashiepattle who ate with the troll for a wager.
Boots who made the princess say, "That's a story." *See* Ashiepattle who made the princess tell the truth at last.
Bopoluchi. Steel. Tales of the Punjab.
Borrowed plumes. *See* Jay and the peacock.
Bosh-bosh oil. Aspinwall. Short stories for short people.
Bostanai. Landa. Aunt Naomi's Jewish fairy tales and legends.
Boston boys of '76. Blaisdell. Child life. 3d reader.
Bottle-hill, Legend of. Olcott. Book of elves and fairies.
Peck. Stories for good children. (Two bottles.)
See also Table, the ass and the stick.
Bottle neck. Andersen. Fairy tales (Lucas tr.).
Andersen. Fairy tales (Paull tr.).
Andersen. Stories and tales.
Bottle of brains. *See* Pottle o'brains.
Bound boy. Eggleston. Queer stories for boys and girls.
Bow. Bryce. Fables from afar.
Bow of Eurytus. *See* Arethusa.
Bowl of porridge. *See* Bruce and the bowl of porridge.
Bowmen. Smith. More mystery tales.
Box on the ear. Guerber. Legends of the Rhine.
Box with something pretty in it. Asbjörnsen. Folk and fairy tales. (Box with the funny thing in it.)
Asbjörnsen. Tales from the fjeld.
Wiggin and Smith. Tales of laughter.
See also Short story; Tail.
Box with the funny thing in it. *See* Box with something pretty in it.
Boy afraid of dark. Storytellers' magazine. June 1916, p. 355.
See also White Hawk, the lazy.
Boy and his mother. Æsop. Fables (Black ed.).
Boy and mosquito. *See* How not to hit an insect.
Boy and the blacksmith (poem). Lindsay. Joyous travelers. (Tale told by the chapman.)
See also Weland's sword.

Boy and the dragon. Macmillan. Canadian fairy tales.
Boy and the echo. Sly. World stories retold.
Boy and the elf. My Bookhouse. v. 3.
Boy and the filberts. Æsop. Fables (Burt ed.).
Æsop. Fables (Stickney).
*Blaisdell. Child life. 2d reader. (Boy and the nuts.)
Sly. World stories retold. (Boy and the nuts.)
Wiggin and Smith. Talking beasts.
Boy and the giant bird. Partridge. Story telling in home and school.
Boy and the goat. *Treadwell. Reading-literature: primer.
Boy and the mud pony. Olcott. Red Indian fairy book. (Mud pony.)
Tappan. Folk stories and fables.
Boy and the nettle. Æsop. Fables (Burt ed.).
Æsop. Fables (Stickney).
Scudder. Children's book.
Scudder. Fables and folk stories.
Boy and the nuts. *See* Boy and the filberts.
Boy and the porridge. Pitman. Chinese fairy stories.
Boy and the river. Blaisdell. Child life. 2d reader.
Boy and the robbers. *See* Little Persian.
Boy and the spirits of things. Nixon-Roulet. Japanese folk stories and fairy tales.
Boy and the violin. Eells. Tales of giants from Brazil.
Boy and the wolf. I. *See* Boy who cried "Wolf."
Boy and the wolf. II. Baldwin. Fifty famous people.
Boy and the wolves. I. Forty famous fairy tales.
* Judd. Wigwam stories. (Little wolf brother.)
Lang. Beauty and the beast, and other stories.
Lang. Yellow fairy book.
Patten. Junior classics. v. 1.
Boy and the wolves. II. Kennedy. New world fairy book. (Wolf boy.)
Boy and the wolves. I and II. *See also* Sheem the forsaken boy.
Boy bathing. Æsop. Fables (Stickney).
Boy-beautiful, the golden apples and the were-wolf. Kunos Turkish fairy tales.
Boy brought up in the woods. *See* Kintaro, the golden boy.
Boy hero. *See* Leak in the dyke.
Boy hero of Harlem. See Leak in the dyke.
Boy hunting locusts. Æsop. Fables (Burt ed.)
Boy in the jug. Olcott, Red Indian fairy book.
Boy in the land of shadows. Macmillan. Canadian fairy tales.
Boy in the moon. I. *See* Why the moon waxes and wanes.
Boy in the moon. II. Judson. Myths and legends of Alaska. (Boy in the moon—Athapascan.)
Judson. Old Crow and his friends. (Real moon.)
Olcott. Red Indian fairy book.
Boy-man. Wade. Indian fairy tales.

Boy martyr. Darton. Tales of the Canterbury pilgrims. (Prioress's tale: The boy martyr.)
Boy of perfect disposition. Davis and Chow-Leung. Chinese fables and folk stories.
Boy of the red twilight sky. Macmillan. Canadian fairy tales.
Boy Pu-nia and the king of the sharks. Colum. At the gateways of the day.
Boy stood on the burning deck. *See* Casabianca.
Boy that let the giant's child fall into the well. Thorpe. Yule-tide stories.
Boy that stole apples. *See* Boy who stole apples.
Boy that stole the giant's treasure. Dasent. Popular tales from the Norse.
Thorpe. Yule-tide stories.
Boy that the eagle stole. See Ganymede.
Boy that visited fairyland. *See* Elidore.
Boy that was named Trouble. *See* Badger in the bag.
Boy that was scaret of dying. Slosson. Story-tell Lib.
Boy who always said the wrong thing. Bosschère. Christmas tales of Flanders.
See also Stupid's cries.
Boy who became a Hsao-tsze. Davis and Chow-Leung. Chinese fables and folk stories.
Boy who became a robin. *See* How the robin came.
Boy who became chief. Nixon-Roulet. Indian folk tales.
Boy who became emperor. Pitman. Chinese fairy stories.
Boy who caught flies. Olcott. Wonder garden.
Boy who contended with the giant in eating. Thorpe. Yule-tide stories.
See also Ashiepattle who ate with the troll for a wager.
Boy who could keep a secret. Lang. Crimson fairy book.
Lang. Little Wildrose.
Boy who could not tell a lie. Nyblom. Jolly Calle.
Storytellers' magazine. May 1914, p. 545.
Boy who cried "Wolf." Æsop. Fables (Black ed. Shepherd's boy.)
Æsop. Fables (Burt ed. Shepherd boy and the wolf.)
Æsop. Fables (Jacobs. Shepherd's boy.)
Æsop. Fables (Stickney. Shepherd's boy.)
*Alderman. Classics. old and new. First reader.
Arnold. Stepping stones to literature. v. 3. (Boy and the wolf.)
Baker and Carpenter. Language reader. 3d year. (Shepherd boy and the wolf.)
*Blaisdell. Child life. 2d reader.
Bryant. Stories to tell to children.
Coe and Christie. Story hour readers. Book 3.
Coussens. Child's book of stories.
(play). Dyer and Brady. Merrill readers. 3d reader.
*Hall and Gillman. Story land. 2d reader.
My Bookhouse. v. 1.

Boy who cried "Wolf"—*continued.*
Patten. Junior classics. v. 1. (Shepherd's boy.)
Scudder. Children's book. (Shepherd boy and the wolf.)
Sly. World stories retold. (Shepherd boy and the wolf.)
Tappan. Folk stories and fables. (Shepherd boy and the wolf.)
Welsh. Stories children love. (Shepherd boy and the wolf.)
Wiggin and Smith. Talking beasts. (Boy and the wolf.)
Boy who discovered the spring. Alden. Why the chimes rang.
Bailey. Stories children need.
Skinner. Emerald story book.
Boy who drew cats. *See* Painter of cats.
Boy who found fear at last. Lang. Olive fairy book.
Boy who found the king. Alden. Boy who found the king and other stories.
Boy who found the pots of gold. Olcott. Book of elves and fairies.
Boy who had a moon on his forehead and a star on his chin. Jacobs. Indian fairy tales.
Boy who hated trees. Faulkner. Story lady's book. (Teddy's tree planting.)
Skinner. Turquoise story book.
*Sly. World stories retold.
Wickes. Happy holidays. (Little boy who hated trees.)
Boy who lived with grizzlies. Sexton. Gray wolf stories.
Boy who lost his head. English. Fairy stories and wonder tales.
Boy who loved fun. *See* Hermes and Apollo.
Boy who made friends by the way. *See* Anton's errand.
Boy who overcame the giants. Macmillan. Canadian fairy tales.
Boy who rescued his brother. Partridge. Glooscap the great chief.
Boy who saw A-ti-us. Grinnell. Pawnee hero stories.
Boy who set a snare for the sun. *See* Sun a prisoner. I.
Boy who slept. Pitman. Chinese fairy stories.
Boy who stole apples. Scudder. Children's book.
Scudder. Fables and folk stories.
Boy who teased, Story of the. Bellamy. Wonder children.
Boy who wanted more cheese. Griffis. Dutch fairy tales.
Boy who wanted the impossible. Davis and Chow-Leung. Chinese fables and folk stories.
My Bookhouse. v. 1.
Boy who wanted to marry. Singleton. Wild flower fairy book.
Boy who was called "Thick-head." Macmillan. Canadian fairy tales.
See also Rat's wedding; Travels of a fox.
Boy who was changed into a flower. *See* Hyacinthus.
Boy who was made a king. *See* King Arthur's coming.

Boy who was sacrificed. Grinnell. Pawnee hero stories.
Boy who was saved by thoughts. Macmillan. Canadian fairy tales.
Boy who went out of the world. Alden. Why the chimes rang.
Boy who went to the north wind. *See* Lad and the north wind.
Boy who went under the earth. Alden. Boy who found the king.
Boy who would not tell a lie. Davis and Chow-Leung. Chinese fables and folk stories.
Boy whose wings fell off. *See* Daedalus and Icarus.
Boy with the box. Curtiss. Christmas stories and legends.
Boyhood of Cuhulain. *See* Cuhulain, Boyhood of.
Boyhood of Finn MacCoul. *See* Finn MacCool.
Boyking islands. Henderson. Sea yarns for boys.
Boys and frogs. *See* Boys and the frogs.
Boys and the frogs. Æsop. Fables (Stickney. Boys and frogs.)
Scudder. Children's book.
Scudder. Fables and folk stories.
Sly. World stories retold.
Tappan. Folk stories and fables.
Wiggin and Smith. Talking beasts.
Boy's drive on the sun-chariot. *See* Phaeton.
Boy's visit to Santa Claus. Storytellers' magazine. Dec. 1913, p. 332.
Boys who left trouble behind. Armfield. Wonder tales.
Boys who met the trolls in Hedal woods. *See* Trolls in Hedale wood.
Boys with the golden stars. Lang. Violet fairy book.
Brabo and the giant. Griffis. Dutch fairy tales.
Bracket bull. Graves. Irish fairy book.
See also Billy Beg and his bull.
Bradamante, Adventures of. Arnold and Gilbert. Stepping stones to literature. v. 5.
Lang. Red romance book. (How Bradamante conquered the wizard; Ring of Bradamante; Fulfilling of the prophecy.)
Brahmadatta and Mallika. *See* Lesson for kings.
Brahmadatta and the prince. Burlingame. Grateful elephant.
Brahman, the tiger, and the six judges. *See* Brahmin, the tiger and the jackal.
Brahmin and his wife. Bradley-Birt. Bengal fairy tales.
Brahmin and the goat. Wiggin and Smith. Talking beasts.
Brahmin, the tiger and the jackal. *Bowen. Second story reader. (Way of the world.)
Bryant. Stories to tell to children.
(play). Doheny. Play awhile.
Frere. Old Deccan days. (Brahmin, the tiger and the six judges.)

Brahmin, the tiger and the jackal—*continued.*
Jacobs. Indian fairy tales. (Tiger, the Brahman, and the jackal.)
Lansing. Dramatic readings. (Brahman, the tiger and the six judges.)
(play). Lansing. Quaint old stories. (Brahman, the tiger and the six judges.)
Patten. Junior classics. v. 1. (Tiger, the Brahman, and the jackal.)
Steel. Tales of the Punjab. (Tiger, the Brâhman, and the jackal.)
Storytellers' magazine. Jan. 1915, p. 20. (Brahmin, the tiger and the six judges.)
Tappan. Folk stories and fables. (Brahmin, the tiger and the six judges.)
Wiggin and Smith. Fairy ring. (Brahmin, the tiger and the six judges.)
See also Reward of the world; Way of the world. I.
Brains in his toes. Baring-Gould. Crock of gold.
Bramble bushes and the lamb. Boston collection of kindergarten stories.
Bran the blessed. *See* Branwen, the daughter of Llyr.
Branwen, the daughter of Llyr. Brooke. Wonder stories from the Mabinogion.
Higginson. Tales of the enchanted islands of the Atlantic. (Bran the blessed.)
Lanier. Knightly legends of Wales.
Brave against his will. Bay. Danish fairy and folk tales.
See also Brave little tailor.
Brave bobtails. Lummis. Pueblo Indian folk stories.
Brave knight and a craven. Guerber. Legends of the Rhine.
Brave laborer. Polevoi. Russian fairy tales.
Brave little bowman. Babbitt. More Jataka tales.
Brave little mole. *See* Sun a prisoner. I.
Brave little tailor. Coe and Christie. Story hour readers. Book 3. (Magic girdle.)
Coussens. Child's book of stories.
Forty famous fairy tales.
Grimm. Fairy tales (Lucas tr. Valiant tailor.)
Grimm. Fairy tales (Paull tr.).
Grimm. Household stories (Crane tr. Gallant tailor.)
Grimm. Household tales (Burt ed.).
Grimm. Household tales. (Everyman's ed. Gallant tailor.)
Jacobs. Europa's fairy book. (Dozen at a blow.)
Lang. Blue fairy book.
Lang. Little Red Riding Hood and other stories.
Lang. Magic book.
Patten. Junior classics. v. 1.
Quiller-Couch. Fairy tales far and near. (Valiant tailor.)
Storytellers' magazine. Apr. 1915. p. 105.

Brave little tailor—*continued.*
Wiggin and Smith. Tales of laughter (Seven at a blow.)
See also Brave against his will; Giant and the tailor; Johnny Gloke; Kara Mustapha, the hero; Little weaver of Duleek gate; Valiant Vicky.
Brave little white rabbit. Donaldson. Little papoose listens.
Brave old Bruin. *See* Bruin Goodfellow.
Brave Seventee-Bai. Frere. Old Deccan days.
Brave three hundred. Baldwin. Fifty famous stories.
Haaren and Poland. Famous men of Greece. (Leonidas at Thermopylae.)
Murray. Story book treasure. (Stories of Leonidas.)
Brave tin soldier. *Andersen. Best fairy tales (Henderson tr. Constant tin soldier.)
Andersen. Fairy tales (Lucas tr. Steadfast tin soldier.)
Andersen. Fairy tales (Paull tr.).
Andersen. Fairy tales (Turpin ed. Steadfast tin soldier.)
Andersen. Fairy tales and stories (Toksvig. Steadfast tin soldier.)
Andersen. Stories (Riverside ed. Constant tin soldier.)
Andersen. Wonder stories. Constant tin soldier.)
Bailey and Lewis. For the children's hour.
Coussens. Child's book of stories.
Dyer. What-happened-then stories.
Field. Famous fairy tales. (Hardy tin soldier.)
Forty famous fairy tales. (Steadfast tin soldier.)
Jerrold. Big book of fairy tales. (Little tin soldier.)
Johnson. Elm-tree fairy book.
Lang. Blue parrot. (Steadfast tin-soldier.)
Lang. Yellow fairy book. (Steadfast tin soldier.)
Lansing. Fairy tales. v. 1. (Steadfast tin soldier.)
Norton. Heart of oak books. v. 3.
O'Grady and Throop. Teacher's story teller's book. (Constant tin soldier.)
Patten. Junior classics. v. 1. (Constant tin soldier.)
Scudder. Children's book. (Constant tin soldier.)
Singleton. Wild flower fairy book.
Tappan. Folk stories and fables. (Constant tin soldier.)
Van Sickle and Seegmiller. Riverside readers. 4th reader. (Constant tin soldier.)
Welsh. Stories children love. (Hardy tin soldier.)
Winnington. Outlook fairy book.
Bravest flower. Donahey. Tales to be told to children.
Brazen brogues; or, Too many to marry. Campbell. Beyond the border.
Douglas. Scottish fairy tales (Burt ed.).
Brazen head. *See* Friar Bacon and the brazen head.
Brazier and his dog. Æsop. Fables (Burt ed.).
Breakfast bell. Potter. Pinafore pocket story book.
Breakfast that flew away. *Grover. Folk-lore readers. v. 1.

Bregenz, Legend of (poem). Arnold and Gilbert. Stepping stones to literature. v. 5.
Baldwin. Fifty famous rides. (Maid of Bregenz.)
(poem). Haaren. Ballads and tales.
Bremen town musicians. Adams. Folk story and verse.
Allison and Perdue. Story in primary instruction. (Street musicians.)
Blaisdell. Child life. 2d reader. (Town musicians.)
*Bowen. Second story reader. (The singers.)
Burchill. Progressive road to reading. Book 2. (Robbers.)
Coe. First book of fairy stories.
Dyer. What-happened-then stories.
Gibbon. In the reign of King Cole. (Waits of Bremen.)
Grimm. Fairy tales (Lucas tr.).
Grimm. Fairy tales (Wiltse. Musicians of Bremen.) v. 1.
Grimm. Household stories (Crane tr.).
Grimm. Household tales (Burt ed. Town musicians.)
Grimm. Household tales (Everyman's ed. Traveling musicians.)
Hodgkins. Atlantic treasury of childhood stories.
Jacobs. Celtic fairy tales. (Jack and his comrades.)
Johnson. Oak-tree fairy book. (Four musicians.)
Johonnot. Grandfather's stories.
Lang. Grey fairy book. (Street musicians.)
Mulock. Fairy book.
O'Grady and Throop. Teachers' story teller's book. (Street musicians.)
Perkins. Twenty best fairy tales.
Pyle. Mother's nursery tales. (Town musicians.)
Scudder. Children's book. (Traveling musicians.)
Scudder. Fables and folk stories. (Traveling musicians.)
(play). Van Sickle and Seegmiller. Riverside readers. 2d reader. (Donkey and his company.)
Wiggin and Smith. Tales of laughter.
See also Choristers of St. Gudule; How Jack went to seek his fortune; Pet lamb.
Brer. *See* Brother.
Owing to the inconsistent use of the terms "Brer" and "Brother" in the same books, and because the same stories appear in different books under different titles, it has been decided to enter them all under "Brother."
See also entries under "Mister."
Brewery of eggshells. Jacobs. Celtic fairy tales.
Yeats. Irish fairy tales.
Success library. v. 3.
See also Changeling.
Briam the fool. *See* Briam, the king's fool.
Briam, the king's fool. Laboulaye. Fairy tales. (Story of Briam, the king's fool.)
Laboulaye. Last fairy tales. (Briam the fool.)
Brian Boru. Crommelin. Famous legends.

Brian Boru—*continued.*
Tappan. Adventures and achievements (Brian of Munster, the boy chieftain.)
Brian of Munster, the boy chieftain. *See* Brian Boru.
Briar rose. *See* Sleeping beauty. I.
Briareus. Pratt. Myths of old Greece. v. 1.
Bridal of the pigmy king. Canton. Reign of King Herla.
See also Ossian in the land of youth.
Bridal of weeping torches. *See* Orpheus and Eurydice.
Bride from the red lake. Griffis. Welsh fairy tales. (Touch of clay.)
Thomas. Welsh fairy book.
Bride of the dragon king. Pitman. Chinese fairy stories.
Bride of the wind. * Cowles. Indan nature myths. (Why the wind wails.)
Holbrook. Nature myths. (Why the face of the moon is white.)
Nixon-Roulet. Indian folk tales.
Bridegroom for Miss Mole. Griffis. Unmannerly tiger, and other Korean tales.
Griffis. Korean fairy tales.
See also Rats and their son-in-law.
Bride's venture. *See* Twelve huntsmen.
Bridge. I. *See* Endless tale. IV.
Bridge. II. Ingelow. Stories told to a child. v. 2.
Bridge of crocodiles. *See* Eighty-one brothers.
Bridge of the gods. Judson. Myths and legends of the Pacific Northwest.
Brier Rose. *See* Sleeping Beauty.
Bright-Hawk's feather. Curtin. Wonder-tales from Russia. (Feather of Bright Finist the Falcon.)
Dole. White duckling and other stories.
Polevoi. Russian fairy tales. (Little feather of Fenist the bright falcon.)
Wheeler. Russian wonder tales. (Feather of Finist the falcon.)
See also East o' the sun and west o' the moon.
Bright sun brings it to light. Grimm. Fairy tales (Paull tr.).
Brighteyes. Burchill. Progressive road to reading. Book 3.
Brighton cats. Dodge. Land of pluck.
Bringing of the light by Raven. *See* Daylight, Origin of. II.
Brittle-legs. *See* Rumpelstiltskin.
Broad man, the tall man, and the man with eyes of flame.
Chodzko. Fairy tales of the Slav.
Lang. Grey fairy book. (Long, Broad and Quickeye.)
Lang. Little King Loc. (Long, Broad and Quickeye.)
Mabie. Folk tales every child should know. (Long, Broad and Sharpsight.)
Marshall. Fairy tales of all nations. (Broadman, Longfellow and Sharpeyes.)

Broad man, the tall man, and the man with eyes of flame —*continued.*
Ortoli. Evening tales. (Enchanted princess.)
Pyle. Wonder tales retold. (Long, Broad and Sharpsight.)
Broadman, Longfellow and Sharpeyes. *See* Broad man, the tall man, and man with eyes of flame.
Broken flower pot. Cabot. Ethics for children.
Broken moon. Allen. Indian fairy tales.
Broken pot. Jacobs. Indian fairy tales.
See also Milkmaid and her pail.
Broken promise. *See* Boy and the wolves. I.
Broken vow. Guerber. Legends of the Rhine.
Broken wing. Schoolcraft. Indian fairy book. (Gray Eagle and his five brothers.)
Wilson. Nature study reader.
Brokerina, Story of. Fairy tales from Brentano.
Bronze boar. Andersen. Fairy tales (Lucas tr.).
Andersen. Fairy tales (Paull tr.).
Bronze ring. Lang. Blue fairy book.
Lang. Sleeping beauty.
Brook in the king's garden. Alden. Why the chimes rang.
Brook that helped. Bailey. Stories for Sunday telling.
Broom fairies. Gate. Broom fairies and other stories.
Brooklet's story. *See* Silly little brook.
Brother and his sisters. Dasent. Popular tales from the Norse.
Brother and sister. I. Field. Famous fairy tales. (Enchanted stag.)
Grimm. Fairy tales (Paull tr. Little brother and sister.)
Grimm. Household stories (Crane tr.).
Grimm. Household tales (Burt ed. Enchanted stag.)
Grimm. Household tales (Everyman's ed.).
*Heller and Bates. Little Golden-Hood.
Ketchum and Jorgensen. Kindergarten gems. (Little brother and sister.)
Mabie. Fairy tales every child should know. (Enchanted stag.)
Mabie. Heroes and fairies. (Enchanted stag.)
Mulock. Fairy book.
Wiggin and Smith. Fairy ring. (Little brother and sister.)
See also Little sister and little brother.
Brother and sister. II. Æsop. Fables (Burt ed.).
Æsop. Fables (Black ed.).
Brother and sister. III. Kunos. Forty-four Turkish fairy tales.
Brother and sister. IV. Olcott Red Indian fairy book.
See also Lost children.
Brother Barnabas. Richards. Silver crown.
Brother Bear and the honey orchard. Harris. Uncle Remus and his friends.
Brother Billy Goat eats his dinner. Harris. Uncle Remus and his friends.

Brother Buzzard's first friend. Young. Plantation bird legends. (Brer Buzzard's fust friend.)
Brother Buzzard's first taste. Young. Plantation bird legends. (Brer Buzzard's fust taste.)
Brother Buzzard's hat. Young. Plantation legends. (Brer Buzzard's hat.)
Brother Buzzard's three-cornder hat 'n' feather. Young. Plantation bird legends. (Brer Buzzard's three-cornder hat 'n' feather.)
Brother Deer an' King Sun's daughter. Harris. Told by Uncle Remus.
Brother Fox and little Mr. Cricket. Harris. Uncle Remus and the little boy. (Story of Brer Fox and little Mr. Cricket.)
See also How the fox and the crab ran a race.
Brother Fox and the white muscadines. Harris. Nights with Uncle Remus.
Brother Fox, Brother Rabbit, and King Deer's daughter. Harris. Nights with Uncle Remus.
Brother Fox catches Mr. Horse. Harris. Nights with Uncle Remus.
Brother Fox covets the quills. Harris. Nights with Uncle Remus.
Brother Fox follows the fashion. Harris. Told by Uncle Remus.
Brother Fox makes a narrow escape. Harris. Nights with Uncle Remus.
Brother Fox smells smoke. Harris. Uncle Remus and his friends.
Brother Fox still in trouble. Harris. Uncle Remus and his friends.
Brother Fox's diamond mine. Harris. Plantation pageants.
Brother Fox's fish-trap. Harris. Nights with Uncle Remus.
Brother Hawk an Brother Buzzard. Young. Plantation bird legends. (Brer Hawk and Brer Buzzard.)
Brother Hawk and de flint rock. Young. Plantation bird legends. (Brer Hawk and de flint rock.)
Brother Jay. Young. Plantation bird legends. (Brer Jay.)
Brother Lizard's strength and wealth. Young. Behind the dark pines.
Brother Loggerhead and Brother Conch. Tappan. Folk stories and fables. (B'Loggerhead and B'Conch.)
Brother Mud Turtle's trickery. Harris. Uncle Remus and his friends.
Brother of Christ. Magnus. Russian folk-tales.
Brother Possum gets in trouble. Harris. Nights with Uncle Remus.
Brother Possum routs Brother Lion. Young. Behind the dark pines. (Brer Possum routs Brer Lion.)
Brother Rabbit. I. *See* White rabbit. I.
Brother Rabbit. II. *See* Mr. Fox is again victimized.

Brother Rabbit and Brother Bull-frog. Harris. Told by Uncle Remus.

Brother Rabbit and Brother Goat. *See* Tar-baby. II.

Brother Rabbit and de' chewin' gum. Storytellers' magazine. July 1916, p. 425. (Brer Rabbit and de chewin' gum.)

Brother Rabbit and his famous foot. Harris. Nights with Uncle Remus.

Brother Rabbit and Miss Nancy. Harris. Told by Uncle Remus.

Brother Rabbit and Mr. Wildcat. Harris. Nights with Uncle Remus.

Brother Rabbit and the brier patch. Harris. Uncle Remus. (How Mr. Rabbit was too sharp for Mr. Fox.)

See also Why turtles stay near the water.

Brother Rabbit and the chickens. Harris. Told by Uncle Remus.

Brother Rabbit and the gizzard eater (poem). Harris. Tar-baby and other rhymes. (De 'Gater and de rabbit gizzard.)

Harris. Told by Uncle Remus.

Brother Rabbit and the goobers. Harris. Plantation pageants. (Brer Rabbit and the goobers.)

Brother Rabbit and the little girl. Harris. Nights with Uncle Remus.

Brother Rabbit and the mosquitoes. Harris. Nights with Uncle Remus.

Brother Rabbit and the pimmerly plum (poem). Harris Uncle Remus and the little boy. (Brer Rabbit and the pimmerly plum.)

See also Pimmerly plum.

Brother Rabbit and the tar-baby. *See* Tar-baby.

Brother Rabbit breaks up a party. Harris. Nights with Uncle Remus.

Brother Rabbit, Brother Fox and the two fat pullets. Harris. Uncle Remus returns.

Brother Rabbit causes Brother Fox to lose his hide. Harris. Uncle Remus and the little boy. (Brer Rabbit causes Brer Fox to lose his hide.)

Brother Rabbit conquers Brother Lion. Harris. Uncle Remus and his friends.

See also Lion and the hare.

Brother Rabbit frightens Brother Tiger. Harris. Uncle Remus and his friends.

See also Elephant has a bet with the tiger.

Brother Rabbit gets Brother Fox's dinner. Harris. Nights with Uncle Remus.

Brother Rabbit gets the provisions. Harris. Nights with Uncle Remus.

Brother Rabbit goes looking for trouble. Young. Behind the dark pines. (Brer Rabbit goes looking for trouble.)

Brother Rabbit has fun at the ferry. Harris. Uncle Remus and his friends.

Brother Rabbit has trouble with the moon. Harris. Uncle Remus and the little boy. (Brer Rabbit has trouble with the moon.)

Brother Rabbit lays in his beef supply. Harris. Nights with Uncle Remus.

Brother Rabbit outdoes Mr. Man. Harris. Nights with Uncle Remus.

Brother Rabbit pretends to be poisoned. Harris. Nights with Uncle Remus.

Brother Rabbit rescues Brother Terrapin. Harris. Nights with Uncle Remus.

Brother Rabbit secures a mansion. Harris. Nights with Uncle Remus.

Brother Rabbit submits to a test. Harris. Nights with Uncle Remus.

Brother Rabbit takes a walk. Harris. Nights with Uncle Remus.

Brother Rabbit takes some exercise. Harris. Nights with Uncle Remus.

Brother Rabbit ties Mr. Lion. Harris. Nights with Uncle Remus.

Brother Rabbit's astonishing prank. Harris. Nights with Uncle Remus.
Olcott and Pendleton. Jolly book.
Tappan. Book of humor.

Brother Rabbit's bear hunt. Harris. Uncle Remus returns.

Brother Rabbit's cool air swing. Patten. Junior classics. v. 2. (Brer Rabbit's cool air swing.)

Brother Rabbit's cradle. Harris. Told by Uncle Remus.

Brother Rabbit's laughing place (poem). Harris. Tar-baby and other rhymes. (Brer Rabbit's gigglin'-place.)
Harris. Told by Uncle Remus.

Brother Rabbit's love-charm. Harris. Nights with Uncle Remus.

Brother Rabbit's money mint. Harris. Uncle Remus and his friends.

Brother Rabbit's riddle. Harris. Nights with Uncle Remus.

Brother Rabbit's riding-horse. Harris. Uncle Remus. (Mr. Rabbit grossly deceives Mr. Fox.)
See also Buffalo and the rabbit; Elephant and the frog; Owl with the great head and eyes.

Brother Rabbit's story. Van Sickle and Seegmiller. 3d reader.

Brother Terrapin deceives Brother Buzzard. Harris. Nights with Uncle Remus.

Brother Terrapin's fiddle string. Harris. Little Mr. Thimblefinger.

Brother Tiger and Daddy Sheep. Cary. French fairy tales. (Papa Tiger and Papa Sheep.)

Brother Tiger and Daddy Sheep—*continued.*
Johnson. Elm-tree fairy book. (Mr. Goat and Mr. Tiger.)
Ortoli. Evening tales.
Pyle. Wonder tales retold. (Why the animals no longer fear the sheep.)
See also Wolves and the deer.
Brother Wolf and the horned cattle. Harris Nights with Uncle Remus.
Brother Wolf and the rock. Bailey. Firelight stories.
Bailey. Once upon a time animal stories.
See also Coyote and rolling rock; Iktomi's blanket; Why the night-hawk's wings are beautiful.
Brother Wolf falls a victim. Harris. Nights with Uncle Remus.
Brother Wolf gets in a warm place. Harris. Nights with Uncle Remus.
Brother Wolf says grace. Harris. Nights with Uncle Remus.
Brother Wolf still in trouble. Harris. Nights with Uncle Remus.
Brother Wolf's two big dinners. Tappan. Book of humor.
Brothers. *See* Two brothers. II.
Brown bear of Norway. Lang. Lilac fairy book.
Lang. Magic book.
Brown bear, Strange tale of. Brady. Green forest fairy tales.
Brown dwarf. *See* John Dietrich, Adventures of.
Brown dwarf of Rügen. *See* John Dietrich, Adventures of.
Brown-eyed Susans, Origin of. Bigham. Overheard in fairyland.
Brown hen. *See* Sky is falling.
Brownie, Adventures of a. Patten. Junior classics. v. 6 (Abridged).
Stone. Children's stories that never grow old.
Brownie and the princess. Alcott. Lulu's library. v. 2.
Brownie and the thievish maids. Douglas. Scottish fairy book.
Brownie in the house. Bailey. Seven peas in the pod.
Brownie of Blednock. Grierson. Children's tales from Scottish ballads.
Olcott. Book of elves and fairies.
Skinner. Merry tales.
Wickes. Happy holidays.
See also How Olaf brought the brownie back.
Brownie of Bodsbeck. Douglas. Scottish fairy tales.
Brownie o' Ferne-Den. Grierson. Scottish fairy book.
Brownie of the lake. Lang. Lilac fairy book.
Lang. Snake prince.
Brownie who wanted the moon. Bailey. Friendly tales.
Brownies on Halloween. Storytellers' magazine. June 1917, p. 295.
Bruce, Robert. Mabie. Heroes and fairies.

Bruce and the bowl of porridge. Chambers' miscellany. v. 9. (King Robert's bowl. *In* Scottish traditionary stories.)
Storytellers' magazine. Oct. 1913, p. 231. (Bowl of porridge.)
Bruce and the spider. Baker and Carpenter. Language readers. 6th year.
Baldwin. Fifty famous stories.
Faulkner. Story lady's book. (Spider story.)
*Jones. 2d reader.
*Sly. World stories retold.
See also Persevering carp Tamerlane.
Bruin and Reynard. *See* Bruin and Reynard partners. I.
Bruin and Reynard partners. I. Asbjörnsen. Fairy tales from the far north. (Bear and the fox go into partnership.)
Asbjörnsen. Tales from the fjeld.
Dasent. Norse fairy tales.
Dasent. Popular tales from the Norse. (Bruin and Reynard.)
Faulkner. Story lady's book. (How the fox fooled the bear.)
Patten. Junior classics. v. 1. (Bear and the fox.)
Skinner. Merry tales.
Thorne-Thomsen. East o' the sun and west o' the moon.
Wiggin and Smith. Tales of laughter.
Bruin and Reynard partners II. Fillmore. Mighty Mikko. (Harvest.)
See also Bear, the boar and the wolf.
Bruin Goodfellow. Asbjörnsen. Folk and fairy tales. (Brave old Bruin.)
Asbjörnsen. Tales from the fjeld.
Gade. Norwegian fairy tales. (Good old Bruin.)
Johnson. Book of fairy-tale bears. (Bruin's ride.)
Bruin outwitted. *See* Slip root, catch Reynard's foot.
Bruin's ride. *See* Bruin Goodfellow.
Brunhilda. Guerber. Myths of northern lands. (*In* Sigurd Saga.)
McSpadden. Stories from great operas. (War Maidens.)
McSpadden. Stories from Wagner. (Ring of the curse.)
Maud. Wagner's heroines.
Patten. Junior classics. v. 2. (Story of Brunhilda and Siegfried.)
See also Horse who rode through fire. Nibelungenlied; Ring: War maidens; Ring: Siegfried; Ring: Twilight of the gods; Siegfried; Sigurd the Volsung; Valkyries.
Bruno's story. Wiggin and Smith. Tales of laughter.
Bubbly boy. Nyblom. Jolly Calle.
Buccoleon. *See* Turk, turban, tulip and dragon.
Bucephalus. *See* Alexander the Great.
Buchettino. Skinner. Nursery tales from many lands.
Buckwheat (The). Andersen. Fairy tales (Paull tr.).

Buckwheat—*continued.*
Andersen. Wonder stories.
Bryant. How to tell stories.
Olcott. Wonder garden. (Proud buckwheat.)
Stebbins. 3d reader.
Buddhist Henny-Penny. *See* Timid hare.
Buddhist Tar-baby. *See* Demon with the matted hair.
Buddy and the buried bone. * Bryant. New stories to tell to children.
Budhibanta, the boy weaver. Bradley-Birt. Bengal fairy tales.
Budulinek. Fillmore. Shoemaker's apron.
Buffalo and the field-mouse. Eastman. Wigwam evenings.
Buffalo and the rabbit. Stanley. Animal folk tales.
See also Brother Rabbit's riding-horse; Elephant and the frog.
Buffoon and the countryman. *See* Actor and the pig.
Builder of ability and the builder of haste. Wiggin and Smith. Talking beasts.
Builders of the pyramids. Brooksbank. Legends of ancient Egypt.
Builders of Troy. *See* Trojan war.
Building of Asgard. *See* Giant builder.
Building of the Wrekin. *See* Wrekin.
Bulat the Brave. *See* Ivanczarovitch and Bulat the Brave.
Bulat the brave companion, Story of. Steele. Russian garland of fairy tales.
See also Ivanczarovitch; Little fool Ivan.
Buleman's house. Noyes. Twilight stories.
Bull. Sologub. Sweet-scented name.
Bull and the bullfinch. Rouse. Talking thrush.
Bull and the calf. Æsop. Fables (Stickney).
Bull and the goat. Æsop. Fables (Black ed.).
Æsop. Fables (Burt ed.).
Bull and the princess at the glass mountain. Bay. Danish fairy and folk tales.
Bull of Norroway. *See* Red bull of Norroway.
Bull-Runs-Round, Adventure of. Borland Rocky Mountain tipi tales. (Bull-Runs-Round and the under-water people.)
Borland. Rocky Mountain tipi tales. (Bull-Runs-Round saves his people.)
Grinnell. Blackfoot lodge tales. (Adventures of Bull Turns Round.)
Bull that demanded fair treatment. Babbitt. Jataka tales. (Ox who won the forfeit.)
Shedlock. Eastern stories and legends.
Bull that proved his gratitude. Shedlock. Eastern stories and legends.
Bullfrogs, Origin of. *See* Glooskap and the bullfrog.
Bullockeen. Gregory. Kiltartan wonder book.

Bun. *Carrick. Picture tales from the Russian.
See also Pancake.
Bundle of sticks. Æsop. Fables (Burt ed. Old man and his sons.)
Æsop. Fables (Black ed. Old man and his sons.)
Æsop. Fables (Jacobs).
Æsop. Fables (Stickney).
Arnold and Gilbert. Stepping stones to literature. v. 2.
Baldwin. Fairy stories and fables. (Farmer and his sons.)
Hall and Gilman. Story land. 2d reader. (Farmer and his sons.)
Hartwell. Story hour readings. 7th year. (Adventure in brotherhood.)
Norton. Heart of oak books. v. 2. (Union gives stength.)
Scudder. Children's book. (Farmer's sons.)
Scudder. Fables and folk stories. (Farmer's sons.)
Welsh. Stories children love. (Old man and his sons.)
Wiggin and Smith. Talking beasts. (Old man and his sons.)
Bunny and the Easter eggs. *See* Easter rabbit. III.
Bunny Bobtail builds a road. Bailey. Friendly tales.
Bunny Bobtail's Easter. Bailey. Stories for Sunday telling.
Bunny Bobtail's merry Christmas. Bailey. Stories for Sunday telling.
Bunnytail, Tale of. Storytellers' magazine. Jan. 1917, p. 52.
Bunyip. Lang. Aladdin and other stories.
Lang. Brown fairy book.
Burg Hill's on fire. *See* Good housewife and her night labours.
Burghers of Ghent refuse to be hanged. Evans. Old time tales.
Burial of poor Cock Robin. *See* Cock Robin.
Buried moon. Jacobs. More English fairy tales.
Wiggin and Smith. Tales of wonder.
Buried treasure. I. *See* Gold in the orchard.
Buried treasure. II. Gate. Fortunate days.
Burning house. Richards. Silver crown.
Burning of the rice fields. Bryant. How to tell stories.
Sly. World stories retold. (Japanese and the earthquake.)
Van Sickle and Seegmiller. Riverside readers. v. 3.
Burnt Njal, Story of. *See* Death of Gunnar; Njal's burning; Slaying of Hallgerda's husbands.
Burnt rock. Sylva and Strettell. Legends from river and mountain. (Piatra arsa, burnt rock.)
Bushy bride. Dasent. Popular tales from the Norse.
Dasent. Norse fairy tales.
*Esenwein and Stockard. Children's stories. (Three heads.)
Jerrold. Big book of fairy tales.
Lang. Blue parrot.
Lang. Red fairy book.
Bushy's bravery. Skinner. Topaz story book.
Butcher. Guerber. Legends of the Rhine.

Butcher bird's board bill. Young. Plantation bird legends.
Butter and eggs. Seton. Woodland tales. (Wicked hoptoad and the little yellow dragon.)
Buttercup. *See* Little Butterkin.
Butterfirefly. Potter. Pinafore pocket story book.
Butterflies. I. Donaldson. Moons of long ago.
See also How butterflies came.
Butterflies. II. *See* Lesson of faith.
Butterfly. I. Andersen. Fairy tales (Paull tr.).
Andersen. Stories and tales.
Butterfly. II. Mulock. Fairy book.
Wiggin and Smith. Magic casements.
Butterfly. III. *See* Lesson of faith.
Butterfly and the clover. *See* Prince Butterfly and Clover-blossom.
Butterfly-blue and Butterfly-dear and what became of them. Tales for bedtime.
Butterfly that stamped. Kipling. Just so stories.
Butterflyflutterby and Flutterbybutterfly. Howells. Christmas every day.
Butterfly's diamond. Field third reader.
Olcott. Book of elves and fairies.
Butterwops. Skinner. Garnet story book.
Button crop. Richards. More five minute stories.
Buz and Hum. Skinner. Emerald story book.
By command of Prince Daniel. Magnus. Russian folk-tales.

C

Cactus, Legend of (poem). Storytellers' magazine. Nov. 1917, p. 471.
Cadi and the roguish Mohammedan monk. Butterworth. Zigzag journeys in the Orient. (*In* Ch. 3.)
Cadi's decisions. Alderman. Classics old and new. 4th reader.
Cadmus and the dragon's teeth. *Bailey. Wonder stories. (Cadmus the alphabet king.)
Baldwin. Old Greek stories. (Cadmus and Europa.)
Guerber. Myths of Greece and Rome. (*In* Jupiter.)
Haaren and Poland. Famous men of Greece.
Hartley. Stories from the Greek legends. (How Cadmus founded a city.)
Hawthorne. Tanglewood tales. (Dragon's teeth.)
Hutchinson. Orpheus with his lute. (Prince Cadmus of Phoenicia.)
Hyde. Favorite Greek myths. (Why Cadmus founded a city.)
Johonnot. Stories of heroic deeds. (Dragon's teeth.)
Mabie. Myths every child should know.
McFee. Treasury of myths. (Cadmus and Europa.)
Pratt. Myths of old Greece. v. 2. (Dragon's teeth.)

Cadmus and the dragon's teeth—*continued.*
Shaw. Stories of the ancient Greeks. (Sowing dragon's teeth.)
Tappan. Myths from many lands. (Dragon's teeth.)
Storr. Half a hundred hero tales.
See also Europa.
Cadwaladr and his goat. Thomas. Welsh fairy book.
Cadwallon. Baring-Gould. Old English fairy tales.
Caedmon the herdsman poet, Story of. Baldwin. Fifty famous people. (Cowherd who became a poet.)
Storytellers' magazine. July 1913, p. 91. (Story of England's first poet.)
Wilmot-Buxton. Stories of early England.
Caesar, Julius. Baldwin. Fifty famous stories.
Baldwin. Thirty more famous stories. (Crossing the Rubicon.)
Guerber. Story of the Romans. (Crossing the Rubicon.)
Caesar and the slave. Æsop. Fables (Black ed.).
Æsop. Fables (Burt ed.).
Cahal, son of King Conor, in Erin, and Bloom of Youth, daughter of the King of Hathony. Curtin. Hero tales from Ireland.
Cailleac-na-Cearc. Gregory. Kiltartan wonder book.
Cake. Richards. Silver crown.
Cake and the seven hungry children. *See* Pancake.
Cake in a basket. Potter. Pinafore pocket story book.
Cake shop on the wooden bridge. Singleton. Goldenrod fairy book.
Calabash man. Finger. Tales from silver lands.
Calais. *See* Siege of Calais.
Caliph and the gardener. Baldwin. Fifty famous people.
Caliph and the poet. Baldwin. Fifty famous people.
Caliph for one day. *See* Abou Hassan.
Caliph Haroun-al-Raschid, Adventures of. Arabian nights (Dodge ed.).
Arabian nights (Lang. Adventures of Haroun-al-Raschid.)
Arabian nights (Townsend).
Ketcham. Oriental fairy tales. (Haroun-al-Raschid.)
Scudder. Children's book (Caliph Haroun Alraschid.)
Caliph Stork. Coussens. Jade story book. (Story of Caliph Stork.)
Hauff. Caravan tales.
Hauff. Fairy tales. (Caliph turned stork.)
Jenks. Tales of fantasy.
Lang. Green fairy book.
Lang. Magician's gifts.
Noyes. Twilight stories.
Success library. v. 3.
Wiggin and Smith. Tales of wonder. (Storks and the night owl.)
See also Blondina.
Caliph the fisherman, Story of. Arabian nights (Olcott).

Caliph turned stork. *See* Caliph Stork.
Callisto and Arcis. *Bailey. Wonder stories. (How a huntress became a bear.)
*Dyer and Brady. Merrill readers. 2d reader. (Great bear and the little bear.)
Faulkner. Story lady's book. (Great dipper.)
Judd. Classic myths.
Kupfer. Stories of long ago. (Great bear and the little bear.)
Pratt. Greek myths. v. 2. (Callisto.)
Shaw. Stories of the ancient Greeks. (*In* Among the stars.)
*Wilson. Nature study reader. (White bear.)
Cally Coo-Coo o' the woods. Storytellers' magazine. Oct. 1913, p. 202.
See also East o' the sun and west o' the moon; King Valemon the white bear; Mysterious prince.
Calydonian hunt. Baldwin. Hero tales told in school. (Hunt in the woods of Calydon.)
Baldwin. Old Greek stories. (Hunt in the forest.)
Baldwin. Story of the golden age. (*In* Two famous boar hunts.)
Buckley. Children of the dawn. (Hunting the Calydonian boar.)
Carpenter. Long ago in Greece. (Hunt in Calydon.)
Cole. Heroes of the olden time. (Meleager and Atalanta.)
Cox. Tales of ancient Greece. (Althea and the burning brand.)
Guerber. Myths of Greece and Rome. (Calydonian hunt.)
Lang. All sorts of stories book. (Meleager and Atalanta.)
Patten. Junior classics. v. 3. (Hunting the Calydonian boar.)
Peabody. Old Greek folk stories.
Storr. Half a hundred hero tales. (Meleager and Atalanta.)
Ca-mee-no-wa-sit, the hairy man. Linderman. Indian Old-man stories.
Camaralzaman, and Badoura, Princess of China. Arabian nights (Lang).
Arabian nights (Townsend).
Arabian nights, More tales. (Olcott. Story of Prince Camaralzaman and the Princess Badoura.)
Cambuscan bold, Story of. Darton. Tales of the Canterbury pilgrims. (Squire's tale: Story of Cambuscan bold.)
Storr and Turner. Canterbury chimes. (Squire's tale: Canace.)
Camel. Æsop. Fables (Stickney).
Bryce. Fables from afar.
Camel and his master. *See* Arab and his camel.
Camel and the jackal. *See* Tit for tat.
Camel and the pig. Baldwin. Another fairy reader.
Dyer and Brady. Merrill readers. 2d reader.

Camel and the pig—*continued.*
Elson and Runkel. Elson readers. Book I.
Patten. Junior classics. v. 1.
Tappan. Folk stories and fables.
Wiggin and Smith. Talking beasts.
See also Elephant and the ape.
Camel driver and the adder. Bidpai. Tortoise and the geese.
See also Way of the world. I.
Camel in the tent. *See* Arab and his camel.
Camelback mountain, Legend of the. *See* In the desert of waiting.
Camel's neck. Rouse. Talking thrush.
Camouflage, Origin of. Griffis. Belgian fairy tales. (Red caps and the hunters; Split-tailed lion.)
Camp robber. Judson. Myths and legends of Alaska.
Can and could. Ingelow. Stories told to a child. v. 1.
Canace. *See* Cambuscan bold, Story of.
Candle. *See* Candles.
Candlemas. *See* How it happens Johnny Chuck sleeps all winter; Why the woodchuck comes out in midwinter.
Candles. I. Andersen. Fairy tales (Turpin).
Andersen. Stories (Riverside ed.).
Andersen. Stories and tales (Author's ed. Candle.)
Bailey and Lewis. For the children's hour. (Candle.)
Candles. II. Sologub. Sweet scented name.
Candles of life. Fillmore. Shoemaker's apron.
Candy-boy. Storytellers' magazine. Sept. 1917, p. 344.
Candy country. Alcott. Lulu's library. v. 1.
Murray. Story book treasures.
Candy stick, Story of. Bailey. Stories for Sunday telling.
Cannetella. Lang. Grey fairy book.
Lang. Invisible prince and other stories.
Success library. v. 3.
Canoe race. Donaldson. Little papoose listens.
Cañon flowers. Olcott. Good stories for great holidays.
Canon's yeoman's tale. *See* Alchemist.
Canonbie Dick and Thomas of Ercildoune. Grierson. Scottish fairy book.
Canova, Antonio. Alderman. Classics old and new. 4th reader. (Scullion who became a sculptor.)
Baldwin. Fifty famous stories.
Canute, King. Baldwin. Fifty famous stories. (King Canute on the seashore.)
Blaisdell. English history story book.
Johonnot. Stories of the olden time.
Cap o' rushes. Armfield. Wonder tales.
Jacobs. English fairy tales.
Wiggin and Smith. Magic casements.
Cap that mother made. *See* Ander's new cap.
Captain John's travels. Laboulaye. Fairy tales.
Captive. Eastman. Indian legends retold.

Caraiman. Storytellers' magazine. May 1915, p. 136.
Sylva and Strettell. Legends of river and mountain.
Carasoyn. MacDonald. Light princess and other fairy tales.
Cardinal flower. McFee. Treasury of flower stories.
See also Prince Scarlet.
Careful child. Bailey. Stories for Sunday telling.
Caribou. Riggs. Animal stories from Eskimo land.
Carlanco. Caballero. Spanish fairy tales.
See also Wolf and the seven little kids.
Carmen. McSpadden. Stories from great operas.
Pleasanton. Fairyland of opera.
Carnation, white and black. Quiller-Couch. Fairy tales far and near.
Carnation youth. Eells. Tales of enchantment from Spain.
Carousing army. Guerber. Legends of the Rhine.
Carpenter and the ape. Bidpai. Tortoise and the geese.
Carpenter builds shelter for some animals. * Dillingham and Emerson. Tell it again stories.
Carving of MacDatho's boar. Rolleston. High deeds of Finn.
Casabianca. Baldwin. Fifty famous stories.
Blaisdell. Child life. 4th reader.
(poem). Tappan. Old-fashioned stories.
Casperl. Fairy stories from St. Nicholas.
Cassim. Peck. Stories for good children.
See also Magic ring. I.
Castle Fortune. Skinner. Merry tales.
Bryant. Stories to tell to children.
Castle hung in the air. Cary. French fairy tales.
Castle in the air. *See* Palace in the clouds.
Castle in the clouds. Stewart. Once upon a time.
Castle of Bim. Stockton. Floating prince.
Castle of delight. Gate. Fortunate days.
Castle of gems. May. Little Prudy's fairy book.
Castle of Kerglas. *See* Perronik, Adventures of.
Castle of life. Laboulaye. Fairy book.
Castle of Montauban. *See* Sons of Aymoun.
Castle of the active door. *See* Sir Peredur.
Castle of the hawk. Griffis. Swiss fairy tales.
Castle on the mountain. Storytellers' magazine. March 1914, p. 469.
Castle Silence. Hackländer. Enchanting and enchanted.
Castle Terrible and the pinetree. Alden. Boy who found the king.
Castle that stood on golden pillars. *See* Palace that stood on golden pillars.
Castle under the sea. Alden. Why the chimes rang.
Castles in Spain. Arnold and Gilbert. Stepping stones to literature. v. 7. (My chateaux.)
Curtis. Prue and I.
Castor and Pollux. Baldwin. Story of the golden age. (*In* Long live the king!)

Castor and Pollux—*continued.*
Hutchinson. Golden porch. (Heavenly twins.)
Judd. Classic myths.
Cat. Bailey. Stories children need.
Cat and his servant. *See* Fox and the cat. IV.
Cat and the bat. Æsop. Fables (Burt ed.).
Cat and the birds. Æsop. Fables (Stickney).
Spaulding and Bryce. Aldine readers. 2d reader.
Cat and the cock. Æsop. Fables (Burt ed.).
Æsop. Fables (Stickney).
Cat and the cradle. Griffis. Dutch fairy tales.
Cat and the dream man. Finger. Tales from silver lands.
Cat and the fox. *See* Fox and the cat. I.
Cat and the hen. I. Stafford. Animal fables.
Cat and the hen. II. Bryce. Fables from afar.
Cat and the mice. Æsop. Fables (Black ed.).
Æsop. Fables (Burt ed.).
Scudder. Children's book.
Scudder. Fables and folk stories.
Wiggin and Smith. Talking beasts.
Cat and the monkey. *See* Cat, the monkey and the chestnuts.
Cat and the mouse. I. Arnold and Gilbert. Stepping stones to literature. v. 1.
Bailey. Firelight stories.
*Bailey. Folk stories and fables.
Bailey and Lewis. For the children's hour.
*Burchill. Progressive road to reading: story steps.
Coussens. Child's book of stories.
Darton. Wonder book of beasts.
Faulkner. Old English nursery tales.
*Haaren. Songs and stories. 2d reader.
Jacobs. English fairy tales.
Mother Goose rhymes and fairy tales (Altemus ed.).
Mother Goose's nursery rhymes, tales and jingles (Warne ed.).
My Bookhouse. v. 1.
O'Grady and Throop. Teachers' story teller's book.
Wiggin and Smith. Tales of laughter.
* Wiltse Kindergarten stories. (Story of a mouse.)
See also Grain of corn; How the mouse got into his hole; Little Tuppen; Munachar and Manacher; Nanny who wouldn't go home to supper; Old woman and her pig; Piece of liver; Sparrow and the bush.
Cat and the mouse. II. James. Cat and the mouse.
Cat and the mouse in partnership. Baldwin. Another fairy reader. (A queer partnership.)
Carrick. Kitty cat tales. (Cat who married a mouse.)
Darton. Wonder book of beasts. (All-gone.)
Field. Famous fairy tales.
Grimm. Fairy tales (Lucas tr.).
Grimm. Household stories (Crane tr.).

Cat and the mouse in partnership—*continued.*
Grimm. Household tales (Burt ed. Cat who married a mouse.)
Johnson. Birch-tree fairy book.
Lang. Magic ring and other stories.
Lang. Yellow fairy book.
(play). Stevenson. Plays for the home. (Cat and the mouse.)
Wiggin and Smith. Tales of laughter.
See also Compair Lapin's godchild; Fox and the wolf; Fox as partner. I; Fox cheats the bear out of his Christmas fare; Wolf's butter; Two friends and the barrel of grease.
Cat and the parrot. Bryant. Best stories to tell to children.
Bryant. How to tell stories to children.
Keyes. Five senses.
Keyes. Stories and story-telling.
Rouse. Talking thrush.
See also Greedy cat; Kuratko the Terrible; Wolf. II.
Cat and the sparrows. I. Æsop. Fables (Burt ed.).
(poem). Wiggin and Smith. Talking beasts. (Cat and the two sparrows.)
Cat and the sparrows. II. Rouse. Talking thrush.
Cat and the two sparrows. See Cat and the sparrows. I.
Cat-cat and Mouse-mouse. Burchill. Progressive road to reading. Book I.
Cat-kin and the Queen mother. Griffis. Korean fairy tales.
Cat-maiden. *See* Venus and the cat.
Cat on the Dovrefell. *See* Bear and Skrattel.
Cat that could not be killed. Bailey. In the animal world.
Darton. Wonder book of beasts.
Cat that waited. Van Sickle and Seegmiller. Riverside readers. 1st reader.
Cat that walked by himself. Kipling. Just so stories.
See also How some wild animals became tame ones.
Cat that winked. Sholl. Faery tales of Weir.
Cat, the cock and the fox. I. Bain. Cossack fairy tales.
Johnson. Book of fairy-tale foxes. (How the cat outwitted the fox.)
Wiggin and Smith. Tales of laughter.
See also Cat, the cock and the fox. II.
Cat, the cock and the fox. II. *Carrick. Picture tales from the Russian.
*Skinner. Nursery tales from many lands. (Peter, Basil and the fox.)
Cat, the monkey and the chestnuts. Æsop. Fables (Stickney. Monkey and the cat.)
Hall and Gilmore. Story land. 2d reader. (Cat and the monkey.)
Scudder. Children's book.
Scudder. Fables and folk stories.
(poem). Wiggin and Smith. Talking beasts. (Monkey and the cat.)

Cat, the monkey and the chestnuts—*continued.*
Tappan. Folk stories and fables.
See also Mr. Thomas Cat's chestnuts.
Cat, the rat and the fox. Stafford. Animal fables.
Cat, the weasel and the young rabbit.
Scudder. Children's book.
Scudder. Fables and folk stories.
Cat who adopted a fox. Donahey. Tales to be told to children.
Cat who could eat so much. *See* Greedy cat.
Cat who kept Christmas. Bailey. In the animal world.
Cat who lost herself. Bailey. Stories and rhymes for a child.
Cat who married a mouse. *See* Cat and the mouse in partnership.
Cat who served the lion, Story of. Success library. v. 3.
Cat witches. Griffis. Welsh fairy tales. (Two cat witches.)
Thomas. Welsh fairy book.
Catalina of Dumaguete. Miller. Philippine folklore stories.
Cathedral of Aix-la-Chapelle. Guerber. Legends of the Rhine. (Cathedral legend.)
Cathedral of Cologne. Guerber. Legends of the Rhine. (Cathedral legend; Devil's wager.)
Cathedral of Strasburg. Guerber. Legends of the Rhine. (Cathedral legends.)
Catherine and Frederick. *See* Frederick and Catherine.
Catherine and her destiny. Fairy tales retold from St. Nicholas.
Lang. Golden mermaid and other stories.
Lang. Pink fairy book.
Catnip and catnap. Bacon. True philosopher.
Cats and the mice. Æsop. Fables (Burt ed.).
Cat's elopement. Johnson. Birch-tree fairy book. (Runaway cats.)
Lang. Pink fairy book.
Lang. Snow-queen and other stories.
Cat's house under the hill. Potter. Pinafore pocket story book.
See also Woman who forgot her cat.
Cat's pilgrimage. Hartwell. Story hour readings. 6th year.
Cats that wouldn't catch mice. Nordau. Dwarf's spectacles.
Cats, the monkey and the cheese. *See* Matter of arbitration.
Catskin. I. Baring-Gould. Old English fairy tales.
Jacobs. More English fairy tales.
Macleod. Book of ballad stories.
Rhys. Fairy gold.
Catskin. II. *See* Many-furred creature.
Cattie sits in the kiln-ring spinning (poem). Douglas. Scottish fairy tales.
See also Mouse and mouser.
Cattle raide of Cooley. Wilmot-Buxton. Stories of early

Cattle raide of Cooley—*continued.*
England. (Tale of the white-horned.)
Cattle that came. Armfield. Wonder tales.
Cauld lad of Hilton. Hartland. English folk and fairy tales.
Jacobs. English fairy tales.
Rhys. Fairy gold.
Cause of Brer Buzzard's red head. Young. Plantation bird legends. ('Caze of Brer Buzzard's red head.)
Cause of tides. I. Farmer. Nature myths.
Van Sickle and Seegmiller. Riverside readers. 3d reader. (Crab and the moon.)
See also Crab that played with the sea; Old woman and the tides; Why the tide runs out.
Cause of Tides. II. Judson. Myths and legends of Alaska. (Origin of the tides—Tsetsaut version.)
Cave fairy. Patterson. Enchanted bird.
Cave of emeralds. Segovia. Spanish fairy book.
Cave of Jalomitza. Sylva and Strettell. Legends from river and mountain.
Cave of the beasts. Martens. Chinese fairy book.
Cave of the Cyclops. See Ulysses and Polyphemus.
Cave of the winds. Stewart. Once upon a time.
Cave of the young men of Snowdonia. Thomas. Welsh fairy book.
Cavern of Steenfoll. Smith. More mystery tales.
Cedar tree's reward. *See* Why the evergreen trees keep their leaves in winter.
Celestial runaway. *See* Phaeton.
Celestial sisters. *See* Star wife.
Centaur. *See* Chiron.
Cephalus and Procris. Guerber. Myths of Greece and Rome.
Storr. Half a hundred hero tales.
Ceres. *See* Proserpina.
Ceres and Proserpina. *See* Proserpina.
Ceyx and Halcyone. *See* Halcyon birds.
Chácopee and the grandfather giant. *See* White Feather.
Chacopee the giant killer. *See* White Feather.
Chain of fools. Macdonell. Italian fairy book.
Chaining of the wolf. *See* Binding of the Fenris wolf.
Chairs in council. Eggleston. Queer stories for boys and girls.
Chameleon. Æsop. Fables (Burt ed.).
(poem). Tappan. Old-fashioned stories.
Wiggin and Smith. Talking beasts.
Champion of Athens. *See* Theseus.
Chandra's vengeance. Frere. Old Deccan days.
Tappan. Myths from many lands.
Change of coats. Gruelle. Friendly fairies.
Change of time. Guerber. Legends of the Rhine.
Changeling. Grimm. Fairy tales (Paull tr. Elves. III.)
Grimm. Household stories (Crane tr. Elves. III.)

Changeling—*continued.*
Grimm. Household tales (Burt ed.).
Grimm. Household tales (Everyman's ed.).
See also Brewery of egg-shells.
Changeling and the bagpipes. Frost. Fairies and folk of Ireland. (*In* Ch. 5.)
Chanina and the angels. Friedlander. Jewish fairy book.
Chanticleer. *See* Cock and the fox.
Chanticleer and Partlett. Allison and Perdue. Story in primary instruction. (Death of the cock.)
Darton. Wonder book of beasts.
Grimm. Fairy tales (Lucas tr.).
Grimm. Fairy tales (Paull tr. Death of the little hen.)
Grimm. Household stories (Crane tr. Death of the hen.)
Grimm. Household tales (Everyman's ed.).
Wiggin and Smith. Tales of laughter.
See also Vagabonds; Herr Korbes; Cock and the hen in the nut wood.
Chapman's tale. *See* Boy and the blacksmith; Barnaby's goose.
Charcoal-burner. I. Asbjörnsen. Folk and fairy tales.
Asbjörnsen. Tales from the fjeld.
Charcoal-burner. II. *See* Charcoal burner and fuller.
Charcoal-burner. III. *See* How Ralph the charcoal-burner entertained King Charles and afterwards went to court.
Charcoal burner and fuller. Æsop. Fables (Black ed. Collier and the fuller.)
Æsop. Fables (Burt ed. Collier and the fuller.)
Æsop. Fables (Stickney).
Arnold and Gilbert. Stepping stones to literature. v. 2. (Charcoal-burner.)
Charcoal man and the king. Baldwin. Fifty famous people.
Charcoal Nils and the troll-woman. Stroebe and Martens. Swedish fairy book.
Chariot race. *See* Orestes.
Charitable girl. Guerber. Legends of the Rhine.
See also Minstrel's ride.
Charlemagne. Baldwin. Hero tales told in school. (How Charlemagne crossed the Alps.)
Evans. Old time tales. (Charlemagne and the magic ring; Charlemagne and the robber.)
Guerber. Legends of the middle ages. (Charlemagne and his Paladins.)
Herbertson. Heroic legends. (How Oliver fought for France and the faith.)
Johonnot. Stories of the olden time.
Stebbins. Sunken city. (Charlemagne's generosity; Magic ring; Silver bridge.)
Tappan. Stories of legendary heroes. (How Fierabras defied King Charles.)
Charlemagne and Elbegast. Guerber. Legends of the Rhine.

Charlemagne and the magic ring. Guerber. Legends of the Rhine. (Magic ring.)
Noyes. Twilight stories. (Magic ring.)
Charles. II. *See* Royal Oak Day.
Charles the Great and the snake. Froelicher. Swiss stories.
Charlotte and the ten dwarfs. Fairy stories from St. Nicholas. (Ten little dwarfs.)
Ketchum and Jorgensen. Kindergarten gems.
St. Nicholas. Dec. 1873, p. 70. (Ten little dwarfs.)
Storytellers' magazine. Feb. 1917, p. 70. (Ten workmen of Mother Watergreen.)
Wiltse. Kindergarten stories.
See also Ten fairies.
Charmed ring. Jacobs. Indian fairy tales.
See also Wonderful ring.
Charming. *See* Beauty of form and beauty of mind.
Charybdis. *See* Scylla and Charybdis.
Chase of Slieve Culinn. Joyce. Old Celtic romances.
Chase of Slieve Fuad. Joyce. Old Celtic romances.
Chase of the Gilla Dacar. Rolleston. High deeds of Finn.
See also Finn MacCool.
Chaucer's tale. *See* Sir Gamelyn.
Cheer-heart, Story of. *See* How pansies came.
Cheerful glacier. Austin. Basket woman.
Cheerful temper. Andersen. Fairy tales (Lucas tr.).
Andersen. Fairy tales (Paull tr.).
Andersen. Stories and tales (Author's ed. Good humor.)
Cheese house. Bigham. Merry animal tales.
See also Rats and the cheese.
Cheesemaker and the monkeys. Field second reader.
Cheeses that ran away. Johnson. Oak-tree fairy book.
See also Luckhinarain the idiot; Wise men of Gotham.
Cheiron. *See* Chiron.
Chenoo. Leland. Algonquin legends of New England.
Partridge. Glooscap the great chief. (Adventure with a Chenoo.)
Cherry. *See* Cherry of Zennor, Adventures of.
Cherry feast of Naunberg. Skinner. Very little child's book of stories. (Feast of cherries.)
Cherry of Zennor, Adventures of. Hartland. English folk and fairy tales.
Pyle. Fairy tales. (Cherry.)
Cherry the frog-bride. Grimm. Household tales (Everyman's ed.).
See also Three feathers. I.
Chess players. Armfield. Wonder tales.
Chest of the lady Zobeide. *See* Sultan's steward's story.
Chestnut kettle. Olcott. Red Indian fairy book.
Chestnut tree. *See* Finette Cendron.
Chevalier Fortuné. *See* Belle-Belle.
Chevy Chace. *See* Chevy Chase.
Chevy Chase. Greenwood. Stories from famous ballads.

Chevy Chase—*continued.*
Johonnot. Stories of the olden time.
(poem). Lanier. Boy's Percy. (Ancient ballad of Chevy Chace.)
(poem). Lanier. Boy's Percy. (More modern ballad of Chevy Chace.)
Mabie. Legends every child should know.
Macleod. Book of ballad stories. (Hunting of the Cheviot.)
Scudder. Children's book. (Hunting of the Cheviot.)
Chib, Adventures of. Kennedy. New world fairy book.
My Bookhouse. v. 3. (Strong boy.)
Chick-a-dee returns from sky-land. Judson. Old Crow and his friends.
Chicken-diddle. See Chicken-Little.
Chicken-Grethe's family. Andersen. Stories and tales.
Chicken-Licken. See Chicken-Little.
Chicken-Little. Arnold and Gilbert. Stepping stones to literature. v. 2.
Asbjörnsen. Fairy tales from the far north. (Hen who went to Dovrefjeld to save the world.)
Bailey. Firelight stories.
* Bailey. Folk stories and fables.
Bailey. Stories and rhymes for a child. (Chicken Little and the baby.)
Bailey and Lewis. For the children's hour.
*Blaisdell. Child life. 2d reader.
*Bowen. Second story reader. (When the sky began to fall.)
Chisholm and Steedman. Staircase of stories. (Henny Penny.)
Coussens. Child's book of stories. (Henny Penny.)
Darton. Wonder book of beasts.
Dasent. Popular tales from the Norse. (Cock and hen that went to Dovrefell.)
Dyer. What-happened-then stories.
Faulkner. Old English nursery tales.
Forty famous fairy tales. (Henny Penny.)
*Grover. Folk lore readers. v. 1.
*Howard. Banbury Cross stories. (Chicken-Licken.)
Jacobs. English fairy tales. (Henny Penny.)
Jerrold. Big book of fairy tales. (Little Chicken Kluk.)
Johnson. Oak-tree fairy book. (Story of Chicken-Licken.)
Klingensmith. Household stories for little readers.
Lansing. Rhymes and stories.
Mother Goose's nursery rhymes, tales and jingles (Warne ed. Chicken Licken.)
Norton. Heart of oak books. v. 1. (Henny Penny.)
O'Grady and Throop. Teachers' story teller's book. (Chicken-Licken.)
*Old, old tales retold. (Chicken Licken.)
Pyle. Mother's nursery tales. (Chicken-diddle.)
Quiller-Couch. Fairy tales far and near. (Little Chicken Cluck.)

Chicken-Little—*continued.*
Rhys. Fairy gold.
Scudder. Book of folk stories. (Story of Chicken Licken.)
Scudder. Children's book. (Story of Chicken Licken.)
Tappan. Folk stories and fables. (Chicken Licken.)
Thorpe. Yule-tide stories. (Little Chicken Kluk and his companions.)
*Treadwell. Reading literature: primer.
Welsh. Stories children love. (Story of Chicken-Licken.)
Wiggin and Smith. Tales of laughter. (Henny Penny.)
Wiltse. Folklore stories and proverbs. (Chicken Licken.)
See also End of the world; Hungry fox; Sky is falling; Timid hare.
Chief Duck sends rain. Borland. Rocky Mountain tipi tales.
Chief in the moon. Judson. Myths and legends of Alaska.
Chief mourner. *See* Fox as chief mourner.
Chief of the healing waters. *See* Hidden waters.
Chief Xat. Allen. Indian fairy tales.
Chief's daughter. Lang. Strange story book.
Chief's son and the maidens. Macnair. Animal tales from Africa.
Child and the world. Wiggin and Smith. Story hour.
Child in the grave. Andersen. Fairy tales (Paull tr.).
Andersen. Stories and tales.
Child of Elle. Macleod. Book of ballad stories.
(poem). Lanier. Boy's Percy.
Child of Mary. *See* Lassie and her godmother.
Child of the forest. *See* Kintaro.
Child of the mist. Baldwin. Another fairy reader.
Olcott. Book of elves and fairies. (Little Niebla.)
Child of the roses. Ortoli. Evening tales.
Child of the sun. Baldwin. Second fairy reader.
Child of the thunder. Griffis. Japanese fairy tales.
James. Green willow. (Good thunder.)
Johnson. Birch-tree fairy book. (Son of the Thunder-god.)
Tappan. Myths from many lands. (Rai-taro, the son of the Thunder God.)
Wiggin and Smith. Tales of wonder.
Child or fairy. Brown. Star jewels.
Child Rowland. *See* Childe Rowland.
Child who came from an egg. Lang. Violet fairy book.
Lang. Marvellous musician.
Child who forgot to wash his face. Bailey. Stories for Sunday telling.
Childe Charity, Story of. Browne. Granny's wonderful chair.
Hodgkins. Atlantic treasury of childhood stories.
Olcott. Book of elves and fairies.
Childe Horne. Mabie. Legends every child should know.
Childe Rowland. Jacobs. English fairy tales.
Lansing. Tales of old England.
Singleton. Wild flower fairy book. (Child Rowland.)

Childe Rowland—*continued.*
Success library. v. 3.
Tyler. Twenty-four unusual stories.
* Young and Field. Literary readers. Book 2.
Children and the dog. Davis and Chow-Leung. Chinese fables and folk stories.
Children and the loon magician. Partridge. Glooscap the great chief.
Children in the moon. I. Blaisdell. Child life. 2d reader.
Judd. Classic myths. (Jack and Jill on the moon mountains.)
Olcott. Wonder garden. (Story of Jack and Jill.)
Children in the moon. II. Holbrook. Book of nature myths.
Children in the moon. III. Esenwein and Stockard. Children's stories. (Jack and Jill's visit to the moon.)
Children in the woods. *See* Babes in the wood.
Children of King Pellicano. Winnington. Outlook fairy book.
Children of Lir. *See* Fate of the children of Lir.
Children of the cloud. Eastman. Indian legends retold.
Children of wind and the clan of peace. Skinner. Emerald story book.
Storytellers' magazine. Dec. 1915, p. 504.
Children with one eye. Macmillan. Canadian fairy tales.
Children's festival. Keyes. Five senses.
Children's prattle. Andersen. Fairy tales (Paull tr.).
Andersen. Stories and tales.
Child's dream of a star. Mabie. Famous stories every child should know.
Olcott. Good stories for great holidays.
Child's grave. Grimm. Fairy tales (Paull tr. Shroud.)
Child's play. Murray. Story book treasures.
My Bookhouse. v. 2.
Richards. Golden windows.
Chilkat blanket, Origin of. *See* Blankets, Indian.
Chimæra. *See* Pegasus.
Chimborazo. Richards. Joyous story of Toto.
See also Oh dear.
Chin-chin Kobakama. Hearn. Japanese fairy tales.
Wiggin and Smith. Tales of laughter.
China Rabbit family. Poulsson. In the child's world.
Chinese beauty and the beast. I. Goddard. Fairy tales in other lands.
Chinese beauty and the beast. II. Fielde. Chinese fairy tales. (Fairy serpent.)
Chinese mandarin's story. Harrison. Bric-a-brac stories.
Chinese prodigal son. Davis and Chow-Leung. Chinese fables and folk stories.
Chinese story. *See* Lantern and the fan.
Ching Yuh and Kyain Oo. *See* Trials of two heavenly lovers.
Chinook ghosts. *See* Blue Jay visits the ghosts.

Chinook wind. Judson. Myths and legends of the Pacific Northwest.
Chipmunk who chattered too much. *See* Chipmunk's stripes. III.
Chipmunk's stripes. I. Cooke. Nature myths. (How the chipmunk got its stripes.)
Stanley. Animal folk tales. (Chipmunk's black stripes, as told by the Hindoos.)
See also Squirrel's devotion; Why striped chipmunk is proud of his stripes.
Chipmunk's stripes. II. Dyer and Brady. Merrill readers. 3d reader. (Stripe on the chipmunk's back.)
Judd. Wigwam stories. (Chipmunk's black stripes.)
Judson. Old Crow stories. (How Grizzly Bear stole the light.)
Stanley. Animal folk tales. (Chipmunk's black stripes, as told by the Indians.)
Storytellers' magazine. May 1914, p. 575. (How the chipmunk got his stripes.)
Tanner. Legends from the red man's forest. (Chipmunk's black stripe.)
Chipmunk's stripes. III. Bailey. Once upon a time animal stories. (Chipmunk who chattered too much.)
Olcott, Red Indian fairy book. (Noisy chipmunk.)
Chipmunk's stripes. IV. Borland. Rocky Mountain tipi tales. (Chipmunk gets his stripes.)
Chipmunk's stripes. V. Linderman. Indian why stories. (Why the chipmunk's back is striped.)
Chiron. Bailey. In the animal world. (Horse who kept school.)
Baldwin. Story of the golden age. (At old Cheiron's school.)
Choctaw mound. Allen. Indian fairy tales.
Choice. Lindsay. More mother stories.
Choice of Hercules. *See* Hercules and his labors.
Choice of the princess. *See* Eighty-one brothers.
Chop-Chin and the golden dragon. Richards. Toto's merry winter.
Choristers of St. Gudule. Bosschère. Fairy tales of Flanders.
Christ and folk-songs. Magnus. Russian folk-tales.
Christ and the geese. Magnus. Russian folk-tales.
Christ-child. I. Dickinson and Skinner. Children's book of Christmas stories.
Christ-child. II. Cowles. Art of story telling.
Christ-child. III. Proudfoot. Child's Christ tales.
Christ-child and the boy. Guerber. Legends of the Rhine.
Christ-child and the clay birds. Lagerlöf. Christ legends. (In Nazareth.)
Pitrè. Swallow book. (Creation of the swallow.)

Christ-child and the clay birds—*continued.*
Proudfoot. Child's Christ tales. (Birds.)
Storytellers' magazine. April 1916, p. 250. (Joyous miracle.)
Christening of a king. Guerber. Legends of the Rhine.
Christian merchant. Arabian nights (Townsend. Story told by the Christian merchant.)
Arabian nights, More tales (Olcott. Story told by the Christian merchant: The left hand.)
Christmas. *See* *After-Christmas reindeer; Animals' Christmas tree; Babe in the manger; Bunny Bobtail's merry Christmas; Candles; Cat who kept Christmas; Christ-child; Coming of the prince; Cratchit's Christmas dinner; Christie: Doll who was sister to a princess; Emperor's vision; Fir tree I; First Christmas presents; First Christmas tree; Forest Christmas tree; Forest witch; Fulfilled; Golden cobwebs; Holly; Holy night; Horse who hung up his shoe; How Christmas came to Bertie's house; How the camel unbent; How the cat kept Christmas; How the pixy kept warm; How the umbrella ran away with Ellie; Jar of Rosemary; Jerusalem Artie's Christmas dinner; Jimmy Scarecrow's Christmas; * Kate Woodenshoe; King Wencelaus; Legend of mercy; Little cake bird; Little fir tree that blossomed; Little girl's Christmas; Little gray lamb; Little green elf's Christmas; Little Gretchen and the wooden shoe; Little Lodewyk and Annie the witch; Little match girl; Little red candle; Little Roger's night in church; Little silver hen; Little tree that never grew up; Luck boy of Toy Valley; Magic sword; Man in the moon; Mercy, Legend of; *Mice's Christmas party; Mother's excuse; Mouse and the moonbeam; Nest that hung on the Christmas tree; Night with Santa Claus; Olaf and Astrid's Christmas eve; Paulina's Christmas; Penitence of Blazenko; Piccola; Pine tree's dress of gold; Promise; Robin's Christmas song; St. Nicholas; Shepherd maiden's gift; Shepherd who did not go; Shepherd who turned back; Shepherd's gift; Silver cones; Silver porringer; Sir Cleges; Star tree; Story of little half-cock; Story of the candy stick; Symbol and the saint; Three kings of Cologne; Three purses; Three little Christmas trees that grew on the hill; Thunder oak; Tilly's Christmas; Tiniest star; Toinette and the elves; Tree in the dark wood; Voyage of the wee red cap; White rabbit and the Christmas tree; Why the chimes rang; * Work basket egg; Worker in sandalwood.
See also Titles beginning Christmas; Santa Claus.
Christmas angel. Storytellers' magazine. Dec. 1916, p. 646.
See also Golden cobweb.
Christmas apple of Hermann the clockmaker. Sawyer. This way to Christmas. (David goes seeking the way to Christmas.)

Christmas before last; or, Fruit of the fragile palm. Stockton. Bee-man of Orn.
Stockton. Queen's museum.
Christmas bells. *See* Why the chimes rang.
Christmas cake. Lindsay. More mother stories.
Christmas candle. Pumphrey. Stories of the pilgrims.
Christmas council of the winter folk. Children's story garden.
Christmas cuckoo. Browne. Granny's wonderful chair.
* Field second reader.
Olcott. Good stories for great holidays.
Tyler. Twenty-four unusual stories.
Christmas dream. Alcott. Lulu's library. v. 1.
Christmas eve in Startown. Potter. Pinafore pocket story book.
Christmas eve, Story of a. Bellamy. Wonder children.
Christmas every day. Howells. Christmas every day.
Christmas fairy. *Elson and Runkel. Elson readers. Book 1.
Christmas fairy of Strasburg. Olcott. Good stories for great holidays.
Christmas gift. I. *See* Piccola.
Christmas gift. II. * Bryant. New stories to tell to children.
Christmas gift. III. Chandler. Pan the piper.
Christmas masquerade. Dickinson and Skinner. Children's book of Christmas stories.
Wilkins. Pot of gold.
Christmas monks. Wilkins. Pot of gold.
Christmas of the little rich child. Bailey. Stories for Sunday telling.
Christmas promise of the three Kings. Sawyer. This way to Christmas. (Locked out fairy again leads the way.)
Christmas rose, Legend of. I. Harper. Story-hour favorites.
Christmas rose, Legend of. II. Olcott. Good stories for great holidays. (Christmas rose.)
Storytellers' magazine. Dec. 1915, p. 452.
Christmas rose, Legend of. III. Baumbach. Tales from wonderland.
Chisholm. Enchanted land.
McFee. Treasury of flower stories.
Christmas rose. IV. *See* Forest witch.
Christmas seals. Storytellers' magazine. Dec. 1917, p. 538. (Fairy seals.)
Christmas star. Dickinson and Skinner. Children's book of Christmas stories.
Pyle. Prose and verse for children.
Christmas stocking. Lindsay. More mother stories.
Christmas stocking with a hole in it. Scudder. Seven little people.
Christmas story. Silver fairy book.

Christmas that was nearly lost. Sawyer. This way to Christmas.
Christmas thorn of Glastonbury. *See* Thorn of Glastonbury.
Christmas town. Bailey. Friendly tales. (In Christmas town.)
Christmas tree. I. Bailey and Lewis. For the children's hour. (Legend of the Christmas tree.)
Curtiss. Christmas stories and legends. (Legend of the Christmas tree.)
Dickinson and Skinner. Children's book of Christmas stories. (First Christmas tree.)
*Dillingham and Emerson. Tell it again stories. (Christmas legend.)
Olcott. Good stories for great holidays. (Stranger child.)
Sly. World stories retold. (Legend of the Christmas tree.)
Christmas tree. II. * Bailey. Folk stories and fables. (How the fir tree became the Christmas tree.)
Bailey and Lewis. For the children's hour. (How the fir tree became the Christmas tree.)
Curtiss. Christmas stories and legends. (How the fir tree became the Christmas tree.)
Christmas tree. III. Austin. Basket woman.
Christmas tree. IV. *See* Thunder oak.
Christmas tree. V. Field. Christmas tales. (First Christmas tree.)
Field. Little book of profitable tales. (First Christmas tree.)
Christmas tree. VI. Van Dyke. Blue flower. (First Christmas tree.)
See also Thunder oak.
Christmas tree fairy. Patterson. Enchanted bird.
Christmas tree for cats. Bailey. Stories children need.
Christmas tree friends. Bailey. Friendly tales.
Christmas tree that grew. Storytellers' magazine. Dec. 1917, p. 528.
Christmas trees. Edey. Six giants and a griffin.
Christmas truants. Stockton. Fanciful tales.
Stockton. Queen's museum.
Christmas turkey and how it came. Alcott. Lulu's library. v. 3.
Christmas visitors. Esenwein and Stockard. Children's stories.
Storytellers' magazine. Dec. 1913, p. 355. (Christmas visitor.)
See also Christmas tree. I.
Christmas wishes. Skinner. Garnet story book.
Chrysanthemum children. Olcott. Wonder garden.
Chrysanthemums. *See* Maiden white and maiden yellow.
Chufil-Filyushka. Magnus. Russian folk-tales.
Chun Yang. *See* Faithful dancing-girl wife.

Chundun Rajah. Frere. Old Deccan days.
Singleton. Goldenrod fairy book. (Sandal-wood necklace.)
Success library. v. 3.
Chunks of daylight. *See* Daylight, Origin of. II.
Church clock and the sun-dial. *See* Clock and the dial.
Church of the apostles. Guerber. Legends of the Rhine.
Church pillar. Guerber. Legends of the Rhine.
Ciad, son of the king of Norway, Adventures of. MacManus. Donegal fairy stories.
Ciccu. Lang. Elf maiden.
Lang. Pink fairy book.
Cicely and the bears (poem). Storytellers' magazine. Jan. 1917, p. 20.
Cid, The. Crommelin. Famous legends.
Evans. Old time tales. (The Cid wins his name; The last days of the Cid.)
Guerber. Legends of the middle ages.
Haaren and Poland. Famous men of the middle ages.
Herbertson. Heroic legends. (How my Cid the Campeador won the favor of his king.)
Lang. Red romance book.
Mabie. Heroes and fairies.
Mabie. Heroes every child should know.
My Bookhouse. v. 5. (Tale of the Cid and his daughters.)
Patten. Junior classics. v. 4. (Spanish chronicle of the Cid.)
Tappan. Stories of legendary heroes.
See also Babieca, the booby.
Cincinnatus, Story of. Baldwin. Fifty famous stories.
Johonnot. Stories of the olden time.
Cinder-Maid. *See* Cinderella.
Cinder Youth. Kunos. Forty-four Turkish fairy tales. (Simpleton.)
Kunos. Turkish fairy tales.
Cinderboy and the witch. *See* Golden lantern, the golden goat and the golden cloak.
Cinderella; or, The little glass slipper. Adams. Folk-story and verse.
Allison and Perdue. Story in primary instruction.
Aunt Louisa's book of fairy tales.
Baldwin. Fairy stories and fables.
Bates. Once upon a time.
Burke. Fairy tales.
Canton. Reign of King Herla.
Chaplin. Treasury of fairy tales.
Chisholm. In fairyland.
Coe. First book of stories.
Coe and Christie. Story hour readers. Book 3.
Coussens. Child's book of stories.
Cruikshank. Cruikshank's fairy book.
*Dillingham and Emerson. Tell it again stories.

Cinderella;—*continued.*
Douglas. Favourite French fairy tales.
Dyer. What-happened-then stories.
*Dyer and Brady. Merrill readers. 3d reader.
Favorite fairy tales.
Forty famous fairy tales.
Grimm. Fairy tales (Lucas tr. Ashenputtel.)
Grimm. Fairy tales (Paull tr.).
Grimm. Household stories (Crane tr. Aschenputtel.)
Grimm. Household tales (Burt ed.).
Grimm. Household tales (Everyman's ed. Aschenputtel.)
Harris. Favorites from fairyland.
Hodgkins. Atlantic treasury of childhood stories.
*Howard. Dick Whittington and other stories.
Hoxie. Kindergarten story book.
Jacobs. Europa's fairy book. (Cinder-Maid.)
Jerrold. Big book of fairy tales.
Johnson. Oak-tree fairy book.
Ketchum and Jorgensen. Kindergarten gems.
*Lang. Cinderella and other fairy tales.
Lang. Blue fairy book.
Lansing. Fairy tales. v. 1.
Larned. Fairy tales from France.
Mabie. Fairy tales every child should know.
Mabie. Heroes and fairies.
Marshall. Fairy tales of all nations.
Mother Goose rhymes, jingles and fairy tales (Altemus ed.).
Mulock. Fairy book.
My Bookhouse. v. 2.
Norton. Heart of oak books. v. 2.
Nursery tales.
Olcott. Book of elves and fairies.
Patten. Junior classics. v. 1.
Perkins. Twenty best fairy tales.
Perrault. Fairy tales.
Perrault. Old-time stories.
Perrault. Tales of Mother Goose.
Perrault. Tales of passed times.
Pyle. Mother's nursery tales.
Quiller-Couch. Sleeping beauty.
Rhys. Fairy gold.
Scudder. Book of folk stories.
Scudder. Children's book.
Scudder. Fables and folk stories.
*Stone. Children's stories that never grow old.
Success library. v. 3.
Tappan. Folk stories and fables.
Thorpe. Yule-tide stories. (Little gold shoe.)
Tweed. Fairy tales everyone should know.
Valentine. Old, old fairy tales (Warne ed.)
Welsh. Fairy tales children love.

Cinderella;—*continued.*
See also Conkiajgharuna; Fair, Brown, and Trembling; Finette Cendron; Huron Cinderella; Kari Woodengown; Little Sosana and her gold wrought shoe; Nippit fit and Clippit fit; Pigling and her proud sister; Red slipper; Rhodopsis and her little gilded sandals; Rushen Coatie I and II; Tattercoats.
Cinderlad. *See* Princess on the glass hill.
Circe's palace. *See* Ulysses.
Circling of cranes. Judson. Myths and legends of Alaska.
Circus parade. Bigham. Merry animal tales.
See also Rat and the elephant.
Citizen of the world. Friedlander. Jewish fairy book.
City child and the country child. Bailey. Stories for Sunday telling.
City mouse and the country mouse. *See* Country mouse and the city mouse.
City of brass. Arabian nights (Olcott ed.).
Arabian nights. Wiggin and Smith.
City of the sea king. Harrison. Prince Silverwings.
City rat and the country rat (poem). Wiggin and Smith. Talking beasts.
City that never was reached. Stocking. City that never was reached and other stories.
City under the sea. Beston. Firelight fairy book.
Claus and his wonderful staff. Pyle. Pepper and salt.
Cleft mountain. Brown. Tales of the red children.
Cleobis and Biton. Guerber. Myths of Greece and Rome. (*In* Juno.)
Cleomene. Baring-Gould. Crock of gold.
Cleopatra. Brooksbank. Legends of ancient Egypt. (Glory of sunset.)
Clerk's tale. *See* Patient Griselda.
Clergyman's ghost. Hartland. English folk and fairy tales.
Clever Alice. Grimm. Fairy tales (Lucas tr. Clever Elsa.)
Grimm. Fairy tales (Paull tr. Clever Bess.)
Grimm. Household fairy tales (Burt ed. Clever Elfe.)
Grimm. Household stories (Crane tr. Clever Else.)
Lansing. Fairy tales. v. 2.
Mulock Fairy book.
Scudder. Children's book.
Scudder. Fables and folk stories.
See also Three sillies.
Clever Bess. *See* Clever Alice.
Clever cat. Lang. Orange fairy book.
Clever chicken. Bailey. In the animal world. (Fox outwitted.)
Grayl. Fairy tales from foreign lands.
See also Bird, the fox and the dog.
Clever companions. Armfield. Wonder tales.
Clever Elfe. *See* Clever Alice.
Clever Elsa. *See* Clever Alice.

Clever Else. *See* Clever Alice.
Clever Elsie. *See* Clever Alice.
Clever folk. Grimm. Fairy tales (Paull tr.).
See also All women are alike.
Clever geese. *See* Fox and the geese.
Clever girl. *See* Peasant's clever daughter.
Clever goat. Fillmore. Mighty Mikko.
Rouse. Talking thrush.
Clever Grethel. Grimm. Fairy tales (Lucas tr.).
Grimm. Fairy tales (Paull tr. Clever Maggie.)
Grimm. Household stories (Crane tr.).
Grimm. Household tales (Everyman's ed. Hans and his wife Grettel, pt. 1.)
See also Two chickens; or, Two ears.
Clever Hans. *See* Prudent Hans.
Clever jackal. *See* Little jackal and the alligator.
Clever lass. *See* Peasant's clever daughter.
Clever Maggie. *See* Clever Grethel.
Clever Manka. Fillmore. Shoemaker's apron.
Clever Maria. Lang. Crimson fairy book.
Lang. Magic ring and other stories.
Clever Peter and the two bottles. Pyle. Pepper and salt.
Clever prince. Grundtvig. Fairy tales from afar.
Wiggin and Smith. Fairy ring.
Clever prince and the stupid brother. Jewett. Wonder tales from Tibet.
Clever rat. *See* Rat's wedding.
Clever shepherd. Johnson. Birch-tree fairy book.
Clever shepherdess. Lindsay. Joyous travelers. (Tale told by the older sister.)
Clever student and the master of black arts. Pyle. Wonder clock.
Clever tailor. Johnson. Book of fairy-tale bears. (Bear and the tailor.)
Lang. Green fairy book.
Lang. Three dwarfs and other stories.
Clever turtle. Skinner. Merry tales.
Clever weaver. Lang. Olive fairy book.
Clever wife. I. *See* Gobborn seer.
Clever wife. II. Friedlander. Jewish fairy tales.
Clever young girl. Stroebe and Martens. Danish fairy book.
See also Clever Alice; Three sillies.
Climbing alone. Cabot. Ethics for children.
Climbing the mountain. Seton. Woodland tales.
Clock. Fyleman. Rainbow cat.
Clock and the dial. Æsop. Fables (Burt ed.).
Curry. Little classics. (Church clock and the sun-dial.)
Clocks and no clocks. Storytellers' magazine. Feb. 1914, p. 453.
Clocks of Rondaine. My Bookhouse. v. 4.
Stockton. Queen's museum.

Close alliance. Steel. Tales of the Punjab.
Closing door. Cross and Statler. Story-telling.
Lindsay. Mother stories.
Cloud. Bryant. Stories to tell to children.
Cabot. Ethics for children.
Skinner. Turquoise story book.
Sly. World stories retold.
See also Rain cloud; Water drop. II.
Cloud-cuckoo-borough. Carpenter. Long ago in Greece.
Cloud-fairy's grandchildren. Patterson. Enchanted bird.
Cloud maidens. Harrison. Prince Silverwings.
Clouds and waves. My Bookhouse. v. 1.
Clover-blossom (poem). Alcott. Flower fables.
Clover leaf. Baumbach. Tales from wonderland.
Clovis' vow. Guerber. Legends of the Rhine.
Clytie. *Alderman. Classics old and new. 1st reader.
Bailey and Lewis. For the children's hour.
*Beckwith. In mythland. v. 1.
Cooke. Nature myths and stories.
*Dyer and Brady. Merrill readers. 2d reader.
*Elson and Runkel. Elson readers. Book 2. (Girl who was changed to a sunflower.)
Firth. Stories of old Greece. (Helios and Clytie.)
Francillon. Gods and heroes. (Sun-flower.)
Holbrook. 'Round the year in myth and song.
Hyde. Favorite Greek myths.
Judd. Classic myths. (Girl who was changed into a sunflower.)
McFee. Treasury of flower stories.
My Bookhouse. v. 2.
Olcott. Good stories for great holidays. (Clytie, the heliotrope.)
Olcott. Wonder garden. (Clytie, the heliotrope. Adapted.)
*Poulsson. In the child's world.
Pratt. Greek myths. v. 2.
Skinner. Turquoise story book. (Origin of the sunflower.)
*Skinner. Very little child's book of stories.
Sly. World stories retold. (Story of the sunflower.)
Wilson. Nature study reader.
Coach in the forest. Bailey. Friendly tales.
Coal. *See* Gnome's wish.
Coal-black steed. *See* Fairy's midwife.
Coat o' clay. Jacobs. More English fairy tales.
Coat of all colors. *See* Many-furred creature.
Cobble-stone, Adventures of. Sologub. Sweet-scented name.
Cobbler. Cowles. Art of story telling.
Cobbler and the brownies. Nursery tales.
Cobbler and the fairies. *See* Elves and the shoemaker.
Cobbler and the ghosts. Ewing. Old-fashioned fairy tales.
Cobbler and the king, Merry history of. Lansing. Tales of old England.

Cobbler and the king, Merry history of—*continued.*
Skinner. Garnet story book. (Merry tale of the king and the cobbler. Adapted.)
Cobbler turned doctor. Æsop. Fables (Burt ed.).
Cobbler's lad. Grundtvig. Danish fairy tales.
Cobbler's luck. Macdonell. Italian fairy book.
Cobblers of Bruges. Bouvé. Lamp-light tales.
Cobbler's song. Bryce. Fables from afar.
Cock-a-doo-dle-do. Bryant. Stories to tell to children.
Cock-alu and Hen-alie. Darton. Wonder book of beasts.
Dyer and Brady. Merrill readers. 3d reader.
Cock and hen a-nutting. *See* Cock and hen in the nut wood.
Cock and hen that went to Dovrefell. *See* Chicken-Little.
Cock and his combats (poem). Success library. v. 3.
Cock and the crested hen. Djurklo. Fairy tales from the Swedish.
Wiggin and Smith. Tales of laughter.
Cock and the diamond. *See* Cock and the jewel.
Cock and the fox. I. Æsop. Fables (Black ed.).
Æsop. Fables (Burt ed. Fox and the cock.)
Æsop. Fables (Stickney).
Cock and the fox. II. Æsop. Fables (Black ed.).
Æsop. Fables (Burt ed.).
Æsop. Fables. (Jacobs. Fox, the cock and the dog.)
(poem). Æsop. Fables (Stickney. Supplement).
Bosschère. Fairy tales of Flanders.
*Elson and Runkel. Elson readers. Book 1.
(play). Lansing. Quaint old stories.
(poem). Wiggin and Smith. Talking beasts.
See also Cock and fox. VI.; Mr. Fox and the Turkey tree.
Cock and the fox. III. Asbjörnsen. Fairy tales from the far north.
Asbjörnsen. Tales from the fjeld. (Reynard and Chanticleer.)
*Bowen. Second story reader. (Fox and the rooster.)
Field. Famous fairy tales.
Houghton. Russian grandmother's wonder tales. (Master Reinicke and Gockeling the cock.)
Thorne-Thomsen. East o' the sun and west o' the moon. (Reynard and the cock.)
Wiggin and Smith. Tales of laughter. (Reynard and Chanticleer.)
Cock and the fox. IV. *Burchill. Progressive road to reading. Book 2.
Curry. Little classics. (Chanticleer.)
Darton. Tales of the Canterbury Pilgrims. (Nun's priest's tale: Cock and the fox.)
Esenwein and Stockard. Children's stories. (Fox and the cock.)
McSpadden. Stories from Chaucer. (Priest's tale: Cock and the fox.)

Cock and the fox—*continued.*
Skinner. Merry tales. (Chanticleer.)
Storr and Turner. Canterbury chimes. (Nun's priest's tale: Cock and the fox.)
Storytellers' magazine. Sept. 1916, p. 479. (Tale of Chanticleer.)
Cock and the fox. V. Baldwin. Fairy stories and fables. (Fox outwitted.)
Douglas. Scottish fairy tales. (Fox and the cock.)
Johnson. Birch-tree fairy book. (Fox and the rooster.)
Johnson. Book of fairy-tale foxes. (Fox and the boastful rooster.)
O'Grady and Throop. Teachers' story tellers' book. (Fox and the rooster.)
Cock and the fox. VI. Æsop. Fables. (Stickney. Dog, the cock and the fox.)
Cock and the goose. Caballero. Spanish fairy tales.
Cock and the hen. I. *See* Vagabonds.
Cock and the hen. II. Dasent. Popular tales from the Norse.
Dasent. Norse fairy tales.
Houghton. Russian grandmother's wonder tales.
See also Drakesbill and his friends.
Cock and the hen in the nut wood. Dasent. Popular tales from the Norse. (Cock and hen a-nutting.)
Thorpe. Yule-tide stories.
See also Chanticleer and Partlett; Vagabonds.
Cock and the horses. Æsop. Fables (Burt ed.).
Cock and the jewel. Æsop. Fables (Black ed.).
Æsop. Fables (Burt ed.).
Æsop. Fables (Jacobs. Cock and the pearl.)
Æsop. Fables (Stickney).
Bryce. Fables from afar. (Cock and the diamond.)
Patten. Junior classics. v. 1.
Wiggin and Smith. Talking beasts.
Cock and the pearl. *See* Cock and the jewel.
Cock Robin (poem). Haaren. Songs and stories. 2d reader. (Who killed Cock Robin.)
Jerrold. Big book of nursery rhymes. (Death and burial of Cock Robin.)
Lansing. Rhymes and stories.
Mother Goose rhymes, jingles and fairy tales (Altemus ed.).
O'Shea. Six nursery classics. (Burial of poor Cock Robin.)
O'Shea. Six nursery classics. (Courtship, marriage and dinner of Cock Robin and Jenny Wren and death of Cock Robin.)
See also Robin's Christmas song.
Cock, the cuckoo, and the blackcock. Dasent. Popular tales from the Norse.
Dasent. Norse fairy tales.
Wiggin and Smith. Tales of laughter.

Cock, the mouse and the little red hen. Hodgkins. Atlantic treasury of childhood stories.
My Bookhouse. v. 1.
Skinner. Very little child's book of stories.
*Van Sickle and Seegmiller. Riverside readers. 2d reader.
See also Little red hen. III.
Cock who fell into the brewing vat. *See* Death of Chanticleer.
Cock's kraal. Bourhill and Drake. Fairy tales from South Africa.
Cock's stone. Macdonell. Italian fairy book.
Cock's wife. Cary. French fairy tales.
See also Drakesbill and his friends.
Cockyloo. Alcott. Lulu's library. v. 1.
Coco. *See* Half-Chick.
Codadad and his brothers, History of. Arabian nights (Townsend).
Arabian nights (Housman. Wicked half-brothers, Story of.)
Arabian nights (Wiggin and Smith).
Coffee, Discovery of. Cather. Educating by story telling. (Dervish of Mocha.)
Coffee-mill which grinds salt. *See* Why the sea is salt. III.
Cogia Hassan Alhabbal, History of. Arabian nights (Dodge ed.).
Arabian nights (Townsend).
Ketcham. Oriental fairy tales.
Scudder. Children's book.
Coins of Elijah. Friedlander. Jewish fairy tales.
Cold heart. *See* Stone-cold heart.
Cold lady. James. Green willow.
Cold princess. Kennedy. New world fairy book.
Coldfeet and the Queen of Lonesome Land. Curtin. Hero tales from Ireland.
Colin and Mary. Gibbon. Reign of King Cole.
Collector of lies. Seton. Woodmyth and fable.
Colman Grey. Hartland. English folk and fairy tales.
See also King of the cats.
Colony of cats. Lang. Crimson fairy book.
Lang. Snow-queen and other stories.
See also Why the cat scratches.
Colt and the farmer (poem). Æsop. Fables (Burt ed.).
Colours of the rainbow. Olcott. Wonder garden.
Columbine and Pierrot. My Bookhouse. v. 3. (Columbine and her play-fellows.)
Columbus and the eclipse. Johonnot. Stories of heroic deeds.
Columbus and the egg. Baldwin. Thirty more famous stories.
Olcott. Good stories for great holidays.
Wickes. Happy holidays. (Simplest thing in the world.)

Comanche Chief, the peace-maker. Grinnell. Pawnee hero stories.
Comatos and the honey bee. Hyde. Favorite Greek myths.
See also Rhœcus and the oak.
Comb and the collar. Lang. Olive fairy book.
Lang. White doe.
Comet. Andersen. Stories and tales.
Coming of Angus and Bride. Hodgkins. Atlantic treasury of childhood stories.
Coming of Benten Sama. Nixon-Roulet. Japanese folk stories and fairy tales.
Coming of Finn. *See* Finn MacCool.
Coming of Galahad. *See* Sir Galahad.
Coming of Ki-Ki. Nixon-Roulet. Indian folk tales.
Coming of Seegwun. *See* Old Winter Man and the Spring. II.
Coming of the god and goddess. *See* Isis and Osiris, Story of.
Coming of the king. I. Bailey and Lewis. For the children's hour.
My Bookhouse. v. 2.
Richards. Golden windows.
Coming of the king. II. Storytellers' magazine. Oct. 1917, p. 395.
Coming of the prince. Field. Christmas tales.
Field. Little book of profitable tales.
Harper. Story-hour favorites.
Coming of the wonder tree. Cather. Educating by story telling.
Compair Lapin and Mr. Turkey. Tappan. Folk stories and fables.
Compair Lapin's godchild. Tappan. Folk stories and fables.
See also Cat and the mouse in partnership.
Companion. Asbjörnsen. Fairy tales from the far north.
Asbjörnsen. Tales from the fjeld.
See also Traveling companion.
Companions of the forest. Macdonell. Italian fairy book.
Compliment to the vizier. Success library. v. 3.
Comrade. Stroebe and Martens. Norwegian fairy book.
Comrades. *See* Manstin, the rabbit.
Conal and Donal and Taig. MacManus. Donegal fairy stories.
Olcott and Pendleton. Jolly book.
Conall Yellowclaw. Jacobs. Celtic fairy tales.
Conceited apple-branch. Andersen. Fairy tales (Paull tr.).
Andersen. Fairy tales (Turpin. There is a difference.)
Andersen. Stories and tales. ("There's a difference.")
Baker and Carpenter. Language readers. 3d year.
Conceited grasshopper. Keyes. Stories and story-telling.
Sly. World stories retold.
Storytellers' magazine. July 1916, p. 420.

Conceited owl. Æsop. Fables (Burt ed.).
Conflicting customs. Guerber. Legends of the Rhine.
Confucius, Legend of. Martens. Chinese fairy book.
Conjuration for a fairy. Rhys. Fairy gold.
Conjure wives. Wickes. Happy holidays.
Young. Plantation bird legends. (Owls.)
Conkiajgharuna. Wardrop. Georgian folk tales.
See also Cinderella.
Conn-Eda, Story of. Pyle. Fairy tales from far and near.
Yeats. Irish fairy and folk tales.
Connla and the fairy maiden. Forty famous fairy tales.
Jacobs. Celtic fairy tales.
Joyce. Old Celtic romances. (Connla of the golden hair and the fairy maiden.)
Connla of the golden hair and the fairy maiden. *See* Connla and the fairy maiden.
Constable. Martens. Chinese fairy book.
Constance. *See* Faithful Constance.
Constans the emperor. Wilmot-Buxton. Stories from old French romance. (Story of Constans the emperor.)
See also King who would be stronger than fate; Fore-ordained match; Fish and the ring.
Constant tin soldier. *See* Brave tin soldier.
Constantes and the Dhrako. Byrne. Modern Greek fairy tales.
Constantine's cross. Guerber. Legends of the Rhine.
Contrary woman. *See* Goody 'Gainst-the-Stream.
Convenient whale. Henderson. Sea yarns for boys.
Convent free from care. Bosschère. Christmas tales of Flanders.
Tyler. Twenty-four unusual stories.
See also King and the miller; Emperor and the abbott.
Conversion of King Laoghaire's daughter. Yeats. Irish fairy and folk tales.
Coo-my-doo. Richards. Little master.
Cookies. Bailey. Stories for Sunday telling.
Cook's tale. *See* Sir Gamelyn.
Cooky. Bryant. How to tell stories.
Richards. Golden windows.
Cooky nut trees. Fairy tales retold from St. Nicholas.
Cooky valentine. Bailey. Stories for Sunday telling.
Coolnajoo the stupid. Partridge. Glooscap the great chief.
Copper canoe. Judson. Myths and legends of the Pacific Northwest.
Coquerico. See Half-Chick.
Corday, Charlotte. Evans. Old time tales. (Crime of Charlotte Corday.)
Coriolanus. Baldwin. Fifty famous people. (Story of old Rome.)
Guerber. Story of the Romans.
Haaren. Famous men of Rome.

Coriolanus—*continued.*
Olcott. Good stories for great holidays. (Revenge of Coriolanus.
Corkscrews. Guerber. Legends of the Rhine.
Cormac. Rolleston. High deeds of Finn.
This includes: Birth of Cormac; Judgment of Cormac; Marriage of Cormac; Instructions of the king; Cormac sets up the first mill in Erinn; Pleasant story of Cormac's Brehon; Judgment concerning Cormac's sword; Disappearance of Cormac; Description of Cormac; Death and burial of Cormac.
Cormorant and the fishes. Æsop. Fables (Burt ed.).
Cormorants of Udröst. Asbjörnsen. Folk and fairy tales.
Gade. Norwegian fairy book. (Ut-Röst cormorants.)
Corn chooses a mate. Borland. Rocky Mountain tipi tales.
See also First corn. IX.
Corn, Legend of. *See* First corn.
Corn-smut girl. Curtis. Indian days of the long ago.
Storytellers' magazine. Nov. 1916, p. 574. (Tales of an Indian grandfather.)
See also Man who married the moon.
Cornelia and her jewels. *See* Cornelia's jewels.
Cornelia's jewels. Baldwin. Fifty famous stories.
Faulkner. Story lady's book. (Mother love.)
Olcott. Good stories for great holidays.
Sly. World stories retold. (Cornelia and her jewels.)
Cornflower youth. Olcott. Wonder garden.
Corpse watchers. Graves. Irish fairy book.
Cottager and his cat. Lang. Crimson fairy book.
Lang. Snow-queen and other stories.
See also Fortune seekers. I.
Cotton, Origin of. *See* Fairy spinner.
Council held by rats. *See* Belling the cat.
Council of horses (poem). Æsop. Fables (Burt ed.).
Wiggin and Smith. Talking beasts.
Count Gismond. Storytellers' magazine. March 1917, p. 141.
Count of the empty pockets. Mendel. Our little Austrian cousin.
Countess Itha. Guerber. Legends of the Rhine.
Countess Kathleen O'Shea. Yeats. Irish fairy and folk tales.
Counting your chickens before they hatch. *See* Barber's fifth brother; Broken pot; Lad and the fox; Maid with her basket of eggs; Milkmaid with her pail of milk.
Country cat. Cowles. Art of story telling.
Country fellow and the river. Scudder. Children's book.
Scudder. Fables and folk stories.
Wiggin and Smith. Talking beasts.
Country maid and her milk-pail. *See* Milkmaid and her pail of milk.
Country maid and the milk pail. *See* Milkmaid and her pail of milk.

Country mouse and the city mouse. *See* Country mouse and the town mouse.
Country mouse and the town mouse. Æsop. Fables (Black ed. Country mouse and the city mouse.)
Æsop. Fables (Burt ed. Town mouse and the country mouse.)
Æsop. Fables (Jacobs. Town mouse and the country mouse.)
Æsop. Fables (Stickney).
Asbjörnsen. Fairy tales (Town mouse and the country mouse.)
Asbjörnsen. Tales from the fjeld. (Town mouse and the fell-mouse.)
Baker and Carpenter. Language readers. 3d year. (Town mouse and the country mouse.)
(play). Bailey. For the story teller. (Town mouse and the country mouse.)
Blaisdell. Child life. 2d reader.
Bryant. Stories to tell to children.
*Burchill. Progressive road to reading. Book 1. (Country mouse and the city mouse.)
(play). Dyer and Brady. Merrill readers. 3d reader. (City mouse and the country mouse.)
Gade. Norwegian fairy tales. (Housemouse and the field-mouse.)
Norton. Heart of oak books. v. 2. (Field mouse and the town mouse.)
Patten. Junior classics. v. 1.
Scudder. Children's book.
Scudder. Fables and folk stories.
(poem). Success library. v. 3. (Town and country mouse.)
Wiggin and Smith. Tales of laughter. (Town mouse and country mouse.)
*Young and Field. Literary readers. Book 2. (Town mouse and the country mouse.)
See also Littlest mouse; Mr. Blackrat's house party.
Country of swindlers. Bradley-Birt. Bengal fairy tales.
Country where the mice eat iron. Tappan. Folk stories and fables.
Countryman and his pet jay. Success library. v. 3.
Countryman and the merchant. Wardrop. Georgian folk tales.
See also Little Claus and Big Claus.
Countryman and the snake. Æsop. Fables (Black ed.).
Æsop. Fables (Burt ed.).
Æsop. Fables (Jacobs. Woodman and the serpent.)
Æsop. Fables (Stickney. Farmer and snake.)
Patten. Junior classics. v. 1. (Woodman and the serpent.)
(poem). Wiggin and Smith. Talking beasts. (Countryman and the serpent.)

Count's leap. Guerber. Legends of the Rhine.
Count's vision. Guerber. Legends of the Rhine.
Court ball. Guerber. Legends of the Rhine.
Court cards. Andersen. Wonder stories.
Court of death (poem). Æsop. Fables (Burt ed.).
Courteous King Jamie. Grierson. Scottish fairy book.
Courtship and marriage of Cock Robin and Jenny Wren. *See* Cock Robin; Robin's Christmas song.
Cousin Greylegs the great red fox and Grandfather Mole. Pyle. Wonder clock.
Cousin Mattie. Douglas. Scottish fairy tales.
Covan the Brown-haired, Adventures of. Lang. Orange fairy book.
Lang. Fairy nurse.
Covetous man. I. Bay. Danish fairy and folk stories.
Covetous man. II. *See* Miser.
Covetous neighbor. Dyer and Brady. Merrill readers. 3d reader.
Cow. Bailey. Stories children need.
Cow and the ass (poem). Arnold and Gilbert. Stepping stones to literature. v. 4.
(poem). Scudder. Children's book.
Cow that lost her tail. Poulsson. In the child's world.
Cow with golden horns. Wilkins. Pot of gold.
Coward heart. *See* Thor and Hrungnir.
Cowardly bat. *See* Bat, birds and beasts.
Cowslip. I. Boston collection of kindergarten stories.
Wiltse. Kindergarten stories.
Cowslip. II. Bosschère. Christmas tales of Flanders. (Key flower.)
Olcott. Wonder garden. (Fairy cowslips.)
See also Primrose, Legend of.
Coyote. I. *See* How fire was brought to the Indians; How the animals secured salmon.
Coyote. II. Lummis. Pueblo Indian folk stories.
Curtis. Indian days of the long ago. (Adventures of Coyote.)
Coyote and Grizzly. Judson. Myths and legends of the Pacific Northwest.
Coyote and rolling rock. Sexton. Gray wolf stories.
See also Brother Wolf and the rock; Coyote steals a blanket; Rolling rock; Wolverine and the rock.
Coyote and the bear. Lummis. Pueblo Indian folk stories.
Coyote and the blackbirds. Lummis. Pueblo Indian folk stories.
Coyote and the cedar tree. Judson. Old Crow stories.
Coyote and the crow. Lummis. Pueblo Indian folk stories.
Coyote and the dragon. Judson. Myths and legends of the Pacific Northwest.
Coyote and the Indian fire bringer. *See* Fire bringer.
Coyote and the salmon. *See* How the animals secured salmon.

Coyote and the thunder knife. Lummis. Pueblo Indian folk stories.
Coyote and the woodpecker. Lummis. Pueblo Indian folk stories.
Coyote in the buffalo country. Judson. Myths and legends of the Pacific Northwest.
Coyote lives with ten grizzlies. Sexton. Gray wolf stories.
Coyote marries the daughter of Thunder. Sexton. Gray wolf stories.
Coyote pushes in Mountain Lion's face. Borland. Rocky Mountain tipi tales.
Coyote puts fire in sticks. Borland. Rocky Mountain tipi tales.
Coyote-spirit and the weaving woman. Austin. Basket woman.
Coyote steals a blanket. Borland. Rocky Mountain tipi tales.
Coyote steals fire. I. Borland. Rocky Mountain tipi tales.
Coyote steals fire. II. Young. Algonquin Indian tales. (*In* Ch. 9. How coyote obtained fire.)
Coyote takes a ride. *See* Coyote's ride on a star.
Coyote the hungry. Olcott. Red Indian fairy book.
Coyote the proud. *See* Bluebird and Coyote.
Coyote the trickster, tries to become a creator. Bayliss. Treasury of Indian tales.
Coyote transforms a monster. Sexton. Gray wolf stories.
Coyote's last adventure. Sexton. Gray wolf stories.
Coyote's ride on a star. Chandler. In the reign of coyote.
Judson. Old Crow stories. (Coyote takes a ride.)
Crab and his mother. Æsop. Fables (Black ed. Two crabs.)
Æsop. Fables (Burt ed. Two crabs.)
Æsop. Fables (Jacobs. Two crabs.)
Æsop. Fables (Stickney. Crab and its mother.)
Grover. Folklore stories. v. 1.
Hall and Gilman. Story land. 2d reader.
My Bookhouse. v. 1. (Two crabs.)
Scudder. Children's book.
Scudder. Fables and folk stories.
Wiggin and Smith. Talking beasts. (Crab and its mother.)
Crab and its mother. *See* Crab and his mother.
Crab and the crane. *See* Crane and the crab.
Crab and the fox. *See* How the fox and the crab ran a race.
Crab and the monkey. Bailey. Stories and rhymes for a child. (How the crab got even.)
Blaisdell. Child life in many lands. (Ape and the crab.)
Chisholm and Steedman. Staircase of stories. (Monkey and the crab.)
Griffis. Japanese fairy tales. (Ape and the crab.)
Lang. Crimson fairy book.
Lang. Little Wildrose.

Crab and the monkey—*continued.*
Ozaki. Japanese fairy book. (Quarrel of the monkey and the crab.)
Wiggin and Smith. Tales of laughter. (Battle of the mon key and the crab.)
Crab and the moon. *See* Cause of tides.
Crab that played with the sea. Kipling. Just so stories. *See also* Cause of tides.
Crabs in plenty. Fielde. Chinese fairy tales.
Cradle song. Judson. Myths and legends of Alaska.
Crafty fox and industrious goose. Caballero. Spanish fairy tales. (Fox and the goose.)
Johnson. Book of fairy-tale foxes.
Wiggin and Smith. Tales of laughter. (Fox and the goose.)
Crafty lover. Macleod. Book of ballad stories.
Crafty Mister Man outwits Brer B'ar and Cuffey. Young. Behind the dark pines.
Crane. Young. Plantation bird legends.
Crane and the crab. Babbitt. Jataka tales. (Crab and the crane.)
Bidpai. Tortoise and the geese.
Coussens. Jade story book.
Jacobs. Indian fairy tales. Cruel crane outwitted.)
Crane and the crow. *See* Why the crow is black. III.
Crane and the crows. See Farmer and the stork.
Crane and the fool. Wiggin and Smith. Talking beasts.
Crane and the heron. *Carrick. Picture tales from the Russian.
Crane and the humming bird. Eastman. Indian legends retold.
Crane express. Poulsson. In the child's world.
Crane in the wheatfields. Johnson. Oak-tree fairy book.
Crane Tribe, Origin of. Judd. Wigwam stories.
Crane's gratitude. Stories of classic myths.
Cratchit's Christmas dinner. Bailey and Lewis. For the children's hour.
Blaisdell. Child life. 4th reader. (Tiny Tim's Christmas dinner.)
Judson and Bender. Graded literature readers. Book 6.
Patten. Junior classics. v. 6.
Tappan. Modern stories.
Creaking wheel. Æsop. Fables (Black ed.).
Æsop. Fables (Burt ed.).
Creation of man (Eskimo). Bayliss. Treasury of Eskimo tales. (First man; First woman.)
Bayliss. Treasury of Eskimo tales. (What the Eskimo believes.)
Judson. Myths and legends of Alaska. (Origin of mankind.)
Creation of man (Greek). *Bailey. Wonder stories. (What Prometheus did with a bit of clay.)

Creation of man—*continued.*
See also Deucalion and Pyrrha.
Creation of man (Indian). Bayliss. Treasury of Indian tales. (How the animal-men became real men.)
Chandler. In the reign of coyote.
Judson. Old Crow stories. (Remaking of real people.)
Judson. Old Crow stories. (When real people were baked.)
Judson. Myths and legends of the Pacific Northwest. (Creation of mankind.)
Lansing. Dramatic readings. (How all the animals tried to make man.)
Creation of man (Turkish). Kunos. Forty-four Turkish fairy tales.
Creation of mankind. *See* Creation of man.
Creation of the killer whale. Judson. Myths and legends of Alaska.
Creation of the porcupine. Judson. Myths and legends of Alaska.
Creation of the swallow. *See* Christ-child and the clay birds.
Creation of the world (Egyptian). Brooksbank. Legends of ancient Egypt. (Beginning of all things.)
Creation of the world (Eskimo). Judson. Myths and legends of Alaska. (Origin of land and people.)
Creation of the world (Greek). Francillon. Gods and heroes. (Saturn.)
Guerber. Myths of Greece and Rome.
Hutchinson. Orpheus with his lute. (Dawn of the world.)
Pratt. Myths of old Greece. v. 2.
See also Deucalion and Pyrrha.
Creation of the world (Indian). Borland. Rocky Mountain tipi tales. (How the world was made.)
Chandler. In the reign of coyote.
Chandler. Pan the piper. (*In* How color came to the world.)
Grinnell. Blackfoot lodge tales. (Blackfoot Genesis.)
Judson. Myths and legends of the Pacific Northwest. (How Kemush created the world.)
Judson. Myths and legends of the Pacific Northwest. (How Silver Fox created the world.)
Judson. Myths and legends of the Pacific Northwest. (How Qawaneca created the world.)
Nixon-Roulet. Indian folk tales. (Spider woman's mistake.)
See also Indians' flood.
Creation of the world (Norse). Brown. In the days of giants. (Beginning of things.)
Mabie. Norse stories. (Making of the world.)
Patten. Junior classics. v. 2. (Northmen's story of how all things began.)
Pratt. Legends of Norseland. (The beginning.)
Wickes. Beyond the rainbow bridge. (Tale of the beginning.)

Creation of the world—*continued.*
Wilmot-Buxton. Stories of Norse heroes. (How all things began.)
Creation of the world (Philippine). Miller. Philippine folk-lore stories. (How the world was made.)
Creep-Mouse. St. Nicholas. Feb. 1917, p. 378.
Cricket and the cougar. Chandler. In the reign of coyote.
Cricket and the poet. Bailey and Lewis. For the children's hour.
Crimson ribbon. Sologub. Sweet-scented name.
Crimson sleeve. *See* Sir Lancelot and Elaine.
Cristobal. May. Little Prudy's fairy book.
Critic. *See* Midas. II.
Critics silenced. Guerber. Legends of the Rhine.
Noyes. Twilight stories. (Statue.)
See also Actor and the pig; Owl critic.
Crœsus. Baldwin. Thirty more famous stories. (As rich as Crœsus.)
Haaren and Poland. Famous men of Greece. (*In* Draco and Solon.)
Scudder. Children's book. (Story of King Crœsus.)
Crooked fir. Austin. Basket woman.
Crooked Jack. Eggleston. Queer stories for boys and girls.
Cross, Legend of. Guerber. Legends of the Rhine.
Cross purposes. Macdonald. Dealings with fairies.
Macdonald. Light princess and other fairy tales.
Crosses on the wall (poem). Alexander. Hidden servants.
Crossing of the ford. Guerber. Legends of the Rhine.
Crossing the rubicon. *See* Cæsar, Julius.
Crow. Forty famous fairy tales.
Lang. Invisible prince and other stories.
Lang. Yellow fairy book.
Success library. v. 3.
Crow and Mercury. Æsop. Fables (Burt ed.).
Crow and the daylight. Riggs. Animal stories from Eskimo land.
See also Raven brings light.
Crow and the dove. Bryce. Fables from afar.
Crow and the fox. *See* Fox and the crow.
Crow and the lobster. Carrick. Picture tales from the Russian.
Crow and the mussel. Æsop. Fables (Burt ed.).
Wiggin and Smith. Talking beasts.
Crow and the owl. *See* Why the crow is black. II.
Crow and the partridge. Wiggin and Smith. Talking beasts.
Crow and the pitcher. Æsop. Fables (Black ed.).
Æsop. Fables (Burt ed.).
Æsop. Fables (Jacobs).
Æsop. Fables (Stickney).
Arnold and Gilbert. Stepping stones to literature. v. 2.
Bailey. Folk stories and fables.

Crow and the pitcher—*continued.*
Bailey and Lewis. For the children's hour.
Baldwin. Fairy stories and fables. (Wise crow.)
Coussens. Child's book of stories.
Grover. Folk-lore readers. v. 1.
My Bookhouse. v. 1.
Patten. Junior classics. v. 1.
Scudder. Children's book.
Scudder. Fables and folk stories.
Sly. World stories retold.
Wiggin and Smith. Talking beasts.
Wiltse. Kindergarten stories.
Crow-child. Dodge. Land of Pluck.
Crow children. Nixon-Roulet. Indian folk tales.
Olcott. Wonder garden. (Why crows caw.)
Crow feet. Brown. Tales of the red children.
Crow is a crow forever. Rouse. Talking thrush.
Crow-Peri. Kunos. Turkish fairy tales.
Kunos. Forty-four Turkish fairy tales.
Pyle. Wonder tales retold.
Crow talk. Gruelle. Friendly fairies.
Crow that thought it knew. Shedlock. Eastern stories and legends.
Crow, the jackal, the wolf and the camel. Bidpai. Tortoise and the geese.
Crown. Danielson. Story telling time.
Crown of white roses. Baring-Gould. Old English fairy tales.
Crows and the windmill. Bryce. Fables from afar.
Crow's children (poem). Wilson. Nature study reader.
See also One's own children are always the prettiest.
Cruel crane outwitted. *See* Crane and the crab.
Cruel father. Guerber. Legends of the Rhine.
Cruel parents. Guerber. Legends of the Rhine.
Cruel sister. Guerber. Legends of the Rhine.
See also Binnorie; Singing bone.
Cruel stepmother. MacMillan. Canadian fairy tales.
Cruel tribute. *See* Theseus.
Crumbs on the table. Grimm. Fairy tales (Paull tr.).
Cry-because-he-had-no-wife. Judson. Myths and legends of the Pacific Northwest.
Cry fairy. Brown. One-footed fairy.
Crystal coffin. Lang. Green fairy book.
Lang. Three dwarfs and other stories.
Crystal mirror. I. Storytellers' magazine. July 1917, p. 330.
Crystal mirror. II. Storytellers' magazine. Nov. 1917, p. 478.
Crystal palace. Guerber. Legends of the Rhine.
Stebbins. Sunken city.
Cub's triumph. Wiggin and Smith. Tales of laughter.
Cuchulain. *See* Cuhulain.

Cuckoo. Olcott. Wonder garden. (Why the little bird that brags cries cuckoo!)
Cuckoo and the cock. Æsop. Fables (Stickney. Supplement).
Wiggin and Smith. Talking beasts.
Cuckoo and the eagle. Æsop. Fables (Stickney. Supplement).
Wiggin and Smith. Talking beasts.
Cuckoo and the turtle-dove. Wiggin and Smith Talking beasts.
Cuckoo, the hedge-sparrow and the owl. Æsop. Fables (Burt ed.).
Cuculin. *See* Cuhulain.
Cud, Cad, Micad, three sons of the king of Urhu. Curtin. Hero tales from Ireland.
Cuhulain. Bryant. Treasury of hero tales. (How Cuchulain got his name.)
Curtin. Myths and folk-lore of Ireland. (Cuculin.)
Graves. Irish fairy book. (Boyhood of Cuhulain.)
Graves. Irish fairy book. (Cuchulain of Muirthemne.)
My Bookhouse. v. 5. (Cuchulain the Irish hound).
Stewart. Tell me a hero story. (How a boy prince took arms.)
Cunning apprentice. Baring. Blue rose fairy book.
Cunning Arab. Hartwell. Story hour readings. 5th year.
Cunning hare. Lang. Brown fairy book.
Lang. Elf Maiden.
Cunning jackal; or, The biter bit. Rouse. Talking thrush.
Cunning man in Hilltown. Bay. Danish fairy and folk tales.
Cunning of Fin's wife. *See* Knockmany, Legend of.
Cunning old man and the Demi. Wardrop. Georgian folk tales.
Cunning shoemaker. Lang. Golden mermaid and other stories.
Lang. Pink fairy book.
Cunning snake. Harris. Nights with Uncle Remus.
Cunning wolf. Babbitt. More Jataka tales.
Cup of Thanksgiving. Olcott. Wonder garden.
Cupid. Olcott. Wonder garden. (Adventures of Cupid among the roses; Lost, lost; Cupid punished.)
Cupid and Psyche. Almost true tales.
*Bailey. Wonder stories. (How Psyche reached Mount Olympus.)
Bailey and Lewis. For the children's hour.
*Beckwith. In mythland. v. 2.
Buckley. Children of the dawn. (Eros and Psyche.)
Carpenter. Long ago in Greece.
Firth. Stories of old Greece. (Psyche.)
Francillon. Gods and heroes. (Love and the soul.)
Guerber. Myths of Greece and Rome. (*In* Venus.)
Holbrook. Round the year in myth and song.

Cupid and Psyche—*continued.*
Hyde. Favorite Greek myths. (Psyche.)
Lang. Red romance book.
Olcott. Good stories for great holidays.
Patten. Junior classics. v. 2. (Story of Cupid and Psyche.)
Peabody. Old Greek folk stories.
*Poulsson. In the child's world. (Psyche's tasks.)
Pratt. Greek myths. v. 2.
Pyle. Fairy tales from far and near. (Eros and Psyche.)
Tappan. Myths from many lands.
Cupid's darts. Olcott. Wonder garden.
Cure for story-telling. Magnus. Russian folk tales.
Curious impertinent. Success library. v. 3.
Curious woman. Gregory. Kiltartan wonder book.
Curious young man. Lang. Twelve huntsmen and other stories.
Curly-tailed lion. Griffis. Dutch fairy tales.
Curmudgeon's skin. Olcott. Book of elves and fairies.
Curse of Echo. *See* Echo and Narcissus.
Curse of Pantannas. Thomas. Welsh fairy book.
Curtius. Guerber. Story of the Romans. (Two heroes.)
Cusheen Loo (poem). Yeats. Irish fairy tales.
"Cutta cord-la!" Harris. Nights with Uncle Remus.
Cyane. *See* Weeping waters.
Cyclops. I. *See* Ulysses and Polyphemus.
Cyclops. II. *See* Titans.
Cydippe and Acontius. Carpenter. Long ago in Greece.
Cynewulf and Cyneherd. Wilmot-Buxton. Stories of early England.
Cypress tree, Story of the. Kupfer. Stories of long ago. (How a boy loved a stag.)
Cyrus and his grandfather. Baldwin. Fifty famous people. (Young cupbearer.)
Johonnot. Stories of the olden time.
Cyrus and the Armenians. Johonnot. Stories of the olden time.
Czar. *See* Tsar.
Czar and the angel. Bain. Cossack fairy tales.

D

Dædalus and Icarus. *Bailey. Wonder stories. (Where the labyrinth led.)
Baldwin. Old Greek stories. (Wonderful artisan.)
*Beckwith. In mythland. v. 3. (Man that learned to fly.)
Burt and Ragozin. Herakles and other heroes. (Dædalos, a hero of invention.)
Carpenter. Long ago in Greece.
Francillon. Gods and heroes. (Lost secret.)
Guerber. Myths of Greece and Rome. (*In* Theseus.)

Dædalus and Icarus—*continued.*
Hartwell. Story hour readings. 7th year. (Wonderful artisan.)
Kupfer. Stories of long ago. (Artisan's wonderful wings.)
Merrill readers. 3d reader. (Flight through the sky.)
Olcott. Wonder garden. (Boy whose wings fell off.)
Peabody. Old Greek folk stories.
Pratt. Myths of old Greece. v. 3.
Shaw. Stories of the ancient Greeks. (Wings of wax.)
Stories of classic myths.
Storr. Half a hundred hero tales.
Tappan. Stories from the classics.
See also Hunter who could fly; Why the partridge stays near the ground.
Dagda's harp. Bryant. Best stories to tell to children.
Bryant. Stories to tell to children.
Dahul. Bassett. Wander ships.
See also Flying Dutchman.
Dai Sion's homecoming. Thomas. Welsh fairy book.
Dairywoman and the pot of milk. *See* Milkmaid and her pail of milk.
Daisy. Andersen. Fairy tales (Paull tr.).
Andersen. Fairy tales (Turpin).
Andersen. Stories (Riverside ed.).
Andersen. Wonder stories.
Arnold and Gilbert. Stepping stones to literature. v. 3. (Daisy and the lark.)
Bailey and Lewis. For the children's hour.
Curry. Little classics.
Ketchum and Jorgensen. Kindergarten gems.
Scudder. Children's book.
Daisy and the lark. *See* Daisy.
Daisy, Legend of the. Chisholm. Enchanted land.
Noyes. Twilight stories. (Story of the daisy.)
Daisy's first winter. Curry. Little classics.
Dalbec, Adventures of. Storytellers' magazine. Sept. 1917, p. 354.
Dalimkumar. Bradley-Birt. Bengal fairy tales.
Dalles. Judson. Myths and legends of the Pacific Northwest.
Dama's jewels. Cabot. Ethics for children.
Dambeck bells. Thorpe. Yule-tide stories.
Dame cricket's story. Walker. Sandman's goodnight stories.
Dame Fortune and Don Money. Caballero. Spanish fairy tales.
Dame Grumble and her curious apple-tree. Brady. Green forest fairy tales.
Dame Gudbrand. Asbjörnsen. Fairy tales from the far north. (Gudbrand on the hill-side.)
Chisholm and Steedman. Staircase of stories. (Gudbrand on the hillside.)
Dasent. Norse fairy tales. (Gudbrand on the hillside.)

Dame Gudbrand—*continued.*
Dasent. Popular tales from the Norse. (Gudbrand on the hillside.)
Laboulaye. Fairy tales. (Good woman.)
Laboulaye. Last fairy tales.
Olcott and Pendleton. Jolly book. (Gudbrand on the hillside.)
Storytellers' magazine. Feb. 1915, p. 47. (Gudbrand on the hillside.)
Tappan. Folk stories and fables. (Gudbrand on the hillside).
Thorne-Thomsen. East o' the sun and west o' the moon. (Gudbrand on the hillside.)
Thorpe. Yule-tide stories. (Gudbrand on the hillside.)
Wiggin and Smith. Tales of laughter. (Gudbrand on the hillside.)
See also Hans in luck; Mr. Vinegar; "What the good man does is sure to be right."
Dame Martha's stepdaughter; or, Grandmother of the gnomes. Harrison. Old-fashioned fairy book.
Dame Pridgett and the fairies. *See* Fairy ointment.
Dame Weasel and her husband. Laboulaye. Fairy tales. (Weasel and her husband. *In* Captain John's travels.)
Laboulaye. Last fairy tales.
Dame Wiggins of Lee and her seven wonderful cats. (poem). Bailey. In the animal world.
(poem). My Bookhouse. v. 2.
(poem). Norton. Heart of oak books. v. 2.
O'Shea. Six nursery classics.
Damocles: Sword of Damocles. Baldwin. Fifty famous stories.
Damon and Pythias. Baldwin. Fifty famous stories.
Cabot. Ethics for children.
Coe. Second book of stories.
Johonnot. Stories of the olden time.
Sly. World stories retold.
Yonge. Book of golden deeds. (Two friends of Syracuse.)
Danae. *See* Perseus.
Dance in a buffalo skull. Zitkala-Sa. Old Indian legends.
Dance of the fairies. Pitman. Chinese fairy tales.
Dancers cursed. Guerber. Legends of the Rhine.
Dancing cat. *See* Cat-cat.
Dancing gang. Dasent. Popular tales from the Norse.
Dancing horses of Sybaris. Baldwin. Horse fair.
Dancing shoes. I *See* Twelve dancing princesses.
Dancing shoes. II. *See* Red shoes.
Dancing water, singing stone and talking bird. *See* Three sisters. I.
Dancing water, the singing apple, and the speaking bird. *See* Three sisters. I.
Dandelion. I. Bailey and Lewis. For the children's hour.
Dandelion. II. *See* Prairie dandelion.

Dandelion fairies. Olcott. Wonder garden.
Dandelion, Legend of. I. Bailey and Lewis. For the children's hour.
Dandelion, Legend of. II. *See* Dandelion stars.
Dandelion maiden. *See* Prairie dandelion.
Dandelion stars. Farmer. Nature myths.
Strong. All the year round. v. 3. Spring. (Legend of the dandelion.)
Dandelions, Story of. Donahey. Tales to be told to children.
See also Elf's flower; Goldenrod, Legend of I; Sun princess.
Dando and his dogs. Hartland. English folk and fairy tales.
Dandy Beaver and Sippy Woodchuck Messer. Next time stories.
Danes. Gregory. Kiltartan wonder book.
Dangerous reward. Martens. Chinese fairy book.
Dangerous ride. *See* Phaethon.
Daniel O'Rourke. Graves. Irish fairy book.
Johnson. Birch-tree fairy book. (Visit to the moon.)
My Bookhouse. v. 3.
Olcott and Pendleton. Jolly book. (Astounding voyage of Daniel O'Rourke.)
Tappan. Folk stories and fables.
Yeats. Irish fairy tales.
See also Dream of Owen Mulready.
Danilo the unfortunate. Magnus. Russian folk-tales.
Danish popular legends. Andersen. Stories and tales.
Danny's Halloween. Bouvé. Lamplight fairy tales.
Daphne. Adams. Myths of old Greece.
*Bailey. Wonder stories. (Wonder the frogs missed.)
Baldwin. Old Greek stories. (*In* Lord of the silver bow.)
Coe. Second book of stories. (Story of the laurel tree.)
Cooke. Nature myths.
Farmer. Nature myths. (Laurel tree.)
Firth. Stories of old Greece.
Francillon. Gods and heroes. (Laurel.)
Guerber. Myths of Greece and Rome. (*In* Apollo.)
Hartley. Stories from the Greek legends. (Story of Apollo and Daphne; or, The first laurel tree.)
Hyde. Favorite Greek myths. (Apollo and Daphne.)
Judd. Classic myths. (Little maiden who became a laurel tree.)
Olcott. Good stories for great holidays.
Olcott. Wonder garden.
Patten. Junior classics. v. 2. (Daphne, child of the morning.)
Pratt. Myths of old Greece. v. 1.
Pratt. Myths of old Greece. v. 2. (Apollo and Daphne.)
Storr. Half a hundred hero tales.
Wilson. Nature study reader. (Apollo and Daphne.)
Dapplegrim. Dasent. Popular tales from the Norse.
Dasent. Norse fairy tales.

Dapplegrim—*continued.*
Lang. Forty thieves and other stories.
Lang. King of the waterfalls.
Lang. Red fairy book.
Pyle. Wonder tales retold.
Thorpe. Yule-tide stories. (Grimsbork.)
Wiggin and Smith. Tales of wonder.
Dark day. Baldwin. Fifty famous stories.
Darling, Grace. Baldwin. Fifty famous stories.
Darning needle. Andersen. Best fairy tales (Hendersen tr.).
Andersen. Fairy tales (Paull tr.).
Andersen. Fairy tales (Turpin).
Andersen. Fairy tales and stories (Toksvig).
Andersen. Stories (Riverside ed.).
Andersen. Wonder stories.
Boys' and girls' fairy book.
Johnson. Fir-tree fairy book.
Lang. Twelve huntsmen and other stories.
Lang. Yellow fairy book.
Patten. Junior classics. v. 1.
Scudder. Children's book.
Tappan. Folk stories and fables.
Wiggin and Smith. Tales of laughter.
Dashing captain. Birch. Green-faced toad.
Date palm, Origin of. Cather. Educating by story telling. (Coming of the wonder tree.)
Daughter of a Samurai. Nixon-Roulet. Japanese folk stories and fairy tales.
Daughter of Buk Ettemsuch. Lang. Grey fairy book.
Lang. Invisible prince and other stories.
Daughter of the King of Ku-ai-he-laui. Colum. At the gateways of the day.
Daughter of the laurel. Olcott. Wonder garden.
Daughter of the Padishah of Kandahar. Kunos. Forty-four Turkish fairy tales.
See also Faithful John.
Daughter of the stars. *See* Star-wife.
Daughter of the sultan. Gate. Fortunate days.
Daughter of Tiogaughwa. Nixon-Roulet. Indian folk tales.
See also Sun princess.
David and the good health elves. Storytellers' magazine. June, July 1916, Feb., Mar., 1917.
David and the insects. Friedlander. Jewish fairy book.
David, King of Israel. *See* From shepherd boy to king.
Davy and the goblin. Van Sickle and Seegmiller. Riverside readers. 4th reader. (Believing voyage.)
Daw and peacocks. *See* Jay and the peacocks.
Dawn of the world. *See* Creation of the world (Greek).
Day. Richards. Golden windows.
Day and night. I. Gatty. Parables from nature.
Day and night. II. Judd. Wigwam stories. (How light, fire and water first came to the world.)

Day and night—*continued.*
Judson. Old Crow stories. (Grizzly Bear is at it again.)
See also Daylight, Origin of.
Day-dreaming. *See* Barber's fifth brother; Counting your chickens before they hatch.
Day the sun ran away. Potter. Pinafore pocket story book.
Day there were no mothers. Potter. Pinafore pocket story book.
Day with the capercailzies. Asbjörnsen. Folk and fairy tales.
Daylight, Origin of. I. Judson. Myths and legends of the Pacific Northwest.
Judson. Old Crow stories. (How Raven brought the light.)
Daylight, Origin of. II. Bayliss. Treasury of Eskimo tales. (Chunks of daylight.)
Judson. Myths and legends of Alaska. (Bringing of the light by Raven.)
Judson. Old Crow stories. (When the real people stole sun.)
Daylight, Origin of. III. Eastman. Indian legends retold (How the daylight came.)
Daylight, Origin of. IV. Holbrook. Book of nature myths. (How the raven helped men.)
Nixon-Roulet. Indian folk tales. (How fire came to the earth.)
Daylight, Origin of. V. My Bookhouse. v. 3. (Adventures of Yehl and the beaming maiden.)
Daylight, Origin of. For other versions *See* Sun, moon and stars; Day and night; Lost light.
Day's a'-breakin'. Young. Plantation bird legends.
Days of the week. Andersen. Stories and tales.
Deacon's dream. Bay. Danish fairy and folk tales.
Deacon's wife. Bay. Danish fairy and folk tales.
Dead mother. Canton. Reign of King Herla.
See also Tender mother.
Dead, Tales of. Magnus. Russian folk-tales.
Dead wife. Lang. Yellow fairy book.
Dear departed. Mendes. Fairy spinning wheel.
Dear little hen. * Fillmore. Shoemaker's apron.
See also Chanticleer and Partlett.
Dear-my-soul. Fairy tales from Brentano.
Death and burial of Cock Robin. *See* Cock Robin.
Death and burial of the poor hen-sparrow. Steel. Tales of the Punjab.
See also Death of Chanticleer; Spider and the flea; Titty Mouse and Tatty Mouse.
Death and Cupid. Æsop. Fables (Black ed.).
Æsop. Fables (Burt ed.).
Death and the doctor. *See* Lad with the beer keg.
Death and the negro man. Harris. Uncle Remus and his friends.

Death and the three revellers. *See* Three revellers and death.
Death and the woodman. Æsop. Fables (Black ed. Old man and death.)
Æsop. Fables (Burt ed. Old man and death.)
Æsop. Fables (Jacobs. Old man and death.)
Æsop. Fables (Stickney. Supplement).
Scudder. Children's book. (Old man and death.)
Death of Abu Nowas and his wife. Lang. Crimson fairy book.
Lang. Little Wildrose.
See also Abou Hassan; or, The sleeper awakened.
Death of Chanticleer. Asbjörnsen. Fairy tales from the far north. (Cock who fell into the brewing-vat.)
Asbjörnsen. Tales from the fjeld.
Wiggin and Smith. Tales of laughter.
See also Death and burial of poor hen-sparrow; Spider and the flea; Titty Mouse and Tatty Mouse.
Death of Grettir the Strong. Lang. Tales of romance.
Death of Gunnar. Lang. Red romance book.
Death of Koschei the Deathless. *See* Marya Morevna.
Death of the cock. *See* Chanticleer and Partlett.
Death of the hen. *See* Chanticleer and Partlett.
Death of the innocent. Guerber. Legends of the Rhine.
Death of the little hen. *See* Chanticleer and Partlett.
Death of the Sun-Hero. Lang. Three dwarfs and other stories.
Lang. Yellow fairy book.
Death ship. Hauff. Caravan tales.
Deborah's book. Ingelow. Stories told to a child. v. 1.
Deceived eagle. Æsop. Fables (Burt ed.).
Deceiver and the thief. Kunos. Forty-four Turkish fairy tales.
Deep-sea violets. Harrison. Old-fashioned fairy book.
Deer. *See* Stag at the lake.
Deer and the lion. I. Æsop. Fables (Black ed.).
Æsop. Fables (Burt ed.).
Deer and the lion. II. *See* Stag at the lake.
Deer and the rabbit. Coe and Christie. Story hour readers. 3d book. (Swift runner.)
Eastman. Indian legends retold. (How the deer got his horns.)
Farmer. Nature myths.
(play). *Field first reader. (How the deer got his horns.)
Olcott. Wonder garden. (Why the deer have antlers.)
Stanley. Animal folk tales. (Deer's horns.)
Deer and the rainbow. *See* Animals in the sky.
Deer gets antelope's dew claws. *See* Fast runners.
Deer of the five colors. Singleton. Wild flower fairy book.
Deer prince. Stroebe and Martens. Danish fairy book.
Deereeree the wagtail and the rainbow. Success library. v. 3.

Deer's horns. I. *See* Deer and the rabbit.
Deer's horns. II. *See* Stag at the lake.
Defeat of Hrungner. Pratt. Legends of Norseland.
Defeat of time. Rhys. Fairy gold.
Deianeira. *See* Hercules and Deianeira.
Deirdre. Chisholm. Enchanted land. (Star-eyed Deirdre.)
Jacobs. Celtic fairy tales.
Delenda est Carthago. Baldwin. Thirty more famous stories.
Delicate child. Sologub Sweet-scented name.
Delphi. Baldwin. Story of the golden age. (*In* Centre of the earth.)
Delphian oracle. Baldwin. Story of the golden age. (*In* Centre of the earth.)
Guerber. Story of the Romans. (Oracle of Delphi.)
Deluge. *See* Deucalion and Pyrrha; Indians' flood.
Deluge, and how it came about, Story of the. Harris. Uncle Remus, his songs and his sayings.
See also Indians' flood.
Delusive whispers. Guerber. Legends of the Rhine.
Demeter. *See* Proserpina.
Demian's fish soup. Æsop. Fables (Stickney. Supplement).
Wiggin and Smith. Talking beasts.
Demon cat. Graves. Irish fairy book.
Demon lover. Tappan. Old ballads in prose.
Demon of the mountain. Pyle. Tales of wonder and magic.
Demon Tregeagle. Hartland. English folk and fairy tales.
Demon with the matted hair. Burlingame. Grateful elephant. (Buddhist Tar-baby.)
Jacobs. Indian fairy tales.
Demon's marriage. Friedlander. Jewish fairy book.
Demon's mother-in-law. Caballero. Spanish fairy tales.
Derido; or, The giant's quilt. Stockton. Floating prince.
Dervish. Wardrop. Georgian folk tales.
Dervish and the lost camel. *See* Lost camel.
Dervish of Mocha. Cather. Educating by story telling.
Desecrated tombs. Guerber. Legends of the Rhine.
Desert. Richards. Golden windows.
Deserted children. Partridge. Glooscap the great chief.
See also Brother and sister. IV; Lost children.
Deserted city. Guerber. Legends of the Rhine.
Deserted wife of Boppart. Guerber. Legends of the Rhine.
Deserted wife of Godesberg. Guerber. Legends of the Rhine.
Deserter. Houghton. Russian grandmother's wonder tales.
Wiggin and Smith. Tales of wonder.
Desideratus. Baring-Gould. Old English fairy tales.
Desolate things. Birch. Green-faced toad.
Despot and the wag. Wiggin and Smith. Talking beasts.
Destiny. I. Cary. French fairy tales.

Destiny. II. Laboulaye. Fairy book.
Wiggin and Smith. Tales of wonder.
Destruction of Da Derga's hostel (play). Colum. Boy in Eirinn.
Deucalion and Pyrrha. Baldwin. Old Greek stories. (The flood.)
Baldwin. Story of the golden age. (*In* Children of Prometheus.)
Burt and Ragozin. Herakles and other heroes. (Deukalion, the champion of a new race.)
Francillon. Gods and heroes. (Great flood.)
Guerber. Myths of Greece and Rome. (*In* Beginning of all things.)
Haaren and Poland. Famous men of Greece. (Deucalion and the flood.)
Hartley. Stories from the Greek legends. (Story of the great deluge; or, The ark of Deucalion.)
Hutchinson. Orpheus with his lute. (Deucalion's flood.)
Hyde. Favorite Greek myths. (Great deluge.)
Peabody. Old Greek folk stories. (The deluge.)
Pratt. Myths of old Greece. v. 2. (Great flood; New creation.)
Shaw. Stories of the ancient Greeks. (Deucalion's flood.)
Storr. Half a hundred hero tales.
See also Creation of the world (Greek).
Deucalion's flood. *See* Deucalion and Pyrrha.
Devil and the blacksmith. *See* Smith and the devil. III.
Devil and the donkey. Guerber. Legends of the Rhine.
Devil and the rooster. Guerber. Legends of the Rhine.
Devil and the wind. Guerber. Legends of the Rhine.
Devil in the dough-pan. Magnus. Russian folk-tales.
Devil worsted. *See* Evil one and Kitta Grau; Gentle Dora; Katcha and the devil; Old Nick and Kitty.
Devil's bridge. I. Thomas. Welsh fairy book.
Devil's bridge. II. Froelicher. Swiss stories.
Devil's gifts. Fillmore. Shoemaker's apron.
Wenig. Beyond the giant mountains.
See also Table, the ass and the stick.
Devil's hide. Fillmore. Mighty Mikko.
See also Keep cool; Jack and his master; Hans Humdrum.
Devil's imprint. Guerber. Legends of the Rhine.
Devil's kindness. Stroebe and Martens. Danish fairy book.
Devil's ladder. Evans. Old time tales.
Guerber. Legends of the Rhine.
Devil's little brother-in-law. Fillmore. Shoemaker's apron.
Devil's match. Fillmore. Shoemaker's apron.
Devil's mill. I. Thorpe. Yule-tide stories.
Devil's mill. II. Wenig. Beyond the giant mountains.
Devil's pulpit. Guerber. Legends of the Rhine.
Devil's stone. Guerber. Legends of the Rhine.
Devoted friend. Wilde. Fairy tales.

Dew Mother's gift to the rose. *See* Moss rose, Legend of.
Dewdrop. *See* Drop of rain.
Diablo and the dogwood. Seton. Woodland tales.
Diamond. Murphy. Necklace of jewels.
Diamond and the glow-worm. Æsop. Fables (Burt ed.).
Bryce. Fables from afar. (Glowworm and the diamond.)
Diamond cut diamond. Lang. Olive fairy book.
Diamonds and roses and pearls. *See* Diamonds and toads.
Diamonds and toads. Arnold and Gilbert. Stepping stones to literature. v. 3.
Bates. Once upon a time (Toads and diamonds.)
Blaisdell. Child life. 3d reader.
Boston collection of kindergarten stories.
Coussens. Child's book of stories.
Douglas. Favourite French fairy tales.
Jerrold. Reign of King Oberon. (Fairy at the well.)
Lang. Blue fairy book. (Toads and diamonds.)
Lang. Little Red Riding-Hood and other stories. (Toads and diamonds.)
Lansing. Fairy tales. v. 1.
My Bookhouse. v. 2. (Toads and diamonds.)
Norton. Heart of oak books. v. 2.
Nursery tales.
Olcott. Book of elves and fairies. (Toads and diamonds.)
Perrault. Fairy tales. (Fairies.)
Perrault. Tales of Mother Goose. (Toads and diamonds.)
Perrault. Tales of passed times. (Fairies.)
Pyle. Fairy tales from many lands. (Diamonds and roses and pearls.)
Sly. World stories retold.
Success library. v. 3. (Toads and diamonds.)
Valentine. Old, old fairy tales.
Welsh. Fairy tales children love.
Young and Field. Literary readers. Book 2. (Fairy.)
See also Patty and her pitcher; Three gifts. I.
Diana. Judd. Classic myths.
Peabody. Old Greek folk stories. (Apollo's sister.)
See also Endymion; Orion; Queres Diana.
Diana and Actæon. Guerber. Myths of Greece and Rome. (*In* Diana.)
Hartley. Stories from the Greek legends. (Story of Artemis, the queen huntress, and the death of Actæon the bold hunter.)
Peabody. Old Greek folk stories.
Pratt. Myths of Old Greece. v. 2. (Actæon.)
Dick and his cat. *See* Dick Whittington and his cat.
Dick o' the cow. Grierson. Children's tales from Scottish ballads.
Dick the fiddler's money. Thomas. Welsh fairy book.
Dick Whittington. *See* Dick Whittington and his cat.
Dick Whittington and his cat. Bailey. Stories children need.

Dick Whittington and his cat—*continued.*
Baker and Carpenter. Language readers. 3d year. (Dick and his cat.)
Baldwin. Fifty famous stories. (Whittington and his cat.)
Blaisdell. Child life. 3d reader. (Dick Whittington.)
Carrick. Kitty cat tales. (Dick Whittington and his wonderful cat.)
Coussens. Child's book of stories.
Haaren. Ballads and tales.
Hartland. English folk and fairy tales. (Whittington and his cat.)
*Howard. Dick Whittington and other stories.
Jacobs. English fairy tales.
Jerrold. Big book of fairy tales.
Johnson. Elm-tree fairy book. (Whittington and his cat.)
Johonnot. Grandfather's stories.
Lang. Blue fairy book. (History of Whittington.)
Lansing. Tales of old England.
Mother Goose rhymes, jingles and fairy tales (Altemus ed. Whittington and his cat.)
My Bookhouse. v. 2.
Nursery tales.
Norton. Heart of oak books. v. 2. (History of Sir Richard Whittington and his cat.)
O'Shea. Old world wonder stories. (Whittington and his cat.)
Rhys. Fairy gold.
Scudder. Book of folk stories.
Scudder. Children's book. (History of Sir Richard Whittington and his cat.)
Scudder. Fables and folk stories.
Sly. World stories retold.
Stone. Children's stories that never grow old.
Tappan. Folk stories and fables. (Whittington and his cat.)
Tweed. Fairy tales everyone should know.
Welsh. Stories children love. (History of Sir R. Whittington and his cat.)
See also Honest penny.
Dick Whittington and his wonderful cat. *See* Dick Whittington and his cat.
Dickey's friend. Donahey. Tales to be told to children.
Dicky Dare. Burchill. Progressive road to reading: Story steps. (Dicky Dare; Dicky Dare and his sheep.)
See also Goats in the turnip field.
Dicky Smiley's birthday. Wiggin and Smith. Story hour.
Didoze. English. Fairy stories and wonder tales.
Dietrich von Bern. Guerber. Legends of the middle ages.
Different kind of bundles. Slosson. Story-tell Lib.
Dill. Patten. Junior classics. v. 6.
Wilkins. Pot of gold.
Dilly dally. *Dillingham and Emerson. Tell it again stories.

Dining with a merman. Henderson. Sea yarns for boys.
Diogenes the wise man. Baldwin. Fifty famous stories.
Haaren and Poland. Famous men of Greece. (*In* Aristotle.)
Diomed's man-eating mares. Baldwin. Horse fair. (Man-eaters.)
See also Hercules and his labors.
Dipper. Bailey and Lewis. For the children's hour. (Legend of the dipper.)
*Elson and Runkel. Elson readers. Book 2. (Star dipper.)
Esenwein and Stockard. Children's stories. (Legend of the dipper.)
Faulkner. Story lady's book. (Great dipper.)
Wiltse. Kindergarten stories. (Legend of the great dipper.)
Dirty shepherdess. Lang. Green fairy book.
Lang. Pretty Goldilocks and other stories.
Disappointed bear. *See* Bear and the little old woman.
Discontented ass. Æsop. Fables (Burt ed.).
Wiggin and Smith. Talking beasts.
Discontented blacksmith (play). Lansing. Quaint old stories.
Discontented cat. Carrick. Kitty cat tales.
Discontented chickens. Esenwein and Stockard. Children's stories.
Discontented coffee pot. Bailey. Firelight stories.
Discontented dewdrop. Walker. Sandman's goodnight stories.
Discontented grass plant. I. *Coe and Christie. Story hour readers. Book 2. (Unhappy grass stalk.)
Discontented grass plant. II. Bayliss. Treasury of Eskimo tales. (Even a grass plant can become some one if it tries.)
Judson. Myths and legends of Alaska.
Discontented mermaid. Stewart. Once upon a time.
Discontented mill window. Harrison. In storyland.
Discontented pendulum. Arnold and Gilbert. Stepping stones to literature. v. 5.
Cabot. Ethics for children.
Edgeworth. Waste not, want not.
Hartwell. Story hour readings. 7th year.
(play). Lansing. Quaint old stories. (One minute at a time.)
Poulsson. In the child's world.
Scudder. Children's book.
Smith. Good old stories.
Tappan. Folk stories and fables.
Welsh. Stories children love.
Discontented pig. Cather. Educating by story telling.
Discontented pine. *See* Little pine tree who wished for new leaves.
Discontented pine tree. *See* Little pine tree who wished for new leaves.

Discontented pumpkin. Skinner. Topaz story book.
Discontented rock. Olcott. Red Indian fairy book.
See also Stone-cutter.
Discontented tadpole. Donahey. Tales to be told to children.
Discontented Teg. Williams. Fairy tales from folklore.
Discontented tree. *See* Little pine tree who wished for new leaves.
Discontented weather cock. Boston collection of kindergarten stories.
Discreet Hans. *See* Prudent Hans.
Disease, Origin of. Cornyn. When the camp fire burns. (Last great council fire.)
Eastman. Indian legends retold. (Origin of sickness and medicine.)
Young. Algonquin Indian tales. (*In* Ch. 11.)
Disenchantment of the werwolf. Lang. Red romance book.
See also William of Palermo.
Disobedient Dicky bird. Children's story garden.
Disobedient ducklings. Danielson. Story telling time.
Disobedient island. Aspinwall. Short stories for short people.
Disobedient little snake. Donaldson. Little papoose listens.
Disobedient rooster. * Fillmore. Shoemaker's apron.
Disowned princess. Martens. Chinese fairy book.
Dissertation upon roast pig. *See* Roast pig, Origin of.
Divers. Success library. v. 3.
Divided Island. Allen. Indian fairy tales.
Divided sea-serpent. Henderson. Sea yarns for boys.
Divine musician. *See* Orpheus and Eurydice.
Divine pilgrim. Guerber. Legends of the Rhine.
Djun, Story of. Lang. Strange story book.
Dmitri, the pretender. Evans. Old time tales.
Do-as-you-likes. Johonnot. Stories of heroic deeds.
Do-not-know. Magnus. Russian folk-tales.
Do what you can. Bailey and Lewis. For the children's hour.
Poulsson. In the child's world.
Dobbin's Thanksgiving. Bailey. Friendly tales.
Doctor and detective. Bay. Danish fairy and folk tales.
See also Dr. Know-all; Harisarman.
Doctor Dog. *See* Strange tale of Doctor Dog.
Doctor Field-mouse. Lummis. Pueblo Indian folk stories.
Doctor-fish. Kennedy. New world fairy book.
Doctor Goldsmith. Baldwin. Fifty famous stories retold.
Dr. Johnson and his father. Baldwin. Thirty more famous stories retold.
Doctor Know-all. Grimm. Fairy tales (Lucas tr.).
Wiggin and Smith. Tales of laughter.
See also Doctor and detective; Harisarman.
Dog and cat from the sky. Bailey. In the animal world.
Dog and his image. *See* Dog and his shadow.

Dog and his shadow. Æsop. Fables (Black ed. Dog and the reflection.)
Æsop. Fables (Burt ed.).
Æsop. Fables (Jacobs).
Æsop. Fables (Stickney).
Arnold and Gilbert. Stepping stones to literature. v. 2. (Dog and his image.)
Bailey. Folk stories and fables.
Bailey and Lewis. For the children's hour.
Baldwin. Fairy stories and fables. (Dog and the shadow.)
Boston collection of kindergarten stories.
Coussens. Child's book of stories. (Dog and his image.)
*Elson and Runkel. Elson readers. Book 1.
*Grover. Folk-lore readers. v. 1.
*Jones. 2d reader.
Patten. Junior classics. v. 1. (Dog and the shadow.)
Scudder. Children's book.
Scudder. Fable and folk stories. (Dog and his image.)
Wiggin and Smith. Talking beasts.
*Young and Field. Literary readers. Book 2.
Dog and the clever rabbit. Stafford. Animal fables.
Dog and the crocodile. Æsop. Fables (Burt ed.).
Wiggin and Smith. Talking beasts.
Dog and the dog dealer. Patten. Junior classics. v. 1.
Dog and the hare. Æsop. Fables (Stickney).
Dog and the image. *See* Dog and his shadow.
Dog and the kingship. Stafford. Animal fables.
Wiggin and Smith. Talking beasts.
Dog and the leopard. Stafford. Animal fables.
Dog and the oyster. Æsop. Fables (Stickney).
Dog and the reflection. *See* Dog and his shadow.
Dog and the shadow. *See* Dog and his shadow.
Dog and the sheep. Æsop. Fables (Black ed.).
Æsop. Fables (Burt ed.).
Dog and the sparrow. Darton. Wonder book of beasts.
Grimm. Fairy tales (Lucas tr.).
Grimm. Household stories (Crane tr.).
Grimm. Household tales (Everyman's ed.).
Lang. Grey fairy book.
Lang. Marvellous musician.
Dog and the stick. *See* Napi and the famine.
Dog and the wolf. I. Æsop. Fables (Black ed.).
Æsop. Fables. (Burt ed. Wolf and the mastiff.)
Æsop. Fables (Jacobs).
Æsop. Fables (Stickney. Wolf and the house dog.)
*Haaren. Songs and stories. 2d reader. (Wolf and the dog.)
Johonnot. Stories of the olden time. (Wolf and the dog.)
Scudder. Children's book.
Wiggin and Smith. Talking beasts. (Wolf and the mastiff.)
Dog and the wolf. II. Baldwin. Fairy stories and fables.
Scudder. Fables and folk stories.

Dog and the wolf. III. *See* Old dog.
Dog, cock and fox. *See* Cock and the fox. VI.
Dog Gellert. *See* Llewellyn and his dog.
Dog in the manger. Æsop. Fables (Black ed.).
Æsop. Fables (Burt ed.).
Æsop. Fables (Jacobs).
Æsop. Fables (Stickney).
Baldwin. Fairy stories and fables.
*Elson and Runkel. Elson readers. Book 2.
*Grover. Folk-lore readers. v. 1.
Hall and Gilman. Story land. 2d reader.
My Bookhouse. v. 1.
Patten. Junior classics. v. 1.
Scudder. Children's book.
Scudder. Fables and folk stories.
Sly. World stories retold.
Van Sickle and Seegmiller. Riverside readers. 2d reader.
Wiggin and Smith. Talking beasts.
Dog invited to supper. Æsop. Fables (Black ed.).
Æsop. Fables (Burt ed.).
Dog of Flanders. Almost true tales.
Dog, the cat and the magic ring. *See* Why dogs wag their tails.
Dog with the green tail. Storytellers' magazine. May 1915, p. 155.
Dogs and the hides. Æsop. Fables (Stickney).
Doll in the grass. Asbjörnsen. Fairy tales from the far north.
Dasent. Norse fairy tales. (Doll i' the grass.)
Dasent. Popular tales from the Norse.
Lansing. Fairy tales. v. 1.
My Bookhouse. v. 2. (Doll i' the grass.)
Patten. Junior classics. v. 1.
Singleton. Wild flower fairy book.
Wiggin and Smith. Fairy ring.
Doll that spoke. *See* Vasilisa the beauty.
Doll under the briar rosebush. My Bookhouse. v. 1.
Thorne-Thomsen. Birch and the star.
Doll who ran away. Donahey. Tales to be told to children.
Doll who was sister to a princess. Bailey. Stories for Sunday telling.
Dolls, Origin of. Bayliss. Treasury of Eskimo tales. (Origin of the wind.)
Dolly, draw the cake. Jerrold. Reign of King Oberon.
Dolorous stroke. *See* Sir Balin.
Domingo's cat. Eells. Tales of giants from Brazil.
See also Puss in boots.
Don Giovanni de la Fortuna. Lang. Elf maiden.
Lang. Pink fairy book.
Success library. v. 3.
See also Fortunatus.

Don Quixote. Baldwin. Fifty famous rides. (Adventure with the windmills.)
Baldwin. Horse fair. (Rozinante.)
Blaisdell. Child life. 5th reader.
Lang. Red romance book.
My Bookhouse. v. 5. (Surprising adventures of Don Quixote of La Mancha.)
Olcott and Pendleton. Jolly book. (Surprising adventures of Don Quixote of La Mancha.)
Patten. Junior classics. v. 4.
Tappan. Stories from seven old favorites.
Don Roderick and the magic tower. Smith. Mystery tales.
Irving. Spanish papers.
Donal that was rich and Jack that was poor. MacManus. Donegal fairy tales.
Donald and his neighbors. See Hudden and Dudden and Donald O'Neary.
Donegal fairy. Yeats. Irish fairy tales.
Donkey and his company. *See* Bremen town musicians.
Donkey and the grasshopper. *See* Ass and the grasshopper.
Donkey and the lap-dog. *See* Ass and the lap-dog.
Donkey and the salt. Æsop. Fables (Burt ed. Ass laden with salt and with sponges.)
Arnold and Gilbert. Stepping stones to literature. v. 2. (Merchant and his donkey.)
Cooke. Nature myths and stories.
Dyer and Brady. Merrill readers. 3d reader. (Pedro and the saddle bags.)
Hall and Gilman. Story land. 2d reader.
Donkey and the wolf. Messer. Next night stories.
Donkey cabbage. Grimm. Fairy tales (Lucas tr. Salad.)
Grimm. Household tales. (Everyman's ed. Donkey-wort.)
Johnson. Fir-tree fairy book.
Lang. Magic ring and other stories.
Lang. Yellow fairy book.
Donkey in the lion's skin. *See* Ass in the lion's skin.
Donkey Skin. Lang. Grey fairy book.
Lang. Trusty John and other stories.
See also Many-furred creature.
Donkey, the cock and the lion. Bryce. Fables from afar.
Donkey, the table and the stick. *See* Table, the ass and the stick.
Donkey's long ears. Farmer. Nature myths.
Donkey's spring. Baumbach. Tales from wonderland.
Donkey's tail, Tale of a. Storytellers' magazine. Sept. 1916, p. 457.
Doodang, Story of. Harris. Uncle Remus and the little boy.
Doom of the children of Lir. *See* Fate of the children of Lir.
Doom of the mischief-maker. *See* Loki.
Doomed prince. *See* Prince and the three fates.
Doomed rider. Douglas. Scottish fairy tales.

Door. Richards. Golden windows.
Dorani. Lang. Olive fairy book.
Dorigen. *See* Rocks removed.
Dormouse's tale. Blaisdell. Child life. 4th reader.
Doubting lover. Sylva and Strettell. Legends from river and mountain.
Dove and the ant. *See* Ant and the dove.
Dove maiden. Grayl. Fairy tales from foreign lands.
Dove who spoke truth. Olcott. Good stories for great holidays.
Down the rat-hole. Pyle. Counterpane fairy.
Downfall of the gods. *See* Ring: Twilight of the gods.
Dozen at a blow. *See* Brave little tailor.
Dragon after his winter sleep. Martens. Chinese fairy book.
Dragon and his grandmother. Lang. Magic ring and other stories.
Lang. Yellow fairy book.
Dragon and the prince. Fillmore. Laughing prince. (Dragon's strength.)
Lang. Crimson fairy book. (Prince and the dragon.)
Lang. Little Wildrose. (Prince and the dragon.)
Mabie. Folk tales every child should know.
Dragon fly. Children's story garden. (Not lost but gone before. Adapted.)
Gatty. Parables from nature. (Not lost but gone before.)
Skinner. Emerald story book.
Wickes. Happy holidays. (Pond world and the wide world.)
See also Grubbiest grub.
Dragon Jewel-neck. Burlingame. Grateful elephant.
Dragon of China. Gate. Fortunate days.
Dragon of Hushby. Brown. Kisington town.
Dragon of the north. Lang. Elf maiden.
Lang. Yellow fairy book.
Dragon of Wantley (poem). Scudder. Children's book.
Dragon-prince and the step-mother. Kunos. Forty-four Turkish fairy tales.
Dragon-princess. Martens. Chinese fairy book.
Dragon Sin. Olcott. Wonder garden.
Dragon slayer. Grayl. Fairy tales from foreign lands.
Dragon's strength. *See* Dragon and the prince.
Dragon's teeth. *See* Cadmus and the dragon's teeth.
Dragon's treasure. Alden. Boy who found the king.
Draiglin' Hoguey. Grierson. Scottish fairy book.
Drak, the fairy. Jokai. Golden fairy book.
Wiggin and Smith. Fairy ring.
Drake, Francis: Upon a peak in Darien. Baldwin. Thirty more famous stories.
Drakesbill and his friends. Bailey. Firelight stories. (How Drakestail went to the king.)

Drakesbill and his friends—*continued.*
Bailey. Once upon a time animal stories. (How Drakestail went to the king.)
Baldwin. Fairy stories and fables.
Bates. Once upon a time. (Drakestail.)
*Dyer and Brady. Merrill readers. 2d reader. (Drakestail.)
Hodgkins. Atlantic treasury of childhood stories. (Drakestail.)
Lang. King of the waterfalls. (Drakestail.)
Lang. Red fairy book. (Drakestail.)
O'Grady and Throop. Teachers' story teller's book.
Storytellers' magazine. May 1914, p. 557. (Drakesbill.)
Wiggin and Smith. Fairy ring.
See also Cock's wife; Little half cock; Medio Pollito; Teenchy Duck; Valiant blackbird.
Drakestail. *See* Drakesbill and his friends.
Drawing of the sword. *See* King Arthur's coming.
Dreadful boar. Fielde. Chinese fairy tales.
Patten. Junior classics. v. 1.
Wiggin and Smith. Tales of laughter.
Dream. Magnus. Russian folk-tales.
Dream and a story. Harris. Nights with Uncle Remus.
Dream inspired. Fielde. Chinese fairy tales.
Dream of freedom. *See* Kosciusko.
Dream of Maxen Wledig. Brooks. Wonder stories from the Mabinogion.
Lanier. Knightly legends of Wales.
Smith. More mystery tales.
Dream of Owen O'Mulready. Jacobs. More Celtic fairy tales.
See also Daniel O'Rourke.
Dream of Rhonabwy. Brooks. Wonder stories from the Mabinogion.
Lanier. Knightly legends of Wales.
Dream of the golden box. Nixon-Roulet. Japanese folk stories and fairy tales.
Dream that came true. *See* Halcyon birds.
Dreamer. Pyle. Fairy tales from far and near.
Dreamer in the wood. Shedlock. Eastern stories and legends.
Dreams. I. Grundtvig. Fairy tales from afar.
Dreams. II. Linderman. Indian why stories.
Dress of scraps. Spaulding and Bryce. Aldine readers. Book 3.
See also Flax leavings.
Dress of the lily and of the cabbage. Sologub. Sweet-scented name.
Dress with spangles. Bailey. Friendly tales.
Drones and the workers. *See* Bees, the drones and the wasp.
Drop of rain (poem). Æsop. Fables (Burt ed.).

Drop of rain—*continued.*
Bryce. Fables from afar. (Dewdrop.)
Wiggin and Smith. Talking beasts.
Drop of water. Andersen. Stories and tales.
Wiltse. Kindergarten stories.
Drop of water, Story of. *See* Water-drop.
Drowning of Mr. Leghorn. *See* Mr. and Mrs. Leghorn.
Drowning of Pecos. Lummis. Pueblo Indian folk stories.
Drowning of the bottom hundred. Thomas. Welsh fairy book.
Drum and vase of sweet herbs. Æsop. Fables (Stickney).
Drum full of bees. Bosschère. Fairy tales of Flanders.
Drummer. Grimm. Fairy tales (Paull tr.).
Drummer of the wheatfield.* Bailey. Friendly tales.
Drums of Raiden. Bouvé. Lamp-light fairy tales.
Drunken husband. Æsop. Fables (Black ed.).
Æsop. Fables (Burt ed.).
Drunken rooks. Bosschère. Fairy tales of Flanders.
Dry grass and fire. Storytellers' magazine. Jan. 1916, p. 22.
Dryad. Andersen. Wonder stories.
Dryad of the old oak. *See* Rhœcus.
Dryope. Guerber. Myths of Greece and Rome. (*In* Minor divinities.)
Pratt. Myths of old Greece. v. 3.
Dschang Liang. Martens. Chinese fairy book.
Dschemil and Dschemila. Lang. Grey fairy book.
Lang. Trusty John and other stories.
Duck and the serpent (poem). Success library. v. 3.
Wiggin and Smith. Talking beasts.
Duck-feather man. Olcott. Wonder garden.
Duck freezes Coyote. Borland. Rocky Mountain tipi tales.
Duck with golden eggs, Story of the. Steele. Russian garland of fairy tales.
Duel between the fox and the wolf. Tappan. Folk stories and fables.
Dulcetta. Byrne. Modern Greek fairy tales.
Duldul and his master. Baldwin. Horse fair.
Dumb book. Andersen. Fairy tales (Paull tr.).
Dumb plaintiff. *See* Bell of Atri.
Dumb princess. Bailey. Seven peas in the pod.
Dumb queen. Grundtvig. Danish fairy tales.
Dumb witness. Bryce. Fables from afar.
Dummburg. Thorpe. Yule-tide stories.
Dummling and the toad. *See* Three feathers. I.
Dumpy, the pony. Lindsay. More mother stories.
Van Sickle and Seegmiller. Riverside readers. 2d reader.
Dun cow. Magnus. Russian folk-tales.
Dun horse. Grinnel. Pawnee hero stories.
Hartwell. Story hour readings. 5th year. (Slayer of the spotted calf.)
Mabie. Folk tales every child should know.

Dun horse—*continued.*
Nixon-Roulet. Indian folk tales. (Slayer of the spotted calf; Winner of Talking Bird.)
Dun Kenneth. Grierson. Scottish fairy book.
Dunnohoo. English. Fairy and wonder tales.
Duration of life. Judson. Myths and legends of the Pacific Northwest.
Judson. Myths and legends of Alaska.
Duration of winter. Judson. Myths and legends of Alaska.
See also Seasons.
Dusk of the gods. *See* Twilight of the gods. I; Ring: Twilight of the gods.
Dust under the rug. Coe. Second book of stories.
Lindsay. Mother stories.
Wickes. Happy holidays.
Dutchman's Breeches. Seton. Woodland tales.
Dutiful children. Storytellers' magazine. July 1915, p. 253.
Dutiful daughter. Allen. Korean tales. (Sim Chung; or, The dutiful daughter.)
Pyle. Fairy tales from far and near.
Dwarf and his confectionery. Griffis. Swiss fairy tales.
Dwarf and the blacksmith. Bosschère. Christmas tales of Flanders.
See also Shoemaker and the elves.
Dwarf Long Nose. *See* Longnose, the dwarf.
Dwarf people. Bayliss. Treasury of Eskimo tales.
Dwarf Roots' story of the pumpkin seed. Keyes. Five senses.
Keyes. Stories and story-telling.
Dwarf, the witch, and the magic slippers. *See* Ha'penny, Adventures of.
Dwarf with the golden beard. Pyle. Wonder stories retold.
Dwarf with the long beard. Chodzko. Fairy tales of the Slav.
Tappan. Myths from many lands.
Dwarfie stone. Grierson. Scottish fairy book.
Dwarfs. Messer. Next night stories.
Dwarfs and the bottle of wine. Froelicher. Swiss stories.
Dwarfs and the fairies. Patten. Junior classics. v. 2.
Dwarf's banquet. Gibbon. Reign of King Cole.
Dwarf's daughter. Grundtvig. Fairy tales from afar.
Dwarf's gifts. Arnold and Gilbert. Stepping stones to literature. 5th reader. (Thor.)
Bradish. Old Norse stories. (Sif's hair.)
Brown. In the days of giants.
*Burchill. Progressive road to reading. Book 3. (Loki and the dwarfs.)
Edmison. Stories from the Norseland. (Magic gifts of the elves.)
Foster and Cummings. Asgard stories. (Hammer of Thor.)
Guerber. Myths of northern lands. (*In* Thor.)

Dwarf's gifts—*continued.*
Jerrold. Reign of King Oberon. (Gifts of the dwarfs.)
Klingensmith. Old Norse wonder tales (Loki).
Litchfield. Nine worlds. (Loki makes trouble between the artists and the gods.)
Mabie. Norse stories. (Making of the hammer.)
Pratt. Legends of Norseland. (Loke's theft; Thor's hammer.)
Tappan. Myths from many lands.
Wilmot-Buxton. Stories of Norse heroes. (How Loki made a wager with the dwarfs.)
See also Freyja.
Dwarf's great adventure. Bailey. Friendly tales.
Dwarf's nest. Hackländer. Enchanted and enchanting.
Dwarf's revenge. Storytellers' magazine. Sept. 1913, p. 176.
Dwarf's secret. Griffis. Swiss fairy tales.
Dwarfs' tailor. Gask. Folk tales from many lands. (Silence.)
Gask. Treasury of folk tales. (Silence.)
Noyes. Twilight stories. (Value of silence.)
Underhill. Dwarfs' tailor and other fairy tales.
Dweller in the Ilsenstein. Dasent. Popular tales from the Norse.
Thorpe. Yule-tide stories.
Dyed jackal. *See* Blue jackal.
Dyeermud Ulta and the king in south Erin. Curtin. Hero tales from Ireland.

E

Each in his own place. *See* Mouse, the bird and the sausage.
Eagle. *See* Paup-Puk-Keewis.
Eagle and the arrow. Æsop. Fables (Burt ed.).
Æsop. Fables (Jacobs).
Æsop. Fables (Stickney).
Arnold and Gilbert. Stepping stones to literature. v. 2. (Wounded eagle.)
Scudder. Children's book. (Archer and the eagle.)
Scudder. Fables and folk stories. (Eagle shot with an eagle's arrow.)
(poem). Success library. v. 3. (Bird wounded by an arrow.)
(poem). Wiggin and Smith. Talking beasts.
Eagle and the beaver. Eastman. Wigwam evenings.
Eagle and the beetle. Æsop. Fables (Burt ed.).
Eagle and the crow. Æsop. Fables (Black ed.).
Æsop. Fables (Burt ed.).
Bryce. Fables from afar.
Eagle and the fox. I. Æsop. Fables (Black ed.)
Æsop. Fables (Burt ed.).

Eagle and the fox—*continued.*
Æsop. Fables (Stickney).
Eagle and the fox. II. Coe and Christie. Story hour readers. 3d book.
Eagle and the man. Æsop. Fables (Burt ed.).
Curry. Little classics.
Eagle and the mole. Wiggin and Smith. Talking beasts.
Eagle and the owl. Æsop. Fables (Burt ed.).
Wiggin and Smith Talking beasts.
(poem). Wiggin and Smith. Talking beasts.
See also Old Mrs. Owl's children.
Eagle and the rice birds. Davis and Chow-Leung. Chinese fables and folk stories.
Eagle and the tortoise. *See* Foolish tortoise.
Eagle and the wren. Douglas. Scottish fairy tales.
Eagle crest. Eastman. Indian legends retold.
Eagle makes the valleys. Borland. Rocky Mountain tipi tales.
Eagle shot with an eagle's arrow. *See* Eagle and the arrow.
Eagle, the cat, and the sow. Æsop. Fables (Black ed.).
Æsop. Fables (Burt ed.).
(poem). Success library. v. 3.
Eagle, the jackdaw, and the magpie. Æsop. Fables (Burt ed.).
Wiggin and Smith. Talking beasts.
Eagles. Glinski. Polish fairy tales.
See also Wild swans.
Ear of corn and the twelve men. Dasent. Popular tales from the Norse.
Ear of wheat. Bakewell. True fairy stories.
Earl Gerald. Frost. Fairies and folk of Ireland. (*In* Ch. 2.)
Yeats. Irish fairy and folk tales. (Enchantment of Gearoidh Iarla.)
See also Emperor's sleep.
Earl Mar's daughter. Grierson. Children's tales from Scottish ballads.
Jacobs. English fairy tales.
Tappan. Old ballads in prose.
Earl of Cattenborough. *See* Puss in boots.
Early Spring Fairy. Potter. Pinafore pocket story book.
Ears of the hare (poem). Wiggin and Smith. Talking beasts.
Ears of wheat. Olcott. Good stories for great holidays.
Earth and the sky. Holbrook. Book of nature myths.
Earthen pot and the iron pot. *See* Earthen pot and the pot of brass.
Earthen pot and the pot of brass. Æsop. Fables (Black ed. Two pots.)
Æsop. Fables (Burt ed.).
Æsop. Fables (Jacobs. Two pots.)
Æsop. Fables (Stickney. Two pots.)
(poem). Success library. v. 3. (Earthen pot and the pot of iron.)

Earthen pot and the pot of brass—*continued.*
(poem). Wiggin and Smith. Talking beasts. (Earthen pot and the iron pot.)
Earthen pot and the pot of iron. *See* Earthen pot and the pot of brass.
Earthworm twins. Donaldson. Moons of long ago.
East Light and the bridge of fishes. Griffis. Unmannerly tiger and other Korean tales.
Griffis. Korean fairy tales.
East o' the sun and west o' the moon. Asbjörnsen. Folk and fairy tales.
Dasent. Norse fairy tales.
Dasent. Popular tales from the Norse.
Jerrold. Reign of King Oberon.
Lang. Blue fairy book.
Lang. Sleeping beauty.
My Bookhouse. v. 3.
Stroebe and Martens. Norwegian fairy book.
Success library. v. 3.
Thorne-Thomsen. East o' the sun and west o' the moon.
Wiggin and Smith. Fairy ring.
Young and Field. Literary readers. Book 2.
See also Cally Coo-Coo o' the woods; King Valemon, the white bear; King who slept; Mysterious prince.
East of the sun and north of the earth. Canton. Reign of King Herla.
East wind and north wind. Judson. Myths and legends of Alaska.
Easter. *See* Almond blossom; Awakening; Beauty of the lily; Boy who brought spring; Child's dream of a star; Daisy's first winter; Dragon fly; Handful of clay; Harold's happy Easter; Horse that brought the spring; Lesson in faith; Lilac bush; Little blue hen; Loveliest rose in the world; Maple; Mrs. Stump's Easter bonnet; Mixed Easter eggs; Moon's message; Nettle gatherer; Proserpina; Selfish giant; Springtime; Two pilgrims; White blackbird; White lily; Why the robin says "cheer up".
See also Titles commencing with the word "Easter".
Easter eggs. *See* Easter rabbit. II.
Easter hares. *See* Easter rabbit. II.
Easter lily. Faulkner. Story lady's book.
Easter rabbit. I. Bailey and Lewis. For the children's hour. (Herr Oster Hase.)
Cather. Educating by story telling. (Rabbit and the Easter eggs.)
Easter rabbit. II. Blaisdell. Child life. 3d reader. (Easter hares.)
Cather. Educating by story telling. (Easter eggs.)
Easter rabbit. III. Brown. Stories of woods and fields. (Bunny and the Easter eggs.)
*Elson and Runkel. Elson readers. Book 2.
Skinner. Emerald story book.

Easter rabbit. IV. Storytellers' magazine. April 1916, p. 261. (Tale of the Easter rabbit.)
Easter rabbit. V. Baumbach. Tales from wonderland.
Easter rabbit. VI. Faulkner. Story lady's book. (Easter rabbit and what he brought.)
Easter surprise. Danielson. Story telling time.
Skinner. A very little child's book of stories.
Eatyoup. Walker. Sandman's goodnight stories.
Eavesdropper, the ugly dwarf. Bailey and Lewis. For the children's hour.
Children's story garden.
Echeola. Rhys. Fairy gold.
Echo and Narcissus. Arnold and Gilbert. Stepping stones to literature. v. 3. (Echo.)
Bailey. Stories children need. (Story of Echo.)
Baker and Carpenter. Language readers. 3d year. (Narcissus.)
*Beckwith. In mythland. v. 3. (Echo; Narcissus.)
Buckley. Children of the dawn. (Curse of Echo.)
Carpenter. Long ago in Greece. (Narcissus and his shadow.)
Coe. Second book of stories. (Why the narcissus grows by the water.)
Farmer. Nature myths. (Narcissus.)
Francillon. Gods and heroes. (Narcissus.)
Guerber. Myths of Greece and Rome. (*In* Venus.)
Harper. Story-hour favorites. (Fate of Echo.)
Hartley. Stories from the Greek legends.
Holbrook. 'Round the year in myth and song. (Narcissus; Echo and Narcissus.)
Hyde. Favorite Greek myths. (Echo; Narcissus.)
Judd. Classic myths. (Echo, the air maiden; Why the narcissus grows by the water.)
Kupfer. Stories of long ago. (Echo and Narcissus; How Narcissus loved his image.)
Olcott. Good stories for great holidays.
Olcott. Wonder garden.
*Poulsson. In the child's world. (Story of Echo.)
Pratt. Fairyland of flowers. (Legend of Narcissus.)
Pratt. Myths of old Greece. v. 2.
Stebbins. 3d reader.
Stories of classic myths. (Story of Narcissus.)
Storr. Half a hundred hero tales.
Storytellers' magazine. April 1917, p. 195. (Curse of Echo.)
Tyler. Twenty-four unusual stories. (Curse of Echo.)
Echo god and the Northern Lights. Judd. Wigwam stories.
Echo, the cave fairy. Olcott. Book of elves and fairies.
Eclipse. Æsop. Fables (Burt ed.).
Eddystone light. Van Sickle and Seegmiller. Riverside readers. 4th reader. (Light of the Eddystone.)
Ederland the poultry-maid. Stroebe and Martens. Danish fairy book.

Ederland the poultry-maid—*continued.*
See also Esben and the witch.
Education of the lion. Æsop. Fables (Stickney).
Wiggin and Smith. Talking beasts.
Edward the Black Prince. *See* Black Prince.
Edwin and Sir Topaz (poem). Hartland. English folk and fairy tales.
See also Knockgrafton, Legend of.
Ee-aw! Ee-aw! Grundtvig. Fairy tales from afar.
Eginhard and Emma. Guerber. Legends of the Rhine.
Egóri the brave and the gipsy. Magnus. Russian folk-tales.
Egyptian puss-in-boots. Goddard. Fairy tales in other lands.
Eight-headed serpent. Williston. Japanese fairy tales. 1st series.
Eight immortals. Martens. Chinese fairy book.
Eight roads. Gate. Broom fairies.
Eighty-one brothers. Griffis. Japanese fairy tales. (Bridge of crocodiles.)
Hearn. Japanese fairy tales. (Hare of Inaba.)
Lyman. Story telling. (White hare and the crocodiles. Adapted.)
Nixon-Roulet. Japanese folk stories and fairy tales. (Choice of the princess.)
Olcott. Wonder garden. (White hare of Inaba.)
Ozaki. Japanese fairy book. (White hare and the crocodiles.)
St. Nicholas. Aug. 1910, p. 892. (Little hare of Oki.)
Williston. Japanese fairy tales. 2d series.
Einion and the Fair Family. Thomas. Welsh fairy book.
Einion and the lady of the greenwood. Thomas. Welsh fairy book.
Eisenkopf. Lang. Crimson fairy book.
Elaine's valentines. *Dillingham and Emerson. Tell it again stories.
Elan the armourer. Rhys. Fairy gold.
Elder brother. Bailey and Lewis. For the children's hour.
Elder mother. Wicks. Happy holidays.
Elder-tree mother. I. Andersen. Fairy tales (Paull tr.).
Andersen. Stories and tales.
Singleton. Goldenrod fairy book.
Elder-tree mother. II. Bakewell. True fairy stories.
Eldest daughter of the king (poem). Alexander. Hidden servants.
Eldest sister. Gate. Broom fairies.
Election day. Cocke. Bypaths in Dixie.
Elephant. Bryce. Fables from afar.
Elephant and the ape. *See* Elephant and the monkey.
Elephant and the assembly of animals. Æsop. Fables (Burt ed.).
Elephant and the bookseller (poem). Success library. v. 3.

Elephant and the dog. *See* Elephant who was lonely.
Elephant and the frog. Bailey. Firelight stories. (Mr. Elephant and Mr. Frog.)
Bailey. Once upon a time animal stories. (Mr. Elephant and Mr. Frog.)
Stafford. Animal fables. (Frog and the elephant.)
Wiggin and Smith. Talking beasts. (Elephant and frog.)
See also Brother Rabbit's riding-horse; Buffalo and the rabbit.
Elephant and the jackal. Wiggin and Smith. Talking beasts.
Elephant and the monkey. Bryce. Fables from afar. (Elephant and the ape.)
Elson and Runkel. Elson readers. Book 2.
See also Camel and the pig.
Elephant and the rats. Bryce. Fables from afar.
See also Lion and the mouse.
Elephant and the tailor. Sly. World stories retold.
Elephant and the ungrateful forester. Bailey. In the animal world. (White elephant.)
Burlingame. Grateful elephant.
Griswold. Hindu fairy tales. (Good elephant and the ungrateful man.)
Elephant as governor. Wiggin and Smith. Talking beasts.
Elephant Girly-Face. Babbitt. Jataka tales.
Elephant has a bet with the tiger. Patten. Junior classics. v. 2.
Stanley. Animal folk tales. (Elephant's bet with the tiger.)
Tappan. Folk stories and fables.
Wiggin and Smith. Talking beasts.
See also Brother Rabbit frightens Brother Tiger; Clever goat. I.
Elephant in favor. Æsop. Fables (Stickney. Supplement).
Wiggin and Smith. Talking beasts.
Elephant that spared life. Shedlock. Eastern stories and legends.
Elephant that was honored in old age. Shedlock. Eastern stories and legends.
Elephant who was lonely. Babbitt. More Jataka tales. (Elephant and the dog.)
Bailey. In the animal world.
Shedlock. Eastern stories and legends. (Faithful friend.)
Elephant's bet with the tiger. *See* Elephant has a bet with the tiger.
Elephant's child. Kipling. Just so stories.
Elf and the dormouse. Bailey and Lewis. For the children's hour. (How we first came to have umbrellas.)
*Elson and Runkel. Elson readers. Book 2. (First umbrella.)
(poem). Keyes. Five senses.
(poem). Van Sickle and Seegmiller. Riverside readers. 2d reader.

Elf and the squirrels. Bailey. In the animal world. (Elf.)
Elf child. Nordau. Dwarf's spectacles.
Elf-dog. Olcott. Whirling king.
Elf-hill. Andersen. Fairy tales (Lucas tr.).
Andersen. Fairy tales (Paull tr. Elfin hill.)
Andersen. Wonder stories. (Elfin mound.)
Haaren. Fairy life. (Elfin-mount.)
Jerrold. Reign of King Oberon.
Elf maiden. Lang. Brown fairy book.
Lang. Elf maiden and other stories.
Elf of light. May. Little Prudy's fairy book.
Elf of the rose. Andersen. Fairy tales (Lucas tr. Rose elf.)
Andersen. Fairy tales (Paull tr.).
Andersen. Stories and tales. (Rose-elf.)
See also Pot of basil.
Elfin grove. Canton. Reign of King Herla. (Elves.)
*Grimm. Fairy tales (Wiltse). v. 2.
Grimm. Household tales (Everyman's ed.).
Williams. Fairy tales from folklore. (Elves of the Rhineland.)
Elfin hill. *See* Elf-hill.
Elfin knight. Grierson. Scottish fairy book.
Elfin mound. *See* Elf-hill.
Elfin-mount. *See* Elf-hill.
Elfin-tree. Hackländer. Enchanting and enchanted.
Elf's flower. Bryce. That's why stories.
Elidore. Griffis. Welsh fairy tales. (Boy that visited fairyland.)
Jacobs. More Celtic fairy tales.
Olcott. Book of elves and fairies. (Elidore and the golden ball.)
Thomas. Welsh fairy book. (Elidyr's sojourn in fairyland.)
Eliduc and Guilliadun. Harrison. Old-fashioned fairy book.
Elidyr's sojourn in fairyland. *See* Elidore.
Elijah the prophet and St. Nicholas. Magnus. Russian folk tales.
Elin Gow, the swordsmith from Erin and the cow Glas Gainach. *See* Wonderful cow.
Elk. Borland. Rocky Mountain tipi tales. (Grass grows on the hills.)
Elk and the moose people and their contests. Young. Algonquin Indian tales. (*In* Ch. 25.)
Storytellers' magazine. Feb. 1917, p. 94.
Elopement. Guerber. Legends of the Rhine.
Elphin Irving. Douglas. Scottish fairy tales.
Elsa and the ten elves. My Bookhouse. v. 2.
Olcott. Book of elves and fairies.
See also Charlotte and the ten dwarfs; Ten fairies.
Elves. I. *See* Elves and the shoemaker.
Elves. II. *See* Maiden's visit.

Elves. III. *See* Changeling.
Elves. IV. Grimm. Fairy tales (Paull tr.).
Elves. V. *See* Elfin grove.
Elves. VI. Olcott. Good stories for great holidays.
Olcott. Red Indian fairy book.
Elves. VII. Haaren. Fairy life.
Elves and the cobbler. *See* Elves and the shoemaker.
Elves and the envious man. *See* Man with the wen.
Elves and the envious neighbor. *See* Man with the wen.
Elves and the shoemaker. Bailey and Lewis. For the children's hour.
Bryant. Stories to tell the children.
*Chisholm and Steedman. Staircase of stories. (Industrious goblins.)
Coussens. Child's book of stories.
Curry. Little classics. (Shoemaker and the fairies.)
Dyer. What-happened-then stories.
Esenwein and Stockard. Children's stories. (Shoemaker and the elves.)
Grimm. Fairy tales (Lucas tr.).
Grimm. Household stories (Crane. Elves.)
Grimm. Household tales (Burt ed. Industrious manikins.)
Grimm. Household tales (Everyman's ed. Elves and the cobbler.)
Haaren. Fairy life.
Hodgkins. Atlantic treasury of childhood stories. (Elves.)
Johnson. Oak-tree fairy book.
Ketchum and Jorgensen. Kindergarten gems.
Keyes. Five senses.
Lansing. Fairy tales. v. 2.
My Bookhouse. v. 1. (Shoemaker and the elves.)
Norton. Heart of oak books. v. 3.
Olcott. Good stories for great holidays.
Pyle. Mother's nursery tales. (Cobbler and the fairies.)
Scudder. Book of folk stories.
Scudder. Children's book.
Scudder. Fables and folk stories.
Storytellers' magazine. May 1914, p. 553.
Van Sickle and Seegmiller. Riverside readers. 3d reader.
Welsh. Fairy tales children love.
Wiggin and Smith. Tales of laughter.
See also Dwarf and the blacksmith.
Elves and their antics. *See* Starch.
Elves' gift. St. Nicholas. Jan. 1874, p. 108.
Elves of the haunted ships. Douglas. Scottish fairy tales. (Haunted ships.)
Johnson. Birch-tree fairy book.
Elves of the Rhineland. *See* Elfin grove.
Embellishment. Patten. Junior classics. v. 6.
Emelyan, the fool. Steele. Russian garland of fairy tales.
Emerald. Murphy. Necklace of jewels.
Emerald book. *See* Goose girl at the well.

Emergency mistress. Stockton. Floating prince.
Emigrant mice. Æsop. Fables (Burt ed.).
Emperor and the abbot. Gask. Folk tales from many lands.
Guerber. Legends of the Rhine. (Emperor's riddles.)
Noyes. Twilight stories.
See also King John and the Abbot of Canterbury; Priest and the clerk.
Emperor and the bird's nest. Sly. World stories retold.
Emperor and the goose boy. Baldwin. Fifty famous stories. (Maximilian and the goose boy.)
*Elson and Runkel. Elson readers. Book 2. (King and the goose herd.)
Sly. World stories retold.
Emperor and the school children. *See* Kingdoms.
Emperor Trojan's ears. Patten. Junior classics. v. 1.
See also Midas. II; March's ears.
Emperor's ducking. Guerber. Legends of the Rhine.
Emperor's friend. Guerber. Legends of the Rhine.
Emperor's new clothes. *Andersen. Best fairy tales (Hendersen tr. New clothes of the Emperor.)
Andersen. Fairy tales (Lucas tr.).
Andersen. Fairy tales (Paull tr.).
Andersen. Fairy tales and stories (Toksvig).
*Andersen. Fairy tales (Turpin).
Andersen. Stories (Riverside ed.).
Andersen. Wonder stories.
Canton. Reign of King Herla.
Forty famous fairy tales. (Story of the emperor's new clothes.)
Lang. Yellow fairy book.
Lang. Magic ring and other stories. (Story of the emperor's new clothes.)
Lansing. Fairy tales. v. 2.
My Bookhouse. v. 5.
Scudder. Children's book.
Thomas. Young folk's book of mirth.
Welsh. Stories children love.
Van Sickle and Seegmiller. Riverside readers. 4th reader.
Emperor's nightingale. See Nightingale.
Emperor's parrot. Bosschère. Christmas tales of Flanders.
Emperor's riddles. *See* Emperor and the abbot.
Emperor's ride. Guerber. Legends of the Rhine.
Emperor's sin. Guerber. Legends of the Rhine.
Emperor's sleep. Baldwin. Thirty more famous stories. (Frederick Barbarossa.)
Crommelin. Famous legends.
Guerber. Legends of the Rhine. (Barbarossa's sleep.)
See also King Arthur's cave; Sleeping king.
Emperor's test (play). Stevenson. Plays in the home.
Emperor's vision. Cather. Educating by story telling.
Cross and Statler. Story-telling.
Lagerlöf. Christ legends.

Emperor's vision.—*continued.*
Tyler. Twenty-four unusual stories.
Emperor's wooing. Guerber. Legends of the Rhine.
Empress Janqwi and the magicians. Coussens. Jade story book.
Empty bottles. Pyle. Twilight land.
Empty drum. Tolstoi. Twenty three tales.
Enano. Finger. Tales from silver lands. (El Enano.)
Enchanted apple-tree. Bosschère. Christmas tales of Flanders.
Enchanted bird. Patterson. Enchanted bird.
Enchanted bride. Asbjörnsen. Folk and fairy tales. (Evening in the squire's kitchen.)
Gade. Norwegian fairy tales.
Enchanted buck. Bourhill and Drake. Fairy tales from South Africa.
Enchanted canary. Field. Famous fairy tales.
Lang. Blue parrot.
Lang. Forty thieves and other stories.
Lang. Red fairy book.
Enchanted castle in the sea. Eells. Tales of enchantment from Spain.
Enchanted cave. I. Bellamy. Wonder children.
Enchanted cave. II. Leamy. Golden spears.
Enchanted crutch. Bouvé. Lamp-light tales.
Enchanted deer. Lang. Lilac fairy book.
Enchanted doe. Macdonell. Italian fairy book.
Enchanted doll. Jenks. Tales of fantasy.
Enchanted donkey. I. Johnson. Fir-tree fairy book.
Enchanted donkey. II. Aunt Naomi. Jewish fairy tales.
Enchanted dragon. *See* Laidly worm of Spindleston.
Enchanted duckling. Pearson. Laughing lion.
Enchanted elm. Beston. Firelight fairy book.
Enchanted forest. I. Andrews. Enchanted forest.
Enchanted forest. II. Wiggin and Smith. Magic casements.
Enchanted forest. III. Segovia. Spanish fairy book.
Enchanted grouse. Fillmore. Mighty Mikko.
Enchanted head. Lang. Brown fairy book.
Lang. Magician's gifts.
Enchanted hind. *See* Hind in the wood.
Enchanted hog. *See* Enchanted pig.
Enchanted horse. Arabian nights (Lang).
Arabian nights. (Colum. Story of the magic horse.)
Arabian nights (Housman. Story of the magic horse.)
Arabian nights (Olcott. Story of the magic horse.)
Arabian nights (Townsend).
Baldwin. Horse fair.
Marshall. Fairy tales of all nations. (Magic horse.)
My Bookhouse. v. 4. (Magic horse.)
Scudder. Children's book.

Enchanted horse—*continued.*
Tappan. Stories from seven old favorites. (Ride on the wooden horse.)
Enchanted island. My Bookhouse. v. 4.
Pyle. Twilight land.
Enchanted knife. Lang. Trusty John and other stories.
Lang. Violet fairy book.
Enchanted knight. *See* Ogier the Dane.
Enchanted lake. Eastman. Indian legends retold.
Enchanted lambs. Houghton. Russian grandmother's wonder tales.
Enchanted mirror. *See* Little gray grandmother.
Enchanted moccasins. Schoolcraft. Indian fairy book.
Enchanted mule. Johnson. Elm-tree fairy book.
Enchanted necklace; or. Legend of the bleeding hearts. Johnston. Little Colonel's house-party.
Enchanted peafowl. *See* Nine pea-hens and the golden apples.
Enchanted pig. Field. Famous fairy tales.
Kunos. Turkish fairy tales. (Enchanted hog.)
Lang. Red fairy book.
Wiggin and Smith. Magic casements.
Enchanted pomegranate branch and the beauty. Kunos. Forty-four Turkish fairy tales.
Enchanted princess. I. *See* Broad man, the tall man and the man with eyes of flame.
Enchanted princess. II. Curtin. Wonder-tales from Russia.
Enchanted princess. III. Storytellers' magazine. Oct. 1914, p. 689.
Enchanted princesses. Baudis. Czech folk tales.
Enchanted ring. I. Lang. Green fairy book.
Lang. Pretty Goldilocks and other stories.
Enchanted ring. II. Polevoi. Russian fairy tales.
Wheeler. Russian wonder tales. (Martin, the peasant's son.)
See also Cassim; Wonderful ring.
Enchanted ring. III. Cary. French fairy tales.
Enchanted shirt (poem). Brown. Stories of childhood and nature.
Enchanted snake. Lang. Green fairy book.
Lang. Forty thieves and other stories.
Enchanted stag. *See* Brother and sister.
Enchanted sugar maple. *See* Mishosha.
Enchanted swine. *See* Ulysses at Circe's palace.
Enchanted toad. Thorpe. Yule-tide stories.
Enchanted trunks. Molesworth. Fairies afield.
Enchanted Tsarévich. Magnus. Russian folk-tales.
Enchanted valley. Kennedy. New world fairy book.
Enchanted watch. Lang. Green fairy book.
Lang. Magician's gifts.
Macé. Home fairy tales.

Enchanted watch—*continued.*
Olcott. Book of elves and fairies.
Enchanted waterfall. *See* Waterfall which flowed saké.
Enchanted whistle. Jokai. Golden fairy book.
Larned. Fairy tales from France. (Magic whistle.)
Wiggin and Smith. Magic casements.
Enchanted windmill. Griffis. Belgian fairy tales.
Enchanted wine jug. *See* Why the cat and dog are enemies.
Enchanted wood. Stewart. Once upon a time
Enchanted wreath. Lang. Orange fairy book.
Lang. Satin surgeon.
Enchanted youth. Wade. Indian fairy tales.
Enchantment of Gearoidh Iarla. *See* Earl Gerald.
End of Mr. Bear. Harris. Uncle Remus, his songs and his sayings.
End of the world. Bosschère. Fairy tales of Flanders.
Endless story. *See* Water-drop.
Endless tale. I. Baldwin. Fifty famous stories.
Bowen. Second story reader. (Long story.)
Skinner. Merry tales. (Story that had no end.)
Sly. World stories retold. (Story without an end.)
(play). Van Sickle and Seegmiller. Riverside readers. 3d reader.
Endless tale. II. Lansing. Dramatic readings for schools. (Story that had no end.)
Endless tale. III. Baldwin. Another fairy reader. (Storyteller.)
Tappan. Folk stories and fables. (Lion, the fox and the storyteller.)
Wiggin and Smith. (Talking beasts. (Lion, the fox and the storyteller.)
Endless tale. IV. Fillmore. Czechoslovak fairy tales (Story that never ends.)
Houghton. Russian grandmother's wonder tales. (Bridge.)
See also Sleepy story.
Endymion. Guerber. Myths of Greece and Rome. (*In* Diana.)
Hartley. Stories from the Greek legends. (Story of the sleep of Endymion.)
Hyde. Favorite Greek myths. (Endymion's sleep.)
Peabody. Old Greek folk stories. (Diana and Endymion.)
Pratt. Myths of old Greece. v. 1. (Sleep of Endymion.)
Shaw. Stories of the ancient Greeks. (*In* In the moonlight.)
Storytellers' magazine. July 1913, p. 82.
Engine that wouldn't stop. * Bryant. New stories to tell to children.
England's first poet, Story of. See Caedmon the herdsman poet, Story of.
English merchant and the Saracen lady. Greenwood. Stories from famous ballads.
Enoch Arden in China. *See* Wife with two husbands.

Entangled mermaid. Griffis. Dutch fairy tales.
Envious glow-worm. Æsop. Fables (Burt ed.).
Envious man and him who was envied. Arabian nights (Lang).
Arabian nights (Townsend).
Envious neighbor. *See* Old man who made withered trees to flower.
Envy burns itself. Thomas. Welsh fairy book.
Epaminondas and his auntie. Bryant. Best stories to tell to children.
Bryant. Stories to tell to children.
Cabot. Ethics for children. (Story of Epaminondas and his auntie.)
Tappan. Book of humor.
Van Sickle and Seegmiller. Riverside readers. 2d reader.
See also Lazy Jack; Prudent Hans; Silly Matt.
Epimetheus. *See* Pandora; Prometheus.
Equality. Sologub. Sweet-scented name.
Erisichthon. *See* King and the oak.
Ermine. Wiltse. Kindergarten stories.
Ermine and the hunter. Macmillan. Canadian fairy tales.
Eros. *See* Cupid and Psyche.
Erysichthon the hungry. See King and the oak.
Esben and the witch. Lang. Aladdin and other stories.
Lang. Pink fairy book.
See also Cinderboy and the witch; Ederland, the poultry-maid.
Escape of Juanita (poem). Miller. Philippine folk lore stories.
Escape of the mouse. Baring-Gould. Old English fairy tales. (Four friends.)
Brooks. Wonder stories from the Mabinogion. (Manawyddan and the mice.)
Lang. Lilac fairy book.
Lanier. Knightly legends of Wales. (Manawyddan and the mice.)
Patten. Junior classics. v. 4. (How Manawyddan caught a thief.)
Tappan. Stories of legendary heroes. (Manawyddan and the seven enchanted cantrevs.)
Etain and Midir, Story of. Rolleston. High deeds of Finn.
Ethelinda; or, The ice-king's bride. Harrison. Old-fashioned fairy book.
Ettrick shepherd. Baldwin. Fifty famous people.
Eumaeus. Baldwin. Story of the golden age. (*In* Swineherd.)
Eunuch's stratagem. Storytellers' magazine. Sept. 1917, p. 320.
Eureka! Baldwin. Thirty more famous stories.
Europa. Baldwin. Old Greek stories. (Cadmus and Europa.)

Europa—*continued.*
Carpenter. Long ago in Greece. (Europa's wedding journey.)
Chisholm and Steedman. Staircase of stories. (Quest.)
Guerber. Myths of Geece and Rome. (*In* Jupiter.)
Hartley. Stories from the Greek legends. (Loss of Europa.)
Hawthorne. Tanglewood tales. (Dragon's teeth.)
Hutchinson. Orpheus with his lute. (Prince Cadmus of Phœnicia.)
McFee. Treasury of myths. (Cadmus and Europa.)
Olcott. Wonder garden. (Snow-white bull.)
Storr. Half a hundred hero tales. (Europa and the God-bull.)
Tappan. Myths from many lands. (Dragon's teeth.)
See also Cadmus and the dragon's teeth.
Eurydice. *See* Orpheus and Eurydice.
Eurytus, *See* Arethusa.
Evangeline, Story of. Scudder. Bodley's telling stories. (*In* Wanderers.)
Eva's visit to fairyland. Alcott. Flower fables.
Alcott. Lulu's library. v. 2.
Eve of St. Mark. Laboulaye. Last fairy tales.
Even a grass plant can become someone if it tries. *See* Discontented grass plant. II.
Evergreen tree and the wilderness marigold. Davis and Chow-Leung. Chinese fables and folk stories.
Every cloud has its silver lining. Young. Behind the dark pines.
Everything for nothing. Bailey. Little man with one shoe.
Everything in its right place. Anderson. Fairy tales (Paull tr.).
Andersen. Stories and tales.
Evil allures but good endures. Cabot. Ethics for children.
Tolstoi. Twenty three tales.
Evil one and Kitta Grau. Stroebe and Martens. Swedish fairy book.
See also Katie Gray.
Evil one and the rat. Nixon-Roulet. Japanese folk stories and fairy tales.
Evil one who married three sisters. Pyle. Fairy tales from many lands.
See also Bluebeard.
Excalibur. *See* King Arthur's sword.
Exchange. Guerber. Legends of the Rhine.
Excuse for the rogue. Young. Plantation bird legends.
Executioner ennobled. Guerber. Legends of the Rhine.
Eya, the devourer. *See* Iya, the camp-eater.
Eyes of the king. Danielson. Story telling time.

F

Fa-Nien-Ts'ing and the Mön-Tien-Sing. Davis and Chow-Leung. Chinese fables and folk stories.

Face of the Manito. Holbrook. Book of nature myths.
Faery surprise party. Scudder. Seven little people.
Fair and the dark Isolde. Hall. Icelandic fairy tales.
Fair, Brown and Trembling. Curtin. Myths and folklore of Ireland.
Jacobs. Celtic fairy tales.
Pyle. Tales of wonder and magic.
See also Cinderella.
Fair Catherine and Pif-paf Poltrie. Wiggin and Smith. Tales of laughter.
See also Piff-paff; or, The art of government.
Fair Circassians. Lang. Grey fairy book.
Lang. Marvellous musician.
This is a continuation of "Three sons of Hali."
Fair-flower. Caballero. Spanish fairy tales.
See also Prince Darling.
Fair Goldilocks. *See* Fair one with golden locks.
Fair maid of Astolat. *See* Sir Lancelot and Elaine.
Fair Melusina. Scudder. Book of legends.
Fair one with golden locks. Aulnoy. Fairy tales. (Fair with golden hair.)
Aunt Louisa's book of fairy tales.
Coussens. Child's book of stories. (Story of Pretty Goldilocks.)
Douglas. Favourite French fairy tales. (Goldenlocks.)
Jerrold. Big book of fairy tales.
Lang. Blue fairy book. (Story of Pretty Goldilocks.)
Lang. Pretty Goldilocks and other stories. (Pretty Goldilocks.)
*Lang. Princess on the glass hill. (Story of Pretty Goldilocks.)
Lansing. Fairy tales. v. 1. (Fair Goldilocks.)
Larned. Fairy tales from France. (King's messenger.)
Mabie. Fairy tales every child should know.
Mabie. Heroes and fairies.
Mulock. Fairy book.
Nursery tales.
Patten. Junior classics. v. 1.
Perkins. Twenty best fairy tales.
Scudder. Children's book.
Singleton. Wild flower fairy book. (Fair Goldilocks.)
Success library. v. 3. (Story of Pretty Goldilocks.)
Valentine. Old, old fairy tales (Warne ed.).
Wiggin and Smith. Fairy ring.
See also Golden Hair.
Fair unknown. Patten. Junior classics. v. 4. (Fair unknown; Fight with two giants; Castle of the sorcerers.)
See also Sir Gareth.
Fair white city; or, Story of the past, present and future. Harrison. In story-land.
Fair with golden hair. *See* Fair one with golden locks.

Fairer-than-a-fairy. Lang. Beauty and the beast, and other stories.
Lang. Yellow fairy book.
Valentine. Old, old fairy tales.
Fairies. I. Bigham. Overheard in fairyland.
Fairies. II. Brown. Star jewels.
Fairies. III. *See* Diamonds and toads.
Fairies and the fiddler. Harrison. Old-fashioned fairy book.
Fairies and the two hunchbacks. *See* Knockgrafton.
Fairies' caldron. Hartland. English folk and fairy tales.
Fairies' cobbler (poem). Haaren. Fairy life.
Fairies' frolic (play). Rhys. Fairy gold.
Fairies' gold. *Burchill. Progressive road to reading. Book 3
Fairies in the mountain of the moon. Griswold. Hindu fairy tales.
Fairies of Merlin's crag. Grierson. Scottish fairy book.
Johnson. Fir-tree fairy book.
Fairies of Pesth. Field. Little book of profitable tales.
Fairies of the bracken. Patterson. Enchanted bird.
Fairies of the Caldon Low (poem). Haaren. Fairy life.
(poem). O'Grady and Throop. Teachers' story teller's book.
Rolfe. Fairy tales in prose and verse.
(poem). Smith. Good old stories.
Winnington. Outlook fairy book.
Fairies of the kitchen. Griffis. Belgian fairy tales.
Fairies of the mill. Patterson. Enchanted bird.
Fairies' passage. I. (poem.) Graves. Irish fairy book.
(poem). Haaren. Fairy life.
(poem). Olcott. Book of elves and fairies.
Fairies' passage. II. Kipling. Puck of Pook's Hill. (Dymchurch flit.)
Fairies' ship. Cary. French fairy tales.
Fairies' weather. Alden. Boy who found the king.
Fairy. *See* Diamonds and toads.
Fairy and the daughter of the earth. Cary. French fairy tales.
Fairy and the miller's wife. Douglas. Scottish fairy tales.
Fairy and the poor man (play). Doheny. Play awhile.
Fairy and the prince. Segovia. Spanish fairy book.
Fairy at the well. *See* Diamonds and toads.
Fairy ball. Patterson. Enchanted bird.
Fairy banquet. Hartland. English folk and fairy tales.
Rhys. Fairy gold.
Fairy bird. Bourhill and Drake. Fairy tales from South Africa.
Partridge. Story-telling in home and school.
Fairy borrowing. Thomas. Welsh fairy book.
Fairy box. Alcott. Lulu's library. v. 1.
Fairy boy of Leith. Douglas. Scottish fairy tales.
Fairy butterflies. Donaldson. Little papoose listens.

Fairy candle. Storytellers' magazine. June 1917, p. 275.
Fairy caught. Hartland. English folk and fairy tales.
Fairy congress. Griffis. Welsh fairy tales.
Fairy cow. Johnson. Oak-tree fairy book.
Fairy cowslips. *See* Cowslips. II.
Fairy crawfish. Laboulaye. Last fairy tales.
Rolfe. Fairy tales in prose and verse.
See also Fisherman and his wife; Golden fish.
Fairy-Do-Nothing and Giant Snap-'Em-Up. Olcott. Book of elves and fairies.
Fairy dog. Thomas. Welsh fairy book.
Fairy dust. Jokai. Golden fairy book.
Fairy fair. Hartland. English folk and fairy tales.
Rhys. Fairy gold.
Fairy fish. Rhys. Fairy gold.
Fairy flower. I. *See* Little Annie's dream.
Fairy flower. II. Skinner. Emerald story book.
Fairy folk. (poem). Olcott. Book of elves and fairies.
Fairy food. Rhys. Fairy gold.
Fairy friar. Caballero. Spanish fairy tales.
Fairy frog. Bourhill and Drake. Fairy tales from South Africa.
Landa. Aunt Naomi's Jewish fairy tales and legends.
Fairy funeral. Hartland. English folk and fairy tales.
Fairy garland. McFee. Treasury of flower stories.
Fairy gifts. Haaren. Fairy life.
Lang. Green fairy book.
Lang. Magician's gifts.
Fairy guardian. *See* Pigeon and the dove.
Fairy harp. Griffis. Welsh fairy tales. (Golden harp.)
·Thomas. Welsh fairy book.
Fairy hen. Caballero. Spanish fairy tales.
Fairy horn. Hartland. English folk and fairy tales.
Olcott. Good stories for great holidays. (Benevolent goblin.)
Rhys. Fairy gold.
Fairy horseshoe. Keyes. Stories and story-telling.
Fairy huntsmen. Peck. Stories for good children.
Fairy in the cuckoo clock. Griffis. Swiss fairy tales.
Fairy in the mirror. Boston collection of kindergarten stories.
Ketchum and Jorgensen. Kindergarten gems.
Fairy island. Olcott. Book of elves and fairies.
Fairy lamps. Seton. Woodland tales.
Seton. Woodmyth and fable.
Fairy linen. * Dillingham and Emerson. Tell it again stories.
Fairy minstrel of Glenmalure. Leamy. Fairy minstrel of Glenmalure.
Fairy names. Judson. Flower fairies.
Fairy nurse. Lang. Lilac fairy book.

Fairy nurse—*continued.*
Lang. Fairy nurse and other stories.
See also Fairy's midwife; Fairy ointment; How Dame Margery Twist saw more than was good for her.
Fairy nursling. *See* "Fary" nursling.
Fairy of the dawn. Lang. Violet fairy book.
Fairy of the edelweiss. Griffis. Swiss fairy tales.
Fairy of the lily. Patterson. Enchanted bird.
Fairy of the poppies. Griffis. Belgian fairy tales.
Fairy ointment. Duncan-Jones. English folk-lore stories. (Ointment.)
Jacobs. English fairy tales.
Pyle. Tales of folks and fairies. (Dame Pridgett and the fairies.)
Thomas. Welsh fairy book.
See also Fairy's midwife; How Dame Margery Twist saw more than was good for her.
Fairy Old Boy and the tiger. Pitman. Chinese fairy stories.
Fairy Palace of the Quicken Trees. Joyce. Old Celtic romances.
Fairy party. Judson. Flower fairies.
Fairy password. Thomas. Welsh fairy book.
Fairy pinafores. Alcott. Aunt Jo's scrapbag. v. 3.
Fairy-prince and griffin. Burlingame. Grateful elephant.
Fairy princess of Ergetz. Landa. Aunt Naomi's Jewish fairy tales and legends.
Fairy queen. *See* Una and the Red Cross knight.
Fairy queen and the carrier doves. Griffis. Belgian fairy tales.
Fairy Red Breast. Canton. Reign of King Herla.
Fairy reward. Thomas. Welsh fairy book.
Fairy ring. I. Gruelle. Friendly fairies.
Fairy ring. II. Meyer. Little green door.
Fairy Rosy-Wings, Adventure of. Patterson. Enchanted bird.
Fairy seals. *See* Christmas seals.
Fairy serpent. Fielde. Chinese fairy tales.
Fairy shoemaker. I. *See* Lepracaun.
Fairy shoemaker. II. Gate. Punch and Robinetta.
Fairy shoes. Hoxie. Kindergarten story book.
Fairy sleeping beauty. *See* Lilybell and Thistledown.
Fairy spinner. Skinner. Turquoise story book.
Fairy spring. Alcott. Lulu's library. v. 2.
Fairy steeds. Wickes. Happy holidays.
Fairy story. I. Arnold and Gilbert. Stepping stones to literature.
Fairy story. II. Cooke. Nature myths and stories.
Fairy story-shop. Storytellers' magazine. July 1915, p. 237.
Fairy swan song. Olcott. Wonder garden.
Fairy tale of a fox. * Heller and Bates. Little Golden Hood.
Fairy-tale teller. Haaren. Fairy life.
Fairy tankard. Hackländer. Enchanting and enchanted.

Fairy Tell-True. Field. Famous fairy tales.
*Grimm. Fairy tales (Wiltse. Woodcutter's child.) v. 2.
Grimm. Household tales (Burt ed.).
Welsh. Fairy tales children love.
Wiggin and Smith. Magic casements. (Woodcutter's child.)
See also Lassie and her god-mother.
Fairy tempter. Rolfe. Fairy tales in prose and verse.
Fairy thieves. Hartland. English folk and fairy tales.
Rhys. Fairy gold.
Fairy thimble. *See* Princess Girlikin.
Fairy thorn. Yeats. Irish fairy tales.
Fairy tree. *See* Bones of Djulung.
Fairy tree of Dooros. Leamy. Golden spears.
Fairy tulips. *See* Tulip bed.
Fairy walking stick. Thomas. Welsh fairy book.
Fairy wand. Spaulding and Bryce. Aldine readers. Book 3.
Fairy wedding. Olcott. Book of elves and fairies.
Fairy well of Lagnanay (poem). Yeats. Irish fairy tales.
Fairy who came to our house. Bailey and Lewis. For the children's hour.
Fairy who judged her neighbors. Bailey. Stories children need.
Curry. Little classics. (Lark and his spurs.)
Ingelow. Stories told to a child. v. 2.
Ingelow. Three fairy tales.
My Bookhouse. v. 2.
Smith. Good old stories.
Fairy wife. *See* Touch of iron.
Fairy wishes nowadays. St. Nicholas. Jan. 1883, p. 166.
Fairyfoot. Browne. Granny's wonderful chair.
*Dyer and Brady. Merrill readers. 3d reader. (How Fairyfoot met Robin Goodfellow; Finding of the Princess Maybloom; Fair fountain and the growing well.)
My Bookhouse. v. 3. (Story of Fairyfoot.)
Patten. Junior classics. v. 6.
Peck. Stories for good children. (Prince Fairyfoot.)
Skinner. Garnet story book.
Welsh. Fairy tales children love.
See also Green-faced toad.
Fairy's birthday gift. *See* Little Blessed-Eyes.
Fairy's blunder. Lang. Grey fairy book.
Fairy's day. Judson. Flower fairies. (Just a beginning.)
Fairy's midwife. Hartland. English fairy and folk tales.
Olcott. Book of elves and fairies. (Coal-black steed.)
See also Fairy ointment; Fairy nurse; How Dame Margery Twist saw more than was good for her.
Fairy's New Year gift. Olcott. Good stories for great holidays.
Poulsson. In the child's world.
Fairy's servants. Olcott. Book of elves and fairies.
Faithful and Faithless. *See* True and Untrue.

Faithful and Unfaithful. Stroebe and Martens. Swedish fairy book.
Faithful Argus. *See* Ulysses's return.
Faithful beasts. *See* Grateful beasts. I and II.
Faithful Constance. Darton. Tales of the Canterbury pilgrims. (Man of law's tale: Faithful Constance.)
McSpadden. Stories from Chaucer. (Lawyer's tale: Constance.)
Storr and Turner. Canterbury chimes. (Man of law's tale: Constance.)
Faithful dancing-girl wife. Allen. Korean tales. (Chun Yang; or, The faithful dancing-girl wife.)
Faithful dog. *See* Old man who made withered trees to flower.
Faithful friend. *See* Elephant who was lonely.
Faithful friends. *See* Beg and the fox.
Faithful John. Grimm. Fairy tales (Lucas tr.).
Grimm. Household stories (Crane tr.).
Grimm. Household tales (Burt ed.).
Grimm. Household tales (Everyman's ed.).
Jacobs. Europa's fairy book. (John the true.)
Lang. Blue fairy book. (Trusty John.)
*Lang. Dick Whittington, and other stories. (Trusty John.)
Lang. Trusty John and other stories. (Trusty John.)
Singleton. Goldenrod fairy book.
Tappan. Folk stories and fables.
Wiggin and Smith. Fairy ring. (Faithful John, the king's servant.)
See also Daughter of the Padishaw; Golden steed; Log; Lucky Luck.
Faithful lover. Guerber. Legends of the Rhine.
Faithful minstrel. *See* Richard Coeur de Leon.
Faithful prince. Steel. Tales of the Punjab.
Faithful purse-bearer. Campbell. Beyond the border.
Douglas. Scottish fairy tales (Burt ed.).
Johnson. Elm-tree fairy book. (Faithful steward.)
Faithful Rajpoot. Coussens. Jade story book.
Faithful steward. *See* Faithful purse-bearer.
Faithful Svend. Grundtvig. Danish fairy tales.
See also Fridolin at the forge.
Faithful wife. I. *See* Savitri, the faithful wife.
Faithful wife. II. Johnson. Elm-tree fairy book.
Faithlessness of Sinogo. Miller. Philippine folklore stories.
Falcon and the capon. Æsop. Fables (Burt ed.).
Wiggin and Smith. Talking beasts.
Falcon and the duck. Eastman. Wigwam evenings.
Falcon-king. Harrison. Old-fashioned fairy book.
Falconer and the partridge. *See* Partridge and the fowler
Fall of Polobulac. Miller. Philippine folklore stories.
Fall of the spider man. Macmillan. Canadian fairy tales.
Fall of Troy. *See* Trojar war.

Falling stars. Donaldson. Moons of long ago.
Falls of the Willamette. Judson. Myths and legends of the Pacific Northwest.
False bride. *See* Goose girl.
False Caliph. *See* Mahomed Ali the jeweller.
False collar. *See* Shirt collar.
False economy. Fielde. Chinese fairy tales.
False Foodrage. Tappan. Old ballads in prose.
False knight. Tappan. Old ballads in prose.
Tappan. Book of humor.
False prince. *See* Sham prince.
False prince and the true. Lang. Lilac fairy book.
Lang. Little King Loc.
Falsehood and truth. Laboulaye. Last fairy tales.
Falsehood and wickedness. Friedlander. Jewish fairy tales.
Family servants. Wiggin and Smith. Tales of laughter.
Famine. *See* St. Nicholas and the children.
Fanch Scouarnec. Cary. French fairy tales.
See also Jack and his master; Keep cool.
Fancha and the magpie. Griffis. Korean fairy tales.
Fanchon. Hodgkins. Atlantic treasury of childhood stories.
Far Darrig in Donegal. Yeats. Irish fairy tales.
Far famed Oriental. Griffis. Belgian fairy tales.
Farm that ran away and came back. Griffis. Dutch fairy tales.
Farm-yard cock and the weather-cock. Andersen. Fairy tales (Paull tr.).
Andersen. Wonder stories (Author's ed.).
Farmer and his dog. Æsop. Fables (Burt ed.).
Wiggin and Smith. Talking beasts.
See also Beth Gellert; King and his falcon.
Farmer and his sons. I. *See* Buried treasure.
Farmer and his sons. II. *See* Bundle of sticks.
Farmer and his three enemies. Æsop. Fables (Burt ed.).
Farmer and the badger. Ballard. Fairy tales from far Japan. (Kachi Kachi mountain.)
Ozaki. Japanese fairy book.
Farmer and the boggart. *See* Boggart.
Farmer and the fox. Patten. Junior classics. v. 1.
Farmer and the hill-man. Haaren. Fairy life. (Farmer and the troll.)
Van Sickle and Seegmiller. Riverside readers. 3d reader.
Wiggin and Smith. Tales of laughter. (Farmer and the troll.)
Farmer and the humming bird. Bryce. Fables from afar.
See also Nightingale and the pearl.
Farmer and the money lender. Jacobs. Indian fairy tales.
Patten. Junior classics. v. 1.
Steel. Tales of the Punjab.
Wiggin and Smith. Tales of laughter.
Farmer and the noses. *See* Are you not satisfied?

Farmer and the pixy. Pyle. Wonder tales retold.
Farmer and the stork. Æsop. Fables (Black ed. Husbandman and the stork.)
Æsop. Fables (Burt ed. Husbandman and the stork.)
Æsop. Fables (Stickney. Husbandman and the stork.)
Arnold and Gilbert. Stepping stones to literature. v. 2. (Crane and the crows.)
Scudder. Children's book.
Scudder. Fable and folk stories.
Wiggin and Smith. Talking beasts.
Farmer and the troll. *See* Farmer and the hill-man.
Farmer Broom, Farmer Leaves, and Farmer Iron. Bosschère. Christmas tales of Flanders.
See also Three little pigs. II.
Farmer Mybrow and the fairies. Olcott. Wonder garden.
Farmer Grigg's boggart. Pyle. Pepper and salt.
Farmer of Liddesdale. Jacobs. More Celtic fairy tales.
Wiggin and Smith. Tales of wonder.
Farmer, the sheep and the robbers. Bidpai. Tortoise and the geese.
Farmer Weatherbeard. Asbjörnsen. Fairy tales from the far north.
Baldwin. Another fairy reader.
Dasent. Norse fairy tales. (Farmer Weathersky.)
Dasent. Popular tales from the Norse. (Farmer Weathersky.)
Lang. Red fairy book.
See also Magician's pupil; Master and pupil.
Farmer Weathersky. *See* Farmer Weatherbeard.
Farmer's ass. Rouse. Talking thrush.
Farmer's sons. *See* Bundle of sticks.
Farmer's tale. *See* Gaffer Wiseman's choice.
Farmer's wife and the raven (poem). Æsop. Fables (Burt ed.).
Wiggin and Smith. Talking beasts.
Farmer's wife of Deloraine. Douglas. Scottish fairy book.
Farquhar MacNeill. Grierson. Scottish fairy book.
Farrukruz the favorite of fortune, History of. Olcott. Tales of the Persian genii.
Farther south than south, and farther north than north, and in the great hill of gold. Stroebe and Martens. Norwegian fairy book.
Farthing rushlight. Æsop. Fables (Stickney).
"Fary" nursling. Rhys. Fairy gold.
Fast runners. Borland. Rocky Mountain tipi tales. (Deer gets antelope's dew claws.)
Grinnell. Blackfoot lodge tales.
Grinnell. Pawnee hero stories. (How the deer lost his gall.)
Linderman. Indian why stories. (Why the deer has no gall.)
Fatal courtship. Æsop. Fables (Burt ed.).

Fatal marriage. Æsop. Fables (Black ed.).
Fatal wish. Mendes. Fairy spinning wheel.
Fate. I. Laboulaye. Fairy tales. (*In* Captain John's travels.)
Fate. II. Wardrop. Georgian folk tales.
Fate of a little old woman. *See* Sir Gammer Vans.
Fate of Echo. *See* Echo and Narcissus.
Fate of Erisichthon. *See* King and the oak.
Fate of Mamondagokwa. Nixon-Roulet. Indian folk tales.
Fate of Mr. Jack Sparrow. Harris. Uncle Remus, his songs and his sayings.
Fate of the children of Lir. Canton. Reign of King Herla. (Doom of the children of Lir.)
Chisholm. Enchanted land. (Four white swans.)
Chisholm and Steedman. Staircase of stories. (Sorrows of Finola.)
Colum. Boy in Eirinn. (Children of Lir.)
Frost. Fairies and folk of Ireland. (*In* Ch. 2.)
Grierson. Children's book of Celtic stories.
Higginson. Tales of the enchanted islands of the Atlantic. (Swan-children of Lir.)
Jacobs. More Celtic fairy tales.
Joyce. Old Celtic romances. (Fate of the children of Lir; or, The four white swans.)
Mabie. Legends every child should know.
Rolleston. High deeds of Finn. (Story of the children of Lir.)
Wilmot-Buxton. Stories of early England. (Children of Lir.)
Yeats. Irish fairy tales.
Fate of the children of Turenn. Joyce. Old Celtic romances. (Fate of the children of Turenn; or, The quest for the eric-fine.)
Rolleston. High deeds of Finn. (Quest of the sons of Turenn.)
Fate of the sons of Usna. Joyce. Old Celtic romances.
Fate of the turtle. *See* Talkative tortoise.
Fates. Richards. Silver crown.
Father and his two daughters. Æsop. Fables (Burt ed.).
Welsh. Stories children love.
Father Bruin in the corner. Asbjörnsen. Fairy tales from the far north. (Old Father Bruin in the wolf pit.)
Asbjörnsen. Tales from the fjeld.
Dasent. Norse fairy tales.
Johnson. Book of fairy-tale bears. (Bear in a forest pitfall.)
Stanley. Animal folk tales. (Father Bruin in the wolf pit.)
Thorne-Thomsen. East o' the sun and west o' the moon. (Father Bruin.)
Wiggin and Smith. Tales of laughter.
Father Frost. *See* King Frost.

Father Grumbler. Lang. Aladdin and other stories.
Lang. Brown fairy book.
Father "Lime-Stick" and the flower-picker. Wiggin and Smith. Talking beasts.
Father of the family. Asbjörnsen. Folk and fairy tales. (Seven fathers in the house.)
Asbjörnsen. Tales from the fjeld.
*Klingensmith. Just stories.
Father of the house. Noyes. Twilight stories. (Master of the house.)
Father's legacies. *See* Fortune seekers. I.
Father's legacy. Guerber. Legends of the Rhine.
Father's prophecy. Wardrop. Georgian folk tales.
Fatma. Silver fairy book.
Fause fable of the Lord Lathom. Hartland. English folk and fairy tales.
Faust. McSpadden. Stories from great operas.
Pleasanton. Fairyland of opera.
Favorite of fortune and the child of ill luck. Martens. Chinese fairy book.
Favorite of the gods. *See* Tantalus.
Fawn and his mother. Æsop. Fables (Stickney).
Fawn and the little tiger. Wiggin and Smith. Talking beasts.
Fear. Kunos. Forty-four Turkish fairy tales.
Fearless boy. Bay. Danish fairy and folk tales.
Feast. Richards. Silver crown.
Feast of cherries. *See* Cherry feast of Naunberg.
Feast of lanterns. Coe. Second book of stories.
Coussens. Jade story book. (Feast of the lanterns.)
Wiggin and Smith. Tales of wonder.
See also Rip Van Winkle.
Feast of the dead. Magnus. Russian folk-tales.
Feast of the mountain goats. Eastman. Indian legends retold.
Feather Head, Story of. Donahey. Tales to be told to children.
Feather of Bright Finist the Falcon. *See* Bright-Hawk's feather.
Feather of Finist the Falcon. *See* Bright-Hawk's feather.
Feather of the Zhar bird. Bain. Cossack fairy tales. (Tremsin, the bird Zhar, and Nastasia, the lovely maid of the sea.)
Pyle. Fairy tales from many lands.
Featherbird. *See* Forbidden room.
Feathered barbers. Lummis. Pueblo Indian folk stories.
Feats of the giants. *See* Thor and his journey to Jötunheim.
Felicia and the pot of pinks. *See* Fortunée.
Female Solomon. *See* Maiden who was wiser than an emperor.

Fenris wolf. *See* Binding of the Fenris wolf.
Ferdinand Faithful, and Ferdinand Unfaithful. Grimm. Fairy tales (Paull tr.).
Ferré. *See* Big Ferré.
Fertram and Hildur. Hall. Icelandic fairy tales.
Festival of the little people. Eastman. Wigwam evenings.
Festivities at the house of Conan of Crann Sleibhe. Graves. Irish fairy book.
Fetching a halter. Thomas. Welsh fairy book.
Fiddi-wow-wow-wow. Underhill. Dwarfs' tailor and other fairy tales.
Fiddle-diddle-dee. Van Sickle and Seegmiller. Riverside readers. 2d reader.
Fiddler in the fairy ring. Ewing. Old-fashioned fairy tales.
Fiddler's well. Douglas. Scottish fairy tales.
Fidelio. McSpadden. Stories from great operas.
Field lark and partridge. Young. Plantation bird legends.
Field mouse and the town mouse. *See* Country mouse and the town mouse.
Field of Boiiauns. Jacobs. Celtic fairy tales.
Quiller-Couch. Fairy tales far and near. (Boliawns.)
Singleton. Goldenrod fairy book.
Field of the cloth of gold. Evans. Old time tales.
Fierabras. *See* Charlemagne.
Fight at Brihtnoth. Wilmot-Buxton. Stories of early England.
Fighting cocks. Æsop. Fables (Black ed.).
Æsop. Fables (Burt ed.).
Fighting cocks and the turkey. Æsop. Fables (Burt ed.).
Fighting hare. *See* Sun a prisoner. IV.
Filial girl. *See* Mirror of Matsuyama.
Filial piety. *See* Parrot that fed his parents.
Fin MacCumhail. *See* Finn MacCool.
Finding a dark place. O'Grady and Throop. Teachers' story teller's book.
Finding dreams in the Land of Sleep. Donaldson Moons of long ago.
Finding of the hammer. *See* Thor: Quest of the hammer.
Fine plan. *See* Belling the cat.
Finest liar in the world. Lang. Violet fairy book
Lang. Satin surgeon.
Finette Cendron. Aulnoy. Fairy tales.
*Aulnoy. Children's fairy tales. (Chestnut tree.)
See also Cinderella.
Fingers. Ketchum and Jorgensen. Kindergarten gems.
Finikin and his golden pippins. Skinner. Garnet story book.
Finn and the fairy shoemaker. Skinner. Merry tales.
Finn MacCool. Colum. Boy in Eirinn. (Boyhood of Finn MacCoul.)
Curtin. Myths and folklore of Ireland.

Finn MacCool—*continued.*
This includes: Birth of Fin MacCumhail and the origin of the Fenians of Erin; Fin MacCumhail and the Fenians of Erin in the castle of Fear Dubh; Fin MacCumhail and the knight of the full axe; Fin MacCumhail and the son of the king of Alba; Fin MacCumhail, the seven brothers and the king of France; Gilla Na Grakin and Fin MacCumhail.
Graves. Irish fairy book. (Coming of Finn.)
Grierson. Children's book of Celtic stories.
This includes: Finn, the son of Cumhal; How Finn obtained the tooth of knowledge; How Finn found Bran; Finn's ransom.
Jacobs. More Celtic fairy tales. (How Fin went to the kingdom of the big men.)
Rolleston. High deeds of Finn.
This includes: Boyhood of Finn; Coming of Finn; Finn's chief men; Chase of the Gilla Dacar.
See also Black, Brown and Gray; Kilwch and Olwen; Knockmany, Legend of; Last of the Feni.
Finn the giant and the minister of Lund. Stroebe and Martens. Swedish fairy book.
Finn's ransom. *See* Finn MacCool.
Fir-apple. *See* Fundevogel.
Fir tree. I. *Alderman. Classics old and new. (Little fir tree.)
Allison and Perdue. Story in primary instruction.
Andersen. Fairy tales (Paull tr.).
Andersen. Fairy tales (Turpin ed.).
Andersen. Stories (Riverside ed. Pine tree.)
Andersen. Wonder stories.
Bailey and Lewis. For the children's hour. (Pine tree.)
*Baldwin. Fairy reader. (Little fir tree.)
Blaisdell. Child life. 3d reader. (Little fir tree.)
Boston collection of kindergarten stories.
Coe. First book of stories.
Coussens. Child's book of stories.
Curtiss. Christmas stories and legends. (Adapted.)
Dickinson and Skinner. Children's book of Christmas stories.
Field. Famous fairy tales.
Johnson. Fir-tree fairy book.
Ketchum and Jorgensen. Kindergarten gems. (Pine tree.)
Klingensmith. Household stories for little readers. (Little fir tree.)
Lang. Pink fairy book.
Lang. Snow-queen and other stories.
Lansing. Fairy tales. v. 2.
Olcott. Good stories for great holidays. (Pine tree.)
Patten. Junior classics. v. 1.
Scudder. Children's book.
Singleton. Goldenrod fairy book.

Fir tree. I.—*continued.*
Sly. World stories retold. (Adapted.)
Strong. All the year round. v. 2. Winter.
Success library. v. 3.
Tappan. Folk stories and fables.
Welsh. Stories children love.
Fir tree. II. Bryant. Best stories to tell to children. (Little fir tree. Adapted.)
Bryant. Stories to tell to children. (Little fir tree. Adapted.)
Van Sickle and Seegmiller. Riverside readers. 2d reader.
Wiggin and Smith. Story hour. (Story of the forest.)
Fir tree and the bramble. Æsop. Fables (Burt ed.).
Æsop. Fables (Black ed.).
Arnold and Gilbert. Stepping stones to literature. v. 2.
Fire bell. Guerber. Legends of the Rhine.
Fire bird. *See* How fire was brought to the Indians. V.
Fire-bird, the horse of power and the Princess Vasilissa. Chisholm and Steedman. Staircase of stories.
Fire bringer. Austin. Basket woman.
Bryant. Best stories to tell to children.
Bryant. How to tell stories to children.
Sly. World stories retold. (Coyote and the Indian fire-bringer.)
See also How fire was brought to the Indians. I and II.
Fire-drill's son. Lang. Strange story book.
Fire flower. Judson. Flower fairies. (Fire.)
Fire Glow and Fire Gloom. *See* Ambitious hunter and skilful fisher.
Fire-god. Martens. Chinese fairy book.
Fire-leggings. Grinnell. Blackfoot lodge tales. (Theft from the sun.)
Linderman. Indian why stories.
See also Old-Man steals the sun's leggings.
Fire, Origin of. Judson. Myths and legends of Alaska.
See also How fire was brought to the Indians; Secret of fire.
Fire-plume. Schoolcraft. Indian fairy book.
Wade. Indian fairy tales.
Fire quest. *See* Firefly's lovers.
Fire-test. Harris. Nights with Uncle Remus.
Firebird. *See* How fire was brought to the Indians. V.
Fireflies, Origin of. *See* Butterfirefly; Light of the fly.
Firefly. Bryce. That's why stories.
Firefly of Matsui. Nixon-Roulet. Japanese folk stories and fairy tales.
Firefly's lovers. Griffis. Japanese fairy tales.
James. Green willow. (Fire quest.)
Olcott. Wonder garden. (Prince Golden-Firefly.)
Skinner. Turquoise story book. (Princess Fire-Fly.)
First ants. Holbrook. Book of nature myths.
First battle. Eastman. Wigwam evenings.

First bears. *See* Giant bear.
First birds. *See* How the birds came.
First born, first wed. Stroebe and Martens. Swedish fairy book.
First buttercups. Bryce and Spaulding. Aldine language series. Book 1.
Wade and Sylvester. Language readers. 2d reader.
First butterflies. Holbrook. Book of nature myths.
First Calender. Arabian nights (Lang).
Arabian nights (Olcott. Story of the first royal mendicant.)
Arabian nights (Townsend.)
First camel. *Bryce. That's why stories. (How we got the first camel.)
First Christmas present. I. Wiltse. Kindergarten stories.
First Christmas present. II. Sawyer. This way to Christmas. (Trapper's tale of the first birthday.)
First Christmas tree. *See* Christmas tree. I and V.
First corn. I. Farmer. Nature myths.
First corn, II. Brooks. Stories of the red children. (Little Red Plume.)
Coe and Christie. Story hour readers. 3d reader. (Gift of corn.)
Compton. American Indian fairy tales. (Adventures of Living Statue.)
Hartwell. Story hour readings. 5th year. (Gift of Mondamin.)
Judd. Wigwam stories. (Mondahmin, who gave the corn.)
Nixon-Roulet. Indian folk tales. (Gift of Mondamin.)
See also Living Statue, Adventures of.
First corn. III. Bailey and Lewis. For the children's hour.
Baker and Carpenter. Language reader. 3d year. (Legend of the Indian corn.)
*Cowles. Indian nature myths. (Gift of Indian corn.)
Olcott. Good stories for great holidays. (How Indian corn came into the world.)
Olcott. Red Indian fairy book. (How Indian corn came into the world.)
Patten. Junior classics. v. 2. (Wunzh, the father of Indian corn.)
Schoolcraft. Indian fairy book. (Wunzh, the father of Indian corn.)
Tanner. Legends from the red man's forest. (Maize.)
First corn. IV. Borland. Rocky Mountain tipi tales. (Redheaded stranger.)
First corn. V. Grinnell. Punishment of the stingy.
Tyler. Twenty-four unusual stories.
First corn. VI. Skinner. Topaz story book.
First corn. VII. Olcott. Wonder garden. (Legend of the corn.)
First corn. VIII. (poem). Alexander. Hidden servants. (Origin of Indian corn.)

First corn. IX. Powers. Around the Iroquois story fire. (How corn and beans came to be.)
See also Corn chooses a mate.
First day of vacation. Bailey. Stories for Sunday telling
First diamonds. Holbrook. Book of nature myths.
First emeralds. Holbrook. Book of nature myths.
First fire. I. Eastman. Indian legends retold.
First fire. II. Judson. Myths and legends of Alaska. (Origin of fire.)
See also How fire was brought to the Indians.
First frogs. Holbrook. Book of nature myths.
See also Latona and the frogs.
First grasshopper. *See* Aurora and Tithonus.
First horse. *See* Pegasus.
First humming bird. Cowles. Indian nature myths. (Story of the humming bird.)
Holbrook. Book of nature myths.
First laurel tree. *See* Daphne.
First man. I. *See* Prometheus.
First man. II. Bayliss. Treasury of Eskimo tales.
First man and woman. Judd. Wigwam stories.
First medicine lodge. *See* Scarface. III.
First men. Borland. Rocky Mountain tipi tales.
First mocking-bird. Holbrook. Book of nature myths.
First moles. *See* Mole, Origin of.
First moon. *See* Sun, moon and stars.
First mosquitoes. Farmer. Nature myths.
First of the rattlesnakes. *See* First rattlesnake. I.
First old man and the hind. Arabian nights (Dodge ed.).
Arabian nights (Lang).
Arabian nights (Townsend).
Jenks. Tales of fantasy.
Scudder. Children's book.
First peace pipe. Borland. Rocky mountain tipi tales.
First pearls. Holbrook. Book of nature myths.
First pine trees. *See* Glooscap and the magic gifts. II.
First printer. *See* Gutenberg.
First rabbits. Farmer. Nature myths. (White hares.)
Holbrook. Book of nature myths. (Why the white hares have black ears.)
Olcott. Wonder garden. (Snowball hares.)
Williston. Japanese fairy tales. 2d series.
First rattlesnake. I. Lummis. Pueblo Indian folk stories. (First of the rattlesnakes.)
First rattlesnake. II. Farmer. Nature myths. (First rattlesnakes.)
First rattlesnakes. *See* First rattlesnake. II.
First snow storm. *See* Princess lost in the snow.
First snowdrops. I. Holbrook. Book of nature myths.
See also Old Winter Man and the Spring. II.

First snowdrops. II. Bryce. That's why stories. (How we got the first snowdrop.)
Olcott. Wonder garden. (How the first snowdrop came.)
First strawberries. Borland. Rocky Mountain tipi stories.
Eastman. Indian legends retold. (First strawberry.)
See also Battle that never was fought.
First tears. Judson. Myths and legends of Alaska.
First totem pole. Judson. Myths and legends of the Pacific Northwest.
First tree frog. Hyde. Favorite Greek myths. (Hylas.)
Olcott. Wonder garden. (Little Hylas.)
First umbrella. *See* Elf and the dormouse.
First vineyard. Friedlander. Jewish fairy book.
See also Giant of the flood.
First wife's wedding ring. Ewing. Old-fashioned fairy tales.
First whitefish. Holbrook. Book of nature myths.
First winter. *See* How the winter came.
First woman. I. Bayliss. Treasury of Eskimo tales. (What happened to the lone woman of St. Michael.)
Judson. Myths and legends of Alaska.
First woman. II. Bayliss. Treasury of Eskimo tales.
First woodpecker. *See* Woodpecker.
Fish and the fishermen. *See* Three fish. I.
Fish and the flowers. Davis and Chow-Leung. Chinese fables and folk stories.
Peck. Stories for good children.
Fish and the ring. Duncan-Jones. English folk-lore stories.
Jacobs. English fairy tales.
See also Constans, the emperor; Foreordained match; King who would be stronger than fate.
Fish-hook of pearl. Colum. At the gateways of the day.
Fish-peri. Kunos. Forty-four Turkish fairy tales.
Fish prince. I. James. Enchanted castle.
Fish prince. II. James. Magic bed.
Fish prince. III. *See* Muchie Lal.
Fish story. Lang. Lilac fairy book.
Fish which wanted a bath. Potter. Pinafore pocket story book.
Fish who helped Saint Gudwall. Brown. Book of saints and friendly beasts.
Fisher. Æsop. Fables (Burt ed.).
Æsop. Fables (Jacobs).
Fisher and the little fish. Æsop. Fables (Black ed. Angler and the little fish.)
Æsop. Fables (Burt ed. Angler and the little fish.)
Æsop. Fables (Jacobs).
Æsop. Fables (Stickney. Fisherman and the little fish.)
Cowles. Art of story telling. (Fisherman.)
Grover. Folk-lore readers. v. 1. (Fisherman and the fish.)
Scudder. Fables and folk stories. (Fisherman and the sprat.)

Fisher boy. *See* Uraschimataro and the turtle.
Fisher-boy Urashima. *See* Uraschimataro and the turtle.
Fisher who let out summer. *See* How summer came to the earth. I.
Fisherman. I. *See* Fisherman and the genie.
Fisherman. II. Æsop. Fables (Black ed.).
Fisherman. III. *See* Fisherman and the little fish.
Fisherman. IV. Meigs. Kingdom of the winding road.
Fisherman and his soul. Wilde. Fairy tales.
Fisherman and his wife. Bailey. Stories children need.
Baldwin. Fairy tales.
*Benson. Really truly fairy tales.
Boys' and girls' fairy book.
*Burchill. Progressive road to reading. Book 2.
Chandler. Pan the piper. (*In* Pan's frolic with the bronze folk.)
Field. Famous fairy tales.
Grimm. Fairy tales (Lucas tr.).
Grimm. Fairy tales (Paull tr.).
*Grimm. Fairy tales (Wiltse). v. 2.
Grimm. Household stories (Crane tr.).
Grimm. Household tales (Burt ed.).
Grimm. Household tales (Everyman's ed.).
*Haaren. Songs and stories. 2d reader.
Hodgkins. Atlantic treasury of childhood stories.
Johnson. Oak-tree fairy book.
Lang. Beauty and the beast and other stories.
Lang. Green fairy book.
My Bookhouse. v. 2.
Noyes. Twilight stories.
Scudder. Children's book.
Scudder. Fables and folk stories.
Wiggin and Smith. Tales of laughter.
See also Fairy crawfish; Golden fish; Old woman who lived in a vinegar bottle; Sea king's gift; Wonderful fish.
Fisherman and the fish. *See* Fisher and the little fish.
Fisherman and the genie Arabian nights (Colum. Story of the fisherman.)
Arabian nights (Dodge ed. Story of the fisherman.)
Arabian nights (Housman).
Arabian nights (Lang. Story of the fisherman.)
Arabian nights (Olcott).
Arabian nights (Townsend. History of the fisherman.)
Arabian nights (Wiggin and Smith).
Baker and Carpenter. Language readers. 5th year. (Story of the fisherman.)
Johnson. Elm-tree fairy book.
Pyle. Where the wind blows.
Scudder. Children's book. (History of the fisherman.)
Welsh. Fairy tales children love.
Fisherman and the little fish. *See* Fisher and the little fish.

Fisherman and the merman. Douglas. Scottish fairy tales.
Fisherman and the piskies. Hartland. English folk and fairy tales.
Fisherman and the sprat. *See* Fisher and the little fish.
Fisherman and troubled water. Æsop. Fables (Burt ed.).
Fisherman who caught the sun. *See* Sun a prisoner. V.
Fisherman's son, Adventures of. Eells. Tales of giants from Brazil.
Fisherman's son and the Gruagach of tricks. Curtin. Myths and folklore of Ireland.
See also Oh; Magician's pupil; Wizard and his pupil.
Fishes. *Dillingham and Emerson. Tell it again stories.
Fishes of the boiling spring. Nixon-Roulet. Japanese folk stories and fairy tales.
Fishing party. *See* Moon in the millpond.
Fishsave. Welsh. Stories children love.
Fitna and the cow. Armfield. Wonder tales.
Five brothers. Hall. Icelandic fairy tales.
Johnson. Elm-tree fairy book.
Five companions. Noyes. Saints of Italy.
Five in one pod. *See* Pea blossom.
Five little pigs. Coussens. Child's book of stories.
*Skinner. Very little child's book of stories.
Five little seed babies. Bakewell. True fairy stories.
Five little white heads. Bryant. How to tell stories to children.
Five out of one pod. *See* Pea blossom.
Five out of one shell. *See* Pea blossom.
Five peas in a pod. *See* Pea blossom.
Five queer brothers. Fielde. Chinese fairy tales.
Patten. Junior classics. v. 1.
Wiggin and Smith. Tales of wonder.
Five servants. Grimm. Household tales (Everyman's ed.).
Wiggin and Smith. Tales of laughter.
See also How six traveled through the world.
Five wise words of the Guru. Lang. Olive fairy book.
Lang. Magic book.
Flail which came from the clouds. Grimm. Fairy tales (Paull tr. Flail from Heaven.)
Wiggin and Smith. Tales of laughter.
Flaming horse. Fillmore. Czechoslovak fairy tales.
Flat Tail the Beaver. Eggleston. Queer stories for boys and girls.
Flax.
Andersen. Fairy tales (Paull tr.).
Andersen. Fairy tales (Turpin).
Andersen. Stories (Riverside ed.).
Andersen. Wonder stories.
Arnold and Gilbert. Stepping stones to literature. v. 3.
Bailey and Lewis. For the children's hour.
Blaisdell. Child life. 3d reader.
Curry. Little classics.

Flax—*continued.*
Ketchum and Jorgensen. Kindergarten gems.
Keyes. Five senses.
Poulsson. In the child's world.
Scudder. Children's book.
Van Sickle and Seegmiller. Riverside readers. v. 5.
Wiltse. Kindergarten stories.
See also How flax was given to men.
Flax leavings. Grimm. Fairy tales (Paull tr.).
Keyes. Stories and story telling. (Odds and ends.)
Storytellers' magazine. June, 1917, p. 300. (Idleness and industry.)
Wiggin and Smith. Tales of laughter. (Shreds.)
Flayed piper. *See* Marsyas and Apollo.
Fleece of gold. Laboulaye. Fairy tales.
Laboulaye. Last fairy tales.
Fleetfoot and Billy. Bigham. Merry animal tales.
See also Two goats.
Flibbertigibbit. Bailey. Friendly tales.
Flies and the honey-pot. Æsop. Fables (Burt ed.).
Scudder. Children's book. (Flies and the pot of honey.)
Scudder. Fables and folk stories. (Flies and the pot of honey.)
Wiggin and Smith. Talking beasts.
Flies and the pot of honey. *See* Flies and the honey-pot.
Flight into Egypt. Lagerlöf. Christ legends.
Flight of the beasts. Lansing. Quaint old tales.
Flight of the dolls. Patten. Junior classics. v. 6.
Flight of the golden ram. *See* Argonauts.
Flight through the air. *See* Daedalus and Icarus.
Flight to the moon. Bayliss. Treasury of Eskimo tales.
Flint and the steel (poem). Success library. v. 3.
Wiggin and Smith. Talking beasts.
Flitting day. Andersen. Stories and tales (Author's ed.).
Floating prince. Stockton. Floating prince.
Flood. I. *See* Deucalion and Pyrrha.
Flood. II. Judson. Myths and legends of Alaska.
See also Indians' flood; Deluge; Olelbis.
Florian, Adventures of. Beston. Firelight fairy book.
Florinda and Yoringal. *See* Jorinde and Joringel.
Flory Cantillon's funeral. Yeats. Irish fairy tales.
Flower basket. *Dillingham and Emerson. Tell it again stories.
Fower de luce. Baring-Gould. Crock of gold.
Flower elves. Martens. Chinese fairy book.
Flower fairies. Olcott. Book of elves and fairies.
Flower fairy. *See* Mignonette fairy.
Flower legend. *See* Angel of the flowers. II.
Flower legends. Bigham. Overheard in fairyland.
Flower of beauty. Eells. Tales of enchantment from Spain.
Flower of joy. Richards. Silver crown.
Flower of the peony. *See* Princess Peony.

Flower of the rainbow. Olcott. Wonder garden.
Flower pixies. Bigham. Overheard in fairyland.
Flower-pot trees. *See* Hachi-no-ki.
Flower princess. I. Brown. Flower princess.
Flower princess. II. Donahey. Tales to be told to children.
Flower prison. Nordau. Dwarf's spectacles.
Flower queen's daughter. Lang. Three dwarfs.
Lang. Yellow fairy book.
Flower that lives above the clouds. Children's story garden.
Flowers, Legend of. Skinner. Turquoise story book.
Flower's lesson (poem). Alcott. Flower fables.
Flower's story. Alcott. Lulu's library. v. 2.
Flower's thanks. Skinner. Turquoise story book.
Flowers that fly. Donaldson. Moons of long ago.
Flowers with hoods. Donaldson. Little papoose listens.
Flute. James. Green willow.
See also Singing bone.
Flutter-wheel. Eggleston. Queer stories for boys and girls.
Fly. Success library. v. 3.
Fly and the moth. Æsop. Fables (Stickney).
Fly and the draught-mule. Æsop. Fables (Burt ed.).
Fly in St. Paul's cupola. Æsop. Fables (Burt ed.).
Flyaway hat. * Bryant. New stories to tell to children.
Flying carpet, the invisible cap, the gold-giving ring, and the smiting club. Chodzko. Slav fairy tales.
Flying castle. Sylva and Strettell. Legends from river and mountain.
Flying Dutchman. Chapin. Wonder stories from Wagner.
Scudder. Book of legends.
(poem). Smith. More mystery tales.
Van Sickle and Seegmiller. Riverside readers. 4th reader.
Wheelock. Stories of Wagner opera.
See also Dahul.
Flying head (poem). Wilson. Myths of the red children.
Flying lion. James. Man elephant.
Flying ogre. Martens. Chinese fairy book.
Flying ship. Lang. Three dwarfs.
Lang. Yellow fairy book.
My Bookhouse. v. 3. (Good comrades of the flying ship.)
Polevoi. Russian fairy tales.
Flying trunk. Andersen. Fairy tales (Lucas tr.).
Andersen. Fairy tales (Paull tr.).
Andersen. Wonder stories (Author's ed.).
Forty famous fairy tales.
Johnson. Birch-tree fairy book.
Lang. Pink fairy book.
Nursery tales.
Patten. Junior classics. v. 1.
Flying wizard. Olcott. Whirling king.
Followers of the sun. Eastman. Indian legends retold.
Folly of panic. *See* Timid hare.

Food that belonged to all. Armfield. Wonder tales of the world.
Fool for luck. Harris. Uncle Remus and his friends.
Fool of Athina. Aunt Naomi. Jewish fairy tales.
Fool of the family. Fielde. Chinese fairy tales.
Fool who tried to be like his brother-in-law. Fielde. Chinese fairy tales.
Foolhardy frogs and the stork. Coussens. Child's book of stories.
Foolhardy wolf. Babbitt. More Jataka tales.
Foolish bears. Storytellers' magazine. March 1914, p. 464.
Foolish Brahmin. Olcott and Pendleton. Jolly book.
Foolish crow. *See* Fox and the crow. I.
Foolish fish. Rouse. Talking thrush.
Foolish flies (play). *Doheny. Play awhile.
Foolish fox. Donaldson. Moons of long ago.
Foolish frog. *See* Frog and the ox.
Foolish Frolic. Faulkner. Story lady's book.
Foolish goose. *See* Rich goose.
Foolish grumbling. *See* Jane, Jane, don't complain.
Foolish Jim and Clever James. Johnson. Oak-tree fairy book.
Foolish little air-current. Alderman. Classics old and new. 4th reader.
Foolish men and scolding wives. *See* Silly men and cunning wives.
Foolish monkey and the wise turtle. *Fee. First year book.
Foolish, timid, little hare. *See* Timid hare.
Foolish tortoise. I. Æsop. Fables (Black ed. Tortoise and the eagle.)
Æsop. Fables (Burt ed. Tortoise and the eagle.)
Æsop. Fables (Jacobs. Tortoise and the birds.)
Arnold and Gilbert. Stepping stones to literature. v. 2. (Tortoise and the eagle.)
Baldwin. Fairy stories and fables.
Scudder. Children's book. (Tortoise and the eagle.)
Scudder. Fables and folk stories. (Tortoise and the eagle.)
Foolish tortoise. II. *See* Talkative tortoise.
Foolish weathercock. Blaisdell. Child life. 2d reader. (Foolish weathervane.)
Van Sickle and Seegmiller. Riverside readers. 2d reader.
Foolish weathervane. *See* Foolish weathercock.
Foolish weaver. Lang. Orange fairy book.
Foolish wishes. Ketchum and Jorgensen. Kindergarten gems.
Foolish wolf. Rouse. Talking thrush.
Foolish wolf and the shrewd fox. Caballero. Spanish fairy tales.
Fools and the drum. Patten. Junior classics. v. 1.
Fool's good fortune. Wardrop. Georgian folk tales.

Footless and blind champions. I. Curtin. Wonder-tales from Russsia.
Magnus. Russian folk-tales. (Legless knight and the blind knight.)
Footless and blind champions. II. Curtin. Wonder-tales from Russia. (Footless and the blind.)
Footsteps in the air. Griswold. Hindu fairy tales.
For three shillings. Grundtvig. Danish fairy tales.
For you and me. Richards. Silver crown.
Forbidden fountain. Thomas. Welsh fairy book.
Forbidden room. Grimm. Household tales (Everyman's ed.).
Some editions of Grimm not indexed here use the title "Featherbird" for this story.
See also Pig.
Foreordained match. Fielde. Chinese fairy tales.
See also Constans the emperor; Fish and the ring; King who would be stronger than fate.
Forest. *See* Fir tree. II.
Forest bailiff. *See* Fox and the cat. IV.
Forest bride. Fillmore. Mighty Mikko.
See also Three feathers; White cat.
Forest Christmas tree. Faulkner. Story lady's book.
Forest elemental. Success library. v. 3.
See also Rumpelstiltskin.
Forest fairy. I. Olcott. Whirling king.
Forest fairy. II. Tales for bedtime.
Forest full of friends. Alden. Why the chimes rang.
Van Sickle and Seegmiller. Riverside readers. 3d reader.
Forest lad and the wicked giant. Eells. Tales of giants from Brazil.
See also Vitazko.
Forest maiden. Leland. Algonquin legends of New England. (Mournful mystery of the Partridge-witch.)
Partridge. Glooscap the great chief.
Forest man. Winnington. Outlook fairy book.
Forest mill. Darton. Wonder book of beasts.
Forest of rainbow colors. Harrison. Star fairies.
Forest Rover. * Coe and Christie. Story hour readers. Book I.
See also Little black Sambo.
Forest witch. Poulsson. Top of the world stories.
See also How the oak leaves came to have notches.
Forester and the lion. *See* Man and the lion.
Forester Etin. Tappan. Old ballads in prose.
Forget-me-not. I. Bryce. That's why stories.
Farmer. Nature myths.
Judd. Classic myths.
McFee. Treasury of flower stories. (Legends of the forget-me-not.)
Pratt. Fairyland of flowers.
Forget-me-not. II. Cather. Educating by story telling.
Olcott. Wonder garden.

Forget-me-not. III. Skinner. Emerald story book.
Forget-me-not. IV. Donaldson. Moons of long ago.
Forget-me-not. V. Judson. Flower fairies.
Forging of the hammer. *See* Thor: Quest of the hammer.
Forlorn princess. Kunos. Forty-four Turkish fairy tales.
Forseti. Guerber. Myths of northern lands.
Wickes. Beyond the rainbow bridge.
Fortuitous application. Fielde. Chinese fairy tales.
Fortunatus.
Lang. Grey fairy book. (Fortunatus and his purse.)
Lang. Little King Loc. (Fortunatus and his purse.)
Mulock. Fairy book.
Rhys. Fairy gold. (Old Fortunatus.)
Scudder. Children's book.
Valentine. Old, old fairy tales. (Fortunatus and the wishing cap. Warne ed.).
This version is much longer than the others.
See also Don Giovanni de la Fortuna.
Fortunatus and his purse. *See* Fortunatus.
Fortunatus and the wishing cap. *See* Fortunatus.
Fortune. Richards. Golden windows.
Fortune and knowledge. Bay. Danish fairy and folk tales.
Fortune and misfortune. Caballero. Spanish fairy tales.
Fortune and the beggar. Young and Field. Literary readers. Book 2.
Fortune and the booby. Macdonell. Italian fairy book.
Fortune and the boy. Æsop. Fables (Black ed.).
Æsop. Fables (Burt ed.).
Fortune and the wood-cutter. Lang. Brown fairy book.
Fortune seekers. I. Grimm. Fairy tales (Paull tr.).
*Grimm. Fairy tales (Wiltse. Three luck children.) v. 2.
Grimm. Household tales (Burt ed. Father's legacies.)
Grimm. Household tales (Everyman's ed. Three children of fortune.)
Ortoli. Evening tales. (Rooster, the cat, and the reaphook.)
Wiggin and Smith. Tales of laughter. (Three luck children.)
See also Cottager and his cat; Three brothers. III.
Fortune seekers. II. *See* Knapsack, the hat and the horn.
Fortune teller. I. Æsop. Fables (Burt ed.).
Fortune teller. II. Kunos. Forty-four Turkish fairy tales.
Fortunée. Aulnoy. Fairy tales.
Lang. Blue fairy book. (Felicia and the pot of pinks.)
Lang. Princess on the glass hill. (Felicia and the pot of pinks.)
Singleton. Wild flower fairy book. (Pinks.)
Fortune's feather. *See* Sunshine stories.
Fortunes of Shrikantha. Jewett. Wonder tales from Tibet.
See also Grateful beasts. II.
Fortunio. *See* Belle-Belle; or, The Chevalier Fortuné.
Forty-first brother. Bain. Cossack fairy tales.

Forty-nine dragons. Johnson. Fir-tree fairy book.
See also Ali Baba and the forty thieves.
Forty princes and the seven-headed dragon. Kunos. Forty-four Turkish fairy tales.
Kunos. Turkish fairy tales.
Forty robbers. *See* Ali Baba and the forty thieves.
Forty thieves. *See* Ali Baba and the forty thieves.
Fostering of Aslaug. *See* Aslaug and Ragnar.
Foundling prince. Magnus. Russian folk-tales.
Fountain of beauty. Macdonell. Italian fairy book.
Fountain of Giant Land. Eells. Tales of giants from Brazil.
See also Three sisters. I.
Fountain of the genii. Olcott. Tales of the Persian genii.
Fountain of youth. *See* Ponce de Leon and the fountain of youth.
Four accomplished brothers. *See* Four clever brothers.
Four ages. Baldwin. Old Greek stories. (Golden age.)
Guerber. Myths of Greece and Rome. (Four ages and the flood.)
Four brothers. I. James. Enchanted castle.
Four brothers. II. James. Magic bed.
Four bulls and the lion. *See* Lion and the four bulls.
Four clever brothers. Grimm. Fairy tales (Lucas tr.).
Grimm. Household tales (Everyman's ed. Four craftsmen.)
Johnson. Fir-tree fairy book.
Norton. Heart of oak books. v. 3.
Ruskin. King of the golden river. (Four skilful brothers.)
Welsh. Fairy tales children love.
Four cords that hold the earth. Borland. Rocky Mountain tipi tales.
Four craftsmen. *See* Four clever brothers.
Four friends. I. *See* Escape of the mouse.
Four friends. II. *See* True friendship.
Four gifts. Lang. Lilac fairy book.
Lang. King of the waterfalls.
Four grizzly bears capture the camp. Sexton. Gray wolf stories.
Four hundred. Finger. Tales from silver lands.
Four-leaf clover. Bryce. That's why stories.
Four-leaved clover. I. *See* Abdallah.
Four-leaved clover. II. Olcott. Book of elves and fairies.
Four little children who went round the world. Wiggin and Smith. Tales of laughter.
Four little pigs. *Dillingham and Emerson. Tell it again stories.
Four musicians. *See* Bremen town musicians.
Four oxen and the lion. *See* Lion and the four bulls.
Four riddles. Bradley-Birt. Bengal fairy tales.
Four seasons. *See* Twelve months. I.
Four-shilling piece. *See* Honest penny.
Four swindlers. Bradley-Birt. Bengal fairy tales.

Four white swans. *See* Fate of the children of Lir.
Four winds. Eastman. Indian legends retold.
Four wishes. Pyle. Wonder tales retold.
Fourth of July surprise. Bailey. Friendly tales.
Fowler and the birds. Æsop. Fables (Burt ed.).
Fowler and the blackbird. Æsop. Fables (Black ed.).
Æsop. Fables (Burt ed.).
Fowler and the lark. Æsop. Fables (Black ed.).
Æsop. Fables (Burt ed.).
Fowler and the ringdove. Æsop. Fables (Black ed.).
Æsop. Fables (Burt ed.).
Fowler, the hawk and the lark (poem). Wiggin and Smith. Talking beasts.
Fowls and the bees. Bryce. Fables from afar.
Fox and a crab. Æsop. Fables (Stickney).
Fox and his adventures. *See* Fox and his five hungry comrades; Mikko the fox; Reynard and Bruin; Russet dog.
Fox and his five hungry comrades. Fillmore. Mighty Mikko. (Animals take a bite.)
Johnson. Book of fairy-tale foxes.
Lang. Crimson fairy book. (Six hungry beasts.)
Lang. Little Wildrose. (Six hungry beasts.)
Fox and his friends. *See* Beg and the fox.
Fox and the ape. Æsop. Fables (Black ed.).
Æsop. Fables (Burt ed.).
Fox and the ass. *See* Ass in the lion's skin.
Fox and the badger. Houghton. Russian grandmother's wonder tales.
Fox and the bear. *See* Why the bear has a stumpy tail.
Fox and the boar. Æsop. Fables (Black ed.).
Æsop. Fables (Burt ed.).
Fox and the boastful rooster. *See* Fox and the cock. II.
Fox and the bramble. Æsop. Fables (Black ed.).
Æsop. Fables (Burt ed.).
Fox and the cat. I. Æsop. Fables (Black ed. Cat and the fox.)
Æsop. Fables (Burt ed. Cat and the fox.)
Æsop. Fables (Jacobs).
Æsop. Fables (Stickney. Cat and the fox.)
Arnold and Gilbert. Stepping stones to literature. v. 4.
Baker and Carpenter. Language readers. 3d year.
*Baldwin. Fairy reader. (Cat and the fox.)
Carrick. Kitty cat tales. (Cat and the fox.)
*Elson and Runkel. Elson readers. Book 1. (Cat and the fox.)
Grimm. Fairy tales (Lucas tr.).
*Grimm. Fairy tales (Wiltse). v. 2.
Grimm. Household tales (Burt ed.).
Johnson. Book of fairy-tale foxes. (Fox with a sackful of tricks.)
Patten. Junior classics. v. 1.
Sly. World stories retold. (One good trick.)

Fox and the cat. I.—*continued.*
(poem). Wiggin and Smith. Talking beasts. (Cat and the fox.)
See also Mr. Fox and Mr. Thomas Cat.
Fox and the cat. II. Æsop. Fables (Burt ed.).
Wiggin and Smith. Tales of laughter. (Fox and the cat. German.)
Fox and the cat. III. Bain. Cossack fairy tales.
Storytellers' magazine. Nov. 1915, p. 391.
Wiggin and Smith. Tales of laughter. (Fox and the cat. Cossack.)
See also Old Sultan.
Fox and the cat. IV. Bailey. In the animal world. (How the cat became head forester.)
*Burchill. Progressive road to reading. Book 2. (Cat and his servant.)
Skinner. Merry tales. (Forest bailiff.)
See also Fox and the cat. V; Mr. Samson cat; Old Sultan; War of the fox and the wolf; Whiteling's war with Isegrim.
Fox and the cat. V. Fillmore. Mighty Mikko. (Fox's servant.)
See also Fox and the cat. IV; Old Sultan; War of the fox and the wolf; Whiteling's war with Isegrim.
Fox and the cock. I. *See* Cock and the fox. IV and V.
Fox and the cock. II. *See* Peter, Basil and the fox.
Fox and the colt. Van Sickle and Seegmiller. Riverside readers. 2d reader.
See also Reinecke's revenge on Isegrim.
Fox and the countryman. Æsop. Fables (Black ed.).
Æsop. Fables (Burt ed.).
Wiggin and Smith. Talking beasts.
Fox and the coyote. Chandler. In the reign of coyote.
Fox and the crab. *See* How the fox and the crab ran a race.
Fox and the crabs. Wiggin and Smith. Talking beasts.
Fox and the crafty crab. *See* How the fox and the crab ran a race.
Fox and the crane. Baldwin. Fairy stories and fables.
Fox and the crow. I. Æsop. Fables (Black ed.).
Æsop. Fables (Burt ed.).
Æsop. Fables (Jacobs).
Æsop. Fables (Stickney).
Arnold and Gilbert. Stepping stones to literature. v. 2.
Bailey. Folk stories and fables. (Crow and the fox.)
Bailey and Lewis. For the children's hour. (Crow and fox.)
*Bowen. Second story reader.
(play). *Dyer and Brady. Merrill readers. 2d reader. (Foolish crow.)
Norton. Heart of oak books. v. 2.
Patten. Junior classics. v. 1.
Scudder. Children's book. (Crow and the fox.)

Fox and the crow. I.—*continued.*
(play). Stevenson. Plays for the home. (Crow and the fox.)
Wiggin and Smith. Talking beasts.
See also Fox and the raven.
Fox and the crow. II. Fillmore. Mighty Mikko.
Riggs. Animal stories from Eskimo land. (Robin, the crow and the fox.)
See also Fox and the dove; Jackal and the heron; Tricks of the fox.
Fox and the dove. Bryce. Fables from afar. (Fox, the raven and the dove.)
Houghton. Russian grandmother's wonder tales.
Wiggin and Smith. Tales of laughter.
See also Fox and the crow. II.
Fox and the drum. Wiggin and Smith. Talking beasts.
Fox and the farmer. Byrne. Modern Greek fairy tales.
Fox and the fireflies. Stanley. Animal folk tales.
Fox and the geese. Grimm. Fairy tales (Paull tr.).
Johnson. Fir-tree fairy book. (Praying geese.)
Keyes. Stories and story-telling. (Clever geese.)
Fox and the goat. Æsop. Fables (Black ed.).
Æsop. Fables (Burt ed.).
Æsop. Fables (Jacobs).
Æsop. Fables (Stickney).
(poem). Æsop. Fables (Stickney. Supplement).
Patten. Junior classics. v. 1.
Fox and the goose. I. *See* Crafty fox and the industrious goose.
Fox and the goose. II. *See* Fox outwitted. I.
Fox and the grapes. Æsop. Fables (Black ed.).
Æsop. Fables (Burt ed.).
Æsop. Fables (Jacobs).
Æsop. Fables (Stickney).
(poem). Æsop. Fables (Stickney. Supplement).
Boston collection of kindergarten stories.
Coussens. Child's book of stories.
Hall and Gilman. Story land. 2d reader.
*Jones. First reader.
Patten. Junior classics. v. 1.
Scudder. Children's book.
Scudder. Fables and folk stories.
Sly. World stories retold.
Tappan. Folk stories and fables.
Wiggin and Smith. Talking beasts.
Young and Field. Literary readers. Book 2.
Fox and the hedgehog. I. Houghton. Russian grandmother's wonder tales.
Wiggin and Smith. Tales of laughter.
Fox and the hedgehog. II. *See* Fox and the mosquitoes.
Fox and the horse. Arnold and Gilbert. Stepping stones to literature. v. 4.

Fox and the horse—*continued.*
*Baldwin. Fairy reader.
Grimm. Fairy tales (Lucas tr.).
Grimm. Household tales (Everyman's ed.).
Johnson. Fir-tree fairy book. (Old horse.)
Wiggin and Smith. Tales of laughter.
Fox and the jackal. Success library. v. 3.
Fox and the king's son. Wardrop. Georgian folk tales.
See also Beg and the fox.
Fox and the Lapp. Lang. Brown fairy book.
Fox and the leopard. Æsop. Fables (Stickney)
Fox and the lion. Æsop. Fables (Black ed.).
Æsop. Fables (Burt ed.).
Æsop. Fables (Jacobs).
Æsop. Fables (Stickney).
Scudder. Children's book.
Scudder. Fables and folk stories.
Fox and the little red hen. *See* Little red hen. II.
Fox and the mask. Æsop. Fables (Black ed.).
Æsop. Fables (Burt ed.).
Æsop. Fables (Jacobs).
Fox and the mosquitoes. Æsop. Fables (Black ed. Fox and the hedgehog.)
Æsop. Fables (Burt ed. Fox and the hedgehog.)
Æsop. Fables (Jacobs).
Fox and the old cat and dog. *See* War of the wolf and the fox.
Fox and the piece of meat. Bidpai. Tortoise and the geese.
Fox and the pot. * Carrick. Picture tales from the Russian.
Fox and the rabbit. *See* Mr. Fox goes a-hunting but Mr. Rabbit bags the game.
Fox and the raven. Friedlande Jewish fairy tales.
Martens. Chinese fairy book.
See also Fox and the crow. I.
Fox and the rooster. I. *See* Cock and fox. III.
Fox and the rooster. II. *See* Fox and the cock. II.
Fox and the sheep. *See* Fox as herdsboy.
Fox and the sick lion. Æsop. Fables (Black ed.).
Æsop. Fables (Burt ed.).
Fox and the small red hen. *See* Little red hen. II.
Fox and the stork. Æsop. Fables (Black ed.)
Æsop. Fables (Burt ed.).
Æsop. Fables (Jacobs).
Æsop. Fables (Stickney).
Baker and Carpenter. Language readers. 3d year.
Cooke. Nature myths and stories.
My Bookhouse. v. 1.
Patten. Junior classics. v. 1.
Scudder. Children's book.
Scudder. Fables and folk stories.
Success library. v. 3.

Fox and the stork—*continued.*
Tappan. Folk stories and fables.
Wiggin and Smith. Talking beasts.
See also Mr. Fox and his dinner party; Mr. Heron's dinner-party; One bad turn begets another.
Fox and the tiger. I. Æsop. Fables (Black ed.).
Æsop. Fables (Burt ed.).
Farmer. Nature myths.
Fox and the tiger. II. Martens. Chinese fairy book.
Fox and the villagers. Wiggin and Smith. Talking beasts.
Fox and the wicked wolf. Johnson. Book of fairy-tale foxes.
Fox and the wolf. I. Æsop. Fables (Black ed.).
Æsop. Fables (Burt ed.).
Fox and the wolf. II. *See* Fox as partner. I.
Fox and the wolf. III. *See* Fox, the wolf and the cheese.
Fox and the wolf. IV. Storytellers' magazine. Sept. 1917, p. 353.
Fox and the wolf's daughter. Johnson. Book of fairy-tale foxes.
Fox and the wrens. Douglas. Scottish fairy tales.
Spaulding and Bryce. Aldine readers. Book 3. (Russet dog.)
Fox as a shepherd. *See* Fox as herdsboy.
Fox as chief mourner. Fillmore. Mighty Mikko. (Chief mourner.)
Johnson. Book of fairy-tale foxes. (Fox and his five hungry comrades.)
Fox as herdsboy. Asbjörnsen. Fairy tales from the far north.
Bailey. Firelight stories. (How the fox played herdsman.)
Bailey. Once upon a time animal stories. (How the fox played herdsman.)
*Burchill. Progressive road to reading. Book 2. (Fox and the sheep.)
Coussens. Child's book of stories. (Fox as herdsman.)
Dasent. Norse fairy tales. (Fox as herdsman.)
Dasent. Popular tales from the Norse. (Fox as herdsman.)
*Dyer and Brady. Merrill readers. 2d reader. (How the fox took care of the herds.)
Farmer. Nature myths. (Fox's white-tipped tail.)
Gade. Norwegian fairy tales. (Fox as a shepherd.)
Holbrook. Book of nature myths. (Why the tail of the fox has a white tip.)
Johnson. Book of fairy-tale foxes. (Fox who became a shepherd.)
Lansing. Rhymes and stories.
Storytellers' magazine July 1917, p. 315. (Norse folk tales.)
Wiggin and Smith. Tales of laughter. (Fox turned shepherd.)
Fox as herdsman. *See* Fox as herdsboy.

Fox as partner. I. Dasent. Popular tales from the Norse. (Bruin and Reynard.)
Grierson. Scottish fairy book. (Fox and the wolf.)
Jacobs. More Celtic fairy tales. (*In* Russet dog.)
Thorpe. Yule-tide stories. (Fox cheats the bear out of his Christmas fare.)
See also Cat and mouse in partnership; Two friends and the barrel of grease; Wolf's butter.
Fox as partner. II. Jacobs. Europa's fairy book. (*In* Reynard and Bruin.)
Fox as partner. III. Fillmore. Mighty Mikko. (Partners.)
Jacobs. More Celtic fairy tales. (*In* Russet dog.)
See also Bruin and Reynard partners.
Fox cheats the bear out of his Christmas fare. *See* Fox as partner. I.
Fox fire. Martens. Chinese fairy book.
Fox in gloves. Olcott. Wonder garden.
Fox in the ice. Young and Field. Literary readers. Book 2.
See also Fox that lost his tail.
Fox in the well. I. Æsop. Fables (Black ed.).
Æsop. Fables (Burt ed.).
Baldwin. Fairy stories and fables.
Scudder. Children's book.
Scudder. Fables and folk stories.
Tappan. Folk stories and fables.
Van Sickle and Seegmiller. Riverside readers. 3d reader.
Wiggin and Smith. Talking beasts.
Fox in the well. II. Patten. Junior classics. v. 1.
Wiggins and Smith. Talking beasts.
See also Old Mr. Rabbit, he's a good fisherman; Ups and downs.
Fox maiden. James. Green willow. (Tamamo, the fox maiden.)
Fox outwitted. I. Bryce. Fables from afar. (Fox and the goose.)
Douglas. Scottish fairy tales.
Johnson. Book of fairy-tale foxes. (Fox who did not want to be a heathen.)
Fox outwitted. II. *See* Cock and the fox. II.
Fox outwitted. III. *See* Clever chicken.
Fox story. Riggs. Animal stories from Eskimo land.
Fox that lost his tail. Æsop. Fables (Black ed. Fox without a tail.)
Æsop. Fables (Burt ed. Fox without a tail.)
Æsop. Fables (Jacobs. Fox without a tail.)
Æsop. Fables (Stickney. Fox who had lost his tail.)
(poem). Æsop. Fables (Stickney. Supplement. Fox with his tail cut off.)
Baldwin. Fairy stories and fables. (Fox who lost his tail.)
*Grover. Folk-lore readers. v. 1.

Fox that lost his tail—*continued.*
Patten. Junior classics. v. 1. (Fox without a tail.)
Scudder. Children's book.
Scudder. Fables and folk stories.
Sly. World stories retold. (Fox without a tail.)
Wiggin and Smith. Talking beasts. (Fox without a tail.)
See also Fox in the ice.
Fox, the bear and the poor farmer. Fillmore. Mighty Mikko. (Last of Osmo.)
Jacobs. Europa's fairy book. (*In* Reynard and Bruin.)
Johnson. Book of fairy-tale bears.
Spaulding and Bryce. Aldine readers. Book 3. (Fox, the bear and the farmer.)
See also Man, the hare, the fox and the bear; Well done, ill paid.
Fox, the cock and the dog. *See* Cock and the fox. II.
Fox, the eagle and the wolf. Byrne. Modern Greek fairy tales.
Fox, the hen and the drum. Bidpai. Tortoise and the geese.
Fox, the monkey and the animals (poem). Wiggin and Smith. Talking beasts.
Fox, the old cat and dog. *See* War of the wolf and the fox.
Fox, the raccoon and the bear. Messer. Next night stories.
Fox, the raven and the dove. *See* Fox and the dove.
Fox, the weasel, and the rabbit. Æsop. Fables (Burt ed.).
Fox, the wolf, and the cheese. Johnson. Book of fairy-tale foxes.
Lang. Orange fairy book.
Fox, the wolf and the horse. Æsop. Fables (Burt ed.).
(poem). Wiggin and Smith. Talking beasts.
Fox turned shepherd. *See* Fox as herdsboy.
Fox who became a shepherd. *See* Fox as herdsboy.
Fox who did not want to be a heathen. *See* Fox outwitted. I.
Fox who had lost his tail. *See* Fox that lost his tail.
Fox who lost his tail. *See* Fox that lost his tail.
Fox with a sackful of tricks. *See* Fox and the cat. I.
Fox with his tail cut off. *See* Fox that lost his tail.
Fox without a tail. *See* Fox that lost his tail.
Fox, wolf and hare (poem). Æsop. Fables (Stickney. Supplement).
Fox's brush. *See* Golden bird. II.
Fox's son. Darton. Wonder book of beasts.
Fox's white-tipped tail. *See* Fox as herdsboy.
Fragolette. Laboulaye. Fairy tales.
Laboulaye. Last fairy tales.
Lang. Grey fairy book. (Prunella.)
Fragrant tulip bed. *See* Tulip bed. II.
Frail wildflower, Legend of. *See* Anemone. II.
Francis and Martin. Baudis. Czech folk tales.
Frank Martin and the fairies. Yeats. Irish fairy tales.
Frankenstein, Jewish. *See* Rabbi's bogey-man.

Franklin's whistle. *See* Whistle.
Franklin's tale. *See* Rocks removed.
Frau Hütte. Mendel. Our little Austrian cousin.
See also Girl that trod upon bread.
Fred and Kate. *See* Frederick and Catherine.
Frederick and Catherine. Grimm. Fairy tales (Lucas tr. Fred and Kate.)
Grimm. Fairy tales (Paull tr.).
Grimm. Household stories (Crane tr. Fred and Kate.)
Grimm. Household tales (Everyman's ed.).
Frederick Barbarossa. *See* Emperor's sleep.
Freeing of the prince. Spaulding and Bryce. Aldine readers. Book 3.
Freischütz. *See* Sharpshooter.
French Puck. Lang. Lilac fairy book.
French tar-baby. *See* Tar-baby. II.
Frenchman's visit to Prague. Laboulaye. Fairy tales.
Fresh-air Tubby. Bailey. Friendly tales.
Fresh Airs' Fourth of July. Bailey. Stories for Sunday telling.
Freshet. Guerber. Legends of the Rhine.
Frey. *See* Wooing of Gerd.
Freya. *See* Freyja.
Freyja. Bradish. Old Norse stories. (Freya).
Foster and Cummings. Asgard stories. (Freyja's necklace.)
Guerber. Myths of northern lands. (*In* Freya.)
Keary. Heroes of Asgard. (Necklace Brisingamen.)
Wickes. Beyond the rainbow bridge. (Jewelled necklace.)
See also Dwarf's gifts.
Friar Bacon and the brazen head. Baldwin. Thirty more famous stories.
Scudder. Book of legends. (Brazen head.)
Smith. More mystery tales.
Friar of orders gray (poem). Lanier. Boy's Percy.
Macleod. Book of ballad stories.
Friar's tale. *See* Summoner and the fiend.
Fridolin at the forge. Guerber. Legends of the Rhine. (Jealous husband.)
See also Faithful Svend.
Friendly cowslip bells. Skinner. Turquoise story book.
Friendly frog. *See* Benevolent frog.
Friends in life and death. Asbjörnsen. Tales from the fjeld.
Frigga. Guerber. Myths of northern lands.
See also Freyja.
Frightened fawn. Faulkner. Story lady's book.
Friquet and Friquette. Macé. Home fairy tales.
Frisk. *Dillingham and Emerson. Tell it again stories.
Frisky Wisky, Story of. Fairy tales from Brentano.
Frithiof. Crommelin. Famous legends.
Guerber. Legends of the middle ages.
Holbrook. Northland heroes.

Frithiof—*continued.*
Klingensmith. Old Norse wonder tales.
My Bookhouse. v. 5.
Tappan. Stories of legendary heroes.
Wilmot-Buxton. Stories of Norse heroes.
Fritz and his friends. *See* Grateful beasts. II.
Frog. Lang. Beauty and the beast.
Lang. Violet fairy book.
See also Puddocky.
Frog and crow. Douglas. Scottish fairy tales.
Frog and his clothes. Eells. Tales of enchantment from Spain.
Frog and the elephant. *See* Elephant and the frog.
Frog and the fox. *See* Quack frog.
Frog and the hen. Æsop. Fables (Burt ed.).
Frog and the leopard. Stafford. Animal fables.
Frog and the lion fairy. *See* Benevolent frog.
Frog and the mouse. Æsop. Fables (Black ed.).
Æsop. Fables (Burt ed.).
Frog and the ox. Æsop. Fables (Black ed. Proud frog.)
Æsop. Fables (Burt ed. Frog who wished to be as big as an ox.)
Æosp. Fables (Jacobs).
Æsop. Fables (Stickney. Ox and the frog.)
Arnold and Gilbert. Stepping stones to literature. v. 2. (Frog who tried to be as big as an ox.)
Baker and Carpenter. Language readers. 3d year.
Bryant. How to tell stories to children.
*Elson and Runkel. Elson readers. Book 2. (Foolish frog.)
*Grover. Folk-lore readers. v. 1.
My Bookhouse. v. 1.
Patten. Junior classics. v. 1.
Scudder. Children's book.
Scudder. Fables and folk stories.
Tappan. Folk stories and fables.
Wiggin and Smith. Talking beasts. (Frog who wished to be as big as an ox.)
Frog and the snake. Rouse. Talking thrush.
Frog and the tadpole. Æsop. Fables (Burt ed.).
Frog crest, Origin of. Judson. Myths and legends of Alaska.
Frog for a husband. Griffis. Unmannerly tiger and other Korean tales.
Griffis. Korean fairy tales.
Frog girl. Messer. Next night stories.
Frog he would a-wooing go. Jerrold. Big book of nursery rhymes.
(poem). Mother Goose rhymes and fairy tales (Altemus ed.).
Frog in the moon. Chandler. In the reign of coyote.
Curtis. Indian days of the long ago. (*In* Strange trail.)

Frog in the moon—*continued.*
See also Making the moon.
Frog king. I. *See* Frog prince.
Frog king. II. *See* Frogs who asked for a king.
Frog prince. Bailey. Stories children need.
Bates. Once upon a time.
Chisholm. Enchanted land.
*Dillingham and Emerson. Tell it again stories. (Princess and her golden ball. Adapted.)
Field. Famous fairy tales.
Grimm. Fairy tales (Lucas tr.).
Grimm. Fairy tales (Paull tr.).
*Grimm. Fairy tales (Wiltse). v. 1.
Grimm. Household stories (Crane tr.).
Grimm. Household tales (Burt ed.).
Grimm. Household tales (Everyman's ed.).
Jerrold. Big book of fairy tales.
Lansing. Fairy tales. v. 1.
Mulock. Fairy book.
Norton. Heart of oak books. v. 3.
Perkins. Twenty best fairy tales.
Pyle. Mother's nursery tales.
Scudder. Children's book.
Singleton. Goldenrod fairy book.
Sly. World stories retold. (Frog king.)
Tappan. Folk stories and fables. (Frog king.)
Welsh. Fairy tales children love.
Wiggin and Smith. Fairy ring.
See also Maiden and the frog; Well of the world's end.
Frog princess. I. Byrne. Modern Greek fairy tales.
See also Three feathers. I.
Frog princess. II. Martens. Chinese fairy book.
Frog princess. III. *See* Frog queen.
Frog queen. Blumenthal. Folk tales from the Russian. (Tsarevna frog.)
Dole. White duckling and other stories.
Glinski. Polish fairy tales. (Frog princess.)
O'Grady and Throop. Teachers' story teller's book. (Tsarevna frog.)
Polevoi. Russian fairy tales. (Frog-tsarevna.)
Pyle. Tales of folks and fairies. (Frog princess.)
Wheeler. Russian wonder tales. (Frog-tzarevna.)
Frog, the crab and the serpent. Bidpai. Tortoise and the geese.
Frog travellers. Armfield. Wonder tales. (*In* Lazy Taro.)
Blaisdell. Child life. 3d reader.
Coe and Christie. Story hour readers. Book 3. (Frogs' travels.)
Griffis. Japanese fairy tales. (Travels of the two frogs.)
Harper. Story-hour favorites. (Two frogs.)
Lang. Violet fairy book. (Two frogs.)
Shedlock. Art of the storyteller. (Two frogs.)

Frog travellers—*continued.*
Tappan. Book of humor. (Travels of the two frogs.)
Frog-tsarevna. *See* Frog queen.
Frog who tried to be as big as an ox. *See* Frog and the ox.
Frog who wished to be as big as an ox. *See* Frog and the ox.
Frogs. Sologub. Sweet-scented name.
Frogs and the crane. Eastman. Wigwam evenings.
Frogs and the fairies. Walker. Sandman's goodnight stories.
Frogs and the fighting bulls. Æsop. Fables (Black ed.).
Æsop. Fables (Burt ed.).
See also Kerchunk's sisters.
Frogs and the rain. Stanley. Animal folk tales.
Frogs ask for a king. *See* Frogs who asked for a king.
Frogs desiring a king. *See* Frogs who asked for a king.
Frogs, Origin of. *See* Latona and the frogs.
Frog's skin. Wardrop. Georgian folk tales.
Frogs' travels. *See* Frog travelers.
Frogs who asked for a king. Æsop. Fables (Black ed. Frogs desiring a king.)
Æsop. Fables (Burt ed. Frogs desiring a king.)
Æsop. Fables (Jacobs. Frogs desiring a king.)
Æsop. Fables (Stickney).
Bryant. Stories to tell to children. (Frog king.)
Cowles. Art of story telling. (King of the frogs.)
Patten. Junior classics. v. 1. (Frogs desiring a king.)
Scudder. Children's book. (Frogs ask for a king.)
Scudder. Fables and folk stories. (Frogs ask for a king.)
Wiggin and Smith. Talking beasts. (Frogs desiring a king.)
Frolic of the wild things. Skinner. Nursery tales from many lands.
Frolicsome duke. Macleod. Book of ballad stories.
From a far country. Richards. Golden windows.
From a window in Vartou. Andersen. Stories and tales (Author's ed.).
From castle to cot. Guerber. Legends of the Rhine.
From shepherd boy to king. Landa. Aunt Naomi's Jewish fairy tales and legends.
Frost giants and the sunbeam fairies. Griffis. Swiss fairy tales.
Frost king; or, The power of love. Alcott. Flower fables.
Alcott. Lulu's library. v. 2. (Frost king and how the fairies conquered him.)
Frozen heart. *See* Heart of ice. I.
Frozen hearth-fairy. Harrison. Old-fashioned fairy book.
Frozen princess. Gate. Broom fairies.
Fruit of happiness. Pyle. Twilight land.
Fruit of the fragile palm. *See* Christmas before last.
Fruit on the rose-bush. Olcott. Wonder garden.
Frying-pan. Bosschère. Christmas tales of Flanders.

Fulfilled. Bryant. How to tell stories.
Grundtvig. Fairy tales from afar.
Wiggin and Smith. Magic casements.
See also Poor man and the rich man.
Fundevogel. Grimm. Fairy tales (Lucas tr.).
Grimm. Household tales (Burt ed. Birdie and her friend.)
Funeral of Tom Grimalkin. Carrick. Kitty cat tales.
Funny fellow. Bay. Danish fairy and folk tales.
Funny little old woman. Eggleston. Queer stories for boys and girls.
Funny story. Frere. Old Deccan days.
Furball. *See* Many-furred creature.
Furious host. Gibbon. Reign of King Cole.
See also Three cows.
Furnica. Sylva and Strettell. Legends from river and mountain.
Further adventures of the fisherman. Arabian nights (Townsend).
Future. Sologub. Sweet-scented name.
Future life. Judson. Myths and legends of Alaska.

G

Gadfly. Guerber. Legends of the Rhine.
Gaffer Wiseman's choice. Lindsay and Poulsson. Joyous travelers. (Tale told by the farmer.)
Gagliuso; or, The good cat. Laboulaye. Last fairy tales.
Macdonell. Italian fairy book.
See also Puss in boots.
Galafron. *See* Rabican the enchanted.
Galahad. *See* Sir Galahad.
Galatea. I. *See* Acis and Galatea.
Galatea. II. *See* Pygmalion and Galatea.
Galileo. Baldwin. Thirty more famous stories. (Galileo and the lamps.)
Gallant tailor. *See* Brave little tailor.
Galoshes of fortune. *See* Goloshes of fortune.
Game of chess. Guerber. Legends of the Rhine.
Gamelyn. *See* Sir Gamelyn.
Ganem, son of Abou Ayoub, and known by the surname of Love's Slave. Arabian nights (Townsend).
Ganymede. Hyde. Favorite Greek myths.
Olcott. Wonder garden. (Boy that the eagle stole.)
Garden of after dark. Donahey. Tales to be told to children.
Garden of being sick. Donahey. Tales to be told to children.
Garden of childhood. Bay. Danish fairy and folk tales.
Garden of frost flowers. Olcott. Wonder garden.
Garden of lonely hours. Donahey. Tales to be told to children.

Garden of mistakes. Donahey. Tales to be told to children.
Garden of misunderstanding. Donahey. Tales to be told to children.
Garden of paradise. Andersen. Fairy tales (Lucas tr.).
Andersen. Fairy tales (Paull tr.).
Johnson. Birch-tree fairy book.
Garden of rainy days. Donahey. Tales to be told to children.
Garden of sulky times. Donahey. Tales to be told to children.
Garden of tears and smiles. Meigs. Kingdom of the winding road.
Garden of the Hesperides. Baldwin. Golden fleece.
Garden of the sorceress. *See* Rapunzel.
Gardener. Andersen. Fairy tales (Paull tr.).
Gardener and his dog. Æsop. Fables (Black ed.).
Æsop. Fables (Burt ed.).
Gardener and his landlord. Æsop. Fables (Burt ed.).
Gardener and his master. Æsop. Fables (Burt ed.).
Gardener and the bear. Bidpai. Tortoise and the geese.
Gardener prince. Baring-Gould. Old English fairy tales.
Gareth. *See* Sir Gareth.
Gareth and Lynette. *See* Sir Gareth.
Gargantua. Fuller. Book of friendly giants.
Griffis. Swiss fairy tales. (Mountain giants.)
Guerber. Legends of Switzerland. (Legends of Vaud).
Rabelais. Three good giants.
Gargoyles. *See* Oni on his travels.
Garret adventure. Dodge. Land of pluck.
Gate of the giant scissors. *See* Giant scissors.
Gater and de rabbit gizzard. *See* Brother Rabbit and the gizzard eater.
Gathering of the birds. Success library. v. 3.
Gathering of the fays. Rolfe. Fairy tales in prose and verse.
Gau-wi-di-ne and Go-hay, winter and spring. *See* Old Winter Man and the Spring. II.
Gawaine. *See* Sir Gawain.
Gawayne. See Sir Gawain.
Gay Goshawk. Grierson. Children's tales from Scottish ballads.
Macleod. Book of ballad stories. (Gay Goss Hawk.)
Richards. Little master. (Jolly Goshawk.)
Gay Goss Hawk. *See* Gay Goshawk.
Gay little king. Skinner. Topaz story book.
Gazelle. Bateman. Zanzibar tales. (Haamdaanee.)
Lang. Violet fairy book.
Pyle. Fairy tales from many lands. (Haamdaanee and the wise gazelle.)
Geese. Success library. v. 3.
Geese and the cranes. Æsop. Fables (Black ed.).
Æsop. Fables (Burt ed.).

Geese and the tortoise. *See* Talkative tortoise.
Geese save Rome. Guerber. Story of the Romans. (Sacred geese.)
Haaren. Famous men of Rome. (*In* Camillus.)
Gierlaug, the king's daughter. Lang. Olive fairy book.
Lang. Little King Loc.
Geirrod and Odin. Edmison. Stories from the Norseland. (Geirrod and Agnar.)
Guerber. Myths of northern lands. (*In* Odin.)
Klingensmith. Old Norse wonder tales. (Geirrod.)
Mabie. Norse stories. (Odin in Geirrod's palace.)
Wickes. Beyond the rainbow bridge. (Kingly guest.)
Wilmot-Buxton. Stories of Norse heroes. (*In* How All-Father Odin became wise.)
Geirrod and Thor. Bradish. Old Norse stories. (Thor and Geirrod.)
Brown. In the days of giants. (In the giant's house.)
Edmison. Stories from Norseland. (Thor's visit to the giant Geirrod.)
Guerber. Myths of northern lands. (*In* Thor.)
Klingensmith. Old Norse wonder tales. (Thor and Geirrod.)
Wilmot-Buxton. Stories of Norse heroes. (Giant's daughters.)
General and the fox. Baldwin. Fifty famous people.
General, the bird and the ant. Davis and Chow-Leung. Chinese fables and folk stories.
Generides. Baring-Gould. Crock o' gold.
Generous deed. Guerber. Legends of the Rhine.
Generous lion. Æsop. Fables (Burt ed.).
Genie of the mountains. Segovia. Spanish fairy book.
Genius, virtue and reputation. Æsop. Fables (Burt ed.).
Genseric. Evans. Old time tales. (Vandal horde.)
Gentian, Legend of. I. Baker and Carpenter. Language readers. 3d year.
Gentian, Legend of. II. *Dillingham and Emerson. Tell it again stories.
McFee. Treasury of flower stories.
Gentian, Legend of. III. Skinner. Topaz story book.
Gentle Dora. Fillmore. Shoemaker's apron.
See also Ghost of the spring and the shrew; Devil worsted.
Gentle folk, Tale of. Finger. Tales of silver lands.
Gentle lady. Meigs. Kingdom of the winding road.
Gentleman pirate. *See* Lafitte, Jean.
George, St. *See* St. George.
George Washington and the cherry tree. *See* Washington and the cherry tree.
George Washington and the colt. *See* Washington and the colt.
George Washington boy. Bailey. Stories for Sunday telling.

George with the goat. Mabie. Folk tales every child should know.
Geraint and Enid. *See* Sir Geraint.
Geraint the son of Erbin. *See* Sir Geraint.
Geranium story. Bailey. Stories and rhymes for a child.
Gerd. *See* Wooing of Gerd.
Gerda's ride to her wedding. Evans. Old time tales.
Geria, the poor man's son. Wardrop. Georgian folk tales.
German patriot and the barley-fields. *See* Honest farmer.
Germelshausen. Noyes. Twilight stories.
Gertrude's bird. *See* Why the woodpecker has a red head. I.
Gertrude's visit to the moon. Edey. Six giants and a griffin.
Get up and bar the door. *See* Barring of the door.
Getting rid of fairies. Thomas. Welsh fairy book.
Ghost bride. Grinnell. Pawnee hero stories.
Ghost feast. Guerber. Legends of the Rhine.
Ghost land. I. Judson. Myths and legends of Alaska.
Ghost land. II. Judson. Myths and legends of the Pacific Northwest. (Memaloose Islands.)
See also Blue Jay visits the ghosts; In the land of souls.
Ghost-laying stories. Hartland. English folk and fairy tales.
Ghost of Rosewarne. Hartland. English folk and fairy tales.
Ghost of Solomon. Success library. v. 3.
Ghost of the spring and the shrew. Kunos. Forty-four Turkish fairy tales. (Imp of the well.)
Kunos. Turkish fairy tales.
See also Gentle Dora.
Ghost story. Harris. Nights with Uncle Remus.
Ghost town. Judson. Myths and legends of Alaska.
Ghost who was foiled. Martens. Chinese fairy book.
Ghost wife. I. Eastman. Wigwam evenings.
Ghost wife. II. Grinnell. Pawnee hero stories.
Ghost wife. III. Grinnell. Blackfoot lodge tales. (Origin of the worm pipe.)
Ghost wife. IV. Judson. Myths and legends of Alaska. (Land of the dead.)
Ghost wife of Craig Aulnaic. Grierson. Scottish fairy book.
Ghostly interview. Guerber. Legends of the Rhine.
Ghostly rehearsal. Thomas. Welsh fairy book.
Ghost of Forefathers' Hill. Alden. Boy who found the king.
Ghvthisavari. Wardrop. Georgian folk tales.
Giant. Bayliss. Treasury of Eskimo tales.
Giant and his drum. Riggs. Animal stories from Eskimo land.
Giant and Johannes Blessom. Asbjörnsen. Folk and fairy tales.
Stroebe and Martens. Norwegian fairy book.

Giant and the herdboy. Fuller. Book of friendly giants.
Lang. Yellow fairy book.
Giant and the tailor. Froelicher. Swiss stories.
Wiggin and Smith. Tales of laughter.
See also Brave little tailor.
Giant bear. Stanley. Animal folk tales.
Giant builder. Brown. In the days of giants.
Edmison. Stories from the Norseland. (Building of Asgard.)
Klingensmith. Old Norse wonder tales. (Building of the Asgard fort.)
Mabie. Myths every child should know.
Tappan. Myths from many lands.
Wilmot-Buxton. Stories of Norse heroes. (How a gian built a fortress for the Asas.)
Giant Crump and Lady Moon. Richards. Joyous story of Toto.
Giant Energy and Fairy Skill. Lindsay. Mother stories.
Giant Giro. *Coe and Christie. Story hour readers. Book 2.
See also Three billy goats gruff.
Giant Golden-Beard. *See* Giant with the golden hair.
Giant in fragments. Fairy stories retold from St. Nicholas.
Giant maiden. *See* Toy of the giant child.
Giant magicians. *See* Good giants.
Giant of Band-Beggars Hall. *Burchill. Progressive road to reading. Book 2.
MacManus. In chimney corners.
Giant of flaming mountain. Kennedy. New world fairy book.
Giant of St. Michaels. Rhys. Fairy gold.
Giant of the black mountains. Johnson. Oak-tree fairy book.
Giant of the causeway. Bosschère. Christmas tales of Flanders.
Giant of the flood. Landa. Aunt Naomi's Jewish fairy tales and legends.
Giant prince. Grayl. Fairy tales from foreign lands.
Giant princess. Storytellers' magazine. Feb. 1915, p. 51.
Giant scissors. Johnston. Giant scissors.
Giant that was a miller. Rhys. Fairy gold.
Giant Thunder Bones. Fairy stories retold from St. Nicholas.
Giant Tom and giant Bluff. Griffis. Welsh fairy tales.
Giant tortoise's golden rule. Quiroga. South American jungle tales.
Giant who became a saint. *See* St. Christopher, Legend of.
Giant who came back. Fuller. Book of friendly giants.
Giant who cracked his heart. Bailey. Friendly tales.
Giant who did not keep his heart in his body. *See* Giant who had no heart.
Giant who had no heart. Absjörnsen. Folk and fairy tales.
Dasent. Norse fairy tales.

Giant who had no heart—*continued.*
Dasent. Popular tales from the Norse. (Giant who had no heart in his body.)
Gade. Norwegian fairy tales. (Giant who did not keep his heart in his body.)
Stroebe and Martens. Norwegian fairy book. (Anent the giant who did not have his heart about him.)
Thorne-Thomsen. East o' the sun and west o' the moon. (Giant who had no heart in his body.)
See also Man without a heart. II.
Giant who had no heart in his body. *See* Giant who had no heart.
Giant who laughed at a dwarf. Patten. Junior classics. v. 2.
Giant who loved a sea nymph. *See* Acis and Galatea.
Giant who rode on the ark. Fuller. Book of friendly giants.
Giant with a belt of stars. *See* Orion.
Giant with nine lives. Kennedy. New world fairy book.
Giant with the golden hair. I. Aunt Louisa's book of fairy tales.
Chisholm. Enchanted land. (Three golden hairs.)
Chisholm and Steedman. Staircase of stories. (Three golden hairs.)
Field. Famous fairy tales. (Three golden hairs.)
Fillmore. Czechoslovak fairy tales. (Three golden hairs.)
Grimm. Household tales (Burt ed. Three golden hairs.)
Grimm. Household tales (Everyman's ed. Giant Golden Beard.)
Johnson. Birch-tree fairy book.
Valentine. Old, old fairy tales. (Giant with the golden hairs.)
Welsh. Fairy tales children love.
Giant with the golden hair. II. Chodzko. Fairy tales of the Slav. (Sun; or, The three golden hairs of the old man Vsévède.)
Silver fairy book. (Three golden hairs of Old Vsévède.)
Tappan. Myths from many lands. (Sun; or, Three golden hairs of the old man Vsévède.)
See also Giant with the golden hair. I; Three wonderful beggars.
Giant with the golden hairs. *See* Giant with the golden hair.
Giant with the grey feathers. Macmillan. Canadian fairy tales.
See also Napi and the famine.
Giantess and the granite boat. *See* Witch in the stone boat.
Giantess' playthings. *See* Toy of the giant child.
Giantess who would not. *See* Wooing of Gerd.
Giants and fairies. Judd. Wigwam stories.
Giants and the herd-boy. *See* Giant and the herdboy.
Giant's cliff. Pyle. Fairy tales from far and near.
Giant's daughters. *See* Geirrod and Thor.

Giants fool Thor. *See* Thor and his journey to Jötunheim.
Giant's heart. Macdonald. Dealings with fairies.
Macdonald. Light princess and other fairy tales.
Giant's house with the roof of sausages. Tappan. Golden goose.
Giant's kitten. Potter. Pinafore pocket story book.
Giant's New Year. Marshall. Fairy tales of all nations.
Giants' pot. Fuller. Book of friendly giants.
Guerber. Legends of the Rhine.
Giant's pupil. Eells. Tales of giants from Brazil.
Giant's quilt. *See* Derido.
Giants' ship. Fuller. Book of friendly giants.
Giant's shoes. Wiggin and Smith. Tales of laughter.
Giant's sock. Potter. Pinafore pocket story book.
Giant's son and the beautiful maiden. Partridge. Glooscap the great chief.
Giant's stairs. Yeats. Irish fairy and folk tales.
Giauna the beautiful. Martens. Chinese fairy book.
Gift of Athene. *See* Athens.
Gift of corn. *See* First corn. II.
Gift of fire. *See* How fire was brought to the Indians.
Gift of flax. *See* How flax was given to men.
Gift of gold lacquer. Griffis. Japanese fairy tales.
Gift of Indian corn. *See* First corn. III.
Gift of Mondamin. *See* First corn. II.
Gift of the birds. Harrison. Star fairies.
Gift of the fairies. Peck. Stories for good children.
See also Knockgrafton, Legend of.
Gift of the olive tree. *See* Athens.
Gift of the white bear. Hartwell. Story hour readings 7th year.
Gift of Tritemius. Johonnot. Stories of the olden times.
Giftie. Richards. Golden windows.
Gifts. *See* In the kitchen garden.
Gifts of the dwarfs. *See* Dwarf's gifts.
Gifts of the magician. Lang. Crimson fairy book.
Lang. Magician's gifts and other stories. (Magician's gifts.)
Gifts the trees gave. I. Donaldson. Moons of long ago.
Powers. Around an Iroquois story fire. (How the tree brothers gave.)
Gifts the trees gave. II. Coe and Christie. Story hour readers. Book 3. (*In* Gray mole and the Indian.)
Compton. American Indian fairy tales. (*In* Fighting hare.)
Gifts the trees gave. III. Seton. Woodmyth and fable. (Doings of a little fib.)
Gigi and the magic ring. Macdonell. Italian fairy book.
My Bookhouse. v. 3.
Gilbert, Sir Humphrey. Baldwin. Fifty famous stories.
Gilla Na Chreck. *See* Lad with the goat-skin.
Gilla Na Grakin and Fin MacCumhail. *See* Finn MacCool.

Gillie Dhu. Olcott. Book of elves and fairies.
Gillyflower gentleman. Richards. Silver crown.
Gingerbread boy (play). Bailey. For the story teller.
Bailey. Folk stories and fables.
Bailey and Lewis. For the children's hour.
Bryant. Best stories to tell to children. (Gingerbread man.)
Bryant. Stories to tell to children. (Gingerbread man.)
*Burchill. Progressive road to reading. Book 1.
Coussens. Child's book of stories. (Gingerbread man.)
Dyer. What-happened-then stories. (Gingerbread man.)
*Dyer and Brady. Merrill readers. 2d reader.
Faulkner. Old English nursery tales.
*Grover. Folk-lore reader. v. 1.
My Bookhouse. v. 1. (Gingerbread man.)
Old, old tales retold.
*Treadwell. Reading literature. Primer.
*Van Sickle and Seegmiller. Riverside readers. First reader.
See also Johnny cake; Pancake; Wee bannock.
Gingerbread cat's adventures. Bailey. Friendly tales.
Gingerbread man. I. *See* Gingerbread boy.
Gingerbread man. II. (poem). Bailey and Lewis. For the children's hour.
Gingerbread man. III. Tales for bedtime. (Little gingerbread man.)
Giotto. Baldwin. Fifty famous people. (Shepherd-boy painter.)
Girl and fly. *See* How not to hit an insect.
Girl and the fish. Dasent. Popular tales from the Norse.
Girl and the snake. Stroebe and Martens. Swedish fairy book.
Girl and the witch people. Curtis. Indian days of the long ago.
Girl clad in mouse-skin. Thorpe. Yule-tide stories.
Girl-fish. Lang. Orange fairy book.
Lang. Little King Loc.
Girl in the chest. Fillmore. Laughing prince.
Girl-monkey and the string of pearls. Babbitt. More Jataka tales.
Girl who always cried. Macmillan. Canadian fairy tales.
Girl who became a pine tree. *See* Leelinau, the lost daughter.
Girl who could spin gold from clay and long straw. Thorpe. Yule-tide stories.
See also Rumpelstiltskin.
Girl who danced with the fairies. Olcott. Book of elves and fairies.
Girl who fell splash in a wash tub. Potter. Pinafore pocket story book.
Girl who married the fire spirit. Eastman. Indian legends retold.
Girl who married the star. Eastman. Wigwam evenings.

Girl who pretended to be a boy. Lang. Beauty and the beast, and other stories.
Lang. Violet fairy book.
Girl who rejected her cousin. Eastman. Indian legends retold.
Girl who trod on the loaf. Andersen. Fairy tales (Lucas tr.).
Andersen. Fairy tales (Paull tr.).
Andersen. Wonder stories. (Girl who trod upon bread.)
Bailey. For the story teller.
Olcott. Wonder garden.
(play). Stevenson. Plays for the home.
Girl who trod upon bread. *See* Girl who trod on the loaf.
Girl who used her wits. *See* Lantern and the fan.
Girl who wanted three husbands. Caballero. Spanish fairy tales.
Girl who was changed into a sunflower. *See* Clytie.
Girl who was stolen by the fairies. Olcott. Book of elves and fairies.
Girl who was the ring. Grinnell. Punishment of the stingy.
Girl with the horse's head; or, The silkworm goddess. Martens. Chinese fairy book.
Gitche O-kok-o-hoo. Seton. Woodmyth and fable.
Seton. Woodland tales. (How the littlest owl came.)
Glass. Richards. Silver crown.
Glass axe. Lang. Beauty and the beast and other stories.
Lang. Yellow fairy book.
Glass coffin. *See* Crystal coffin.
Glass mender. Baring. Blue rose fairy book.
Glass mountain. Lang. Invisible prince.
Lang. Yellow fairy book.
Patten. Junior classics. v. 1.
Glaucon. Johonnot. Stories of the olden time.
Glaucus. *Bailey. Wonder stories.
Baldwin. Story of the golden age. (*In* Voyage on the sea.)
Carpenter. Long ago in Greece.
Glaucus and Scylla. *See* Scylla and Charybdis.
Gleam-o'-Day and Princess Lotus Flower. Olcott. Wonder garden.
Gloaming bucht. Douglas. Scottish fairy tales.
Glob and Alger. Thorpe. Yule-tide stories.
Glooscap. *See* Glooskap.
Glooskap and his people. Roberts. Flying plover. (Gluskap and his people.)
Glooskap and Malsum, the wolf. Wade. Indian fairy tales.
Glooskap and the bullfrog. *Cowles. Indian nature myths. (Why the frogs croak.)
Leland. Algonquin legends. (How Glooskap conquered the great bull frog.)
Skinner. Turquoise story book. (Origin of bullfrogs.)

Glooskap and the bullfrog—*continued.*
Tanner. Legends from the red man's forest. (Things of the water.)
Wade. Indian fairy tales.
Glooskap and the giant's frolic. Wade. Indian fairy tales.
See also Return of Glooscap.
Glooscap and the great wind bird. *See* Wuchowson, the wind blower.
Glooskap and the magic gifts. I. Wade. Indian fairy tales.
Glooskap and the magic gifts. II. Cornyn. When the camp fire burns. (Little Thunder's wedding journey; Magic of Glooskap.)
Olcott. Red Indian fairy book. (Mikumwess.)
Partridge. Glooscap the great chief. (How Glooscap transformed the Indian.)
Glooskap and the magic gifts. III. Olcott. Red Indian fairy book. (Wishes.)
Glooskap and the magic gifts. IV. Olcott. Red Indian fairy book. (First pine trees.)
Pratt. Legends of the red children. (Pine trees.)
Tanner. Legends from the red man's forest. (Pine trees.)
Glooskap and the magic gifts. V. Partridge. Glooscap the great chief. (How the Indians sought the great chief.)
Glooskap and the magic gifts. VI. Kennedy. New world fairy book. (Three wishes.)
Glooskap and the three seekers. Wade. Indian fairy tales.
Glooskap and the tortoise. *See* Return of Glooskap.
Glooskap and the turtle. Wade. Indian fairy tales.
Glooskap and the whale. Wade. Indian fairy tales.
See also How Glooscap conquered his enemies.
Glooskap and the winter giant. *See* How summer came to the earth. II.
Glooskap and the witch maiden. Wade. Indian fairy tales.
See also How Glooscap conquered his enemies.
Glowworm and the diamond. *See* Diamond and the glowworm.
Glowworm and the jackdaw. Patten. Junior classics. v. 1.
Wiggin and Smith. Talking beasts. (Glowworm and the daw.)
Glowworms, Origin of. *See* Butterfirefly.
Gluskap. *See* Glooskap.
Gnat and the bee. Æsop. Fables (Burt ed.).
Gnat and the bull. Æsop. Fables (Burt ed.).
(poem). Æsop Fables. (Burt ed. Ox and the fly.)
Æsop. Fables (Stickney).
Scudder. Fables and folk stories.
Wiggin and Smith. Talking beasts.
Gnomes' road. Guerber. Legends of the Rhine.
Stebbins. Sunken city.
Gnome's wish. Bailey. Friendly tales.

"Go" and "Come." Richards. Golden windows.
Go, I know not whither—fetch, I know not what. Curtin. Wonder-tales from Russia. (Go to the verge of destruction and bring back Shmat—Razum.)
Polevoi. Russian fairy tales.
See also Empty drum.
Go-to-sleep story. *Elson and Runkel. Elson readers. Book 1.
O'Grady and Throop. Teachers' storyteller's book.
Poulsson. In the child's world. (Go-sleep story.)
Skinner. Very little child's book of stories.
Go to the verge of destruction and bring back Shmat-Razum. *See* Go, I know not whither—fetch, I know not what.
Goat and the boy. Arnold and Gilbert. Stepping stones to literature. v. 2.
See also Goat herd and the she-goat.
Goat and the hog. Rouse. Talking thrush.
Goat and the lion. Æsop. Fables (Black ed.).
Æsop. Fables (Burt ed.).
Goat and the pig. *See* Ram and the pig.
Goat-face. *See* Goat-faced girl.
Goat-faced girl. Lang. Grey fairy book.
Storytellers' magazine. June 1915, p. 196. (Goat-face.).
Goat girl. Dasent. Popular tales from the Norse. (Tatterhood.)
Marshall. Fairy tales of all nations.
Goat, the lion, the leopard, and the hyena. Macnair. Animal tales from Africa.
Goatherd. *See* Karl Katz.
Goatherd and his pipe. Macdonell. Italian fairy book.
Goatherd and the goats. Æsop. Fables (Burt ed.).
Goat-herd and the she-goat. Æsop. Fables (Black ed.).
Æsop. Fables (Burt ed.).
See also Goat and the boy.
Goats. Gregory. Kiltartan wonder book.
Goats ask for horns. Success library. v. 3.
Goat's ears of the emperor Trojan. Lang. Violet fairy book.
Goats in the rye field. *See* Goats in the turnip field.
Goats in the turnip field. *Elson and Runkel. Elson readers. Book 1.
Esenwein and Stockard. Children's stories. (Goats in the rye field.)
*Jones. Second reader. (How did he do it?)
My Bookhouse. v. 1. (Johnny and the three goats.)
O'Grady and Throop. Teachers' story teller's book. (Johnny and the three goats.)
Storytellers' magazine. July 1913, p. 97. (Three goats.)
Gobborn seer. Johnson. Oak-tree fairy book. (Clever wife.)
Jacobs. More English fairy tales.
Goblin and the grocer. *See* Nis at the grocer's.

Goblin and the huckster. *See* Nis at the grocer's.
Goblin and the princess. Friedlander. Jewish fairy book.
Goblin market (play). Bone. Children's stories.
Maud. Heroines of poetry. (Good sister.)
Goblin of Adachigahara. Ozaki. Japanese fairy book.
Goblin of Rümmelsburg. Smith. Mystery tales.
Goblin pony. Lang. Grey fairy book.
Lang. Trusty John and other stories.
Goblin spider. Hearn. Japanese fairy tales.
Goblin tree. Nixon-Roulet. Japanese folk stories and fairy tales.
Goblin workman. Duncan-Jones. English folk lore stories.
See also Boggart; Farmer Grigg's boggart.
Goblins turned to stone. Griffis. Dutch fairy tales.
God and the sick princess. *See* Journey of Khensu to Bekhten.
God of fire. *See* Vulcan.
God of the ivy crown. *See* Bacchus and Pentheus.
God of the thundering water. *See* Bended rocks.
God of war. Martens. Chinese fairy book.
Goddess of green-growing things. Nixon-Roulet. Japanese folk stories and fairy tales.
Goddess of light. Williams. Fairy tales from folklore.
Godfather. *See* Wonderful glass.
Godfather Death. *See* Strange godfather.
Godfrey de Bouillon. Landa. Aunt Naomi's Jewish fairy tales and legends. (King for three days.)
Lansing. Page, esquire and knight. (Godfrey, knight of the crusades.)
Godfrey, the little hermit. Gask. Folk tales from many lands.
Godiva. Hartland. English folk and fairy tales. (Lady Godiva.)
Gods and the giants. *See* Jupiter and the Titans.
God's blessing compasses all things. Magnus. Russian folk-tales.
Gods grow old. *See* Iduna's apples.
Gods know. Pitman. Chinese fairy stories.
Pitman. Chinese fairy tales.
God's mercy. Guerber. Legends of the Rhine.
Going to sea. *See* Washington does not go to sea.
Gold beads. *Dillingham and Emerson. Tell it again stories.
Gold-bearded man. Lang. Crimson fairy book.
Lang. Little Wildrose.
Gold-Bethli and Pitch-Babi. Froelicher. Swiss stories.
Gold braids. Nordau. Dwarf's spectacles.
Gold bread. *See* Golden loaf.
Gold bugs. Bailey. Firelight stories.
Cowles. Art of story telling.
Gold children. *See* Golden lads.
Gold egg. *Carrick. Picture tales from the Russian.

Gold-giving serpent. Jacobs. Indian fairy tales.
Gold in the orchard. Æsop. Fables (Black ed. Husbandman and his sons.)
Æsop. Fables (Burt ed. Husbandman and his sons.)
(poem). Æsop. Fables (Stickney. Supplement. Ploughman and his sons.)
Bryant. Stories to tell to children.
Hartwell. Story hour readings. 7th year. (Hidden treasure.)
Scudder. Children's book. (Farmer and his sons.)
Van Sickle and Seegmiller. Riverside readers. 4th reader. (Buried treasure.)
(poem). Wiggin and Smith. Talking beasts. (Ploughman and his sons.)
Gold Maria and Pitch Maria. Underhill. Dwarfs' tailor and other fairy tales.
See also Mother Holle.
Gold-maria and Gold-feather. Jerrold. Big book of fairy tales.
Thorpe. Yule-tide stories.
Gold of Fairnilee. Lang. My own fairy book.
Gold-spinner. *See* Rumpelstilskin.
Gold-spinners. Coussens. Child's book of stories. (Water lily; or, The gold-spinners.)
Lang. Blue fairy book. (Water-lily. Gold spinners.)
Lang. Princess on the glass hill. (Waterlily. Gold spinners.)
Wiggin and Smith. Magic casements.
Gold-tree and Silver-tree. Grierson. Scottish fairy book.
Jacobs. Celtic fairy tales.
See also Snow White and the seven dwarfs.
Golden age. Judson. Myths and legends of the Pacific Northwest.
Golden apple. *See* Paris: Apple of discord.
Golden apple-tree and the nine pea-hens. *See* Nine peahens and the golden apples.
Golden apples. Underhill. Dwarfs' tailor and other fairy tales.
Golden apples of Hesperides. *See* Hercules and his labors.
Golden archer. Sholl. Faery tales of Weir.
Golden arm. Jacobs. English fairy tales.
See also Ghost story; Taily-po.
Golden ball. Jacobs. More English fairy tales.
Golden bees of Mythia. Silver fairy book.
Golden beetle. *See* Why the dog and cat are enemies. I.
Golden beetle that went on his travels. *See* Beetle who went on his travels.
Golden bird. I. Asbjörnsen. Fairy tales from the far north.
Asbjörnsen. Tales from the fjeld.
Gade. Norwegian fairy tales.
Wiggin and Smith. Fairy ring.

Golden bird. I.—*continued.*
See also Golden bird. II; Golden blackbird; Golden mermaid.
Golden bird. II. Bailey. In the animal world.
*Benson. Really truly fairy tales.
Canton. Reign of King Herla.
Grimm. Fairy tales (Lucas tr.).
Grimm. Household stories (Crane tr.).
Grimm. Household tales (Burt ed.).
Grimm. Household tales (Everyman's ed. Fox's brush.)
Marshall. Fairy tales of all nations.
My Bookhouse. v. 3.
Pyle. Mother's nursery tales.
Scudder. Children's book.
Scudder. Fables and folk stories.
Singleton. Goldenrod fairy book.
Tappan. Folk stories and fables.
See also Golden bird. I; Golden blackbird; Golden mermaid; Greek princess and the young gardener; Ivan and the gray wolf; Ohnivak.
Golden blackbird. Baldwin. Fairy stories and fables. (Princet and the golden blackbird.)
Lang. Green fairy book.
Lang. Pretty Goldilocks and other stories.
Patten. Junior classics. v. 1.
Wiggin and Smith. Magic casements.
See also Golden bird. I and II; Golden mermaid.
Golden bough. *See* Golden branch.
Golden branch. Aulnoy. Fairy tales.
Lang. Red fairy book.
Wiggin and Smith. Magic casements. (Golden bough.)
Golden-breasted kootoo. Richards. Joyous story of Toto.
Golden bucket (play). Van Sickle and Seegmiller. Riverside readers. 2d reader.
Golden bull. Baring-Gould. Old English fairy tales.
Golden canister. Martens. Chinese fairy book.
Golden cobwebs. Bryant. Best stories to tell to children.
Bryant. How to tell stories to children.
Dickinson and Skinner. Children's book of Christmas stories.
*Elson and Runkel. Elson readers. Book 2. (Adapted).
Sly. World stories retold.
See also Christmas angel.
Golden cock. Bryce. That's why stories.
Golden comb. James. Green willow. (Strange story of a golden comb.)
Golden crab. Lang. Magic ring, and other stories.
Lang. Yellow fairy book.
Wiggin and Smith. Fairy ring.
Golden dragon of the Boringue. Griffis. Belgian fairy tales.
Golden duck. Fillmore. Czechoslovak fairy tales.
Golden dwarf. Storytellers' magazine. June 1914, p. 587.

Golden eggs. Guerber. Legends of the Rhine.
Golden eggs and cock of gold. Tappan. Folk stories.
Golden fish. I. Gask. Folk tales from many lands.
Gask. Treasury of folk tales.
Patten. Junior classics. v. 1.
See also Fisherman and his wife.
Golden fish. II. Grayl. Fairy tales from foreign lands.
See also Two brothers. III.
Golden fleece. I. *See* Argonauts.
Golden fleece. II. *See* Fleece of gold.
Golden fortune. Austin. Basket woman.
Golden gift of King Midas. *See* Midas. I.
Golden goblet. Stocking. Golden goblet.
Golden goblin. Hume. Chronicles of fairyland.
Golden godmother. Fillmore. Czechoslovak fairy tales.
Golden goose. I. Baldwin. Fairy stories and fables. (Peter and the magic goose.)
Coussens. Child's book of stories.
Golden goose and the three bears.
Grimm. Fairy tales (Lucas tr.).
Grimm. Household stories (Crane tr.).
Grimm. Household tales (Everyman's ed.).
Johnson. Elm-tree fairy book.
Lang. Red fairy book.
Lang. White doe.
Lansing. Fairy tales. v. 2.
Mabie. Fairy tales every child should know.
Norton. Heart of oak books. v. 3.
Pyle. Mother's nursery tales.
*Sly. World stories retold.
Storytellers' magazine. Oct. 1914, p. 683.
Welsh. Fairy tales children love.
Wiggin and Smith. Tales of laughter.
See also Hans who made the princess laugh; Magic swan; Saucy Jesper.
Golden goose. II. *See* Lilla Rosa and Long Leda.
Golden goose. III. Babbitt. More Jataka tales.
Golden grasshopper. Skinner. Turquoise story book.
Golden Hair. Chodzko. Fairy tales of the Slav. (Maid with hair of gold.)
Fillmore. Shoemaker's apron. (Zlatovlaska the golden-haired.)
Singleton. Goldenrod fairy book.
Storytellers' magazine. Feb. 1916, p. 395. (Maid with hair of gold.)
See also Fair one with golden locks; White snake.
Golden Hair and the three bears. *See* Three bears.
Golden-haired children. Kunos. Turkish fairy tales.
Golden harp. *See* Fairy harp.
Golden-headed fish. Lang. Olive fairy book.
Lang. White doe.
Golden helmet. Griffis. Dutch fairy tales.

Go[illegible]r hoard. *See* Siegfried.
Golden Hood. *See* Little Golden Hood.
Golden horse and his rider. Stocking. City that never was reached.
Golden horse, the moon lantern, and the princess in the troll's cage. Pyle. Tales of wonder and magic.
Thorpe. Yule-tide stories.
Golden horseshoe. Gate. Fortunate days.
Golden key. I. Pyle. Mother's nursery tales.
Wiggin and Smith. Tales of laughter.
Golden key. II. Macdonald. Dealings with the fairies.
Macdonald. Light princess and other fairy tales.
Golden key. III. Bellamy. Wonder children.
Golden lads. *Grimm. Fairy tales (Wiltse. Gold children.) v. 1.
Lang. Green fairy book.
Lang. Three dwarfs and other stories.
Golden lantern, the golden goat, and the golden cloak. Jerrold. Reign of King Oberon.
Lang. Blue parrot. (Pinkel the thief.)
Lang. Orange fairy book. (Pinkel the thief.)
Thorpe. Yule-tide stories.
Underhill. Dwarfs' tailor and other fairy tales. (Cinderboy and the witch.)
Wiggin and Smith. Fairy ring.
See also Esben and the witch.
Golden legend. *See* Peasant maid.
Golden lion. Lang. Aladdin and other stories.
Lang. Pink fairy book.
Golden loaf. Laboulaye. Fairy book. (Gold bread.)
Laboulaye. Fairy tales.
Storytellers' magazine. June 1914, p. 594. (Bread of gold.)
Wiggin and Smith. Magic casements. (Gold bread.)
Golden mermaid. Lang. Golden mermaid and other stories.
Lang. Green fairy book.
See also Golden blackbird. I and II.
Golden mountain. Blumenthal. Folk tales from the Russian.
Johnson. Fir-tree fairy book. (Spendthrift merchant's son.)
Polevoi. Russian fairy tales.
Steele. Russian garland of fairy tales.
Golden nugget. Pitman. Chinese wonder book.
Golden palace that hung in the air. Asbjörnsen. Tales from the fjeld.
Golden pears. Keyes. Stories and story-telling
See also Apples of health.
Golden post. Sologub. Sweet-scented name.
Golden purse and the seeing eye. Children's story garden.
Golden river. I. Harrison. Prince Silverwings.
Golden river. II. *See* King of the Golden River.
Golden-rod. *See* Goldenrod, Legend of. III.
Golden serpent. Grayl. Fairy tales from foreign lands.

Golden shoes. Guerber. Legends of the Rhine.
Golden slipper. Bain. Cossack fairy tales.
See also Rashin Coatie. I and II.
Golden spears. Leamy. Golden spears and other stories.
Golden spinning-wheel. I. Silver fairy book.
Golden spinning-wheel. II. Fillmore. Czechoslovak fairy tales.
Golden steed. Byrne. Modern Greek fairy tales.
Golden strawberries. Olcott. Wonder garden.
Golden touch. *See* Midas. I.
Golden treasure. Andersen. Fairy tales (Paull tr.).
Andersen. Stories and tales (Author's ed.).
Golden tripod. Baldwin. Fifty famous people.
Golden tulip. Meigs. Kingdom of the winding road.
Golden whistle. *See* Said, Adventures of.
Golden windows. Richards. Golden windows.
Goldenlocks. I. *See* Goldielocks.
Goldenlocks. II. *See* Fair one with golden locks.
Goldenrod and aster. Bailey and Lewis. For the children's hour.
Cooke. Nature myths and stories.
Hall and Gilman. Story land. 2d reader. (Story of the aster and the goldenrod.)
McFee. Treasury of flower stories. (Story of the goldenrod.)
Pratt. Fairyland of flowers.
Skinner. Topaz story book. (Goldenrod and purple aster.)
Goldenrod, Legend of the. I. Danielson. Story telling time.
Skinner. Topaz story book.
Goldenrod, Legend of the. II. Olcott. Wonder garden.
Goldenrod, Legend of the. III. Bryce. That's why stories. (Golden-rod.)
Goldielocks. Ketchum and Jorgensen. Kindergarten gems. (Goldenlocks.)
Macé. Home fairy tales.
Winnington. Outlook fairy book.
Goldilocks. *See* Three bears.
Goldilocks and the three bears. *See* Three bears.
Goldsmith. Guerber. Legends of the Rhine.
Goldsmith's fortune. Lang. Orange fairy book.
Goloshes of fortune. Andersen. Fairy tales (Lucas tr.).
Andersen. Fairy tales (Paull tr.).
Andersen. Wonder stories. (Galoshes of fortune.)
See also Magic umbrella.
Good advice. Richards. Golden windows.
Good and bad apples. Keyes. Five senses.
Ruskin. King of the Golden River.
Good and bad weather. Riggs. Animal stories from Eskimo land.
Good bargain. Grimm. Fairy tales (Paull tr.).
Grimm. Household tales (Burt ed.).

Good bear and the lost boy. Judd. Wigwam stories.
Good bishop. *See* St. Nicholas.
Good cat. *See* Gagliuso.
Good children. Mabie. Folk tales every child should know.
Good comrades of the flying ship. *See* Flying ship.
Good elephant and the ungrateful man. *See* Elephant and the ungrateful forester.
Good ferryman and the water nymphs. Glinski. Polish fairy tales.
"Good-for-nothing." I. *See* She was good for nothing.
Good-for-nothing. II. Wardrop. Georgian folk tales.
See also Knapsack, the hat and the horn.
Good giants. Fuller. Book of friendly giants. (Wigwam giants.)
Leland. Algonquin legends of New England. (Giant magicians.)
Partridge. Glooskap the great chief. (Giant magicians.)
St. Nicholas. June 1914, p. 694. (Wigwam giants.)
Wilson. Myths of the red children.
Good gifts and a fool's folly. Pyle. Twilight land.
Good housewife and her night labours. Grierson. Children's book of Celtic stories.
Olcott. Good stories for great holidays. (Burg Hill's on fire.)
See also Horned women.
Good humor. *See* Cheerful temper.
Good king. Cowles. Art of story-telling.
Good little Henry. Segur. French fairy tales.
Segur. Old French fairy tales.
Good little mouse. Aulnoy. Fairy tales.
*Heller and Bates. Little Golden-hood.
Lang. Red fairy book. (Little good mouse.)
Wiggin and Smith. Fairy ring. (Little good mouse.)
Valentine. Old, old fairy tales.
Good little spirit. Eastman. Indian legends retold.
Good luck is better than gold. Ewing. Old-fashioned fairy tales.
Good-luck token. Eastman. Wigwam evenings.
Good-natured bear. Skinner. Garnet story book.
St. Nicholas. Dec. 1876, p. 135.
Good-natured dragons. Griffis. Swiss fairy tales.
Good-natured giant. Bouvé. Lamplight fairy tales.
Good of a few words. Pyle. Twilight land.
Good old Bruin. *See* Bruin Goodfellow.
Good practical joke. Curry. Little classics.
Good Sir James. Lang. Strange story book.
Good sister. *See* Goblin market.
Good sword. Stroebe and Martens. Danish fairy book.
Good Thanksgiving (poem). Curry. Little classics.
Good thunder. *See* Child of the thunder.
Good time (poem). Hartwell. Story hour readings. 5th year.

Good woman. *See* Dame Gudbrand.
Good year. Stein. When fairies were friendly.
Goodman of the inn. Campbell. Beyond the border.
Goody Blake and Harry Gill (poem). Arnold and Gilbert. Stepping stones to literature. v. 4.
Scudder. Children's book.
Tappan. Old-fashioned stories.
Goody 'Gainst-the-Stream. Asbjörnsen. Fairy tales from the far north. (Contrary woman.)
Asbjörnsen. Tales from the fjeld.
Dasent. Norse fairy tales.
See also Mary, Mary, so contrary; Scissors.
Goody Two-Shoes. Bailey. For the story teller.
*Blaisdell. Child life readers. 2d reader.
History of the little Goody Two-Shoes.
My Bookhouse. v. 2. (Little Goody Two-Shoes.)
Norton. Heart of oak books. v. 2.
Poulsson. In the child's world.
Scudder. Children's book. (Renowned history of Goody Two-Shoes.)
Tappan. Old-fashioned stories and poems. (Renowned history of Little Goody Two-Shoes.)
Valentine. Old, old fairy tales (Burt ed.).
Welsh. Stories children love. (Renowned history of Little Goody Two-Shoes.)
Goose. Young. Plantation bird legends.
Goose and the golden eggs. *See* Goose that laid golden eggs.
Goose and the swans (poem). Æsop. Fables (Burt ed.).
Wiggin and Smith. Talking beasts.
Goose girl. Bates. Once upon a time.
Coussens. Child's book of stories.
Grimm. Fairy tales (Lucas tr.).
Grimm. Household stories (Crane tr.).
Grimm. Household tales (Burt ed. False bride.)
Grimm. Household tales (Everyman's ed.)
Jerrold. Big book of fairy tales.
Jerrold. Reign of King Oberon.
Lang. Blue fairy book.
Lang. Dick Whittington and other stories.
Patten. Junior classics. v. 1.
Pyle. Mother's nursery tales.
Quiller-Couch. Fairy tales far and near.
Success library. v. 3.
Wiggin and Smith. Fairy ring.
Goose girl and the blue gander. Brady. Green forest fairy tales.
Goose girl at the well. Grimm. Fairy tales (Paull tr.).
*Grimm. Fairy tales (Wiltse). v. 2.
Wiggin and Smith. Magic casements. (Emerald book.)
Goose that laid golden eggs. Æsop. Fables (Black ed. Man and his goose.)
Æsop. Fables (Burt ed.).

Goose that laid golden eggs—*continued.*
Æsop. Fables (Jacobs. Goose with the golden eggs.)
Blaisdell. Child life. 2d reader. (Goose and the golden eggs.)
*Grover. Folk-lore readers. v. 1. (Man and his goose.)
*Klingensmith. Just stories. (Goose that laid the golden egg.)
Scudder. Children's book.
Scudder. Fable and folk stories.
Sly. World stories retold. (Goose with the golden eggs.)
Tappan. Folk stories and fables.
Welsh. Stories children love. (Goose with the golden eggs.)
Wiggin and Smith. Talking beasts. (Goose with the golden eggs.)
See also Mallard that asked too much.
Goose with the golden eggs. *See* Goose that laid golden eggs.
Goosey Grizzel. Dasent. Popular tales from the Norse.
Gordian Knot. *See* Alexander the Great.
Gordy's New Year's dinner party. *Bryant. New stories to tell to children.
Gore-Gorinskoe. Blumenthal. Folk tales from the Russian. (Woe Bogotir.)
Polevoi. Russian fairy tales.
Gorgon's head. *See* Perseus.
Goronwy Tudor and the witches of Llanddona. Thomas. Welsh fairy book.
Goso, the teacher. Bateman. Zanzibar tales.
Gotham men and the cuckoo. Johnson. Oak-tree fairy book.
Götterdämmerung. *See* Ring: Twilight of the gods; Twilight of the gods. I.
Gourd and the pine. Æsop. Fables (Burt ed.).
Æsop. Fables (Stickney).
Bailey. Folk stories and fables.
Bailey and Lewis. For the children's hour. (Gourd and the pine tree.)
See also Oak and the vine.
Gourd and the pine tree. *See* Gourd and the pine.
Grace's well. Thomas. Welsh fairy book.
Gracieuse and Percinet. *See* Graciosa and Percinet.
Graciosa and Percinet. Aulnoy. Fairy tales. (Gracieuse and Percinet.)
Aulnoy. Children's fairy land. (Gracieuse and Percinet.)
Lang. Red fairy book.
Mullock. Fairy tales.
Pyle. Fairy tales from far and near.
Valentine. Old, old fairy tales.
Welsh. Fairy stories children love.
Wiggin and Smith. Fairy ring.
Gradual fairy. Bailey. Stories children need.
Brown. One-footed fairy.

Graham of Morphie. *See* Laird of Morphie and the water kelpie.
Grain of corn. Steel. Tales of the Punjab.
See also Cat and the mouse; How the mouse got into his hole; Little Tuppen; Munachar and Manachar; Nanny who wouldn't go home to supper; Old woman and her pig; Sparrow and the bush.
Grain of wheat. *See* Little red hen. I.
Grain that was like an egg. Tolstoi. Tales.
Grandee. Success library. v. 3.
Grandfather. Bailey. Stories children need.
Grandfather and the fairy. Patterson. Enchanted bird.
Grandfather Skeeterhawk. Gruelle. Friendly fairies.
Grandfather's eyes. Fillmore. Czechoslovak fairy tales.
Grandmother. Andersen. Fairy tales (Paull tr.).
Grandmother of the gnomes. *See* Dame Martha's stepdaughter.
Grandmother Old-Year and the baby. Potter. Pinafore pocket story book.
Grandmother's golden dish. Babbitt. Jataka tales. (Merchant of Seri.)
Shedlock. Eastern stories and legends.
Grandmother's spectacles. Bailey. Stories for Sunday telling.
Grandmother's sunshine. Boston collection of kindergarten stories. (Bennie's sunshine.)
Dyer and Brady. Merrill readers. 2d reader.
Grandmother's Thanksgiving present. Bailey. Stories for Sunday telling.
Grandsire bear and Reynard the fox. *See* Bear and fox make a wager.
Granny Chipmunk's lesson. Messer. Next night stories.
Granny's Blackie. Babbitt. Jataka tales.
Peck. Stories for good children.
Grapes, Origin of. Landa. Aunt Naomi's Jewish fairy tales and legends. (Giant of the flood.)
See also First vineyard.
Grasp all, lose all. Olive fairy book.
Grasshopper. Wade. Indian fairy tales.
Grasshopper and the ant. I. *See* Ant and the grasshopper.
Grasshopper and the ant. II. Wardrop. Georgian folk tales.
Grasshopper, Origin of. *See* Aurora and Tithonus.
Grasshopper, Wonderful exploits of. *See* Paup-Puk-Keewis.
Grasshopper's trip to the city. Aspinwall. Short stories for short people.
Grateful animals and ungrateful man. *See* Prince Wicked and the grateful animals.
Grateful beasts. I. Lang. Yellow fairy book.
Lang. Snake prince.
See also Magic ring: Jack and his golden snuff-box.

Grateful beasts. II. Graves. Irish fairy book.
Grayl. Fairy tales from foreign lands.
Grimm. Household tales. (Everyman's ed. Fritz and his friends.)
*Grimm. Fairy tales. v. 1. (Wiltse. Faithful beasts.)
Johnson. Birch-tree fairy book.
Norton. Heart of oak books. v. 3.
Stebbins. Third reader. (Faithful beasts.)
Young and Field. Literary readers. Book 2. (Faithful beasts.)
See also Fortunes of Shrikantha; Magic ring.
Grateful cobra. Wiggin and Smith. Fairy ring.
Grateful crane. Griffis. Japanese fairy tales.
Wiggin and Smith. Tales of wonder.
Grateful elephant. Babbitt. Jataka tales. (King's white elephant.)
Burlingame. Grateful elephant and other stories.
Stanley. Animal folk tales.
Grateful foxes. Cooke. Nature myths and stories.
Mabie. Folk tales every child should know.
Nixon-Roulet. Japanese folk stories and fairy tales. (Princess and the fox baby.)
Stanley. Animal folk tales.
Tappan. Folk stories and fables.
Wiggin and Smith. Tales of wonder.
Grateful goat. Rouse. Talking thrush.
Grateful prince. Lang. Violet fairy book.
Lang. White doe.
Grateful sparrows. Nordau. Dwarf's spectacles.
Grave diggers. Richards. Silver crown.
Gray Cat and Black Cat. Burchill. Progressive road to reading. Book 1.
Gray cat's tricks. Bigham. Merry animal tales.
Gray Eagle and his five brothers. *See* Broken wing.
Gray fox. *See* Hungry fox.
Gray goat and the fox. Hodgkins. Atlantic treasury of childhood stories.
See also Wolf and the seven little kids.
Gray mole and the Indian. *See* Sun a prisoner. IV.
Graywings, the goose. Hartwell. Story hour readings. 5th year.
Grazier's wife. Johnson. Fir-tree fairy book.
Great bear. I. *See* Callisto and Arcas.
Great bear. II. *See* Great bear in the sky.
Great bear. III. *See* Aurora, the white arch and the great bear.
Great bear in the sky. I. Judd. Wigwam stories.
Tanner. Legends from the red man's forest. (Great bear.)
See also Why the autumn leaves are red. II.
Great bear in the sky. II *See* Callisto and Arcas.
Great bell. Pitman. Chinese wonder book.

Great big beautiful wheel. Storytellers' magazine. July 1916, p. 414.
Great boar hunt. *See* Calydonian hunt.
Great Claus and Little Claus. *See* Little Claus and Big Claus.
Great deluge. *See* Deucalion and Pyrrha.
"Great events from small occasions rise." Storytellers' magazine. March 1916, p. 162.
Great feast. Richards. Golden windows.
Great fire. Guerber. Legends of the Rhine.
Great flood. I. *See* Deucalion and Pyrrha.
Great flood. II. Brown. Tales of the red children.
Great flood. III. Martens. Chinese fairy book.
Great-grandfather. Andersen. Stories and tales (Author's ed.).
Great gray goose. Potter. Pinafore pocket story book.
Great head. Compton. American Indian fairy tales.
Eastman. Indian legends retold.
Great Heart and the three tests. Macmillan. Canadian fairy tales.
See also How six traveled through the world.
Great kettle. *See* Thor's fishing.
Great King Eagle. Stewart. Once upon a time.
Great Panjandrum himself. Eggleston. Queer stories for boys and girls.
Great red dragon of Wales. *See* Why the red dragon is the emblem of Wales.
Great repentance and a great forgiveness. Davis and Chow-Leung. Chinese fables and folk stories.
Great scholar. Macé. Home fairy tales.
Great serpent of the hill. Kennedy. New world fairy book.
Great sorrow. Andersen. Fairy tales (Paull tr.).
Great stone face. Bailey. For the story teller.
Baker and Carpenter. Language readers. 6th year.
Mabie. Famous stories every child should know.
Patten. Junior classics. v. 6.
Sly. World stories retold. (Adapted.)
Tappan. Modern stories.
Welsh. Stories children love.
Great stone fire eater. Griffis. Unmannerly tiger and other Korean tales.
Griffis. Korean fairy tales.
Great white bear. Lindsay. Story-teller.
Great white bear and the trolls. *See* Bear and Skrattel.
Great wizard. *See* Manabozho.
Greatest wealth. Guerber. Legends of the Rhine.
Grecian king and the physician. *See* Grecian king and the physician Douban.)
Grecian king and the physician Douban. Arabian nights (Dodge ed.).
Arabian nights (Lang. Story of the Greek king and the physician Douban.)

Grecian king and the physician Douban—*continued.*
Arabian nights (Olcott. Grecian king and the sage Douban.)
Arabian nights (Townsend. History of the Greek king and Douban the physician.)
Welsh. Fairy tales children love. (Grecian king and the physician.)
Grecian king and the sage Douban, Story of. *See* Grecian king and the physician Douban.
Greedy abbot. Guerber. Legends of the Rhine.
Greedy beggar. *Bowen. Second story reader.
Greedy blackbird. Olcott. Wonder garden.
Greedy cat. Asbjörnsen. Tales from the fjeld.
Bailey. Firelight stories.
Bailey. Once upon a time animal stories.
Johnson. Elm-tree fairy book.
Stroebe and Martens. Norwegian fairy book. (Cat who could eat so much.)
Wiggin and Smith. Tales of laughter.
See also Cat and the parrot; Kuratko the terrible; Wolf. II.
Greedy cobbler. *See* King Arthur's cave.
Greedy fox. Aunt Naomi. Jewish fairy tales.
Greedy geese. Olcott. Good stories for great holidays.
See also St. Werburg and her goose.
Greedy humming bird. Young. Plantation bird legends.
Greedy jackal. Wiggin and Smith. Talking beasts.
Greedy old man. I. *See* Greedy woodcutter and the fairy ring.
Greedy old man. II. Storytellers' magazine. Oct. 1917 p. 405.
Greedy parrot. Bailey. Stories children need.
See also Little red hen. I.
Greedy shepherd. Bailey. Stories children need.
Browne. Granny's wonderful chair.
*Burchill. Progressive road to reading. Book 3. (Kind and Clutch.)
O'Grady and Throop. Teachers' story teller's book.
Greedy woodcutter and the fairy ring. Field third reader.
Olcott. Book of elves and fairies. (Greedy old man.)
Greedy youngster. *See* Grumblegizzard.
Greek king and the physician Douban. *See* Grecian king and the physician Douban.
Greek princess and the young gardener. Jacobs. More Celtic fairy tales.
Yeats. Irish fairy tales.
See also Golden bird. II.
Green bird. Winnington. Outlook fairy book.
Green cap. Brown. Star jewels.
Green cheese and the man in the moon. Donahey. Tales to be told to children.
Green children. Hartland. English folk and fairy tales.
Rhys. Fairy gold.

Green-faced toad. Birch. Green-faced toad.
See also Fairyfoot.
Green gnome. I. (poem). Rolfe. Fairy tales in prose and verse.
Green gnome. II. English. Fairy stories and wonder tales.
Green goblin. Brown. One-footed fairy.
Green isles of ocean. Thomas. Welsh fairy book.
Green jacket. Richards. Toto's merry winter.
Green knight. I. Asbjörnsen. Tales from the fjeld.
Gade. Norwegian fairy tales.
Wiggin and Smith. Magic casements.
Green knight. II. Lang. Olive fairy book.
Lang. Snake prince.
Green knight. III. *See* Sir Gawain and the green knight.
Green monkey. *See* Alphege.
Green serpent. Aulnoy. Fairy tales.
Aulnoy. Children's fairy land.
Green willow. Hearn. Japanese fairy tales.
James. Green willow and other fairy tales.
Greenies. Andersen. Stories and tales (Author's ed.).
Gregory's angels. Johonnot. Stories of the olden time.
Morris. Historical tales: English. (How England became Christian.)
Grendel. *See* Beowulf.
Gretchen and the magic fiddle. *Dillingham and Emerson. Tell it again stories.
Grettir the Strong. Lang. Book of romance.
Lang. Tales of romance. (How Grettir the Strong became an outlaw.)
Grey wizard. English. Fairy stories and wonder tales.
Greybeard. Hall. Icelandic fairy tales.
Greyfoot. Bay. Danish fairy and folk tales.
See also King Thrushbeard.
Griffin and the minor canon. Stockton. Bee-man of Orn and other tales.
Stockton. Fanciful tales.
Stockton. Queen's museum.
Grillo the cricket, Story of. Field third reader.
Grizzly and rattlesnake save coyote's grandchildren. Sexton. Gray wolf stories.
Grizzly bear and the four chiefs. Eastman. Indian legends retold.
Grizzly bear crest, Origin of. Judson. Myths and legends of Alaska.
Grimsbork. *See* Dapplegrim.
Grizzled Peter. *See* Man who was going to mind the house.
Grizzly bear's medicine. Grinnell. Punishment of the stingy.
Groac'h of the Isle of Loc. Lang. Lilac fairy book
Lang. King of the waterfalls.

Groundhog. *See* Why the woodchuck comes out in midwinter.
Growing-up-like-one-who-has-a-grandmother. Lang. Strange story book.
Grubbiest grub. Skinner. Turquoise story book.
See also Dragon fly.
Grumblegizzard. Asbjörnsen. Folk and fairy tales. (Greedy youngster.)
Asbjörnsen. Tales from the fjeld.
Mabie. Folk tales every child should know. (Greedy youngster.)
Stroebe and Martens. Norwegian fairy book. (Murmur-Goose-Egg.)
Grumbling Peter. *Baldwin. Second fairy reader.
Grumpy saint. Richards. Silver crown.
Guardian angel. Patten. Junior classics. v. 2.
Guardian spirits. Caballero. Spanish fairy tales.
Guarinos, Story of. *See* Knight of France.
Gudbrand of the mountain side. *See* Dame Gudbrand.
Gudbrand on the hillside. *See* Dame Gudbrand.
Gude Wallace. Grierson. Children's tales from Scottish ballads.
Gudeman of Ballengeich. Storytellers' magazine. April 1917, p. 213.
Gudra's daughter. Stockton. Floating prince.
Gudrun. Guerber. Legends of the middle ages.
See also Siegfried.
Guenevere. Clay. Stories from Le Morte d'Arthur. (Queen Guenevere.)
Lang. Tales of the Round Table. (Fight for the Queen; Lancelot and Guenevere.)
Guest. I. Bailey. Stories for Sunday telling.
Guest. II. Bayliss. Treasury of Eskimo tales.
Guest in the playhouse. Bailey. Friendly tales.
Guilty brick (poem). Pitman. Chinese fairy tales.
Guineas. Young. Plantation bird legends.
Guinever. *See* Guenevere.
Gulambara and Sulambara. Wardrop. Georgian folk tales.
Guleesh. Frost. Fairies and folk of Ireland. (*In* Ch. 4.)
Jacobs. Celtic fairy tales.
Johnson. Birch-tree fairy book. (Kidnapped princess.)
Pyle. Where the wind blows. (Guleesh na Guss Dhu.)
See also Jamie Freel and the young lady.
Guleesh na Guss Dhu. *See* Guleesh.
Gullible world. Fillmore. Shoemaker's apron.
Gulliver's travels. Jenks. Tales of fantasy. (Gulliver.)
Gulliver's travels: Brobdingnag. Fuller. Book of friendly giants. (Man who went to the giants' country.)
Gibbon. Reign of King Cole. (Gulliver's adventures in Brobdingnag.)
Tappan. Stories from seven old favorites.
Welsh. Stories children love.

Gulliver's travels: Lilliput land. Arnold and Gilbert. Stepping stones to literature. v. 6.
Baldwin. Fifty famous rides. (How Gulliver rode to Lilliput.
Blaisdell. Child life. Fifth reader.
Hartwell. Story hour readings. 7th year. (Voyage to Lilliput.)
Judson and Bender. Graded literature readers. Sixth book.
Lang. Blue fairy book.
Lang. King of the waterfalls. (Voyage to Lilliput.)
Scudder. Children's book.
Tappan. Stories from seven old favorites.
Welsh. Stories children love.
Gulnare of the sea, Story of. Arabian nights (Wiggin and Smith.)
Arabian nights. (Colum. Story of Bedr Basim and Jawharah, the daughter of the king of the sea.)
In some editions of the Arabian Nights not indexed here this story is given under the title "King of Persia and the princess of the sea."
Gunawolf. Harper. Story-hour favorites. (Gunniwolf.)
Storytellers' magazine. May 1915, p. 158.
Gunnar. *See* Brunhilda.
Gunniwolf. *See* Gunawolf.
Gutenburg, John. Baldwin. Thirty more famous stories. (First printer.)
Baldwin. Thirty more famous stories. (John Gutenberg and the voices.)
Guto Bach and the fairies. Thomas. Welsh fairy book.
Guy Fawkes Day. Blaisdell. English history story book. (Gunpowder plot.)
Guy of Warwick. Lang. Red romance book.
(poem). Lanier. Boy's Percy. (Guy and Amarant; Legend of Sir Guy.)
Mabie. Legends every child should know.
Wilmot-Buxton. Stories of early England.
Gwâshbrâri, the glacier-hearted queen. Steel. Tales of the Punjab. (Legend of Gwâshbrâri.)
Gylfe. Mabie. Norse stories. (Gods and men.)

H

Ha-le-ma-no and the Princess Kama, Story of. Colum. At the gateways of the day.
Haamdaanee. *See* Gazelle.
Haamdaanee and the wise gazelle. *See* Gazelle.
Habetrot and Scantlie Mab. Douglas. Scottish fairy tales. (Habitrot.)
Grierson. Scottish fairy book. (Habetrot the spinstress.)

Habetrot and Scantlie Mab—*continued.*
*Haaren. Songs and stories. 2d reader. (Spinners.)
Jacobs. More English fairy tales.
See also Three little crones each with something big. I, II and III; Three spinning fairies; Tom Tit Tot.
Habetrot the spinstress. *See* Habetrot and Scantlie Mab.
Habitrot. *See* Habetrot and Scantlie Mab.
Habogi. Lang. Brown fairy book.
Lang. Invisible prince and other stories.
Hachi-no-ki; or, The flower-pot trees. Storytellers' magazine. Sept. & Oct. 1915, p. 273, 349.
Hackelnberg. Thorpe. Yule-tide stories.
Hacon Grizzlebeard. Dasent. Popular tales from the Norse.
Dasent. Norse fairy tales.
See also King Thrushbeard.
Hafiz the stone-cutter. *See* Stone-cutter.
Hair tree. Nichols and DeMorgan. Princess Girlikin.
Hairy man. Lang. Crimson fairy book.
Lang. Little Wildrose.
Halcyon birds. *Bailey. Wonder stories. (Little errand girl's new dress.)
Firth. Stories of old Greece.
Guerber. Myths of Greece and Rome. (*In* Somnus and Mors.)
Guerber. Myths of Greece and Rome. (Story of Ceyx and Halcyone.)
Hyde. Favorite Greek myths. (Juno and Halcyone.)
Kupfer. Stories of long ago. (Dream that came true.)
Olcott. Wonder garden.
Pratt. Myths of old Greece. v. 3.
Storytellers' magazine. April 1917, p. 242. (*In* God's truth.)
Half-chick. *Bailey. Folk stories and fables. (Little Half Chick.)
Bailey and Lewis. For the children's hour. (Little Half Chick.)
Baldwin. Second fairy reader. (Coco.)
Bryant. Best stories to tell to children. (Little Half-Chick.)
Bryant. Stories to tell to children. (Little Half-Chick.)
Burchill. Progressive road to reading. Book 1. (Little Half-chick.)
Esenwein and Stockard. Children's stories. (Little Half-Chick.)
*Howard. Banbury cross stories.
Keyes. Stories and story-telling. (Coquerico.)
*Klingensmith. Just stories.
Laboulaye. Fairy tales. (Story of Coquerico. *In* Captain John's travels.)
Lang. Green fairy book.

Half-Chick—*continued.*
Lang. Magician's gifts.
My Bookhouse. v. 1. (Little Half-chick.)
O'Grady and Throop. Teacher's story teller's book.
Patten. Junior classics. v. 1.
Success library. v. 3.
Wiggin and Smith. Fairy ring. (Story of Coquerico.)
See also Proud cock.

Half-man-riding-on-the-worse-half-of-a-lame-horse. Kunos Turkish fairy tales.

Halfman. I. Higginson. Tales of the enchanted islands of the Atlantic.

Halfman. II. Lang. Beauty and the beast and other stories.
Lang. Violet fairy book.

Hall of the roses. Patterson. Enchanted bird.

Hallowe'en. *See* Astounding voyage of Daniel O'Rourke; Bear and Skrattel; *Blue calico witch; Boggart; Black cat III; Brownie who wanted the moon; Brownies on Hallowe'en; *Cat's house under the hill; Childe Rowland; Conjure wives; Danny's Hallowe'en; Death and the negro man; *Desolate things; Discontented pumpkin; Dwarf root's story of the pumpkin seed; Fairy horn; Ghost story (Harris); Good housewife and her labors; *Great white bear; Hansel and Grethel; How Jan Brewer was pisky-laden; How peeping Kate was pisky-led; *Jack-o'-lantern; *Judy and the fairy cat; King of the cats; *King's cat; *Little pumpkin; Mister Woodpecker; My grandfather. Hendry Watly; Old witch; Phantom knight of the vandal camp; *Real Hallowe'en witch; Roll-call of the reef; Schippeitaro; Strange visitor; Taily-po; Tam O'Shanter; *Teeny, tiny woman; *Teeny-tiny II; Tom Connor's cat; Wait till Martin comes; Witch cat; Woodman and the goblins.

Hallowe'en story. I. *Dillingham and Emerson. Tell it again stories.
*Field second reader.
*My Bookhouse. v. 1.

Hallowe'en story. II.
Brady. Green forest fairy tales. (Tale for Hallowe'en.

Halos of the saints. Martens. Chinese fairy book.

Hand of glory. Hartland. English folk and fairy tales.

Handful of clay. Van Dyke. Blue flower.
(play). Luetkenhaus. Plays for school children.
Van Sickle and Seegmiller. Riverside readers. 6th reader.

Hang-the-money-up-tree. Nixon-Roulet. Japanese folk stories and fairy tales.

Hans. Hall. Icelandic fairy tales.

Hans and his dog. Coe. Second book of stories.
Lindsay. More mother stories.

Hans and his white pussy cat. *See* Bear and Skrattel.

Hans and his wife Grettel. Grimm. Household tales. (Everyman's ed.).
(Parts 1 and 2 of this story appear in other editions under the titles "Clever Grethel" and "Hans in love.")
See also Hans married.
Hans and the brownie. Burchill. Progressive road to reading. Book 1.
Hans and the four big giants. Allison and Perdue. Story in primary instruction.
Harrison. In story-land.
Hans and the hoop of gold. St. Nicholas. Feb. 1916, p. 337.
Hans and the wonderful flower. Bailey and Lewis. For the children's hour.
Bryce. That's why stories. (Forget-me-not.)
St. Nicholas. Jan. 1882, p. 185. (Max and the wonder flower.)
Wickes. Happy holidays. (Little brown herb.)
Hans Broemser. Guerber. Legends of the Rhine.
Hans Clodhopper. *Andersen. Best fairy tales (Henderson tr.).
Andersen. Fairy tales (Lucas tr.).
Andersen. Fairy tales and stories (Toksvig. Booby Hans.)
Andersen. Wonder stories. (Jack the dullard.)
Lang. Blue parrot. (Blockhead-Hans.)
Lang. Yellow fairy book. (Blockhead Hans.)
See also Three questions. II.
Hans Hecklemann's luck. Pyle. Pepper and salt.
Hans Humdrum. Bay. Danish fairy and folk tales.
See also Keep cool.
Hans in love. *See* Prudent Hans.
Hans in luck. Adams. Folk-story and verse.
Coussens. Child's book of stories.
*Elson and Runkel. Elson readers. Book 2. (Lucky Hans.)
Grimm. Fairy tales (Lucas tr.).
Grimm. Fairy tales (Wiltse) v. 2.
Grimm. Household stories (Crane tr.).
Grimm. Household tales (Everyman's ed.).
*Haaren. Songs and stories. 2d reader.
Johnson. Birch-tree fairy book.
Lansing. Fairy tales. v. 1.
Mabie. Folk tales every child should know.
Marshall. Fairy tales of all nations. (Lucky Jack.)
Norton. Heart of oak books. v. 3.
Pyle. Mother's nursery tales. (Jack in luck.)
Scudder. Book of folk stories.
Scudder. Children's book.
Scudder. Fables and folk stories.
Tappan. Folk stories and fables.
Wiggin and Smith. Tales of laughter.
See also Dame Gubrand; Mr. Vinegar; Monkey's bargains.

Hans married. Grimm. Fairy tales (Paull tr.).
See also Hans and his wife Grettel.
Hans Sachs. Maud. Wagner's heroes.
Hans the hunter. Gibbon. Reign of King Cole.
Hans, the mermaid's son. Lang. Pink fairy book.
Lang. Snow-queen and other stories.
Hans the otherwise. Tappan. Book of humor.
Hans the shepherd boy. Cabot. Ethics for children.
Coe. Second book of stories.
Curry. Little classics. (How Hans was promoted.)
Lansing. Dramatic readings for schools.
See also Little shepherd.
Hans von Waldenburg. Froelicher. Swiss stories. (Origin of the statue of Hans von Waldenburg.)
Hans Wagner and the angel who kept his word. Stocking. City that never was reached.
Hans, who made the princess laugh. Asbjörnsen. Folk and fairy tales.
Asbjörnsen. Tales from the fjeld. (Taper Tom.)
Gade. Norwegian fairy tales. (Taper Tom who made the pricess laugh.)
Mabie. Folk tales every child should know.
Olcott and Pendleton. Jolly book. (Taper Tom.)
Thorne-Thomsen. East o' the sun and west o' the moon. (Taper Tom.)
Van Sickle and Seegmiller. Riverside readers. 3d reader.
See also Golden Goose; Magic swan; Saucy Jesper.
Hansel and Grethel. I. Coe and Christie. Story hour readers. 3d book. (Hansel and Gretel.)
Coussens. Child's book of stories. (Hansel and Gretel.)
Field. Famous fairy tales.
Forty famous fairy tales. (Hansel and Grettel.)
Grimm. Fairy tales (Lucas tr.).
Grimm. Household stories (Crane tr.).
Grimm. Household tales (Burt ed.).
Grimm. Household tales (Everyman's ed.).
Jacobs. Europa's fairy book. (Johnnie and Grizzle.)
Jerrold. Big book of fairy tales.
Jerrold. Reign of King Oberon.
Lang. Blue fairy book. (Hansel and Grettel.)
Lang. Blue parrot. (Hansel and Grettel.)
Lang. Little Red Riding-Hood and other stories. (Hansel and Grettel.)
Mabie. Fairy tales every child should know.
Marshall. Fairy tales of all nations.
My Bookhouse. v. 3.
Olcott. Good stories for great holidays.
Patten. Junior classics. v. 1.
Stone. Children's stories that never grow old.
Success library. v. 3.
Tappan. Folk stories and fables.
Welsh. Fairy tales children love.

Hansel and Grethel. I.—*continued.*
Winnington. Outlook fairy book. (Hansel and Gretel.)
See also Roof of sausages; Sugar candy house.
Hansel and Grethel. II. Bailey. Stories children need.
McSpadden. Stories from great operas. (Hansel and Gretel.)
Ha'penny; or, The dwarf, the witch, and the magic slippers. Harrison. Old-fashioned fairy tales.
Happiness. Andrews. Enchanted forest.
Happy age in the animal world. Stafford. Animal fables.
Happy clothes-dryer. Ruskin. King of the Golden River and other stories.
Happy family. Andersen. Fairy tales (Paull tr.).
Anderson. Stories (Riverside ed.).
Andersen. Wonder stories (Author's ed.).
Wiggin and Smith. Tales of laughter.
Happy hunter and the cheerful fisher. *See* Ambitious hunter and skilful fisher.
Happy hunter and the skillful fisher. *See* Ambitious hunter and the skilful fisher.
Happy little princess. Bailey. Stories for Sunday telling.
Happy-New-Year Man. Storytellers' magazine. Jan. 1917, p. 3.
Happy prince. Bailey. Stories children need.
Harper. Story-hour favorites.
Keyes. Stories and story-telling.
Skinner. Pearl story book.
Wilde. Fairy tales.
Happy princess. Bailey. Friendly tales.
Happy rattle. Gruelle. Friendly fairies.
Hard-headed woman (poem). Harris. Tar baby and other rhymes.
Harris. Told by Uncle Remus.
Hardy tin soldier. *See* Brave tin soldier.
Hardyknute (poem). Lanier. Boy's Percy.
Hare afraid of his ears. Æsop. Fables (Burt ed.).
See also Mr. Rabbit's ears.
Hare and many friends. *See* Hare with many friends.
Hare and the dog. Æsop. Fables (Burt ed.).
Hare and the elephant. *See* Timid hare.
Hare and the fox. Noyes. Twilight stories.
Wiggin and Smith. Tales of laughter.
See also Two foxes and the hot rolls.
Hare and the hedgehog (play). Doheny. Play awhile.
*Dyer and Brady. Merrill readers. 2d reader.
Noyes. Twilight stories. (Race between the hare and the hedgehog.)
Tappan. Folk stories and fables.
Van Sickle and Seegmiller. Riverside readers. 3d reader.
Wiggin and Smith. Tales of laughter. (Race between hare and hedgehog.)
See also Race of the tails.

Hare and the heiress. *See* Hare who had been married.
Hare and the hound. Æsop. Fables (Burt ed.).
Æsop. Fables (Stickney ed.).
Hare and the lion. Bateman. Zanzibar tales.
Hare and the partridge (poem). Wiggin and Smith. Talking beasts.
Hare and the pig. Wiggin and Smith. Talking beasts.
Hare and the tortoise. Æsop. Fables (Black ed.).
Æsop. Fables (Burt ed.).
Æosp. Fables (Jacobs).
Æsop. Fables (Stickney).
Baldwin. Fairy stories and fables.
Boston collection of kindergarten stories.
*Coe and Christie. Story hour readers. Book 1. (Race.)
Coussens. Child's book of stories. (Tortoise and the hare.)
(play). *Dyer and Brady. Merrill readers. 2d reader. (Race of the hare and the tortoise.)
*Elson and Runkel. Elson readers. Book 1. (Race.)
Hall and Gilman. Story land. 2d reader.
*Jones. First reader.
My Bookhouse. v. 1.
Scudder. Children's book. (Tortoise and the hare.)
Scudder. Fables and folk stories. (Tortoise and the hare.)
Sly. World stories retold.
Tappan. Folk stories and fables. (Tortoise and the hare.)
Wiggin and Smith. Talking beasts.
Wiltse. Kindergarten stories.
Hare in the moon. I. Farmer. Nature myths.
Holbrook. Nature myths. (Why there is a hare in the moon.)
Hare in the moon. II. Shedlock. Eastern stories and legends. (Hare that was not afraid to die.)
Shedlock. Art of the storyteller. (True spirit of a festival day.)
Hare in the moon. III. *See* Moon's message.
Hare of Inaba. *See* Eighty-one brothers.
Hare that ran away. *See* Timid hare.
Hare that was not afraid to die. *See* Hare in the moon. II.
Hare that was sent to York. Johnson. Oak-tree fairy book.
Hare, the bear and the fox. Cary. French fairy tales.
See also Two brothers. III.
Hare, the fox, and the wolf. Bidpai. Tortoise and the geese.
Hare who had been married. Asbjörnsen. Fairy tales from the far north.
Asbjörnsen. Tales from the fjeld. (Hare and the heiress.)
Hare who thought the world had come to an end. *See* Timid hare.

Hare with many friends (poem). Æsop. Fables (Burt ed.).
Æsop. Fables (Jacobs).
*(play). Doheny. Play awhile.
(poem). Wiggin and Smith. Talking beasts. (Hare and many friends.)
Hares. *See* Hares and the frogs.
Hares and foxes. Æsop. Fables (Stickney.)
Hares and the frogs. Æsop. Fables (Black ed.).
Æsop. Fables (Burt ed.).
Æsop. Fables (Jacobs).
Æsop. Fables (Stickney. Hares.)
Baldwin. Fairy stories and fables. (Hares.)
Scudder. Fables and folk stories.
Wiggin and Smith. Talking beasts.
Hare's bride. *See* Rabbit's bride.
Harisarman. Jacobs. Indian fairy tales.
Wiggin and Smith. Tales of laughter.
See also Doctor Know-all.
Harka, Story of. *See* White Hawk, the lazy.
Harold the Viking. Higginson. Tales of the enchanted islands of the Atlantic.
Harold's happy Easter. Bailey. Stories for Sunday telling.
Haroun-al-Raschid, Caliph of Bagdad, Adventures of. Haaren and Poland. Famous men of the middle ages. (Harun-al-Rashid.)
See also Caliph Haroun-al-Raschid, Adventures of.
Harper. I. Æsop. Fables (Black ed.).
Æsop. Fables (Burt ed.).
Harper. II. *See* Promise.
Harper's gratuity. Thomas. Welsh fairy book.
Harpies. Patten. Junior classics. v. 3. (*In* Æneas.)
Harriett's dream. Pyle. Counterpane fairy.
Hart and the hunter. *See* Stag at the lake.
Hart and the vine. *See* Stag and the vine.
Hart in the ox-stall. *See* Stag in the ox-stall.
Harvest. *See* Bruin and Reynard partners. II.
Hassan of Balsora. Arabian nights (Olcott. Story of the adventures of Hassan of Balsora.)
Jacobs. Book of wonder voyages. (Journeyings of Hasan of Bassorah to the Islands of Wak-Wak.)
Hassan the Arab and his horse. Hartwell. Story hour readings. 6th year. (Arab and his horse.)
My Bookhouse. v. 2.
Hassebu. Lang. Violet fairy book.
Lang. Snake prince.
Hasteen saves the jewels of the king. Pearson. Laughing lion and other stories.
Hat of the huldres. Stroebe and Martens. Norwegian fairy book.
Hati Sing; or, The vanquisher of an elephant. Bradley-Birt. Bengal fairy tales.

Hatim Tai. Olcott. Tales of the Persian genii. (Hatim the giver.)
Baldwin. Horse fair. (Duldul and his master.)
Hatshepset. *See* Lady of the obelisk.
Hatto, Bishop. *See* Mouse tower.
Hatto the hermit. Skinner. Turquoise story book.
Haughty princess. *See* King Thrushbeard.
Haunted castle of Thurnberg. Guerber. Legends of the Rhine.
Haunted house. Hartland. English folk and fairy tales.
Haunted mill. I. *See* Mill.
Haunted mill. II. Baudis. Czech folk tales.
Haunted ships. *See* Elves of the haunted ships.
Haunted spring (poem). Haaren. Fairy life.
(poem). Rolfe. Fairy tales in prose and verse.
Haunted widower. Hartland English folk and fairy tales.
Havelock and Argentile. *See* Havelok the Dane.
Havelok and Goldborough. *See* Havelok the Dane.
Havelok the Dane. Baring-Gould. Old English fairy tales. (Havelock and Argentile.)
Lang. Red romance book. (Havelok and Goldborough.)
Patten. Junior classics. v. 4. (Havelock hid from the traitor.)
Tappan. Stories of legendary heroes. (Havelok.)
Wilmot-Buxton. Stories of early England.
Hawk. Burlingame. Grateful elephant.
Hawk and the farmer. Æsop. Fables (Black ed.).
Æsop. Fables (Burt ed.).
Hawk and the nightingale. Æsop. Fables (Black ed.).
Æsop. Fables (Burt ed.).
Æsop. Fables (Stickney).
Hawk and the osprey. *See* Hawks and their friends.
Hawk and the rooster. *See* Why the hawk catches chickens.
Hawk, kite and pigeons. Æsop. Fables (Stickney).
Hawks and their friends. Babbitt. More Jataka tales.
Shedlock. Eastern stories and legends. (Hawk and the osprey.)
Hawk's disguise. Young. Plantation bird legends.
Hawk's first quarry. Young. Plantation bird legends.
Hawt; or, The great world contest. Washburn. Indian legends.
Haymo and the devil. Mendel. Our little Austrian cousin.
Hazel-nut child. Lang. Twelve huntsmen and other stories.
Lang. Yellow fairy book.
He of the little shell. *See* Pukwudgee and the morning star.
He who asks little receives much. Armfield. Wonder tales.
He who knew not fear. *See* Youth who could not shiver and shake.
He wins who waits. Lang. Olive fairy book.
He wished to live forever. Coussens. Jade story book.
Head of the princess. Birch. Green-faced toad.

Headless dwarfs. Violet fairy book.
Lang. Fairy nurse.
Headless horseman. *See* Sleepy Hollow.
Healing waters. *See* Hidden waters.
Health and happiness. Grundtvig. Danish fairy tales.
See also Three wishes. I.
Heart of a monkey. Lang. Lilac fairy book.
Lang. Magic book.
See also Monkey and the crocodile.
Heart of hare. Quiller-Couch. Fairy tales far and near.
Heart of ice. I. Lang. Green fairy book.
Lang. Pretty Goldilocks and other stories.
*Olcott. Whirling king. (Frozen heart. Abridged and adapted.)
Wiggin and Smith. Magic casements.
Heart of ice. II. Baring-Gould. Crock of gold.
Heart of the Princess Joan. Chisholm. Enchanted land.
Chisholm. Tales for bedtime.
Heart thread. Nordau. Dwarf's spectacles and other fairy tales.
Heartless husband. Martens. Chinese fairy book.
Heart's ease, Legend of. Olcott. Wonder garden.
Heather fairies. Stewart. Once upon a time.
Heavenly flower man. Pitman. Chinese fairy tales.
Heavenly river with the people who dwell thereon. *See* Sky bridge of birds.
Heavenly stair of the Hus brothers. Bayliss. Treasury of Indian tales.
Heavenly treasures. Friedlander. Jewish fairy book.
Heavenly twins. *See* Castor and Pollux; Leda and the swan.
Hector. Arnold and Gilbert. Stepping stones to literature. v. 4. (Death of Hector.)
Evans. Heroes of Troy.
Storr. Half a hundred hero tales. (Death of Hector.)
Hedge and the vineyard. Bryce. Fables from afar.
Hedley Kow. Hartland. English folk and fairy tales.
Jacobs. More English fairy tales.
Heidelberg castle, Legend of. Guerber. Legends of the Rhine.
Heidelberg tun and the dwarf. Guerber. Legends of the Rhine. (Legends of the tun.)
Heimdall. Guerber. Myths of northern lands. (*In* Heimdall.)
Heimdall and Loki. Guerber. Myths of northern lands. (*In* Heimdall.)
Heinzelmannchen. Guerber. Legends of the Rhine.
Heir of Linne. Greenwood. Stories from famous ballads.
Grierson. Children's tales from Scottish ballads.
(poem). Lanier. Boy's Percy.
Macleod. Book of ballad stories.
(poem). Scudder. Children's book.

Heir of Linne—*continued.*
Wilmot-Buxton. Stories of early England.
See also Ali of Cairo; Merchant.
Helen of Troy. Baldwin. Story of the golden age. (*In* Race for a wife.)
See also Trojan war.
Helga. Hall. Icelandic fairy tales.
Helge-Hal in the Blue Hill. *See* Lord Peter.
Helig's hollow. Thomas. Welsh fairy book.
Helios. *See* Apollo.
Heliotrope. *See* Clytie.
Hell gate. Richards. Silver crown.
Hello, house. *See* Heyo, house.
Help in need. Martens. Chinese fairy book.
Helpful turtles. Donaldson. Moons of long ago.
See also Turtle's shell.
Heming, Story of. Baring-Gould. Crock of gold.
Hen and the bag of flour. *See* Little red hen. I.
Hen and the cat. Wiggin and Smith. Talking beasts.
Hen and the Chinese mountain turtle. Davis and Chow-Leung. Chinese fables and folk stories.
Wiggin and Smith. Talking beasts.
Hen and the falcon. Bidpai. Tortoise and the geese.
Hen and the fox. Æsop. Fables (Black ed.).
Æsop. Fables (Burt ed.).
Wiggin and Smith. Talking beasts.
Hen and the lark. *Burchill. Progressive road to reading. Book 1.
Hen and the squirrel. Elson and Runkel. Elson readers. Book 1.
Hen and the swallow. Æsop. Fables (Black ed.).
Æsop. Fables (Burt ed.).
Æsop. Fables (Stickney).
Hen that hatched ducks. Whittier. Child life in prose.
Hen that ran away. Messer. Next time stories.
Hen, the cat and the bird. Davis and Chow-Leung. Chinese fables and folk stories.
Hen who went to Dovrefjeld to save the world. *See* Chicken-Little.
Hen who went to High Dover. *Elson and Runkel. Elson readers. Book 1.
See also Chicken-Little.
Henny Penny. *See* Chicken-Little.
Henny-Penny, Buddhist. *See* Timid hare.
Hens and the eagles. Success library. v. 3.
Hepatica, Story of. Seton. Woodland tales. (Blue-eyes, the snow child.)
Her majesty's servants. Kipling. Jungle book.
Heracles. *See* Hercules and his labors.
Herald of the beast. Sologub. Sweet-scented name.
Herb shop. Keyes. Five senses.

Herbs that heal. *See* How the Indians came to know medicine.

Hercules and Deianeira. *Bailey. Wonder stories. (Horn of plenty.)

Baldwin. Story of the golden age.

Guerber. Myths of Greece and Rome.

Olcott. Good stories for great holidays. (Horn of plenty.)

Hercules and his labors. Adams. Myths of old Greece. (Hercules.)

Almost true tales. (Three golden apples.)

Arnold and Gilbert. Stepping stones to literature. v. 5. (Pygmies.)

Bailey. Stories children need. (Three golden apples.)

*Bailey. Wonder stories. (Hero with a fairy godmother; Pygmies.)

Baker and Carpenter. Language readers. 5th year. (Hercules and the golden apples.)

Baldwin. Hero tales told in school. (Choice of Hercules.)

Baldwin. Story of the golden age. (How a great hero met his master.)

*Burchill. Progressive road to reading. Book 3.

Burt and Ragozin. Herakles and other heroes.

Church. Greek story and song. (Deeds and death of Hercules.)

Cole. Heroes of the olden time.

Francillon. Gods and heroes. (Hero of heroes.)

Guerber. Myths of Greece and Rome. (Hercules.)

Haaren and Poland. Famous men of Greece.

Hawthorne. Tanglewood tales. (Pygmies.)

Hawthorne. Wonder book. (Three golden apples.)

Hyde. Favorite Greek myths. (Hercules.)

Kingsley. Heroes (Everyman's ed.).

Kupfer. Stories of long ago. (Mighty hero of olden times; Story of a poisoned shirt.)

Lang. All sorts of stories book. (Heracles the dragon-killer.)

Mabie. Heroes every child should know. (Hercules.)

Mabie. Myths every child should know. (Three golden apples.)

My Bookhouse. v. 4. (Labors of Hercules.)

Olcott. Wonder garden.

Patten. Junior classics. v. 2. (Twelve labors of Hercules; Hercules' search for the apples of Hesperides.)

Pratt. Myths of Old Greece. v. 3. (Hercules.)

Scudder. Childrens' book. (Choice of Hercules.)

Shaw. Stories of the ancient Greeks. (What a strong man did.)

Skinner. Topaz story book. (Three golden apples.)

Stories of classic myths. (Diomed's man-eating mares. *In* Some mythological horses.)

Stories of classic myths. (Labors of Hercules.)

Hercules and his labors—*continued.*
Storr. Half a hundred hero tales. (Hercules and the golden apples; Hercules and Nessus.)
Tales for bedtime. (Pygmies.)
Tappan. Myths from many lands. (Pygmies.)
Hercules and Juno. Success Library. v. 3. (Hercules.)
Hercules and Pallas. Æsop. Fables (Burt ed.).
Hercules and Plutus. Æsop. Fables (Burt ed.).
Hercules and the carter. *See* Hercules and the wagoner.
Hercules and the wagoner. Æsop. Fables (Black ed. Hercules and the carter.)
Æsop. Fables (Burt ed.).
Æsop. Fables (Jacobs).
Æsop. Fables (Stickney).
Arnold and Gilbert. Stepping stones to literature. v. 3. (Hercules and the lazy man.)
Coussens. Child's book of stories.
Norton. Heart of oak books. v. 2.
Patten. Junior classics. v. 1.
Scudder. Children's book.
Wiggin and Smith. Talking beasts.
Wiltse. Kindergarten stories.
Hercules' choice. Baldwin. Story of the golden age. (*In* King of cattle thieves.)
Cabot. Ethics for children. (Choice of Hercules.)
Olcott. Good stories for great holidays. (Choice of Hercules.)
See also Hercules and his labors.
Herd boy. Jerrold. Reign of King Oberon.
Thorpe. Yule-tide stories.
Wiggin and Smith. Magic casements.
Herd boy and the giant. Thorpe. Yule-tide stories.
Herd boy and the weaving maiden. Martens. Chinese fairy book.
See also Sky-bridge of birds.
Hereafterthis. Forty famous fairy tales.
Jacobs. More English fairy tales.
Wiggin and Smith. Tales of laughter.
Hermes and Apollo. *Bailey. Wonder stories. (How Mercury gave up his tricks.)
*Beckwith. In mythland. v. 3. (Boy who loved fun.)
Cooke. Nature myths and stories. (Hermes.)
Firth. Stories of old Greece.
Guerber. Myths of Greece and Rome. (*In* Mercury.)
Hartley. Stories from the Greek legends. (Story of how Apollo received his lyre; or, Hermes, the prince of thieves.)
Hyde. Favorite Greek myths. (How Apollo got his lyre.)
Judd. Classic myths. (Little wind-god.)
Pratt. Myths of old Greece. v. 1. (Hermes.)
Wilson. Nature study reader. (Apollo's cows.)

Hermes and Apollo—*continued.*
Young and Field. Literary readers. Book 2. (Wind and the clouds.)
Hermit. Jokai. Golden fairy book.
Wiggin and Smith. Tales of wonder.
Hermit and the bear. Æsop. Fables (Burt ed.).
Hermit and the elf-boy. *See* Boy who found the spring.
Hermit gnome. Brown. Kisington town.
Hermit philosopher. Wardrop. Georgian folk tales.
Hermit sisters. Guerber. Legends of the Rhine.
Hermit, the thief and the demon. Wiggin and Smith. Talking beasts.
Hermit thrush. Donaldson. Moons of long ago.
Hermits of the desert. Noyes. Saints of Italy.
Hermod and Hadvor. Hall. Icelandic fairy tales.
Lang. Yellow fairy book.
Hermod's journey to the underworld. *See* Baldur and the mistletoe.
Hero and Leander. Buckley. Children of the dawn.
Carpenter. Long ago in Greece.
Guerber. Myths of Greece and Rome. (*In* Venus.)
Storr. Half a hundred hero tales.
Hero Makóma. Lang. Orange fairy book. (Story of the Hero Makóma).
Lang. Satin surgeon. (Story of the Hero Makóma.)
Hero of heroes. *See* Hercules and his labors.
Hero twins. I. Finger. Tales from silver lands.
Hero twins. II. Lummis. Pueblo Indian folk tales.
Hero with a fairy godmother. *See* Hercules and his labors.
Heron legs. Bouvé. Lamp-light tales.
Hero's mother. *See* Sohrab and Rustem.
Herr Korbes. Grimm. Household stories (Crane tr. Mr. Korbes.)
Grimm. Household tales (Burt ed. Troublesome visitors.)
See also Chanticleer and Partlett; Cock and the hen in the nut wood; Ito and his friends; Vagabonds.
Herr Lazarus and the Draken. Lang. Grey fairy book.
Lang. Marvellous musician.
Herr Oster Hase. See Easter rabbit. I.
Hesione. Baldwin. Hero tales told in school.
Guerber. Myths of Greece and Rome. (*In* Neptune.)
"Heyo, house." Coe. Second book of stories.
Harris. Uncle Remus and his friends.
(poem). Harris. Uncle Remus and the little boy. (Hello, house.)
See also Jackal and the crocodile; Little jackal and the alligator; Speaking cave.
Hiawatha (poem). Blaisdell Child life. Fourth reader. (Hiawatha's childhood.)
Judd. Wigwam stories. (Hiawatha the wise: how he united the Five Nations.)

Hiawatha—*continued.*
Mabie. Legends every child should know. (Wigwam legend of Hiawatha.)
Pratt. Legends of the red children.
Wade. Indian fairy tales.
Hickory Horn-devil. Seton. Woodland tales.
Hidden servants (poem). Alexander. Hidden servants.
Bryant. Stories to tell to children.
Hidden treasure. *See* Gold in the orchard.
Hidden waters. Cornyn. When the camp fire burns. (Magic waters.)
Donaldson. Moons of long ago. (Legend of the painted leaves.)
Macmillan. Canadian fairy tales. (Song Bird and the healing waters.)
Nixon-Roulet. Indian folk tales. (Chief of the healing waters.)
Olcott, Red Indian fairy book.
Hideous lady. *See* Sir Gawain's marriage.
Hiding of the church bell. Johnson. Oak-tree fairy book.
Higgledy-piggledy palace. Landa. Aunt Naomi's Jewish fairy tales and legends.
High cross. Guerber. Legends of the Rhine.
Hill Mother. Pyle. Prose and verse for children.
Hill-nanny and her kids. Bailey. In the animal world.
See also Wolf and the seven little kids.
Hill of the fairy calf. Winnington. Outlook fairy book.
Hillman and the housewife. Ewing. Old-fashioned fairy tales.
Graves. Irish fairy book.
Hodgkins. Atlantic treasury of childhood stories.
Olcott. Good stories for great holidays.
Skinner. Merry tales.
Hina, the woman in the moon. Colum. At the gateways of the day.
Hind in the forest. Aulnoy. Fairy tales. (Hind in the wood.)
Coussens. Child's book of stories. (Enchanted hind.)
Lang. Orange fairy book. (White doe.)
Lang. White doe and other stories. (White doe.)
Mulock. Fairy book. (Hind of the forest.)
Perkins. Twenty best fairy tales. (Hind of the forest.)
Singleton. Wild flower fairy book. (Hind in the wood.)
Valentine. Old, old fairy tales. (Warne ed. Enchanted hind.)
Wiggin and Smith. Magic casements. (Story of the hind in the forest.)
Hind in the wood. *See* Hind in the forest.
Hind of the forest. *See* Hind in the forest.
Hindu Sykes and the quails. See Quails.
Hinemoa's bath. James. Magic jaw bone.
Hinzelmann. Gibbon. Reign of King Cole.

Hippogriff and the dragon. Brown. One-footed fairy.
Hiram Dorky's berg. Henderson. Sea yarns for boys.
Hiram, King of Tyre. Landa. Aunt Naomi's Jewish fairy tales and legends. (Paradise in the sea.)
Hired lad. Macleod. Book of ballad stories.
Hireman Chiel. Tappan. Old ballads in prose.
History of, etc. *See* the first important word of the title.
Hobyahs. Bailey. Firelight stories.
Bailey. Once upon a time animal stories.
Coe. Second book of stories for the story-teller.
Jacobs. More English fairy tales.
Johnson. Oak-tree fairy book.
Hodge and the raven (poem). Æsop. Fables (Burt ed.).
Hofus the stone cutter. *See* Stone cutter.
Hok Lee and the dwarfs. Lang. Green fairy book.
Lang. Forty thieves and other stories.
Patten. Junior classics. v. I.
Hokey Pokey. Richards. Joyous story of Toto.
Holger Danske. Andersen. Fairy tales (Lucas tr.).
Andersen. Fairy tales (Paull tr.).
Andersen. Stories and tales (Author's ed.).
Scudder. Children's book.
Holger the Dane. *See* Holger Danske.
Holly, Legend of. Skinner. Pearl story book.
Holy Grail. Baldwin. Stories of the king. (Beginning of the great quest; Adventures of Percival; End of the great quest.)
Clay. Stories of King Arthur and the Round Table.
Church. Heroes of chivalry and romance. (Adventures of the Holy Grail; How Sir Galahad found the Holy Grail.)
Cutler. Stories of King Arthur and his knights.
Greene. King Arthur and his court.
Guerber. Legends of the middle ages. (Titurel and the Holy Grail.)
Lang. Book of romance. (Quest of the Holy Grail.)
Lang. Tales of the Round Table. (Quest of the Holy Grail.)
Mabie. Heroes every child should know. (Sir Galahad.)
Patten. Junior classics. v. 4. (How Sir Launcelot saw the Holy Grail; End of the quest.)
Storytellers' magazine. May 1914, p. 563. (Quest of the Holy Grail.)
Storytellers' magazine. June 1914, p. 597. (Achieving of the quest.)
Tappan. Stories of legendary heroes. (Institution of the quest of the Holy Grail.)
See also King Arthur; Knights of the Holy Grail; Lohengrin; Round Table, Founding of; Sir Galahad; Sir Percival.
Holy Night. I. *See* Shepherd's gift.
Holy Night. II. Woman's Home Companion. December 1915. (Christmas story.)

Home. Richards. Golden windows.
Home fairy. Macé Home fairy tales.
Home of the rat. Stafford. Animal fables.
Honeim's magic shoes. Aunt Naomi. Jewish fairy tales.
Honest big-ears. Lummis. Pueblo Indian folk stories.
Honest farmer. Cabot. Ethics for children.
Coe. Second book of stories.
Sly World stories retold. (German patriot and the barley fields.)
Storytellers' magazine. Jan. 1917, p. 19. (Noble old farmer.)
Honest penny. Asbjörnsen. Tales of the fjeld.
Dasent. Norse fairy tales.
Storytellers' magazine. April, 1914, p. 505.
Stroebe and Martens. Norwegian fairy book. (Four shilling piece.)
See also Dick Whittington and his cat.
Honest woodcutter. *See* Honest woodman.
Honest woodman. Æsop. Fables (Black ed. Mercury and the woodman.)
Æsop. Fables (Burt ed. Mercury and the woodman.)
Æsop. Fables (Stickney. Mercury and the woodman.)
Arnold and Gilbert. Stepping stones to literature. v. 3.
Boston collection of kindergarten stories.
Cowles. Art of story-telling.
(play). Doheny. Play awhile.
(play). Lansing. Quaint old stories. (Woodcutter and the fairy.)
My Bookhouse, v. 2.
Noyes. Twilight tales. (Woodchopper.)
Poulsson. In the child's world.
(poem). Wiggin and Smith. Talking beasts. (Woodman and Mercury.)
*Young and Field. Literary readers. Book 2. (Honest woodcutter.)
Honesty is the best policy. Thorpe. Yule-tide stories.
Hong Kil Tong; or, The adventures of an abused boy. Allen. Korean tales.
Honor, prudence, and pleasure. Æsop. Fables (Burt ed.).
Hood of roses. *See* Benevolent frog.
Hoodie-crow. Lang. Lilac fairy book.
Lang. White doe.
Hookedy-Crookedy. MacManus. Donegal fairy stories.
Wiggin and Smith. Tales of wonder.
Hop-about Man. O'Grady and Throop. Teachers' story teller's book.
Hop-o'-my-Thumb. I. Aunt Louisa's book of fairy tales.
Bates. Once upon a time.
Chaplin. Treasury of fairy tales.
Chisholm. In fairyland.
Coe. First book of stories.

Hop-o'-my-Thumb—*continued.*
Coussens. Child's book of stories. (Little Thumb.)
Cruikshank. Criukshank fairy book.
Douglas. Favourite French fairy tales. (Little Thumbling.)
Dyer. What-happened-then stories.
Dyer and Brady. Merrill readers. 3d reader.
Favorite fairy tales.
Jerrold. Big book of fairy tales.
Johnson. Oak-tree fairy book.
*Klingensmith. Just stories.
Lang Blue fairy book. (Little Thumb.)
Lang. Cinderella and other fairy tales. (Little Thumb.)
Lansing. Fairy tales. v. 1.
Marshall. Fairy tales of all nations. (Tom Thumb.
Mullock. Fairy book.
Nursery tales.
Patten. Junior classics. v. 1.
Perkins. Twenty best fairy tales.
Perrault. Fairy tales. (Little Thumbling.)
Perrault. Old-time stories. (Little Tom Thumb.)
Perrault. Tales of Mother Goose. (Little Thumb.)
Perrault. Tales of passed times. (Little Thumb.)
Scudder. Children's book.
Singleton. Goldenrod fairy book.
Tappan. Folk stories and fables.
Tweed. Fairy tales everyone should know.
Valentine. Old, old fairy tales (Warne ed.).
Washburn. Old-fashioned fairy tales.
Welsh. Fairy tales children love. (Little Thumb.)
Hop-o'-my-Thumb. II. Bosschère. Christmas tales of Flanders.
See also Tom Thumb.
Horaizan. James. Green willow.
See also Man who did not wish to die.
Horatii and Curiatii. Guerber. Story of the Romans. (Fight between the Horatii and the Curiatii.)
Haaren. Famous men of Rome.
Laing. Seven kings of the seven hills. (*In* Tullus Hostilius.)
Patten. Junior classics. v. 3. (Story of Alba.)
Horatius at the bridge. Baldwin. Fifty famous stories.
Guerber. Story of the Romans. (Defense of the bridge.)
Haaren. Famous men of Rome. (Horatius.)
Johonnot. Stories of the olden time. (Tarquin the wicked.)
Sly. World stories retold.
Horn-book. Andersen. Stories and tales (Author's ed.).
Horn of plenty. *See* Hercules and Deianeira.
Horned women. Graves. Irish fairy book.
Jacobs. Celtic fairy tales.
Yeats. Irish fairy tales.

Hornets and the bees (poem). Wiggin and Smith. Talking beasts.
See also Wax house.
Horse and foal. Gregory. Kiltartan wonder book.
Horse and his rider. Æsop. Fables (Stickney).
Horse and the ass. Æsop. Fables (Black ed.).
Æsop. Fables (Burt ed.).
Æsop. Fables (Jacobs).
Æsop. Fables (Stickney. War horse and ass.)
Horse and the groom. Æsop. Fables (Burt ed.).
Horse and the hen. Messer. Next night stories.
Horse and the hog. Æsop. Fables (Burt ed.).
Horse and the laden ass. *See* Horse and the loaded ass.
Horse and the lion. Æsop. Fables (Black ed.).
Æsop. Fables (Burt ed.).
Horse and the loaded ass. Æsop. Fables (Black ed.).
Æsop. Fables (Burt ed. Horse and the laden ass.)
Horse and the olive. *See* Athens.
Horse and the stag. Æsop. Fables (Black ed.).
Æsop. Fables (Burt ed.).
Æsop. Fables (Jacobs. Horse, the hunter and the stag.)
Bryce. Fables from afar.
Horse-devil and the witch. Kunos. Forty-four Turkish fairy tales. (Horse-dew and the witch.)
Kunos. Turkish fairy tales.
Horse-dew and the witch. *See* Horse-devil and the witch.
Horse Gullfaxi and the sword Gunnfjoder. Lang. Crimson fairy book.
Lang. Marvellous musician.
Horse of wood. *See* Wooden horse. I.
Horse Shoe Falls. *See* Bended rocks.
Horse that b'leeved he'd get there. Slosson. Story-tell Lib.
Horse that brought the spring. Bailey. In the animal world.
Horse that held out to the end. Shedlock. Eastern stories and legends.
Horse, the hunter and the stag. *See* Horse and the stag.
Horse who hung up his shoe. Bailey. Friendly tales.
Horse who kept school. *See* Chiron.
Horse who rode through fire. Bailey. In the animal world.
See also Nibelungenlied; Ring: Siegfried; Sigurd the Volsung.
Horse with wings. *See* Pegasus.
Horseman and the shoemaker. Noyes. Twilight stories.
Horseshoe nails. *See* Nail. II.
Horseshoe of Luck. St. Nicholas. April 1897, p. 514.
Horseshoes on the church door. Thorpe. Yule-tide stories.
Horus. *See* Isis and Osiris, Story of.
Hospitality. Richards. Silver crown.
Hostile brothers. Guerber. Legends of the Rhine.
Hot porridge. *See* Journey of the porridge pot.
Hottentot moon story. *See* Moon's message.

Hounds in couples. Æsop. Fables (Burt ed.).
House in the garden wall. Bailey. Stories for Sunday telling.
House in the lake. Leamy. Golden spears.
House in the wood. Bailey and Lewis. For the children's hour.
Baldwin. Fairy reader. (Little house in the woods.)
(play). Doheny. Play awhile.
Dyer and Brady. Merrill reader. 3d reader. (House in the forest.)
*Elson and Runkel. Elson readers. Book 2. (House in the woods. Adapted.)
Grimm. Fairy tales (Paull tr.).
Grimm. Fairy tales (Wiltse). v. 1.
Lang. Pink fairy book.
Lang. Snow-queen and other stories.
Wiggin and Smith. Fairy ring.
House Island. Mulock. Fairy book.
House mouse and the field mouse. *See* Country mouse and the town mouse.
House of beautiful days. Stocking. City that never was reached.
House of love. Richards. Golden windows.
House on the hill. *See* Ram and the pig.
House that Jack built. Bailey and Lewis. For the children's hour.
Burchill. Progressive road to reading. Book 1.
Coussens. Child's book of stories.
Gibbon. Reign of King Cole.
Grover. Folk-lore readers. v. 1.
Jerrold. Big book of nursery rhymes.
Lansing. Rhymes and stories.
Mother Goose rhymes, jingles and fairy tales (Altemus ed.).
Norton. Heart of oak books. v. 1.
O'Shea. Six nursery classics.
Welsh. Stories children love. (Story of the house that Jack built.)
Wiltse. Folklore stories and proverbs.
House that needed friends. Bailey. Friendly tales.
House that went downhill. Bailey. Friendly tales.
House that woke up. Dyer and Brady. Merrill readers. 2d reader.
Housekeeper. Richards. Silver crown.
How a bad king became a good one. Æsop. Fables (Burt ed.).
See also Tyrant who became a just ruler.
How a bird turned the world upside down. Powers. Around an Iroquois story fire.
How a boy became first a lamb and then an apple. Lang. All sorts of stories book.
How a boy loved a stag. *See* Cypress tree.
How a boy prince took arms. *See* Cuhulain.

How a crab learned the rights of others. Powers. Around an Iroquois story fire.
How a fish swam in the air and a hare in the water. Fillmore. Mighty Mikko. (Susan Walker, what a talker.)
Lang. Snow-queen and other stories.
Lang. Violet fairy book.
Polevoi. Russian fairy tales. (Woman accuser.)
How a giant built a fortress for the Asas. *See* Giant builder.
How a giant made a mountain. *See* Wrekin.
How a golden apple caused a war. *See* Paris: Apple of discord.
How a great hero met his master. *See* Hercules and his labors.
How a huntress became a bear. *See* Callisto and Arcis.
How a king was found. Van Sickle and Seegmiller. Riverside readers. 4th reader.
How a little boy got a new shirt. Poulsson. In the child's world.
How a little Indian boy first made maple sugar. *See* How maple sugar came. III.
How a mother's pride was humbled. *See* Niobe.
How a prince learned to read. *See* King Alfred.
How a soldier punished the devils. Wenig. Beyond the giant mountains.
See also Knapsack.
How a song changed the world. Powers. Around an Iroquois story fire.
How a troll made a lake. Farmer. Nature myths.
How a turtle outwitted a wolf. Powers. Around an Iroquois story fire.
See also Hare and the hedgehog; Race between a reindeer and a tom-cod; Race of the tails.
How a wicked city was destroyed. *See* Baucis and Philemon.
How a wooden horse won a war. *See* Wooden horse. I.
How a young man served in hell. Wenig. Beyond the giant mountains.
See also Devil's little brother-in-law.
How Ableegumooch retaliated upon the otter. Partridge. Glooscap the great chief.
How Ableegumooch was punished for his laziness. *See* How Master Rabbit went fishing.
How Alexander the king got the water of life. Tyler. Twenty-four unusual stories.
How All-Father Odin became wise. *See* Odin's search for wisdom.
How all things began. *See* Creation of the world (Norse).
How an elf set up housekeeping. Fairy stories retold from St. Nicholas.

How an Indian found his game. Powers. Around an Iroquois story fire.
See also Lost camel.
How an old man lost his wen. *See* Man with the wen.
How an old woman cheated the devil. Wenig. Beyond the giant mountains.
How Arthur was made king. *See* King Arthur's coming.
How Arthur won his sword, his bride and his round table. *See* King Arthur's sword.
How Arthur won his kingdom. *See* King Arthur's coming.
How Ball-Carrier finished his task. Lang. Aladdin and other stories.
Lang. Brown fairy book.
How Beaver stole fire. Judson. Myths and legends of the Pacific Northwest.
See also How fire was brought to the Indians. II.
How Beowulf delivered Heorot. My Bookhouse. v. 5.
How Billy Black turned white. Storytellers' magazine. Nov. 1917, p. 472.
How birds and fairies came to be. *See* How the fairies came.
How Boots befooled the king. Pyle. Wonder clock.
How brave Walter hunted wolves. Lang. Lilac fairy book.
How Brer Coon lost his shoes. Young. Behind the dark pines.
How Brer Flea outwits Brer Rabbit. Young. Behind the dark pines.
How Brer Possum lost his own shoes. Young. Behind the dark pines.
How Brer Rabbit met Brer Tar-Baby. *See* Tar-baby. I.
How Brer Rabbit raises the dust (poem). Harris. Uncle Remus and the little boy.
How Brer Rabbit rid our woods of the elephants. Young. Behind the dark pines.
How Brer Rabbit saved Brer B'ar's life. Harper. Story-hour favorites.
Harris. Uncle Remus and the little boy.
How Brer Tarrypin learned to fly (poem). Harris. Tar-baby and other rhymes.
How Brother Bear's hair was combed. Harris. Little Mr. Thimblefinger.
How Brother Fox failed to get his grapes. Harris. Nights with Uncle Remus.
Tappan. Folk stories and fables.
How Brother Fox was too smart. I. Harris. Nights with Uncle Remus.
How Brother Fox was too smart. II. Harris. Nights with Uncle Remus.
How Brother Rabbit brought family trouble on Brother Fox. Harris. Uncle Remus returns.

How Brother Rabbit fooled the whale and the elephant. *See* How the elephant and the whale were tricked. I.
How Brother Rabbit frightened his neighbors. Harris. Nights with Uncle Remus.
Olcott and Pendleton. Jolly book.
How Brother Rabbit got the meat. Harris. Nights with Uncle Remus.
How Bruin fared with Reynard the fox. *See* Reynard the fox.
How Bruin tried to bring Reynard to court. Johnson. Book of fairy-tale bears.
How buttercups came. *Elson and Runkel. Elson readers. Book 2.
McFee. Treasury of flower stories. (Pot of gold.)
How butterflies came. Skinner. Emerald story book.
See also Butterflies. I.
How careless Brer B'ar lost the goobers. Young. Behind the dark pines.
How cats came to purr. Bailey. In the animal world.
Carter. Cat stories.
St. Nicholas. Oct. 1902, p. 1094.
How Cedric became a knight. Bailey and Lewis. For the children's hour.
Harrison. In storyland. (How little Cedric became a knight.)
How Chicken-Little went fishing. Bailey. Stories and rhymes for a child.
How Christmas came to Bertie's house. Bakewell. True fairy stories.
How Claus won the princess. *See* Princess who said:—
How clay dishes were first made. Judd. Wigwam stories.
How color came to the world. Chandler. Pan the piper.
How come Br'er Buzzard boards. Young. Plantation bird legends.
How Cormac Mac Art went to faery. Jacobs. More Celtic fairy tales.
How corn and beans came to be. *See* First corn. IX.
How coyote got his cunning. Judson. Myths and legends of the Pacific Northwest.
Judson. Old Crow stories.
How coyote stole fire. I. *See* How fire was brought to the Indians. I.
How coyote stole fire. II. Young. Algonquin Indian tales. (*In* Ch. 9.)
How coyote was killed. Judson. Myths and legends of the Pacific Northwest.
How crows became black. *See* Why the crow is black.
How daisy chains came. Bailey. Friendly tales.
How Dame Margery Twist saw more than was good for her. Pyle. Pepper and salt.
See also Fairy's midwife; Fairy ointment; Fairy nurse.

How Decius Mus saved Rome. Baldwin. Thirty more famous stories.
How did he do it. *See* Goats in the turnip field.
How diseases and cares came to men. *See* Pandora.
How dog stole fire. Judson. Myths and legends of the Pacific Northwest.
See also How fire was brought to the Indians. I.
How Doubledarling's old shoes became lady's slippers. St. Nicholas. March 1887, p. 342.
How Drakestail went to the king. *See* Drakesbill and his friends.
How Drummer the woodpecker came by his red cap. Burgess. Mother West Wind "How" stories.
How Ethne quitted fairyland. Rolleston. High deeds of Finn.
How Fair Maid got the last lick. Young. Behind the dark pines.
How fear came. Kipling. Second jungle book.
How Fin went to the kingdom of the big men. *See* Finn MacCool.
How Finn found Bran. *See* Finn MacCool.
How Finn obtained the tooth of knowledge. *See* Finn MacCool.
How fire came to the earth. I. *See* Prometheus.
How fire came to the earth. II. *See* How fire was brought to the Indians. II.
How fire came to the mountaineers. Roberts. Flying plover.
How fire came to the real people. *See* How fire was brought to the Indians. I.
How fire was brought to the Indians. I. Chandler. In the reign of coyote. (How the animals secured fire.)
Compton. American Indian fairy tales. (*In* Coyote.)
Cooke. Nature myths. (How the spark of fire was saved.)
Harper. Story-hour favorites. (How the animals secured fire.)
Holbrook. Book of nature myths.
Judd. Wigwam stories. (How light, fire and water first came to the world.)
Judson. Myths and legends of the Pacific Northwest. (How coyote stole fire.)
Judson. Old Crow stories. (How fire came to the real people.
Lansing. Dramatic readings. (How the Indians got fire.)
See also Secret of fire; Coyote puts fire in sticks.
How fire was brought to the Indians. II. Holbrook. Book of nature myths. (How the raven helped men.)
Macmillan. Canadian fairy tales. (How Raven brought fire to the Indians.)
Nixon-Roulet. Indian folk tales. (How fire came to the earth.)

How fire was brought to the Indians. III. Olcott. Wonder garden. (Little white rabbit.)

Young. Algonquin Indian tales. (*In* Ch. 8. How Nanahboozhoo stole the fire from the old magician.)

How fire was brought to the Indians. IV. Eastman. Indian legends retold.

How fire was brought to the Indians. V. Farmer. Nature myths. (Gift of fire.)

(play). Field second reader. (Fire bird.)

Olcott. Red Indian fairy book. (Firebird.)

How fire was brought to the Indians. I–V.

For other versions *see* Coyote puts fire in sticks; Coyote steals fire; Firebringer; First fire; Fox and the fireflies; How beaver stole fire; How dog stole fire; Secret of fire; Why the robin has a red breast. IV.

How fire was stolen from heaven. *See* Prometheus.

How flax was given to men. Coe and Christie. Story hour readers. Book 3. (Queen Hulda and the flax.)

Cowles. Art of story-telling. (How the queen of the sky gave gifts to men.)

Farmer. Nature myths. (Little blue flowers.)

Foster and Cummings. Asgard stories. (Gift from Frigga.)

Guerber. Myths of northern lands. (*In* Frigga.)

Holbrook. Book of nature myths.

Patten Junior classics. v. 2. (How the queen of the sky gave to men.)

Skinner. Turquoise story book. (Gift of flax.)

Wickes. Beyond the rainbow bridge (Blue flower.)

Wilmot-Buxton. Stories of Norse heroes. (How the queen of the sky gave gifts to men.)

See also Prince Spin Head and Miss Snow White; Princess with twenty petticoats.

How footbinding started. Pitman. Chinese wonder book.

How Geirald the coward was punished. Lang. Brown fairy book.

Lang. Elf maiden.

How giving evil for evil ends. Powers. Around an Iroquois story fire.

How Gladheart went to court. Brown. One-footed fairy.

How Glooscap conquered his enemies. Partridge. Glooscap the great chief.

See also Glooskap and the whale; Glooskap and the witch maiden.

How Glooscap conquered the great bullfrog. *See* Glooskap and the bullfrog.

How Glooscap defeated the sorcerers. Partridge. Glooscap the great chief.

How Glooscap found the summer. *See* How summer came to the earth. II.

How Glooscap made the birds. *See* How the birds came.

How Glooscap transformed the Indian. *See* Glooskap and the magic gifts.

How Glooscap was conquered by Wasis. *See* Why the baby says "goo."

How gosling learned to swim. *Elson and Runkel. Elson readers. Book 1.

How greed for a trifling thing led a man to lose a great one. Martens. Chinese fairy book.

How Grizzly Bear stole the light. *See* Chipmunk's stripes. II.

How Gushtasp won his way. Wilmot-Buxton. Stories of Persian heroes.

How Hans did as he was told. *See* Prudent Hans.

How Hans Roth saved the town of Solothurn. Froelicher. Swiss stories.

How Hans was promoted. *See* Hans the shepherd boy.

How harm came to Mister Buzzard. Young. Plantation bird legends.

How Hermod made a journey to the underworld. *See* Baldur and the mistletoe.

How Howler the wolf got his name. Burgess. Mother West Wind "how" stories.

How I became an admiral. Henderson. Sea yarns for boys.

How Ian Direach got the blue falcon. Lang. Orange fairy book.
Lang. Satin surgeon.

How Indian corn came into the world. *See* First corn. III.

How Indian summer came. *See* Indian summer.

How Isuro the rabbit tricked Gudu. Lang. Orange fairy book.
Lang. Blue parrot.

How it happens Johnny Chuck sleeps all winter. Burgess. Mother West Wind "how" stories.

How Jack found the giant Riverrath. Fuller. Book of friendly giants.
See also Giant of Band-Beggars' Hall.

How Jack o' lantern frightened the Indians. *See* Jack-o'-lantern and the Indians.

How Jack Rabbit was lost. Storytellers' magazine. April 1917, p. 248.

How Jack went to seek his fortune. *Chisholm and Steedman. Staircase of stories. (Jack seeks his fortune.)
Coussens. Child's book of stories.
*Dyer and Brady. Merrill readers. 2d reader.
Jacobs. English fairy tales.
See also Bremen town musicians; White pet.

How Jack won a wife. *See* Jack the cunning thief.

How Jan Brewer was piskey-laden. Tyler. Twenty-four unusual stories.

How Jason brought home the golden fleece. *See* Argonauts.

How jedge Peacock sowed his wild oats. Young. Plantation bird legends.

How Johnny Cricket saw Santa Claus. Gruelle. Friendly fairies.
How June found Massa Linkum. Cross and Statler. Storytelling.
Patten. Junior classics. v. 7.
How Jupiter granted a wish. *See* Baucis and Philemon.
How Kahukura learned to make nets. Olcott. Book of elves and fairies.
How Kemush created the world. *See* Creation of the world (Indian).
How Kilhugh rode to Arthur's hall. *See* Kilwch and Olwen.
How King Midas lost his ears. *See* Midas. II.
How light, fire and water first came to the world. *See* How fire was brought to the Indians. I.
How Lightfoot the Deer learned to jump. Burgess. Mother West Wind "how" stories.
How little Cedric became a knight. *See* How Cedric became a knight.
How little Han Hsin made princes laugh. Stewart. Tell me a hero story.
How Loki made a wager with the dwarfs. *See* Dwarf's gifts.
How Loki was punished at last. *See* Loki.
How Ma-ui fished up the great island. Colum. At the gateways of the day.
How Ma-ui lifted up the sky. Colum. At the gateways of the day.
How Ma-ui overcome Kuna Loa the long eel. Colum. At the gateways of the day.
How Ma-ui snared the sun. *See* Sun a prisoner. V.
How Ma-ui strove to win immortality for men. At the gateways of the day.
How Ma-ui won a place for himself in the house. Colum. At the gateways of the day.
How Ma-ui won fire for men. *See* Secret of fire. II.
How Mad Buffalo fought the thunder-bird. Compton. American Indian fairy tales.
How Mahomet rode to Jerusalem. Baldwin. Fifty famous rides.
Baldwin. Horse fair. (Al Borak.)
How Manahbozho killed the great white sea lion. Young. Algonquin Indian tales.
How Manahbozho stole fire. *See* How fire was brought to the Indians. III.
How Manawydden caught a thief. *See* Escape of the mouse.
How many beans make five. Campbell. Beyond the border.
How maple sugar came. I. Field third reader.
Olcott. Red Indian fairy book.
Young. Algonquin Indian tales. (How the Indians first learned to make maple sugar.)
How maple sugar came. II. Bailey. Once upon a time animal stories.

How maple sugar came. III. *Dyer and Brady. Merrill readers. 3d reader. (How a little Indian boy first made maple sugar.)

How Master Rabbit went fishing. Bailey. Once upon a time animal stories. (How the rabbit tried to coast.)

Olcott. Red Indian fairy book.

Partridge. Glooscap the great chief. (How Ableegumooch was punished for his laziness.)

See also Blue jay the imitator; I know what I have learned; Rabbit and the woodpecker girls.

How Melampos fed the serpent. *See* Melampus.

How Mercury gave up his tricks. *See* Hermes and Apollo.

How Minerva built a city. *See* Athens.

How Mr. Flying Squirrel almost got wings. Burgess Mother West Wind "how" stories.

How Mr. Rabbit lost his fine bushy tail. Harris. Uncle Remus, his songs and his sayings.

How Mr. Rabbit saved his meat. Harris. Uncle Remus, his songs and his sayings.

How Mr. Rabbit succeeded in raising a dust. Harris. Uncle Remus, his songs and his sayings.

How Mister Rabbit was punished for discontent. Young. Behind the dark pines.

How Mr. Rabbit was too sharp for Mr. Fox. Harris. Uncle Remus, his songs and his sayings.

How Mr. Rooster lost his dinner. Harris. Nights with Uncle Remus.

How Mr. Weasel was made an outcast. Burgess. Mother West Wind "how" stories.

How Mrs. Fox married again. *See* Wedding of Mrs. Fox.

How Mrs. White Hen helped Rose. Spaulding and Bryce. Aldine readers. 2d reader.

How Molo stole the lovely Rose-Red. Martens. Chinese fairy book. (Rose Red.)

How Momek rode the firehorse. Storytellers' magazine. May 1914, p. 551.

How mosquitoes came. I. Cornyn. When the camp fire burns.

Tanner. Legends from the red man's forest.

How mosquitoes came. II. Cowles. Indian nature myths. (How mosquitoes came to be.)

How mosquitoes came. III. Young. Algonquin Indian tales. (*In* Ch. 2)

How mosquitoes came. IV. Farmer. Nature myths. (First mosquitoes.)

How mosquitoes came. V. Powers. Around an Iroquois story fire. (Why we have mosquitoes.)

See also Why the mosquito hates smoke.

How moss roses came. *See* Moss rose, Legend of.

How Narcissus loved his image. *See* Echo and Narcissus.

How Nial won the beautiful princess. Stein. When fairies were friendly.

How nice it would be. Bailey. Stories children need.
How night came. My Bookhouse. v. 3.
How Normandy came by its name. *See* Rollo.
How not to hit an insect. Burlingame. Grateful elephant (Boy and mosquito; Girl and fly.)
See also Gardener and the bear.
How Oberon saved Huon. Lang. Red romance book.
How Olaf brought the brownie back. Skinner. Merry tales.
See also Brownie of Blednock.
How old Craney-Crow lost his head. Harris. Told by Uncle Remus.
How old King Eagle won his white head. Burgess. Mother West Wind "how" stories.
How old man above created the world. Judson. Myths and legends of the Pacific Northwest.
See also Creation of the world (Indian).
How old Mr. Crow lost his double tongue. Burgess. Mother West Wind "how" stories.
How old Mr. Heron learned patience. Burgess. Mother West Wind "how" stories.
How old Mr. Mink taught himself to swim. Burgess. Mother West Wind "how" stories.
How old Mr. Otter learned to slide. Burgess. Mother West Wind "how" stories.
How old Mr. Squirrel became thrifty. Burgess. Mother West Wind "how" stories.
How old Mr. Toad learned to sing. Burgess. Mother West Wind "how" stories.
How old Mr. Tree Toad found out how to climb. Burgess. Mother West Wind "How" stories.
How Oliver fought for France and the faith. *See* Charlemagne.
How one turned his troubles to some account. Pyle. Wonder clock.
How one went out to woo. Dasent. Popular tales from the Norse.
Dasent. Norse fairy tales.
Patten. Junior classics, v. 1.
Storytellers' magazine. Sept. 1917, p. 352.
See also Similar diseases.
How opportunity came. Armfield. Wonder tales.
How pansies came; or, The story of Cheer-heart. Hubbard. Chats with Color-kin.
How pansies came colored. Olcott Wonder garden.
How partridge built the birds' canoes. Olcott, Red Indian fairy book.
How peeping Kate was piskey set. Olcott. Book of elves and fairies.
How Peredur became a knight. *See* Sir Peredur.
How Polly saw the aprons grow. St. Nicholas. Feb. 1888, p. 272.

How Porcupine Killer learned still more about the wonderful fire. Roberts. Flying plover.

How preacher Crow makes a start toward being a vegetarian. Young. Plantation legends.

How Prying Joan was served by the piskies. Hodgkins. Atlantic treasury of childhood stories.

How Psyche reached Mount Olympus. *See* Cupid and Psyche.

How Pulowech avenged the sea maiden. Partridge. Glooscap the great chief.

How Pwyll outwitted Gawl. *See* Badger in the bag.

How Qawneca created the world. *See* Creation of the world (Indian).

How Rabbit deceived Fox. Macmillan. Canadian fairy tales.

How Ralph, the charcoal-burner, entertained King Charles, and afterwards went to court. Tappan. Stories of legendary heroes.

Herbertson. Heroic legends. (Charcoal-burner.)

See also King and the miller of Mansfield; Gudeman of Ballengeich.

How Raven brought the light. *See* Daylight, Origin of. I.

How Raven stole the lake. Judson. Myths and legends of Alaska.

Judson. Old Crow stories. (How Raven stole a lake.)

How Raven taught the Chilkats. Judson. Myths and legends of Alaska.

How Reynard fooled Bruin. Aunt Naomi. Jewish fairy tales and fables.

How Reynard outwitted Bruin. *See* Slip root, catch Reynard's foot.

How Rome was founded. *See* Romulus and Remus.

How roses came. Bailey. Friendly tales.

How Rustem rode to Mazinderan. *See* Sohrab and Rustem.

How sense was distributed. Wiggin and Smith. Talking beasts.

How Sigmund fought his last battle. *See* Sigmund.

How Sigurd slew the dragon. *See* Sigurd the Volsung.

How Sigurd won the hand of Brunhild. *See* Sigurd the Volsung.

How Silver Fox created the world. *See* Creation of the world (Indian).

How Sis Wren lost her prize. Young. Behind the dark pines.

How six friends sought adventure. Jewett. Wonder tales from Tibet.

How six men travelled through the wide world. Coussens. Child's book of stories. (Six comrades.)

*Grimm. Fairy tales. (Wiltse. How six traveled through the world.) v. 2.

Grimm. Household stories (Crane, tr. Six soldiers of fortune.)

How six men traveled through the wide world—*continued.*
Johnson. Birch-tree fairy book. (Six comrades.)
Lang. Invisible prince and other stories.
Lang. Yellow fairy book.
Pyle. Mother's nursery tales. (Six companions.)
See also Booby; Five servants; Six-in-one; Youth who would not tell his dream.

How Skadi chose her husband. Bradish. Old Norse stories. (Skadi.)
Brown. In the days of giants. (Skadi's choice.)
Edmison. Stories from the Norseland.
Foster and Cummings. Asgard stories. (Skadi.)
Guerber. Myths of northern lands. (*In* Niord.)

How Smaland and Schonen came to be. Stroebe and Martens. Swedish fairy book.

How some wild animals became tame ones. Lang. Brown fairy book.
See also Cat that walked by himself.

How Starbright found his laugh. Andrews. Enchanted forest.

How Strongheart won his mate. Powers. Around an Iroquois story fire.

How summer came to the earth. I. Brooks. Stories of the red children. (How summer came.)
Brown. Tales of the red children. (How summer came.)
*Cowles. Indian nature myths. (How the seasons came to be.)
*Elson and Runkel. Elson Readers. Book 2. (Summer maker.)
Holbrook. Book of nature myths.
Judson. Old Crow stories. (Summer birds.)
Pratt. Legends of the red children. (How the summer came.)
Skinner. Turquoise story book. (Summer maker.)
Tanner. Legends from the red man's forest. (Summer maker.)
Wilson. Myths of the red children. (Fisher who let out summer.)
Wilson. Nature study reader. (How summer came upon earth.)
See also Summer.

How summer came to the earth. II. Cornyn. When the camp fire burns. (When Glooskap smokes his pipe.)
Farmer. Nature myths. (Summer.)
Hodgkins. Atlantic treasury of childhood stories. (How Glooskap found the summer.)
Leland. Algonquin legends. (How Glooskap found the summer.)
Olcott. Red Indian fairy book. (Summer fairies.)
Partridge. Glooscap the great chief. (How Glooscap found the summer.

How summer came to the earth. II.—*continued.*
Skinner. Turquoise story book. (How summer conquered winter.)
Wilson. Myths of the red children. (Glooskap and the winter giant.)
How summer came to the earth. III. Olcott. Wonder garden. (Old Man Coyote and summer in a bag.)
How summer came upon earth. *See* How summer came to the earth. I.
How summer conquered winter. *See* How summer came to the earth. II.
How sun became so bright. Judson. Old Crow stories.
How sun was made. Judson. Old Crow stories.
How Tatters helped. Bailey. Friendly tales.
How the alphabet was made. Kipling. Just so stories.
How the andirons took a walk (poem). Aspinwall. Short stories for short people.
How the animal-men became real men. *See* Creation of man (Indian).
How the animals got their colors. Chandler. In the reign of coyote.
How the animals secured fire. *See* How fire was brought to the Indians. I.
How the animals secured salmon. Chandler. In the reign of coyote.
Compton. American Indian fairy tales. (Coyote; or, Prairie wolf.)
Judson. Myths and legends of the Pacific Northwest. (Coyote and the salmon.)
How the antelope was caught. Shedlock. Eastern stories and legends.
How the apple-blossoms came back. Bailey and Lewis. For the children's hour.
How the Aristocrats sailed away. Stockton. Floating prince.
How the arrow became winged. Powers. Around an Iroquois story fire.
How the ass became a man again. Lang. Red romance book.
Tyler. Twenty-four unusual stories.
How the badger made Mrs. Bear blind. *See* Lox the mischief maker.
How the badger made the magical fire. Partridge. Glooscap the great chief.
How the bean got its black seam. *See* Straw, the coal, and the bean.
How the bear family got its name. *See* Mooin the bear's child.
How the bear lost his tail. *See* Why the bear has a short tail.

How the bear nursed the little alligator. Harris. Nights with Uncle Remus.

How the bees got their stings. Young. Algonquin Indian tales. (*In* Ch. 3.)

How the beggar boy turned into Count Piro. Lang. Crimson fairy book.

Lang. Little Wildrose.

See also Puss in boots.

How the birds came. Bryce. That's why stories. (First birds.)

Cowles. Indian nature myths. (Beginning of birds.)

Klingensmith. Just stories. (Indian legend.)

Macmillan. Canadian fairy tales. (How Glooskap made the birds.)

Skinner. Emerald story book.

How the birds came to have feathers. Tanner. Legends from the red man's forest.

How the birds got their colors. I. Judson. Old Crow and his friends. (That new idea.)

How the birds got their colors. II. Donaldson. Little papoose listens. (Mountain with summer in its heart.)

How the birds learned to build nests. *See* Magpie's nest. I.

How the birds learned to make their nests. *See* Magpie's nest. I.

How the birds saved the Emperor's life. *See* Nightingale. III.

How the bittern boomed. Armfields' animal book.

How the bloodroot came. Seton. Woodland tales. (Story of the white Dawnsinger.)

How the blossoms came to the heather. Holbrook. Book of nature myths.

How the bluebird came. Seton. Woodland tales.

Seton. Woodmyth and fable. (Origin of the bluebird.)

How the bluebird got its color. Donaldson. Moons of long ago. (Bluebird.)

Grinnell. Birds of song and story.

See also Bluebird and coyote; When Mr. Bluebird won his beautiful coat.

How the bluebird was chosen herald. Skinner. Emerald story book.

Stocking. City that never was reached.

How the Brazilian beetles got their coats. My Bookhouse v. 2.

How the bugs overcame the worms. Powers. Around an Iroquois story fire.

How the buttercup grew yellow. Walker. Sandman's goodnight stories.

How the camel got his hump. Kipling. Just so stories.

How the camel unbent. Armfields' animal book.

How the cardinal grosbeak got its red bill. Grinnell. Birds of song and story.

How the carpenter lost his hump. *See* Knockgrafton, Legend of.

How the cat became head forester. *See* Fox and the cat. IV.

How the cat got all the grain. Keyes. Stories and story-telling.

See also Little red hen. I.

How the cat kept Christmas. Coolidge. New Year's bargain.

How the cat outwitted the fox. *See* Cat, the cock and the fox.

How the chestnut burrs became. Skinner. Topaz story book.

Seton. Woodmyth and fable.

Seton. Woodland tales.

How the child of the sea was made knight. *See* Amadis of Gaul.

How the chipmunk got its stripes. *See* Chipmunk's stripes. II.

How the chipmunk got the stripes on its back. *See* Chipmunk's stripes. I.

How the cliff was clad. Curry. Little classics.

Gatty. Parables from nature.

Ruskin. King of the Golden River and other stories.

How the copper mountain came to fall. Judd. Wigwam stories.

How the crab got even. *See* Crab and the monkey.

How the crane became a fisherman. Field third reader.

How the crickets brought good fortune. Bailey. Stories children need.

Whittier. Child life.

How the Culloo punished the badger. Partridge. Glooscap the great chief.

How the curse of the gold is fulfilled. *See* Siegfried.

How the Cymry land became inhabited. Griffis. Welsh fairy tales.

How the dancing stars got into the sky. *See* Pleiades. II.

How the daylight came. *See* Daylight, Origin of. III.

How the deer got his horns. *See* Deer and the rabbit.

How the deer lost his gall. *See* Fast runners.

How the devil became afraid of a woman. Wenig. Beyond the giant mountains.

See also Gentle Dora; Katcha and the devil; Katie Gray; Old Nick and Kitty.

How the devil contended with man. Wenig. Beyond the giant mountains.

How the dragon was tricked. Lang. Pink fairy book.

How the dryad learned to sing. Bailey. Friendly tales.

How the duck came to have a flat back. Compton. American Indian fairy tales. (*In* Great wizard.)

Patten. Junior classics v. 1. (Why the diver duck has so few tail feathers.)

How the duck came to have a flat back—*continued.*
Schoolcraft. Indian fairy book. (*In* Manabozho the mischief maker.)
Tanner. Legends from the red man's forest.
Wade. Indian fairy tales. (Manabozho and how the diver got a flat back.)
Young. Algonquin Indian tales. (*In* Ch. 21. Why the loon has a flat back.)
Zitkala-Sa. Old Indian legends. (Iktomi and the ducks.)
See also Great wizard.

How the ducks got their fine feathers. Linderman. Indian why stories.

How the eagle made friends. Armfields' animal book.

How the eagle went hungry. Bailey. Once upon a time animal stories.

How the elephant and the whale were tricked. Bryant. Best stories to tell to children. (How Brother Rabbit fooled the whale and the elephant.)
Bryant. Stories to tell to children. (How Brother Rabbit fooled the whale and the elephant.)
Harper. Story-hour favorites.
Pyle. Fairy tales from many lands.

How the elephant and the whale were tricked. II. Lang. Brown fairy book. (*In* Tale of a tortoise and of a mischievous monkey.)
Patten. Junior classics. v. 2. (Which was the stronger, the tortoise, the tapir, or the whale?)
Stanley. Animal folk tales. (Tortoise and the elephant.)
See also When the lamb was a hero.

How the elephant came. Bailey. In the animal world.

How the ermine got its necklace. Judson. Myths and legends of the Pacific Northwest.

How the Evil One was made. Nixon-Roulet. Indian folk tales.

How the eyes of old Mr. Owl became fixed. Burgess. Mother West Wind "how" stories.

How the fairies came. *Cowles. Indian nature myths. (How birds and fairies came to be.)
Judd. Wigwam stories. (Legend of Mackinaw Island.)
Olcott. Red Indian fairy book.
Schoolcraft. Indian fairy book. (Osseo, the son of the evening star.)

How the fairies were changed into mocking-birds. Harrison. Moon princess.

How the Fenris wolf was chained. *See* Binding of the Fenris wolf.

How the finch got her colors. My Bookhouse. v. 2.

How the fir tree became the Christmas tree. *See* Christmas tree. II.

How the firefly got its light. Storytellers' magazine. April 1914, p. 519.

How the first bears came. *See* Why grizzly bear goes on all fours.
How the first letter was written. Kipling. Just so stories.
How the first mayflower came. Bailey. Once upon a time animal stories.
How the first snowdrop came. *See* First snowdrop. II.
How the fishes got their color. Donaldson. Moons of long ago.
How the five ancients became men. Martens. Chinese fairy book.
How the flamingoes got their stockings. Quiroga. South American jungle tales.
How the flowers came. Skinner. Emerald story book.
How the flying squirrel got his wings. Bailey. Once upon a time animal stories. (How the squirrel got wings.)
*Cowles. Indian nature myths.
Olcott. Red Indian fairy book. (Nuts of Jonisgyout.)
See also Birds' ball game.
How the fox and the crab ran a race. Coussens. Jade story book. (Fox and the crafty crab.)
Davis and Chow-Leung. (Proud fox and the crab.)
Johnson. Book of fairy-tale foxes.
Noyes. Twilight tales. (Crab and the fox.)
Partridge. Story telling in home and school. (Fox and the crab.)
Stanley. Animal folk tales. (Fox and the crab.)
Wiggin and Smith. Talking beasts. (Proud fox and the crab.)
See also Brother Fox and little Mr. Cricket; How the turtle won the race.
How the fox became red. *See* Why fox became red.
How the fox fooled the bear. *See* Bruin and Reynard partners.
How the fox played herdsman. *See* Fox as herdsboy.
How the fox took care of the herds. *See* Fox as herdsboy.
How the four winds were named. Olcott. Red Indian fairy book.
How the giants got the best of Thor. *See* Thor and his journey to Jötunheim.
How the giantess Guimara became small. Eells. Tales of giants from Brazil.
How the giraffe became. Seton. Woodmyth and fable.
How the goldfish got his colors. Bosschère. Folk tales of Flanders.
How the good gifts were used by two. Pyle. Wonder clock.
How the grasshoppers honoured the grass. Armfields' animal book. (How the grasshoppers honoured.)
How the Grosbeak got his rose-colored breast. Grinnell. Birds of song and story.

How the hair of O'Neil's head was made to grow. Grierson. Children's book of Celtic stories.

How the hermit helped to win the king's daughter. Lang. Pink fairy book.

Lang. Snow-queen and other stories.

How the hermit thrush got his song. Meyer. Little green door.

How the heron clan song came. Powers. Around an Iroquois story fire.

How the home was built. My Bookhouse. v. 1.

How the horse looked ahead. Armfields' animal book.

How the horses of the sun ran away. *See* Phaeton.

How the humming bird lost her voice. Young. Behind the dark pines.

How the hunter became a partridge. Olcott. Red Indian. fairy book.

How the hunter destroyed the snow. Brown. Stories of childhood and nature.

How the Indian Pipe came. Seton. Woodland tales.

How the Indians came to know medicine plants. Judd. Wigwam stories.

Tanner. Legends from the red man's forest. (Herbs that heal.)

See also Beloved warrior.

How the Indians got fire. *See* How fire was brought to the Indians. I.

How the Indians got tobacco. Young. Algonquin Indian tales. (*In* Ch. 24.)

How the Indians sought the great chief. *See* Glooskap and the three seekers.

How the jelly-fish lost his shell. *See* Monkey and the jelly-fish. II.

How the Kidsadi clan came to Sitka. Judson. Myths and legends of Alaska.

How the king recruited his army. Harris. Uncle Remus and his friends.

See also Monkey's bargains.

How the kingfisher got his ring and his ruffle. Judd. Wigwam stories.

Skinner. Turquoise story book. (Kingfisher's necklace and ruffle.)

Tanner. Legends from the red man's forest. (White spot of the kingfisher.)

Young. Algonquin Indian tales. (Why the kingfisher wears a white collar.)

See also Manabozho and the lake magicians.

How the knight of the sun rescued his father. Lang. Red romance book.

How the lame man and the blind man helped each other. *See* Blind man and the lame man.

How the lark got the crescent on its breast. Grinnell. Birds in song and story.

How the leopard got his spots. Kipling. Just so stories.
How the little brother set free his big brothers. Lang. Brown fairy book.
Lang. Magician's gifts.
How the little demon earned his stolen crust of bread. Tolstoi. Tales.
Tolstoi. Twenty three tales. (Imp and the crust.)
How the little rabbit snared the sun. *See* Sun a prisoner. II.
How the littlest owl came. Seton. Woodland tales.
Seton. Woodmyth and fable. (Gitche O-kok-o-hoo.)
How the lord of beasts and men strove with the mighty Wasis. *See* Why the baby says "goo."
How the man found his mate. Linderman. Indian why stories.
How the mice got out of trouble. Darton. Wonder book of beasts.
How the minstrel saved the king. *See* Richard Coeur de Leon.
How the monkey saved his troop. Babbitt. More Jataka tales.
How the moon became beautiful. Davis and Chow-Leung. Chinese fables and folk stories.
How the moon princess came to earth. Harrison. Moon princess.
How the moon princess was taken captive by the black dwarf. Harrison. Moon princess.
How the mouse got into his hole. Rouse. Talking thrush and other tales from India.
See also Cat and the mouse; Grain of corn; Little Tuppen; Munachar and Manachar; Nanny who wouldn't go home to supper; Old woman and her pig; Sparrow and the bush.
How the Nautilus left his ship. Bakewell. True fairy stories.
Curry. Little classics.
How the news of the wild wood got abroad. Young. Behind the dark pines.
How the nightingale sang out of tune. Storytellers' magazine May 1916, p. 312.
How the oak leaves came to have notches. Bryce. That's why stories.
See also Forest Witch.
How the oak tree became king. Arnold and Gilbert. Stepping stones to literature. v. 3.
How the Okanogans became red. Judson. Myths and legends of the Pacific Northwest.
How the otter skin became great medicine. Linderman. Indian why stories.
How the patient worm saved the children. *See* Rock of the measuring worm.

How the peacock got his tail. *Dillingham and Emerson. Tell it again stories.

How the peepers came to be. Storytellers' magazine. Feb. 1915, p. 43.

How the pig built a house. *See* Ram and the pig.

How the pigs can see the wind. Bailey. Firelight stories.
Bailey. Once upon a time animal stories.

How the pine tree did some good. Skinner. Pearl story book.

How the pixy kept warm. Bailey. Friendly tales.

How the pony was won. *Coe and Christie. Story hour readers. Book 2.

How the poplar leaves were made. Meyer. Little green door.

How the porcupine got its quills. Donaldson. Little papoose listens.

How the pride of Thor was brought low. *See* Thor and his journey to Jötunheim.

How the princess was beaten in a race. Scudder. Book of legends.
See also Atalanta's race.

How the princess' pride was broken. Pyle. Wonder clock.

How the puffin got his "horns." Allen. Indian fairy tales.

How the quail became a snipe. Holbrook. Book of nature myths.

How the queen of the sky gave gifts to men. *See* How flax was given to men.

How the rabbit tried to coast. *See* How Master Rabbit went fishing.

How the rain comes. Brooks. Stories of the red children.
Pratt. Legends of the red children. (Rain and the snow.)
Tanner. Legends from the red man's forest. (Rain and snow.)

How the Raja's son won the princess Labam. Jacobs. Indian fairy tales (Burt ed.).
Tappan. Folk stories and fables.

How the rattlesnake got its rattle. Young. Algonquin Indian tales. (*In* Ch. 24.)

How the raven helped men. *See* How fire was brought to the Indians. II.

How the ravens were fed. Armfields' animal book.

How the rays defended the ford. Quiroga. South American jungle tales.

How the red clover got the white mark on its leaves. Seton. Woodland tales.

How the rhinoceros got his skin. Kipling. Just so stories.

How the river god's wedding was broken off. Martens. Chinese fairy book.

How the rivers were formed. Judson. Myths and legends of Alaska.

How the robin came. Cooke. Nature myths and stories. (Indian story of the robin.)
Cowles. Art of story-telling. (Opeeche, the robin redbreast.)
Judd. Wigwam stories. (Opeeche, the robin redbreast.)
Kennedy. New world fairy book. (Robin Redbreast.)
Olcott. Good stories for great holidays. (Boy who became a robin.)
Olcott. Red Indian fairy book. (Boy who became a robin.)
Pratt. Legends of the red children. (Legend of the Opeeche.)
Schoolcraft. Indian fairy book. (Origin of the robin.)
Stebbins. Third reader. (Why the robin has a red breast. pt. 1.)
Tanner. Legends from the red man's forest. (Opeeche, the robin redbreast.)
Wilson. Nature study reader. (Robin redbreast.)
How the robin got its red breast. *See* Why the robin has a red breast. I.
How the robin's breast became red. *See* Why the robin has a red breast. I.
How the rooster built a house of his own. Keyes. Stories and story telling.
See also Ram and the pig.
How the rose became queen. Skinner. Turquoise story book.
How the sea became salt. *See* Why the sea is salt. I.
How the seasons came to be. I. *See* How summer came to the earth. I.
How the seasons came to be. II. Judson. Old Crow stories. (Coyote and Grizzly again.)
How the shad came and how the chestnut got its burrs. Seton. Woodland tales.
Seton. Woodmyth and fable. (Fretful porcupine.)
Skinner. Topaz story book. (How the chestnut burrs became.)
How the shoes went to the picnic. Pyle. Prose and verse for children.
How the skunk helped the coyote. Linderman. Indian Old-man stories.
How the spark of fire was saved. *See* How fire was brought to the Indians. I.
How the spring comes. Pratt. Legends of the red children.
How the squirrel got wings. *See* How the flying squirrel got his wings.
How the Stalos were tricked. Lang. Orange fairy book.
How the storks came and went. Bakewell. True fairy stories.
Coolidge. Round dozen.
How the summer came. *See* How summer came to the earth.

How the sun and moon came. *See* Sun, moon and stars. IV.
How the sun prince rescued the moon princess. Harrison. Moon princess.
How the sun princess came to earth. Harrison. Moon princess.
How the sun, the moon and the wind went out to dinner. *See* Why all men love the moon.
How the sun was caught and freed. *See* Sun a prisoner. I.
How the swallows learned the song. Armfields' animal book.
How the Swiss came to use the Alpine horn. Cather. Educating by story telling. (Gift of the gnomes.)
Froelicher. Swiss stories.
Griffis. Swiss fairy tales. (Wonderful Alpine horn.)
Guerber. Legends of Switzerland. (Bern.)
How the terrapin beat the rabbit. Eastman. Indian legends retold.
See also Hare and the hedgehog; How a turtle outwitted a wolf.
How the terrible ones lost their caves. Storytellers' magazine. March 1917, p. 155.
How the three clever men outwitted the demons. Frere. Old Deccan days.
How the tortoise outran the deer. Patten. Junior classics. v. 2.
See also Hare and the hedgehog.
How the tree brothers gave. *See* Gifts the trees gave.
How the turkey got his beard. Eastman. Indian legends retold.
How the turtle got his shell. *See* Turtle's shell.
How the turtle saved his own life. Babbitt. Jataka tales.
Storytellers' magazine. Nov. 1914, p. 739.
How the turtle won the race. Powers. Around an Iroquois story fire.
See also How the fox and the crab ran a race.
How the turtles learned to differ. Armfields' animal book.
How the umbrella ran away with Ellie. Coolidge. Mischief's Thanksgiving.
How the water lily came. *See* Star maiden.
How the waterfall came to the thirsting mountain. My Bookhouse. v. 3.
How the west wind saw itself. Meyer. Little green door.
How the whale got his throat. Kipling. Just so stories.
How the white whales happened. Riggs. Animal stories from Eskimo land.
See also Narwahl, Origin of.
How the wicked sons were duped. Jacobs. Indian fairy tales.
Patten. Junior classics. v. 1.
How the wicked Tanuki was punished. Lang. Crimson fairy book.
Lang. Little Wildrose.

How the wild roses got their thorns. *See* Why roses have thorns. II.
How the winter came. Cornyn. Around the wigwam fire. Skinner. Pearl story book. (First winter.)
How the wolf lost his tail. Douglas. Scottish fairy tales.
How the wolverine's legs were shortened. I. *See* Wolverine and the rock.
How the wolverine's legs were shortened. II. Stanley. Animal folk tales. (Mischievous wolverine.)
How the woodchuck helped Menabozho. Judd. Wigwam stories.
How the world was made. *See* Creation of the world.
How the wren became king of the birds. *See* King Wren.
How the youth Kilwch came to King Arthur's court. *See* Kilwch and Olwen.
How they came to have kite day in China. Cather. Educating by story telling.
How they described a camel they had never seen. *See* Lost camel.
How they got Hairlock home. *See* Nanny who wouldn't go home to supper.
How Thiassi captured Loki. *See* Iduna's apples.
How Thomas Connolly met the banshee. Yeats. Irish fairy tales.
How Thor humbled his pride. *See* Thor: Quest of the hammer.
How Thor went to Jötunheim. *See* Thor and his journey to Jötunheim.
How Thor went to the land of giants. *See* Thor and his journey to Jötunheim.
How Thorkill went to the underworld and Eric the Far-travelled to Paradise. Jacobs. Book of wonder voyages.
How Thor's hammer was lost and found. *See* Thor: Quest of the hammer.
How three heroes came by their deaths because of two peaches. Martens. Chinese fairy book.
How three went out into the wide world. Pyle. Wonder clock.
How Timothy won the princess. *See* Bee, the harp, the mouse and the bum-clock.
How to find out a true friend. Lang. Crimson fairy book. Lang. Snow-queen and other stories.
How to tell a real princess. *See* Princess on the pea.
How to tell a true princess. *See* Princess on the pea.
How to win a prince. Asbjörnsen. Tales from the fjeld.
How "To Wut In" made the rainbow. Allen. Indian fairy tales.
How Toda slew the long serpent. Griffis. Japanese fairy tales.
See also Lord Bag of Rice.
How troubles came into the world. *See* Pandora.

How Tufty the lynx happens to have a stump of a tail. Burgess. Mother West Wind "how" stories.
How Twinkle-Toes went to school. Bailey. Friendly tales.
How two beetles took lodgings. Wiggin and Smith. Tales of laughter.
How two looked at a shower. Ketchum and Jorgensen. Kindergarten gems.
How two squaws saved their band. Judd. Wigwam stories.
How two went into partnership. Pyle. Wonder clock.
How Wattle Weasel was caught. Harris. Nights with Uncle Remus.
How we came to have butterflies. Meyer. Little green door.
How we came to have ferns. Meyer. Little green door.
How we came to have pink roses. Bryant. How to tell stories to children.
How we came to have yellow violets. Meyer. Little green door.
How we first came to have umbrellas. *See* Elf and the dormouse.
How we got the first camel. *See* First camel.
How West Wind helped dandelion. Poulsson. In the child's world.
How Wiley Wolf rode in the bag. Harris. Told by Uncle Remus.
How woman came to earth. Grinnell. Birds in song and story.
How woodpecker changed his colors. *See* Woodpecker gray.
How Wry-Face played a trick on One-Eye, the potato wife. Coe. Second book of stories.
Skinner. Merry tales. (Overturned cart.)
How youth and beauty came to Asgard. *See* Iduna's apples.
Hrungner. *See* Thor: Thor and Hrungnir.
Hu Gadarn. *See* Afang the monster.
Huckleberry. Stockton. Floating prince.
Hudden and Dudden and Donald O'Neary. Forty famous fairy tales.
Frost. Fairies and folk of Ireland. (*In* Ch. 6.)
Jacobs. Celtic fairy tales.
Wiggin and Smith. Tales of laughter.
Yeats. Irish fairy and folk tales.
See also Little Claus and Big Claus.
Huffi, the stone-breaker. *See* Stone-cutter.
Humility rewarded and pride punished. Bradley-Birt. Bengal fairy tales.
See also Mother Holle.
Humming bird. *See* First humming bird.
Humming bird and the flower. Finger. Tales from silver lands.

Humming bird's colors. Donaldson. Moons of long ago. (Bird with the sweet wing song.)
Hunchback. I. Caballero. Spanish fairy tales.
Hunchback. II. *See* Little hunchback.
Hunchback and his two brothers. *See* King's three sons.
Hunchback, the pool, and the siver ring. Baring. Blue rose fairy book.
Hundred-headed daffodil. *See* Proserpina.
Hungry cat and the pigeons. Æsop. Fables (Burt ed.).
Hungry fox. Burchill. Progressive road to reading. Book 1. (Hungry fox; Gray fox.)
Hungry fox and his breakfast. Johnson. Book of fairy-tale foxes.
Hungry gleam. Sologub. Sweet-scented name.
Hungry grandfathers. Lummis. Pueblo Indian folk stories.
Hungry jackal and a hungry alligator. *See* Little jackal and the alligator.
Hungry Mr. Mail Box. Potter. Pinafore pocket story book.
Hungry old witch. Finger. Tales from silver lands.
Hungry rabbit's reward. Allen. Indian fairy tales.
Hunt for the beautiful. Alden. Why the chimes rang.
Hunt in Calydon. *See* Calydonian hunt.
Hunt in the forest. *See* Calydonian hunt.
Hunt in the wood of Calydon. *See* Calydonian hunt.
Hunt in the wood of Puelle. Balwin. Hero tales told in school.
Hunted beaver. Æsop. Fables (Black ed.).
Æsop. Fables (Burt ed.).
Hunted hare. Hartland. English folk and fairy tales.
Hunter. Houghton. Russian grandmother's wonder tales.
Hunter and his hounds. Success library. v. 3.
Hunter and the priest. Nixon-Roulet. Japanese folk stories and fairy tales.
Hunter and the ugly dwarf. Froelicher. Swiss stories.
Hunter and the woodcutter. Scudder. Fables and folk stories.
Hunter, the fox, and the leopard. Bidpai. Tortoise and the geese.
Hunter, the fox, and the tiger. Æsop. Fables (Burt ed.).
Hunter, the snipe and the bivalve. Davis and Chow-Leung. Chinese fables and folk stories.
Hunter who became a deer. Eastman. Indian legends retold.
Hunter who could fly. Eastman. Indian legends retold. (Winged hunter.)
Judd. Wigwam stories.
See also Daedalus.
Hunter who forgot. *See* Miser of Takhoma.
Hunter who trapped the sun. *See* Sun a prisoner. III.
Hunting of the boar. Colum. Island of the mighty.
Hunting of the cheviot. *See* Chevy Chase.

Hunting the Calydonian boar. *See* Calydonian hunt.
Huntsman the unlucky. Patten. Junior classics. v. 1.
Singleton. Goldenrod fairy book.
Huntsman's son. Leamy. Golden spears.
Huon of Bordeaux. Guerber. Legends of the middle ages.
Lang. Red romance book. (Meeting of Huon and Oberon; How Oberon saved Huon.)
Huron Cinderella. Kennedy. New world fairy book.
See also Cinderella.
Hurry-up boy. Bailey. Stories for Sunday telling.
Husband and the parrot. Arabian nights (Dodge ed.).
Arabian nights (Lang. Story of the husband and the parrot.)
Arabian nights (Townsend. History of the husband and the parrot.)
Welsh. Fairy tales children love.
Husband and wife. Stroebe and Martens. Danish fairy book.
Husband of the rat's daughter. *See* Rats and their son-in-law.
Husband who was to mind the house. *See* Man who was going to mind the house.
Husbandman and his sons. *See* Gold in the orchard.
Husbandman and the eagle. Æsop. Fables (Burt ed.).
Husbandman and the stork. *See* Farmer and the stork.
Husbandman that lost his mattock. Æsop. Fables (Burt ed.).
Hut in the forest. Hoxie. Kindergarten story book.
O'Grady and Throop. Teachers' story teller's book.
Hyacinth. *See* Hyacinthus.
Hyacinthus. *Bailey. Wonder stories. (How Hyacinthus became a flower.)
Firth. Stories of old Greece.
Francillon. Gods and heroes. (Hyacinth.)
Hartley. Stories from Greek legends. (Story of Apollo and Hyacinthus; or, The boy who was changed into a flower.)
Hyde. Favorite Greek myths.
Kupfer. Stories of long ago.
McFee. Treasury of flower stories. (Hyacinth.)
Olcott. Good stories for great holidays.
Olcott. Wonder garden. (Hyacinth.)
Wilson. Nature study reader. (Apollo and Hyacinthus.)
Hyena's punishment. Stafford. Animal fables.
Hyena's spots. Stafford. Animal fables.
Hylas. *See* First tree frog.
Hymer. *See* Thor: Thor's fishing.
Hynde Etin. Macleod. Book of ballad stories.
Hynde Horn. Grierson. Children's tales from Scottish ballads.
Hypermnestra. Storr. Half a hundred hero tales.
Hyung Bo and Nahl Bo. *See* Swallow-king's rewards.

I

I and we. *See* Travellers and the axe.
I don't care. Coussens. Child's book of stories.
*Elson and Runkel. Elson readers. Book 1.
Welsh. Stories children love.
I have a right. Ingelow. Stories told to a child. v. 1.
I know what I have learned. Lang. Golden mermaid and other stories.
Lang. Pink fairy book.
Stroebe and Martens. Danish fairy book. (To the devil with the money! I know what I know.)
I-kun-uh kah-tsi. *See* Woman who married a buffalo.
I serve. Storytellers' magazine. Jan. 1916, p. 8.
I wonder. *See* Boots and his brothers.
"I won't." Ewing. Old-fashioned fairy tales.
Iagoo, the great story-teller. Compton. American Indian fairy tales. (Story teller himself.)
Judd. Wigwam stories.
Iain, the fisher's son. Grierson. Children's book of Celtic stories.
Ian, the soldier's son. Lang. Orange fairy book.
Lang. King of the waterfalls.
Ianto's chase. Thomas. Welsh fairy book.
Ib and Christine. *See* Ib and little Christina.
Ib and little Christina. Andersen. Fairy tales (Paull tr.).
Andersen. Stories and tales (Author's ed. Ib and Christine.)
Ibbity. Bailey. Firelight stories.
Bailey. Once upon a time animal stories. (Story of Ibbity.)
See also Bridegroom for Miss Mole; Legend of St. Christopher; Rats and their son-in-law.
Icarus. *See* Dædalus and Icarus.
Ice king. Olcott. Red Indian fairy book. (Snow man.)
Partridge. Glooscap the great chief.
Skinner. Pearl story book.
Washburn. Indian legends.
Ice king and his wonderful grandchild. *See* Steam.
Ice king's bride. *See* Ethelinda.
Ice-maiden. Andersen. Fairy tales (Paull tr.).
Andersen. Stories and tales (Author's ed.).
Ice man puts out the fire. *See* Little ice man.
Ice queen's palace. Harrison. Prince Silverwings.
Ichabod Crane. *See* Sleepy Hollow.
Ida and Mrs. Overtheway. Curry. Little classics.
Idas and Marpessa. Guerber. Myths of Greece and Rome. (*In* Neptune.)
Iddly Bung's April Christmas tree. Wiltse. Kindergarten stories.
Idle maiden. *See* Spinning queen.

Idleness and Industry. *See* Flax, leavings.
Idol and the whale. Griffis. Japanese fairy tales.
Idun. *See* Iduna's apples.
Idun and the magic apples. *See* Iduna's apples.
Iduna's apples. Arnold and Gilbert. Stepping stones to literature. v. 5.
Baldwin. Hero tales told in school. (Idun and her apples.)
Bradish. Old Norse stories. (Iduna.)
Brown. In the days of giants. (Magic apples.)
Bryant. Treasury of hero tales. (Apples of youth.)
*Burchill. Progressive road to reading. Book 3. (Magic apples.)
Edmison. Stories from Norseland. (Idun's apples of youth.)
Foster and Cummings. Asgard stories. (Stealing of Iduna.)
Guerber. Myths of northern lands. (Idun.)
Keary. Heroes of Asgard.
Klingensmith. Old Norse wonder tales. (Apples of Idun.)
Litchfield. Nine worlds. (How Thiassi captured Loki; Thiassi carries off Loki; The gods grow old.)
Mabie. Myths every child should know. (Apples of Idun.)
Mabie. Norse stories. (Apples of Idun.)
My Bookhouse. v. 4. (Stealing of Iduna.)
Olcott. Wonder garden. (Idun and the magic apples.)
Patten. Junior classics. v. 2. (Iduna's apples of youth.)
Pratt. Legends of Norseland. (Apples of life.)
Skinner. Emerald story book. (Spring-maiden and the frost giants.)
Storytellers' magazine. March 1916, p. 131. (Spring maiden and the frost giants.)
Tappan. Myths from many lands.
Wicks. Beyond the rainbow bridge. (How youth and beauty came to Asgard.)
Wilmot-Buxton. Stories of Norse heroes. (Apples of youth.)
If Heaven will it. Caballero. Spanish fairy tales.
Wiggin and Smith. Tales of laughter.
If this should be. Richards. Silver crown.
Iktomi and the coyote. Zitkala-Ša. Old Indian legends.
Iktomi and the ducks. Donaldson. Little papoose listens. (Indian singer.)
Zitkala-Ša. Old Indian legends.
See also Unktomee and his bundle of songs.
Iktomi and the fawn. Zitkala-Sa. Old Indian legends.
See also Paup-Puk-Keewis.
Iktomi and the muskrat. Zitkala-Sa. Old Indian legends.
Iktomi and the turtle. Zitkala-Ša. Old Indian legends.
Iktomi's blanket. Zitkala-Ša. Old Indian legends.
See also Why the night-hawk's wings are beautiful.

Il crocifisso della Providenza (poem). Alexander. Hidden servants.
Ildini. Eastman. Indian legends retold.
Iliya of Murom and the robber nightingale. Steele. Russian garland of fairy tales.
I'll do so another time. *See* Lazy Jack.
Ill-luck and the fiddler. Pyle. Twilight land.
Ill-treating a ghost. Henderson. Sea yarns for boys.
Ilyá Múromets and Soyatogór the knight. Magnus. Russian folk-tales.
Ilyá Múromets and the nightingale robber. Magnus. Russian folk tales.
Image and the treasure. Alderman. Classics old and new. 3d reader.
Scudder. Book of legends.
Imitating animals (poem). Æsop. Fables (Burt ed.).
Imitative cat-bird. Young. Plantation bird legends.
Immortal fountain. Olcott. Book of elves and fairies.
Poulsson. In the child's world.
Smith. Good old stories. (Palace of beauty.)
Whittier. Child life in prose.
Imp of the well. *See* Ghost of the spring and the shrew.
Imp tree. Rhys. Fairy gold.
Imperishable. Chodzko. Fairy tales of the Slav.
Impossible enchantment. Lang. Grey fairy book.
Lang. Trusty John and other stories.
Impty-Umpty and the blacksmith. Harris. Uncle Remus returns.
See also Smith and the devil.
In a thousand years. Andersen. Stories and tales (Author's ed.)
In de swamp. *See* Owls, origin of.
In Nazareth. *See* Christ-child and the clay birds.
In safe shelter. Noyes. Twilight stories.
"In some lady's garden." Harris. Nights with Uncle Remus.
In the bear's paws and the eagle's claws. Grundtvig. Fairy tales from afar.
In the desert of waiting; or, The legend of Camelback mountain. Johnston. Little Colonel in Arizona.
In the duck-yard. *See* Portuguese duck.
In the flag house. Bailey. Friendly tales.
In the Forest of Sherwood. *See* Robin Hood.
In the giant's house. *See* Geirrod and Thor.
In the great walled country. Alden. Why the chimes rang.
In the green meadow. *See* Water drop.
In the kingdom of friends. Bailey. Friendly tales.
In the kitchen garden. Gatty. Parables from nature. (Gifts.)
Skinner. Turquoise story book.

In the land of souls. Bassett. Wander ships. (Stone canoe.)
Judd. Wigwam stories. (White stone canoe.)
Lang. Yellow fairy book.
Success library. v. 3.
Tanner. Legends from the red man's forest. (Island of the Blessed.)
Wiggin and Smith. Magic casements. (Journey to the island of souls.)
See also Blue Jay visits the ghosts; Ghost land; Ghost wife. IV.
In the nursery. Andersen. Wonder stories.
In the shaded room. Richards. Silver crown.
In the temple. Lagerlöf. Christ legends.
"In the uttermost parts of the sea." Andersen. Fairy tales (Paull tr.).
Andersen. Stories and tales (Author's ed.).
In the village of lights. Bailey. Friendly tales.
In union is strength. *See* Lion and the mosquitoes.
Inao of the Ainu. Nixon-Roulet. Japanese folk stories and fairy tales.
Inchcape bell. *See* Inchcape rock.
Inchcape rock. Baldwin. Fifty famous stories.
Sly. World stories retold. (Inchcape bell.)
Independent leaves. Sologub. Sweet-scented name.
Indian and the Frenchman. Æsop. Fables (Burt ed.).
Indian brave, Adventures of an. Lang. Orange fairy book.
Indian corn, Legend of. *See* First corn. III.
Indian corn, Origin of. *See* First corn. VI and VIII.
Indian fairy. Brown. Star jewels.
Indian legend. *See* How the birds came.
Indian legend of the water lily. *See* Star maiden.
Indian Orpheus. Brown. When the world was young.
Indian singer. *See* Iktomi and the ducks.
Indian story of the mole. *See* Sun a prisoner. III.
Indian story of the robin. *See* How the robin came.
Indian story of the winds. I. Hall and Gilman. Story land. 2d reader.
Indian story of the winds. II. Faulkner. Story lady's book. (Indian legend of the winds.)
Pratt. Legends of the red children. (Legends of the winds.)
Indian story of the winds. III. Cowles. Indian nature myths. (Keeper of the winds.)
Donaldson. Little papoose listens. (Song of the winds.)
Indian summer. Cornyn. When the camp fire burns. (When Glooskap smokes his pipe.)
Donaldson. Moons of long ago. (How Indian summer came.)
Macmillan. Canadian fairy tales. (Boy in the land of shadows.)

Indian summer—*continued.*
Pratt. Legends of the red children. (Rainbow.)
Seton. Woodland tales.
Young. Algonquin Indian tales. (*In* Ch. 25. Haze of the Indian summer.)
Indian who lost his wife. Patten. Junior classics. v. 1.
See also Wooden wife.
Indian who married the moon. *See* Man who married the moon. II.
Indian who saved his tribe from the Thunderbird. Bayliss. Treasury of Indian tales. (Watogo who saved his tribe from the Thunderbird.)
St. Nicholas. March 1888, p. 376. (Onatoga's sacrifice.)
Indians and the jack o'lanterns. *See* Jack-o'-lantern and the Indians.
Indians' Cinderella. *See* Little Scar Face.
Indian's dream. Hartwell. Story hour readings. 5th year.
Indians' flood. I. Judd. Wigwam stories. (Story of the deluge.)
Nixon-Roulet. Indian folk tales. (*In* Wonderful deeds of Manabozho.)
Schoolcraft. Indian fairy book. (*In* Manabozho the mischief maker.)
Tanner. Legends from the red man's forest.
Indians' flood. II. Linderman. Indian why stories. (Oldman remakes the world.)
Young. Algonquin Indian tales. (*In* Ch. 18.)
Indians' flood. III. Bayliss. Treasury of Indian tales. (Wisakaha slays the cloud manitous.)
Indians' flood. I, II, and III. *See also* Deluge and how it came about; Manabozho and the lake magicians; Olelbis; Wisakaha slays the cloud manitous.
Indian's vow to the thunder gods. Judson. Myths and legends of the Pacific Northwest.
Indian's war dance. *See* Pleiades. II.
Industrious goblins. *See* Elves and the shoemaker.
Industrious manikins. *See* Elves and the shoemaker.
Industry and sloth. Æsop. Fables (Burt ed.).
Ingebjorg. Hall. Icelandic fairy tales.
Ingratitude. I. Coussens. Jade story book.
Ingratitude. II. Noyes. Twilight stories.
See also Way of the world. I.
Innkeeper's wine. Guerber. Legends of the Rhine.
Inquisitive girl. *See* Pandora.
Inquisitive man. Æsop. Fables (Stickney. Supplement).
Inquisitive Mr. Possum. Walker. Sandman's goodnight stories.
Inside again. *See* Way of the world. I.
Intelligence and Luck. *See* Luck and Intelligence.
Interrupted wedding. Guerber. Legends of the Rhine.
Invalid lion. *See* Lion, the fox and the beasts.
Invention of soap bubbles. St. Nicholas. June 1906, p. 698.

Invisible kingdom. Winnington. Outlook fairy book.
Invisible knight. *See* Prince Slugobyl.
Invisible one. *See* Little Scar Face.
Invisible prince. I. Lang. Invisible prince and other stories.
Lang. Yellow fairy book.
Invisible prince. II. Aulnoy. Fairy tales (Prince Sprite).
Mulock. Fairy book. (Prince Sprite.)
Valentine. Old, old fairy tales. (Prince Sprite.)
Invisible wall. Sholl. Faery tales of Weir.
Io. *Bailey. Wonder stories. (How Mercury gave up his tricks.)
Baldwin. Old Greek stories.
Baldwin. Story of the golden age. (*In* Children of Prometheus.)
Guerber. Myths of Greece and Rome. (*In* Mercury.)
Hartley. Stories from the Greek legends. (Story of Io and Argus; or, The watchman with a hundred eyes.)
Holbrook. Book of nature myths. (Why the peacock's tail has a hundred eyes.)
Hyde. Favorite Greek myths. (Mercury and Argus.)
Judd. Classic myths. (Juno's bird, the peacock.)
Kupfer. Stories of long ago.
Pratt. Myths of old Greece. v. 2.
*Wilson. Nature study reader. (Story of the peacock.)
Ion, Story of. Hutchinson. Orpheus with his lute. (*In* In the house of Apollo.)
Iphigenia. Baldwin. Hero tales told in school.
Baldwin. Story of the golden age. (*In* Becalmed at Aulis.)
Church. Greek story and song. (Finding of Iphigenia.)
Haaren. Famous men of Greece. (*In* Agamemnon.)
Storr. Half a hundred hero tales.
Iris. I. *Bailey. Wonder stories. (Little errand girl's new dress.)
Cooke. Nature myths. (Iris' bridge.)
Judd. Classic myths. (Iris, the rainbow princess.)
Pratt. Fairyland of flowers. (Legend of the iris.)
Pratt. Myths of old Greece. v. 3.
Young and Field. Literary readers. Book 2. (Rainbow bridge.)
Iris. II. Olcott. Wonder garden. (Why the iris wears rainbow colours.)
Skinner. Turquoise story book.
Iris. III. McFee. Treasury of flower stories. (Legend of the iris.)
Irish princess and her ship of sod. Griffis. Belgian fairy tales.
Irmgard's cow. Lindsay. More mother stories.
Iron and the trees. Friedlander. Jewish fairy book.
Iron casket. Silver fairy book.
Wiggin and Smith. Tales of wonder.

Iron dog. Aspinwall. Short stories for short people.
Iron eagle. Canton. Reign of King Herla.
Iron Hans. Grimm. Fairy tales (Lucas tr.).
Grimm. Fairy tales (Paull tr.).
Iron kettle, Story of the. *See* Thor: Thor's fishing.
Iron, Origin of. *See* Wicked hornet.
Iron stove. *Grimm. Fairy tales (Wiltse). v. 1.
Lang. Magic ring and other stories.
Lang. Yellow fairy book.
Mulock. Fairy book.
Wiggin and Smith. Fairy ring.
Iron wolf. Bain. Cossack fairy tales.
Wiggin and Smith. Fairy ring.
Ironlaczy. Underhill. Dwarfs' tailor and other fairy tales.
Isaac's loaves. Storytellers' magazine. July 1914, p. 623.
Isabella and the green silk frock. Bailey. Stories children need.
Isis and Osiris, Story of. Brooksbank. Legends of ancient Egypt.
Storytellers' magazine. May 1915, p. 149. (Coming of the god and goddess. Abridged.)
Island fable. *See* Mouse and the elephant.
Island fairies. *See* Laka and the menehunes.
Island of Demons. Higginson. Tales of the enchanted islands of the Atlantic.
Island of skeletons. Compton. American Indian fairy tales.
Island of the Blessed. *See* In the land of souls.
Isle of the rose. Hutchinson. Golden porch.
Isle of Udröst. Stroebe and Martens. Norwegian fairy book.
Isles of the sea fairies (poem). Olcott. Book of elves and fairies.
Isolda. *See* Sir Tristram.
It is quite true. Andersen. Fairy tales (Paull tr.).
Andersen. Stories and tales (Author's ed. "It's quite true!").
Bailey. Stories children need.
Wiggin and Smith. Tales of laughter.
It snows and it blows. Tales for bedtime.
Italian harp's story. Harrison. Bric-a-brac stories.
Ithenhiela, Story of. Brown. Tales of the red children.
Cowles. Art of story telling. (Story of Ithenthiela.)
Ithentheila. *See* Ithenhiela.
Ito and his friends. Peck. Stories for good children.
Van Sickle and Seegmiller. Riverside readers. 2d reader. (Japanese fairy tale.)
See also Dreadful boar; Herr Korbes; Strange friends in time of need.
"It's quite true." *See* It is quite true.
Ivan. Jacobs. Celtic fairy tales. (Tale of Ivan.)
See also Lac of rupees for a piece of advice.

Ivan and the daughter of the sun. Bain. Cossack fairy tales.
Ivan and the gray wolf. Curtin. Wonder tales from Russia. (Ivan Tsarevich, the fire-bird, and the gray wolf.)
Dole. White duckling and other stories.
Gask. Folk tales from many lands. (Prince Ivan and the grey wolf.)
Magnus. Russian folk-tales. (Tale of Ivan Tsarevich, the bird of light, and the gray wolf.
Patten. Junior classics. v. 2. (Prince Ivan and the gray wolf.)
Wheeler. Russian wonder tales. (Tsarevich Ivan, the glowing bird and the gray wolf.)
See also Golden Bird. II.
Ivan Bey of Montenegro. Butterworth. Zigzag journeys in the Orient. (*In* Ch. 7.)
Ivan overcomes the giant. Children's story garden.
Ivan the fool and St. Peter's fife. Bain. Cossack fairy tales.
Ivan the fool, Story of. Tolstoi. More tales.
Tolstoi. Twenty-three tales.
Ivan the peasant's son and the little man, himself one finger tall, his mustache seven versts in length. Curtin. Wonder-tales from Russia.
Steele. Russian garland of fairy tales.
See also Tsarevich Ivan and the harp that harped without a harper.
Ivan Tsarevich, the fire-bird, and the gray wolf. *See* Ivan and the gray wolf.
Ivanczarovitch and Bulat the Brave. Underhill. Dwarfs' tailor and other fairy tales.
Ivango; or, The lost sister. Riggs. Animal stories from Eskimo land.
Ivanoushka the simpleton. *See* Little Fool Ivan.
Iváshko and the wise woman. Magnus. Russian folk-tales.
Ivory city and its fairy princess. Jacobs. Indian fairy tales.
Ixion. Pratt. Myths of old Greece. v. 1.
Iya, the camp-eater. Eastman. Wigwam evenings. (Eya. the devourer.)
Zitkala-Sä. Old Indian legends.

J

Jack and his brothers. *See* Boots and his brothers.
Jack and his comrades. Jacobs. Celtic fairy tales.
Spaulding and Bryce. Aldine readers. Book 3. (Jack and his companions.)
Tappan. Folk stories and fables.
See also Bremen town musicians.

Jack and his golden snuff-box. Jacobs. English fairy tales.
Marshall. Fairy tales of all nations.
Jack and his master. Jacobs. Celtic fairy tales.
Tappan. Folk stories and fables.
See also Devil's hide; Fanch Scouarnec; Keep cool.
Jack and Jill. *See* Children in the moon. I.
Jack and Jill on the moon mountains. *See* Children in the moon. I.
Jack and Jill's visit to the moon. *See* Children in the moon. III.
Jack and the bean-stalk. Adams. Folk story and verse.
Aunt Louisa's book of fairy tales.
Baldwin. Fairy stories and fables.
Bates. Once upon a time.
*Bowen. Second story reader.
Boys' and girls' fairy book.
Chaplin. Treasury of fairy tales.
Chisholm. In fairyland.
Coe. First book of stories.
Coussens. Child's book of stories.
Crane. Red Riding Hood's picture book.
Cruikshank. Fairy book.
Dyer. What-happened-then stories.
*Elson and Runkel. Elson readers. Book 2.
Favorite fairy tales.
Forty famous fairy tales.
Gibbon. Reign of King Cole.
Harris. Favorites from fairyland.
Hartland. English folk and fairy tales.
*Heller and Bates. Little Golden Hood and other stories.
*Howard. Dick Whittington and other stories.
Jacobs. English fairy tales.
Jerrold. Big book of fairy tales.
Johnson. Oak-tree fairy book.
Ketchum and Jorgensen. Kindergarten gems.
Lang. Red fairy book.
Lansing. Tales of old England in prose and verse.
Mabie. Fairy tales every child should know.
Mabie. Heroes and fairies.
Mother Goose rhymes, jingles and fairy tales (Altemus ed.).
Mulock. Fairy book.
My Bookhouse. v. 2.
Norton. Heart of oak books. v. 2.
Nursery tales.
O'Shea. Old world wonder stories.
Patten. Junior classics. v. 1.
Perkins. Twenty best fairy tales.
Pyle. Mother's nursery tales.
Rhys. Fairy gold.
Scudder. Book of folk stories.

Jack and the bean-stalk—*continued.*
Scudder. Children's book.
Scudder. Fables and folk stories.
Sly. World stories retold.
Stone. Children's stories that never grow old.
Success library. v. 3.
Tappan. Folk stories and fables.
Tweed. Fairy tales everyone should know.
Valentine. Old, old fairy tales (Warne ed.).
Welsh. Fairy tales children love.
Wiltse. Hero folk of ancient Britain.
Jack and the giant. *See* Jack the giant-killer.
Jack and the king who was a gentleman. MacManus. In chimney corners.
Olcott and Pendleton. Jolly book.
Wiggin and Smith. Tales of laughter.
See also Shepherd who won the king's daughter by a single word.
Jack and the Troll have an eating match. *See* Ashiepattle who ate with the troll for a wager.
Jack Frost and his work. Poulsson. In the child's world.
Jack Frost's frolic. Storytellers' magazine. Nov. 1916, p. 563.
Jack Hannaford. Jacobs. English fairy book
Jack Hornby, the ready boy. Welsh. Stories children love.
Jack Horner. Baring-Gould. Crock of gold.
Jack in luck. *See* Hans in luck.
Jack-in-the-box. *See* Squeaky and the scare box.
Jack in the pulpit. Donaldson. Moons of long ago.
Jack my Hedgehog. Lang. Green fairy book.
Lang. Three dwarfs and other stories.
See also Prince Hedgehog.
Jack-o'-lantern (play). Field third reader.
Jack-o'-lantern and the glow worm. Cocke. Bypaths in Dixie.
Jack-o'-lantern and the Indians. I. Blaisdell. American history story book. (Timely jack o' lantern.)
Blaisdell. Child life. 3d reader. (Jack o' lantern.)
Hartwell. Story hour readings. 5th year. (Obed's pumpkins.)
Jack-o'-lantern and the Indians. II. Pumphrey. Stories of the pilgrims. (Indians and the jack-o'-lanterns.)
Jack Rabbit's wisdom spot. *See* Rabbit and the animal wizard.
Jack seeks his fortune. *See* How Jack went to seek his fortune.
Jack Sprat, his wife and the cat (poem). Rhys. Fairy gold.
Jack the cunning thief. Forty famous fairy tales.
Jacobs. More Celtic fairy tales.
Johnson. Elm-tree fairy book. (How Jack won a wife.)
See also Master thief; Shifty lad, the widow's son.

Jack the dullard. *See* Hans Clodhopper.

Jack the giant-killer. Adams. Folk story and verse.
Aunt Louisa's book of fairy tales.
Bates. Once upon a time.
Chisholm. In fairyland.
Coe. First book of stories.
Coussens. Child's book of stories.
Favorite fairy tales.
Forty famous fairy tales. (History of Jack the giant-killer.)
Gibbon. Reign of King Cole.
Hartland. English folk and fairy tales.
Jacobs. English fairy tales.
Jerrold. Big book of fairy tales.
Johnson. Birch-tree fairy book.
Keyes. Five senses.
Keyes. Stories and story-telling.
Lang. Blue fairy book.
Lang. History of Jack the giant killer, and other stories. (History of Jack the giant killer.)
Mabie. Fairy tales every child should know.
Mabie. Heroes and fairies.
Marshall. Fairy tales of all nations.
Mother Goose rhymes, jingles and fairy tales (Altemus ed.).
Mother Goose's nursery rhymes, tales and jingles (Warne ed. Jack and the giant.)
Mulock. Fairy book.
Norton. Heart of oak books. v. 3. (History of Jack the giant killer.)
Nursery tales.
O'Shea. Old world wonder stories.
Patten. Junior classics. v. 1.
Perkins. Twenty best fairy tales.
Pyle. Mother's nursery tales.
Scudder. Children's book.
Sly. World stories retold.
Success library. v. 3.
Tappan. Folk stories and fables.
Tweed. Fairy tales everyone should know.
Valentine. Old, old fairy tales (Warne ed.).
Welsh. Fairy tales children love.
Wiggin and Smith. Fairy ring.
Wiltse. Hero folk of ancient Britain.
See also Scandinavian Jack the giant killer; Simple-minded giant.

Jack the giant-killer, Indian. *See* Boy who overcame the giants.

Jack the preacher. Walker. Sandman's goodnight stories.

Jack the terrible. English. Fairy stories and wonder tales.

Jack with the golden hair. Stroebe and Martens. Danish fairy book.

Jackal. Lang. Orange fairy book. (Adventures of a jackal.)
Jackal and the alligator. I. *See* Jackal and the crocodile.
Jackal and the alligator. II. *See* Little jackal and the alligator.
Jackal and the camel. Rouse. Talking thrush.
Jackal and the cat. Wiggin and Smith. Talking beasts.
Jackal and the crocodile. Darton. Wonder book of beasts. (Jackal and the alligator.)
Patten. Junior classics. v. 1.
Steel. Tales of the Punjab.
See also Little jackal and the alligator; "Heyo, house."
Jackal and the heron. Stafford. Animal fables.
See also Fox and the crow. II; Fox and the dove; Tricks of the fox.
Jackal and the hyena. Stafford. Animal fables.
Jackal and the iguana. Patten. Junior classics. v. 1.
Steel. Tales of the Punjab.
See also Pride shall have a fall.
Jackal and the leopard. Stafford. Animal fables.
Jackal and the partridge. Patten. Junior classics. v. 1.
Steel. Tales of the Punjab.
Jackal and the pea hen. Steel. Tales of the Punjab.
Jackal and the spring. *Field second reader.
Lang. Grey fairy book.
Jackal, deer and the crow. Coussens. Jade story book.
Jackal king. *See* Blue jackal.
Jackal or tiger? Lang. Olive fairy book.
Lang. Little King Loc.
Jackal that lost his tail. Rouse. Talking thrush and other tales from India.
Jackal, the barber and the Brahmin. Frere. Old Deccan days. (Jackal, the barber and the Brahmin who had seven daughters.)
Singleton. Wild flower fairy book.
Wiggin and Smith. Tales of wonder.
Jackal, the barber and the Brahmin who had seven daughters. *See* Jackal, the barber and the Brahmin.
Jackal, the dove and the panther. Lang. Aladdin and other stories.
Lang. Pink fairy book.
Jackal, the schoolmaster. Bradley-Birt. Bengal fairy tales.
Jackal's eldest son. Lang. Orange fairy book. (Adventures of the jackal's eldest son.)
Jackal's younger son. Lang. Orange fairy book. (Adventures of the younger son of the jackal.)
Jackdaw. Yeats. Irish fairy and folk tales.
Jackdaw and the doves. Scudder. Children's book.
Scudder. Fables and folk stories.
Jackdaw and the pigeons. Æsop. Fables (Black ed.).
Æsop. Fables (Burt ed.).

Jackdaw and the sheep. Æsop. Fables (Black ed.).
Æsop. Fables (Burt ed.).
Æsop. Fables (Stickney).
Jackdaw with borrowed plumes. *See* Vain Jackdaw.
"Jacky-my-Lantern." Harris. Uncle Remus, his songs and his sayings.
Jade, Origin of. Pearson. Laughing lion. (Saddler's son and the dragon.)
Jahkarpasse, Adventures of. Brown. Tales of the red children.
James, the huntsman. Bay. Danish fairy and folk tales.
Jamie Freel and the young lady. Graves. Irish fairy book.
Yeats. Irish fairy tales.
See also Guleesh.
Jamie Watt and his grandmother's tea kettle. *See* Watt and the teakettle.
Jan and the magic pencil. Fyleman. Rainbow cat.
Jan the animal judge. Stafford. Animal fables.
Jane and the bears. Edey. Six giants and a griffin.
Jane, Jane, don't complain. Fillmore. Mighty Mikko.
Noyes. Twilight stories. (Foolish grumbling.)
Janni and the Draken. Lang. Grey fairy book.
Lang. Little King Loc.
Japanese and the earthquake. *See* Burning of the rice fields.
Japanese boy, Story of. *See* Blind boy's fall.
Japanese fairy tale. *See* Ito and his friends.
Japanese fisherman. *See* Uraschimataro and the turtle.
Japanese ogre. *See* Ito and his friends.
Japanese Red Riding Hood. Goddard. Fairy tales in other lands.
Jar of olives. *See* Ali Cogia.
Jar of Rosemary. *Lindsay. Story-teller.
Jarro, the wild duck. Hartwell. Story hour readings. 5th year.
Jason. *See* Argonauts.
Jay and the peacock. Æsop. Fables (Jacobs).
Æsop. Fables. (Stickney. Supplement. Jay in feathers of a peacock.)
My Bookhouse. v. 1.
Patten. Junior classics. v. 1.
See also Proud crow; Two foolish birds; Vain jackdaw.
Jay in feathers of a peacock. *See* Jay and the peacock.
Jealous courtiers. Bryant. Stories to tell to children.
Jealous husband. *See* Fridolin at the forge.
Jean Malin and the bull-man. Pyle. Tales of folk and fairies.
See also Why Brother Bull growls and grumbles.
Jean Valjean in Cathay. Fielde. Chinese fairy tales.
Jeannot and Colin. Storytellers' magazine. July 1917, p. 507.

Jelly fish and the monkey. *See* Monkey and the jelly-fish.
Jellyfish takes a journey. *See* Monkey and the jelly-fish.
Jerome. *See* St. Jerome.
Jesper who herded the hares. Lang. Trusty John and other stories.
Lang. Violet fairy book.
Pyle. Tales of folks and fairies. (Magic pipe.)
Skinner. Merry tales. (King's rabbit keeper.)
See also Ashiepattle and the king's hares; Enchanted whistle.
Jester's sword. Johnston. Mary Ware, the Little Colonel's chum.
Jew. Pleasanton. Fairyland of opera. (La Juive.)
Jew among the thorns. Gibbon. Reign of King Cole. (Jew in the bush.)
Grimm. Fairy tales (Lucas tr.).
Grimm. Fairy tales (Paull tr.).
Grimm. Household tales (Everyman's ed. Jew in the bush.)
Scudder. Children's book. (Jew in the bush.)
See also Little Freddy and his fiddle; Magic fiddle.
Jew in the bush. *See* Jew among the thorns.
Jewel in the toad's head. *See* Toad. I; Toad's jewel.
Jewel of great price. *See* Man who obeyed orders.
Jewel tears. Olcott. Wonder garden.
Jeweled beach. Harrison. Moon princess. (Story of the jeweled beach.)
Jeweled sea. James. Jeweled sea.
Jewelled necklace. *See* Freyja.
Jewish doctor. Arabian nights (Townsend. Story told by the Jewish doctor.)
Arabian nights. More tales (Olcott. Story told by the Jewish physician: The necklace of jewels.)
Jewish girl. *See* Jewish maiden.
Jewish maiden. Andersen. Fairy tales (Paull tr.).
Andersen. Stories and tales (Author's ed. Jewish girl.)
Jimmy Gnat. Bigham. Merry animal tales.
Jimmy Scarecrow's Christmas. Dickinson and Skinner. Children's book of Christmas.
Jipi. Sylva and Strettell. Legends from river and mountain.
Jippy and Jimmy (poem). Young and Field. Literary readers. Book 2.
Joan of Arc. Evans. Old time tales.
Joan of Arc of China. *See* Dance of the fairies.
Joblilies. Eggleston. Queer stories for boys and girls.
Joel's talk with Santa Claus. Field. Christmas tales.
Jogi's punishment. Lang. Lilac fairy book.
Lang. Magic book.
John Bit-of-a-man. Cary. French fairy tales.
John Dietrich, Adventures of (poem). Arnold and Gilbert. Stepping stones to literature. v. 4. (Brown dwarf of Rügen.)
Mulock. Fairy book.

John Dietrich, Adventures of—*continued.*
(poem). Olcott. Book of elves and fairies. (Brown dwarf.)
(poem). Whittier. Poetical works. (Brown dwarf of Rügen.)
John Gethin and the candle. Thomas. Welsh fairy book.
John Gilpin. Baldwin. Horse fair. (Calender's nag.)
John Grumlie (poem). Lansing. Tales of old England.
John Lydgate's tale. *See* Thebes: Destruction of Thebes.
John the conjurer. Caballero. Spanish fairy tales.
John the true. *See* Faithful John.
Johnnie and Grizzle. *See* Hansel and Grethel.
Johnny and the golden goose. Nursery tales.
Johnny and the three goats. *See* Goats in the turnip field.
Johnny Appleseed. Bailey and Lewis. For the children's hour. 1918 ed. (Apple-seed John.)
Forbush. Young folks' book of ideals.
Harrison. In story land.
My Bookhouse. v. 2. (Old Johnny Appleseed.)
(poem). Poulsson. In the child's world. (Apple-seed John.)
(poem). St. Nicholas. June 1880, p. 604-5. (Apple-seed John.)
Skinner. Topaz story book.
Johnny-cake. I. Bailey. Firelight stories.
*Baldwin. Second fairy reader. (Nimble Johnny-cake.)
*Bowen. Second story reader.
*Burchill. Progressive road to reading. Book 2.
*Elson and Runkel. Elson readers. Book 1.
Jacobs. English fairy tales.
Johnson. Oak-tree fairy book.
O'Grady and Throop. Teachers' story teller's book.
Spaulding and Bryce. Aldine readers. Book 3.
Storytellers' magazine. June 1913, p. 10.
Wiggin and Smith. Tales of laughter.
See also Gingerbread boy; Pancake; Wee bannock; Wonderful cake.
Johnny-cake. II (poem). Boston collection of kindergarten stories.
Johnny Chuck finds the best thing in the world. Bailey. Stories children need.
Johnny Gloke. Jacobs. More English fairy tales.
Johnson. Fir-tree fairy book.
See also Brave little tailor.
Johnny Reed's cat. Johnson. Birch-tree fairy book.
See also King of the cats.
Joke or no joke. Campbell. Beyond the border.
Joker. Kennedy. New world fairy book.
Jokkoree. English. Fairy stories and wonder tales.
St. Nicholas. Jan. 1875, p. 143.
Jolly beggar. Gibbon. Reign of King Cole.
Jolly Calle. Nyblom. Jolly Calle.

Jolly Goshawk. Richards Little master.
See also Gay Goshhawk.
Jolly harper. *See* Lochmaben harper.
Jolly Mr Wind. *Storytellers' magazine. April 1917, p. 223.
Jorinda and Joringel. *See* Jorinde and Joringel.
Jorinde and Joringel. Grimm. Fairy tales (Lucas tr.).
Grimm. Household tales (Burt ed. Florinda and Yoringal.)
Grimm. Household tales (Everyman's ed. Jorinda and Jorindel.)
Lang. Green fairy book. (Jorinda and Joringal.)
Scudder. Children's book.
Singleton. Goldenrod fairy book. (Florinda and Yoringal.)
Joseph, the Sabbath lover. Friedlander. Jewish fairy book.
Jötunheim. *See* Thor and his journey to Jötunheim.
Joudar, Story of. Arabian nights, More tales (Olcott).
Journey of Khensu to Bekhten. Brooksbank. Legends of ancient Egypt.
Jewett. Egyptian tales of magic. (God and the sick princess.)
Journey of the porridge pot. Guerber. Legends of the Rhine. (Hot porridge.)
Noyes. Twilight stories.
Stebbins. Sunken city. (Pot of hot porridge.)
Journey to Jerusalem. Magnus. Russian folk-tales.
Journey to the island of souls. *See* In the land of souls.
Journey to the sun and the moon. Chodzko. Fairy tales of the Slav.
Journeyings of Hasan of Bassorah to the Islands of Wak-Wak. *See* Hassan of Balsora.
Jowiis and the eagles. Olcott. Red Indian fairy book.
Joyous miracle. *See* Christ-child and the clay birds.
Juan, Adventures of. Coussens. Jade story book.
See also Table, the ass and the stick.
Juan Holgado and death. Caballero. Spanish fairy tales.
Judas tree. *See* Red-bud tree.
Judge and the beetle. Arnold and Gilbert. Stepping stones to literature. v. 3.
Judge's debt. Curry. Little classics.
Judge's nose. Macdonell. Italian fairy book.
Judgment. Richards. Silver crown.
Judgment of Midas. *See* Midas. II.
Judgment of Paris. *See* Paris: Apple of discord.
Judgment of Shemyaka. Steele. Russian garland of fairy tales.
Judgment of the fox. Bailey. In the animal world. (Adapted.)
See also Way of the world I and II.
Judgment of the jackal. Rouse. Talking thrush.
Judgment seat of Vikramaditya. Partridge. Story telling in home and school.
Judicious lion. Æsop. Fables (Black ed.).

Judy and the fairy cat. Olcott. Book of elves and fairies.
Juliet; or, The little white mouse. Harrison. Old-fashioned fairy book.
"Jump in my sack!" Ortoli. Evening tales.
See also Table, the ass and the stick.
Jumpers. *See* Leaping match.
Jungfrau Maleen. Wiggin and Smith. Magic casements.
Jungfrau Svanhvita and Jungfrau Räfrumpa. Thorpe. Yule-tide stories.
Juniper tree. Grimm. Household stories (Crane tr. Almond tree.)
Grimm. Household tales (Everyman's ed.).
Mulock. Fairy book.
See also Milk white doo'; Rose tree.
Juno and Halcyone. *See* Halcyon birds.
Juno and the peacock. *See* Peacock and Juno.
Juno's bird, the peacock. *See* Io.
Jupiter and a bee. Æsop. Fables (Burt ed.).
Æsop. Fables (Stickney).
Bryce. That's why stories. (Jupiter and the bee.)
Jupiter and his mighty company. Baldwin. Old Greek stories.
Jupiter and Pallas. Æsop. Fables (Black ed.).
Jupiter and the animals. Æsop. Fables (Burt ed.).
Jupiter and the ass. Æsop. Fables (Black ed.).
Æsop. Fables (Burt ed.).
Jupiter and the camel. Æsop. Fables(Black ed.).
Æsop. Fables (Burt ed.).
Jupiter and the herdsman. Æsop. Fables (Black ed.).
Æsop. Fables (Burt ed.).
Jupiter and the Titans. *See* Titans.
Jupiter and the two wallets. *See* Jupiter's two wallets.
Jupiter, Neptune, Minerva and Momus. Æsop. Fables (Burt ed.).
Æsop. Fables (Stickney).
Jupiter's lottery. Æsop. Fables (Burt ed.).
Jupiter's two wallets. Æsop. Fables (Burt ed.).
Æsop. Fables (Stickney. Jupiter and the two wallets.)
Wiggin and Smith. Talking beasts.
Just as well. Arnold and Gilbert. Stepping stones to literature. v. 4.
Brown. Stories of childhood and nature.
Coussens. Child's book of stories. (So-so.)
Just-for-fun story from Spain. *See* Put it on my bill.
Just judge. Lansing. Dramatic readings.
Jutlander and his stockings. Bay. Danish fairy and folk tales.

K

Kaa's hunting. Kipling. Jungle book.
Kabouters and the bells. Griffis. Dutch fairy tales.

Kachi Kachi mountain. *See* Farmer and the badger.
Kai Kaoos. Wilmot-Buxton. Stories of Persian heroes. (Seven labors of Rustem.)
Kai Khosroo. Wilmot-Buxton. Stories of Persian heroes. (Coming of Kai Khosroo; How Kai Khosroo found his rest.)
Kalevala, land of heroes. My Bookhouse. v. 5.
See also Sampo.
Kalopaling. Bayliss. Treasury of Eskimo tales.
Kamer-Taj, the moon-horse. Kunos. Forty-four Turkish fairy tales.
Kana, the youth who could stretch himself upwards, Story of. Colum. At the gateways of the day.
Kanchanmala, the golden wreath. Bradley-Birt. Bengal fairy tales.
Kara Mustafa the hero. Kunos. Forty-four Turkish fairy tales.
See also Brave little tailor.
Kari Woodengown. Dasent. Popular tales from the Norse. (Katie Woodencloak.)
Dasent. Norse fairy tales. (Katie Woodencloak.)
Gade. Norwegian fairy tales. (Kari Wooden-skirt.)
Lang. Marvellous musician.
Lang. Red fairy book.
Stroebe and Martens. Norwegian fairy book. (Kari Woodencoat.)
See also Cinderella.
Kari Wooden-skirt. *See* Kari Woodengown.
Karl and the dryad. Brown. Star jewels.
Karl Katz. Baldwin. Thirty more famous stories. (Peter Klaus the goat-herd.)
Dasent. Popular tales from the Norse. (Goatherd.)
Grimm. Household tales (Everyman's ed.).
Haaren. Songs and stories. 2d reader. (Peter Klaus.)
Jerrold. Reign of King Oberon.
Thorpe. Yule-tide stories. (Goatherd.)
See also Rip Van Winkle.
Karma. James. Green willow.
Katcha and the devil. Baudis. Czech folk tales. (Old Nick and Kitty.)
Fillmore. Czechoslovak fairy tales.
Tyler. Twenty-four unusual stories.
See also Evil One and Kitta Grau; Gentle Dora; How the devil became afraid of a woman.
Kate Crackernuts. *See* Katherine Crackernuts.
Kate, Katak, and Kataky. Campbell. Beyond the border.
Kate Mary Ellen and the fairies. Colum. Boy in Eirinn.
Kate Woodenshoe. Potter. Pinafore pocket story book.
Katharine Altmüller and the three dwarfs. Froelicher. Swiss stories.
Katherine Crackernuts. Grierson. Scottish fairy book.
Jacobs. English fairy tales. (Kate Crackernuts.)

Katie Gray. Djurklo. Fairy tales from the Swedish.
See also Evil One and Kitta Grau.
Katie Woodencloak. *See* Kari Woodengown.
Katmanush; or, The human being who was made of wood. Bradley-Birt. Bengal fairy tales.
Katy-did weather. Potter. Pinafore pocket story book.
Katy's queer gift. St. Nicholas. June 1901, p. 698.
Kazha-ndü. Wardrop. Georgian folk tales.
"Keen-point," "cob-handle," and "butch." Harris. Little Mr. Thimblefinger.
Keep cool. Jacobs. Europa's fairy book.
See also Fanch Scouarnec; Jack and his master; Devil's hide; Hans Humdrum.
Keep tryst. Johnson. Little Colonel's Christmas vacation.
Keepers of the winds. Cowles. Indian nature myths.
Keesh, the bear hunter. Tales for bedtime.
Kempion. Pyle. Fairy tales from many lands.
Kenelm and the red leaf. Eliot. House on the edge of things.
Storytellers' magazine. July 1915, p. 229.
Kenneth, the Yellow. Grierson. Children's book of Celtic stories.
See also Nose-tree.
Kentsham bell. Hartland. English folk and fairy tales.
Kept close is not forgotten. Andersen. Stories and tales (Author's ed.).
Kerchunk. Bigham. Merry animal tales.
See also Talkative tortoise.
Kerchunk's sisters. Bigham. Merry animal tales.
See also Frogs and the fighting bulls.
Kettle and the engines. Dyer and Brady. Merrill readers. 3d reader.
Kettle that would not walk. Johnson. Oak-tree fairy book.
Key flower. I. McFee. Treasury of flower stories. (Legends of the forget-me-not.)
Key flower. II. *See* Cowslips. II.
Key flower. III. *See* Primrose, Legend of.
Keys. Sologub. Sweet-scented name.
Khoodeh, the youngest born. Bradley-Birt. Bengal fairy tales.
Kid and the tiger. Rouse. Talking thrush.
Kid and the wolf. I. Æsop. Fables (Stickney).
Kid and the wolf. II. Æsop. Fables (Black ed.).
Æsop. Fables (Jacobs. Wolf and the kid.)
Æsop. Fables (Stickney).
Baldwin. Fairy tales and fables. (Silly kid.)
Hall and Gilman. Story land. 2d reader.
Scudder. Fables and folk stories.
Kid who would not go. Bailey. Firelight stories.
Bailey. Once upon a time animal stories.
Hoxie. Kindergarten story book.
See also Old woman and her pig.

Kidnapped princess. *See* Guleesh.
Kield. Thorpe. Yule-tide stories.
Kil Arthur. Curtin. Myths and folk-lore of Ireland.
Kila's ride on the shark. Pope. Hawaii.
Kildare pooka. Graves. Irish fairy book.
Yeats. Irish fairy tales.
Kilhwch and Olwen. *See* Kilwch and Olwen.
Killer whale. I. Judson. Myths and legends of Alaska.
Killer whale. II. Judson. Myths and legends of Alaska. (Orgin of the killer whale crest.)
Killing of Cabrakañ. Finger. Tales of silver lands.
Kilwch and Olwen. Baldwin. Fifty famous rides. (How Kilhugh rode to Arthur's hall.)
Brooks. Wonder stories from the Mabinogion.
Colum. Island of the mighty. (How the youth Kilwch came to King Arthur's court.)
Hartwell. Story hour readings. 7th year. (How Kilhugh rode to Arthur's hall.)
Jacobs. Celtic fairy tales. (Wooing of Olwen.)
Lang. Lilac fairy book. (Winning of Olwen.)
Lang. Red romance book. (Pursuit of Diarmid.)
Lang. White doe. (Winning of Olwen.)
Lanier. Knightly legends of Wales; or, The boy's Mabinogion. (Kilwch and Olwen.)
Wilmot-Buxton. Stories of early England. (Story of the quest of the seven champions.)
Kind and Clutch. *See* Greedy shepherd.
Kind cranes. Elson and Runkel. Elson readers. Book 1.
Kind hawk. Olcott. Red Indian fairy book.
Kind heart. Donaldson. Moons of long ago.
Kind hearted boy. *See* Queen bee.
Kind old oak. *Elson and Runkel. Elson readers. Book 2.
Poulsson. In the child's world.
Skinner. Topaz story book.
Kindly magician. Martens. Chinese fairy book.
King Alexander's adventures. *See* Alexander the Great.
King Alfred. Baldwin. Fifty famous people. (How a prince learned to read.)
Blaisdell. English history story book.
*Burchill. Progressive road to reading. Book 3. (Alfred the great.)
Dyer and Brady. Merrill readers. 2d reader. (How Alfred learned to read; How Alfred baked the cakes.)
Haaren and Poland. Famous men of the middle ages.
Mabie. Heroes and fairies.
Mabie. Heroes every child should know.
Stewart. Tell me a hero story. (Minstrel, soldier and king.)
King Alfred and Guthrum. Wilmot-Buxton. Stories of early England. (Alfred and Guthrum.)
King Alfred and the cakes. Sly. World stories retold.
King and boar. Burlingame. Grateful elephant.

King and de peafowl. Patten. Junior classics. v. 1.
King and his hawk. Baldwin. Fifty famous stories.
Wiggin and Smith. Talking beasts.
See also Beth Gellert; King, the falcon and the drinking cup.
King and his three sons. I. Brown. Stories of childhood and nature.
King and his three sons. II. Cary. French fairy tales.
See also Singing bone.
King and queen of the dead. *See* Proserpina.
King and the ant's tree. Dasent. Popular tales from the Norse.
King and the apple. Wardrop. Georgian folk tales.
King and the bees. *See* King Solomon's answer.
King and the country girl. Danielson. Story telling time.
King and the fisherman. James. Cat and the mouse.
King and the goose herd. *See* Emperor and the goose boy.
King and the kites. Rouse. Talking thrush.
King and the lapwings. Ortoli. Evening tales.
King and the miller. Bay. Danish fairy and folk tales.
See also King John and the Abbot of Canterbury; Priest and the clerk.
King and the miller of Mansfield. Greenwood. Stories from famous ballads.
Macleod. Book of ballad stories. (King Henry and the miller of Mansfield.)
Tappan. Book of humor.
Tappan. Old ballads in prose.
See also Cobbler and the king; Gudeman of Ballengeich; How Ralph the charcoal burner entertained King Charles; Soldier and the Tsar in the forest.
King and the oak. Bailey. Wonder stories. (Ploughman who brought famine.)
*Beckwith. In mythland. v. 3. (Fate of Erisichthon.)
Hyde. Favorite Greek myths.
Olcott. Wonder garden. (Erysichton the hungry.)
Shaw. Stories of the ancient Greeks. (In the woods.)
King and the page. Baldwin. Fifty famous people.
King and the sage. Wardrop. Georgian folk tales.
King Arthur. Arnold. Stepping stones to literature. v. 8.
Baldwin. Stories of the king.
Church. Heroes of chivalry and romance.
Crommelin. Famous legends.
Greene. King Arthur and his court.
Guerber. Legends of the middle ages. (Round Table.)
Haaren. Ballads and tales.
Lang. Book of romance.
Mabie. Heroes and fairies.
Mabie. Heroes every child should know.
Patten. Junior classics. v. 4.
Storytellers' magazine. July 1913, p. 61. (Merlin and his prophecies.)
Tappan. Stories of legendary heroes.

King Arthur—*continued.*
See also Holy Grail; Round Table, Founding of.
King Arthur's cave. Cather. Educating by story telling. (Greedy cobbler.)
Griffis. Welsh fairy tales.
Shedlock. Art of the story teller. (Arthur in the cave.)
Thomas. Welsh fairy book.
See also Emperor's sleep; Sleeping king.
King Arthur's coming. Bailey. Stories children need. (Boy who was made king.)
Bryant. How to tell stories to children. (Arthur and the sword.)
*Burchill. Progressive road to reading. Book 3. (How Arthur was made king.)
Clay. Stories from Le Morte d'Arthur.
Cowles. Art of story telling.
Cutler. Stories of King Arthur and his knights.
*Dillingham and Emerson. Tell it again stories. (Arthur and the sword.)
Herbertson. Heroic legends. (Sword in the stone.)
Lang. Book of romance. (Drawing of the sword.)
Lang. Tales of the Round Table. (Drawing of the sword.)
Lansing. Dramatic readings for schools. (How England found her king.)
Lansing. Page, esquire and knight. (Drawing of the sword.)
Storytellers' magazine. Sept. 1913, p. 155. (How Arthur won his kingdom.)
King Arthur's death. Baldwin. Stories of the King. (Passing of Arthur.)
Blaisdell. Child life. 5th reader. (Death of Arthur.)
Clay. Stories from Le Morte d'Arthur. (Morte d'Arthur.)
Higginson. Tales of the enchanted islands of the Atlantic. (King Arthur at Avalon.)
Lang. Tales of the Round Table. (End of it all.)
Lansing. Page, esquire and knight. (Passing of Arthur.)
Norton. Heart of oak books. v. 4. (Death of Arthur.)
Storytellers' magazine. July 1914, p. 627. (Passing of Arthur.)
King Arthur's sword. Blaisdell. Child life, 5th reader. (King Arthur wins Excalibur.)
*Bowen. Second story reader. (King Arthur's sword.)
Clay. Stories from Le Morte d'Arthur. (Of the finding of Excalibur.)
Cutler. Stories of King Arthur and his knights. (How Arthur got his sword Excalibur.)
Griffis. Welsh fairy tales. (Sword of Avalon.)
Lang. Book of romance. (Sword Excalibur.)
Lang. Tales of romance.
Storytellers' magazine. Oct. 1913, p. 214. (How Arthur won his sword, his bride, and his Round Table.)

King Azad and the two royal sheykhs, History of. Olcott. Tales of the Persian genii.
King Bizarre and Prince Charming. Laboulaye. Fairy book.
King Canute. *See* Canute.
King Clovis. Evans. Old time tales. (King Clovis becomes a Christian.)
King Cophetua and the beggar maid. Macleod. Book of ballad stories.
Scudder. Book of legends.
King-crow and the water-snail. Wiggin and Smith. Talking beasts.
King Dragon. Stroebe and Martens. Danish fairy book.
See also King Lindorm.
King Edmund. *See* Aslaug and Ragnar.
King Edward IV and the tanner of Samworth (poem). Lanier. Boy's Percy.
King Estmere (poem). Lanier. Boy's Percy.
Macleod. Book of ballad stories.
King Falcon, King Dolphin and King Stag. Macdonell. Italian fairy book.
King for three days. Landa. Aunt Naomi's Jewish fairy tales and legends.
King Fortrager, Story of. Wilmot-Buxton. Stories of early England.
King Frost. Blumenthal. Folk tales from the Russian. (Father Frost.)
Lang. Three dwarfs and other stories. (Story of King Frost.)
Lang. Yellow fairy book.
Polevoi. Russian fairy tales (Morozko).
Success library. v. 3. (Story of King Frost.)
King Frost and King Winter. Skinner. Pearl story book.
King Gram. Dasent. Popular tales from the Norse.
King Grizzle-Beard. *See* King Thrushbeard.
King Hawksbeak. *See* King Thrushbeard.
King Henry and the miller of Mansfield. *See* King and the miller of Mansfield.
King Horn. Baring-Gould. Old English fairy tales.
Patten. Junior classics. v. 4.
King Iubdan and King Fergus. Rolleston. High deeds of Finn.
King James V of Scotland. *See* Gudeman of Ballengeich.
King John and Prince Arthur. Baldwin. Thirty more famous stories.
King John and the abbot. *See* King John and the Abbot of Canterbury.
King John and the Abbot of Canterbury. Baldwin. Fifty famous stories. (King John and the abbot.)
*Burchill. Progressive road to reading. Book 3. (King John and the merchant.)
Forty famous fairy tales.

King John and the Abbot of Canterbury—*continued.*
Jacobs. More English fairy tales.
(poem). Lanier. Boy's Percy.
(play). Lansing. Dramatic readings.
Lansing. Tales of old England. (King John and the abbot.)
Scudder. Children's book. (King John and the abbot.)
Tappan. Old ballads. (King John and the abbot.)
See also Emperor and the abbot; King and the miller; Little tailor; Priest and the clerk.
King John and the charter. *See* King John and the Magna Charta.
King John and the knight. Curry. Little classics.
King John and the Magna Charta. Baldwin. Thirty more famous stories.
Johonnot. Stories of the olden time. (King John and the charter.)
King John and the merchant. *See* King John and the Abbot of Canterbury.
King Kojata. Baudis. Czech folk tales. (Kojata.)
Cather. Educating by story telling. (Prince Unexpected.)
Jokai. Golden fairy book. (Kojata.)
Lang. Forty thieves and other stories.
Lang. Green fairy book.
Success library. v. 3.
King Khufu and the magicians. Jewett. Egyptian tales of magic.
King Lear. Canton. Reign of King Herla.
Macleod. Book of ballad stories. (King Lear and his three daughters.)
King Lear and his three daughters. *See* King Lear.
King Lindorm. Lang. Aladdin and other stories.
Lang. Pink fairy book.
See also King Dragon.
King Log and King Stork. *See* Frogs who asked for a king.
King Lud, Story of. Wilmot-Buxton. Stories of early England.
King Midas. *See* Midas.
King Mocking Bird. Stewart. Once upon a time.
King Mu of Dschou. Martens. Chinese fairy book.
King Mungo. James. Man elephant.
King Oberon's library. Hume. Chronicles of fairy land.
King of Candy Castle. Potter. Pinafore pocket story book.
King of England and his three sons. Jacobs. More English fairy tales.
King of Erin and the queen of the Lonesome Island. Curtin. Myths and folklore of Ireland.
King of Ethiopia. Laboulaye. Fairy tales. (Story of the king of Ethiopia.)
King of flowers. Griffis. Korean fairy tales.
King of France's daughter. Greenwood. Stories from famous ballads.
King of Huai Nan. Martens. Chinese fairy book.

King of Persia and the princess of the sea. *See* Gulnare of the sea, Story of.
King of Put. Birch. Green-faced toad.
King of Spain and his queen. Thorpe. Yule-tide stories.
King of the ants. Martens. Chinese fairy book.
King of the birds. I. *See* Setuli.
King of the birds. II. *See* King Wren.
King of the black desert. Graves. Irish fairy book.
King of the Black Isles. *See* Young king of the Black Isles, History of.
King of the buffaloes. Pyle. Wonder tales retold.
Schoolcraft. Indian fairy book. (Man with his leg tied up.)
See also Woman who married a buffalo.
King of the cats. Carrick. Kitty cat tales.
Hartland. English folk and fairy tales.
Jacobs. More English fairy tales.
Lansing. Dramatic readings.
Lansing. Fairy tales. v. 2.
Olcott. Good stories for great holidays.
Rhys. Fairy gold.
See also Colman Grey; Johnny Reed's cat.
King of the Clinkers. Van Sickle and Seegmiller. Riverside readers. 4th reader.
King of the crocodiles. Steel. Tales of the Punjab.
King of the Ebony Isles. *See* Young king of the Black Isles, History of.
King of the field-mice. Carrick. Kitty cat tales.
King of the fishes. Jacobs. Europa's fairy book.
King of the forest. Danielson. Story telling time.
King of the frogs. *See* Frogs who asked for a king.
King of the gnomes. Orcutt. Princess Kallisto.
King of the golden geese. Griswold. Hindu fairy tales.
King of the golden mountain. Grimm. Fairy tales (Lucas tr.).
Grimm. Fairy tales (Paull tr.).
Grimm. Household tales (Everyman's ed.).
Johnson. Oak-tree fairy book.
Scudder. Children's book.
King of the Golden River; or, The black brothers. Arnold and Gilbert. Stepping stones to literature. v. 1.
Bailey. Stories children need.
Blaisdell. Child life. 5th reader. (River of gold.)
Bryant. How to tell stories. (Golden river.)
Field. Famous fairy tales.
Lansing. Dramatic readings. (Strange visitor. Abridged.)
Mabie. Famous stories.
Patten. Junior classics. v. 6.
Ruskin. King of the Golden River and other stories.
Sly. World stories retold. (Abridged.)
Smith. Good old stories.
Tappan. Modern stories.

King of the golden woods. Fairy stories retold from St. Nicholas.
King of the hawks. Johnson. Elm-tree fairy book.
King of the kites. Rouse. Talking thrush.
King of the lions. Ortoli. Evening tales.
King of the mice. Rouse. Talking thrush.
King of the mineral kingdom. Johnson. Birch-tree fairy-book.
King of the peacocks. *See* Princess Rosette. I.
King of the servants. *See* Language of beasts.
King of the sparrows. *See* Swallow king's rewards.
King of the tigers is sick. Tappan. Folk stories and fables.
King of the vipers. Rhys. Fairy gold.
King of the waterfalls. Lang. Lilac fairy book.
Lang. King of the waterfalls and other stories.
King Olaf. Evans. Old time tales. (Olaf, the boy viking of Norway.)
Klingensmith. Old Norse wonder tales. (Saga of King Olaf.)
King O'Toole and his goose. Graves. Irish fairy tales. (King O'Toole and St. Kevin.)
Johnson. Oak-tree fairy book.
Jacobs. Celtic fairy tales.
Success library. v. 3.
Yeats. Irish fairy tales.
King O'Toole and St. Kevin. *See* King O'Toole and his goose.
King Picus. Hyde. Favorite Greek myths. (Circe.)
Olcott. Wonder garden. (King Picus the woodpecker.)
King Richard and Blondel. *See* Richard Coeur de Leon.
King Robert of Sicily. Bryant. Best stories to tell to children.
Bryant. Stories to tell to children.
*Burchill. Progressive road to reading. Book 3. (Proud king.)
Crommelin. Famous legends. (Legend of King Robert of Sicily.)
Hartwell. Story hour readings. 6th year.
Patten. Junior classics. v. 2.
See also Beggar king; Proud king; Tsar Angey and how he suffered for pride: Tsar and the angel.
King Roughbeard. *See* King Thrushbeard.
King Ryence's challenge (poem). Lanier. Boy's Percy.
King Schahriar and Scheherazade. Arabian nights (Colum. Beginning of the stories: Sharazad.)
Arabian nights (Lang. Introduction.)
Arabian nights (Olcott. Story of King Shahriar and Sheherazade.)
King Setnan and the Assyrians. Jewett. Egyptian tales of magic.
Brooksbank. Legends of ancient Egypt. (*In* Reign of the twelve kings.)

King Solomon. Coe. Second book of stories.
Gregory. Kiltartan wonder book.
See also Parable of the pomegranate.
King Solomon and the ants. Cooke. Nature myths and stories.
King Solomon and the demon. Byrne. Modern Greek fairy tales.
King Solomon and the owl. Rouse. Talking thrush.
King Solomon and the worm. Friedlander. Jewish fairy tales.
King Solomon's answer. Aunt Naomi. Jewish fairy tales and fables. (King, the queen and the bee.)
Baldwin. Fifty famous people. (King and the bees.)
Cooke. Nature myths and stories. (Wise king and the bee.)
Tyler. Twenty-four unusual stories. (King, the queen and the bee.)
Van Sickle and Seegmiller. Riverside readers. 3rd reader.
King Solomon's carpet. *See* Palace of Eagles.
King Stork. Pyle. Wonder clock.
King Suleyman and the nightingale. Olcott. Wonder garden.
King Tawny Mane, Story of. Boys' and girls' fairy book.
King that talked biggity. Harris. Uncle Remus and his friends.
King, the falcon, and the drinking cup. Bidpai. Tortoise and the geese.
Van Sickle and Seegmiller. Riverside readers. 4th reader.
See also King and his hawk.
King, the hermit, and the two princes. Bidpai. Tortoise and the geese.
King, the queen and the bee. *See* King Solomon's answer.
King Thrushbeard. Bates. Once upon a time. (King Hawksbeak.)
Grimm. Fairy tales (Lucas tr.).
Grimm. Fairy tales (Paull tr.).
Grimm. Household stories (Crane tr.).
Grimm. Household tales (Burt ed. King Roughbeard.)
Grimm. Household tales (Everyman's ed. King Grizzle-Beard.)
Olcott and Pendleton. Jolly book. (Haughty princess.)
Tappan. Folk stories and fables. (Haughty princess.)
Yeats. Irish fairy and folk tales. (Haughty princess.)
Wiggin and Smith. Tales of laughter.
See also Greyfoot; Hacon Grizzlebeard; Peter Redhat.
King Tongue. Aunt Naomi. Jewish fairy tales and fables.
Wiggin and Smith. Tales of wonder.
King Valemon, the white bear. Asbjörnsen. Tales from the fjeld.
Johnson. Book of fairy tale bears. (Bear who was an enchanted king.)
See also East o' the sun and west o' the moon; Mysterious prince.

King Waldemar. Dasent. Popular tales from the Norse.
Thorpe. Yule-tide stories.
King Wenceslaus, Legend of. Skinner. Pearl story book.
Storytellers' magazine. Feb. 1916, p. 77.
King who saw the truth. Shedlock. Eastern stories and legends.
King who slept. Eells. Tales of enchantment from Spain.
See also Stone-patience and knife-patience.
King who was fried. Steel. Tales of the Punjab.
King who would be stronger than fate. Lang. Brown fairy book.
Lang. Magician's gifts.
See also Constans the emperor; Foreordained match; Fish and the ring; Giant with golden hair.
King who would have a beautiful wife. Lang. Golden mermaid and other stories.
Lang. Pink fairy book.
King who would see paradise. Lang. Orange fairy book.
King Wichtel the first. St. Nicholas. April 1879, p. 398.
King William and the water sprite. Ewing. Old-fashioned fairy tales.
King Winter's harvest. Skinner Pearl fairy book.
King Wren. Bosschère. Folk tales of Flanders. (King of the birds.)
Grimm. Fairy tales (Paull tr.).
Johonnot. Grandfather's stories.
Klingensmith. Household stories.
Olcott. Good stories for great holidays. (King of the birds.)
Seton. Woodland tales. (How the wren became king of the birds.)
Wiggin and Smith. Tales of laughter.
See also Why the wren flies close to the earth.
Kingdom of little care. Meigs. Kingdom of the winding road.
Kingdom of the greedy. Harper. Story-hour favorites.
Storytellers' magazine. Dec. 1916, p. 672.
Kingdom of the mind's eye. Storytellers' magazine. May 1916, p. 299.
Kingdom of the ogres. Martens. Chinese fairy book.
Kingdoms. Baldwin. Fifty famous stories.
Sly. World stories retold. (Emperor and the school children.)
Kingfisher's necklace and ruffle. *See* How the kingfisher got his ring and ruffle.
Kingly children. *See* King's children.
Kingly guest. *See* Geirrod and Odin.
Kings and queens and peasant folk. Brady. Green forest fairy book.
King's ankus. Kipling. Second jungle book.
See also Three revellers and death.
King's bell. *See* Bell of Atri.

King's candles. Skinner. Topaz story book.
King's cat. Pearson. Laughing lion and other stories.
King's children. Bailey. Stories children need. (Kingly children.)
McSpadden. Stories from great operas.
King's counsellor. Wardrop. Georgian folk tales.
King's foot holder. Griffis. Welsh fairy tales.
King's hares. *See* Ashiepattle and the king's hares.
King's jewel. Bailey. Stories and rhymes for a child.
Danielson. Story telling time.
King's messenger. *See* Fair one with golden locks.
King's mistake; or, The prince who had no fairy godmother. Brown. Mermaid's gift.
Kings of Kilakkari. Alden. Boy who found the king.
King's page. Bailey. Stories for Sunday telling.
King's pie. Brown. Kisington town.
King's power. Caballero. Spanish fairy tales.
King's rabbit keeper. *See* Jesper who herded the hares.
King's servant. Lindsay. Story-teller.
King's son. I. Meigs. Kingdom of the winding road.
King's son. II. Wardrop. Georgian folk tales.
King's son and Messeria. Thorpe. Yule-tide stories.
King's son and the magic song, Story of the. Bourhill and Drake. Fairy tales from South Africa.
King's son and the painted lion. Æsop. Fables (Burt ed.).
See also Young man and the lion.
King's son and the Princess Singorra. Thorpe. Yule-tide stories.
King's son and the white-bearded Scolog. Curtin. Hero tales from Ireland.
King's son and Ubongopu. Gibbon. Reign of King Cole.
King's son from Erin, the Sprisawn, and the dark king. Curtin. Hero tales from Ireland.
King's three sons. I. Cary. French fairy tales. (King's three sons; or, The hunch-back and his two brothers.)
See also Three feathers.
King's three sons. II. Hall. Icelandic fairy tales.
King's treasure. James. Cat and the mouse.
King's white elephant. *See* Grateful elephant.
Kinkach Martinko. Chodzko. Fairy tales of the Slav.
See also Rumpelstiltskin.
Kinmont Willie. Grierson. Children's tales from Scottish ballads.
Kintaro, the golden boy. Griffis. Japanese fairy tales. (Boy brought up in the woods.)
Olcott. Wonder book of elves and fairies.
Ozaki. Japanese fairy book. (Adventures of Kintaro the golden boy.)
Tappan. Myths from many lands. (Child of the forest.)
Kirunmala; or, The wreath of light. Bradley-Birt. Bengal fairy tales.
See also Three sisters. I.

Kirwan's search for Hy-Brasail. Higginson. Tales of the enchanted islands of the Atlantic.
Kisa, the cat. Lang. Brown fairy book.
Lang. White doe.
Kiss of the unborn. Sologub. Sweet-scented name.
Kitchen family party. Storytellers' magazine. May 1917, p. 266.
Kite and the butterfly. *Elson and Runkel. Elson readers. Book 1.
Kite and the pigeons. Æsop. Fables (Black ed.).
Æsop. Fables (Burt ed.).
Scudder. Children's book.
Scudder. Fables and folk stories.
Wiggin and Smith Talking beasts.
Kite, Tale of. Faulkner. Story lady's book.
Kite that played a joke. Bailey. Friendly tales.
Kites and the crows. Bateman. Zanzibar tales.
Kitpooseagunow the Avenger. Partridge. Glooscap the great chief.
Kitten that wanted to be a Christmas present. *Dillingham and Emerson. Tell it again stories.
Kitten who forgot. Burchill Progressive road to reading: story steps.
Kitten who had no name. Bailey. In the animal world.
Kitten's tailor. Bacon. True philospher.
Kiviung. Bayliss. Treasury of Eskimo tales.
Klein-Else. Success library. v. 3.
Klickitat basket, Legend of the. Judson. Myths and legends of the Pacific Northwest.
Knapsack. Bay. Danish fairy and folk tales.
See also How a soldier punished the devils.
Knapsack, the hat and the horn. Canton. Reign of King Herla. (Luck of the youngest son.)
Grimm. Households stories (Crane tr.).
Grimm. Household tales (Burt ed. Fortune-seekers.)
See also Good-for-nothing. II.
Knave and fool. Ewing. Old-fashioned fairy tales.
Knavish little bird. Caballero. Spanish fairy tales.
Knight and his charger. Æsop. Fables (Burt ed.).
Knight and his story. Jenks. Tales of fantasy.
Knight Bambus. Baudis. Czech folk tales.
Knight betrayed. Guerber. Legends of the Rhine.
Knight of France. Storytellers' magazine. Sept. 1913, p. 172.
Knight of the ill-shapen coat. Herbertson. Heroic legends.
Knight of the green vesture, Adventures of. Grierson. Scottish fairy book.
Knight of the mermaid. Grierson. Scottish fairy book.
Knight of the Sun. Lang. Red romance book.
Knight, the lady, and the falcon. Cutler Stories of King Arthur and his knights.

Knight who married a water nymph. Guerber. Legends of the Rhine. (Spectral foot.)
See also Undine.
Knight Yaroslav Lasarevich and the Princess Anastasia, Story of. Steele. Russian garland of fairy tales.
Knightly waste-paper man. Nixon-Roulet. Japanese folk stories and fairy tales.
Knights and the good child. Bakewell. True fairy stories.
Knights and the naughty child. Bakewell. True fairy stories.
Knights' cellar. Thorpe. Yule-tide stories.
Knights of the fish. Caballero. Spanish fairy tales.
Lang. Brown fairy book.
Lang. Trusty John and other stories.
Singleton. Goldenrod fairy book.
Wiggin and Smith. Tales of wonder.
Knights of the Holy Grail. Patten. Junior classics. v. 2.
Knights of the silver shield. Alden. Why the chimes rang.
My Bookhouse. v. 4.
Van Sickle and Seegmiller. Riverside readers. 3d reader.
Knight's tale. *See* Palamon and Arcite.
Knocker's diamonds. Olcott. Book of elves and fairies.
Knockgrafton, Legend of. *Burchill. Progressive road to reading. Book 3. (How the carpenter lost his hump.)
Cary. French fairy tales. (Fairies and the two hunchbacks.)
Frost. Fairies and folk of Ireland. (*In* Ch. 6.)
Graves. Irish fairy book.
Jacobs. More Celtic fairy tales. (Legend of Knockgrafton.)
Olcott. Book of elves and fairies. (Monday! Tuesday!)
Yeats. Irish fairy tales.
See also Edwin and Sir Topaz; Elves and the envious man; You must not work on Sunday.
Knockmany, Legend of. Fuller. Book of friendly giants. (Cunning of Fin's wife.)
Graves. Irish fairy book.
Jacobs. Celtic fairy tales.
Yeats. Irish fairy tales.
See also Finn MacCool.
Knös. Stroebe and Martens. Swedish fairy book.
Knot-grass. Houghton. Russian grandmother's wonder tales.
Knut Spelevink. Poulsson. Top of the world stories.
Kojata. *See* King Kojata.
Königskinder. *See* King's children.
Koschei, the deathless. *See* Marya Morevna.
Kosciusko, Thaddeus. Stewart. Tell me a hero story. (Dream of freedom.)
Koshchéi without death. Curtin. Wonder-tales from Russia.
See also Marya Morevna; Tsarevna Loveliness-Inexhaustible.
Kovlad. Chodzko. Slav fairy tales.

Kron the mighty. Orcutt Princess Kallisto.
Kulooskap. Bayliss. Treasury of Indian tales. (*In* Sunbright heroes.)
Kunterbunt. Kunos. Forty-four Turkish fairy tales.
Kupti and Imani. Lang. Olive fairy book.
Lang. Snake prince.
Kuratko the terrible. Fillmore. Shoemaker's apron.
See also Cat and the parrot; Greedy cat; Wolf II.
Kutoyis, the avenger. Grinnell. Blackfoot lodge tales.
Nixon-Roulet. Indian folk tales. (Strange deeds of Kutoyis.)
Kuz'ma Skorobogaty. Polevoi. Russian fairy tales.
Kvasir's blood. *See* Odin and the mead.
Kwannon, Legend of. James. Green willow.
Kweedass and Kindawiss. Kennedy. New world fairy book.

L

Labor Day. *See* Elf's flower; Four-leaf clover; Only a penny.
Labourer and the nightingale. Æsop. Fables (Jacobs).
Lac of rupees. *See* Lac of rupees for a piece of advice.
Lac of rupees for a piece of advice. Jacobs. Indian fairy tales.
Wiggin and Smith. Tales of wonder. (Lac of rupees.)
See also Ivan.
Laconic answer. Baldwin. Fifty famous stories.
Lad and Luck's house. St. Nicholas. Ap. 1916, p. 529.
Lad and the devil. Asbjörnsen. Folk and fairy tales.
Dasent. Popular tales from the Norse. (Lad and the de'il.)
Mabie. Folk tales every child should know. (Lad and the de'il.)
Stroebe and Martens. Norwegian fairy book. (Young fellow and the devil.)
Lad and the fox. Djurklo. Fairy tales from the Swedish.
Johnson. Book of fairy-tale foxes. (Sleeping fox and the boy with a stone.)
Storytellers' magazine. June 1916, p. 355.
Wiggin and Smith. Tales of laughter.
Lad and the north wind. *See* Lad who went to the north wind.
Lad who made the princess say "That's a story." *See* Ashiepattle who made the princess tell the truth at last.
Lad who rode sidesaddle. Baldwin. Fifty famous people.
Lad who went to the north wind. Asbjörnsen. Folk and fairy tales.
Bay. Danish fairy and folk tales. (Boy who went to the north wind.)
Dasent. Norse fairy tales.
Dasent. Popular tales from the Norse.
*Elson and Runkel. Elson readers. Book 2.
Judd. Classic myths. (A legend of the north wind.)

Lad who went to the north wind—*continued.*
Mabie. Folk tales every child should know.
Patten. Junior classics. v. 1.
Storytellers' magazine. March 1914, p. 461.
Tappan. Folk stories and fables.
Thorne-Thomsen. East o' the sun and west o' the moon.
Thorpe. Yule-tide stories. (Youth who went to the north wind and demanded his flour again.)
See also Little old woman who went to the north wind.

Lad who went wooing the daughter of old Mother Corner. *See* Mother Roundabout's daughter.

Lad with one sandal. *See* Argonauts.

Lad with the beer keg. Asbjörnsen. Fairy tales from the far north.
Asbjörnsen. Tales from the fjeld. (Death and the doctor.)
Gade. Norwegian fairy tales.
See also Strange godfather.

Lad with the goat-skin. Graves. Irish fairy book. (Adventures of Gilla Na Chreck.)
Jacobs. Celtic fairy tales.

Ladder of lions. Harris. Little Mr. Thimblefinger.

Ladle that fell from the moon. Fielde. Chinese fairy tales.
Wiggin and Smith. Tales of laughter.

Ladronius, the prince of thieves. Tappan. Stories from the classics.

Lads who met the trolls in the Hedale Wood. *See* Trolls in Hedale Wood.

Lady and the fountain. *See* Sir Owain and the lady of the fountain.

Lady and the lion. *See* Soaring lark.

Lady and the wasp (poem). Success library. v. 3.

Lady-bird and little fly. *See* Spider and the flea.

Lady-bird and the fly. *See* Spider and the flea.

Lady Brown Owl. Potter. Pinafore pocket story book.

"Lady-bug, lady-bug." Potter. Pinafore pocket story book.

Lady Cicely went a-maying. Lindsay and Poulsson. Joyous travelers. (Second tale told by the older sister.)

Lady Dunya, History of. Arabian nights, More tales (Olcott).

Lady Featherflight. Johnson. Oak-tree fairy book.
See also Nix nought nothing.

Lady from the silver moon. *See* Bamboo-cutter and the moon-child.

Lady Godiva's ride. Guerber. Story of the English
Hortland. English folk and fairy tales.

Lady in fetters. Sologub. Sweet-scented name.

Lady in the mist. Storytellers' magazine. July 1916, p. 416.

Lady mole. Rhys. Fairy gold.

Lady of Kynast. Patten. Junior classics. v. 2.

Lady of Pintorp. Stroebe and Martens. Swedish fairy book.

Lady of Shalott. *See* Sir Lancelot and Elaine.

Lady of snow. Aspinwall. Short stories for short people.
Lady of solace. Lang. Red romance book.
Lady of Stavoren. *See* Sunken city.
Lady of the fountain. *See* Sir Owain and the lady of the fountain.
Lady of the lake. I. Baldwin. Stories of the king.
Lady of the lake. II. Griffis. Welsh fairy tales.
Pyle. Tales of wonder and magic.
Thomas. Welsh fairy book.
Lady of the moon. Martens. Chinese fairy book.
See also Moon's message.
Lady of the obelisk. Brooksbank. Legends of ancient Egypt.
Lady slipper orchid. Bryce. That's why stories.
Lady White and Lady Yellow. *See* Maiden White and Maiden Yellow.
Lady who was murdered by her husband. Arabian nights (Townsend. History of the lady who was murdered by her husband.)
Lady with the lantern. Hartland. English folk and fairy tales.
Ladybird! ladybird! Olcott. Wonder garden.
Lafitte, Jean. Stewart. Tell me a hero story. (Gentleman pirate.)
Laidley worm of Spindleston. *See* Laidly worm of Spindleston.
Laidly worm of Spindleston. Jacobs. English fairy tales. (Laidly worm of Spindleston Heugh.)
Marshall. Fairy tales of all nations. (Enchanted dragon.)
(poem). Rhys. Fairy gold. (Laidley worm of Spindleston.)
See also Lambton worm.
Laidly worm of Spindleston Heugh. *See* Laidly worm of Spindleston.
Laird and the man of peace. Ewing. Old-fashioned fairy tales.
Laird o' Co'. Douglas. Scottish fairy tales.
Laird o' Logie. Grierson. Children's tales from Scottish ballads.
Laird of Morphie and the water kelpie. Douglas. Scottish fairy tales. (Graham of Morphie.)
Grierson. Scottish fairy book.
Laka and the menehunes. Pope. Hawaii. (Island fairies.)
Colum. At the gateways of the day. (*In* Me-ne-hu-ne.)
Lake of gems. Wiggin and Smith. Tales of wonder.
Lake of Issarles, Legend of. Cary. French fairy tales.
Lake that walked, Story of. Storytellers' magazine. June 1915, p. 179.
See also Two old women and the lake.
Lakshmi's gift. Bradley-Birt. Bengal fairy tales.
Lamb and the fish. Grimm. Fairy tales (Paull tr.).
Lamb that went to fairyland. Fyleman. Rainbow cat.

Lambikin. Bailey. Firelight stories.
Bailey. Once upon a time animal stories. (Story of Lambikin.)
Baldwin. Another fairy reader.
Bryant. Stories to tell to children.
Coussens. Child's book of stories.
(play). Doheny. Play awhile.
*Elson and Runkel. Elson readers. Book 1.
Jacobs. Indian fairy tales.
(play). Lansing. Quaint old stories.
Patten. Junior classics. v. 1.
Skinner. Nursery tales from many lands.
*Spaulding and Bryce. Aldine readers. 2d reader.
Steel. Tales of the Punjab.
Wiggin and Smith. Tales of laughter.
Lambkin. *See* Lambikin.
Lambton worm. Hartland. English folk and fairy tales.
Jacobs. More English fairy tales.
Johnson. Elm-tree fairy book.
Rhys. Fairy gold.
See also Laidly worm of Spindleston.
Lame angel. Mendes. Fairy spinning wheel.
Lame boy. Cabot. Ethics for children.
Lame dog. Stroebe and Martens. Swedish fairy book.
Lame duck. *Carrick. Picture tales from the Russian.
Lame man and the blind man. *See* Blind man and the lame man.
Lame Molly. Johnson. Birch-tree fairy-book.
Lame squirrel's Thanksgiving. Bailey. Stories and rhymes for a child.
Lamia. I. *See* Serpent woman.
Lamia. II. Pyle. Tales of wonder and magic.
Lamp and the sun. Arnold and Gilbert. Stepping stones to literature. v. 2.
Lamp of Aladdin. *See* Aladdin.
Lampblack. Keyes. Stories and story-telling.
Lancelot. *See* Sir Lancelot.
Land and people, Origin of. *See* Creation of the world (Eskimo).
Land crab. Seton. Woodmyth and fable.
Land of discontented children. Storytellers' magazine. March 1917, p. 166.
Land of Jibbity Joo. Storytellers' magazine. Oct. 1917, p. 374.
Land of Nod. Castella. Sandman: his fairy tales.
Land of the dead. *See* Ghost wife. IV.
Land of the Hereafter. Pratt. Legends of the red children.
Land of the northern lights. Olcott. Red Indian fairy book.
Land of the polar star. Harrison. Star fairies.
Land of Yomi. James. Green willow.
Land of youth. I. Silver fairy book.

Land of youth. II. *See* Last of the Feni.
Land otter. Judson. Myths and legends of Alaska.
Land-Otter the Indian. Lang. Strange story book.
Land without common folks. Brown. One-footed fairy.
Landlord's mistake. Baldwin. Fifty famous people.
Language of animals. *See* Language of beasts.
Language of beasts. Grimm. Household tales (Burt ed. Language of animals).
Jacobs. Europa's fairy book. (Language of animals.)
Laboulaye. Fairy tales. (Language of animals. *In* Captain John's travels.)
Laboulaye. Last fairy tales. (King of the serpents.)
Lang. Crimson fairy book.
Lang. Magic ring and other stories.
Patten. Junior classics. v. 1. (Language of animals.)
Language of the birds. I. Blumenthal. Folk tales from the Russian.
Magnus. Russian folk tales.
O'Grady and Throop. Teachers' story teller's book.
Storytellers' magazine. Oct. 1914, p. 697.
Language of the birds. II. Olcott and Pendleton. Jolly book.
Language of the birds. I and II. *See also* Ravens; Three languages.
Lantern and the fan. Hall and Gilman. Story land. 2d reader. (Chinese story.)
Holbrook. Book of nature myths.
My Bookhouse. v. 2. (Girl who used her wits.)
Van Sickle and Seegmiller. Riverside readers. 2d reader.
See also Young head of the family.
Lanty O'Hoolahan and the little people. St. Nicholas. Oct. 1884, p. 929.
Laocoön. Baldwin. Thirty more famous stories. (Doom of Laocoön; Fall of Troy.)
Laomedon and the building of Troy. Baldwin. Story of the golden age. (*In* Cause of war.)
See also Trojan war.
Laotsze. Martens Chinese fairy book.
Lapwing and the owl. Storytellers' magazine. Jan. 1914, p. 384.
Lariboo. Smith. Good old stories.
Lark and her little ones. *See* Lark and her young ones. I.
Lark and her nest. *See* Lark and her young ones. I.
Lark and her young ones. I. Æsop. Fables (Black ed.).
Æsop. Fables (Burt ed.).
Æsop. Fables (Stickney).
Arnold and Gilbert. Stepping stones to literature. v. 2. (Lark's nest.)
Baldwin. Fairy stories and fables. (Lark and the farmer.)
Blaisdell. Child life. 2d reader. (Lark and her little ones.)
Boston collection of kindergarten stories.

Lark and her young ones. I.—*continued.*
Bryant. Stories to tell children. (Larks in the cornfield.)
Faulkner. Story lady's book.
Hall and Gilman. Story land. 2d reader. (Lark and the farmer.)
*Jones. 2d reader
Norton. Heart of oak books. v. 2.
Scudder. Children's book.
Scudder. Fables and folk stories.
Sly. World stories retold. (Larks in the wheat field.)
Tappan. Folk stories and fables.
Wiggin and Smith. Talking beasts.
*Young and Field. Literary readers. Book 2. (Lark and her nest.)
See also Wee birdies.
Lark and her young ones. II. Olcott. Good stories for great holidays. (Lark and its young ones.)
Lark and his spurs. Curry. Little classics.
See also Fairy who judged her neighbors.
Lark and the caterpillar. *See* Lesson of faith.
Lark and the child. *Dyer and Brady. Merrill readers. 2d reader.
See also Maribel and Mrs. Lark; Trading babies.
Lark and the farmer. *See* Lark and her young ones. I.
Lark, the fox, the cat and the snake. *See* Sun is shining.
Larks in the cornfield. *See* Lark and her young ones. I.
Larks in the wheat field. *See* Lark and her young ones. I.
Lark's nest. *See* Lark and her young ones. I.
"Lars, my lad!" Djurklo. Fairy tales from the Swedish.
Stroebe and Martens. Swedish fairy book. (Lasse, my thrall.)
Wiggin and Smith. Fairy ring.
Lass of Söndervand. Grundtvig. Danish fairy tales.
Lasse, my thrall. *See* "Lars. my lad!"
Lassie and her godmother. Dasent. Popular tales from the Norse.
Dasent. Norse fairy tales.
Gade. Norwegian fairy tales. (Virgin Mary as godmother.)
Stroebe and Martens. Norwegian fairy book. (Child of Mary.)
See also Fairy Tell-True.
Last abbot. Guerber. Legends of the Rhine.
Last dream of the old oak. Andersen. Fairy tales (Paull tr.).
Andersen. Stories and tales (Author's ed. Old oak-tree's last dream).
Last great council fire. *See* Disease, Origin of; Medicines, Origin of.
Last lesson. *See* Last lesson in French.
Last lesson in French. Blaisdell. Child life. 3d reader.
Bryant. How to tell stories to children. (Last lesson.)
Last of Osmo. *See* Fox, the bear and the poor farmer.

Last of the dragons. Faulkner. Story lady's book.
Last of the fairies. I. Coolidge. New Year's bargain.
Last of the fairies. II. Mendes. Fairy spinning wheel.
Last of the Feni; or, The man who went to the land of youth. Curtin. Myths and folk-lore of Ireland. (Oisin in Tir na n-Og.)
Frost. Fairies and folk of Ireland. (*In* Ch. 9.)
Graves. Irish fairy book. (Lay of Oisin in the land of youth.)
Grierson. Children's book of Celtic stories.
Higginson. Tales of the enchanted islands of the Atlantic. (Usheen in the island of youth.)
Joyce. Old Celtic romances. (Oisin in Tirnanoge; or, Last of the Fena.)
Rolleston. High deeds of Finn. (Birth of Oisin; Oisin in the lands of youth.)
See also Finn MacCool.
Last of the Picts. Douglas. Scottish fairy tales (Pechs).
Last of the serpents. Olcott. Wonder garden.
Last of the Templars. Guerber. Legends of the Rhine.
Last of the thunderbirds. Bayliss. Treasury of Eskimo tales.
Judson. Myths and legends of Alaska.
Last peacemaker queen. Nixon-Roulet. Indian folk tales.
Last pearl. Andersen. Fairy tales (Paull tr.).
Andersen. Stories and tales (Author's ed.).
Last year's fly. Nordau. Dwarf's spectacles.
Latona and the frogs. *Bailey. Wonder stories. (Wonder the frogs missed.)
Bailey and Lewis. For the children's hour. (Latona and the rustics.)
Beckwith. In mythland. v. 1. (Latona.)
Farmer. Nature myths. (Origin of frogs.)
Guerber. Myths of Greece and Rome. (*In* Apollo.)
Hartley. Stories from the Greek legends. (Childhood of Apollo and Artemis.)
Johonnot. Stories of heroic deeds. (Latona and the rustics.)
Judd. Classic myths. (Where the frogs came from.)
Kupfer. Stories of long ago. (Childhood of Diana and Apollo.)
Shaw. Stories of the ancient Greeks. (*In* In the moonlight.)
Wilson. Nature study reader. (Apollo's mother.)
See also First frogs.
Laugh-maker. Eastman. Wigwam evenings.
Laughing apple and the weeping apple. Kunos. Forty-four Turkish fairy tales.
Laughing dumpling. Hearn. Japanese fairy tales. (Old woman who lost her dumplings.)
Nixon-Roulet. Japanese folk stories and fairy tales.
Wiggin and Smith. Tales of laughter. (Old woman who lost her dumpling.)

Laughing Eye and Weeping Eye; or, The limping fox. Fillmore. Laughing prince. (Little lame fox.)
Johnson. Book of fairy-tale foxes. (Limping fox.)
Lang. Grey fairy book.
Lang. Invisible prince and other stories.
Success library. v. 3.
Laughing Ingibjorg. Hall. Icelandic fairy tales.
Laughing lion. Pearson. Laughing lion and other stories.
Laughing prince. Fillmore. Laughing prince.
Laughing water. *See* Minnehaha, Laughing water.
Launcelot. *See* Sir Lancelot.
Laurel. *See* Daphne.
Laurel tree, Story of. *See* Daphne.
Laurustinus and the rose-tree. Æsop. Fables (Burt ed.).
Law of the wood. Gatty. Parables from nature.
Wilson. Nature study reader.
Lawkamercyme (poem). Jacobs. More English fairy tales.
Lawn Dyarrig. Curtin. Hero tales from Ireland.
Graves. Irish fairy book.
Lawyer as a debtor. Fielde. Chinese fairy tales.
Lawyer's advice. Bay. Danish fairy and folk tales.
Lazy beauty and her aunts. *See* Three little crones each with something big. III.
Lazy bee. Quiroga. South American jungle tales.
Lazy boys who became the Pleiades. *See* Pleiades. II.
Lazy Coomarasawmy. St. Nicholas, March 1904, p. 403.
Lazy giant. Bailey. Friendly tales.
Lazy Harry. Grimm. Fairy tales (Paull tr.).
Lazy Jack. Chisholm and Steedman. Staircase of stories. (Lazy John.)
Coussens. Child's book of stories.
Hartland. English folk and fairy tales.
*Howard. Banbury cross stories.
Jacobs. English fairy tales.
Johnson. Oak-tree fairy book.
Keyes. Stories and story-telling.
Lansing. Rhymes and stories.
Mother Goose's nursery rhymes, tales and jingles (Warne ed.).
Rhys. Fairy gold.
Welsh. Stories children love. (Lazy Jack; or, I'll do so another time.)
See also Epaminondas and his auntie; Prudent Hans; Silly Matt.
Lazy Lizette. Underhill. Dwarfs' tailor and other fairy tales.
Lazy people, Tale of. Finger. Tales from silver lands.
Lazy raccoon. Bryce. That's why stories.
Lazy spinner. Grimm. Fairy tales (Paull tr.).
Lazy Taro. Armfield. Wonder tales.
Lazy white chicken. Storytellers' magazine. June 1917, p. 293.

Leaf from Heaven. Andersen. Fairy tales (Paull tr.).
Andersen. Stories and tales (Author's ed. Leaf from the sky).
Leaf from the sky. *See* Leaf from Heaven.
Leak in the dyke. Arnold and Gilbert. Stepping stones to literature. v. 3. (Boy hero.)
Bailey. Stories children need. (Little hero of Holland.)
Blaisdell. Child life. 3d reader.
Bryant. Best stories to tell to chidren. (Little hero of Haarlem.)
Bryant. How to tell stories to children. (Little hero of Haarlem.)
Cabot. Ethics for children. (Little hero of Haarlem.)
My Bookhouse. v. 2. (Boy hero of Harlem.)
Poulsson. In the child's world. (Little hero of Haarlem.)
Sly. World stories retold. (Boy hero of Holland.)
(poem). Smith. Good old stories.
Lean cat and the fat cat. *See* Old woman's cat.
Leap frog. *See* Leaping match.
Leap of Roushan Beg. Baldwin. Fifty famous stories.
Leaping match. Andersen. Best fairy tales (Henderson tr.).
Andersen. Fairy tales (Paull tr. Jumpers.)
Andersen. Wonder stories. (Leap frog.)
Darton. Wonder book of beasts. (Three jumpers.)
Skinner. Merry tales.
Leaping Rock in the Pipestone Valley. Judd. Wigwam stories.
Learn to wait. Ketchum and Jorgensen. Kindergarten gems.
Learned hunter. Grimm. Fairy tales. (Paull tr.).
Learned man, Story of. Gate. Fortunate days.
Learned owl. *See* Rama and Luxman.
"Learned princess." Maud. Heroines of poetry.
Leda and the swans. Hutchinson. Golden porch. (Heavenly twins.)
Lee penny. Douglas. Scottish fairy tales.
Leeching of Kayn's leg. Jacobs. More Celtic fairy tales.
Yeats. Irish fairy and folk tales.
Leelinau, the fairy girl. *See* Leelinau, the lost daughter.
Leelinau, the lost daughter. Judd. Wigwam stories. (Girl who became a pine tree.)
Olcott. Red Indian fairy book. (Leelinau the fairy girl.)
Schoolcraft. Indian fairy book.
Skinner. Pearl story book. (Pine tree maiden.)
Leezie Lindsay. Richards. Little master.
Left hand. *See* Christian merchant's story.
Legend of, etc. *See* the first important word of the title.
Legless knight and the blind knight. *See* Footless and blind champions. I.
Leilani the rainbow girl. Pope. Hawaii. (Rainbow girl.)

Lemon tree and the pumelo. Davis and Chow-Leung. Chinese fables and folk stories.
Leo the slave. Johonnot. Stories of the olden time.
Leonidas at Thermopylae. *See* Brave three hundred.
Leopard and the fox. Æsop. Fables (Black ed.).
Æsop. Fables (Burt ed.).
Leopard and the other animals. Wiggin and Smith. Talking beasts.
Leperhaun. *See* Lepracaun. II.
Lepracaun. I (poem). Graves. Irish fairy tales.
(poem). Book of elves and fairies. (Leprechaun; or, Fairy shoemaker.)
(poem). Winnington. Outlook fairy book. (Fairy shoemaker.)
(poem). Yeats. Irish fairy and folk tales. (Lepracaun; or, Fairy shoemaker.)
Lepracaun. II. Harrison. Old fashioned fairy book. (Leperhaun.)
Lepracaun. III. * Elson and Runkle. Elson readers. Book 2. (Fairy shoemaker.)
See also Bad boy and the Leprechaun; Boy who found the pots of gold; Field of Bolianus; Finn and the fairy shoemaker; Ragweed.
Leprechaun. *See* Lepracaun.
Less inequality than men deem. Frere. Old Deccan days.
Lesson for kings. Burlingame. Grateful elephant. (Brahmadatta and Mallika.)
Cabot. Ethics for children.
Jacobs. Indian fairy tales.
Lesson in humility. Baldwin. Fifty famous people.
Lesson in justice. Baldwin. Fifty famous people.
Lesson in manners. Baldwin. Fifty famous people.
Lesson in politeness. Van Sickle and Seegmiller. Riverside readers. 3d reader.
Lesson of faith. Boston collection of kindergarden stories.
Cowles. Art of story telling.
Esenwein and Stockard. Children's stories. (Wondrous change. Adapted.)
Gatty. Parables from nature.
Ketchum and Jorgensen. Kindergarten gems. (Lark and the caterpillar.)
Olcott. Good stories for great holidays.
Poulsson. In the child's world.
Skinner. Emerald story book. (Butterfly.)
Wickes. Happy holidays.
See also Nettle gatherer; Prince Butterfly and Cloverblossom; Small green caterpillar.
Lesson of the leaves. *See* Sibyl.
Leto. *See* Apollo: Birth of Apollo.
Letting in the jungle. Kipling. Second jungle book.
Leucothea. *See* Ulysses.

Liar, Adventures of. Storytellers' magazine. Nov. 1917, p. 444. (This includes: Liar and the bin-long nuts; Liar and the pigs feet; Golden stick; Liar and Buddha.)
Liban the mermaid. *See* Overflowing of Lough Neagh.
Lichens, Origin of. Young. Algonquin Indian tales. (*In* Ch. 21.)
Life and death. Nordau. Dwarf's spectacles.
Life that was lost. Storytellers' magazine. Sept. 1916, p. 463.
Lifelong penance. Guerber. Legends of the Rhine.
Life's secret. Pyle. Tales of folks and fairies.
Light-house lamp. Aspinwall. Short stories for short people.
Light of the fly. Miller. Philippine folklore stories.
Light princess. Mabie. Fairy tales every child should know.
Mabie. Heroes and fairies.
Macdonald. Dealings with fairies.
Macdonald. Light princess and other fairy tales.
Lightning. Brooks. Stories of the red children.
Pratt. Legends of the red children. (Legend of lightning.)
Lightning gold. Kennedy. New world fairy book.
Lightning trees. Pratt. Fairyland of flowers.
Like seeks like. Nordau. Dwarf's spectacles.
Lil' Hannibal, Story of. *See* Little Hannibal.
Lilac bush. Van Sickle and Seegmiller. Riverside readers. 4th reader.
Lilies white. Olcott. Wonder garden.
Lilla Rosa. *See* Lilla Rosa and Long Leda.
Lilla Rosa and Long Leda. Canton. Reign of King Herla. (Lilla Rosa.)
Tappan. Golden goose. (Golden goose.)
Thorpe Yule-tide stories.
See also Princess Rosette. I.
Lillekort. *See* Shortshanks.
Lilliput land. *See* Gulliver's travels: Lilliput land.
Lilly Etta and wee bruin. Coe and Christie. Story hour readers. Book 2.
Lily and the bear. Eells. Tales of enchantment from Spain.
Lily and the lion. *See* Soaring lark.
Lily-bell and Thistledown; or, Fairy sleeping beauty.
Alcott. Flower fables.
Alcott. Lulu's library. v. 2.
Lily maid of Astolat. *See* Sir Lancelot and Elaine.
Lily of the valley. I. Pratt. Fairyland of flowers.
Skinner. Turquoise story book.
Lily of the valley. II. *See* Dragon Sin.
Lily-star. *See* Star maiden.
Limestone broth. *See* Stone broth.
Limping fox. *See* Laughing Eye and Weeping Eye.
Lincoln, Abraham. Faulkner. Story lady's book. (Our American knight.)

Lincoln and the little birds. Baldwin. Fifty famous people. (Saving the birds.)
Cabot. Ethics for children. (Lincoln's unvarying kindness.)
My Bookhouse. v. 2. (Two little birds and a great man.)
Wickes. Happy holidays. (Lincoln's kindness to animals.)
Lincoln and the pig. Keyes. Stories and story telling. (Abraham Lincoln's kindness.)
Sly. World stories retold. (Abraham Lincoln and the pig.)
Lincoln and the woodchopper. Wickes. Happy holidays.
Lincoln's birthday. *See* How June found Massa Linkum; Man who made giants.
Linden and the oak. *See* Baucis and Philemon.
Line of golden light; or, The little blind sister. Harrison. In story land.
McFee. Treasury of flower stories. (Line of light and what it brought.)
Lineik and Laufey. Hall. Icelandic fairy tales.
Linton Church, Legend of. Douglas. Scottish fairy tales.
Lion and mouse. *See* Lion and the mouse.
Lion and other beasts. *See* Lion's share.
Lion and the ass. Æsop. Fables (Burt ed.).
Lion and the ass hunting (poem). Wiggin and Smith. Talking beasts.
Lion and the asses and hares. Æsop. Fables (Burt ed.).
Lion and the badger. Stanley. Animal folk tales.
Lion and the bear. Æsop. Fables (Black ed. Lion, the bear and the fox.)
Æsop. Fables (Burt ed. Lion, the tiger and the fox).
Baldwin. Fairy stories and fables. (The quarrel.)
Scudder. Fables and folk stories.
Lion and the cat. Lang. Brown fairy book.
Lion and the council of beasts. Æsop. Fables (Burt ed.).
Lion and the crane. Jacobs. Indian fairy tales.
Lion and the echo (poem). Æsop. Fables (Burt ed.).
Wiggin and Smith. Talking beasts.
Lion and the elephant. I. Æsop. Fables (Burt ed.).
Welsh. Stories children love.
Lion and the elephant. II. Wiltse. Folklore stories and proverbs.
Lion and the four bulls. Æsop. Fables (Black ed.).
Æsop. Fables (Burt ed. Lion and the four oxen.)
Æsop. Fables (Jacobs).
Scudder. Fables and folk stories. (Four bulls and the lion.)
Lion and the four oxen. *See* Lion and the four bulls.
Lion and the fox. *See* Lion, the fox and the beasts.
Lion and the frog. Æsop. Fables (Black ed.).
Æsop. Fables (Burt ed.).
Lion and the gadfly. Wiggin and Smith. Talking beasts.
See also Lion and the mouse.

Lion and the gnat. I. Æsop. Fables (Burt ed.).
(poem). Wiggin and Smith. Talking beasts.
Lion and the gnat. II. Bryce. Fables from afar.
See also Gnat and the bull.
Lion and the goat. Patten. Junior classics. v. 1.
Wiggin and Smith. Talking beasts.
Lion and the hare. Bidpai. Tortoise and the geese.
Coussens. Jade story book.
Rouse. Talking thrush.
Wiggin and Smith. Talking beasts. (Lion and the rabbit.)
See also Brother Rabbit conquers Brother Lion; Little jackals and the lion.
Lion and the jackals. *See* Little jackals and the lion.
Lion and the man. *See* Man and the lion.
Lion and the mosquitoes. Coussens. Jade story book. (In union is strength.)
Davis and Chow-Leung. Chinese fables and folk stories.
Stanley. Animal folk tales.
Wiggin and Smith. Talking beasts.
Lion and the mouse. Æsop. Fables (Black ed.).
Æsop. Fables (Burt ed.).
Æsop. Fables (Jacobs).
Æsop. Fables (Stickney).
Arnold and Gilbert. Stepping stones to literature. v. 2.
Baker and Carpenter. Language readers. Book 3.
Baldwin. Fairy stories and fables. (Mouse and the lion.)
Boston collection of kindergarden stories.
*Bowen. Second story reader. (Lion and the mouse.)
*Burchill. Progressive road to reading: Story steps.
Coussens. Child's book of stories.
(play). *Dyer and Brady. Merrill readers. 2d reader.
Esenwein and Stockard. Children's stories.
Grover. Folk-lore readers. v. 1.
Hall and Gilman. Story land. 2d reader.
Ketchum and Jorgensen. Kindergarten gems. (Lion and mouse.)
My Bookhouse. v. 1.
Patten. Junior classics. v. 1.
Scudder. Children's book.
Scudder. Fables and folk stories.
Sly. World stories retold.
Tappan. Folk stories and fables.
Wiggin and Smith. Talking beasts.
Wiltse. Folklore stories and proverbs.
Wiltse. Kindergarten stories.
*Young and Field. Literary readers. Book 2.
See also Elephant and the rats; Lion and the gadfly; Mr. Lion.
Lion and the mule. *See* Mule and the lion.
Lion and the old hare. Storytellers' magazine. Dec. 1913, p. 357. (Story of the lion and the old hare.)
Lion and the rabbit. *See* Lion and the hare.

Lion and the snake. Æsop. Fables (Burt ed.).
Lion and the statue. *See* Man and the Lion.
Lion and the two jackals. Success library. v. 3.
Lion and the wild dog. Wiggin and Smith. Talking beasts.
Lion going to war. *Bowen. Second story reader.
(poem). Wiggin and Smith. Talking beasts.
Lion hunting with other beasts. Æsop. Fables (Burt ed.)
Lion in bad company. Babbitt. More Jataka tales.
Lion in his den. *See* Lion, the fox and the beasts.
Lion in love. Æsop. Fables (Black ed.).
Æsop. Fables (Burt ed.).
Æsop. Fables (Jacobs).
Scudder. Children's book.
Scudder. Fables and folk stories.
Lion of Lucerne. Noyes. Twilight stories.
Lion passant. Brown. Kisington town.
Lion, Story of. *See* Androclus and the lion.
Lion, the ass and the fox. I. *See* Lion, the fox and the ass.
Lion, the ass and the fox. II. *See* Lion's share.
Lion, the bear and the fox. *See* Lion and the bear.
Lion, the bear, the monkey and the fox. Æsop. Fables (Burt ed.).
Wiggin and Smith. Talking beasts.
Lion, the fox and the ass. Æsop. Fables (Black ed. Lion, the ass and the fox.)
Æsop. Fables (Burt ed.).
Lion, the fox and the beasts. Æsop. Fables (Jacobs).
Baldwin. Fairy stories and fables. (Old lion.)
Coussens. Child's book of stories. (Lion in his den.)
Scudder. Children's book.
Scudder. Fable and folk stories. (Lion and the fox.)
Sly. World stories retold. (Lion and the fox.)
Wiggin and Smith. Talking beasts. (Invalid lion.)
Lion the fox and the storyteller. *See* Endless tale. III.
Lion, the fox, and the wolf. Æsop. Fables (Burt ed.).
Lion, the goat and the baboon. Dasent. Popular tales from the Norse.
Lion, the hyena and the rabbit. Bateman. Zanzibar tales.
Lion, the mouse and the cat. Wiggin and Smith. Talking beasts.
Lion, the tiger and the fox. *See* Lion and the bear.
Lionbruno. Macdonell. Italian fairy book.
Lioness and the bear (poem). Wiggin and Smith. Talking beasts.
Lioness and the fox. Æsop. Fables (Burt ed.).
Scudder. Children's book.
Lions in the way. Lindsay. Story-teller.
Lion's secret. Ortoli. Evening tales.
Lion's share. Æsop. Fables (Black ed. Lion and other beasts.)
Æsop. Fables (Burt ed. Lion, the ass and the fox.)

Lion's share—*continued.*
Æsop. Fables (Jacobs).
Baldwin. Fairy stories and fables.
Coe and Christie. Story hour readers. 3d book.
Patten. Junior classics. v. 1.
Scudder. Children's book. (Lion, the ass and the fox.)
Scudder. Fables and folk stories. (Lion, the ass and the fox.)
(poem). Wiggin and Smith. Talking beasts.
Litigious cats. *See* Matter of arbitration.
Litill Tritill, the bird and the peasant lad. Hall. Icelandic fairy tales.
Little acorn. Dillingham and Emerson. Tell it again stories.
Skinner. Emerald story book.
Little alligator and the jackal (play). Doheny. Play awhile. (Alligator and the jackal.)
Little and good. Gate. Broom fairies.
Little Anklebone. Steel. Tales of the Punjab.
Little Annie the goose-girl. Dasent. Popular tales from the Norse.
Little Annie's dream; or, The fairy flower. Alcott. Flower fables.
Little ant. I. Caballero. Spanish fairy tales.
See also Spider and the flea; Little black ant.
Little ant. II. *See* Little ant that was going to Jerusalem.
Little ant that was going to Jerusalem. Cary. French fairy tales. (Little ant that was going to Jerusalem, and the snow.)
Skinner. Very little child's book of stories. (Little ant.)
See also House that Jack built; Who is strongest?
Little bear. Bailey. Firelight stories.
Bailey. Once upon a time animal stories.
Brown. Kisington town.
Little Bear's-Son. Wheeler. Russian wonder tales.
Little bee Trunkhosie. Bailey. Firelight stories.
Storytellers' magazine. July. 1917, p. 334.
Little Beta and the lame giant. Harrison. In story land.
Little big man. My Bookhouse. v. 1.
Little bird, Story of the. *See* Monk and the bird's song.
Little bird told me. *See* What the birds said.
Little birds who lived in a cave, Story of the. Bourhill and Drake. Fairy tales from South Africa.
Little black ant. Skinner. Nursery tales from many lands.
See also Spider and the flea.
Little Black Mingo. Wiggin and Smith. Tales of laughter.
Little Black Sambo, Story of. Stone. Children's stories that never grow old.
Little blacksmith Verholen. Bosschère. Christmas tales of Flanders.
See also Smith and the devil.

Little Blessed Eyes; or, The fairy's birthday gift. Harrison. In story land.
Little blind boy. Bailey. Stories for Sunday telling.
Little blind sister. *See* Line of golden light.
Little blue apron. Potter. Pinafore pocket story book.
Little blue bag. Tales for bedtime.
Little blue flowers. *See* How flax was given to men.
Little blue hen. Bailey. Friendly tales.
Little boy and big cow. Bailey. Firelight stories. (Wee, wee man.)
Jacobs. More English fairy tales. (Wee, wee mannie.)
Johnson. Fir-tree fairy book.
My Bookhouse. v. 1. (Wee, wee mannie and the big, big coo.)
Wiggin and Smith. Tales of laughter. (Wee, wee mannie.)
Little boy and the little dog, Story of. Keyes. Stories and story-telling.
Little boy man. I. Eastman. Wigwam evenings.
Little boy-man. II. Schoolcraft. Indian fairy book.
Little boy man returns. Eastman. Wigwam evenings. (Return of the little boy man.)
See also Manabozho and the lake magicians.
Little boy who forgot to wash his hands. Cowles. Art of story telling.
Little boy who found his fortune. *See* Old hag's long leather bag.
Little boy who wanted to be a soldier. Storytellers' magazine. Feb. 1914, p. 444.
Little brave heart. Donaldson. Little papoose listens.
Little brother and sister. *See* Brother and sister.
Little brothers of the air. *See* St. Francis of Assisi.
Little brown bantam. Faulkner. Story lady's book.
Little brown bear and big billy goat. Skinner. Very little child's book of stories.
See also Little white rabbit. II.
Little brown berry. Bailey. Stories and rhymes for a child.
Little brown fairy. Storytellers' magazine. June 1914, p. 611.
Little brown hen. Brown. One-footed fairy.
Little brown herb. *See* Hans and the wonderful flower.
Little Brown Lady. Danielson. Story telling time.
Little brown man. Brady. Green forest fairy tales.
Little brown path. Bailey. Stories for Sunday telling.
Little bud. Alcott. Flower fables.
Alcott. Lulu's library. v. 2.
Little bull-calf. Jacobs. More English fairy tales.
Little Burnt-face. *See* Little Scar-face.
Little Butterkin. Asbjörnsen. Fairy tales from the far north.
Dasent. Norse fairy tales. (Buttercup.)
Dasent. Popular tales from the Norse. (Buttercup.)
Pyle. Fairy tales. (Buttercup.)

Little Butterkin—*continued.*
Tappan. Folk stories and fables.
Little cabin boy. Armfield. Wonder tales.
Little cake-bird. Hodgkins. Atlantic treasury of childhood stories.
Litte Carl's Christmas. *See* Sabot of Little Wolff.
Little castaways. Scudder. Seven little people.
Little chick that didn't like to go to bed. Storytellers' magazine. Sept. 1916, p. 490.
Little chicken Kluk. *See* Chicken-Little.
Little chicken Kluk and his companions. *See* Chicken-Little.
Little child and the pumpkin tree. Dasent. Popular tales from the Norse.
Little Childeric's bees. Canton. Reign of King Herla.
Little china shepherdess. Walker. Sandman's goodnight stories.
Little Chinese rose. Davis and Chow-Leung. Chinese fables and folk stories.
Little Claus and Big Claus. Andersen. Fairy tales (Lucas tr. Great Claus and Little Claus.)
Andersen. Fairy tales (Paull tr.).
Andersen. Fairy tales and stories (Toksvig).
Andersen. Wonder stories (Author's ed.).
Dasent. Popular tales from the Norse. (Big Peter and Little Peter.)
Lang. Twelve huntsmen and other stories. (Story of Big Klaus and Little Klaus.)
Lang. Yellow fairy book. (Story of Big Klaus and Little Klaus.)
Scudder. Children's book.
See also Countryman and the merchant; Hudden and Dudden and Donald O'Neary.
Little clay boy. *See* Lutoschenka.
Little cookie boy. Wiltse. Kindergarten stories.
Little corn-bringer. Olcott. Red Indian fairy book.
Little cowherd brother. Bailey. Stories children need.
Children's story garden.
Partridge. Story telling in home and school.
Little cripple (poem). Lindsay and Poulsson. Joyous travelers. (Second tale told by the scholar.)
Little cup of tears. Dasent. Popular tales from the Norse.
Thorpe. Yule-tide stories.
Little Czar Novishny, the false sister, and the faithful beasts. Bain. Cossack fairy tales.
Little Daffydowndilly. Bailey. Stories children need.
Benson. Really truly fairy tales.
Curry. Little classics. (Abridged.)
Hartwell. Story hour readings. 5th year.
Hawthorne. Little Daffydowndilly.
Little darner. Ewing. Old-fashioned fairy tales.

Little dawn boy and the rainbow trail. Field third reader.
Olcott. Red Indian fairy book.
Little Daylight. Bailey. Stories children need.
Bryant. How to tell stories to children.
Macdonald. Light princess and other fairy tales.
Storytellers' magazine. March, 1916, p. 142.
Little Dear-me. Potter. Pinafore pocket story book.
Little Diamond and the north wind. My Bookhouse. v. 3.
Little dog and big dog. Lindsay. Story garden.
Little duchess. Maud. Heroines of poetry.
Little Duckling tries his voice. *Skinner. Very little child's book of stories.
Little dwellers in the marsh. Harrison. Moon princess.
Little engine that could. My Bookhouse. v. 1.
See also Little steam engine; Royal engine.
Little errand girl's new dress. *See* Iris.
Little eyes. *See* Matariki.
Little farmer. Grimm. Fairy tales (Lucas tr. Little peasant.)
Grimm. Household stories (Crane tr.).
Little fawn. Wilson. Myths of the red children.
Little feather of Fenist the bright falcon. *See* Bright-Hawk's feather.
Little field mouse, Adventures of. Bryant. Stories to tell to children.
Little field mice. Bailey. Folk stories and fables.
Little Fingerling. Macdonell. Italian fairy book.
Little fir tree. *See* Fir-tree.
Little fir tree that blossomed. Bailey. Stories for Sunday telling.
Little fish and the fisher (poem). Æsop. Fables (Stickney. Supplement).
Little-flower-that-hides-in-the-snow. Donaldson. Moons of long ago.
Little folk of the glass hills. Canton. Reign of King Herla.
Little folks' presents. Grimm. Fairy tales (Paull tr.).
Little fool Ivan. Blumenthal. Folk tales from the Russian. (Ivanoushka, the simpleton.)
Polevoi. Russian fairy tales.
Little footsteps upon the water. Bailey. Firelight stories.
Bailey. Once upon a time animal stories.
Little Forget-me-not. Gibbon. Reign of King Cole.
Little Fred and his fiddle. Asbjörnsen. Fairy tales from the far north.
Asbjörnsen. Tales from the fjeld. (Little Freddy with his fiddle.)
Dasent. Norse fairy tales. (Little Freddy with his fiddle.)
Field. Famous fairy tales.
Gade. Norwegian fairy tales.

Little Fred and his fiddle—*continued.*
Thorne-Thomsen. East o' the sun and west o' the moon. (Little Freddy with his fiddle.)
See also Jew among the thorns.
Little Freddy with his fiddle. *See* Little Fred and his fiddle.
Little friend. Brown. Flower princess.
Little friend coyote. Grinnell. Punishment of the stingy.
Little friend sparrow. *See* Swallow king's rewards.
Little gingerbread man. *See* Gingerbread man. III.
Little girl and the hare. *See* Rabbit's bride.
Little girl and the serpent. Stroebe and Martens. Danish fairy book.
Little girl of snow. *See* Snowflake. I.
Little girl who traveled on a big ship. Nordau. Dwarf's spectacles.
Little girl who wanted the stars. *See* Stars in the sky.
Little girl's Christmas. Dickinson and Skinner. Children's book of Christmas stories.
Little Glass-man. *See* Stone-cold heart.
Little glass shoe. Jerrold. Reign of King Oberon.
Little glass slipper. *See* Cinderella.
Little gold apple. Bailey. Stories for Sunday telling.
Little gold shoe. *See* Cinderella.
Little Golden Hair. *See* Three bears.
Little Goldenhood. Coussens. Child's book of stories. (History of little Golden-Hood.)
*Heller and Bates. Little Golden Hood.
Lang. Red fairy book. (True history of Little Goldenhood.)
See also Little Red Riding Hood.
Little good mouse. *See* Good little mouse.
Little Goody Two-Shoes. *See* Goody Two-Shoes.
Little grain of wheat, Story of. Skinner. Emerald story book.
Little gray grandmother; or, The enchanted mirror.
Bailey and Lewis. For the children's hour.
Harrison. In story land.
Little gray lamb. Bailey. Stories for Sunday telling.
Little gray man. I. Jokai. Golden fairy book.
Laboulaye. Fairy tales.
Laboulaye. Last fairy tales.
Storytellers' magazine. Nov. 1916, p. 588.
Little gray man. II. Lang. Grey fairy book.
Lang. Marvellous musician.
Little gray mouse. Segur. French fairy tales.
Segur. Old French fairy tales.
Little gray pony. Bailey. Stories children need.
Burchill. Progressive road to reading: story steps.
Lindsay. Mother stories.
My Bookhouse. v. 1.
O'Grady and Throop. Teachers' story teller's book.

Little green door. Meyer. Little green door and other stories.
Little green elf's Christmas. Bailey. Stories and rhymes for a child.
Little green field. Potter. Pinafore pocket story book.
Little green frog. Lang. Elf maiden.
Lang. Yellow fairy book.
Little Gretchen and the wooden shoe. Curtiss. Christmas stories and legends.
Dickinson and Skinner. Children's book of Christmas stories.
Storytellers' magazine. Dec. 1914, p. 747.
See also Piccola.
Little Gretchen's lily. Danielson. Story telling time.
Little guards of the night. Donaldson. Moons of long ago.
Little Gulliver. My Bookhouse. v. 4.
Little Gustava. Elson and Runkel. Elson Readers. Book 1.
Little Half Chick. *See* Half-Chick.
Little half-cock, Story of. Bosschère. Christmas tale of Flanders.
See also Drakesbill and his friends.
Little Hannibal. Coe. Second book of stories. (Story of Lil' Hannibal.)
My Bookhouse. v. 2. (Story of Li'l' Hannibal.)
Skinner. Merry tales. (Story of Li'l' Hannibal.)
Wickes. Happy holidays. (Story of Li'l' Hannibal.)
Little Hannibal's Christmas. Wickes Happy holidays. (Li'l' Hannibal's Christmas.)
Little Hans and the star of Bethlehem. Gibbon. Reign of King Cole.
Little hare. Lang. Elf maiden.
Lang. Pink fairy book.
Little hare of Oki. *See* Eighty-one brothers.
Little heartsease. *See* Pansies. II.
Little hero of Haarlem. *See* Leak in the dyke.
Little hero of Holland. *See* Leak in the dyke.
Little horse and his kind master. Johnson. Oak-tree fairy book.
Little house. *Carrick. Picture tales from the Russian.
Little house in the woods. *See* House in the wood.
Little house neighbors. Bailey. Friendly tales.
Little humpbacked horse. Wheeler. Russian wonder tales.
Little hunchback. I. Arabian nights (Lang).
Arabian nights (Townsend. Story of the little hunchback.)
Arabian nights, More tales (Olcott. Story of the hunchback.)
Chisholm. Enchanted land. (Hunchback.)
Olcott and Pendleton. Jolly book. (Story of the hunchback.)
Scudder. Children's book. (Story of the little hunchback.)
Little hunchback. II. Cary. French fairy tales.
See also Golden bird. II.

Little hunting dog. Martens. Chinese fairy book.
See also Sick-bed elves.
Little Hyacinth's kiosk. Kunos. Forty-four Turkish fairy tales.
Little Hylas. *See* First tree frog.
Little ice man. Eastman. Indian legends retold. (Ice man puts out the fire.)
Wilson. Myths of the red children.
Little Ida's flowers. Andersen. Fairy tales (Paull tr.).
Andersen. Fairy tales and stories (Toksvig.)
Andersen. Wonder stories (Author's ed.).
Lyman. Story telling.
Singleton. Wild flower fairy book.
Little In-a-minute. Bailey. For the story teller.
Little Jack Roll-a-Round. Bryant. Best stories to tell to children.
Bryant. Stories to tell to children.
Little Jackal and the alligator. Bryant. Best stories to tell to children.
Bryant. Stories to tell to children.
*Coe and Christie. Story hour readers. Book I. (Clever jackal.)
(play). Doheny. Play awhile (Alligator and the jackal.)
*Dyer and Brady. Merrill readers. 2d reader. (Hungry jackal and a hungry alligator. Abridged.)
Frere. Old Deccan days. (Alligator and the jackal.)
Pyle. Wonder tales retold. (Jackal and the alligator.)
Skinner. Merry tales.
Stanley. Animal folk tales. (Alligator and the jackal.)
Van Sickle and Seegmiller. Riverside readers. 2d reader.
Wiggin and Smith. Tales of laughter. (Alligator and the jackal.)
See also "Heyo, house"; Jackal and the crocodile.
Little jackal and the camel. *See* Tit for tat.
Little jackals and the lion. Bryant. Best stories to tell to children.
Bryant. Stories to tell to children.
*Burchill. Progressive road to reading. Book 2.
Darton. Wonder book of beasts. (Singh Rajah and the cunning litte jackals.)
Frere. Old Deccan days. (Singh Rajah and the cunning little jackals.)
Peck. Stories for good children. (Lion and the jackals.)
Tappan. Folk stories and fables. (Singh Rajah and the cunning little jackals.)
Wiggin and Smith. Tales of laughter. (Singh Rajah and the cunning little jackals.
See also Lion and the hare.
Little Jack's playthings. *Dillingham and Emerson. Tell it again stories.
Little Jacob and the sugar-plum tree. Underhill. Dwarfs' tailor and other fairy tales.

Little Jewel. *See* Young head of the family.
Little Joe Otter's slippery slide. Murray. Story book treasures.
Little Karen and her baby. Coolidge. Round dozen.
Little King Loc. Lang. Olive fairy book.
Lang. Little King Loc and other stories.
Little king's rabbits. Lindsay. Story garden.
Little lame fox. *See* Laughing Eye and Weeping Eye.
Little lame prince. Bailey. For the story teller.
Blaisdell. Child life. 4th reader.
Stone. Children's stories that never grow old.
Little Lasse. Lang. Lilac fairy book.
Lang. Magic book.
Little leaf's Thanksgiving. Bailey. Stories for Sunday telling.
Little lights. Bryce. Fables from afar.
Little loaf. Cabot. Ethics for children.
Little Lodewyk and Annie the witch. Bosschère. Christmas tales of Flanders.
Little Long-tail. Hoxie. Kindergarten story book.
Little lost stars, Story of. Donahey. Tales to be told to children.
Little Maia. *See* Thumbelina.
Little maid Hildegarde. Lindsay. Story-teller.
Little maiden who became a laurel tree. *See* Daphne.
Little man. Laboulaye. Last fairy tales.
Little man as big as your thumb with mustaches seven miles long. *See* Tsarevitch Ivan and the harp that harped without a harper.
Little mare. Bay. Danish fairy and folk tales.
Little martyr. Guerber. Legends of the Rhine.
Little match girl. *Andersen. Best fairy tales (Henderson tr.).
Andersen. Fairy tales (Lucas tr.).
Andersen. Fairy tales (Paull tr. Little match-seller.)
Andersen. Fairy tales (Turpin).
Andersen. Stories (Riverside ed.).
Andersen. Stories and tales (Author's ed.).
Bailey. Stories children need.
Baker and Carpenter. Language readers. 3d. year. (Little match-seller.)
Blaisdell. Child life. 2d reader.
Coe. First book of stories.
Curtiss. Christmas stories and legends.
Jerrold. Big book of fairy tales.
Ketchum and Jorgensen. Kindergarten gems. (Little match-seller.)
Klingensmith. Household stories for little readers. (Little match seller.)
Noyes. Twilight stories.
Olcott. Good stories for great holidays.
Scudder. Children's book.
Storytellers' magazine. Jan. 1916, p. 5.

Little match seller. *Sec* Little match girl.
Little May. Stroebe and Martens. Danish fairy book.
Little mermaid. Andersen. Fairy tales (Lucas tr. Mermaid.)
Andersen. Fairy tales (Paull tr.).
Andersen. Fairy tales and stories (Toksvig.)
Andersen. Fairy tales (Turpin ed.).
Andersen. Wonder stories (Author's ed. Little sea-maid.)
Chisholm. In fairyland.
Marshall. Fairy tales of all nations.
Singleton. Wild flower fairy book.
Winnington. Outlook fairy book.
Little Millie. Ketchum and Jorgensen. Kindergarten gems.
Little Miss Magpie. Bigham. Merry animal tales.
Little Miss Magpie at Madison Square. Bigham. Merry animal tales.
Little Miss Mouse and her friends. Rouse. Talking thrush.
Little Mister Cricket and the other creatures. Harris. Told by Uncle Remus.
Little Mook. Hauff. Caravan tales.
Hauff. Fairy tales. (History of the little Mook.)
Little mouse and the strangers. *See* Mouse, the cat and the cock.
Little mouse pie. Storytellers' magazine. Oct. 1913, p. 199.
Little mouse's mistake. *See* Mouse, the cat and the cock.
Little Nell and Mrs. Jarley's wax works. Bailey. Stories children need.
Little Never-upset. Walker. Sandman's goodnight stories.
Little Niebla. *See* Child of the mist.
Little No-Cap. Potter. Pinafore pocket story book.
Little nymph who loved bright colours. Olcott. Wonder garden.
Little nymph who rang the bells. Olcott. Wonder garden.
Little old man and his gold. Danielson. Story telling time.
Little old woman. Macdonell. Italian fairy book.
Little old woman and her pig. *See* Old woman and her pig.
Little old woman who lived in a vinegar bottle. Chisholm and Steedman. Staircase of stories.
Little old woman who went to the north wind. Bailey. Firelight stories.
See also Lad who went to the north wind.
Little One-eye, little Two-eyes, and little Three-eyes. *See* One-eye, Two-eyes, Three-eyes.
Little One-eye, Two-eyes, Three-eyes. *See* One-eye, Two-eyes, Three-eyes.
Little owl boy. Olcott. Red Indian fairy book.
Little peach child. *See* Momotaro.
Little peach man. Potter. Pinafore pocket story book.
Little Peachling, Adventures of. *See* Momotaro.
Little peasant. *See* Little farmer.

Little people of the Senecas. Judd. Wigwam stories.
Little Persian. Arnold and Gilbert. Stepping stones to literature. v. 3. (Truthful little Persian.)
Baldwin. Fifty famous people. (Boy and the robbers.)
Field third reader. (Boy and the robbers.)
Whittier. Child life in prose.
Little Persian princess. St. Nicholas. Aug. 1889, p. 757.
Wilkins. Young Lucretia.
Little Piccola. *See* Piccola.
Little pig. Burchill. Progressive road to reading: story-steps.
Lindsay. More mother stories.
Little pig that went to see the world. Field first reader.
Little pigeon. Burchill. Progressive road to reading: story-steps.
Little pine tree. *See* Little pine tree who wished for new leaves.
Little pine tree who wished for new leaves. *Bailey. Folk stories and fables.
Bailey and Lewis. For the children's hour.
Blaisdell. Child life. 2d reader. (Little pine tree.)
*Elson and Runkel. Elson readers. Book 1. (Pine tree and its needles.)
Ketchum and Jorgensen. Kindergarten gems. (Discontented tree.)
Klingensmith. Household stories for little readers. (Discontented pine tree.)
O'Grady and Throop. Teachers' story teller's book. (Discontented tree.)
Olcott. Good stories for great holidays. (Little tree that longed for other leaves.)
(poem). Pratt. Fairyland of flowers. (Little pine tree.)
(poem). Strong. All the year round. v. 2. Winter. (Discontented pine.)
Young and Field. Literary readers. Book 2. (Little pine tree.)
Little pink rose. Bryant. Best stories to tell to children.
Bryant. Stories to tell to children.
Little pitcher-man. Walker. Sandman's goodnight stories.
Little Portunes. Rhys. Fairy gold.
Little Princess White Chicory. Olcott. Wonder garden.
Little pumpkin. Skinner. Topaz story book.
Little rabbit who wanted red wings. Bailey. For the story teller.
Bailey. Once upon a time animal stories. (Rabbit who wanted red wings.)
Elson and Runkel. Elson readers. Book 2. (Rabbit who wanted wings.)
Field first reader. (Rabbit who wanted red wings.)
Harper. Story-hour favorites.
My Bookhouse. v. 1.

Little rabbits. Coe. Second book of stories.
Harris. Uncle Remus, his songs and his sayings. (Story about the little rabbits.)
My Bookhouse. v. 2. (Story about the little rabbits.)
See also Why Brother Wolf didn't eat the little rabbits.
Little Ravageot. Macé. Home fairy tales.
Little red apple. Bailey. Stories and rhymes for a child.
Storytellers' magazine. July 1917, p. 333.
Little red candle. Storytellers' magazine. Dec. 1917, p. 536. (*In* Little storyteller.)
Little Red-cap. *See* Little Red Riding Hood.
Little red hen. I. Bailey. Folk stories and fables.
Blaisdell. Child life. 2nd reader. (Little red hen and the grain of wheat.)
Bowen. Second story reader. (Grain of wheat.)
Bryant. Stories to tell to children. (Little red hen and the grain of wheat.)
*Burchill. Progressive road to reading. Book 1. (Rat, the hen, the pig and the duck; Hen and the bag of flour.)
Coe. First book for story-tellers.
Coussens. Child's book of stories. (Little red hen and the grain of wheat.)
*Elson and Runkel. Elson readers. Book 1.
Faulkner. Old English nursery tales.
Johnson. Oak-tree fairy book. (Little red hen and the wheat.)
*Lansing. Rhymes and stories. (Little red hen and the grain of wheat.)
My Bookhouse. v. 1. (Little red hen and the grain of wheat.)
O'Grady and Throop. Teachers' story teller's book. (Little red hen and the grain of wheat.)
Old, old tales retold.
*Treadwell and Free. Reading literature: primer.
*Van Sickle and Seegmiller. Riverside readers. 1st reader.
See also How the cat got all the grain; Wonderful cake.
Little red hen. II. Bryant. Stories to tell to children. (Another little red hen.)
(poem). Bryant. Stories to tell to children. (Story of the little red hen.)
Coussens. Child's book of stories. (Fox and the little red hen.)
Dyer. What-happened-then stories.
Faulkner. Old English nursery tales. (Little red hen and the fox.)
Johnson. Book of fairy-tale foxes. (Robber fox and the little red hen.)
Johnson. Oak-tree fairy book. (Fox and the little red hen.)
*Jones. Second reader. (Fox and the small red hen.)
Klingensmith. Household tales.
Klingensmith. Just stories.
*Lansing. Rhymes and stories.

Little red hen. II.—*continued.*
O'Grady and Throop. Teacher's story tellers' book. (Little red hen and the fox.)
(poem). Scudder. Doings of the Bodley family in town and country.
Sly. World stories retold.
Whitney. Faith Gartney's girlhood. (*In* Ch. 5.)
Little red hen. III. Bailey and Lewis. For the children's hour.
Klingensmith. Household stories.
Little red hen. III. includes both I and II.
Little red hen. IV. *See* Cock, the mouse and the little red hen.
Little red hen and the fox. *See* Little red hen. II.
Little red hen and the grain of wheat. *See* Little red hen. I.
Little red hen and the wheat. *See* Little red hen. I.
Little red house with no doors. Bailey. Stories for Sunday telling.
Little red juggler. Leamy. Fairy minstrel of Glenmalure.
Little Red Plume. *See* First corn. II.
Little Red Riding Hood. Adams. Folk-story and verse.
Allison and Perdue. Story in primary instruction.
Aunt Louisa's book of fairy tales.
Baldwin. Fairy stories and fables.
Bates. Once upon a time.
Blaisdell. Child life. 2d reader.
*Burchill. Progressive road to reading. Book 2.
Burke. Fairy tales.
Chaplin. Treasury of fairy tales. (Red Riding Hood.)
Chisholm. In fairy land. (Red Riding Hood.)
Coe. First book of stories.
Coussens. Child's book of stories.
Crane. Red Riding Hood's picture book.
*(play). Doheny. Play awhile.
Douglas. Favourite French fairy tales.
Dyer. What-happened-then stories.
Favorite fairy tales.
Forty famous fairy tales.
Grimm. Fairy tales (Lucas tr. Red Riding Hood.)
Grimm. Fairy tales (Paull tr. Little Red Cap.)
Grimm. Household stories (Crane tr. Little Red-cap.)
Grimm. Household tales (Burt ed.).
Jerrold. Big book of fairy tales.
Johnson. Oak-tree fairy book.
Ketchum and Jorgensen. Kindergarten gems.
Klingensmith. Household stories. (Red Riding Hood.)
Lang. Blue fairy book.
Lang. Little Red Riding Hood and other stories.
Lansing. Rhymes and stories.
Mabie. Fairy tales every child should know.
Mabie. Heroes and fairies.

Little Red Riding Hood —*continued.*
Mother Goose rhymes, jingles and fairy tales (Altemus ed.).
Mulock. Fairy book.
Norton. Heart of oak books. v. 2.
Nursery tales.
Patten. Junior classics. v. 1.
Perkins. Twenty best fairy tales.
Perrault. Fairy tales.
Perrault. Old-time stories.
Perrault. Tales of Mother Goose.
Perrault. Tales of passed times.
Pyle. Mother's nursery tales.
Rhys. Fairy gold.
Scudder. Book of folk stories.
Scudder. Children's book.
Scudder. Fables and folk stories.
Sly. World stories retold. (Red Ridinghood.)
Stone. Children's stories that never grow old.
Success library. v. 3.
Tappan. Folk stories and fables.
Tweed. Fairy tales everyone should know.
Valentine. Old, old fairy tales (Warne ed.).
Washburn. Old-fashioned fairy tales.
Welsh. Stories children love. (Story of Little Red Riding Hood.)
See also Little Goldenhood.
Little red tortoise. Stanley. Animal folk tales.
Little red wagon. Bailey. Stories for Sunday telling.
Little Redcap. Olcott. Book of elves and fairies.
Little rid hin. *See* Little red hen. II.
Little Roger's night in the church. Coolidge. Mischief's Thanksgiving.
Little rooster. I. *Bailey. Folk stories and fables. (Alarm clock that was alive.)
Bailey and Lewis. For the children's hour (1920 ed. Live alarm clock.)
Bailey and Lewis. For the children's hour (5th ed. Living alarm clock.)
*Elson and Runkel. Elson readers. Book 1.
Little rooster. II. Boston collection of kindergarten stories.
Little Ruby Fish. *See* Muchie Lal.
Little Scar Face. Leland. Algonquin legends of New England. (Invisible one.)
Olcott. Red Indian fairy book. (Little Burnt-face.)
Partridge. Glooscap the great chief. (Oochigeaskw, the little scarred girl.)
Storytellers' magazine. Nov. 1913, p. 265. (Oochigeaskw, the little scarred girl.)
Tanner. Legends from the red man's forest. (Indians' Cinderella.)
Wilson. Myths of the red children.
Young and Field. Literary readers. Book 2.

Little sea-maid. *See* Little mermaid.
Little shepherd. Curtiss. Christmas stories and legends.
Lindsay. More mother stories.
(play). Van Sickle and Seegmiller. Riverside readers. 2d reader.
Little shepherd boy. *See* Shepherd boy and the king.
Little silver hen. Storytellers' magazine. Jan. 1916, p. 25.
Wilkins. Pot of gold. (Silver hen.)
Little Silver's dreams. Griffis. Japanese fairy tales.
Little Simpleton, Story of. *See* Silver saucer and the crystal apple.
Little singing frog. Fillmore. Laughing prince.
Little Sister. Fillmore. Mighty Mikko.
See also Seven ravens.
Little sister and little brother. Dole. White duckling.
Storytellers' magazine. March 1916, p. 137.
See also Brother and sister. I.
Little Sister Kindness and the loving stitches. Cowles. Art of story-telling.
Little sister of the giants. Eells. Tales of giants from Brazil.
See also Snow-White and the seven dwarfs.
Little Snow-Flake. *See* Twelve months. II.
Little Snow maiden. *See* Snowflake. I.
Little Snow-White. *See* Snow-White and the seven dwarfs.
Little Snowdrop. *See* Snow-White and the seven dwarfs.
Little soldier. Bailey. Stories for Sunday telling.
Lang. Green fairy book.
See also Magic apples II; Nose-tree.
Little Sosana and her gold-wrought shoe. Goddard. Fairy tales in other lands.
See also Cinderella.
Little spirit of Massawunk. Kennedy. New world fairy book.
Little star flower. Donaldson. Moons of long ago.
Little steam engine. Van Sickle and Seegmiller. Riverside readers. 2d reader.
See also Little engine that could; Royal engine.
Little stepmother. Cather. Educating by story telling.
Little stick. Sologub. Sweet-scented name.
Little Sunshine. I. Bay. Danish fairy and folk tales. (Sunshine.)
Little Sunshine. II. Bailey and Lewis. For the children's hour.
Blaisdell. Child life. 2d reader.
Little Surya Bai. Frere. Old Deccan days.
Pyle. Fairy tales from far and near.
Singleton. Wild flower fairy book. (Sun-lady, Surya Bai.)
Wiggin and Smith. Tales of wonder.
Little tadpole. Skinner. Emerald story book.
Little tailor (play). *Elson and Runkel. Elson readers. Book 2.

Little tailor—*continued.*
See also King John and the Abbot of Canterbury.
Little Tavwots, Story of. *See* Sun a prisoner. II.
Little ten minutes. Sly. World stories retold.
Little thief. Scudder. Book of legends.
Little Thumb. I. *See* Thumbling.
Little Thumb. II. *See* Hop-o'-my-Thumb.
Little Thumb. III. *See* Thumbelina.
Little Thumb. IV. Burke. Fairy tales.
Little Thumbkin's good deed. Gruelle. Friendly fairies.
Little Thumbling. *See* Hop-o'-my-Thumb.
Little Thunder's wedding journey. *See* Glooskap and the magic gifts. II.
Little tin soldier. *See* Brave tin soldier.
Little Tiny. *See* Thumbelina.
Little Tom Thumb. *See* Hop-o'-my-Thumb.
Little Totty. *See* Thumbelina.
Little tree that longed for other leaves. *See* Little pine tree who wished for new leaves.
Little tree that never grew up. Brady. Green forest fairy book.
Little Tuk. Andersen. Fairy tales (Lucas tr.).
Andersen. Fairy tales (Paull tr.).
Andersen. Stories and tales (Author's ed.).
Bailey. For the story teller.
Forty famous fairy tales.
Little Tuppen. Baldwin. Fairy stories and fables.
Old, old tales retold.
Treadwell and Free. Reading literature: primer. (Little Tuppens.)
Wiggin and Smith. Tales of laughter.
See also Cat and the mouse; Grain of corn; How the mouse got into his hole; Munachar and Manachar; Nanny who wouldn't go home to supper; Old woman and her pig; Sparrow and the bush.
Little Tuppens. *See* Little Tuppen.
Little Two-eyes *See* One-eye, Two-eyes, Three-eyes.
Little Ugly Boy. Wilson. Myths of the red children.
Little Warrior's counsel. Grinnell. Pawnee hero stories.
Little weaver. *See* Arachne.
Little weaver of Duleek gate, Legend of. Graves. Irish fairy book.
Quiller-Couch. Fairy tales far and near. (*In* Appendix.)
See also Brave little tailor.
Little Wee Duck. *See* Teenchy Duck.
Little wee pumpkin's Thanksgiving. Wickes. Happy holidays.
Little weed. Skinner. Topaz story book.
Little white blossom. Storytellers' magazine. Nov. 1917, p. 474.
Little white cat. Leamy. Golden spears.
Little white daisy. Olcott. Wonder garden.

Little white dove. Coolidge. Round dozen.
Little white mouse. *See* Juliet.
Little white rabbit. I. Olcott. Wonder garden.
See also How fire was brought to the Indians III; How Manabozho stole fire.
Little white rabbit. II. Skinner. Nursery tales from many lands.
See also Little brown bear and big billy goat.
Little wild duck. I. Stroebe and Martens. Danish fairy book.
See also Jungfrau Svanhita and Jungfrau Rafrumpa; Maiden Bright-eye; Princess Rosetta; White duck.
Little wild duck. II. *See* North Wind and the duck.
Little wild man. Tappan. Golden goose.
Little Wildrose. Lang. Crimson fairy book.
Lang. Little Wildrose and other stories.
Little wind-god. *See* Hermes and Apollo.
Little wolf brother. *See* Boy and the wolves. I.
Little Wolff's wooden shoes. *See* Sabot of little Wolff.
Littlest mouse, Tale of the. Bailey and Lewis. For the children's hour.
See also Country mouse and the town mouse.
Live alarm clock. *See* Little rooster. I.
Live potato. Keyes. Five senses.
Liver. *See* Piece of liver.
Living alarm clock. *See* Little rooster. I.
Living Statue, Adventures of. *See* First corn. II.
Lizard's friendship. Farmer. Nature myths.
Lizbeth and the heart of gold. Storytellers' magazine. Sept. 1917, p. 324.
Lizzie Lindsay. Macleod. Book of ballad stories.
Richards. Little Master. (Leezie Lindsay.)
Tappan. Old ballads in prose.
Llanfabon changeling. Thomas. Welsh fairy book.
Llew Llaw and his wife. Brooks. Wonder stories from the Mabinogion.
Llewellyn and his dog. *See* Beth Gellert.
Lludd and Llevelys, Story of. Brooks. Wonder stories from the Mabinogion.
Lanier. Knightly legends of Wales.
Patten. Junior classics. v. 4.
Llyn Cwm Llwch. Thomas. Welsh fairy book.
Llyn Llech Owen. Thomas. Welsh fairy book.
Lo-Sun, the blind boy. Pitman. Chinese fairy stories.
Lobsters. Æsop. Fables (Burt ed.).
Lochmaben harper. Grierson. Children's tales from Scottish ballads.
Macleod. Book of ballad stories. (Jolly harper.)
Lock of purple hair and what came of it. *See* Scylla, daughter of Nisus.
Locked-out fairy. Sawyer. This way to Christmas.
Locusts and the grasshopper. Æsop. Fables (Burt ed.).

Log. Fillmore. Mighty Mikko.
See also Faithful John.
Lohengrin. Curry. Little classics.
Chapin. Wonder stories from Wagner.
Griffis. Belgian fairy tales. (Swan Maidens, and the silver knight.)
Guerber. Legends of the Rhine. (Swan knight.)
McSpadden. Stories from great operas.
Maud. Wagner's heroes.
Patten. Junior classics. v. 2. (Story of Lohengrin.)
Pleasanton. Fairyland of opera.
Sologub. Sweet-scented name.
*Stebbins. Sunken city. (Swan knight.)
Wheelock. Stories of Wagner operas.
Loke. *See* Loki.
Loke's wolf. *See* Binding of the Fenris wolf.
Loki. Baldwin. Hero tales told in school. (Doom of the mischief-maker.)
Bradish. Old Norse stories. (Loki's punishment).
Brown. In the days of giants. (Punishment of Loki.)
Edmison. Stories from the Norseland. (Loki—The cause of all mischief.)
Foster and Cummings. Asgard stories. (Punishment of Loki.)
Guerber. Myths of northern lands. (*In* Loki.)
Klingensmith. Old Norse wonder tales. (Loke's punishment.)
Litchfield. Nine worlds. (Loki at Ægir's feast; Capture of Loki.)
Mabie. Norse stories. (How Loki was punished.)
Pratt. Legends of Norseland. (Punishment of Loki.)
Wickes. Beyond the rainbow bridge. (Binding of Loki.)
Wilmot-Buxton.. Stories of Norse heroes. (How Loki was punished at last.)
See also Binding of the Fenris wolf; Dwarf's gifts; Giant builder: Skrymsli.
Loki and his children. *See* Binding of the Fenris wolf.
Loki and the dwarfs. *See* Dwarf's gifts.
Lombardy poplar. *See* Poplar tree. II.
Lone chief. Grinnell. Pawnee hero stories.
Lonesome lake, Legend of. Storytellers' magazine. Oct. 1917, p. 405.
Long bow story. Lang. Olive fairy book.
Lang. White doe.
Long, Broad and Quickeye. *See* Broad man, tall man and man with eyes of flame.
Long, Broad and Sharpsight. *See* Broad man, tall man and man with eyes of flame.
Long leather bag. *See* Old hag's long leather bag.
Long spoon. Yeats. Irish fairy and folk tales.
Long story. *See* Endless tale. I.
Long time. Cary. French fairy tales.

Long winter. Eastman. Indian legends retold.
Long yacht race. Henderson. Sea yarns for boys.
Longka, the dancing girl. Griffis. Korean fairy tales.
Longnose the dwarf. Hauff. Caravan tales. (Wonder child.)
Hauff. Fairy tales.
Lang. Trusty John and other stories. (Dwarf Long Nose.)
Lang. Violet fairy book. (History of Dwarf Long Nose.)
Wiggin and Smith. Tales of wonder.
Longshanks, Girth and Keen. Fillmore. Czechoslovak fairy tales.
Looks-at-the-stars. Linderman. Indian Old-man stories.
Loony John. Ortoli. Evening tales.
Lora, the goddess of love. Dasent. Popular tales from the Norse.
Thorpe. Yule-tide stories.
Lord and master. Fillmore. Laughing prince.
Lord Bag of Rice. Hearn. Japanese fairy tales. (My Lord Bag-o'-Rice.)
Ozaki. Japanese fairy book. (My Lord Bag of Rice.)
Stewart. Tell me a hero story. (My Lord Bag of Rice.)
Williston. Japanese fairy tales. 2nd series.
See also How Toda slew the long serpent.
Lord Beichan. Macleod. Book of ballad stories.
Lord Cuttle-fish's concert. Griffis. Japanese fairy tales.
Lord Long-legs' procession. Griffis. Japanese fairy tales.
Lord of death. Steel. Tales of the Punjab.
Lord of Pengerswick. Hartland. English folk and fairy tales.
Lord of the hill and John Blessom. *See* Giant and Johannes Blessom.
Lord of the silver bow. *See* Apollo.
Lord Peter. Asbjörnsen. Fairy tales from the far north. (Squire Peter.)
Dasent. Norse fairy tales.
Dasent. Popular tales from the Norse.
Stroebe and Martens. Norwegian fairy book. (Helge-Hal in the Blue Hill.)
See also Puss in boots.
Lord Roland's grief. Mendes. Fairy spinning wheel.
Lord Soules. Grierson. Children's tales from Scottish ballads.
Lord Thomas and Fair Annet (poem). Lanier. Boy's Percy.
Lords of the white and gray castles. Browne. Granny's wonderful chair.
Lorelei. I. Crommelin. Famous legends.
Griffis. Swiss fairy tales. (Siren of the Rhine.)
Guerber. Legends of the Rhine. (Fisherman; Magic spell.)
Mabie. Legends every child should know.
Noyes. Twilight stories.

Lorelei. II. Evans. Old time tales.
See also Lorelei. III.
Lorelei. III. Guerber. Legends of the Rhine. (Unhappy beauty.)
Lost and found. Bay. Danish fairy and folk tales.
Lost bell. Gibbon. Reign of King Cole.
Lost camel. Arnold and Gilbert. Stepping stones to literature. v. 3.
Butterworth. Zigzag journeys in the orient. (*In* Ch. 3.)
Curry. Little classics. (Dervis and the lost camel.)
Sly. World stories retold.
Welsh. Stories children love.
See also How an Indian found his game.
Lost charm. *See* Why the dog and cat are enemies. II.
Lost child. I. Chodzko. Fairy tales of the Slav.
Johnson. Elm-tree fairy book.
Lost child. II. *See* Proserpina.
Lost children. Grinnell. Blackfoot lodge tales.
See also Brother and sister. IV.
Lost city of the sea. Harrison. Star fairies.
Lost crown. Underhill. Dwarfs' tailor and other fairy tales.
Lost fiddle. *Burchill. Progressive road to reading. Book 3.
See also Thirst of the standing stones. I.
Lost goat. *See* Oeyvind and Marit.
Lost half-hour. Beston. Firelight fairy book.
Lost kernel. Chisholm and Steedman. Staircase of stories.
Lost lamb. Boston collection of kindergarten stories.
Lost legs. Johnson. Oak-tree fairy book.
Lost light. Judson. Myths and legends of Alaska.
Lost! lost! *See* Cupid.
Lost nail. *See* Nail. I.
Lost ocean. Harrison. Moon princess.
Lost paradise. Lang. Lilac fairy book.
Lang. Fairy nurse.
Lost prince of the poles. Richards. Joyous story of Toto.
Lost purse (play). Van Sickle and Seegmiller. Riverside readers. 3d reader.
Lost secret. *See* Dædalus and Icarus.
Lost son. I. *See* Pink.
Lost son. II. Riggs. Animal stories from Eskimo land.
Lost spear. Jokai. Golden fairy book.
My Bookhouse. v. 3.
Wiggin and Smith. Magic casements.
Lost spindle. *See* Mother Holle.
Lost Sylphid. May. Little Prudy's fairy book.
Lost talisman, Story of. Jewett. Egyptian tales of magic.
Lost wand. Ingelow. Stories told to a child. v. 2.
Patten. Junior classics. v. 6.
Lost wife. Johnson. Birch-tree fairy book.
Lothian farmer's wife. Douglas. Scottish fairy tales.
Lothian Tom. Douglas. Scottish fairy tales.

Lotus eaters. Evans. Heroes of Troy.
McFee. Treasury of flower stories. (Lotus blossoms.)
Patten. Junior classics. v. 3.
Loughleagh (Lake of Healing). Yeats. Irish fairy and folk tales.
Loutish peasant. Stroebe and Martens. Danish fairy book.
Love and the soul. *See* Cupid and Psyche.
Love or a snow-white fox. Johnson. Fir-tree fairy book.
Love of the dryad. Canton. Reign of King Herla.
See also Rhœcus and the oak.
Lovek and Seranak. Riggs. Animal stories from Eskimo land.
Loveliest rose in the world. Andersen. Fairy tales (Paull tr.).
Andersen. Stories and tales (Author's ed.).
Olcott. Good stories for great holidays.
Loveliness of duty. Storytellers' magazine. May 1916, p. 294.
Lovely Ilonka. Lang. Crimson fairy book.
Lang. Magic ring and other stories.
Lover of men. Baldwin. Fifty famous people. (Lover of men.)
Lovers. I. *See* Top and ball.
Lovers. II. Guerber. Legends of the Rhine.
Loving cup which was made of iron. Harrison. In story land.
Loving Laili. Jacobs. Indian fairy tales.
Lower than the beasts. Keyes. Five senses.
Lowri Dafydd earns a purse of gold. Thomas. Welsh fairy book.
Lox and the bear. Partridge. Story-telling in home and school.
Lox, the michief maker. Partridge. Glooscap the great chief. (How the badger made Mrs. Bear blind.)
Wade. Indian fairy tales.
Lox, the mischief maker and the three fires. Wade. Indian fairy tales.
Loyal John, Story of. Storytellers' magazine. March 1914, p. 475.
Loyal knight. Alderman. Classics old and new. 4th reader.
Lu-San, daughter of heaven. Pitman. Chinese wonder book.
Lucia di Lammermoor. Pleasanton. Fairyland of opera.
Lucia, the organ-maiden. Aspinwall. Short stories for short people.
Lucifer's ear. Caballero. Spanish fairy tales.
Luck and Intelligence. Mabie. Folk tales every child should know. (Intelligence and luck.)
Luck and Wealth. Spaulding and Bryce. Aldine readers. Book 3.
See also Cogia Hassan.

Luck boat of Lake Geneva. Cather. Educating by story telling.
Griffis. Swiss fairy tales. (Fairies' palace car.)
Luck boy of Toy Valley. Cather. Educating by story telling.
My Bookhouse. v. 3.
Luck fairies. Eells. Tales of enchantment from Spain.
Luck may lie in a pin. *Andersen. Best fairy tales (Henderson tr. Luck may lie in a stick.)
Andersen. Stories (Riverside ed.).
Andersen. Stories and tales (Author's ed.).
Luck may lie in a stick. *See* Luck may lie in a pin.
Luck-mouse. Kennedy. New world fairy book.
See also Magic little animal.
Luck of the youngest son. *See* Knapsack, the hat and the horn.
Luck-penny. *See* Lucky penny.
Luckhinarain, the idiot. Bradley-Birt. Bengal fairy tales.
See also Cheeses that ran away.
Lucky Andrew. Gade. Norwegian fairy tales. (Tufte-people on Sandflaesen.)
Stroebe and Martens. Norwegian fairy book.
Lucky coin. Jokai. Golden fairy book.
Wiggin and Smith. Tales of wonder.
Lucky dog, Legend of. Storytellers' magazine. Sep. 1917, p. 316.
Lucky Hans. *See* Hans in luck.
Lucky hunter and skillful fisher. *See* Ambitious hunter and skilful fisher.
Lucky hunter and the skilful fisherman. *See* Ambitious hunter and skilful fisher.
Lucky Jack. *See* Hans in luck.
Lucky Luck. Lang. Crimson fairy book.
Lang. Magic ring and other stories.
See also Faithful John.
Lucky penny. Storytellers' magazine. Feb. 1916, p. 90. (Luck-penny.)
Thorpe. Yule-tide stories.
Lucky two shoes. Bailey. Friendly tales.
Lucretia, Story of. Guerber. Story of the Romans. (Death of Lucretia.)
Haaren. Famous men of Rome.
Laing. Seven kings of the seven hills.
Lucy on May morning (poem). Lindsay and Poulsson. Joyous travelers. (Tale told by the younger sister.)
Ludwig and Marleen. Hoxie. Kindergarten story book.
Lumawig on earth. Coussens. Jade story book.
Lump of gold. *See* Bar of gold.
Lump of sugar. Sologub. Sweet-scented name.
Lupins (poem). Alexander. The Hidden servants.
Lusmore and his hump. *See* Knockgrafton, Legend of.

Lute player. Lang. Violet fairy book.
Lang. Snake prince.
Lutoschenka, the little clay boy. Storytellers' magazine. Jan. 1917, p. 7.
Lyderic, the orphan. Griffis. Belgian fairy tales.
Lynx and the mole. Æsop. Fables (Burt ed.).
Lyubim Tsarevich and the winged wolf, Story of. Steele. Russian garland of fairy tales.

M

McCarthy of Ballinacarthy. Frost. Fairies and folk of Ireland. (*In* Ch. 3.)
Mabel on Midsummer Day (poem). O'Grady and Throop. Teachers' story teller's book.
(poem). Olcott. Book of elves and fairies.
(poem). Poulsson. In the child's world.
(poem). Smith. Good old stories.
(poem). Tappan. Old-fashioned stories and poems.
McAndrew family. Jacobs. More Celtic fairy tales. (Story of the McAndrew family.)
Macbeth. Johonnot. Stories of the olden time. (Legend of Macbeth.)
Mackerel trolling. *See* Storm magic.
Mackinaw Island, Legend of. *See* How the fairies came.
Macquorquodale. Campbell. Beyond the border.
Mad cow. Macé. Home fairy tales.
Winnington. Outlook fairy book.
Mad goose and the tiger forest. Pitman. Chinese wonder book.
Mad Mehmed. Kunos. Forty-four Turkish fairy tales. (Mahomet, the bald-head.)
Kunos. Turkish fairy tales.
Mad pudding. *See* Pudding bewitched.
Mad tea party. Bailey. Stories children need.
Madame Butterfly. Pleasanton. Fairyland of opera.
Madhumala, the wreath of sweetness. Bradley-Birt. Bengal fairy tales.
"Madjun." *See* Madschun.
Madonna of the goldfinch. Chisholm and Steedman. Staircase of stories.
Madschun. Kunos. Forty-four Turkish fairy tales. ("Madjun.")
Lang. Olive fairy book.
Maelduin's voyage. *See* Voyage of Maelduin.
Magi in the west and their search for the Christ. Curtiss. Christmas stories and legends.
Magic apples. I. *See* Iduna's apples.
Magic apples. II. Stroebe and Martens. Norwegian fairy book.
See also Little soldier.

Magic apples. III. Friedlander. Jewish fairy book.
Magic arrows. Eastman. Wigwam evenings.
Magic axe and the white cat. Macé. Home fairy tales.
Magic ball. Finger. Tales from silver lands.
Magic bed. I. James. Enchanted castle.
Magic bed. II. James. Magic bed.
Magic book. Lang. Orange fairy book.
Lang. Magic book and other stories.
Magic bottles. Jerrold. Reign of King Oberon.
Johnson. Fir-tree fairy book. (Bewitched bottles.)
Magic bow. Baumbach. Tales from wonderland.
Magic candles. Chisholm. Enchanted land.
Magic cap. Bosschère. Folk tales of Flanders.
Magic carpet of old Persia. *See* Sohrab and Rustem.
Magic carpets. *See* Flying carpet; Little lame prince; Magic turban; Phœnix and the carpet; Prince Ahmed.
Magic cask. Martens. Chinese fairy book.
Magic circus. Pyle. Counterpane fairy.
Magic coffee mill. *See* Annette.
Magic crocodile. Jewett. Egyptian tales of magic.
Magic deer ball. Stanley. Animal folk tales.
Magic dog. Finger. Tales from silver lands.
Magic egg. Bain. Cossack fairy tales.
Wiggin and Smith. Fairy ring.
Magic feather. *See* White Feather and the six giants.
Magic ferns. Olcott. Book of elves and fairies.
Magic fiddle. Jacobs. Indian fairy tales.
Johnson. Oak-tree fairy book.
See also Jew among the thorns.
Magic flower. Lindsay. Story-teller.
Magic frog. Griffis. Japanese fairy tales.
Magic gifts. Segovia. Spanish fairy book.
Magic gifts of the elves. *See* Dwarf's gifts.
Magic girdle. *See* Brave little tailor.
Magic gold. *See* Siegfried.
Magic hair pins. Kunos. Forty-four Turkish fairy tales.
Magic hat. Stroebe and Martens. Danish fairy book.
Magic hide-and-seek. Lummis. Pueblo Indian folk stories.
Magic horn. Johnson. Fir-tree fairy book.
Magic horse. *See* Enchanted horse.
Magic iron pot. *See* Wonderful pot.
Magic jar. Ewing. Old-fashioned fairy tales.
Magic jaw bone. James. Magic jaw bone.
Magic kettle. *See* Accomplished and lucky teakettle.
Magic key. Bouvé. Lamp-light tales.
Magic knot. Finger. Tales from silver lands.
Magic lamp. Friedlander. Jewish fairy book.
Magic leaf. Friedlander. Jewish fairy book.
Magic little animal. Stanley. Animal folk tales.
See also Luck mouse.
Magic mackerel. Rhys. Fairy gold.
Magic mask. Cabot. Ethics for children.

Magic mead. *See* Odin and the mead.
Magic mirror. I. Lang. Orange fairy book.
Magic mirror. II. *See* Snow-White and the seven dwarfs.
Magic mirror. III. Bellamy. Wonder children. (Story of the magic mirror.)
Magic mirror. IV. Kunos. Forty-four Turkish fairy tales.
Magic mirror. V. *See* Mirror of Matsuyama.
Magic mirror. VI. Olcott. Whirling king.
Magic moccasins. Judd. Wigwam stories.
Wade. Indian fairy tales.
Magic music. Thomas. Welsh fairy book.
Magic of Glooskap. *See* Glooskap and the magic gifts. II.
Magic packet. Schoolcraft. Indian fairy book.
Magic palace. Friedlander. Jewish fairy book. (Wonderful slave.)
Landa. Aunt Naomi's Jewish fairy tales and legends.
Magic peach. Griffis. Korean fairy tales.
Magic perfume. Judson. Flower fairies.
Magic pipe. *See* Jesper who herded the hares.
Magic porcupine quills. Nixon-Roulet. Indian folk tales.
Magic pot. *See* Wonderful pot.
Magic prison. *See* Prince Harweda and the magic prison.
Magic quern. *See* Why the sea is salt. I.
Magic rice kettle. *See* Why the dog and cat are enemies. II.
Magic ring. I. Lang. Magic ring and other stories.
Lang. Yellow fairy book.
Wiggin and Smith. Fairy ring.
See also Fritz and his friends; Jack and his snuffbox; Stone in the cock's head.
Magic ring. II. *See* Prince Darling.
Magic ring. III. *See* Charlemagne and the magic ring.
Magic seeds. Winnington. Outlook fairy book.
Magic spell. *See* Lorelei. I.
Magic strawberries. Olcott. Wonder garden.
Magic swan. *Coe and Christie. Story hour readers. Book 2. (Princess Lilly.)
Coussens. Child's book of stories.
Field. Famous fairy tales.
Lang. Green fairy book.
Lang. Pretty Goldilocks and other stories.
See also Golden Goose. I.
Magic sword. I. (play). Pyle. Prose and verse for children.
Magic sword. II. *See* Sigmund.
Magic sword of Kenaz. Friedlander. Jewish fairy book.
Magic table. Molesworth. Fairies afield.
Magic teapot. St. Nicholas. July 1906, p. 792.
Magic tears. Sholl. Faery tales of Weir.
Magic thimble. Potter. Pinafore pocket story book.
Magic turban, the magic whip and the magic carpet. Kunos. Forty-four Turkish fairy tales.
Kunos. Turkish fairy tales.

Magic turban, the magic whip and the magic carpet—*continued.*
Pyle. Tales of folk and fairies. (Magic turban, the magic sword and the magic carpet.)
Magic umbrella. Fyleman. Rainbow cat.
See also Goloshes of fortune.
Magic waters. *See* Hidden waters.
Magic well. Gibbon. Reign of King Cole. (Spring water.)
Johnson. Birch-tree fairy book.
Magic whistle. *See* Enchanted whistle.
Magic wigwam. Wilson. Myths of the red children.
Magic windpipe. Olcott. Red Indian fairy book.
Magical belt. Partridge. Glooscap the great chief.
Magical dancing doll. Partridge. Glooscap the great chief.
Magical hair string. Partridge. Glooscap the great chief.
Magical music. Stockton. Ting-a-ling tales.
Magician and the courtiers. Guerber. Legends of the Rhine.
Magician and the sultan's son. Bateman. Zanzibar tales.
Magician Palermo. Eells. Tales of enchantment from Spain.
Magician turned mischief maker. Ewing. Old-fashioned fairy tales.
Magician's daughter and the highborn boy. Stockton. Floating prince.
Magician's gifts. Ewing. Old-fashioned fairy tales.
Magician's horse. Lang. Grey fairy book.
Lang. Trusty John and other stories.
Magician's pupil. Dasent. Popular tales from the Norse.
Thorpe. Yule-tide stories.
See also Farmer Weatherbeard; Fisherman's son and the Gruagach of tricks; Master and pupil; Oh; Wizard and his pupil.
Magnus and the white bear. Goddard. Fairy tales in other lands.
Magpie and her children. Wiggin and Smith. Tales of laughter.
Magpie maidens. Olcott. Wonder garden.
Magpie's lesson. *See* Magpie's nest. I.
Magpie's nest. I. Baldwin. Fairy stories and fables. (Nest builders.)
Bowen. Second story reader. (How the birds learned to make their nests.)
Elson and Runkel. Elson Readers. Book 2.
Faulkner. Story lady's book. (Birds' buildings.)
Hall and Gilman. Story land. 2d reader. (Nest builders.)
Jacobs. English fairy tales.
*Klingensmith. Just stories.
My Bookhouse. v. 1.
O'Grady and Throop. Teachers' story teller's book. (Nest builders.)
Olcott. Good stories for great holidays.

Magpie's nest. I.—*continued.*
Skinner. Emerald story book. (How the birds learned to build nests.)
Spaulding and Bryce. Aldine readers. 2d reader. (Magpie's lesson.)
Wiggin and Smith. Tales of laughter.
Magpie's nest. II. Coussens. Child's book of stories.
Holbrook. Book of nature myths. (Why the magpie's nest is not well built.)
Jonnson. Fir-tree fairy book.
Keyes. Stories and story-telling. (Why the magpie's nest is badly made.)
See also Birds and their nests.
Mahala Joe. Austin. Basket woman.
Tappan. Modern stories.
Mahomed Ali. Arabian nights, More tales (Olcott. Story of Mahomed Ali the jeweller; or, The false caliph.)
Mahomet, the bald-head. *See* Mad Mehmed.
Maid and the pail of milk. *See* Milkmaid and her pail of milk.
Maid Lena. Grundtvig. Fairy tales from afar.
Wiggin and Smith. Magic casements.
Maid of Bregenz. *See* Bregenz, Legend of.
Maid of the swan-skin. Maud. Heroines of poetry.
Maid who married the morning star. Cornyn. Around the wigwam fire.
Olcott. Red Indian fairy book. (Star bride.)
See also Star boy.
Maid with hair of gold. *See* Golden Hair.
Maid with her basket of eggs. Arnold and Gilbert. Stepping stones to literature. v. 2.
See also Barber's fifth brother; Lad and the fox; Milkmaid and her pail of milk.
Maiden and the frog. Mother Goose's nursery rhymes, tales and jingles (Warne ed.).
See also Frog prince.
Maiden Bright-eye. Lang. Pink fairy book.
Lang. Satin surgeon.
See also Little wild duck.
Maiden in the moon. Olcott. Wonder garden.
Maiden of the green forest. Griffis. Welsh fairy tales.
Maiden of the white camellias. Olcott. Wonder garden.
Maiden of Unai. James. Green willow.
Maiden White and Maiden Yellow. Olcott. Wonder garden.
Skinner. Topaz story book. (Lady White and Lady Yellow.)
Maiden who loved a fish. Wiggin and Smith. Magic casements.
Maiden who was stolen away. Martens. Chinese fairy book.
Maiden who was wiser than an emperor. Laboulaye.

Maiden who was wiser than an emperor—*continued.*
Fairy tales. (*In* Captain John's travels.)
Laboulaye. Last fairy tales. (Female Solomon.)
Patten. Junior classics. v. 1. (Maiden who was wiser than the king.)
Pyle. Tales of folks and fairies. (Wise girl.)
See also Peasant's clever daughter; Sage damsel; Wise queen; Young head of the house.
Maiden who was wiser than the king. *See* Maiden who was wiser than an emperor.
Maiden with golden hair. *See* Prairie dandelion.
Maiden with the wooden helmet. Hearn. Japanese fairy tales. (Wooden bowl.)
James. Green willow. (Black bowl.)
Lang. Violet fairy book.
Storytellers' magazine. May 1915, p. 137. (Beautiful bride.)
Maiden without hands. Grimm. Household tales (Burt ed.).
Maiden's rock. Sylva and Strettell. Legends from river and mountain.
Maiden's visit. Grimm. Fairy tales (Paull tr. Elves.)
Grimm. Household stories (Crane tr. Elves. pt. 2.)
Grimm. Household tales (Burt ed.).
Mail-coach passengers. Andersen. Fairy tales (Paull tr.).
Andersen. Wonder stories (Author's ed. Twelve by the mail.)
Olcott. Good stories for great holidays.
Maize. *See* First corn. III.
Makatah the war maiden. Bayliss. Treasury of Indian tales.
Maker of the thunder knives. Lummis. Pueblo Indian folk stories.
Making a fairy story. St. Nicholas. May 1877, p. 428.
Making of the hammer. *See* Dwarf's gifts.
Making of the sword. *See* Norseman's sword.
Making of the world. *See* Creation of the world (Norse).
Making the best of it. Bailey and Lewis. For the children's hour.
(play). Elson and Runkel. Elson readers. Book 1. (Thanksgiving in the hen-house.)
Skinner. Merry tales.
Making the moon. Tanner. Legends from the red man's forest.
See also Frog in the moon.
Makóma. Lang. Orange fairy book.
Malanchamala, the wreath in a flower garden. Bradley-Birt. Bengal fairy tales.
Mallard that asked too much. Shedlock. Eastern stories and legends.
See also Goose that laid golden eggs.
Man and his boots. Harris. Uncle Remus and his friends.
Man and his goose. *See* Goose that laid golden eggs.

Man and his piece of cloth. Tappan. Folk stories and fables.
Wiggin and Smith. Talking beasts.
Man and his shadow. Æsop. Fables (Stickney. Supplement).
Success library. v. 3.
Man and his two wives. Æsop. Fables (Black ed.).
Æsop. Fables (Burt ed.).
Man and his wooden god. Æsop. Fables (Black ed.).
Æsop. Fables (Burt ed.).
Æsop. Fables (Jacobs. Man and the wooden god.)
Man and the alligator (play). Stevenson. Plays for the home.
See also Brahmin, the tiger and the jackal; Way of the world. I.
Man and the donkey. *See* Man, the boy and the donkey.
Man and the doukana tree. Dasent. Popular tales from the Norse.
Man and the foxes. Æsop. Fables (Burt ed.).
Man and the gnat. Æsop. Fables (Black ed.).
Æsop. Fables (Burt ed.).
Man and the lion. Æsop. Fables (Black ed. Forester and the lion.)
Æsop. Fables (Burt ed.).
Æsop. Fables (Jacobs. Lion and the statue.)
Arnold and Gilbert. Stepping stones to literature. v. 3.
Scudder. Fables and folk stories.
Success library. v. 3. (Lion and the man.)
Wiggin and Smith. Talking beasts.
Man and the rain. Bryce. Fables from afar.
Man and the satyr. *See* Satyr and the traveller.
Man and the snake (poem). Success library. v. 3.
See also Way of the world. I.
Man and the stone. Æsop. Fables (Burt ed.).
Man and the weasel. Æsop. Fables (Black ed.).
Æsop. Fables (Burt ed.).
(poem). Success library. v. 3.
Man and the wild cattle. Harris. Uncle Remus and his friends.
Man and the wood. *See* Woodman and the trees.
Man and the wooden god. *See* Man and his wooden god.
Man and turtle. Wiggin and Smith. Talking beasts.
Man bitten by a dog. Æsop. Fables (Black ed.).
Æsop. Fables (Burt ed.).
Man elephant. James. Man elephant.
Man from Ringerige and the three women. *See* Such women are.
Man, his son and his ass. *See* Man, the boy and the donkey.
Man in a shell. Fielde. Chinese fairy tales.
Man in the bag. *See* Turnip.
Man in the iron mask. Baldwin. Thirty more famous stories.

Man in the iron mask—*continued.*
Evans. Old time tales. (Man with the iron mask.)
Man in the moon. Cather. Educating by story telling.
Dasent. Popular tales from the Norse.
Headland. Chinese boy and girl.
Holbrook. Book of nature myths. (Why there is a man in the moon.)
Judd. Classic myths.
Olcott. Wonder garden.
Sly. World stories retold.
Tappan. Folk stories and fables. (Why there is a man in the moon.)
Thorpe. Yule-tide stories.
Man in the moon and the orphan boy. Bayliss. Treasury of Eskimo tales. (What the man in the moon did.)
Young. Algonquin Indian tales. (*In* Ch. 23. Man in the moon and the Indian boy.)
Man, lion and statue. *See* Lion and statue.
Man of brass. Baldwin. Golden fleece.
Man of Gotham and the cheeses. Bailey. Firelight stories.
Man of law's tale. *See* Faithful Constance.
Man of luck and the man of pluck. Wiggin and Smith. Talking beasts.
Man of snow. Skinner. Garnet story book.
Man on the chimney. Boston collection of kindergarten stories.
Coe. Second book of stories.
Man that learned to fly. *See* Dædalus and Icarus.
Man that served the sea. Gregory. Kiltartan wonder book.
Man, the boy and the donkey. Æsop. Fables (Black ed. Old man, his son and the ass.)
Æsop. Fables (Burt ed. Old man, his son and the ass.)
Æsop. Fables (Jacobs).
Æsop. Fables (Stickney. Man, his son and his ass.)
Arnold and Gilbert. Stepping stones to literature. v. 3. (Old man and his donkey.)
*Elson and Runkel. Elson readers. Book 2. (Pleasing everybody.)
Lansing. Dramatic readings.
Noyes. Twilight stories. (Man and the donkey.)
Patten. Junior classics. v. 1. (Man, boy and donkey.)
Scudder. Children's book. (Miller, his son and their ass.)
Scudder. Fables and folk stories. (Miller, his son and their ass.)
Sly. World stories retold. (Miller and his donkey.)
(play). Stevenson. Plays for the home. (Miller, his son and their donkey.)
Wiggin and Smith. Talking beasts. (Old man, his son and the ass.)
Man, the hare, the fox, and the bear. Houghton. Russian grandmother's wonder tales.
See also Fox, the bear and the poor farmer.

Man who became a serpent. Nixon-Roulet. Japanese folk stories and fairy tales.

Man who brought fire. *See* Prometheus.

Man who did not like to work. *Jones. Second reader.

Man who did not wish to die. I. Ozaki. Japanese fairy book.

Man who did not wish to die. II. Cather. Educating by story-telling. (Why the Japanese love the stork.)

See also Horaizan.

Man who died on Holy Innocents' Day. Stroebe and Martens. Swedish fairy book.

Man who entertained bears. Eastman. Indian legends retold.

Man who lived in the middle. Storytellers' magazine. Sept. 1915, p. 307.

Man who loved Hai Quai. *See* Miser of Takhoma.

Man who loved money better than life. Davis and Chow-Leung. Chinese fables and folk stories.

Man who made giants. Bailey. Friendly tales.

Man who made time. Potter. Pinafore pocket story book.

Man who made trees blossom. *See* Old man who made withered trees to flower.

Man who married a goose. Success library. v. 3.

Man who married the moon. I. Lummis. Pueblo Indian folk stories.

Man who married the moon. II. Judd. Wigwam stories. (Indian who married the moon.)

Man who married the thunder's sister. Eastman. Indian legends retold.

Man who met misery. Baudis. Czech folk tales.

Man who never died. *See* Aurora and Tithonus.

Man who obeyed orders. Dyer and Brady. Merrill readers. 3d reader.

(play). Dyer and Brady. Merrill readers. 3d reader. (Jewel of great price.)

Man who ticked. Potter. Pinafore pocket story book.

Man who told a lie. Shedlock. Eastern stories and legends.

Man who wanted to chain the sea. Wiltse. Kindergarten stories.

Man who was a hundred years young. Aunt Naomi. Jewish fairy tales and fables.

Storytellers' magazine. April 1914, p. 522.

Man who was enriched by accident. Bradley-Birt. Bengal fairy tales.

Man who was going to mind the house. Asbjörnsen. Folk and fairy tales.

Dasent. Norse fairy tales. (Husband who was to mind the house.)

Dasent. Popular tales from the Norse. (Husband who was to mind the house.)

Laboulaye. Fairy tales. (*In* Good woman. pt. 2. Neighbor Peter who was determined to rule his own house.)

Man who was going to mind the house—*continued.*
Laboulaye. Last fairy tales. (Grizzled Peter.)
Patten. Junior classics. v. 1. (Husband who was to mind the house.)
Tappan. Folk stories and fables. (Husband who was to mind the house.)
Thorne-Thomsen. East o' the sun and west o' the moon (Husband who was to mind the house.)
See also Seppy, Story of; Wife of Auchtermuchty.
Man who was only a finger and a half in stature. Bradley-Birt. Bengal fairy tales.
See also Thumbling. I.
Man who went home with a grizzly. Sexton. Gray wolf stories.
Man who went to the giant's country. *See* Gulliver's travels: Brobdingnag.
Man who went to the land of youth. *See* Last of the Feni.
Man who worked to give alms. Shedlock. Eastern stories and legends.
Man who would not scold. Pitman. Chinese wonder book.
Man who wouldn't keep Sunday. Lummis. Pueblo Indian folk stories.
Man with his leg tied up. *See* King of the buffaloes.
Man with the bell. Baring-Gould. Old English fairy book.
Man with the green weeds. Thomas. Welsh fairy book.
Man with the iron mask. *See* Man in the iron mask.
Man with the wen. Ballard. Fairy tales from far Japan.
Bryce. Fables from afar. (Elves and the envious man.)
Hearn. Japanese fairy tales. (Old man and the devils.)
Ozaki. Japanese fairy book. (How an old man lost his wen.)
Tappan. Myths from many lands. (Elves and the envious neighbor.)
Wiggin and Smith. Tales of laughter. (Old man and the devils.)
Williston. Japanese fairy tales. 2d series. (Old man with a wart.)
Man without a heart. I. Bay. Danish fairy and folk tales.
Man without a heart. II. Dasent. Popular tales from the Norse.
Lang. Golden mermaid and other stories.
Lang. Pink fairy book.
Thorpe. Yule-tide stories.
See also Giant who had no heart.
Manabozho. Bayliss. Treasury of Indian tales. (*In* Sunbright heroes.)
Compton. American Indian fairy tales. (Great wizard.)
Judd. Wigwam stories. (Menabozho and his three brothers; Menabozho: or. the great white hare.)
Nixon-Roulet. Indian folk tales. (Wonderful deeds of Manabozho.)

Manabozho—*continued.*
Patten. Junior classics. v. 1.
Schoolcraft. Indian fairy book. (Manabozho, the mischief maker.)
Young. Algonquin Indian tales. (Nanahboozhoo.)
See also Glooskap; Iktomi.
Manabozho and his toe. Judd. Wigwam stories. (*In* Menabozho and his three brothers.)
Wiggin and Smith. Tales of laughter.
Manabozho and how the diver got a flat back. *See* How the duck came to have a flat back.
Manabozho and the lake magicians. Compton. American Indian fairy tales. (*In* Great Wizard.)
Johnson. Book of fairy-tale bears. (Bears and the magician.)
Schoolcraft. Indian fairy book. (*In* Manabozho, the mischief maker.)
Young. Algonquin Indian tales. (*In* Ch. 18. How Nanahboozhoo killed the great white sea lion.)
See also Little boy man returns.
Manabozho and the squirrels. *See* Why the squirrel barks.
Manabozho and the wolf pack. Compton. American Indian fairy tales. (*In* Great Wizard.)
Grinnell. Blackfoot lodge tales. (Bears.)
Johnson. Book of fairy-tale bears. (Bears and the magician.)
Patten. Junior classics. v. 1. (Manabozho is changed into a wolf.)
Schoolcraft. Indian fairy tales. (*In* Manabozho, the mischief maker.)
Manabozho and the woodpecker. Patten. Junior classics. v. 1.
Schoolcraft. Indian fairy tales. (*In* Manabozho, the mis chief maker.)
See also Blue jay, the imitator; Rabbit and the woodpecker girls.
Manabozho caught. Judd. Wigwam stories. (Menabozho caught.)
Judson. Old Crow stories. (When coyote was hard to please.)
Patten. Junior classics. v. 1. (Manabozho is robbed by wolves.)
Manabozho swallowed by a large fish. Judd. Wigwam stories.
Wade. Indian fairy tales. (Manabozho's fishing.)
Young. Algonquin Indian tales. (*In* Ch. 17. How Nanahboozhoo destroyed Mooshekinnebik.)
Manabozho's fishing. *See* Manabozho swallowed by a large fish.
Manawyddan and the mice. *See* Escape of the mouse.
Manawyddan and the seven enchanted cantrevs. *See* Escape of the mouse.

Manciple's tale. *See* Why the crow is black.
Mandarin's promise. Bouvé. Lamp-light tales.
Mangita and Larina. Miller. Philippine folklore stories.
Manis the besom man. MacManus. In chimney corners.
Manis the miller. MacManus. Donegal fairy stories.
Manitou and the squirrels. *See* Why the squirrel barks.
Mannanoit and the big red sun. Storytellers' magazine. Oct. 1915, p. 329.
Man's boot (play). Lansing. Quaint old stories.
Welsh. Stories children love.
Young and Field. Literary readers. Book 2. (Shoe.)
Man's daughter and the woman's daughter. Asbjörnsen. Fairy tales.
*Burchill. Progressive road to reading. Book 2. (Two sisters.)
Dasent. Norse fairy tales. (Two stepsisters.)
Dasent. Popular tales from the Norse. (Two step-sisters.)
Lang. Orange fairy book. (Two caskets.)
Lang. Twelve huntsmen and other stories. (Two caskets.)
Thorpe. Yule-tide stories. (Two caskets.)
See also Gold Maria and Pitch Maria; Mother Holle; Two caskets.
Man's first grief. Bayliss. Treasury of Eskimo tales.
Manstin, the rabbit. Eastman. Wigwam evenings. (Comrades.)
Wiggin and Smith. Tales of wonder.
Zitkala-Ša. Old Indian legends.
Mantle of king's beards. Thomas. Welsh fairy book.
Manus. Lang. Orange fairy book. (Story of Manus.)
Many-furred creature. Bates. Once upon a time. (Furball.)
Cather. Educating by story telling. (Coat of all colors.)
Gibbon. Reign of King Cole. (Princess in disguise.)
Grimm. Fairy tales (Paull tr. Princess in disguise.)
Grimm. Household tales (Burt ed. Princess in disguise.)
Grimm. Household tales (Everyman's ed. Catskin.)
Lang. Forty thieves and other stories. (Allerleirauh.)
Lang. Green fairy book. (Allerleirauh; or, The many-furred creature.)
Singleton. Wild flower fairy book. (Princess in disguise.)
Wiggin and Smith. Fairy ring.
Maple. *See* Maple seed!
Maple-leaf and the violet. Wiggin and Smith. Story hour.
Maple leaf for ever. Olcott. Wonder garden.
Maple, Legend of (poem). Stone and Fickett. Trees in prose and poetry.
Maple seed. Arnold and Gilbert. Stepping stones to literature. v. 3. (Maple.)
Skinner. Emerald story book.
Mara's starling. Bailey. Friendly tales.

March and the shepherd. Storyteller's magazine. Jan. 1914, p. 408.
March's ears. Thomas. Welsh fairy book.
See also Emperor Trojan's ears;. Midas. II.
Marco Polo. Evans. Old time tales. (Prince of travelers.)
Margaret: A pearl. Field. Little book of profitable tales.
Margery White Coats. Grierson. Children's book of Celtic stories.
Maribel and Mrs. Lark. Skinner. Very little child's book of stories.
See also Lark and the child; Trading babies.
Maria Morevna. *See* Marya Morevna.
Marianna. Beston. Firelight fairy book.
Marigold arrows. Olcott. Wonder garden.
Mariora Floriora. Olcott. Wonder garden.
Mark of the marten. I. Judson. Myths and legends of Alaska.
Mark of the marten. II. Young. Algonquin Indian tales. (*In* Ch. 20. Why the marten has a white spot.)
Mark the rich. Magnus. Russian folk tales.
See also Giant with the golden hair I and II; Three wonderful beggars.
Marko the rich and Vasily the luckless. *See* Three wonderful beggars.
Marmot and the raven. *See* Raven and Marmot.
Marriage of Cock Robin and Jenny Wren. *See* Robin's Christmas song.
Marriage of King Herla. Canton. Reign of King Herla.
Marriage of Mrs. Reynard. *See* Wedding of Mrs. Fox.
Marriage of Mondahmin. Judd. Wigwam stories.
Marriage of Peleus and Thetis. *See* Paris: Apple of discord.
Marriage of Robin Redbreast and the wren. *See* Robin's Christmas song.
Marriage of Robin Redbreast and Jenny Wren. *See* Robin's Christmas song.
Marrying a simpleton. Field. Chinese fairy tales.
See also Prudent Hans.
Mars. *Bailey. Wonder stories. (How Mars lost a battle.)
Marsh king's daughter. Andersen. Fairy tales (Lucas tr.).
Andersen. Fairy tales (Paull tr.).
Andersen. Wonder stories (Author's ed.).
Marsyas and Apollo. Francillon. Gods and heroes. (Flayed piper.)
Guerber. Myths of Greece and Rome. (*In* Apollo.)
Marten and the white rabbit. Judd. Wigwam stories.
Martha. McSpadden. Stories from great operas.
Martin, the peasant's son. *See* Enchanted ring. II.
Martyred hound. *See* Beth Gellert.
Marvelous dog and the wonderful cat. Beston. Firelight fairy book.

Marvelous musician. *See* Wonderful musician.
Marvelous pot. *See* Wonderful pot.
Marvelous sword. *See* St. Galgano.
Marvelous tower. Judson and Bender. Graded literature readers. 6th book.
Mary Ambree (poem). Lanier. Boy's Percy.
Mary, Mary, so contrary. Fillmore. Mighty Mikko.
See also Goody 'Gainst-the-Stream.
Marya Morevna. Curtin. Wonder-tales from Russia.
Dole. White duckling.
Lang. Red fairy book. (Death of Koschei the deathless.)
Magnus. Russian folk-tales.
Wheeler. Russian wonder tales. (Maria Morevna.)
Marziale the robber chief. Chisholm and Steedman. Staircase of stories.
Masoy and the ape. Stanley. Animal folk tales.
Master. Nordau. Dwarf's spectacles.
Master and his pupil. I. Jacobs. English fairy tales.
Johnson. Fir-tree fairy book.
Master and his pupil. II.
Lang. Golden mermaid and other stories. (Master and pupil.)
Lang. Pink fairy book. (Master and pupil.)
Success library. v. 3.
Wardrop. Georgian folk tales. (Master and pupil.)
See also Farmer Weatherbeard; Fisherman's son and the Gruagach of tricks; Magician's pupil; Oh; Wizard and his pupil.
Master and his scholar. Æsop. Fables (Black ed.).
Æsop. Fables (Burt ed.).
Master and man. Yeats. Irish fairy tales.
Master and pupil. *See* Master and his pupil.
Master cat. *See* Puss in boots.
Master Chanticleer and Dame Hen. Bailey. Firelight stories.
See also Spider and the flea.
Master fool. Bay. Danish fairy and folk tales.
Master fox. Lindsay and Poulsson. Joyous traveler. (Tale of the young lord's servant.)
Master girl. *See* Master maid.
Master Jacob. Pyle. Wonder clock.
Master-maid. I. Dasent. Popular tales from the Norse.
Dasent. Norse fairy tales.
Grundtvig. Danish fairy tales. (Prince Irregang and Maid Miseri.)
Lang. Blue fairy book.
Lang. Dick Whittington and other stories.
Stroebe and Martens. Norwegian fairy book. (Master girl.)
See also Prince Fernando; Prince of golden land; Yvon and Finnette.
Master maid. II. *See* Battle of the birds.

Master makes a bagain. St. Nicholas. March 1916, p. 422.
Master Mariner. Beston. Firelight fairy book.
Master of all masters. Jacobs. English fairy tales.
Johnson. Oak-tree fairy book.
My Bookhouse. v. 2.
Olcott and Pendleton. Jolly book.
Wiggin and Smith. Tales of laughter.
Master of magic. Bailey. Little man with one shoe.
Master of the harvest. Gatty. Parables from nature.
Olcott. Good stories for great holidays.
Master of the house. *See* Father of the family.
Master Rabbit. Stebbins. 3d reader.
Van Sickle and Seegmiller. Riverside readers. 4th reader. (Master Rabbit as a fisherman.)
Wade. Indian fairy tales.
Master Rabbit as a fisherman. *See* Master Rabbit.
Master Redvest. Pyle. Prose and verse for children.
Master Reinecke and Gockeling the cock. *See* Cock and the fox. III.
Master singers of Nuremburg. Wheelock. Stories of Wagner operas.
Chapin. Wonder stories from Wagner.
Master-smith. *See* Smith and the devil.
Master thief. Dasent. Popular tales from the Norse.
Jacobs. Europa's fairy book.
Lang. Red fairy book.
Thorpe. Yule-tide stories.
See also Jack the cunning thief.
Master Tobacco. Asbjörnsen. Tales from the fjeld.
Wiggin and Smith. Fairy ring.
Master weaver. James. Man elephant.
Mastiff and the curs. Æsop. Fables (Burt ed.).
Mastiff and the goose. Æsop. Fables (Burt ed.).
Matariki; or, The little eyes. Success library. v. 3.
See also Pleiades.
Matchless hunter. *See* Ambitious hunter and the skilful fisher.
Matsuyama mirror. *See* Mirror of Matsuyama.
Matter of arbitration. Æsop. Fables (Burt ed. Litigious cats).
Sly. World stories retold. (Monkey and the cats.)
Wiggin and Smith. Talking beasts.
See also Otters and the wolf.
Matter of importance. Richards. Golden windows.
Matthias the hunter's stories. Asbjörnsen. Folk and fairy tales.
Maui gets fire. *See* Secret of fire.
Maui makes the sun go slowly. *See* Sun a prisoner. V.
Max and the wonder flower. *See* Hans and the wonderful flower.
Maximilian and the goose boy. *See* Emperor and the goose boy.

May Blossom. *See* Sleeping beauty.
May-day queen. Faulkner. Story lady's book.
May party. Bailey. Stories for Sunday telling.
May you live a hundred years. Griswold. Hindu fairy tales.
Mayor Rat's niece. *See* Rats and their son-in-law.
Mazeppa, the chief of the Cossacks. Evans. Old time tales.
Me-ne-hu-ne. Colum. At the gateways of the day.
Measure of rice. Babbit. Jataka tales.
Shedlock. Eastern stories and legends. (Rice measure.)
Meadow dandelion. *See* Prairie dandelion.
Meadow lark's concert. Coe and Christie. Story hour readers. Book 2.
Measuring worm, Legend of. *See* Rock of the measuring worm.
Medea. *See* Argonauts.
Medea's cauldron. Bailey. Wonder stories.
See also Argonauts.
Medicine pipe. Grinnell. Blackfoot lodge tales. (Origin of the medicine pipe.)
Medicines, Origin of. Cornyn. When the camp fires burn. (Last great council fire.)
Eastman. Indian legends retold. (Origin of sickness and medicine.)
Young. Algonquin Indian tales. (*In* Ch. 12.)
See also How the Indians came to know medicine plants.
Medio Pollito. Macé. Home fairy tales.
See also Drakesbill and his friends.
Medusa. *See* Perseus.
Meester Stoorworm. *See* Ashiepattle and the stoorworm.
Meeting of Huon and Oberon. Lang. Red romance book.
Melampus. *Bailey. Wonder stories. (How Melampos fed the serpent.)
*Beckwith. In mythland. v. 3. (Melampus, the wise one.)
Lang. All sorts of stories book. (Serpent's gifts.)
Melangell's lambs. Griffis. Welsh fairy tales. (Welsh rabbits and haunted hares.)
Thomas. Welsh fairy book.
Meleager and Atalanta. *See* Calydonian hunt.
Melilot. My Bookhouse. v. 3.
Rhys. Fairy gold.
Mellidora. Fyleman. Rainbow cat.
Melodious napkin. Byrne. Modern Greek fairy tales.
Melon and the professor. Davis and Chow-Leung. Chinese fables and folk stories.
Memaloose Islands. *See* Ghost land. II.
Men learn the buffalo dance. *See* Woman who married a buffalo.
Men learn to make tipis. Borland. Rocky Mountain tipi tales.
Men of Ardudwy. Thomas. Welsh fairy book.

Men of Gotham and the watch. Johnson. Oak-tree fairy book.
Menabozho. *See* Manabozho.
Merchant. Bay. Danish fairy and folk tales.
See also Ali of Cairo; Heir of Linne.
Merchant and his donkey. *See* Donkey and the salt.
Merchant and his iron. Bidpai. Tortoise and the geese.
Merchant and the genie. Arabian nights (Dodge ed.).
Arabian nights (Lang. Story of the merchant and the genius.)
Arabian nights (Townsend. Story of the merchant and the genie.)
Jenks. Tales of fantasy.
Scudder. Children's book.
Merchant and the genius. *See* Merchant and the genie.
Merchant of Seri. *See* Grandmother's golden dish.
Merchant who overcame all obstacles. Shedlock. Eastern stories and legends.
Merchant's daughter. Baring. Blue rose fairy book.
Merchant's daughter of Bristol. Macleod. Book of ballad stories.
Merchant's fortune. Segovia. Spanish fairy book.
Merchant's tale. *See* Beryn.
Mercury. *See* Hermes and Apollo.
Mercury and the carver. Æsop. Fables (Black ed.).
Æsop. Fables (Burt ed.).
Mercury and woodman. *See* Honest woodman.
Mercy, Legend of. Poulsson. Top of the world stories.
Merlin the enchanter. Baldwin. Stories of the king. (Beguiling of Merlin.)
Cutler. Story of King Arthur and his knights. (Wise Merlin's foolishness.)
Guerber. Legends of the middle ages.
Higginson. Tales of the enchanted islands of the Atlantic.
Lang. Book of romance. (Passing of Merlin.)
Lang. Tales of the Round Table.
Merlin's crag. Skinner. Merry tales.
Mermaid. I. *See* Little mermaid.
Mermaid. II. Rhys. Fairy gold.
Mermaid. III. Bosschère. Christmas tales of Flanders.
Mermaid and the boy. Lang. Beauty and the beast, and other stories.
Lang. Brown fairy book.
Mermaid wife. Douglas. Scottish fairy tales.
Mermaids. Alcott. Lulu's library. v. 2.
Mermaid's child. Brown. Flower princess.
Mermaid's gift. Brown. Mermaid's gift, and other stories.
Mermaids, Origin of. *See* How Alexander the king got the water of life.
Merry-Andrew and the countryman. *See* Actor and the pig.

Merry clown. Lindsay and Poulsson. Joyous travelers. (Tale told by the scholar.)
Merry tale of the king and the cobbler. *See* Cobbler and the king.
Merry Twinkle and the dwarf. Cross and Statler. Storytelling.
Merry wives. Lang. Aladdin and other stories.
Lang. Pink fairy book.
Merrymind, Story of. Bailey. Stories children need.
Browne. Granny's wonderful chair.
Skinner. Garnet story book.
Message of the lady moon. *See* Moon's message.
Message of the stars. Storytellers' magazine. Oct. 1914, p. 706.
Messenger bird. Donaldson. Little papoose listens.
Metal king. Olcott. Good stories for great holidays.
Metal pig. Andersen. Fairy tales (Paull tr.).
Meteor. Judson. Myths and tales of Alaska.
Mi-e-rak-puk. Riggs. Animal stories from Eskimo land.
Mice and the cat. *See* Belling the cat.
Mice and the trap. Æsop. Fables (Burt ed.).
*Bryce. Fables from afar.
Mice in council. *See* Belling the cat.
Mice's Christmas party. Potter. Pinafore pocket story book.
Michael Scott. Douglas. Scottish fairy tales.
See also Warlock o' Oakwood.
Micky and the maccaroni. Macdonell. Italian fairy book.
See also Old woman and her pig.
Midas. I. Almost true tales. (Golden touch.)
Arnold and Gilbert. Stepping stones to literature. v. 2. (King Midas.)
*Bailey. Stories children need. (Golden touch.)
*Benson. Really truly fairy stories. (Golden touch.)
Blaisdell. Child life. 2d reader. (King Midas.)
*Bowen. Second story reader. (There are better things than gold.)
Chisholm and Steedman. Staircase of stories. (Golden touch.)
*Dillingham and Emerson. Tell it again stories. (Golden touch.)
(play). Doheny. Play awhile. (Golden touch.)
Esenwein and Stockard. Children's stories. (Golden touch.)
Francillon. Gods and heroes. (Too much gold.)
Guerber. Myths of Greece and Rome. (*In* Bacchus.)
Hartley. Stories from the Greek legends. (Story of King Midas.)
Hawthorne. Wonder book. (Golden touch.)
Hyde. Favorite Greek myths. (King Midas and the golden touch.)
Judd. Classic myths. (Why rivers have golden sands.)

Midas. I.—*continued.*
Mabie. Myths every child should know. (Golden touch.)
My Bookhouse. v. 3. (Golden touch.)
Olcott. Wonder garden. (Golden gift of King Midas.)
Patten. Junior classics. v. 3. (Turning everything into gold.)
Pratt. Myths of old Greece. v. 2. (King Midas.)
Shaw. Stories of the ancient Greeks. (*In* Golden girl.)
*Skinner. Very little child's book of stories. (King Midas.)
Sly. World stories retold. (Golden touch.)
Storr. Half a hundred hero tales.
Tappan. Stories from the classics. (Golden touch.)
Wiltse. Kindergarten stories. (Story of King Midas.)
See also Wicked fairies.

Midas. II. *Bailey. Wonder stories. (How King Midas lost his ears.)
Bryant. How to tell stories. (Judgment of Midas.)
Bryant. Best stories to tell to children. (Judgment of Midas.)
Cowles. Art of story telling. (King Midas' ears.)
Francillon. Gods and heroes. (The critic.)
Guerber. Myths of Greece and Rome. (*In* Apollo.)
Hartley. Stories from the Greek legends. (Story of King Midas.)
Hyde. Favorite Greek myths. (King Midas; Why King Midas had asses' ears.)
Olcott. Wonder garden. (Reeds that told a secret.)
Peabody. Old Greek folk stories. (Judgment of Midas.)
Pratt. Myths of old Greece. v. 2. (King Midas.)
Shaw. Stories of the ancient Greeks. (*In* Golden girl.)
Storr. Half a hundred hero tales.
Storytellers' magazine. Feb. 1915, p. 35. (Judgment of Midas.)
See also Emperor Trojan's ears; March's ears; Pan; Secret of Labra; Secret of the Khan's barber.

Midgard serpent. *See* Thor: Thor's fishing.

Midnight dance. Magnus. Russian folk-tales.
See also Twelve dancing princesses.

Midnight ride. Baldwin. Fifty famous people.

Midridge, Myth of. Hartland. English folk and fairy tales.

Midsummer's eve. Meyer. Little green door.

Midsummer night's dream. Rolfe. Fairy tales in prose and verse.
(play). Skinner. Turquoise story book. (Quarrel in fairyland. Adapted.)
(play). Storytellers' magazine. April 1916. (Abridged and adapted.)

Midsummer's night dance. Stewart. Once upon a time.

Might of the cow-headed club. Wilmot-Buxton. Stories of Persian heroes.

Mighty-Arm and Mighty-Mouth. Pyle. Tales of wonder and magic.

Mighty fisherman. *See* Thor: Thor's fishing.
Mighty hero of olden times. *See* Hercules and his labors.
Mighty Mikko. Fillmore. Mighty Mikko.
Mighty monster Afang. *See* Afang the monster.
Mignon. Baldwin. Fifty famous stories.
McSpadden. Stories from great operas.
Mignonette. Skinner. Turquoise story book.
Mignonette fairy. *Field second reader. (Flower fairy.)
Olcott. Wonder garden.
Mikko the fox. Fillmore. Mighty Mikko.
Mikumwess. *See* Glooskap and the magic gifts. II.
Mild man and his cantankerous wife. Steele. Russian garland of fairy tales.
Milk-white calf and the fairy ring. Olcott. Book of elves and fairies.
Milk-white doo. Douglas. Scottish fairy tales.
Grierson. Scottish fairy book.
See also Juniper tree.
Milkmaid and her pail. *See* Milkmaid and her pail of milk.
Milkmaid and her pail of milk. Æsop. Fables (Burt ed. Maid and her pail of milk.)
Æsop. Fables (Jacobs).
Æsop. Fables (Stickney).
Baldwin. Fairy stories and fables. (Milkmaid and her pail.)
*Elson and Runkel. Elson readers. Book 1. (Molly and the pail of milk.)
My Bookhouse. v. 1. (Milkmaid and her pail.)
Patten. Junior classics. v. 1.
Scudder. Children's book. (Country maid and her milk pail.)
Scudder. Fables and folk stories. (Country maid and her milk pail.)
Tappan. Folk stories and fables. (Country maid and the milkpail.)
Welsh. Stories children love. (Maid and the pail of milk.)
Wiggin and Smith. Talking beasts. (Dairywoman and the pot of milk.)
See also Broken pot; Lad and the fox; Barber's fifth brother; Maid with her basket of eggs.
Milkweed fairies. Bakewell. True fairy stories.
Milky way. Judd. Classic myths.
Mill. Asbjörnsen. Folk and fairy tales. (Legends of the mill.)
Asbjörnsen. Tales from the fjeld. (Haunted mill; Another haunted mill.)
See also Tailor and the witch.
Mill at the bottom of the sea. *See* Why the sea is salt. IV.
Miller and his donkey. *See* Man, the boy and the donkey.
Miller at the Professor's examination. Hartland. English folk and fairy tales.

Miller, his son and their ass. *See* Man, the boy and the donkey.
Miller of the Dee. Baldwin. Fifty famous stories.
Miller's boy and his cat. Grimm. Fairy tales (Paull tr.).
Ruskin. King of the Golden River and other stories. (Poor miller's boy and the cat.)
Storytellers' magazine. Feb. 1915, p. 56.
See also White cat.
Miller's daughter. I. Gibbon. Reign of King Cole.
Miller's daughter. II. *See* Rumpelstiltskin.
Millet thief. Thorpe. Yule-tide stories.
Mimic and the countryman. *See* Actor and the pig.
Mimkudawogoosk, the moosewood man. Partridge. Glooscap the great chief.
Mind the crooked finger. Douglas. Scottish fairy tales.
Mineral springs, Origin of. Judson. Myths and legends of the Pacific Northwest.
Minerva. *See* Arachne; Athens.
Minerva and the owl. Æsop. Fables (Burt ed.).
Minerva's olive. Æsop. Fables (Burt ed.).
Mink and the wolf. Lang. Orange fairy book.
Minkin Mouse, Amiable adventures of. Bailey. Little man with one shoe.
Minnehaha, Laughing-water. Maud. Heroines of poetry.
Minnikin. *See* Shortshanks.
Minnows with silver tails. Alderman. Classics old and new. 4th reader.
Hartwell. Story hour readings. 5th year.
Ingelow. Stories told to a child. v. 1.
Minotaur. *See* Theseus.
Minstrel. Baring. Blue rose fairy book.
Minstrel, soldier and king. *See* King Alfred.
Minstrel's ride. Guerber. Legends of the Rhine.
Minstrel's song. Lindsay. Mother stories.
Miracle of Purun Bhagat. Kipling. Second jungle book.
Miracle of the white wolf. Smith. More mystery tales.
Miraculous hen. Magnus. Russian folk-tales.
Miraculous pitcher. *See* Baucis and Philemon.
Mirri the cat. Fillmore. Mighty Mikko.
See also Fox and the cat. IV.
Mirror. I. Bouvé. Lamplight fairy tales.
Mirror. II. Mendes. Fairy spinning wheel.
Mirror of Matsuyama. Baker and Carpenter. Language reader. 3d year. (Wonderful mirror.)
Ballard. Fairy tales from far Japan. (Magic mirror.)
Hearn. Japanese fairy tales. (Matsuyama mirror.)
Lyman. Story telling.
Ozaki. Japanese fairy book.
Welsh. Stories children love. (Filial girl.)
Wiggin and Smith. Magic casements. (Matsuyama mirror.)
Williston. Japanese fairy tales. 1st series.
See also Reflections.

Mirror of the sun-goddess. James. Green willow. (*In* Susa the impetuous.)
Nixon-Roulet. Japanese folk and fairy tales.
Skinner. Turquoise story book. (Sun-goddess. Adapted.)
Mirror that made trouble. Griffis. Korean fairy tales.
See also Reflections.
Mis' Mocking-bird's chillen. Young. Plantation bird legends.
Mis' Swallow. Young. Plantation bird legends.
Misapplied wit. Fielde. Chinese fairy tales.
Mischievous boy. *See* Naughty boy.
Mischievous dog. Æsop. Fables (Black ed.).
Æsop. Fables (Burt ed.).
Æsop. Fables (Stickney).
Mischievous knix. St. Nicholas. Sept. 1888, p. 856.
Mischievous wolverine. *See* How the wolverine's legs were shortened. II.
Miser. Æsop. Fables (Black ed. Covetous man.)
Æsop. Fables (Burt ed.).
Æsop. Fables (Jacobs. Miser and his gold.)
Æsop. Fables (Stickney).
Miser and his gold. *See* Miser.
Miser and his wife. Welsh. Stories children love.
Miser and Plutus (poem). Success library. v. 3.
Miser and the magpie. Æsop. Fables (Burt ed.).
Miser and the mess of pottage. Griswold. Hindu fairy tales.
Miser of Takhoma. Cowles. Art of story-telling.
Judd. Wigwam stories. (A Rip Van Winkle.)
Judson. Myths and legends of the Pacific Northwest.
My Bookhouse. v. 3. (Man who loved Hai Quai.)
Nixon-Roulet. Indian folk tales. (Man who loved Hai Quai.)
Young and Field. Literary readers. Book 2. (Hunter who forgot.)
Miserly farmer. Martens. Chinese fairy book.
Miserly squire. Grundtvig. Danish fairy tales.
Mish-Queey Enin. Allen. Indian fairy tales.
Mishosha. Bayliss. Treasury of Indian tales. (Panigwun, who outmatched the magician.)
Olcott. Red Indian fairy book. (Mishosha; or, The enchanted sugar maple.)
Pyle. Fairy tales from many lands. (Mishosha, the magician of the lake.)
See also Sheem, the forsaken boy.
Miss Careless. Macé. Home fairy tales.
Miss Cow falls a victim to Mr. Rabbit. Harris. Uncle Remus, his songs and his sayings.
Miss Lilly Dove. Cocke. Bypaths in Dixie.
Miss Peggy and the frog. Harrison. Old-fashioned fairy book.
Miss Queen Bee. Cocke. Bypaths in Dixie.

Miss Rabbit's wedding dress. Young. Behind the dark pines.
Miss Race Hoss an' de fleas. Cocke. Bypaths in Dixie.
Miss Race Hoss's party. Cocke. Bypaths in Dixie.
Miss Woodpecker's bonnet. Young. Behind the dark pines.
Missing man found. Dyer and Brady. Merrill readers. 3d reader. (Wise men of Gotham.)
Johnson. Oak-tree fairy book.
Missing shoes. Butterworth. Zigzag journeys in the Orient. (*In* Ch. 10.)
Mistake of the apes. Fielde. Chinese fairy tales.
Mistakes of Old-Man. Linderman. Indian why stories.
Mr. *See also* Brother.
Owing to the inconsistent use of these terms, entries under both heads should be consulted.
Mr. and Mrs. Leghorn. Spaulding and Bryce. Aldine readers. 2d reader. (Drowning of Mr. Leghorn; Starving of Mrs. Leghorn; Mr. and Mrs. Leghorn to the rescue.)
Mr. and Mrs. Leghorn to the rescue. *See* Mr. and Mrs. Leghorn.
Mr. and Mrs. Spikky Sparrow. Van Sickle and Seegmiller. Riverside readers. 2d reader.
Mr. and Mrs Thumbkins. Gruelle. Friendly fairies.
Mr. and Mrs. Vinegar. *See* Mr. Vinegar.
Mister Bad 'Simmon Tree. Cocke. Bypaths in Dixie.
Mr. Bear catches old Mr. Bull-frog. Harris. Uncle Remus, his songs and his sayings.
Mr. Benjamin Ram and his wonderful fiddle. Harris. Nights with Uncle Remus.
Mr. Benjamin Ram defends himself. Harris. Nights with Uncle Remus.
Mr. Blake's walking-stick. Eggleston. Queer stories for boys and girls.
Mister Bluebird and Mister Mocking-bird. Young. Plantation bird legends.
Mister Bluebird's debt. Young. Plantation bird legends.
Mr. Bull-frog's party (poem). Curry. Little classics.
Mr. Crow goes and tells. Walker. Sandman's goodnight stories.
Mr. E. and the spelling man. Potter. Pinafore pocket story book.
Mr. Eagle and old Mrs. Owl. Bigham. Merry animal tales.
Mr. Elephant and Mr. Frog. *See* Elephant and frog.
Mr. Fox. Hartland. English folk and fairy tales.
Jacobs. English fairy tales.
Mother Goose's nursery rhymes, tales and jingles (Warne ed.).
Rhys. Fairy gold.
See also Robber bridegroom; Sweetheart in the wood.
Mr. Fox and his dinner party. Bigham. Merry animal tales.
See also Fox and the stork.

Mr. Fox and Miss Goose. *Field second reader.
Harris. Nights with Uncle Remus.
Mr. Fox and Mr. Thomas Cat. Bigham. Merry animal tales.
See also Fox and cat. I.
Mr. Fox and the deceitful frogs. Harris. Uncle Remus, his songs and his sayings.
Mr. Fox and the turkey tree. Bigham. Merry animal tales.
See also Cock and the fox. II.
Mr. Fox cuts the Cottontails. Walker. Sandman's good-night stories.
Mr. Fox figures as an incendiary. Harris. Nights with Uncle Remus.
Mr. Fox gets into serious business. Harris. Uncle Remus, his songs and his sayings.
Mr. Fox goes a-hunting, but Mr. Rabbit bags the game.
Coussens. Child's book of stories. (Fox and the rabbit.)
Harris. Uncle Remus, his songs and his sayings.
Mr. Fox is again victimized. Dyer and Brady. Merrill readers. 3d reader. (Story about Brer Rabbit.)
Harris. Uncle Remus, his songs and his sayings.
Mr. Fox is "outdone" by Mr. Buzzard. Harris. Uncle Remus, his songs and his sayings.
Mr. Fox's housewarming. Walker. Sandman's goodnight stories.
Mr. Goat and Mr. Tiger. *See* Brother Tiger and Daddy Sheep.
Mister Grab-all Spider. Cocke. Bypaths in Dixie.
Mr. Gray-squirrel talks. *Bryant. New stories to tell to children.
Mr. Hawk and Brother Buzzard. Harris. Nights with Uncle Remus.
Mr. Hawk and Brother Rabbit. Harris. Nights with Uncle Remus.
Mr. Heron's dinner party. Bigham. Merry animal tales.
See also Fox and the stork.
Mr. Jim Crack. Potter. Pinafore pocket story book.
Mr. Korbes. *See* Herr Korbes.
Mr. Lion. Bigham. Merry animal tales.
See also Lion and the mouse.
Mr. Lion hunts for Mr. Man. Harris. Nights with Uncle Remus.
Mr. Lion's sad predicament. Harris. Nights with Uncle Remus.
Mr. Man has some meat. Harris. Nights with Uncle Remus.
Mr. Maple and Mr. Pine. Stone and Fickett. Trees in prose and poetry.
Mr. Miacca. Coussens. Child's book of stories.
Jacobs. English fairy tales.
Johnson. Oak-tree fairy book. (Mr. Micrawble.)
O'Grady and Throop. Teachers' story teller's book.

Mr. Micrawble. *See* Mr. Miacca.
Mr. Rabbit and Mr. Bear. Harris. Uncle Remus, his songs and his sayings.
Mr. Rabbit as a rain-maker. Harris. Little Mr. Thimble-finger.
Van Sickle and Seegmiller. Riverside readers. 4th reader. (Rain-maker: Brother Rabbit's story.)
Mr. Rabbit finds his match at last. Harris. Uncle Remus, his songs and his sayings.
Mr. Rabbit grossly deceives Mr. Fox. Harris. Uncle Remus, his songs and his sayings.
Mr. Rabbit meets his match again. Harris. Uncle Remus, his songs and his sayings.
Mr. Rabbit nibbles up the butter Harris. Uncle Remus, his songs and his sayings.
Mr. Rabbit's ears. Bigham. Merry animal tales.
See also Hare afraid of his ears.
Mr. Rat and Mr. Ratte. Storytellers' magazine. March 1916, p. 189.
Mister Rattlesnake. Cocke. Bypaths in Dixie.
Mr. Salt and Mrs. Pepper. Potter. Pinafore pocket story book.
Mr. Samson Cat. *Carrick. Picture tales from the Russian.
See also Fox and the cat. IV.
Mr. Sin, the carp. Coussens. Jade story book.
Mr. Snail and Brother Wolf. Ortoli. Evening tales.
Mister Tall Pine's Christmas tree. Cocke. Bypaths in Dixie.
Mr. Terrapin appears upon the scene. Harris. Uncle Remus, his songs and his sayings.
Mr. Terrapin shows his strength. Harris. Uncle Remus, his songs and his sayings.
Mr. Thomas Cat's chestnuts. Bigham. Merry animal tales.
See also Cat, the monkey and the chestnuts.
Mr. Vinegar. Bailey. Firelight stories. (Mr. and Mrs. Vinegar.)
Baldwin. Another fairy reader. (Mr. Vinegar and his fortune.)
Coussens. Child's book of stories.
Hartland. English folk and fairy tales.
Hodgkins. Atlantic treasury of childhood stories. (Story of Mr. Vinegar.)
Howard. Banbury Cross stories.
Jacobs. English fairy tales.
Johnson. Oak-tree fairy book.
Mother Goose's nursery rhymes, tales and jingles (Warne ed.).
Rhys. Fairy gold. (Mr. and Mrs. Vinegar.)
Welsh. Stories children love. (Story of Mr. Vinegar.)
See also Dame Gudbrand; Hans in luck.
Mr. Vinegar and his fortune. *See* Mr. Vinegar.
Mr. Wind and Madam Rain. Lansing. Dramatic readings.

Mr. Wolf makes a failure. Harris. Uncle Remus, his songs and his sayings.
Mr. Wolf tackles Old Man Tarrypin. Harris. Uncle Remus, his songs and his sayings.
Mister Woodpecker. Young. Plantation bird legends.
Mister Woodpecker's work. Young. Plantation bird legends.
Mistletoe. *See* Baldur and the mistletoe.
Mrs. Beaver's shop. Potter. Pinafore pocket story book.
Mrs. Blackrat's house party. Bigham. Merry animal tales.
Mrs. Bunny's dinner party. Skinner. Topaz story book.
Mrs. Chinchilla. Wiggin and Smith. Story hour.
Mistress Flynn and the pot of gold. St. Nicholas. June 1904, p. 689.
Mrs. Fox. *See* Wedding of Mrs Fox.
Mrs. Grasshopper Gay. Bigham. Merry animal tales.
See also Ant and the grasshopper.
Mrs. Gray's family. Stocking. Golden goblet.
Mrs. Margery Two Shoes. *See* Goody Two-Shoes.
Mistress Merciless. Field. Christmas tales.
Mrs. Mouse's rummage sale. Potter. Pinafore pocket story book.
Mrs. November's dinner party. Hartwell. Story hour readings. 6th year.
Mrs. Partridge has a fit. Harris, Uncle Remus and his friends.
Mrs. Partridge's errand. Van Sickle and Seegmiller. Riverside reader. 3d reader.
Mistress Peafowl's bad luck. Young. Plantation bird legends.
Mrs. Santa Claus. Bailey and Lewis. For the children's hour.
Mrs. Speckley Hen. Lindsay. More mother stories.
Mrs. Stump's Easter bonnet. Bailey. Friendly tales.
Mrs. Tabby Gray. My Bookhouse. v. 1.
Mrs. Thrifty-ant's fall. Bigham. Merry animal tales.
See also Ant and the dove.
Mrs. Zippy Zero. Potter. Pinafore pocket story book.
Misunderstanding. Richards. Golden windows.
Mixed Easter eggs. Bailey. Friendly tales.
Mkaaah Jeechonee, the boy hunter. Bateman. Zanzibar tales.
Mo-e Mo-e, Story of. Colum. At the gateways of the day.
Mocking bird. I. Æsop. Fables (Burt ed.).
Mocking bird. II. Young. Plantation bird legends.
Mocking bird's singing-school. Eggleston. Queer stories for boys and girls.
Mocking bird's theft. Young. Plantation bird legends.
Mogarzea and his son. Lang. Beauty and the beast, and other stories.
Lang. Violet fairy book.

Mohammed. Baldwin. Fifty famous rides. (How Mahomet rode to Jerusalem.)
Baldwin. Horse fair. (Al Borak.)
Evans. Old time tales (A camel driver becomes a prophet.)
See also Red geranium.
Mohammed with the magic finger. Lang. Trusty John.
Lang. Violet fairy book.
Mole and her mother. Æsop. Fables (Black ed.).
Æsop. Fables (Burt ed. Mole and her dam.)
Mole and her dam. *See* Mole and her mother.
Mole and the sun. *See* Sun a prisoner. III.
Mole, Origin of. Bain. Cossack fairy tales.
Holbrook. Nature myths. (First moles.)
Molly and the pail of milk. *See* Milkmaid and her pail of milk.
Molly Ann's valentines. Bailey. Friendly tales.
Molly Whuppie. Jacobs. English fairy tales.
See also Smallhead and the King's son.
Moment in heaven. Stroebe and Martens. Danish fairy book.
Momotaro; or, The story of the son of a peach. I. Ballard. Fairy tales from far Japan. (Momotaro; or, The peach boy.)
Field. Famous fairy tales.
Finnemore. Peeps at many lands. Japan.
*Hearn. Japanese fairy tales.
Hodgkins. Atlantic treasury of childhood stories. (Adventures of Momotaro.)
*Olcott. Wonder garden. (Peach Boy's rice cakes.)
Ozaki. Japanese fairy book.
Patten. Junior classics. v. 1. (Adventures of Little Peachling.)
St. Nicholas. May 1874, p. 386. (Peach-boy.)
Stewart. Tell me a hero story. (Momotaro, Son-of-a-peach.)
Storytellers' magazine. Nov. 1915, p. 408. (Little peach child.)
Tappan. Folk stories and fables. (Adventures of Little Peachling.)
Williston. Japanese fairy tales. 2d series. (Peach Darling.)
Momotaro; or, The story of the son of a peach. II. Skinner. Nursery tales from many lands. (Monotaro.)
See also Ito and his friends.
Momotaro. III. Dyer and Brady. Merrill readers. 3d reader. (Stone-cutter.)
Mondahmin. *See* First corn. II.
Monday! Tuesday! *See* Knockgrafton, Legend of.
Money box. I. *See* Money-pig.
Money box. II. Mendes. Fairy spinning wheel.
Money-pig. Andersen. Fairy tales (Paull tr. Money box.)
Andersen. Wonder stories (Author's ed.).

Money-pig—*continued.*
Wiggin and Smith. Tales of laughter. (Money-box.)
Money will buy everything. Bay. Danish fairy and folk tales.
Monk and the bird. *See* Monk and the bird's song.
Monk and the bird of paradise. *See* Monk and the bird's song.
Monk and the bird's song. Crommelin. Famous legends.
Cross and Statler. Storytelling. (Monk and the bird.)
Frost. Fairies and folk of Ireland. (*In* Ch. 9.)
Gask. Folk tales from many lands. (Monk and the bird of paradise.)
Guerber. Legends of the Rhine. (Bird of paradise.)
Lyman. Story telling. (Monk and the bird.)
Scudder. Book of legends. (Monk and the bird.)
Stebbins. Sunken city. (Bird of paradise.)
Storytellers' magazine. Nov. 1915, p. 418. (Monk and the bird of paradise.)
Yeats. Irish fairy and folk tales. (Story of the little bird.)
See also Abbot of Innisfalen.
Monk of the Yangtze-Kiang. Martens. Chinese fairy book.
Monkey, Adventures of. Chisholm and Steedman. Staircase of stories.
Monkey and the camel. Bryce. Fables from afar.
Monkey and the cat. *See* Cat, the monkey and the chestnuts.
Monkey and the cats. *See* Matter of arbitration.
Monkey and the crab. *See* Crab and the monkey.
Monkey and the crocodile. Babbitt. Jataka tales.
Peck. Stories for good children.
Shedlock. Eastern stories and legends.
Skinner. Merry tales.
See also Heart of a monkey; Monkey and the jelly fish; Rabbit's eyes.
Monkey and the crows. Rouse. Talking thrush.
Monkey and the jelly-fish. Hearn. Japanese fairy tales. (Silly jelly fish.)
Griffis. Japanese fairy tales. (How the jelly fish lost his shell.)
James. Green willow. (Jellyfish takes a journey.)
Lang. Twelve huntsmen and other stories.
Lang. Violet fairy book.
Ozaki. Japanese fairy book. (Jelly fish and the monkey.)
Singleton. Wild flower fairy book. (Silly jelly fish.)
Wiggin and Smith. Tales of laughter. (Silly jelly fish.)
See also Monkey and the crocodile; Rabbit's eyes.
Monkey and the leopard (poem). Wiggin and Smith. Talking beasts.
Monkey and the tortoise. Storytellers' magazine. June 1916, p. 382.
Monkey as nurse. Guerber. Legends of the Rhine.

Monkey captain. Henderson. Sea yarns for boys.
Monkey finds worry. Stafford. Animal fables.
Monkey-gardeners. Babbitt. More Jataka tales. (Stupid monkeys.)
Burlingame. Grateful elephant.
Patten. Junior classics. v. 2. (Watering of the saplings.)
Monkey princess. Aulnoy. Children's fairy tales.
Monkey that saved the herd. *See* Monkeys and the hollow canes.
Monkey, the shark and the washerman's donkey. Bateman. Zanzibar tales.
See also Heart of a monkey.
Monkey tricks in the jungle. Aspinwall. Short stories for short people.
Monkey who brought Thanksgiving. Bailey. In the animal world.
Monkey who had seen the world (poem). Æsop. Fables (Burt ed.).
Wiggin and Smith. Talking beasts.
Monkeys and the hollow canes. Griswold. Hindu fairy tales.
Shedlock. Eastern stories and legends. (Monkey that saved the herd.)
Monkeys and the moon. Bryce. Fables from afar.
See also Moon in the millpond.
Monkey's bargains. Rouse. Talking thrush.
See also Hans in luck.
Monkey's rebuke. Rouse. Talking thrush.
Monotaro. *See* Momotaro.
Mons Tro. Grundtvig. Fairy tales from afar.
Wiggin and Smith. Magic casements.
Monster fish. Brown. Tales of the red children.
Monster in the sun. Æsop. Fables (Burt ed.).
Month of March. Faulkner. Italian fairy book.
My Bookhouse. v. 3.
Wiggin. Tales of laughter. (Months.)
See also March and the shepherd; Old woman who met the months; Two brothers, II.
Months. I. *See* Month of March.
Months. II. *See* Twelve months. I.
Mooin, the bear's child. Partridge. Glooscap the great chief.
Washburn. Indian legends. (How the bear family got its name.)
Mooly's Thanksgiving. Bailey. Friendly tales.
Moon and her mother. Hall and Gilman. Story land. 2d reader.
Moon and stars. *See* Sun, moon and stars. III.
Moon and the boy. *See* What the moon saw.
Moon and the cuckoo. Nixon-Roulet. Japanese folk stories and fairy tales.

Moon and the great snake. Linderman. Indian why stories.
Moon cake. Fielde. Chinese fairy tales.
Hall and Gilman. Story land. 2d reader.
Wiggin and Smith. Tales of laughter.
Moon-calf. Richards. Toto's merry winter.
Moon fairy. Patterson. Enchanted bird.
Moon fancies. Hume. Chronicles of fairyland.
Moon flowers and morning glories, Origin of. Bigham. Overheard in fairyland.
Moon hare. James. Jewelled sea.
Moon in the mill-pond. Harris. Nights with Uncle Remus.
Skinner. Merry tales. (Fishing party.)
Wiltse. Folklore stories.
See also Monkeys and the moon.
Moon maiden. I. Nixon-Roulet. Indian folk tales.
Moon maiden. II. *See* Princess Moonbeam.
Moon maiden. III. *See* Bamboo cutter and the moon child.
Moon path. Allen. Indian fairy tales.
Moon stories. *See* Boy in the moon; Children in the moon; Bride of the wind; Daylight, Origin of; Chief in the moon; Frog in the moon; Hare in the moon; Hina, the woman in the moon; Jack and Jill's trip to the moon; Lady in the moon; Man in the Moon; Maiden in the moon; Man who married the moon; Mother moon. Sun, moon and stars; What the children see in the moon; Why sunshine follows rain; Why the moon waxes and wanes; Why the moon's face is smutty.
See also Titles beginning with the word moon.
Moonlight dance. Donaldson. Little papoose listens.
Moonlight sonata, Story of. Cross and Statler. Story-telling. (Beethoven's Moonlight sonata.)
Storytellers' magazine. July 1913, p. 72. (Beethoven's moonlight sonatá.)
Moon's message. Bailey. In the animal world. (Message of the Lady Moon.)
Griffis. Belgian fairy tales. (Belgian bunny.)
Holbrook. Book of nature myths. (Why the rabbit is timid.)
Wilson. Nature study reader. (Hottentot moon story.)
Moon's story. *See* What the moon saw: 31st evening.
Moorish dish, Story of the. Harrison. Bric-a-brac stories.
Moor's legacy, Legend of the. Arnold and Gilbert. Stepping stones to literature. v. 7.
Irving. Alhambra.
Judson and Bender. Graded literature readers. v. 7.
Smith. Mystery tales.
Mop servant. Grierson. Children's book of Celtic stories.
Moqui boy and the eagle. Lummis. Pueblo Indian folk stories.
More modern ballad of Chevy Chase. *See* Chevy Chase.

More trouble for Brother Wolf. Harris. Nights with Uncle Remus.

More ways than one. Pyle. Prose and verse for children.

Morgan le Fay. Cutler. Stories of King Arthur and his knights. (Treachery of Morgan Le Fay.)

Lang. Tales of the Round Table.

Morning and the evening star. Martens. Chinese fairy book.

Morning-dew. Houghton. Russian grandmother's wonder tales.

See also Faithful and Faithless; True and Untrue; Three tasks; Vilas' spring.

Morning-glory. Walker. Sandman's goodnight stories.

Morning-glory fan. Olcott. Wonder garden.

Morning glory seed, Story of the. Arnold and Gilbert. Stepping stones to literature. v. 3.

Dyer and Brady. Merrill readers. 2d reader.

Morning-glory trumpets. Judson. Flower fairies.

Morning star. I. Brooks. Stories of the red children.

Cowles. Indian nature myths. (Puckwudjee and the morning star.)

Farmer. Nature myths. (Legend of the morning star.)

Judd. Wigwam stories. (Where the morning star came from.)

Pratt. Legends of the red children. (Legend of the morning star.)

Schoolcraft. Indian fairy book. (He of the little shell.)

Tanner. Legends from the red man's forest.

Morning star. II. Olcott. Red Indian fairy book. (Legend of the morning star.)

Morning star. III. *See* Maid who married the morning star.

Moro's ears. Caballero. Spanish fairy tales.

Morozko. *See* King Frost.

Morraha. Graves. Irish fairy book.

Jacobs. More Celtic fairy tales.

Yeats. Irish fairy tales.

Mor's sons and the herder from under the sea. Curtin. Hero tales from Ireland.

Moses. Landa. Aunt Naomi's Jewish fairy tales and legends. (Water-babe.)

Mosquitoes, Origin of. Young. Algonquin Indian tales. (*In* Ch. 2. Wakonda and the origin of mosquitoes.)

See also How mosquitoes came.

Moss-back sinner in every meeting house. Young. Behind the dark pines.

Moss-green princess. Bourhill and Drake. Fairy tales from South Africa. (Nya-nya Bulembu; or. The moss-green princess.)

Moss rose, Legend of. Donaldson. Moons of long ago. (Moss roses.)

Olcott. Wonder garden. (How moss roses came.)

Moss rose, Legend of—*continued.*
Pratt. Fairyland of flowers.
Skinner. Turquoise story book. (Dew mother's gift to the rose.)
Most beautiful bird in the world. Harris. Uncle Remus returns.
Most beautiful princess. Eells. Tales of giants from Brazil.
Most beautiful thing in the world. Meyer. Little green door.
Most cunning animal. Bosschère. Folk tales of Flanders.
See also Wolf and the man.
Most extraordinary thing. Andersen. Stories and tales (Author's ed.).
Most frugal of men. Fielde. Chinese fairy tales.
Wiggin and Smith. Tales of laughter.
Most obedient wife. Bay. Danish fairy and folk tales. (Bend the bough in time.)
Grundtvig. Danish fairy tales.
Grundtvig. Fairy tales from afar.
Most powerful husband in the world. Cary. French fairy tales.
See also Rats and their son-in-law.
Most wonderful and noble self-playing harp, Story of. Steele. Russian garland of fairy tales.
Most wonderful thing in the green forest. Meyer. Little green door.
Moth and rust. Hartwell. Story hour readings. 6th year.
Mother and daughter who worshipped the sun. Steel. Tales of the Punjab.
Mother and maid. *See* Proserpina.
Mother Bertha's stories. Asbjörnsen. Folk and fairy tales.
Mother Frost. *See* Mother Holle.
Mother Goose's party. Edey. Six giants and a griffin.
Mother Hildegarde. Pyle. Wonder clock.
Mother Holle. Allison and Perdue. Story in primary instruction. (Mother Frost.)
*Baldwin. Fairy reader. (Lost spindle.)
Blaisdell. Child life. 3d reader.
(play). Doheny. Play awhile. (Two sisters.)
Grimm. Fairy tales (Lucas tr. Mother Hulda.)
Grimm. Household stories (Crane tr. Mother Hulda.)
Grimm. Household tales (Burt ed. Widow's two daughters.)
Grimm. Household tales (Everyman's ed.).
Haaren. Fairy life.
Keyes. Stories and story-telling.
Lang. Red fairy book.
Pyle. Mother's nursery tales. (Mother Hulda.)
Singleton. Wild flower fairy book.
Welsh. Fairy tales children love. (Mother Hulda.)
See also Black box and red box; Gold Maria and Pitch

Mother Holle—*continued.*
Maria; Humility rewarded; Man's daughter and the woman's daughter; Old witch; Sister and half-sister; Talking eggs.
Mother Hotty and the little Hotties. *Bryant. New stories to tell to children.
Mother Hubbard and her wonderful dog. *See* Old Mother Hubbard.
Mother Hulda. *See* Mother Holle.
Mother in paradise. Field. Second book of tales.
Mother love. *See* Cornelia's jewels.
Mother Michel and her cat. Carrick. Kitty cat tales.
Mother Moon. Lummis. Pueblo Indian folk stories.
Mother of the sea. Byrne. Modern Greek fairy tales.
Mother Roundabout's daughter. Asbjörnsen. Fairy tales from the far north. (Lad who went wooing the daughter of old Mother Corner.)
Asbjörnsen. Tales from the fjeld.
Stroebe and Martens. Norwegian fairy book. (Youth who wanted to win the daughter of the mother in the corner.)
Storytellers' magazine. Dec. 1916, p. 665. (Lad who went wooing the daughter of Old Mother Corner.)
Wiggin and Smith. Fairy ring.
Mother Spider. My Bookhouse, v. 1.
Wickes. Happy holidays.
Mother, Story of a. Andersen Fairy tales (Lucas tr.).
Andersen. Fairy tales (Paull tr.).
Andersen. Stories and tales (Author's ed.).
See also Mother's love.
Mother, the nurse, and the fairy (poem). Æsop. Fables (Burt ed.).
Mother's day. *See* Ander's new cap; *Are you hopping along behind?; Coriolanus; Cornelia's jewels; *Day there were no mothers; Lark and its young ones; Tender mother; Washington does not go to sea.
Mother's love. Andersen. Fairy tales (Paull tr.).
See also Mother, Story of a.
Mother's pet. Bay. Danish fairy and folk tales.
Moti. Lang. Lilac fairy book.
Lang. Little King Loc.
Moti Guj. Alderman. Classics old and new. 3d reader.
Motikatika. Lang. Crimson fairy book.
Lang. Little Wildrose.
Moufflou. Alderman. Classics old and new. (Mufflu.)
Wiggin and Smith. Story hour.
Mouldy penny. Griffis. Dutch fairy tales.
Mount Edgecomb, Alaska, Legend of. Judson. Myths and legends of the Pacific Northwest.
Mount of the Golden Queen. Stroebe and Martens. Swedish fairy book.
Mount Tutokanula. *See* Rock of the measuring worm.

Mountain and the sea. Field. Little book of profitable tales.
Mountain and the squirrel (poem). Murray. Story book treasures. (Fable.)
Mountain ash, Legend of. I. Bryce. That's why stories.
Stone and Fickett. Trees in prose and poetry.
Mountain ash, Legend of. II. Cooke. Nature myths.
Mountain dweller. Eastman. Indian legends retold.
Mountain giants. Griffis. Swiss fairy tales.
Mountain in labor. Æsop. Fables (Burt ed. Mountains in labor.)
Æsop. Fables (Jacobs. Mountains in labor.)
Welsh. Stories children love.
Mountain rose. Nixon-Roulet. Japanese folk stories and fairy tales.
Mountains in labor. *See* Mountain in labor.
Mouse and mouser (poem). Jacobs. English fairy tales.
See also Cattie sits in the kiln-ring spinning.
Mouse and the elephant (poem). Fairy stories retold from St. Nicholas. (An island fable.)
Mouse and the frog. Æsop. Fables (Burt ed.).
Wiggin and Smith. Talking beasts.
Mouse and the lion. *See* Lion and the mouse.
Mouse and the moonbeam. Field. Christmas tales.
Field. Little book of profitable tales.
*Klingensmith. Just stories. (Naughty little mouse. Adapted.)
Mouse and the sausage. *Bailey. Stories children need.
Keyes. Five senses.
Keyes. Stories and story-telling.
Wiggin and Smith. Tales of laughter.
Mouse and the weasel. Æsop. Fables (Black ed.).
Æsop. Fables (Burt ed.).
See also Blackie's picnic.
Mouse-deer's shipwreck. Wiggin and Smith. Talking beasts.
Mouse family, Adventures of a. Ketchum and Jorgensen. Kindergarten gems.
Mouse, the bird and the sausage. Darton. Wonder book of beasts.
Grimm. Fairy tales (Lucas tr.).
Grimm. Household stories (Crane tr.).
Grimm. Household tales (Burt ed.).
Grimm. Household tales (Everyman's ed.).
(play). Stevenson. Plays for the home. (Each in his own place.)
Mouse, the cat and the cock. Æsop. Fables (Burt ed. Young mouse, the cock and the cat.)
Æsop. Fables (Stickney).
Bryce. Fables from afar. (Little mouse's mistake.)
*Elson and Runkel. Elson readers. Book 2. (Little mouse and the strangers.)

Mouse, the cat and the cock—*continued.*
Grover. Folklore reader. v. 1. (Mouse, the cat and the rooster.)
Wiggin and Smith. Talking beasts. (Young mouse, the cock and the cat.)
See also Blackie's fright.
Mouse, the cat and the rooster. *See* Mouse, the cat and the cock.
Mouse, the cricket and the bee. *Elson and Runkel. Elson readers. Book 1.
Mouse, the frog and the hawk. Æsop. Fables (Stickney).
See also Blackie and Mr. Bullfrog.
Mouse tower. Evans. Old time tales.
Gask. Folk tales from many lands.
Gask. Treasury of folk tales.
Guerber. Legends of the Rhine. (Rat tower.)
Noyes. Twilight stories. (Rat tower.)
(poem). Southey. Poems. (God's judgment on a wicked bishop.)
Mouse who became a tiger. Wiggin and Smith. Talking beasts.
Mouse with wings. St. Nicholas. July 1900, p. 780.
Mouse's revenge. Aspinwall. Short stories for short people.
Mouseskin. Jerrold. Big book of fairy tales.
Mowgli's brothers. Kipling. Jungle book.
Much and more. Stocking. Golden goblet.
Much from little. St. Nicholas. Dec. 1915, p. 132.
Much shall have more and little shall have less. Pyle. Twilight land.
Muchie Lal. Frere. Old Deccan days.
Pyle. Wonder tales retold. (Fish prince.)
Singleton. Goldenrod fairy book. (Little Ruby fish.)
Tappan. Myths from many lands.
Wiggin and Smith. Fairy ring.
Muckle-mou'ed Meg. Grierson. Children's tales from Scottish ballads.
Mud pony. *See* Boy and the mud pony.
Mud wasp. Children's story garden.
Mudjee Monedo. *See* Bird lover.
Muff, the fan and the parasol (poem). Success library. v. 3.
Wiggin and Smith. Talking beasts.
Muinwa the rain fairy. Danielson. Story telling time.
Mulberries. *See* Pyramus and Thisbe.
Mule. I. Æsop. Fables (Black ed.).
Æsop. Fables (Burt ed.).
Mule. II. Gregory. Kiltartan wonder book.
Mule and the lion. Davis and Chow-Leung. Chinese fables and folk stories.
Stanley. Animal folk tales. (Lion and the mule.)
Wiggin and Smith. Talking beasts.
Mule, jackal and lion. Wiggin and Smith. Talking beasts.

Mule laden with corn and the mule laden with gold. Æsop. Fables (Burt ed.).
Mules and the robbers. Æsop. Fables (Stickney).
Munachar and Manachar. Bailey. Firelight stories.
Jacobs. Celtic fairy tales.
Skinner. Nursery tales from many lands.
Wiggin and Smith. Fairy ring.
Yeats. Irish fairy tales (Burt ed.).
See also Cat and the mouse; Grain of corn; How the mouse got into his hole; Little Tuppen; Nanny who wouldn't go home to supper; Old woman and her pig; Sparrow and the bush.
Munchausen, Baron. *See* Travels of Baron Munchausen.
Murdered wife. Guerber. Legends of the Rhine.
Murdoch McBrian and the King of Albain. Grierson. Scottish fairy book.
Murdoch's rath. Ewing. Old-fashioned fairy tales.
Hodgkins. Atlantic treasury of childhood stories.
Smith. Good old stories.
Murmur-Goose-Egg. *See* Grumblegizzard.
Murroghoo-More and Murroghoo-Beg. MacManus. In chimney corners.
Murtough and the witch-woman. Graves. Irish fairy book.
Muse of the coming age. Andersen. Stories and tales (Author's ed.).
Music of the sea. Farmer. Nature myths.
Musicians of Bremen. *See* Bremen town musicians.
Mussel and the crow. *Bowen. Second story reader.
Muzhichek-as-big-as-your-thumbs-with-mustaches-seven-versts-long. Polevoi. Russian fairy tales.
My flannel rooster. Aspinwall. Short stories for short people.
My grandfather, Hendry Watty. Tyler. Twenty-four unusual stories.
My Lord Bag of Rice. *See* Lord Bag of Rice.
My own self. Forty famous fairy tales.
Hartland. English folk and fairy tales. (Ainsel.)
Jacobs. More English fairy tales.
Lansing. Fairy tales. v. 1. (Ainsel.)
Olcott. Book of elves and fairies. (Ownself.)
Myles McGarry and Donald McGarry. MacManus. In chimney corners.
Myrtle Maiden, Story of the. Fairy tales from Brentano.
Mysterious books. *See* Sibyl.
Mysterious garden. *See* Mystic garden.
Mysterious island. Ortoli. Evening tales.
Mysterious prince. Williams. Fairy tales from folklore.
See also East o' the sun and west o' the moon; King Valemon, the white bear.
Mysterious servant. Fillmore. Mighty Mikko.
Mysterious voice. Johnson. Fir-tree fairy book.
Mystery of the Sphinx. Jewett. Egyptian tales of magic.

Mystic garden. Coussens. Jade story book. (Mysterious garden.)
Laboulaye. Fairy tales. (Mysterious garden.)
Laboulaye. Last fairy tales.

N

N. S. bicycle. Aspinwall. Short stories for short people.
Na-Ha the fighter. Finger. Tales from silver lands.
Nahum Prince. Bailey. Stories children need.
Poulsson. In the child's world.
Nail. I. Dyer and Brady. Merrill readers. 3d reader. (Lost nail.)
Grimm. Fairy tales (Paull tr.).
Keyes. Stories and story-telling.
Olcott. Good stories for great holidays.
Pyle. Mother's nursery tales.
Van Sickle and Seegmiller. Riverside readers. 4th reader.
Wiggin and Smith. Tales of laughter.
Nail. II. Baldwin. Fifty famous people. (Horseshoe nails.)
Nail broth. *See* Old woman and the tramp.
Naming of a great city. *See* Athens.
Naming of the birds. Judson. Myths and legends of Alaska.
Naming the winds. Skinner. Pearl story book.
Nanahboozhoo. *See* Manabozho.
Nancy Etticoat's ring. Esenwein and Stockard. Children's stories.
Nancy Fairy. Dasent. Popular tales from the Norse.
Nancy's New Year gifts. Bailey. Stories for Sunday telling.
Nanny and Conn. MacManus. In chimney corners.
Nanny who wouldn't go home to supper. Asbjörnsen. Fairy tales from the far north.
Asbjörnsen. Tales from the fjeld. (How they got Hairlock home.)
Bailey. Firelight stories. (How they brought Hairlock home.)
Bailey. Once upon a time animal stories. (How they brought Hairlock home.)
Wiggin and Smith. Tales of laughter.
See also Cat and the mouse; Grain of corn; How the mouse got into his hole; Little Tuppen; Munachar and Manachar; Old woman and her pig; Sparrow and the bush.
Nansi Llwyd and the dog of darkness. Thomas. Welsh fairy book.
Napi and the famine. Grinnell. Blackfoot lodge stories. (Dog and the stick.)
Nixon-Roulet. Indian folk tales.
See also Giant with the grey feathers.

Napoleon. Baldwin. Fifty famous stories. (How Napoleon crossed the Alps.)
Napoleon and the corporal. Guerber. Legends of the Rhine. (Noble deaths.)
Napoleon and the drummer-boy. Sly. World stories retold.
Narcissus. I. *See* Echo and Narcissus.
Narcissus. II. McFee. Treasury of flower stories. (Legend of the Narcissus.)
Narwhal, Origin of. Bayliss. Treasury of Eskimo tales.
Naughty boy. Andersen. Fairy tales (Lucas tr.).
Andersen. Fairy tales (Paull tr. Mischievous boy.)
Andersen. Wonder stories (Author's ed.).
Naughty brother and clever sister. Nordau. Dwarf's spectacles.
Naughty comet. Richards. Toto's merry winter.
Naughty grandchildren. Eastman. Indian legends retold.
Naughty Jocko. Alcott. Lulu's library. v. 1.
Naughty little Cupid. Olcott. Wonder garden.
Naughty little gold finger. Boston collection of kindergarten stories.
Naughty little mouse. *See* Mouse and the moonbeam.
Naughty Nick. Donahey. Tales to be told to children.
Nayang-wite, the first rabbit drive. Austin. Basket woman.
Neck. Ewing. Old-fashioned fairy tales.
Necklace Brisingamen. *See* Freyja.
Necklace of jewels. *See* Jewish doctor's story.
Necklace of Princess Fiorimonde. Chisholm. In fairy land.
Necklace of truth. Boys' and girls' fairy book.
Coe. Second book of stories.
Lansing. Dramatic readings.
Macé. Home fairy tales.
Nectanabus. Jewett. Egyptian tales of magic.
Ned Dog and Billy Goat. Cocke. Bypaths in Dixie.
Ned Puw's farewell. Thomas. Welsh fairy book.
Nedzumi. *See* Rats and their son-in-law.
Neighbor. Richards. Silver crown.
Neighbor Peter who was determined to rule his own house. *See* Man who was going to mind the house.
Neighbor underground. Stroebe and Martens. Norwegian fairy book.
Neighboring families. Andersen. Fairy tales. (Paull tr. Roses and the sparrows.)
Andersen. Wonder stories (Author's ed.).
Nengnie. Andrews. Enchanted forest.
Neptune. Francillon. Gods and heroes.
Guerber. Myths of Greece and Rome. (Neptune.)
Judd. Classic myths.
*Poulsson. In the child's world.
See also Athens.
Ness king. Thorpe. Yule-tide stories.

Nessus. *See* Hercules and his labors.
Nest builders. *See* Magpie's nest. I.
Nest that hung on the Christmas tree. Bailey. Stories and rhymes for a child.
Nettle-gatherer. Whittier. Child life in prose.
See also Lesson of faith.
Nettle spinner. Lang. Red fairy book.
Never mind the money. Bay. Danish fairy and folk tales.
Never-Wash. Magnus. Russian folk-tales.
New clothes of the emperor. *See* Emperor's new clothes.
New day. Bailey. Stories for Sunday.
New kind of circus. Tales for bedtime.
New Santa Claus. *See* Animals' Christmas tree. II.
New voices. Elson and Runkel. Elson readers. Book 2.
New Year, Story of the. Faulkner. Story lady's book.
Ketchum and Jorgensen. Kindergarten gems.
New Year's bell. Proudfoot. Child's Christ tales.
Skinner. Pearl story book.
New Year's Day. *See* Fairy's New Year gift; Good year; Gordy's New Year's dinner party; *Grandmother Old-Year and the baby; Little match girl; Mail-coach passengers; Nancy's New Year gifts; New day; Twelve months, I; Year, Story of.
New Year's day in the garden. Scudder. Seven little people.
New Year's dinner party. Hartwell. Story hour readings. 7th year.
New Year's message. Proudfoot. Child's Christ tales.
News. Jacobs. More English fairy tales.
(play). Lansing. Quaint old stories.
Nezumi the beautiful. *See* Rats and their son-in-law.
Niagara and the Great Lakes, Legend of. Olcott. Red Indian fairy book.
Niagara Falls. *See* Bended rocks.
Nianga Dia Ngenga and Leopard. Wiggin and Smith. Talking beasts.
Nibelungenlied. Baldwin. Hero tales told in school.
Church. Heroes of chivalry and romance.
Guerber. Legends of the middle ages.
Guerber. Legends of the Rhine. (Story of Siegfried.)
Haaren and Poland. Famous men of the middle ages. (Nibelungs.)
Klingensmith. Old Norse wonder tales. (Stories of the Nibelungen).
Mabie. Heroes and fairies. (Siegfried.)
Partridge. Story-telling in home and school. (Making of the sword. Adapted.)
Tappan. Stories of legendary heroes. (Siegfried.)
See also Andvare's golden ring; Horse who rode through fire; Ring: Siegfried; Ring: Twilight of the gods; Ring: War maidens; Sigurd the Volsung.
Nick Bluster's trick. Storytellers' magazine. April 1917, v. 5.

Nickerman's wife. Fillmore. Shoemaker's apron.
Niels and the giants. Lang. Crimson fairy book.
Niflheim. *See* Odin's search for wisdom.
Night and day. Gatty. Parables from nature.
Night before Christmas. Harris. Nights with Uncle Remus.
Night bird. Farmer. Nature myths.
Night on the battlefield. Martens. Chinese fairy book.
Night with Santa Claus. Coe. Second book of stories.
Skinner. Pearl story book.
Nightingale. I. Andersen. Fairy tales (Lucas tr.).
Andersen. Fairy tales (Paull tr.).
Andersen. Fairy tales (Turpin).
Andersen. Fairy tales and stories (Toksvig.)
Andersen. Stories (Riverside ed.).
Andersen. Wonder stories (Author's ed.).
Bryant. Best stories to tell to children.
Bryant. Stories to tell to children.
Johnson. Fir-tree fairy book.
Keyes. Five senses.
Lang. Snake prince.
Lang. Yellow fairy book.
Noyes. Twilight stories.
Scudder. Children's book.
Shedlock. Art of the storyteller.
Wiggin and Smith. Tales of wonder. (Emperor's nightingale.)
See also Nightingale. III.
Nightingale. II. Bakewell. True fairy stories.
Nightingale. III. Coussens. Jade story book. (How the birds saved the emperor's life.)
Nightingale and his cage. Æsop. Fables (Burt ed.).
Nightingale and the glow-worm (poem). Wiggin and Smith. Talking beasts.
Nightingale and the peacock. Bryce. Fables from afar.
Nightingale and the pearl. Olcott and Pendleton. Jolly book.
Storytellers' magazine. Feb. 1916, p. 70. (Nightingale's lesson.)
See also Farmer and the humming bird.
Nightingale and the rose. I. Olcott. Wonder garden.
See also Ant and the grasshopper.
Nightingale and the rose. II. Wilde. Fairy tales.
Nightingale in the mosque. Fillmore. Laughing prince.
Nightingale's lesson. *See* Nightingale and the pearl.
Night's divining glass. Ingelow, Stories told to a child. v. 2.
Nikita the tamer. Magnus. Russsian folk-tales.
Nils, Adventures of. *See* Boy and the elf; Elf and the squirrels; Jarro the wild duck; Nils and the bear.
Nils and the bear. Cowles. Art of story telling.
Hodgkins. Atlantic treasury of childhood stories. (Thumbietot and the bears.)

Nimble-foot and the crystal slippers. Patterson. Enchanted bird.
Nimble Johnny-cake. *See* Johnny-cake.
Nimmo, the trap maker. Allen. Indian fairy tales.
Nimmy Nimmy Not. *See* Tom Tit Tot.
Nine at one blow. Baudis. Czech folk tales.
See also Seven at one blow; Valiant Vicky.
Nine brothers, who were changed to sheep, and their sister. Cary. French fairy tales.
Nine pea-hens and the golden apples. Fillmore. Laughing prince. (Enchanted peafowl.)
Houghton. Russian grandmother's wonder tales. (Golden apple-tree and the nine pea-hens.)
Lang. Marvellous musician.
Lang. Violet fairy book.
See also Seven golden pea-hens.
Nine sister Pierides. *See* Magpie maidens.
Nineteen hundred and seventy-two. Ingelow. Stories told to a child. v. 2.
Ninny Noddy, Story of. Fairy tales from Brentano.
Niobe. Francillon. Gods and heroes. (Stories of Latona and Niobe.)
Guerber. Myths of Greece and Rome. (*In* Diana.)
Hartley. Stories from the Greek legends. (Story of Niobe and the Lady Latona; or, How a mother's pride was humbled.)
Olcott. Wonder garden. (Stone that shed tears.)
Patten. Junior classics. v. 2. (Niobe, a victim of Latona's jealousy.)
Peabody. Old Greek folk stories.
Pratt. Myths of Old Greece. v. 1. (Niobe's children.)
Tappan. Stories from the classics.
Nipon and the king of the Northland. Skinner. Topaz story book.
Nippie Nutcracker. Coolidge. New Year's bargain.
Nippit fit and Clippit fit. Grierson. Scottish fairy book.
See also Cinderella; Rashin Coatie. I and II.
Nis and the dame. Andersen. Wonder stories (Author's ed.).
Nis at the grocer's. Andersen. Fairy tales (Lucas tr. Goblin and the huckster.)
Andersen. Fairy tales (Paull tr. Goblin and the huckster.)
Andersen. Wonder stories (Author's ed.).
Lang. Pink fairy book. (Goblin and the grocer.)
Lang. Snow-queen and other stories. (Goblin and the grocer.)
Nisus and Euryalus. Storr. Half a hundred hero tales.
Nix in mischief. Ewing. Old-fashioned fairy tales.
Nix in the pond. Grimm. Fairy tales (Paull tr. Sprite of the mill pond.)
Grimm. Household tales. (Everyman's ed. Water fairy.)
Lang. Invisible prince and other stories. (Nixy.)

Nix in the pond—*continued.*
Lang. Yellow fairy book. (Nixy.)
Wiggin and Smith. Magic casements. (Nixy.)
Nix Nought Nothing. Forty famous fairy tales.
Jacobs. English fairy tales.
Johnson. Elm-tree fairy book.
See also Battle of the birds; Lady Featherflight.
Nixie. Guerber. *Legends of the Rhine.
Nixies' cleft. Sylva and Strettell. Legends from river and mountain.
Nix's fiddlebow. Noyes. Twilight stories.
Nixy. *See* Nix in the pond.
Njal's burning. Lang. Red romance book.
No ears. Macdonell. Italian fairy book.
Noble old farmer. *See* Honest farmer.
Nodding tiger. Pitman. Chinese wonder book.
Noisy chipmunk. *See* Chipmunk's stripes. III.
None Sae Pretty. Campbell. Beyond the border.
Norka. Lang. Red fairy book.
Normandy. Evans. Old time tales. (How Normandy came by its name.)
Nornagesta. Guerber. Myths of northern lands. (*In* Norno.)
Norse folk tale. *See* Fox as herdsboy.
Norseman's sword. Guerber. Legends of the Rhine. (Story of Siegfried.)
Johonnot. Stories of the olden time.
Partridge. Story-telling in school and home. (Making of the sword.)
North Pole discovered. Henderson. Sea yarns for boys.
North star. Cowles. Art of story-telling.
Judd. Wigwam stories.
North wind. Judson. Myths and legends of Alaska.
North wind and Star boy. Eastman. Wigwam evenings.
North wind and the duck. Blaisdell. Child life. 3d reader. (North wind's defeat.)
Brooks. Stories of the red children.
*Field second reader. (Little wild duck.)
Judd. Wigwam stories. (North wind's defeat.)
Judson. Old Crow and his friends. (Shingebiss and the northwest wind.)
My Bookhouse. v. 1. (Shingebiss.)
Olcott. Red Indian fairy book. (Shingebiss.)
Pratt. Legends of the red children. (Shingebiss.)
North wind and the south wind. Lummis. Pueblo Indian folk stories.
North wind at play. *Elson and Runkel. Elson readers. Book 1.
Poulsson. In the child's world.
North wind, Legend of the. *See* Lad who went to the north wind.
North wind's defeat. *See* North wind and the duck.

North wind's frolic. Skinner. Pearl story book.
North wind's little sister. Storytellers' magazine. March 1915, p. 67.
Northern Lights. Judson. Myths and legends of the Pacific Northwest.
Northland kingdom. Brady. Green forest fairy book.
Northland, Legend of the. *See* Why the woodpecker's head is red.
Northmen's story of how all things began. *See* Creation of the world (Norse).
Northumberland betrayed by Douglas (poem). Lanier. Boy's Percy.
Norwegian wedding crown's story. Harrison. Bric-a-brac stories.
Nose. *See* Nose-tree.
Nose and the eyes (poem). Arnold and Gilbert. Stepping stones to literature. v. 1.
(poem). Scudder. Children's book.
Nose-tree. Coussens. Child's book of stories. (Nose.)
Grimm. Household tales (Everyman's ed.).
Jerrold. Reign of King Oberon.
Norton. Heart of oak books. v. 3. (Nose.)
Scudder. Children's book. (Nose.)
Valentine. Old, old fairy tales. (Three soldiers and the dwarf.)
Welsh. Fairy tales children love. (Nose.)
Wiggin and Smith. Tales of laughter.
See also Kenneth the Yellow; Little soldier; Princess Long-nose; Tiidu the piper.
Noses. *See* Are you not satisfied?
Not a pin to choose. Pyle. Twilight Land.
Not a pin to choose between them. *See* All women are alike.
Not lost, but gone before. *See* Dragon fly.
Nothing child. Grinnell. Punishment of the stingy.
Notorious glutton (poem). Scudder. Children's book.
Notscha. Martens. Chinese fairy book.
Noureddin Ali and his son. Arabian nights (Townsend. Story of Noureddin Ali and his son.)
Noureddin and the beautiful Persian. Arabian nights (Lang. Noureddin and the fair Persian.)
Arabian nights (Townsend. History of Noureddin and the beautiful Persian.)
Noureddin and the fair Persian. *See* Noureddin and the beautiful Persian.
November eve. Hodgkins. Atlantic treasury of childhood stories.
Novice. Guerber. Legends of the Rhine.
Nuckelavee. Douglas. Scottish fairy tales.
Nuisance. Taylor. Thrings of the dark mountain.
Numan and Naan. *See* Old woman who could teach tricks to a fox.

Nunda, eater of people. Lang. Violet fairy book.
Nun's priest's tale. *See* Fox and the cock. II.
Nun's tale. *See* St. Cecilie.
Nuremberg store. My Bookhouse. v. 4.
Nurse. James. Green willow.
Nurse and the wolf. Æsop. Fables (Black ed.).
Æsop. Fables (Burt ed.).
Æsop. Fables (Jacobs).
Æsop. Fables (Stickney).
Nurse Mikko. Fillmore. Mighty Mikko.
Nurse's tale. *See* Wishing well.
Nursling. Richards. Silver crown.
Nut-brown maid (poem). Lanier. Boy's Percy.
Macleod. Book of ballad stories.
Nutcracker and Sugardolly. Bailey. Firelight stories.
Drake. Fairy tales from South Africa.
My Bookhouse. v. 2.
Nutcracker dwarf. Olcott. Good stories for great holidays.
Nutcrackers of Nutcracker Lodge. Skinner. Topaz story book.
Nuts of Jonisgyout. *See* How the flying squirrel got his wings.
Nya-nya Bulembu. *See* Moss-green princess.
Nymph and the dryad. Kennedy. New world fairy book.
Nymph of the well. Wiggin and Smith. Magic casements.

O

Oak and the reed. Æsop. Fables (Black ed.).
Æsop. Fables (Burt ed. Oak and the reeds.)
Æsop. Fables (Jacobs. Tree and the reed.)
Æsop. Fables (Stickney).
Baldwin. Fairy stories and fables. (Tree and the reeds.)
Olcott. Good stories for great holidays. (Proud oak tree.)
Scudder. Fables and folk stories. (Reeds and the oak.)
(poem). Success library. v. 3.
(poem). Wiggin and Smith. Talking beasts.
Oak and the vine. Bryce. Fables from afar.
See also Gourd and the pine.
Oak and the willow. Æsop. Fables (Burt ed.).
Oak-tree and the ivy. Field. Little book of profitable tales.
Oaken settle's story. Harrison. Bric-a-brac stories.
Oat cake. *See* Wee bannock.
Obedient kid. Children's story garden.
Obed's pumpkins. *See* Jack-o'-lantern and the Indians.
Obstinate shoemaker. Bay. Danish fairy and folk tales.
Ocean, Origin of. Harris. Nights with Uncle Remus.
Ocean sleeping beauty. Goddard. Fairy tales in other lands.
See also Sleeping beauty.
Ocean wonders. Brown. Star jewels.
Odds and ends. *See* Flax leavings.

Odin. Judd. Classic myths. (Wodin, god of the northern sky.)
See also Odin's search for wisdom; Odin and the mead; Geirrod and Odin.

Odin and Rinda. Guerber. Myths of northern lands. (*In* Vali.)

Odin and the mead. Bradish. Old Norse stories. (Beginning of poetry.)
Brown. In the days of giants. (Kvasir's blood.)
Edmison. Stories from Norseland.
Guerber. Myths of northern lands. (*In* Bragi.)
Klingensmith. Old Norse wonder tales. (Song mead.)
Mabie. Norse stories. (How Odin brought the mead to Asgard.)
Pratt. Legends of Norseland. (Stolen wine.)
Wilmot-Buxton. Stories of Norse heroes. (Magic mead.)

Odin's search for wisdom. Arnold and Gilbert. Stepping stones to literature. v. 5. (Odin.)
Brown. In the days of giants. (How Odin lost his eye.)
Foster and Cummings. Asgard stories. (Odin's reward.)
Keary. Heroes of Asgard. (Niflheim.)
Litchfield. Nine worlds. (Odin seeks wisdom from Mimir.)
Mabie. Myths every child should know. (How Odin lost his eye.)
Mabie. Norse stories.
Pratt. Legends of Norseland. (Odin at the well of wisdom.)
Wickes. Beyond the rainbow bridge.
Wilmot-Buxton. Stories of Norse heroes. (*In* How All-Father Odin became wise.)

O'Donoghue, The. Frost. Fairies and folk of Ireland. (*In* Ch. 1.)

Odysseus. *See* Ulysses.

Œdipus. *Beckwith. In mythland. v. 3. (A riddle.)
*Bowen. Second story reader. (Story of a riddle.)
Buckley. Children of the dawn. (Riddle of the Sphinx.)
Cole. Heroes of the olden time.
Darton. Tales of the Canterbury pilgrims. (John Lydgate's tale: Destruction of Thebes.)
Guerber. Myths of Greece and Rome. (Œdipus.)
Patten. Junior classics. v. 2. (Riddle of the sphinx.)
Peabody. Old Greek folk stories.
Storr. Half a hundred hero tales. (Œdipus at Colonos.)

Oeyvind and Marit. Bailey. Stories children need.
Hodgkins. Atlantic treasury of childhood stories. (Lost goat.)
Keyes. Stories and story-telling.
My Bookhouse. v. 1.
O'Grady and Throop. Teachers' story teller's book.
Smith. Good old stories.
Storytellers' magazine. June 1916, p. 350.
Whittier. Child life in prose.

Og, King of Bashan. Landa. Aunt Naomi's Jewish fairy tales and legends. (Giant of the flood.)

Ogier the Dane. Baldwin. Hero tales told in school. (Ogier the Dane and the fairies.)
Baldwin. Horse fair. (Black Arabian.)
*Burchill. Progressive road to reading. Book 3. (Olger the Dane.)
Lang. Red romance book.
Patten. Junior classics. v. 4.
Wilmot-Buxton. Stories from old French romance. (Story of the enchanted knight.)
Wilmot-Buxton. Stories of early England. (Olger the Dane.)
See also Holger Danske.
Ogquos, the Cloud Catcher. Allen. Indian fairy tales.
Ogre. I. Bosschère. Christmas tales of Flanders.
Ogre. II. Lang. Grey fairy book.
Marshall. Fairy tales of all nations.
See also Table, the ass and the stick.
Ogre courting. Ewing. Old-fashioned fairy tales.
Ogre in the forest of hazel nuts. Griffis. Belgian fairy tales.
Ogre of Rashomon. Ozaki. Japanese fairy book.
Ogre that played jackstraws. My Bookhouse. v. 3.
Ogre's wife. Johnson. Oak-tree fairy book.
Ogress and the cook. Harrison. Old-fashioned fairy book.
Oh. Bain. Cossack fairy tales.
Field. Famous fairy tales.
Pyle. Tales of folks and fairies.
See also Farmer Weatherbeard; Fisherman's son and the Gruagach of tricks; Master and pupil; Magician's pupil; Wizard and his pupil.
Oh, dear! St. Nicholas. July 1885, p. 646.
Richards. Joyous story of Toto. (Chimborazo.)
Ohnivak. Chodzko. Fairy tales of the Slav.
See also Golden bird. II.
Oisin. *See* Last of the Feni.
Oisin in Tir na n-Og. *See* Last of the Feni.
Ol' Joshway an' de sun (poem). Harris. Uncle Remus and the little boy.
Ola Storbaekkjen. Stroebe and Martens. Norwegian fairy book.
Olaf. *See* King Olaf.
Olaf and Astrid's Christmas eve. Stein. When fairies were friendly.
Olaf of the golden harp. Lindsay and Poulsson. Joyous travelers. (Tale told by the Scotch maid.)
Olaf, the mermaid's son. Grundtvig. Danish fairy tales.
Old bachelor's night-cap. Andersen. Fairy tales (Paull tr.).
Andersen. Stories and tales (Author's ed.).
Old Brother Terrapin gets some fish. Harris. Nights with Uncle Remus.
Old brown coat. Scudder. Seven little people.

Old church bell. Andersen. Fairy tales (Paull tr.).
Andersen. Stories and tales (Author's ed.).
Old dame and her hen. *See* Three sisters trapped in a mountain.
Old deer and old grizzly. Chandler. In the reign of coyote.
Old dog. Bain. Cossack fairy tales.
*Carrick. Picture tales from the Russian. (Dog and the wolf.)
See also Old Sultan.
Old Dragonbeard. Martens. Chinese fairy book. (Dragonbeard.)
Old Dschang. Martens. Chinese fairy book.
Old-fashioned Christmas Eve. Asbjörnsen. Folk and fairy tales.
Old Father Bruin in the wolf pit. *See* Father Bruin in the corner.
Old Father Rhine and the miller. Fairy tales from Brentano.
Old Fortunatus. *See* Fortunatus.
Old German doctor who fell all to pieces. Butterworth. Zigzag journeys in the Orient. (*In* Ch. 5.)
Old grandfather and his grandson. *See* Old man and his grandson.
Old grasshopper gray. *See* Aurora and Tithonus.
Old gravestone. Andersen. Fairy tales (Paull tr.).
Andersen. Stories and tales. (Author's ed.).
Old griffin. Wiggin and Smith. Fairy ring.
Old Grinny-Granny Wolf. Harris. Nights with Uncle Remus.
Old Grizzly and Old Antelope. Judson. Myths and legends of the Pacific Northwest.
Old hag of the forest. Harper. Story-hour favorites.
MacManus. In chimney corners.
See also Two brothers. III.
Old hag's long leather bag. Bailey. Firelight stories. (Little boy who found his fortune.)
Johnson. Oak-tree fairy book. (Two brothers and the old witch.)
Klingensmith. Just stories. (Long leather bag.)
MacManus. Donegal fairy tales.
Wiggin and Smith. Fairy ring (Long leather bag.)
See also Old Witch.
Old hare and the elephants. *See* Rabbits and the elephants.
Old Hopgiant. Stroebe and Martens. Swedish fairy book.
Old horse. *See* Fox and the horse.
Old hound. Æsop. Fables (Black ed.).
Æsop. Fables (Burt ed.).
Æsop. Fables (Stickney).
Old house. Andersen. Fairy tales (Paull tr.).
Andersen. Fairy tales (Turpin).
Andersen. Wonder stories (Author's ed.).
Old iron kettle. *See* Wonderful pot.
Old iron pot. *See* Wonderful pot.

Old Johnny Appleseed. *See* Johnny Appleseed.
Old King Cole. Gibbon. Reign of King Cole.
Old lady of Littledean. Douglas. Scottish fairy tales.
Old lion. I. *See* Sick lion.
Old lion. II. *See* Lion, the fox and the beasts.
Old-Man. Bayliss. Treasury of Indian tales. (*In* Sunbright heroes.)
Old Man Above and the grizzlies. *See* Why grizzly bear goes on all fours.
Old man and death. *See* Death and the woodman.
Old man and his ass (poem). Æsop. Fables (Stickney).
Success library. v. 3. (Sapient ass.)
(poem). Wiggin and Smith. Talking beasts. (Old man and the ass.)
Old-Man and his conscience. Linderman. Indian why stories.
Old man and his donkey. *See* Man, the boy, and the donkey.
Old man and his grandson. Grimm. Fairy tales (Lucas tr.).
Grimm. Fairy tales (Paull tr. Old grandfather and his grandson.)
*Grimm. Fairy tales (Wiltse). v. 1.
*Haaren. Songs and stories. 2d reader.
(play). Stevenson. Plays for the home.
See also Old man and his son.
Old-Man and his new weapons. Linderman. Indian Oldman stories.
Old man and his son. Success library. v. 3.
See also Old man and his grandson.
Old man and his sons. *See* Bundle of sticks.
Old man and the angel. Andersen. Fairy tales (Paull tr.).
Old man and the ass. *See* Old man and his ass.
Old-Man and the bear magicians. Grinnell. Blackfoot lodge tales. (Bears.)
Old man and the devils. *See* Man with the wen.
Old-Man and the fox. Grinnell. Blackfoot lodge tales.
Linderman. Indian why stories.
Old-Man and the lynx. Grinnell. Blackfoot lodge tales.
See also Why the mountain lion is long and lean.
Old-Man and the sun-dance. Linderman. Indian Old-man stories.
Old Man Coyote and summer in a bag. *See* How summer came to the earth. III.
Old Man Gully's hant. Cocke. Bypaths in Dixie.
Old man, his son and the ass. *See* Man, the boy and the donkey.
Old man in the sky. Judd. Wigwam stories.
Old man of the meadow. *See* Aurora and Tithonus.
Old Man Rabbit's Thanksgiving dinner. Bailey. For the story teller.
Esenwein and Stockard. Children's stories.
Wickes. Happy holidays.

Old-Man remakes the world. *See* Indians' flood. II.
Old-Man steals the sun's leggings. Linderman. Indian why stories.
Old man who brought withered trees to life. *See* Old man who made withered trees to flower.
Old man who made the trees blossom. *See* Old man who made withered trees to flower.
Old man who made withered trees to flower. Ballard. Fairy tales from far Japan. (Old man who made the trees blossom.)
Dyer and Brady. Merrill readers. 3d reader. (Old man who made the trees to blossom.)
Johnson. Fir-tree fairy book. (Envious neighbors.)
Lang. Violet fairy book. (Envious neighbor.)
Lyman. Story telling. (Old man who brought withered trees to life.)
Olcott. Wonder garden. (Old man who made the trees to blossom.)
Ozaki. Japanese fairy book. (Story of the old man who made withered trees to flower.)
Peck. Stories for good children. (Man who made trees blossom.)
Pyle. Fairy tales from many lands. (Faithful dog.)
Tappan. Myths from many lands. (Ashes that made trees bloom.)
Old man with a wart. *See* Man with a wen.
Old-Man's courting. Linderman. Indian Old-man stories.
Old-Man's treachery. Linderman. Indian why stories.
Old Mr. Rabbit, he's a good fisherman. Harris. Uncle Remus, his songs and his sayings.
See also Fox in the well II; Ups and downs.
Old Mrs. Owl's children. Bigham. Merry animal tales.
See also Eagle and the owl.
Old Mother Hubbard. Grover. Folk-lore readers. v. 1.
Jerrold. Big book of nursery rhymes.
Lansing. Rhymes and stories.
O'Shea. Six nursery classics. (Mother Hubbard and her wonderful dog.)
Old Mother Wiggle-Waggle. Jacobs. More English fairy tales.
Old Nick and Kitty. *See* Katcha and the devil.
Old Nick and the girl. Djurklo. Fairy tales from the Swedish.
Old Nick and the pedlar. Djurklo. Fairy tales from the Swedish.
Old North Wind. Walker. Sandman's goodnight stories.
Old oak-tree's last dream. *See* Last dream of the old oak.
Old Pipes and the dryad. Cross and Statler. Story-telling.
Lyman. Story-telling.
Stockton. Bee-man of Orn, and other tales.
Stockton. Fanciful tales.
Stockton. Queen's museum.

Old queen, Story of a. *See* Peronnella.
Old rough stone and the gnarled tree. Gruelle. Friendly fairies.
Old street lamp. Andersen. Fairy tales (Paull tr.).
Andersen. Stories and tales (Author's ed.).
Bailey and Lewis. For the children's hour.
Old Sultan. Bailey. In the animal world.
Grimm. Fairy tales (Lucas tr.)
Grimm. Fairy tales (Paull tr. Old Sultan and his friends.)
Grimm. Household stories (Crane tr.).
Grimm. Household tales (Burt ed. Old Sultan and his friends.)
Grimm. Household tales (Everyman's ed.).
Wiggin and Smith. Tales of laughter.
See also Old dog; War of the wolf and the fox; Whiteling's war with Isegrim.
Old Sultan and his friends. *See* Old Sultan.
Old timber top. Griffis. Korean fairy tales.
Old trout, the young trout and the gudgeon. Æsop. Fables (Burt ed.).
Old White Whiskers and Mr. Bunny. Griffis. Unmannerly tiger and other Korean tales.
Griffis. Korean fairy tales.
Old Winter Man and the Spring. I. Bailey and Lewis. For the children's hour. (Legend of the arbutus.)
Brooks. Stories of the red children. (Winter and Spring.)
Cowles. Art of story-telling. (Legend of the arbutus.)
Judd. Wigwam stories. (Legend of the arbutus.)
Olcott. Red Indian fairy book. (Spring beauty.)
Olcott. Wonder garden. (Legend of the trailing arbutus.)
Poulsson. In the child's world. (Indian legend of the arbutus.)
Skinner. Emerald story book. (Legend of trailing arbutus.)
Storytellers' magazine. March 1914, p. 467. (Legend of the trailing arbutus.)
Storytellers' magazine. May 1916, p. 277. (*In* Nature legends. Story of the trailing arbutus.)
Wilson. Myths of the red children. (Old Winter Man and the Spring Maiden.)
Old Winter Man and the Spring. II. *Cowles. Indian nature myths. (Birth of the arbutus.)
Nixon-Roulet. Indian folk tales. (Coming of Seegwun.)
Olcott. Good stories for great holidays. (Spring beauty.)
Patten. Junior classics. v. 2. (Winter spirit and his visitor.)
Schoolcraft. Indian fairy book. (Winter spirit and his visitor.)
Skinner. Pearl story book. (Gau-wi-di-ne and Go-hay. winter and spring. (Adapted.)

Old Winter Man and the Spring. II.—*continued.*
Tanner. Legends from the red man's forest. (Winter and Spring.)
Wilson. Nature study reader. (Legend of the Spring beauty.)
See also First snowdrop I; How summer came to the earth II; Secret of the violet.
Old witch. I. Jacobs. More English fairy tales.
See also Old hag's long leather bag; Mother Holle.
Old witch. II. Olcott. Good stories for great holidays.
Old witch who was a burr. Olcott. Wonder garden.
Old woman and crowbar. Bryce. Fables from afar.
Old woman and her company. *See* Strange visitor.
Old woman and her maids. Æsop. Fables (Black ed.).
Æsop. Fables (Burt ed.).
Æsop. Fables (Stickney. Widow and her little maids.)
Scudder. Children's book. (Woman and her maids.)
Scudder. Fables and folk stories. (Woman and her maids.)
Wiggin and Smith. Talking beasts.
Old woman and her pig. Bailey. Folk stories and fables.
Bailey and Lewis. For the children's hour.
Bryant. Best stories to tell to children.
Bryant. How to tell stories to children.
Chisholm and Steedman. Staircase of stories.
Coe. First book of stories.
*Coe and Christie. Story hour readers. Book 1.
Coussens. Child's book of stories.
Dyer. What-happened-then stories.
Faulkner. Old English nursery tales. (Old woman and the pig.)
Howard. Banbury Cross stories.
Jacobs. English fairy tales.
Johnson. Oak-tree fairy book.
Klingensmith. Household stories.
Lang. Nursery rhyme book.
Lansing. Rhymes and stories.
Mother Goose's nursery rhymes, tales and jingles (Warne ed.).
Norton. Heart of oak books. v. 1.
O'Grady and Throop. Teachers' story teller's book.
*Old, old tales retold.
O'Shea. Six nursery classics.
Pyle. Mother's nursery tales. (Little old woman and her pig.)
Scudder. Book of folk stories.
Skinner. Very little child's book of stories.
*Treadwell. Reading literature: primer.
Welsh. Stories children love. (Story of the old woman and her pig.)
Wiggin and Smith. Tales of laughter.

Old woman and her pig—*continued.*
See also Cat and the mouse; Grain of corn; How the mouse got into his hole; Little Tuppen; Mickey and the maccaroni; Munachar and Manachar; Nanny who wouldn't go home to supper; Sparrow and the bush.

Old woman and the doctor. Æsop. Fables (Burt ed.).
Æsop. Fables (Burt ed. Old woman and the physician.)
Wiggin and Smith. Talking beasts.

Old woman and the empty cask. *See* Old woman and the wine jar.

Old woman and the fish. Djurklo. Fairy tales from the Swedish.
Wiggin and Smith. Tales of laughter.

Old woman and the knight. *See* Sir Gawain's marriage. II.

Old woman and the physician. *See* Old woman and the doctor.

Old woman and the tides. Eastman. Indian legends retold.

Old woman and the tramp. Djurklo. Fairy tales from the Swedish.
Hodgkins. Atlantic treasury of childhood stories. (Tramp and the old woman.)
Wiggin and Smith. Tales of laughter.
See also Stone broth.

Old woman and the wine jar. Æsop. Fables (Black ed. Old woman and the empty cask.)
Æsop. Fables (Burt ed.).
Æsop. Fables (Jacobs).

Old woman in the wood. Grimm. Fairy tales (Paull tr.).
*Grimm. Fairy tales (Wiltse). v. 2.

Old woman Pele. *See* Pele.

Old woman who became a woodpecker. *See* Why the woodpecker's head is red.

Old woman who could teach tricks to a fox, and the wise old doctor. Butterworth. Zigzag journeys in the Orient. (*In* Ch. 8.)

Old woman who lived in a shoe. Gibbon. Reign of King Cole.

Old woman who lived in a vinegar bottle. O'Grady and Throop. Teacher's story teller's book.
See also Fisherman and his wife.

Old woman who lost her dumplings. *See* Laughing dumpling.

Old woman who met the months. Olcott. Wonder garden.
See also Month of March; Twelve months. I.

Old woman who wanted all the cakes. *See* Why the woodpecker's head is red. I.

Old woman's cat. Bidpai. Tortoise and the geese. (Lean cat and the fat cat.)
Wiggin and Smith. Talking beasts.

Older sister's tale. *See* Clever shepherdess; Lady Cicely went a-maying.

Ole-Luk-Oie, the dream-god. Andersen. Fairy tales (Lucas tr. Ole-Luk-Oie, the dustman.)
Andersen. Fairy tales (Paull tr.).
Andersen. Wonder stories (Author's ed. Ole-Shut-Eye.)
Haaren. Songs and stories. 2d reader. (Sandman.)
Hodgkins. Atlantic treasury of childhood stories.
My Bookhouse. v. 1. (Ole-Luk-Oie, the sandman.)

Ole-Shut-Eye. *See* Ole-Luk-Oie, the dream god.

Ole the watchman. Andersen. Stories and tales (Author's ed.).

Olelbis. Bayliss. Treasury of Indian tales. (*In* Sun-bright heroes; Heavenly stair of the Hus brothers.)

Olger the Dane. *See* Ogier the Dane.

Omemee. Cornyn. Around the wigwam fire.

On a pincushion. Nichols and DeMorgan. Princess Girlikin and other fairy tales.

On the other side of the River Mairure. Sologub. Sweet-scented name.

On top of the ark. Coolidge. Mischief's Thanksgiving.

Onatah: the spirit of the corn fields. *See* Spirit of the corn.

Onatoga's sacrifice. *See* Indian who saved his tribe from the Thunderbird.

One bad turn begets another Bosschère. Folk tales of Flanders.

One-eye, Two-eyes, Three-eyes. Chisholm. In fairy land. (Little One-eye, Little Two-eyes and Little Three-eyes.)
*Grimm. Fairy tales (Wiltse). v. 2.
Klingensmith. Household stories for little readers. (Little One-eye, Little Two-eyes and Little Three-eyes.)
Lang. Forty thieves and other stories.
Lang. Green fairy book.
Lansing. Rhymes and stories, (Little One Eye, Two Eyes, and Little Three Eyes.)
Mabie. Fairy tales every child should know.
Mabie. Heroes and fairies.
Marshall. Fairy tales of all nations.
Mulock. Fairy book.
O'Grady and Throop. Teachers' story teller's book.
Scudder. Book of folk stories. (Little One-eye, Two-eyes, Three-eyes.
Scudder. Fables and folk stories. (Little One-eye, Little Two-eyes, and Little Three-eyes.)
Scudder. Children's book. (Little One-eye, Two-eyes, Three-eyes.)
Skinner. Nursery tales from many lands. (Little Two-eyes.)
Tappan. Folk stories and fables. (Little One-eye, Two-eyes, Three-eyes.)
Welsh. Fairy tales children love.

One-eyed doe. Æsop. Fables (Black ed.).
Æsop. Fables (Burt ed.).
Æsop. Fables (Jacobs).
Æsop. Fables (Stickney).
One-eyed prying Joan's tale. Olcott. Book of elves and fairies.
See also How Dame Margery Twist saw more than was good for her.
One-eyed servant. Ingelow. Stories told to a child. v. 1.
One-footed fairy. Brown. One-footed fairy.
One good trick. *See* Fox and the cat. I.
One good turn deserves another. Pyle. Wonder clock.
One-handed girl. Lang. Lilac fairy book.
Lang. Magic book.
See also Pierre and Helène.
One minute at a time. *See* Discontented pendulum.
One of the crowd. Stewart. Tell me a hero story.
One swallow does not make a summer. Norton. Heart of oak books. v. 2.
One way out. Young. Plantation bird legends.
See also Big quar'l.
One who loved him most. Judd. Wigwam stories.
One who travelled to learn what shivering meant. *See* Youth who could not shiver and shake.
One who would harm. Tappan. Old ballads in prose.
One's own children are always the prettiest. Asbjörnsen Fairy tales from the far north.
Dasent. Norse fairy tales.
Dasent. Popular tales from the Norse.
Wiggin and Smith. Tales of laughter.
See also Crow's children.
Oni on his travels. Griffis. Dutch fairy tales.
Only a penny. Dyer and Brady. Merrill readers. 2d reader.
Oochigeaskw, the little scarred girl. *See* Little Scar Face.
Oochigeopch, the scarred young brave. *See* Scar Face. II.
Opal. I. Nichols and DeMorgan. Princess Girlikin and other fairy tales. (Story of the opal.)
Skinner. Topaz story book. (Story of the opal.)
Opal. II. Murphy. Necklace of jewels.
Opal. II. Griffis. Belgian fairy tales. (Society to make fairy tales come true.)
Opeeche, the robin redbreast. *See* How the robin came.
Open door. Richards. Golden windows.
Opossum's tail. *See* Why the possum's tail is bare. I.
Oracle of Delphi. *See* Delphian oracle.
Orange fairy. Johnson. Fir-tree fairy book.
Order and disorder. Edgeworth. Waste not, want not.
Welsh. Stories children love.
Ore-ka-rahr. Grinnell. Pawnee hero stories.
Orestes. Baldwin. Fifty famous rides. (Chariot race.)
Church. Greek story and song.

Orestes and the dragon. Baring. Blue rose fairy book.
Orianne. Walker. Sandman's goodnight stories.
Origin of etc. *See* the first important word of the title; also titles beginning with the word "First."
Oriole. Holbrook. Book of nature myths. (Story of the oriole.)
Oriole's nest. Wiggin and Smith. Story hour.
Orion. *Bailey. Wonder tales. (How Orion found his sight.)
Coe. Second book of stories. (Orion, the starry huntsman.)
Francillon. Gods and heroes. (Diana and the story of Orion.)
Guerber. Myths of Greece and Rome. (*In* Diana.)
Judd. Classic myths. (Giant with a belt of stars.)
Seton. Woodland tales. (Orion the hunter.)
Shaw. Stories of the ancient Greeks. (*In* Among the stars.)
Young and Field. Literary readers. Book 2. (Sun, the moon and the star giant.)
See also Pleiades.
Orphan boy. Riggs. Animal stories from Eskimo land.
Orphan, the dog, and the talking bone. Macnair. Animal tales from Africa.
Orpheus. Judd. Classic myths. (Orpheus, the south wind.)
Orpheus and Eurydice. Adams. Myths of old Greece.
*Bailey. Wonder stories. (Bee man of Arcadia.)
Buckley. Children of the dawn. (Divine musician.)
Burt and Ragozin. Herakles and other heroes. (Orpheus, the hero of the lyre.)
Carpenter. Long ago in Greece.
Firth. Stories of old Greece. (Orpheus, the sweet singer.)
Francillon. Gods and heroes.
Guerber. Myths of Greece and Rome. (*In* Apollo.)
Holbrook. Round the year in myth and song.
Hutchinson. Orpheus with his lute.
Hyde. Favorite Greek myths.
Kupfer. Stories of long ago. (Story of a sweet singer.)
*Olcott. Wonder garden. (Orpheus who made the trees to dance.)
Patten. Junior classics. v. 2. (Orpheus the sweet singer.)
Peabody. Old Greek folk stories.
Pratt. Myths of Old Greece. v. 3.
Shaw. Stories of the ancient Greeks. (Lost by looking back.)
Storr. Half a hundred hero tales.
Tappan. Stories from the classics.
See also Indian Orpheus.
Osborn Boots and Mr. Glibtongue. Asbjörnsen. Tales from the fjeld.
Osborn's pipe. *See* Ashiepattle and the king's hares.
Osiris. *See* Coming of the god and goddess.
Osmo's share. *See* Bear as partner.

Osseo, the son of the evening star. *See* How the fairies came.
Ossian in the land of youth. *See* Last of the Feni.
Other wise man. Harper's magazine. Jan. 1893, p. 277.
Van Dyke. Blue flower.
Other world beneath. Borland. Rocky mountain tipi tales.
Otter Heart of the enchanted forest. Cornyn. When the camp fire burns.
Otters and the wolf. Babbitt. More Jataka tales.
See also Matter of arbitration.
Otilla and the Death's head. Success library. v. 3.
Ouphe of the woods. Ingelow. Stories told to a child. v. 2.
Ingelow. Three fairy tales.
Patten. Junior classics. v. 6.
Our Lord and St. Peter. Lagerlöf. Christ legends.
Our parish clerk. Asbjörnsen. Tales from the fjeld.
Ourson. Segur. French fairy tales.
Segur. Old French fairy tales.
Out of the nest. Lindsay. More mother stories.
Skinner. Emerald story book.
Outcast prince. Landa. Aunt Naomi's Jewish fairy tales. and legends.
Outlaw. Dasent. Popular tales from the Norse.
Thorpe. Yule-tide stories.
Outwitting the devil. Hartland. English folk and fairy tales. (Outwitting the bogie.)
Overflowing of Lough Neagh, and the story of Liban the mermaid. Joyce. Old Celtic romances.
Overturned cart. *See* How Wry-Face played a trick on One-eye, the potato wife.
Owain. *See* Sir Owain and the lady of the fountain.
Owain and the lady of the fountain. *See* Sir Owain and the lady of the fountain.
Owen goes a-wooing. Thomas. Welsh fairy book.
Owl. Grimm. Fairy tales (Paull tr.).
Owl and his friends. Stafford. Animal fables.
Owl and Raven. *See* Why the raven's feathers are black. II.
Owl and the birds. Æsop. Fables (Burt ed.).
Owl and the eagle. Lang. Orange fairy book.
Owl and the grasshopper. Æsop. Fables (Black ed.).
Æsop. Fables (Burt ed.).
Æsop. Fables (Stickney).
Owl and the nightingale. Æsop. Fables (Burt ed.).
Owl and the peacock. Young. Plantation bird legends.
Owl and the raven. *See* Why the crow is black. II.
Owl critic (poem). Arnold and Gilbert. Stepping stones to literature. v. 5.
(poem). Curry. Little classics.
See also Actor and the pig; Critics silenced.
Owl gets married. Eastman. Indian legends retold.
Owl learns to see at night. Borland. Rocky Mountain tipi tales.

Owl monster. Sexton. Gray wolf stories.
Owl, Origin of. I. Lanier. Knightly legends of Wales.
Owl, Origin of. II. Young. Plantation bird legends. (In de swamp.)
See also Conjure wives.
Owl wisdom. Skinner. Turquoise story book.
Owl with the great head and eyes. Macmillan. Canadian fairy tales.
Owls and the gamblesome elf. Pyle. Counterpane fairy.
Owl's answer to Tommy. Keyes. Stories and story-telling.
My Bookhouse. v. 2.
Owls, the bats, and the sun. Æsop. Fables (Burt ed.).
Ownself. *See* My own self.
Ox and the fly. *See* Gnat and the bull.
Ox and the frog. *See* Frog and the ox.
Ox who envied the pig. Babbitt. Jataka tales.
Ox who won the forfeit. *See* Bull that demanded fair treatment.
Oxen and the axle-trees. Æsop. Fables (Burt ed.).
Æsop. Fables (Stickney).
Oxen and the balk of timber. Success library. v. 3.
Oxen and the butchers. Æsop. Fables (Burt ed.).
Oyster and its claimants (poem). Storytellers' magazine. June 1913, p. 29.

P

Pa-hu-ka-tawa. Grinnell. Pawnee hero stories.
P'a-i-shia. Lummis. Pueblo Indian folk stories.
Pack of ragamuffins. *See* Vagabonds.
Pack of vagabonds. *See* Vagabonds.
Paddle-wheel boat. Baldwin. Fifty famous people.
Paddy Corcoran's wife. Yeats. Irish fairy tales.
Paddy O'Kelly and the weasel. Jacobs. More Celtic fairy tales.
Padishah of the forty peris. Kunos. Forty-four Turkish fairy tales. (Padishah of the thirty peris.)
Kunos. Turkish fairy tales.
Padishah of the thirty peris. *See* Padishah of the forty peris.
Padmalochan, the weaver. Bradley-Birt. Bengal fairy tales.
Page boy and the silver goblet. Grierson. Scottish fairy book.
Pagliacci. Pleasanton. Fairyland of opera. (I Pagliacci.)
Painted leaves, Legend of. *See* Hidden waters.
Painter of cats. Hearn. Japanese fairy tales. (Boy who drew cats.)
Nixon-Roulet. Japanese folk stories and fairy tales.
Pair of red mittens. Potter. Pinafore pocket story book.
Pairing time anticipated (poem). Johonnot. Stories of the olden time.

Pairing time anticipated—*continued.*
(poem). Wiggin and Smith. Talking beasts.
Paka: The boy who was reared in the land that the gods have since hidden. Colum. At the gateways of the day.
Palace in the clouds. Friedlander. Jewish fairy book. (Castle in the air).
Landa. Aunt Naomi's Jewish fairy tales and legends.
Palace in the moon. Gate. Fortunate days.
Palace made by music. Alden. Why the chimes rang.
Palace of Alkinoös. Cooke. Nature myths and stories.
Palace of beauty. See Immortal fountain.
Palace of bubbles. Meigs. Kingdom of the winding road.
Palace of clouds. Storytellers' magazine. June 1916, p. 363.
Palace of the eagles. Friedlander. Jewish fairy book. (King Solomon's carpet.)
Landa. Aunt Naomi's Jewish fairy tales and legends.
Palace of the ocean-bed. *See* Ambitious hunter and skillful fisher.
Palace of Vanity. Silver fairy book.
Palace that stood on golden pillars. Pyle. Tales of wonder and magic. (Castle that stood on golden pillars.)
Thorpe. Yule-tide stories.
See also Puss in Boots.
Palace under the waves. Griffis. Swiss fairy tales.
Palamon and Arcita. Darton. Tales of the Canterbury pilgrims. (Knight's tale: Palamon and Arcita.)
McSpadden. Stories from Chaucer. (Knight's tale: Palamon and Arcite.)
Storr and Turner. Canterbury chimes. (Knight's tale: Palamon and Arcite.)
Pambookat. English. Fairy stories and wonder tales.
Pan. Brown. When the world was young. (Pan and his pipes.)
Guerber. Myths of Greece and Rome. (*In* Minor divinities.)
Johonnot. Stories of heroic deeds. (Music of Pan.)
Olcott. Wonder garden. (Reed that was a maiden.)
Peabody. Old Greek folk stories. (Wood-folk.)
Storr. Half a hundred hero tales. (Pan and Syrinx.)
See also Midas II.
Pan and the Babe of Bethlehem. Bone. Children's stories.
Pancake. Asbjörnsen. Folk and fairy tales.
Asbjörnsen. Tales from the fjeld.
Bailey. Stories children need.
Coussens. Child's book of stories.
Hodgkins. Atlantic treasury of childhood stories.
*Klingensmith. Just stories.
Lansing. Rhymes and stories.
Noyes. Twilight stories. (Cake and the seven hungry children.)
*Skinner. Very little child's book of stories. (Mother Goose's pancake.)

Pancake—*continued.*
Sly. World stories retold. (Runaway pancake.)
Stroebe and Martens. Norwegian fairy book. (Chronicle of the pancake.)
Thorne-Thomsen. East o' the sun and west o' the moon.
Treadwell. Reading literature: primer.
Wiggin and Smith. Tales of laughter.
See also Bun; Gingerbread boy; Johnny cake; Wee bannock; Wonderful cake.
Panch-Phul Ranee. Frere. Old Deccan days.
Tappan. Myths from many lands.
Wiggin and Smith. Tales of wonder.
Pandora. Adams. Myths of old Greece. (Prometheus and Epimetheus.)
Almost true tales. (Paradise of children.)
*Bailey. Stories children need. (Wonderful box.)
*Bailey. Wonder stories. (Paradise of children.)
Baldwin. Old Greek stories. (How diseases and cares came to men.)
Carpenter. Long ago in Greece. (Pandora's curiosity.)
*Chisholm and Steedman. Staircase of stories. (Inquisitive girl.)
*Dyer and Brady. Merrill readers. 2d reader. (Pandora's box.)
Francillon. Gods and heroes. (First man.)
Firth. Stories of old Greece. (Epimetheus and Pandora.)
Guerber. Myths of Greece and Rome. (*In* Beginning of all things.)
Hartley. Stories from the Greek legends. (Story of how troubles came into the world; or, Pandora and her box.)
Hawthorne. Wonder book. (Paradise of children.)
Holbrook. Round the year in myth and song.
Hutchinson. Orpheus with his lute. (Prometheus, the fire-bringer.)
Hyde. Favorite Greek myths. (How trouble came into the world.)
*Klingensmith. Just stories.
Mabie. Myths every child should know. (Paradise of children.)
Olcott. Wonder garden. (Man who brought fire.)
Patten. Junior classics. v. 2. (Paradise of children.)
Pratt. Myths of old Greece. v. 2.
Shaw. Stories of the ancient Greeks. (Magic box.)
Storr. Half a hundred hero tales. (Epimetheus and Pandora.)
Tappan. Myths from many lands. (Paradise of children.)
Panigwun, who outmatched the magician. *See* Mishosha.
Pan's frolic with the bronze folk. Chandler. Pan the piper.
Pan's lovely maid. Olcott. Wonder garden.
Pan's song. Olcott. Wonder garden.

Pansies. I. Cather. Educating by story telling. (Little stepmother.)
Pansies. II. Bryce. Fables from afar. (Pansy.)
Skinner. Turquoise story book. (Little heartsease.)
Pansies. III. Baker and Carpenter. Language readers. 3d year. (Legend of the pansies.)
Pansies for thoughts. Judson. Flower fairies.
Pansy. I. Pratt. Fairyland of flowers. (Pansy—an allegory.)
Pansy. II. *See* Pansies. II.
Pansy baby. Hutchinson. Golden porch.
Olcott. Wonder garden. (Pansy-boy.)
Pansy-boy. *See* Pansy baby.
Pantagruel. Rabelais. Three good giants.
Panther. Martens. Chinese fairy book.
Papa Tiger and Papa Sheep. *See* Brother Tiger and Daddy Sheep.
Paper bag. Coussens. Jade story book.
Paper dolls' adventure. Bailey. Friendly tales.
Paper kite (poem). Æsop. Fables (Burt ed.).
Paperarello. Lang. Crimson fairy book.
Lang. Little Wildrose.
Parable of life. Curry. Little classics.
Parable of the pomegranate. Stone and Fickett. Trees in prose and poetry. (Parable.)
Skinner. Emerald story book. (Wonder.)
Paradise in the sea. Landa. Aunt Naomi's Jewish fairy tales and legends.
Paradise of children. *See* Pandora.
Pardoner's tale. *See* Three revellers and death.
Paris: Apple of discord. Adams. Myths of old Greece. (Golden apple.)
Arnold and Gilbert. Stepping stones to literature. v. 4. (Quarrel of the goddesses.)
*Bailey. Wonder stories. (How a golden apple caused a war.)
Baldwin. Hero tales told in school. (Golden apple.)
Baldwin. Story of the golden age.
Evans. Heroes of Troy.
Francillon. Gods and heroes.
Guerber. Myths of Greece and Rome. (*In* Trojan war.)
Haaren and Poland. Famous men of Greece. (*In* Agamemnon.)
Olcott. Wonder garden.
Peabody. Old Greek folk stories.
Pratt. Myths of old Greece. v. 3. (Golden apple.)
Shaw. Stories of the ancient Greeks. (*In* Shepherd prince of Troy.)
Paris: Paris and Œnone. Baldwin. Hero tales told in school.
Baldwin. Story of the golden age. (*In* Golden apple.)
Buckley. Children of the dawn.
Storr. Half a hundred hero tales.

Paris: Paris and Œnone—*continued.*
See also Trojan war.
Parrot. I. Æsop. Fables (Burt ed.).
Parrot. II. Bryce. Fables from afar.
Parrot and his cage. Æsop. Fables (Black ed.).
Parrot and the parson. Rouse. Talking thrush.
Parrot judge. Rouse Talking thrush.
Parrot that fed his parents. Shedlock. Art of the story-teller. (Filial piety.)
Shedlock. Eastern stories and legends.
Parrot that lost its tail. Quiroga. South American jungle tales.
Parrot's story. Richards. Joyous story of Toto.
Parsifal. *See* Sir Percival.
Parsley queen. Welsh. Stories children love.
Parson and the clerk. I. *See* Priest and the clerk.
Parson and the clerk. II. Hartland. English folk and fairy tales.
Parson and the sexton. *See* Priest and the clerk.
Partial judge. Æsop. Fables (Burt ed.).
Parti-colored cow. Thomas. Welsh fairy book.
Parting of the fairies (poem). Rhys. Fairy gold.
Partners. *See* Fox as partner.
Partnership of the thief and the liar. Lang. Grey fairy book.
Lang. Little King Loc.
Partridge and the cocks. Æsop. Fables (Black ed.).
Æsop. Fables (Burt ed.).
Partridge and the crow. Bidpai. Tortoise and the geese.
Partridge and the fowler. Æsop. Fables (Black ed. Falconer and the partridge.)
Æsop. Fables (Burt ed. Falconer and the partridge.)
Æsop. Fables (Stickney).
Partridge and the hawk. Bidpai. Tortoise and the geese.
Partridge, monkey and elephant. Burlingame. Grateful elephant.
Partridge witch. *See* Forest maiden.
Passenger and the pilot. Æsop. Fables (Burt ed.).
*Haaren. Songs and stories. 2d reader.
Wiggin and Smith. Talking beasts.
Passing of Loku. Miller. Philippine folklore stories.
Past, present and future. *See* Fair white city.
Pastor and the sexton. *See* Priest and the clerk.
Pastor's wife. Stroebe and Marten's. Danish fairy book.
Patchwork quilt. Bailey. Stories for Sunday telling.
Patchwork school. Wilkins. Pot of gold.
Patience-stone and patience-knife. *See* Stone-patience and knife-patience.
Patient Annie. Tappan. Old ballads in prose.
Patient Griselda. Darton. Tales of the Canterbury pilgrims. (Clerk's tale: Patient Griselda.)
Greenwood. Stories from famous ballads.

Patient Griselda—*continued.*
Macleod. Book of ballad stories.
McSpadden. Stories from Chaucer. (Clerk's tale: Patient Griselda.)
Patten. Junior classics. v. 4.
Stroebe and Martens. Danish fairy book. (Patient woman.)
Patient woman. I. *See* Patient Griselda.
Patient woman. II. Burlingame. Grateful elephant.
Patrimony. Bacon. True philosopher.
Patroclus. Evans. Heroes of Troy.
Patsy, the calf. Lindsay. More mother stories.
Pattie's new dress. Lindsay. More mother stories.
Pattikins and the sea maiden. Orcutt. Princess Kallisto.
Patty and her pitcher. Valentine. Old, old fairy tales (Burt ed.).
See also Diamonds and toads.
Paulina's Christmas. Curtiss. Christmas stories and legends.
Partridge. Story telling in home and school.
Storytellers' magazine. Dec. 1913, p. 351.
Paup-Puk-Keewis. Bayliss. Treasury of Indian tales.
Kennedy. New world fairy book. (Stormy fool.)
Nixon-Roulet. Indian folk tales. (*In* Wonderful deeds of Manabozho.)
Schoolcraft. Indian fairy book. (Wonderful exploits of Grasshopper.)
Tanner. Legends from the red man's forest. (Eagle.)
See also Iktomi and the fawn.
Pea blossom. Andersen. Fairy tales (Paull tr.).
Andersen. Fairy tales (Turpin. Five in one pod.)
Andersen. Stories and tales (Author's ed. Five out of one shell.)
Arnold and Gilbert. Stepping stones to literature. v. 3.
Baker and Carpenter. Language reader. 3d year.
Blaisdell. Child life. 2d reader. (Five peas in a pod.)
*Boston collection of kindergarten stories. (Five peas in one pod.)
Ketchum and Jorgensen. Kindergarten gems.
Poulsson. In the child's world. (Five peas in a pod.)
Ruskin. King of the golden river and other wonder stories. (Five out of one pod.)
Strong. All the year round. v. 3. Spring.
Wiltse. Kindergarten stories.
Pea that won a princess. Johnson. Elm-tree fairy book.
Peace. *See* Armistice Day; Empty drum.
Peace meeting. Johnson. Fir-tree fairy book.
Peaceful pirates. Henderson. Sea yarns for boys.
Peach-blossom, Plum-blossom and Cinnamon-rose. Griffis. Unmannerly tiger and other Korean tales.
Peach Boy's rice-cakes. *See* Momotaro.
Peach Darling. *See* Momotaro.

Peach, the apple and the blackberry. Æsop. Fables (Burt ed.).
Peaches. Ketchum and Jorgensen. Kindergarten gems.
Peacock. I. *See* Io.
Peacock. II. Æsop. Fables (Burt ed.).
Peacock and Juno. Æsop. Fables (Burt ed.).
Æsop. Fables (Jacobs).
(poem). Wiggin and Smith. Talking beasts. (Peacock complaining to Juno.)
Peacock and the crane. Æsop. Fables (Black ed.).
Æsop. Fables (Burt ed.).
Peacock and the fox. Wiggin and Smith. Talking beasts.
Peacock and the magpie. Æsop. Fables (Black ed.).
Æsop. Fables (Burt ed.).
Peacock butterflies. Walker. Sandman's goodnight stories.
Peacock complaining to Juno. *See* Peacock and Juno.
Peacock's complaint. Æsop. Fables (Black ed.).
Pear tree. Skinner. Nursery tales from many lands.
Pearl. Bailey. Stories and rhymes for a child.
Pearls. Murphy. Necklace of jewels.
See also Drop of water; Pan's song.
Pears and the pudding. *See* Bear's bad bargain.
Peasant and his ass. Bosschère. Folk tales of Flanders.
Peasant and the apple tree. Æsop. Fables (Stickney).
Peasant and the horse. Æsop. Fables (Stickney. Supplement).
Wiggin and Smith. Talking beasts.
Peasant and the laborer. Æsop. Fables (Stickney. Supplement).
Peasant and the robber. Wiggin and Smith. Talking beasts.
Peasant and the Satyr. *See* Satyr and the traveller.
Peasant and the sheep. Æsop. Fables (Stickney. Supplement).
Wiggin and Smith. Talking beasts.
Peasant Demyan. Polevoi. Russian fairy tales. (Tale of the Peasant Demyan.)
Peasant-girl's prisoner. Fielde. Chinese fairy tales.
Peasant maid. Maud. Heroines of poetry.
Peasant Truth. Van Sickle and Seegmiller. Riverside readers. 3d reader.
Peasant's clever daughter. Baudis. Czech folk tales. (Clever lass.)
Grimm. Fairy tales (Paull tr.).
Jacobs. Europa's fairy book. (Clever lass.)
Macdonnell. Italian fairy book. (Clever girl.)
See also Maiden who was wiser than an emperor; Sage damsel; Wise queen; Why the fish laughed; Young head of the family.
Peasie and Beansie. Lansing. Quaint old stories.
Steel. Tales of the Punjab.
Pebble and the diamond. Success library. v. 3.
Wiggin and Smith. Talking beasts.

Pechs. *See* Last of the Picts.
Pechvogel and Glückskind. Winnington. Outlook fairy book.
Peddlar and the serpent. Byrne. Modern Greek fairy tales. *See also* Man and the snake; Way of the world. I.
Peddler's pack. *See* Pedlar's pack.
Pedlar of Swaffham. Hartland. English folk and fairy tales.
Jacobs. More English fairy tales.
Johnson. Fir-tree fairy book.
Pedlar's pack. Chisholm. Enchanted land.
Peck. Stories for good children. (Scarlet blanket.)
Spaulding and Bryce. Aldine readers. Book 3. (Peddler's pack.)
Tales for bedtime. (Pedler's pack.)
Pedler's pack. *See* Pedlar's pack.
Pedro and the saddle bags. *See* Donkey and the salt.
Pedws Ffowk and St. Elian's well. Thomas. Welsh fairy book.
Pee-Wit. Grimm. Household tales (Everyman's ed.).
Perrifool. Grierson. Scottish fairy book.
Pegasus. Baldwin. Fifty famous rides. (Taming of Pegasus.)
Baldwin. Horse fair. (Winged horse of the muses.)
*Bailey. Wonder stories.
*Beckwith. In mythland. v. 3. (Pegasus, the horse with wings.)
Coe. Second book of stories. (Story of Pegasus.)
Guerber. Myths of Greece and Rome. (Bellerophon.)
Hawthorne. Wonder book. (Chimæra.)
Hutchinson. Golden porch. (First horse.)
Hyde. Favorite Greek myths. (Bellerophon.)
Judd. Classic myths. (Pegasus, the horse with wings.)
Lang. All sorts of stories book. (Horse with wings.)
Mabie. Myths every child should know. (Chimæra.)
Olcott. Wonder garden. (Winged horse.)
Patten. Junior classics. v. 3.
*Poulsson. In the child's world.
Pratt. Myths of Old Greece. v. 3. (Pegasus and Bellerophon.)
Shaw. Stories of the ancient Greeks. (Horse with wings.)
Stories of classic myths.
Tappan. Myths from many lands. (Chimæra.)
Peik. Asbjörnsen. Folk and fairy tales.
Asbjörnsen. Tales from the fjeld.
Thorne-Thomsen. East o' the sun and west o' the moon.
Peiter, Peter and Peer. Andersen. Stories and tales (Author's ed.).
Pele. Pope. Hawaii. (Old woman Pele.)
Peleus and the sea-king's daughter. Baldwin. Story of the golden age. (*In* Golden apple.)
Carpenter. Long ago in Greece. (Thetis.)

Peleus and the sea-king's daughter—*continued.*
Hutchinson. Golden porch.
Olcott. Wonder garden. (Wooing of Thetis.)
Pelleas and Ettarde. MacGregor. Stories of King Arthur's knights.
Pellinore. *See* Sir Pellinore.
Pelops. Burt and Ragozin. Herakles and other heroes.
Carpenter. Long ago in Greece. (How Pelops won his bride.)
Hutchinson. Golden porch. (*In* Favorite of the gods.)
Pen and the ink stand. Andersen. Fairy tales (Paull tr.)
Andersen. Wonder stories (Author's ed.)
Patten. Junior classics. v. 1.
Penelope. *See* Ulysses and Penelope.
Penelope's web. Baldwin. Thirty more famous stories.
Peabody. Old Greek folk stories.
Shaw. Stories of the ancient Greeks. (Wanderer's return.)
See also Ulysses.
Penitence of Blazenka. Storytellers' magazine. Dec. 1916, p. 632.
Pennard Castle. Thomas. Welsh fairy book.
Penny-wise monkey. Babbitt. More Jataka tales.
Peonies. Singleton. Wild flower fairy book.
Peony lantern. James. Green willow.
Per Gynt. *See* Peter Gynt.
Peran-Wisa and Afrasiab his king. Wilmot-Buxton. Stories of Persian heroes.
Percival. *See* Sir Percival.
Percy the wizard, nicknamed Snail. Bosschère. Christmas tales of Flanders.
Perdix. *See* Why the partridge stays near the ground.
Peredur, the son of Evrawc. *See* Sir Peredur.
Perfect song. *See* Orpheus and Eurydice.
Perfect little pig. Potter. Pinafore pocket story book.
Pergrin and the mermaiden. Thomas. Welsh fairy book.
Perizad and Perizada. Brown. One-footed fairy.
Perlino. Laboulaye. Fairy book.
Wiggin and Smith. Magic casements.
Peronella. Lansing. Fairy tales. v. 1.
Storytellers' magazine. April 1915, p. 99. (Story of an old queen.)
Welsh. Fairy tales children love.
See also Queen and the peasant girl.
Peronnik, Adventures of. Lang. Lilac fairy book. (Castle of Kerglas.)
Lang. Magic book. (Castle of Kerglas.)
Underhill. Dwarfs' tailor.
Perplexity of Zadig. Lang. Strange story book.
See also Lost camel.
Persephone. *See* Proserpina.

Perseus. Adams. Myths of old Greece.
Almost true tales.
*Bailey. Wonder stories. (How Perseus conquered the sea.)
Baker and Carpenter. Language reader. 5th year. (Perseus and Andromeda.)
Baldwin. Old Greek stories. (Quest of Medusa's head.)
Bryant. Treasury of hero tales. (Gorgon's head.)
Burt and Ragozin. Herakles and other heroes.
Cole. Heroes of the olden time.
Firth. Stories of old Greece. (Perseus, "The Son of the Bright Morning.")
Francillon. Gods and heroes. (Adventures of Perseus.)
Guerber. Myths of Greece and Rome.
Haaren and Poland. Famous men of Greece.
Hartley. Stories from the Greek legends.
Hawthorne. Wonder book. (Gorgon's head.)
Hyde. Favorite Greek myths.
Kingsley. Heroes.
Kupfer. Stories of long ago.
Lang. Blue fairy book. (Terrible head.)
Lang. Princess on the glass hill and other stories. (Terrible head.)
Mabie. Heroes and fairies.
Mabie. Heroes every child should know.
Mabie. Myths every child should know. (Gorgon's head.)
My Bookhouse. v. 4. (Adventures of Perseus.)
Pratt. Myths of old Greece. v. 3. (Perseus and Medusa.)
Pyle. Where the wind blows.
Shaw. Stories of the ancient Greeks. (Men turned to stone.)
Stories of classic myths.
Storr. Half a hundred hero tales. (Perseus and Andromeda.)
Tappan. Myths from many lands. (Gorgon's head.)
Perseverance. Bryce. Fables from afar.
Persevering carp. Storytellers' magazine. March 1917, p. 134.
See also Ambitious carp; Bruce and the spider.
Persian and his three sons. Cabot. Ethics for children.
Sly. World stories retold. (Persian and his sons.)
Persian Jack and the beanstalk. Goddard. Fairy tales in other lands.
Persimmon tree. *See* Why the persimmon tree has its fruit in three colors.
Pert fire engine. My Bookhouse. v. 3.
Pestle and mortar of jade. Coussens. Jade story book.
Pet lamb. *See* White pet.
Pet raven. Cather. Educating by story telling.
Guerber. Legends of the Rhine.
Pet turkey whose feelings were hurt. Olcott. Wonder garden.

Peter and Paul. Macé. Home fairy tales.
Peter and Paul and Espen the cinder-lad. *See* Boots and his brothers.
Peter and the magic goose. *See* Golden goose.
Peter, Basil and the fox. *See* Cat, the cock and the fox. II.
Peter Bull. Lang. Golden mermaid and other stories.
Lang. Pink fairy book.
Peter Cottontail. Murray. Story book treasures. (Peter Rabbit plays a joke.)
My Bookhouse. v. 1. (Peter Rabbit decides to change his name.)
Peter Fiddle-de-dee. Bay. Danish fairy and folk tales.
See also Princess whom nobody could silence.
Peter Gynt. Asbjörnsen. Folk and fairy tales.
Stroebe and Martens. Norwegian fairy book. (Per Gynt.)
Peter Humbug and the white cat. Bay. Danish fairy and folk tales.
See also White cat.
Peter Klaus, the goatherd. *See* Karl Katz.
Peter Muggel. Thorpe. Yule-tide stories.
Peter Pan and the lollipop. Bailey. Friendly tales.
Peter, Paul and Espen. *See* Boots and his brothers.
Peter, Paulina and the pigs. Storytellers' magazine. May 1917, p. 250.
Peter Rabbit decides to change his name. *See* Peter Cottontail.
Peter Rabbit plays a joke. *See* Peter Cottontail.
Peter Rabbit, Story of. Klingensmith. Just stories. (Adapted and abridged.)
My Bookhouse. v. 1. (Tale of Peter Rabbit.)
Stone. Children's stories that never grow old.
Tales for bedtime.
See also Peter Cottontail.
Peter Redhat. Stroebe and Martens. Danish fairy book.
See also King Thrushbeard.
Peter Rugg, the missing man. Mabie. Famous stories every child should know.
Smith. More mystery tales.
Peter Schlemihl. Jenks. Tales of fantasy.
Peter the Great. Evans. Old time tales. (Stories of Peter the Great.)
Klingensmith. Just stories. (Workman king.)
Peter the Hermit. Evans. Old time tales.
Peter the simple. Brown. One-footed fairy.
Peter the stone-cutter. Macdonell. Italian fairy book.
See also Stone cutter.
Peterkin and the little grey hare. Pyle. Wonder clock.
Petrified church. Guerber. Legends of the Rhine.
Petrified mansion. Bradley-Birt. Bengal fairy tales.
Phaethon. *See* Phaeton.
Phaethon's folly. *See* Phaeton.

Phaeton. Adams. Myths of old Greece.
Arnold and Gilbert. Stepping stones to literature. v. 4. (Phaethon.)
*Bailey. Wonder stories. (When Phaeton's chariot ran away.)
Bailey and Lewis. For the children's hour. (Story of Phaeton.)
Baldwin. Fifty famous rides. (Phaethon's folly.)
Baldwin. Story of the golden age. (*In* A voyage on the sea.)
*Beckwith. In mythland. v. 3. (Dangerous ride.)
Burt and Ragozin. Herakles and other heroes. (Phaethon.)
Carpenter. Long ago in Greece. (Celestial runaway.)
Cooke. Nature myths and stories.
Firth. Stories of old Greece. (Phaethon.)
Francillon. Gods and heroes. (Presumption.)
Guerber. Myths of Greece and Rome. (*In* Apollo.)
Hartley. Stories from Greek legends. (Story of Phaethon; or, The boy's drive on the sun-chariot.)
Holbrook. Round the year in myth and song. (Phaethon.)
Hyde. Favorite Greek myths. (Phaethon.)
Judd. Classic myths. (How the horses of the sun ran away.)
McFee. Treasury of myths.
My Bookhouse. v. 3.
Patten. Junior classics. v. 2. (How Phaeton drove the sun.)
Peabody. Old Greek folk stories.
Pratt. Myths of old Greece. v. 1.
Shaw. Stories of the ancient Greeks. (Fiery runaway.)
Skinner. Turquoise story book. (Phaeton's drive in the sun chariot.)
Sly. World stories retold. (Phaethon's wonderful ride.)
Stories of classic myths.
Storr. Half a hundred hero tales. (Story of Phaeton.)
Tappan. Stories from the classics. (Phaethon.)
Wilson. Nature study reader. (Story of Phaethon.)
See also Ixion; When Mink went to sun's house.
Phantom cats. *See* Schippeitaro.
Phantom funeral. Thomas. Welsh fairy book.
Phantom isle. Yeats. Irish fairy and folk tales.
Phantom knight of the Vandal camp. Olcott. Good stories for great holidays.
Phantom vessel. Pitman. Chinese wonder book.
Phika, Story of. *See* Triple crown.
Philemon and Baucis. *See* Baucis and Philemon.
Philomela. *See* Procne and Philomela.
Philopena. Stockton. Bee-man of Orn.
Stockton. Queen's museum.
Philosopher among the tombs. Æsop. Fables (Burt ed.).
Philosopher and the pheasants (poem). Success library. v. 3.

Philosopher, the ants and Mercury. Æsop. Fables (Burt ed.).
Philosopher's scales. Edgeworth. Waste not, want not.
Philosopher's stone. Andersen. Fairy tales (Paull tr.).
Andersen. Wonder stories (Author's ed. Stone of the wise men.)
Phœbus and Boreas. *See* Wind and Sun.
Phœnix. Baker and Carpenter. Language readers. 6th year.
Lang. Red book of animal stories.
Olcott. Wonder garden. (Spice bird.)
Scudder. Seven little people. (*In* Old brown coat.)
Phyrrhus and his elephants. Guerber. Story of the Romans.
Physician's son and the king of the snakes. Bateman. Zanzibar tales.
Physician's tale. *See* Virginia.
Piatra arsa. *See* Burnt rock.
Picciola, the prison flower. Baldwin. Fifty famous stories. (Picciola.)
Chambers' miscellany. v. 1.
Skinner. Emerald story book. (Adapted.)
Sly. World stories retold.
Piccola. Blaisdell. Child life. 3d reader. (Christmas gift.) (poem). Bryant. How to tell stories to children.
Curtiss. Christmas stories and legends. (Little Piccola.)
Hall and Gilman. Story land. 2d reader.
My Bookhouse. v. 2.
Olcott. Good stories for great holidays. (Little Piccola.)
Sly. World stories retold. (Christmas gift.)
Wiggin and Smith. Story hour.
See also Little Gretchen and the wooden shoe.
Pickaninny. Eggleston. Queer stories for boys and girls.
Picture book. Richards. Silver crown.
Picture book without pictures. Andersen. Stories and tales (Author's ed.).
Ruskin. King of the golden river and other wonder stories.
Picture from the castle ramparts. *See* Sunbeam and the captive.
Picture from the ramparts. *See* Sunbeam and the captive.
Picture on the vase, Story of the. Holbrook. Book of nature myths.
Pictures Minerva wove. *See* Arachne.
Picus. *See* King Picus the woodpecker.
Piece of good luck. Pyle. Twilight land.
Piece of liver. Kunos. Forty-four Turkish fairy tales. (Liver.)
Kunos. Turkish fairy tales.
Piece of wood. Æsop. Fables (Burt ed.).
Pied piper of Franchville. *See* Pied piper of Hamelin.
Pied piper of Hamelin (poem). Arnold and Gilbert. Stepping stones to literature. v. 5.
*Benson. Really truly fairy tales.

Pied piper of Hamelin—*continued.*
Blaisdell. Child life. 2d reader.
Browning. Poems.
Bryant. Best stories to tell to children. (Pied piper of Hamelin town.)
Bryant. How to tell stories to children.
*Burchill. Progressive road to reading. Book 2.
Crommelin. Famous legends. (Legend of the pied piper of Hamelin.)
(play). Doheny. Play awhile.
Dyer. What-happened-then stories.
Field. Famous fairy tales. (Rat catcher.)
Jacobs. More English fairy tales. (Pied piper of Franchville.)
Johnson. Fir-tree fairy book. (Pied piper.)
Lang. Red fairy book. (Rat catcher.)
(poem). Rhys. Fairy gold.
(poem). Scudder. Children's book.
Noyes. Twilight stories. (Piper of Hamelin.)
Sly. World stories retold.
(poem). Smith. Good old stories.
Tweed. Fairy tales everyone should know.
Pied piper of Hamelin town. *See* Pied piper of Hamelin.
Pierre and Helene. Cary. French fairy tales.
See also One-handed girl.
Pierre and the pewter cup. Storytellers' magazine. March 1916, p. 165.
Piff-paff; or, The art of government. Laboulaye. Fairy tales.
Pig. Stroebe and Martens. Danish fairy book.
See also Evil one who married three sisters; Forbidden room.
Pig and the dog. Storytellers' magazine. Oct. 1915, p. 366.
Pig brother. Bryant. How to tell stories to children.
Richards. Golden windows.
Pig with gold bristles, the deer with golden horns, and the golden-maned steed with golden tail. Curtin Wonder-tales from Russia.
Pigeon and the crow. Jacobs. Indian fairy tales.
Pigeon and the dove. Aulnoy. Fairy tales.
*Aulnoy. Children's fairy land. (Fairy guardian.)
Pigeon and the painting. Success library. v. 3.
Pigeon house. *Dillingham and Emerson. Tell it again stories.
Pigeon-king and Mouse-king. Coussens. Jade story book.
Pigeon's bride. Fillmore. Laughing prince.
See also Earl of Mar's daughter.
Pigeons of Venice. Cather. Educating by story telling.
Piggy Wig's house. *Coe and Christie. Storyhour readers. Book 1.
Pigling and her proud sister. Griffis. Unmannerly tiger, and other Korean tales.
Griffis Korean fairy tales.

Pigling and her proud sister—*continued.*
My Bookhouse. v. 3.
Pigs, story of the. Harris. Nights with Uncle Remus.
Tappan. Folk stories and fables.
Van Sickle and Seegmiller. Riverside readers. 2d reader.
See also Three little pigs. I and II.
Pike. I. Bay. Danish fairy and folk tales.
Pike. II. Wiggin and Smith. Talking beasts.
Pike and the cat. Wigin and Smith. Talking beasts.
Pikku Matti. *See* Bikku Matti.
Pikoi: The boy who was good at shooting arrows. Colum. At the gateways of the day.
Pilgrim's return. Guerber. Legends of the Rhine.
Pilgrim's secret. Marshall. Fairy tales of all nations.
Pillow dolly. *Dillingham and Emerson. Tell it again stories.
Pimmerly plum. Harris. Nights with Uncle Remus.
See also Brother Rabbit and the pimmerly plum.
Pimpernel. Pratt. Fairyland of flowers.
Pine and the flax. Jones. First reader.
Skinner. Pearl story book.
Pine and the willow. Skinner. Pearl story book.
Pine tree. *See* Fir tree.
Pine tree and its needles. *See* Little pine tree who wished for new leaves.
Pine tree maiden. *See* Leelinau, the lost daughter.
Pine trees. *See* Glooskap and the magic gifts. IV.
Pine tree's dress of gold. Storyteller's magazine. Dec. 1917, p. 524.
Pine trees keep their leaves. *See* Why the evergreen trees keep their leaves all winter. II.
Pineapple and the bee. Wiggin and Smith. Talking beasts.
Pink. Grimm. Fairy tales (Lucas tr.).
Grimm. Fairy tales (Paull tr.).
Grimm. Household tales (Burt ed. Lost son.)
Pinkel, the thief. See Golden lantern, golden goat and golden cloak.
Pinocchio. Harper. Story-hour favorites. (Abridged.)
Lansing. Dramatic readings. (Scenes from Pinocchio.)
Pinocchio's adventure with the cat. Bailey. In the animal world.
Piper and the Puca. Graves. Irish fairy book.
Yeats. Irish fairy tales.
Piper of Hamelin. *See* Pied piper of Hamelin.
Pippa passes. Bailey and Lewis. For the children's hour.
Storytellers' magazine. Oct. 1916, p. 510.
Piskey fine and piskey gay! Olcott. Book of elves and fairies.
Piskies in the cellar. Hartland. English folk and fairy tales.
See also Voyage of the wee red cap.
Pit. Richards. Silver crown.

Pitcher, the witch and the black cats. Olcott. Red Indian fairy book.
Pivi and Kabo. Lang. Brown fairy book.
Lang. Magician's gifts.
Pixies. *See* Pixies' vengeance. I.
Pixies and tulips. *See* Tulip bed. II.
Pixies' thanks. *See* Tulip bed. II.
Pixies' vengeance. I. Olcott. Book of elves and fairies.
Pixies' vengeance. II. Duncan-Jones: English folk-lore stories. (Vengeance of the pixies.)
Hartland. English folk and fairy tales. (Two serving damsels.)
Pixy's clothes. Rhys. Fairy gold.
Plague among the beasts. Æsop. Fables (Burt ed.).
Plaisham. MacManus. Donegal fairy stories.
Plain case. Wilkins. Pot of gold.
Plant. Richards. Silver crown.
Plant that lost it's berry. Slosson. Story-tell Lib.
Plantation witch. Harris. Uncle Remus, his songs and his sayings.
Plate of pancakes. *Lindsay. Story-teller.
Player on the jews-harp. Stroebe and Martens. Norwegian fairy book.
Playful ass. Wiggin and Smith. Talking beasts.
Playroom wedding. Walker. Sandman's goodnight stories.
Please. Van Sickle and Seegmiller. Riverside readers. 2d reader.
Pleasing everybody. I. *See* Man, the boy, and the donkey.
Pleasing everybody. II. Hartwell. Story hour reading. 5th year.
Pleiades. I. Holbrook. Round the year in myth and song.
Hyde. Favorite Greek myths. (Seven sisters.)
See also Orion.
Pleiades. II. Borland. Rocky mountain tipi tales. (Twelve children in the sky.)
Cowles. Indian nature myths. (Stars that dance.)
Eastman. Indian legends retold. (Stars and the pine.)
Judd. Wigwam stories. (Seven stars of Pleiades.)
Olcott. Wonder garden. (Lazy boys who became the Pleiades.)
Powers. Around an Iroquois story fire. (How the dancing stars got into the sky.)
Tanner. Legends from the red man's forest. (Indian's war dance.)
Pleiades. III. Houghton. Russian grandmother's wonder tales. (Seven stars.)
Pleiades. IV. Chandler. In the reign of coyote. (Story of the Pleiades.)
Pleiades. V. Grundtvig. Fairy tales from afar. (Pleiades; or. The seven stars.)
Lansing. Fairy tales. v. 2.

Pleiades. VI. Olcott. Red Indian fairy book. (Singing maidens; Star maiden.)
Plentiful tablecloth, the avenging wand, the sash that becomes a lake, and the terrible helmet, Story of the. Chodzko. Fairy tales of the Slav.
Plight of the brook. Storytellers' magazine. Nov. 1917. p. 469.
Ploughman and Fortune. Æsop. Fables (Black ed.).
Æsop. Fables (Burt ed. Plowman and Fortune.)
Ploughman and his sons. *See* Gold in the orchard.
Ploughman who brought famine. *See* King and the oak.
Plowman and Fortune. *See* Ploughman and Fortune.
Plowman who found content. *See* Wishing ring.
Plucked. Young. Plantation bird legends.
Plucky prince. Skinner. Turquoise story book.
Pluto and Proserpine. *See* Proserpina.
Plutus. Æsop. Fables (Burt ed.).
Po' jay. Young. Plantation bird legends.
Pocahontas and John Smith. Baldwin. Fifty famous stories. (Pocahontas.)
Blaisdell. Child life. 3d reader. (Pocahontas.)
Coe. Second book of stories. (Pocahontas.)
Poet and his little daughter. Whittier. Child life in prose.
Poet, the oyster, and sensitive plant (poem). Wiggin and Smith. Talking beasts.
Poetry, Origin of. *See* Odin and the mead.
Point of view. Richards. Golden windows.
Poisoned shirt, Story of a. *See* Hercules and his labors.
Poisonous trees. Shedlock. Eastern stories and legends.
Pole star. Pratt. Legends of the red children.
See also North star; Star that never moves.
Polite family. *Klingensmith. Just stories.
Polite idiosyncrasy. Field. Chinese fairy tales.
Pollux. *See* Castor and Pollux.
Pollywog. Potter. Pinafore pocket story book.
Polycrates. *See* Ring of Polycrates.
Polyphemus. I. *See* Ulysses.
Polyphemus. II. *See* Acis and Galatea.
Pomegranate. *See* Parable of the Pomegranate.
Pomegranate, apple-tree, and bramble. Æsop. Fables (Burt ed.).
Pomegranate seeds. *See* Proserpina.
Pomona. Bailey. Wonder stories. (When Pomona shared her apples.)
Olcott. Wonder garden. (Wooing of Pomona.)
Skinner. Topaz story book.
Pomona and Vertumnus. Guerber. Myths of Greece and Rome. (*In* minor divinities.)
Ponce de Leon and the fountain of youth. Baldwin. Thirty more famous stories. (Fountain of youth.)
Pond lilies. Allen. Indian fairy tales.
Pond world and the wide world. *See* Dragon fly.

Pontius Pilate, Strange story of. Froelicher. Swiss stories. (Strange story of Pontius Pilate.)
Pony engine. *See* Pony engine and the Pacific Express.
Pony engine and the Pacific express. Alderman. Classics old and new, 3d reader. (Pony engine.)
Howells. Christmas every day.
My Bookhouse. v. 2.
Poor boy in the grave. Grimm. Fairy tales (Paull tr.).
Poor devil. Stroebe and Martens. Swedish fairy book.
Poor diet. Mendes. Fairy spinning wheel.
Poor Hans. Laboulaye. Last fairy tales.
Poor little turkey girl. *See* Turkey maiden.
Poor man and the eagle. Success library. v. 3.
Poor man and the flask of oil. Bidpai. Tortoise and the geese.
Poor man and the rich man. Allison and Perdue. Story in primary instruction. (Wonderful traveler.)
*Benson. Really truly fairy tales. (Three wishes.)
Cather. Educating by story telling.
(play). Lansing. Quaint old stories.
See also Rich woman and the poor woman.
Poor man of Peatlaw. Douglas. Scottish fairy tales.
Poor miller's boy and the cat. *See* Miller's boy and his cat.
Poor Old Good. Skinner. Nursery tales from many lands.
Poor Peter. Bosschère. Folk tales of Flanders.
See also Puss in boots.
Poor-Peter and the princess. Storytellers' magazine. March 1917, p. 150.
Poor turkey girl. *See* Turkey maiden.
Poor widow. Magnus. Russian folk-tales.
Poor woman and the bell. Wiggin and Smith. Talking beasts.
Pope's game of chess. Landa. Aunt Naomi's Jewish fairy tales and legends.
Pope's mule. Olcott and Pendleton. Jolly book.
Poplar blossoms and hickory tassels, Origin of. Bigham. Overheard in fairyland.
Poplar tree. I. Cooke. Nature myths and stories.
Stone and Fickett. Trees in prose and poetry. (Legend of the poplar.)
Strong. All the year round. v. 4. Summer. (Story of the poplar tree.)
Wilson. Nature study reader. (Iris; Story of the poplar.)
Poplar tree. II. Pratt. Fairyland of flowers. (Lombardy poplar.)
Poppies, Origin of. *See* Bad poppy seeds; Fairy of the poppies.
Porcupine. *See* Creation of the porcupine.
Porcupine and the snakes. Æsop. Fables (Black ed.).
Æsop. Fables (Burt ed.).
Æsop. Fables (Stickney).
Wiggin and Smith. Talking beasts.

Porcupine kills coyote. Borland. Rocky Mountain tipi tales.
Pork and honey. *See* Bear and the fox make a wager.
Porridge. Fillmore. Mighty Mikko.
Porter and the ladies of Bagdad and the three royal mendicants. *See* Three calendars, sons of kings and five ladies of Bagdad.
Porter's son. Andersen. Stories and tales (Author's ed.).
Portuguese duck. Andersen. Fairy tales (Paull tr.).
Andersen. Wonder stories. (In the duck-yard.)
Darton. Wonder book of beasts. (In the duck-yard.)
Possum eaten in a dream. Harris. Uncle Remus and his friends. (*In* Acccording to how the drop falls.)
Pot. Richards. Silver crown.
Pot of Basil. Skinner. Myths and legends of flowers and trees. (Basil.)
See also Elf of the rose.
Pot of gold. I. Coe. Second book of stories.
Scudder. Dream children.
Pot of gold. II. Bailey. Stories and rhymes for a child.
Pot of gold. III. *See* How buttercups came.
Pot of gold. IV. Wilkins. Pot of gold and other stories.
Pot of gold at the foot of the rainbow. *See* Pot of gold. I; Poplar tree I and II.
Pot of hot porridge. *See* Journey of the porridge pot.
Potato-choosing boy. Olcott. Wonder garden.
Potato! Potato! Olcott. Wonder garden.
Potato supper. *See* Priest's supper.
Potted sprats, Tale of. Scudder. Children's book.
Potter. I. Magnus. Russian folk-tales.
Potter. II. Richards. Silver crown.
Pottle o' brains. Jacobs. More English fairy tales.
Johnson. Fir-tree fairy book. (Bottle of brains.)
Pouchy Pelican. Coe and Christie. Story hour readers. Book 2.
See also Drakesbill and his friends.
Poucinet. *See* Boots and his brothers.
Poussie Baudrons (poem). Grierson. Scottish fairy book.
Pouting princess. Storytellers' magazine. Oct. 1916, p. 540.
Poveretta. Macé. Home fairy tales.
Powder candle. *See* Christmas candle.
Powell and his bride. *See* Badger in the bag.
Powell, Prince of Dyfed. Colum. Island of the mighty. This includes: Story of Puil, Prince of Dyved; How Puil won Rhiannon for his wife, and how Rhiannon's babe was lost to her; How Puil went into Annwvin, the Realm of Faerie.
See also Badger in the bag.
Power of fables. Æsop. Fables (Burt ed.).
Wiggin and Smith. Talking beasts.
Power of love. I. *See* Frost king.
Power of love. II. *See* Bell of Djoji.

Power of St. Tegla's well. Thomas. Welsh fairy book.
Power of will. Caballero. Spanish fairy tales.
Prairie dandelion. Brooks. Stories of the red children. (South Wind and the dandelion.)
*Cowles. Indian nature myths. (Maiden with golden hair.)
Farmer. Nature myths. (Dandelion maiden.)
Judd. Wigwam stories.
McFee. Treasury of flower stories. (South wind and the dandelion.)
Olcott. Red Indian fairy book. (Meadow dandelion.)
Pratt. Legends of the red children. (Legend of the South Wind.)
Skinner. Turquoise story book. (Origin of the dandelion.)
Storytellers' magazine. May 1916, p. 276. (*In* Nature legends: Story of the dandelion.)
Praying geese. *See* Fox and the geese.
Presents of the little folk. *Grimm. Fairy tales (Wiltse.) v. 2.
Prester John. Mabie. Legends every child should know.
Presumption. *See* Phaeton.
Pretending woodchuck. Skinner. Topaz story book.
See also Blunder.
Pretty Goldilocks. *See* Fair one with golden locks.
Pretty woman. Eastman. Indian legends retold.
Price of a life. Stewart. Tell me a hero story.
Pride goeth before a fall. Jacobs. Indian fairy tales.
Patten. Junior classics, v. 1.
Pride shall have a fall. Rouse. Talking thrush.
See also Jackal and the Iguana.
Priest and the clerk. Asbjörnsen. Folk and fairy tales. (Parson and the clerk.)
Asbjörnsen. Tales from the fjeld.
Djurklo. Fairy tales from the Swedish. (Parson and the clerk.)
Gade. Norwegian fairy tales. (Parson and the sexton.)
Stroebe and Martens. Norwegian fairy book. (Pastor and the sexton.)
Thorne-Thomsen. East o' the sun and west o' the moon. (Parson and the clerk.)
See also Emperor and the abbot; King and the miller; King John and the Abbot of Canterbury.
Priest with the envious eyes. Magnus. Russian folk-tales.
Priest's gate. Guerber, Legends of the Rhine.
Priest's supper. Frost. Fairies and folk of Ireland. (*In* Ch. 10.)
Olcott. Book of elves and fairies. (Potato supper.)
Yeats. Irish fairy tales.
Priest's youngest son. Wardrop. Georgian folk tales.
Primrose, Legend of. Skinner. Turquoise story book.
See also Cowslips. II; Little forget-me-not.
Primrose son. Olcott. Wonder garden.
Prince. Wardrop. Georgian folk tales.

Prince and his servant. Æsop. Fables (Burt ed.).
Prince Agib, Story of. Arabian nights (Wiggin and Smith).
Prince Ahmed. I. Kunos. Forty-four Turkish fairy tales.
Prince Ahmed. II. *See* Prince Ahmed and the fairy Perie Banou.
Prince Ahmed, and the fairy Perie Banou, Story of. Arabian nights (Dodge ed.).
Arabian nights (Townsend).
Arabian nights, More tales (Olcott).
Coussens. Jade story book. (Prince Ahmed.)
Judson and Bender. Graded literature readers. v. 4. (Prince Ahmed.)
Lang. Blue fairy book. (Story of Prince Ahmed and the Fairy Paribanou.)
Lang. Prince Darling and other fairy stories. (Story of Prince Ahmed and the fairy Paribanou.)
Singleton. Wild flower fairy book. (Prince Ahmed and the Fairy Pari Banou.)
Prince Almor and the blind princess. Brown. Mermaid's gift.
Prince Amgiad and Prince Assad, History of. Arabian Nights (Townsend).
Arabian nights, More tales (Olcott. Story of the two princes, Amgiad and Assad.)
Prince and a peasant. Stewart. Tell me a hero story.
Prince and princess in the forest. Lang. Olive fairy book.
Lang. Snake prince.
Prince and the baker's daughter. Fyleman. Rainbow cat.
Prince and the bee. *Jones. 2d reader.
Prince and the dragon. *See* Dragon and the prince.
Prince and the eagle. Armfield. Wonder tales.
Prince and the fakir. Jacobs. Indian fairy tales.
Prince and the foal. Byrne. Modern Greek fairy tales.
Prince and the rabbi. Friedlander. Jewish fairy book.
Prince and the rat. Bryce. Fables from afar.
Prince and the spider. Arnold and Gilbert. Stepping stones to literature. v. 3.
Prince and the three fates. Lang. Brown fairy book.
Jewett, Egyptian tales of magic. (Prince and the three dooms.)
Lang. Pretty Goldilocks and other stories.
Stewart. Tell me a hero story. (Doomed prince.)
Prince Autumn. Skinner. Topaz story book.
Prince Bayaya. Fillmore. Czechoslovak fairy tales.
Prince Beder and the Princess Jehaun-ara, Story of. Arabian nights (Townsend).
Prince Butterfly and Clover-blossom (play). *Field second reader. (Butterfly and the clover.)
Olcott. Wonder garden. (Prince Butterfly and Clover blossom.)
Skinner. Turquoise story book.
Prince Camaralzaman. *See* Camaralzaman

Prince Charming. Perkins. Twenty best fairy tales.
Prince Chéri. *See* Prince Darling.
Prince Cherry. *See* Prince Darling.
Prince Darling. Arnold and Gilbert. Stepping stones to literature. v. 3.
Bryant. Stories to tell to children. (Prince Cherry.)
Curry. Little classics. (Magic ring.)
Douglas. Favourite French fairy tales.
Lang. Blue fairy book.
Lang. Prince Darling and other fairy stories.
Larned. Fairy tales from France.
Mulock. Fairy book. (Prince Cherry.)
My Bookhouse. v. 3. (Prince Cherry.)
Olcott. Book of elves and fairies. (Prince Chéri.)
Rolfe. Fairy tales in prose and verse. (Prince Cherry.)
Scudder. Children's book. (Prince Cherry.)
Success library. v. 3.
Valentine. Old, old fairy tales. (Prince Cherry.)
Welsh. Fairy tales children love. (Prince Cherry.)
Wiggin. Fairy ring. (Prince Cherry.)
See also Fair-flower.
Prince Desire and Princess Mignonetta. Lang. Blue fairy book. (Prince Hyacinth and the dear little princess.)
Lang. History of Jack the giant killer, and other stories. (Prince Hyacinth and the dear little princess.)
Mulock. Fairy book. (Prince with the nose.)
Rolfe. Fairy tales. (Prince with the nose.)
Valentine. Old, old fairy tales.
Prince Evstáfi. Magnus. Russian folk-tales.
Prince Fatal and Prince Fortune. Valentine. Old, old fairy tales.
Prince Featherhead and the Princess Celandine. Lang. Green fairy book.
Lang. Fairy nurse.
Prince Fernando. Eells. Tales of enchantment from Spain.
See also Master Maid.
Prince Fickle and Fair Helena. Lang. Forty thieves, and other stories.
Lang. Green fairy book.
Prince Fireshine and Prince Fireshade. *See* Ambitious hunter and skilful fisher.
Prince Golden-Firefly. *See* Firefly's lovers.
Prince Half-a-son. Steel. Tales of the Punjab.
Prince Harold and the ogre. Winnington. Outlook fairy book.
Prince Harweda and the magic prison. Coe. First book of stories.
Harrison. In storyland.
My Bookhouse. v. 3.
Van Sickle and Seegmiller. Riverside readers. 4th reader. (Magic prison.)

Prince Hassak's march. Stockton. Bee-man of Orn and other tales.
Stockton. Queen's museum.
Prince Hatt under the earth; or, Three singing leaves. Quiller-Couch. Fairy tales far and near.
Thorpe. Yule-tide stories.
Prince Hedgehog. Houghton. Russian grandmother's wonder tales.
Wiggin and Smith. Magic casements.
See also Hans, my Hedgehog.
Prince Hlini. Hall. Icelandic fairy tales.
Prince Hyacinth and the dear little princess. *See* Prince Desire and Princess Mignonetta.
Prince in the dark. Macdonell. Italian fairy book.
Prince Irregang and Maid Miseri. *See* Master Maid.
Prince Isfendiyar. Wilmot-Buxton. Stories of Persian heroes.
Prince Ivan and the grey wolf. *See* Ivan and the gray wolf.
Prince Labour. English. Fairy stories and wonder tales.
Prince Lionheart and his three friends. Steel. Tales of the Punjab.
Prince Malandrach and the Princess Salikalla, Story of. Steele. Russian garland of fairy tales.
Prince Narcissus and the Princess Potentilla. Lang. Green fairy book.
Lang. Fairy nurse.
Prince of golden land. Grayl. Fairy tales from foreign lands.
See also Master Maid. I.
Prince of Naples. Williams. Fairy tales from folklore.
Prince of Wales. Blaisdell. English history story book. (First Prince of Wales.)
See also Black Prince.
Prince of the desert. Gate. Fortunate days.
Prince Peter with the golden keys, and the Princess Magilene, Story of. Steele. Russian garland of fairy tales.
Prince Ponto. Storytellers' magazine. June 1917, p. 290.
Prince Prigio. Jenks. Tales of fantasy.
Lang. My own fairy book.
Prince Rainbow. Olcott. Whirling king.
Prince Ricardo. Lang. My own fairy book.
Prince Ring. Lang. Twelve huntsmen, and other stories.
Lang. Yellow fairy book.
Prince Roland. *See* White Cat.
Prince Sandalwood, the father of Korea. Griffis. Unmannerly tiger and other Korean tales.
Griffis. Korean fairy tales.
Prince Scarlet, Story of. St. Nicholas. July 1912, p. 796.
Stewart. Once upon a time.
Prince Silverwings. Harrison. Prince Silverwings

Prince Sincere. Valentine. Old, old fairy tales.
Prince Slugobyl; or, The invisible knight. Chodzko. Fairy tales of the Slav. (History of Prince Slugobyl; or, The invisible knight.)
Prince Sneeze. Beston. Firelight fairy book.
Prince Spin Head and Miss Snow White. Griffis. Dutch fairy tales.
Prince Sprite. *See* Invisible prince II.
Prince that married a nixie. Bailey. Seven peas in the pod.
Prince Tiresome and Laughing Kitty. Underhill. Dwarfs' tailor, and other fairy tales.
Prince Tito. Valentine. Old, old fairy tales.
Prince Unexpected. *See* King Kojata.
Prince Varna. Coussens. Jade story book.
Prince Vildering and Maid Miseri. Grundtvig. Fairy tales from afar.
Prince Vivien and Princess Placida. Lang. Forty thieves, and other stories.
Lang. Green fairy book.
Prince who befriended the beasts. Wardrop. Georgian folk tales.
Prince who had no fairy godmother. *See* King's mistake.
Prince who hated spiders and flies. Sly. World stories retold.
Prince who wanted to see the world. Lang. Beauty and the beast, and other stories.
Lang. Violet fairy book.
Prince who was a seer. Hutchinson. Golden porch.
Prince who was afraid. Bailey. In the animal world.
Prince who went seeking his sisters. Partridge. Glooscap the great chief.
Prince who would seek immortality. Lang. Crimson fairy book.
Lang. Forty thieves, and other stories.
Prince Wicked, and the grateful animals. Babbitt. More Jataka tales.
Burlingame. Grateful elephant. (Grateful animals and ungrateful man.)
Prince Winter. Skinner. Pearl story book.
Prince Wisewit's return. Browne. Granny's wonderful chair.
Prince with the golden hand. Chodzko. Fairy tales of the Slav.
Jokai and others. Golden fairy book. (Prince with the hand of gold.)
Tappan. Myths from many lands.
Prince with the golden mouth. Jewett. Wonder tales from Tibet.
Prince with the hand of gold. *See* Prince with the golden hand.
Prince with the noble heart. Orcutt. Princess Kallisto.

Prince with the nose. *See* Prince Desire and Princess Mignonetta.
Prince Wolf. Grundtvig. Fairy tales from afar.
Prince Yamato Take. *See* Prince Yamato's adventures.
Prince Yamato's adventures. Griffis. Japanese fairy tales. (Prince Yamato's adventures; Sword that mowed the grass.)
Nixon-Roulet. Japanese folk stories and fairy tales. (Sacrifice to Kompira.)
Ozaki. Japanese fairy book. (Prince Yamato Take.)
See also Sword of the assembled clouds of heaven.
Prince Zeyn Alasnam and the Sultan of the Genii. Arabian nights (Dodge ed.).
Arabian nights (Townsend. History of Prince Zeyn Alsnam and the Sultan of the Genii.)
Coussens. Jade story book.
Singleton. Goldenrod fairy book.
Princes and the friendly animals. Pyle. Fairy tales from far and near.
Princess and the water-sprite. Babbitt. Jataka tales.
Prince's choice. Pyle. Prose and verse for children.
Prince's dream. Ingelow. Stories told to a child.
Ingelow. Three fairy tales.
Patten. Junior classics. v. 6.
Smith. Good old stories.
Princes Fire-flash and Fire-fade. *See* Ambitious hunter and skilful fisher.
Prince's visit. Bailey. For the story teller.
Scudder. Dream children.
Tappan. Modern stories.
Whittier. Child life in prose.
Prince's vow. Guerber. Legends of the Rhine.
Princess. *See* Learned princess.
Princess and the bean. *See* Princess on the pea.
Princess and the beggar. Friedlander. Jewish fairy book.
See also Princess of the tower.
Princess and the Count of Oldenburg. Gibbon. Reign of King Cole.
Princess and the fox baby. *See* Grateful foxes.
Princess and the giant. Johnson. Fir-tree fairy book.
Princess and the glass mountain. *See* Princess on the glass mountain.
Princess and the golden ball. *See* Frog prince.
Princess and the golden blackbird. *See* Golden blackbird.
Princess and the pea. *See* Princess on the pea.
Princess and the rabbi. Aunt Naomi. Jewish fairy tales and fables.
Princess Aubergine. Steel. Tales of the Punjab.
Princess Beautiful. Van Sickle and Seegmiller. Riverside readers. 3d reader.
Princess Bella-Flor. Lang. Orange fairy book.
Lang. Little King Loc.

Princess Belle-Etoile and Prince Cheri. Aulnoy. Fairy tales.
Princess Birdie. Mendes. Fairy spinning wheel.
Princess Carpillon. Aulnoy. Fairy tales.
Princess Dyonetia. Gate. Punch and Robinetta.
Princess Eglantine. Harrison. Old-fashioned fairy book.
Princess Finola and the dwarf. Hodgkins. Atlantic treasury of childhood stories.
Leamy. Golden spears.
Princess Fire-fly. *See* Firefly's lovers.
Princess Gentle. *See* Rondel.
Princess Girlikin; or, The fairy thimble. Nichols and DeMorgan. Princess Girlikin and other fairy tales.
Princess Golden Hair and the great black raven. Pyle. Wonder clock.
Princess Hase, Story of. Ozaki. Japanese fairy book.
Princess Hilda. May. Little Prudy's fairy book.
Princess in disguise. *See* Many-furred creature.
Princess in the cavern. Thorpe. Yule-tide stories.
See also Princess on the island.
Princess in the chest. Lang. Pink fairy book.
Lang. Snow-queen, and other stories.
Princess Kalabutti. Bradley-Birt. Bengal fairy tales.
Princess Kallisto. Orcutt. Princess Kallisto, and other tales.
Princess Kwan-Yin. Pitman. Chinese wonder book.
Princess Lilly. *See* Magic swan.
Princess Lindagull. Poulsson. Top of the world stories.
Princess Longnose. Macdonnell. Italian fairy book.
See also Nose-tree.
Princess lost in the snow. Eliot. House on the edge of things. (First snow storm.)
Storytellers' magazine. Dec. 1915, p. 494. (House on the edge of things: First snow storm.)
Princess Maia. *See* Princess Printaniere.
Princess Mayblossom. *See* Princess Printaniere.
Princess Meadowlark. Stewart. Once upon a time.
Princess Minikin. Valentine. Old, old fairy book.
Princess Minon-Minette. Lang. Golden mermaid, and other stories.
Lang. Pink fairy book.
Princess Miranda and Prince Hero. Glinski. Polish fairy tales.
Princess Moonbeam. Lyman. Story telling.
My Bookhouse. v. 3. (Moon maiden.)
Nixon-Roulet. Japanese folk-stories and fairy tales.
Skinner. Turquoise story book.
See also Bamboo cutter and the moon child.
Princess Moonlight. *See* Bamboo-cutter and the moon-child.
Princess Morgana. Hackländer. Enchanting and the enchanted.
Princess of Babylon. Lang. Strange story book.

Princess of Canterbury. Hartland. English folk and fairy tales.
Jacobs. More English fairy tales.
Mother Goose's nursery rhymes, tales and fables (Warne ed.).
Princess of Colchester. Hartland. English folk and fairy tales.
Rhys. Fairy gold.
Princess of Deryabar, History of. Arabian nights (Townsend).
Arabian nights (Housman).
Princess of the brazen mountain. Glinski. Polish fairy tales.
See also Seven swans.
Princess of the Golden Castle. Pyle. Counterpane fairy.
Princess of the rainbow. Orcutt. Princess Kallisto.
Princess of the sea. *See* Uraschimataro and the turtle.
Princess of the springs. Eells. Tales of giants from Brazil.
Princess of the tower. Landa. Aunt Naomi's Jewish fairy tales and legends.
Princess of Tronkolaine. Cary. French fairy tales.
Williams. Fairy tales from folklore.
Princess on the glass hill. Canton. Reign of King Herla.
Coussens. Child's book of stories.
Dasent. Norse fairy tales.
Dasent. Popular tales from the Norse.
Dyer and Brady. Merrill readers. 3d reader. (Cinderlad; Princess on the glass hill.)
Lang. Blue fairy book.
Lang. Princess on the glass hill, and other stories.
My Bookhouse. v. 3.
Thorne-Thomsen. East o' the sun and west o' the moon.
Wiggin and Smith. Fairy ring.
Princess on the glass mountain. Stroebe and Martens. Swedish fairy book.
Thorpe. Yule-tide stories. (Princess on the glass mountain.)
Princess on the island. Stroebe and Martens. Danish fairy book.
See also Princess in the cavern.
Princess on the pea. Andersen. Best fairy tales (Henderson, tr. Real princess.)
Andersen. Fairy tales (Lucas tr. Real princess.)
Andersen. Fairy tales (Turpin. Princess and the pea.)
Andersen. Fairy tales and stories (Toksvig).
Andersen. Stories (Riverside ed.).
Andersen. Stories and tales (Author's ed.).
Bailey. Stories children need. (Princess and the pea.)
Forty famous fairy tales. (Real princess.)
Johnson. Birch-tree fairy book. (Princess and the bean.)
Lang. Yellow fairy book. (How to tell a true princess.)

Princess on the pea—*continued.*
Lansing. Fairy tales. v. 1. (How to tell a real princess.)
Mabie. Fairy tales every child should know.
Mabie. Heroes and fairies.
Olcott and Pendleton. Jolly book. (Real princess.)
Scudder. Children's book.
Shedlock. Art of the storyteller. (Princess and the pea.)
Wiggin and Smith. Tales of laughter. (How to tell a true princess.)
Princess Peony. James. Green willow. (Flower of the peony.)
Olcott. Wonder garden.
Princess Pepperina. Steel. Tales of the Punjab.
Princess Periezade and the speaking bird, the singing tree and the golden water. *See* Three sisters. I.
Princess Printaniere. Aulnoy. Fairy tales.
Lang. King of the waterfalls. (Princess Mayblossom.)
Lang. Red fairy book. (Princess Mayblossom.)
Valentine. Old, old fairy book. (Princess Maia.)
Princess Red-White-and-Black. Macdonell. Italian fairy tales.
Princess Rosalind. Baring-Gould. Crock of gold.
Princess Rosamund. Bay. Danish fairy and folk tales.
Princess Rosetta and the pop-corn man. Wilkins. Pot of gold.
Princess Rosette. I. Aulnoy. Fairy tales.
Aulnoy. Children's fairy land. (King of the peacocks.)
Jerrold. Reign of King Oberon.
Lang. Red fairy book.
Lang. White doe.
Larned. Fairy tales from France. (King of the peacocks.)
Perrault. Old-time stories.
Pyle. Wonder tales retold. (Princess Rosetta.)
Valentine. Old, old fairy tales.
Wiggin and Smith. Magic casements.
See also Lilla Rosa and Long Leda; True bride. III.
Princess Rosette. II. Segur. French fairy tales.
Segur. Old French fairy tales.
Princess Rosette. III. Perrault. Tales of passed times.
Princess Sorrowful and the Green Knight. Grundtvig. Fairy tales from afar.
Princess Sunset, Story of. Harrison. Moon princess.
Princess Swallow-heart. Colum. Peep-show man.
Princess to be kissed at a charge. Magnus. Russian folk-tales.
Princess White Wings and the Knight of the Robin Red Breast. Stewart. Once upon a time.
Princess who could not be silenced. *See* Princess whom nobody could silence.
Princess who could not cry. Fyleman. Rainbow cat.
Princess who had but one accomplishment. Bailey. Seven peas in the pod.

Princess who hid her shoes. Nyblom. Jolly Calle.
Princess who said:— Bay. Danish fairy and folk tales.
(play). Lansing. Quaint old stories. (How Claus won the princess.)
See also Ashiepattle who made the princess tell the truth at last.
Princess who was dumb. Eells. Tales of enchantment from Spain.
See also Wild swans.
Princess who was hidden underground. Lang. Beauty and the beast and other stories.
Lang. Violet fairy book.
Princess who would not smile. Magnus. Russian folk-tales.
Princess whom nobody could silence. Asbjörnsen. Fairy tales from the far north.
Dasent. Norse fairy tales. (Taming the shrew.)
Dasent. Popular tales from the Norse. (Taming the shrew.)
Olcott and Pendleton. Jolly book.
Spaulding and Bryce. Aldine readers. Book 3.
Storytellers' magazine. Nov. 1914, p. 734.
Thorne-Thomsen. East o' the sun and west o' the moon. (Princess who could not be silenced.)
Wiggin and Smith. Tales of laughter.
See also Peter Fiddle-de-dee.
Princess with the twelve pair of golden shoes. Stroebe and Martens. Danish fairy book.
See also Twelve dancing princesses.
Princess with twenty petticoats. Griffis. Dutch fairy tales.
Princesses who lived in a kailyard. Armfield. Wonder tales.
Princess's garden. Storytellers' magazine. April 1917, p. 250.
Princess's gold shoes. Bailey. Stories for Sunday telling.
Princet and the golden blackbird. *See* Golden blackbird.
Princetta's doll. *Dillingham and Emerson. Tell it again stories.
Prioress's tale. *See* Boy martyr.
Prize ball. Bailey. Friendly tales.
Procne and Philomela. Hyde. Favorite Greek myths.
Procrustes. Baldwin. Old Greek stories.
See also Theseus.
Professor and the wonderful egg. Gibbons. Reign of King Cole.
Profligate prince. Eggleston. Queer stories for boys and girls.
Prometheus. Adams. Myths of old Greece. (Prometheus and Epimetheus.)
Bailey. Wonder stories. (What Prometheus did with a bit of clay.)

Prometheus—*continued.*
Baldwin. Old Greek stories. (Story of Prometheus.)
Baldwin. Story of the golden age. (*In* Children of Prometheus.)
Burt and Ragozin. Herakles and other heroes.
Church. Greek story and song. (Binding of Prometheus.)
Cooke. Nature myths and stories.
Firth. Stories of old Greece.
Francillon. Gods and heroes. (First man.)
Guerber. Myths of Greece and Rome. (*In* Beginning of all things.)
Hartley. Stories from the Greek legends.
Hutchinson. Orpheus with his lute. (Prometheus the fire-bringer; Prometheus unbound.)
Hyde. Favorite Greek myths.
Judd. Classic myths. (How fire came to the earth.)
McFee. Treasury of myths.
Olcott. Wonder garden. (Man who brought fire.)
Peabody. Old Greek folk stories.
Shaw. Stories of the ancient Greeks. (Fire from heaven.)
Sly. World stories retold.
See also Pandora.
Prominent man. Richards. Golden windows.
Promise. I. Caballero. Spanish fairy tales.
Promise II. Lindsay. Story-teller.
Promise of Massang. Jewett. Wonder tales from Tibet.
Promised plant. Proudfoot. Child's Christ tales.
Skinner. Emerald story book.
Prompt retort. Guerber. Legends of the Rhine.
Prophet. McSpadden. Stories from great operas.
Pleasanton. Fairyland of opera.
Prophetic dream. Polevoi. Russian fairy tales.
Proserpina. Adams. Myths of old Greece.
Almost true tales. (Pomegranate seeds.)
Arnold and Gilbert. Stepping stones to literature. v. 4. (Persephone.)
*Bailey. Wonder stories. (When Proserpine was lost.)
Bailey and Lewis. For the children's hour. (Story of Persephone.)
*Beckwith. In mythland. v. 1. (Ceres and Proserpina.)
Burt and Ragozin. Herakles and other heroes (*In* Triptolemos).
Chisholm and Steedman. Staircase of stories. (Lost child.)
Coe. Second book of stories. (Ceres and Proserpina.)
Cooke. Nature myths and stories.
Francillon. Gods and heroes. (King and queen of the dead.)
Guerber. Myths of Greece and Rome. (Ceres and Proserpina.)
Hartley. Stories from the Greek legends. (Story of the springtime.)

Proserpina—*continued.*
Hawthorne. Tanglewood tales. (Pomegranate seeds.)
Holbrook. Round the year in myth and song. (Ceres and Persephone.)
Hutchinson. Orpheus with his lute. (Mother and the maid.)
Hyde. Favorite Greek myths. (Ceres and Proserpine.)
Judd. Classic myths. (Legend of the seed.)
Kupfer. Stories of long ago. (Story of the springtime.)
McFee. Treasury of myths. (Persephone.)
Mabie. Myths every child should know. (Pomegranate seeds.)
Olcott. Wonder garden. (Hundred-headed daffodil.)
Patten. Junior classics. v. 3. (Pomegranate seeds.)
Pratt. Fairyland of flowers. (Why the flowers bloom only half the year.)
Pratt. Myths of old Greece. v. 1. (Persephone.)
Shaw. Stories of the ancient Greeks. (Kingdom under the ground.)
Skinner. Emerald story book. (Proserpina and King Pluto.)
Storr. Half a hundred hero tales. (Pluto and Proserpine.)
Storytellers' magazine. Sept. 1913, p. 148. (Story of Persephone.)
Tappan. Stories from the classics. (Pomegranate seeds.)
Wilson. Nature study reader. (Proserpine.)
Proserpine. *See* Proserpina.
Prospect and retrospect. Fielde. Chinese fairy tales.
Prospero and Miranda. Gibbon. Reign of King Cole.
Tappan. Stories from seven old favorites. (Tempest.)
Protesilaus. Storr. Half a hundred hero tales.
Proteus. Baldwin. Story of the golden age. (*In* Voyage on the sea.)
Harrison. In story land. (*In* Strange story of a wonderful sea-god.)
Storytellers' magazine. Sept. 1914, p. 657. (Strange story of a wonderful sea god.)
Proud and foolish peacock. Messer. Next night stories.
Proud brook-grass. Hubbard. Chats with Color-kin.
Proud buckwheat. *See* Buckwheat.
Proud chicken. Davis and Chow-Leung. Chinese fables and folk stories.
Wiggin and Smith. Talking beasts.
Proud cock. Shedlock. Art of the storyteller.
See also Half-chick.
Proud crow. *Spaulding and Bryce. Aldine readers. 2d reader.
See also Jay and the peacock.
Proud doll. Nordau. Dwarf's spectacles.
Proud fox and the crab. *See* How the fox and the crab ran a race.

Proud fox and the young prairie chicken. Johnson. Book of fairy-tale foxes.
Proud frog. *See* Frog and the ox.
Proud king. I. Scudder. Book of legends.
Proud king. II. *See* King Robert of Sicily.
Proud lady and the caterpiller (poem). Æsop. Fables (Burt ed.)
Proud Lady Margaret. Macleod. Book of ballad stories.
Proud leaves. *Elson and Runkel. Elson readers Book 1.
Proud mouse. Riggs. Animal stories from Eskimo land.
Proud oak tree. *See* Oak and the reed.
Proud poppy and the little blue cornflower. McFee. Treasury of flower stories.
Proud princess and the ugly prince. St. Nicholas. May 1908, p. 627.
Proud wolves. Sexton. Gray wolf stories.
Prudent farmer. Laboulaye. Fairy tales. (*In* Captain John's travels.)
Laboulaye. Last fairy tales.
Prudent Hans. Dyer and Brady. Merrill readers. 2d reader. (How Hans did as he was told.)
Grimm. Fairy tales (Lucas tr. Clever Hans.)
Grimm. Household stories (Crane tr.).
Grimm. Household tales (Everyman's ed. Hans and his wife Grettel; Hans in love.)
Lansing. Dramatic readings.
Wiggin and Smith. Tales of laughter. (Discreet Hans.)
See also Epaminondas and his auntie; Lazy Jack; Silly Hans; Silly Matt.
Prunella. *See* Fragolette.
Psyche. I. Andersen. Stories and tales (Author's ed.).
Psyche. II. *See* Cupid and Psyche.
Psyche's tasks. *See* Cupid and Psyche.
Publishing the truth. Children's story garden.
Puck. *See* French Puck; Midsummer's night dream.
Puckwudjee and the morning star. *See* Morning star. I.
Pudding bewitched. Graves. Irish fairy book. (Mad pudding.)
Yeats. Irish fairy and folk tales.
Pudding stone, Story of the. Cooke. Nature myths and stories.
Puddock, Mousie and Ratton. Jacobs. More English fairy tales.
Puddocky. Lang. Forty thieves, and other stories.
Lang. Green fairy book.
See also Frog; Three feathers; White cat.
Pueblo Bluebeard. Lummis. Pueblo Indian folk stories.
Puil. *See* Powell, Prince of Dyfed.
Pulling up the corners. *Dillingham and Emerson. Tell it again stories.
Pulowech and the sea maiden. Partridge. Glooscap the great chief.

Pumpkin and the acorn. *See* Acorn and the pumpkin.
Pumpkin-eater. Harris. Little Mr. Thimblefinger.
Pumpkin giant. Skinner. Topaz story book.
Wilkins. Pot of gold.
Pumpkin-glory. Howells. Christmas every day.
Pumpkin pirates. Olcott. Good stories for great holidays.
Punch and Judy. My Bookhouse. v. 3. (Renowned and world famous adventures of Punch and Judy.)
Punch and Robinetta. Gate. Punch and Robinetta.
Punchinello. I. Coe and Christie. Story hour readers. Book 2.
Punchinello. II. Brady. Green forest fairy book.
Punchkin. Coussens. Jade story book.
Frere. Old Deccan days.
Jacobs. Indian fairy tales.
Patten. Junior classics. v. 1.
Punishment of greed. Martens. Chinese fairy book.
Punishment of the fairy Gangana. Lang. Olive fairy book.
Punishment of the stingy. Grinnell. Punishment of the stingy and other stories.
Pupil who taught the teacher. Shedlock. Eastern legends and stories.
Puppet-show man. Andersen. Fairy tales (Paull tr.).
Purring when you're pleased. Gatty. Parables from nature.
Pursuit of Dermat and Grania. Joyce. Old Celtic romances.
Pursuit of Diarmid. *See* Kilwch and Olwen.
Pursuit of the Gilla Dacker. Graves. Irish fairy book.
Joyce. Old Celtic romances.
Pushpamala, the wreath of flowers. Bradley-Birt. Bengal fairy tales.
Puss in boots; or, The master cat. Aunt Louisa's book of fairy tales.
Bailey. In the animal world. (Adapted.)
Baldwin. Fairy stories and fables.
Carrick. Kitty cat tales.
Chaplin. Treasury of fairy tales.
Coe. First book of stories.
Coussens. Child's book of stories.
Cruikshank. Cruikshank fairy book.
Douglas. Favourite French fairy tales.
Forty famous fairy tales. (Master cat; or, Puss in boots.)
Jacobs. Europa's fairy book. (Earl of Cattenborough.)
Jerrold. Big book of fairy tales.
Johnson. Fir-tree fairy book.
Lang. Blue fairy book.
Lang. Cinderella and other stories. (Master cat.)
Lang. Pretty Goldilocks and other stories. (Master cat; or, Puss in boots.)
Lansing. Fairy tales. v. 1.
Mabie. Fairy tales every child should know.

Puss in boots—*continued.*
Mabie. Heroes and fairies.
Mother Goose rhymes, jingles and fairy tales (Altemus ed.).
Mother Goose's nursery rhymes, tales and jingles (Warne ed.).
Mullock. Fairy book.
Norton. Heart of oak books. v. 2.
Nursery tales.
Patten. Junior classics. v. 1.
Perkins. Twenty best fairy tales.
Perrault. Fairy tales.
Perrault. Old-time stories.
Perrault. Tales of Mother Goose.
Perrault. Tales of passed times.
Pyle. Mother's nursery tales.
Scudder. Book of folk stories.
Scudder. Children's book.
Scudder. Fables and folk stories.
Tappan. Folk stories and fables.
Tweed. Fairy tales everyone should know.
Valentine. Old, old fairy tales (Warne ed.).
Washburn. Old fashioned fairy tales.
Winnington. Outlook fairy book.
See also Domingo's cat; Egyptian Puss in boots; Gagliuso; How the beggar boy turned into Count Piro; Kuzma Skorobogaty; Lord Peter; Palace that stood on golden pillars; Poor Peter.

"Pussy cat, pussy cat, where have you been?" *See* Black cat's journey.

Pussy Tinker's Thanksgiving. Bailey. Stories for Sunday telling.

Pussy willow. Skinner. Emerald story book.

Pussy willow basket. Bailey. Stories for Sunday teling.

Pussy Willow's furs. Walker. Sandman's goodnight stories.

Pussy Willow's hood. Pratt. Fairyland of flowers.

Pussy willows, Origin of. I. Bigham. Overheard in fairyland.

Pussy willows, Origin of. II. *Dillingham and Emerson. Tell it again stories. (Sybil's pussies.)

Pussy willows, Origin of. III. Donaldson. Moons of long ago. (Pussy willows.)

Put it on my bill. Storytellers' magazine. Feb. 1917, p. 67. (Just-for-fun story from Spain.)

Putnam and the wolf. Baldwin. Fifty famous people. (Another wolf story.)
Hartwell. Story hour readings. 5th year.
Sly. World stories retold.

Putnam's ride. Baldwin. Fifty famous rides. (General Putnam's dashing ride.)

Puzzled executor. Butterworth. Zigzag journeys in the Orient. (*In* Ch. 6.)

Pwca of the Trwyn. Thomas. Welsh fairy book.

Pwyll and Rhiannon. *See* Badger in the bag.
Pwyll and the game of badger in the bag. *See* Badger in the bag.
Pwyll, prince of Dyved. *See* Badger in the bag.
Pygmalion and Galatea. *Bailey. Wonder stories. (Wonders Venus wrought.)
Buckley. Children of the dawn. (Sculptor and the image.)
Guerber. Myths of Greece and Rome. (*In* Venus.)
Kupfer. Stories of long ago. (Wonderful sculptor.)
Peabody. Old Greek folk stories.
Pratt. Myths of old Greece. v. 2.
Storr. Half a hundred hero tales. (Pygmalion and the image.)
Tappan. Myths from many lands.
Pygmies. *See* Hercules and his labors.
Pyramus and Thisbe. Guerber. Myths of Greece and Rome. (*In* Venus.)
Patten. Junior classics. v. 2. (Sad story of Pyramus and Thisbe.)
Peabody. Old Greek folk stories.
Storr. Half a hundred hero tales. (Story of Pyramus and Thisbe.)
Storytellers' magazine. May 1916, p. 315. (Why the mulberry's berry is purple.)
Tappan. Stories from the classics.
Pyrrha. *See* Deucalion and Pyrrha.
Pythia. *See* Delphian oracle.

Q

Quack frog. Æsop. Fables (Black ed. Frog and the fox.)
Æsop. Fables (Burt ed. Frog and the fox.)
Æsop. Fables (Stickney).
Quackalina. Alderman. Classics old and new. 3d reader.
Quail and the fowler. Rouse. Talking thrush.
Quail, crow, fly, frog, and elephants. Burlingame. Grateful elephant.
Quails. Babbitt. Jataka tales. (Quarrel of the quails.)
Burlingame. Grateful elephant. (Quails and fowler.)
Cabot. Ethics for children.
*Coe and Christie. Story hour readers. Book 2. (Hindu Sykes and the quails.)
Olcott. Good stories for great holidays.
Storytellers' magazine. Feb. 1915, p. 45.
Van Sickle and Seegmiller. Riverside readers. 4th reader.
See also Pigeon-king and Mouse-king.
Quaking aspen, Legend of. *See* Why the aspen leaves tremble. IV.
Quare gander. Graves. Irish fairy book.
Quarrel. *See* Lion and the bear.
Quarrel in fairyland. *See* Midsummer's night dream.

Quarrel of Sun and Moon. Judson. Myths and legends of the Pacific Northwest.
Quarrel of the dog and cat. *See* Why the dog and cat are enemies. IV.
Quarrel of the goddesses. *See* Paris: Apple of discord.
Quarrel of the monkey and the crab. *See* Crab and the monkey.
Quarrel of the quails. *See* Quails.
Quarrel of the rainbow colors. Storytellers' magazine. Sept. 1914, p. 676.
Quarrelsome wife. Magnus. Russian folk-tales.
Quartette. Wiggin and Smith. Talking beasts.
Queen and the peasant girl. Haaren. Fairy life.
See also Peronella.
Queen Aster. Alcott. Lulu's library. v. 2.
Skinner. Topaz story book.
Queen bee. Adams. Folk story and verse.
Blaisdell. Child life. 2nd reader.
*Bowen. Second story reader. (Kindhearted boy.)
Grimm. Fairy tales (Lucas tr.).
Grimm. Fairy tales (Paull tr.).
*Grimm. Fairy tales (Wiltse). v. 1.
Grimm. Household stories (Crane tr.).
Grimm. Household tales (Burt ed.).
Grimm. Household tales (Everyman's ed.).
Wiggin and Smith. Fairy ring.
Queen Bertha. Evans. Old time tales. (Bertha with the big foot.)
Queen Crane. Stroebe and Martens. Swedish fairy book.
Queen discovers the silkworm. Jenkins. Interesting neighbors.
Queen Hulda and the flax. *See* How flax was given to man.
Queen Mab (poem). Jerrold. Reign of King Oberon.
(poem). Olcott. Book of elves and fairies.
(poem). Rolfe. Fairy tales in prose and verse.
Queen Mab's horns. Gate. Broom fairies.
Queen Margiana, History of. Arabian nights, More tales (Olcott).
Queen of Heart's banquet. Fyleman. Rainbow cat. (Fourth adventure of the rainbow cat.)
Queen of heaven. Martens. Chinese fairy book.
Queen of Lantern Land. Beston. Firelight fairy book.
Queen of the flowery isles. Lang. Grey fairy book.
Lang. Marvellous musician.
Queen of the Golden Mines. MacManus. In chimney corners.
Wiggin and Smith. Tales of wonder.
Queen Philippa and the citizens of Calais. *See* Siege of Calais.
Queen who wished the flowers away. Storytellers' magazine. Dec. 1917, p. 508.

Queendom of Girlicia. Henderson. Sea yarns for boys.
Queen's cat. Bacon. True philosopher.
Queen's champions. Tappan. Old ballads in prose.
Queen's County witch. Yeats. Irish fairy and folk tales.
Queen's museum. Stockton. Bee-man of Orn and other tales.
Stockton. Queen's museum and other tales.
Queen's necklace. Cowles. Art of story-telling.
Nyblom. Jolly Calle.
Queen's treasure. Olcott. Whirling king.
Queen's tree (poem). Lindsay and Poulsson. Joyous traveler. (Tale told by the young lord.)
Queen's wedding dress. Gate. Fortunate days.
Queen's whim. Wardrop. Georgian folk tales.
Queer blockade runner. Henderson. Sea yarns for boys.
Queer company. *See* Strange visitor.
Queer little baker man. Bailey. Stories children need.
Queer partnership. *See* Cat and the mouse in partnership.
Queres Diana. Lummis. Pueblo Indian folk stories.
Query Queer and the flowers. Stocking. City that never was reached.
Quern at the bottom of the sea. *See* Why the sea is salt. II.
Quest for a magic name. Griswold. Hindu fairy tales.
Quest for the eric-fine. *See* Fate of the children of Turenn.
Quest for the nightingale. Lindsay. Story-teller.
Quest of cleverness. Eells. Tales of giants from Brazil.
Quest of Isis. Jewett. Egyptian tales of magic. (When Isis sought her lord.)
Quest of Medusa's head. *See* Perseus.
Quest of Offero. *See* St. Christopher, Legend of.
Quest of the four leaf clover. *See* Abdallah.
Quest of the hammer. *See* Thor: Quest of the hammer.
Quest of the Holy Grail. *See* Holy Grail.
Quest of the magic bow. Cornyn. When the camp fire burns.
Quest of the seven champions. *See* Kilwch and Olwen.
Quest of the sons of Turenn. Rolleston. High deeds of Finn.
Joyce. Old Celtic romances. (Fate of the children of Turenn.)
Quest of the wild duck. Stewart. Once upon a time.
Questing beast. Lang. Tales of the Round Table.
Quick-running squash. Aspinwall. Short stories for short people.
My Bookhouse. v. 1.
Quicoy and the Onglac. Miller. Philipine folklore stories.
Quill pen's stories. Harrison. Bric-a-brac stories.
Quiquern. Kipling. Second jungle book.
Quo-too-quat, the cripple. Linderman. Indian Old-man stories.

R

Ra and Isis, Story of. Brooksbank. Legends of ancient Egypt.
Jewett. Egyptian tales of magic. (Secret name of Ra.)
Rabbi's bogey man. Landa. Aunt Naomi's Jewish fairy tales and legends.
Rabbit and his ears. I. *See* Tar baby. III.
Rabbit and his ears. II. *See* Hare afraid of his ears.
Rabbit and other legends. *See* Rabbit's eyes.
Rabbit and otter. Judson. Old Crow and his friends. (Rabbit makes a plan.)
Stanley. Animal folk tales.
Rabbit and tar wolf. Judson. Old Crow and his friends.
Rabbit and the alligator. Stafford. Animal fables.
Rabbit and the animal wizard. Stafford. Animal fables.
Stanley. Animal folk tales. (Jack Rabbit's wisdom spot.)
Rabbit and the cabbage leaves. *Field second reader.
Rabbit and the ducks. Judson. Old Crow and his friends.
Rabbit and the Easter eggs. *See* Easter rabbit. I.
Rabbit and the elephant. Stafford. Animal fables.
Rabbit and the girl. Storytellers' magazine. July 1915, p. 261.
Rabbit and the grain buyers. Macmillan. Canadian fairy tales.
Rabbit and the Indian chief. Macmillan. Canadian fairy tales.
Rabbit and the monkey. Johnson. Fir-tree fairy book. (Rabbit and the greedy monkey.)
Rouse. Talking thrush.
Rabbit and the moon. Stafford. Animal fables.
Rabbit and the moon-man. Macmillan. Canadian fairy tales.
See also Sun a prisoner. II.
Rabbit and the other animals. Stafford. Animal fables.
Rabbit and the wild cat. Kennedy. New world fairy book.
Olcott. Red Indian fairy book. (Bad wild cat.)
Rabbit and the woodpecker girls. Olcott. Red Indian fairy book. (Woodpecker girls.)
See also Blue Jay the imitator; How Master Rabbit went fishing; Manabozho and the woodpeckers.
Rabbit escapes the wolf's anger. Stafford. Animal fables.
Rabbit in the cabbages. *See* Rabbit's bride.
Rabbit prince. Bourhill and Drake. Fairy tales from South Africa.
Rabbit that wanted red wings. *See* Little rabbit who wanted red wings.
Rabbit who snared the sun. *See* Sun a prisoner. II.
Rabbit who wanted red wings. *See* Little rabbit who wanted red wings.
Rabbit who wanted wings. *See* Little rabbit who wanted red wings.

Rabbit who was afraid. *See* Timid hare.
Rabbit with curly ears. Potter. Pinafore pocket story book.
Rabbits and the dogs. Bryce. Fables from afar.
Rabbits and the elephants. Wiggin and Smith. Talking beasts.
Patten. Junior classics. v. 2. (Old hare and the elephants.)
Rabbit's bride. *Bailey. Stories children need. (Rabbit's housekeeper.)
Darton. Wonder book of beasts.
Grimm. Fairy tales (Paull tr. Hare's bride.)
Grimm. Household stories (Crane tr.).
Johnson. Elm-tree fairy book. (Rabbit in the cabbages.)
My Bookhouse. v. 1. (Little girl and the hare.)
Rabbit's eyes. Allen. Korean tales. (Rabbit and other legends.)
Griffis. Korean fairy tales.
Griffis. Unmannerly tiger and other Korean tales.
Pyle. Wonder tales retold.
See also Monkey and the crocodile; Monkey and the jellyfish.
Rabbit's housekeeper. *See* Rabbit's bride.
Rabbit's riding horse. *See* Buffalo and the rabbit; Elephant and the frog; Mr. Rabbit grossly deceives Mr. Fox; Owl with the great head and eyes.
Raccoon and the bee-tree. Eastman. Wigwam evenings.
Raccoon and the man-of-tar. Chandler. In the reign of coyote.
See also Tar-baby.
Race. *See* Hare and the tortoise.
Race between a reindeer and a tom-cod. Riggs. Animal stories from Eskimo land.
See also Hare and the hedgehog; How a turtle outwitted a wolf; Race of the tails.
Race between hare and hedgehog. *See* Hare and the hedgehog.
Race for a wife. *See* Atalanta's race.
Race for the boundary. Froelicher. Swiss stories.
Race of the hare and the tortoise. *See* Hare and the tortoise.
Race of the tails. Lummis. Pueblo Indian folk stories.
See also Hare and the hedgehog.
Racers. *See* Swiftest runners.
Rag doll's Christmas. Bailey. Stories and rhymes for a child.
Ragamuffins. *See* Vagabonds.
Ragged head. Grinnell. Punishment of the stingy.
Ragged pedlar. Aunt Naomi. Jewish fairy tales and fables.
My Bookhouse. v. 3.
Raggylug. Bryant. Best stories to tell to children.
Bryant. How to tell stories to children.

Raging host. Guerber. Legends of the Rhine.
See also Emperor's sleep.
Ragnar Lodbrok. Guerber. Legends of the middle ages.
Rags. Andersen. Stories and tales (Author's ed.).
Rags and Tatters. Macdonell. Italian fairy book.
Storytellers' magazine. Oct. 1915, p. 359.
Ragweed. Olcott. Book of elves and fairies.
Rai-taro, the son of the Thunder God. *See* Child of the thunder.
Raid on the wind people. Judson. Myths and legends of Alaska. (Wind people.)
Judson. Old Crow and his friends.
Raiko and his guards. Griffis. Japanese fairy tales.
Raiko slays the demons. Griffis. Japanese fairy tales.
Rain and the snow. *See* How the rain comes.
Rain Bird. *Field second reader.
Rain elves. Walker. Sandman's goodnight stories.
Rain goblins. Eliot. House on the edge of things.
Storytellers' magazine. Oct. 1915, p. 333.
Rain-maker. *See* Mr. Rabbit as a rain-maker.
Rainbow. Brooks. Stories of the red children.
Pratt. Legends of the red children.
Tanner. Legends from the red man's forest.
See also Robe of feathers; Scarf of the lady.
Rainbow and the autumn leaves. *See* Why the autumn leaves are red. I.
Rainbow bridge. *See* Iris.
Rainbow cat and the giantess. Fyleman. Rainbow cat. (Third adventure of the rainbow cat.)
Rainbow cat and the thunder giant. Fyleman. Rainbow cat. (First adventure of the rainbow cat.)
Rainbow children. Pyle. Counterpane fairy.
Rainbow fairies. Bryce. That's why stories.
Rainbow girl. *See* Leilani.
Rainbow sisters. Harrison. Moon princess.
Rainbow snake. Tanner. Legends from the red man's forest. (Another story of the rainbow.)
(poem). Wilson. Myths of the red children.
Raincloud. Æsop. Fables (Stickney. Supplement).
Bryce. Fables from afar.
See also Cloud.
Rairu and the star maiden. Finger. Tales from silver lands.
Raising the flag. Bailey. Friendly tales.
Raja Rasalu. Coussens. Jade story book. (Rajah Rasalu; Rasalu, the fakir and the giants.)
Jacobs. Indian fairy tales.
This includes: How Raja Rasalu went out into the world; How Raja Rasalu journeyed to the city of King Sarkap; How Raja Rasalu swung the seventy fair maidens, daughters of the King; How Raja Rasalu played chaupur with King Sarkap.

Raja Rasalu—*continued.*
Steel. Tales of the Punjab.
This includes: How Raja Rasalu was born; How Raja Rasalu went out into the world; How Raja Rasalu's friends forsook him; How Raja Rasalu killed the giants; How Raja Rasalu became a jogi; How Raja Rasalu journeyed to the city of King Sarkap; How Raja Rasalu swung the seventy fair maidens; How Raja Rasalu played chaupur with King Sarkap.
Rajeb's reward. Jokai and others. Golden fairy book.
Wiggin and Smith. Magic casements.
Rakshas' palace. Frere. Old Deccan days.
Pyle. Fairy tales from many lands. (Two sisters.)
Wiggin and Smith. Tales of wonder. (Rakshas's palace.)
Raleigh's cloak. Baker and Carpenter. Language readers. 6th year. (Queen Elizabeth and Sir Walter Raleigh.)
Baldwin. Fifty famous stories. (Sir Walter Raleigh.)
Blaisdell. Child life. 5th reader.
Blaisdell. English history story book. (Sir Walter Raleigh.)
Lansing. Dramatic readings. (Queen Elizabeth and Sir Walter Raleigh.)
Sly. World stories retold. (Sir Walter Raleigh.)
Welsh. Stories children love.
Ram. Aulnoy. Fairy tales.
Lang. Blue fairy book. (Wonderful sheep.)
Lang. Prince Darling and other fairy stories. (Wonderful sheep.)
Ram and the pig. Asbjörnsen. Fairy tales from the far north. (Ram and the pig who went into the woods to live by themselves.)
Asbjörnsen. Tales from the fjeld. (Sheep and the pig who set up house.)
*Bailey. Folk stories and fables. (Sheep and the pig.)
Bailey and Lewis. For the children's hour. (Sheep and the pig.)
*Burchill. Progressive road to reading: Story steps. (Sheep, the pig, the cow and the goose.)
*Elson and Runkel. Elson readers. Book 2. (Animals that found a home.)
Esenwein and Stockard. Children's stories. (Sheep and the pig who set up housekeeping.)
Gade. Norwegian fairy tales. (Ram and the pig who went into the woods to live by themselves.)
*Grover. Folk-lore stories. v. 1. (How the pig built a house.)
My Bookhouse. v. 1. (Sheep and the pig that made a home.)
O'Grady and Throop. Teachers' story teller's book. (Sheep and the pig that built the house.)
*Old, old tales retold. (House on the hill.)
Peck. Stories for good children. (Goat and the pig.)

Ram and the pig—*continued.*
Thorne-Thomsen. East o' the sun and west o' the moon. (Sheep and the pig who set up housekeeping.)
Wiggin and Smith. Fairy ring. (Ram and the pig who went into the woods to live by themselves.)
Wiltse. Folklore stories and proverbs. (Sheep and the pig.)
See also Piggy Wig's house.
Ram and the pig who went into the woods to live by themselves. *See* Ram and the pig.
Ram with the golden fleece. *See* Argonauts.
Rama. My Bookhouse. v. 5. (Exile of Rama.)
Rama and Luxman; or, The learned owl. Frere. Old Deccan days.
Rapunzel. Bates. Once upon a time.
Chisholm. In fairy land.
Grimm. Fairy tales (Lucas tr.).
Grimm. Fairy tales (Paull tr.).
Grimm. Household stories (Crane tr.).
Grimm. Household tales (Burt ed. Garden of the sorceress.)
Lang. King of the waterfalls.
Lang. Red fairy book.
Lansing. Fairy tales. v. 1.
Wiggin and Smith. Fairy ring.
Rashin-Coatie. I. Baldwin. Another fairy reader. (Rushy-coat.)
Douglas. Scottish fairy tales.
Rashin-Coatie. II. Jacobs. More English fairy tales. (Rushen Coatie.)
See also Cinderella; Nippit-fit and Clippit-fit; Golden slipper.
Rasberry worm. Lang. Lilac fairy book.
Lang. White doe.
Rat and the elephant. Æsop. Fables (Stickney).
(poem). Wiggin and Smith. Talking beasts.
See also Circus parade.
Rat and the king. Burchill. Progressive road to reading. Book 1.
Rat and the oyster (poem). Wiggin and Smith. Talking beasts.
See also Ringtail's journey.
Rat and the toad. Wiggin and Smith. Talking beasts.
Rat catcher *See* Pied piper of Hamelin.
Rat catcher and cats (poem). Wiggin and Smith. Talking beasts.
Rat hall. Douglas. Scottish fairy tales.
Rat meetings. Bigham. Merry animal tales.
See also Belling the cat.
Rat princess. *See* Rats and their son-in-law.
Rat, the hen, the pig and the duck. *See* Little red hen. I.
Rat tower. *See* Mouse tower.
Rata, Legend of. Patten. Junior classics. v. 2.

Rats and the cat. *See* Belling the cat.
Rats and the cheese (poem). Æsop. Fables (Burt ed.).
(poem). Wiggin and Smith. Talking beasts.
See also Cheese house.
Rats and their son-in-law. Bryant. How to tell stories to children. (Rat princess.)
*Coe and Christie. Story hour reader. Book 2. (Mayor Rat's niece.)
James. Green willow. (Espousal of the rat's daughter.)
Johnson. Birch-tree fairy book. (Nezumi the beautiful.)
Lang. Brown fairy book. (Husband of the rat's daughter.)
Lang. Magician's gifts. (Husband of the rat's daughter.)
Storytellers' magazine. Oct. 1915, p. 363. (Two rats.)
Tappan. Myths from many lands. (Nedzumi.)
Wiggin and Smith. Tales of laughter.
See also Bridegroom for Miss Mole; So born, so die.
Rats, the fox and the egg. *Grover. Folk lore readers. v. 1.
(poem). Wiggin and Smith. Talking beasts. (Two rats, the fox and the egg.)
See also Blackie's egg.
Rat's wedding. Esenwein and Stockard. Children's stories. (Clever rat. Adapted.)
Patten. Junior classics. v. 1.
Steel. Tales of the Punjab.
See also Boy who was called Thick-head; Hans in luck; Monkey's bargains.
Rattan vine and the rose tree. Davis and Chow-Leung. Chinese fables and folk stories.
Rattle-rattle-rattle and chink-chink-chink. Fillmore. Czechoslovak fairy tales.
Raven. I. Grimm. Fairy tales (Lucas tr.).
Grimm. Fairy tales (Paull tr.).
Grimm. Household stories (Crane tr.).
Grimm. Household tales (Everyman's ed.).
Raven. II. Allen. Indian fairy tales.
Raven. III. (poem). Wiggin and Smith. Talking beasts.
Raven. IV. *See* Raven and the cattle.
Raven and coot. *See* Why the raven's feathers are black. III.
Raven and his mother-in-law. Eastman. Indian legends retold.
Raven and marmot. Bayliss. Treasury of Eskimo tales. (Marmot and the Raven.)
Judson. Myths and legends of Alaska.
Judson. Old Crow and his friends. (Raven's adventures.)
Raven and Pitch. Judson. Myths and legends of Alaska.
Raven and the cattle. Bryce. Fables from afar. (Raven.)
Tappan. Folk stories and fables.
Raven and the children. Eastman. Indian legends retold.
Raven and the crab. Eastman. Indian legends retold.
Raven and the geese. Bayliss. Treasury of Eskimo tales.
Judson. Myths and legends of Alaska. (Raven's marriage.)

Raven and the gulls. Judson. Myths and legends of Alaska.
See also Raven's adventures.
Raven and the hunters. Eastman. Indian legends retold.
Raven and the salmon woman. Eastman. Indian legends retold.
Raven and the seals. Judson. Myths and legends of Alaska.
Raven and the serpent. Æsop. Fables (Black ed.).
Æsop. Fables (Burt ed.).
Raven and the swan. Æsop. Fables (Stickney).
Raven finds sun. Judson. Old Crow stories.
Raven makes an ocean voyage. Bayliss. Treasury of Eskimo tales.
Raven of Salby. Grundtvig. Danish fairy tales.
Ravens. Storytellers' magazine. Nov. 1915, p. 405.
See also Language of birds.
Raven's adventures. Judson. Myths and legends of Alaska. (Raven myth.)
Judson. Old Crow and his friends.
Raven's dancing blanket. Eastman. Indian legends retold. (Beautiful blanket.)
Judson. Myths and legends of Alaska.
See also Robe of Kemush.
Raven's feast. Judson. Myths and legends of Alaska.
Raven's marriage. *See* Raven and the geese.
Raw recruit. Guerber. Legends of the Rhine.
"Read, and you will know." Baldwin. Fifty famous people.
Real African swell. Henderson. Sea yarns for boys.
Real hallowe'en witch. Bailey. Friendly tales.
Real people vanish. Judson. Old Crow stories.
Real princess. *See* Princess on the pea.
Realm of stone. Magnus. Russian folk-tales.
Realms of copper, silver and gold. Magnus. Russian folk-tales.
Rebellious waters. Friedlander. Jewish fairy book.
Recipe for a happy day. Gruelle. Friendly fairies.
Red bandits of Montgomery. *See* Sili go Dwt.
Red bear. Bayliss. Treasury of Eskimo tales.
Red-boots. Aspinwall. Short stories for short people.
Red-bud tree. Babbitt. More Jataka tales.
Shedlock. Eastern legends and stories. (Judas tree.)
See also Blind men and the elephant; Two sides to every question.
Red bull of Norroway. Mother Goose's nursery rhymes, tales and jingles (Warne ed. Bull of Norroway.)
Singleton. Goldenrod fairy book.
See also Black bull of Norroway.
Red cloud. Storytellers' magazine. April 1914, p. 513.
Red crowned warbler. Young. Plantation bird legends.
Red dog. I. Kipling. Second jungle book.
Red dog. II. Allen. Indian fairy tales.
Red elf. Hume. Chronicles of fairyland.

Red-Etin. *See* Red-Ettin.
Red-Ettin. Grierson. Scottish fairy book. (Red-Etin.)
Jacobs. English fairy tales.
Lang. Blue fairy book.
Red geranium. Farmer. Nature myths.
Skinner. Turquoise story book. (Legend of the red geranium.)
Red-headed stranger. *See* First corn. IV.
Red-headed woodpecker. *See* Why the woodpecker's head is red.
Red King and his wife. Grierson. Scottish fairy book.
Red pony. Graves. Irish fairy book.
Red Riding Hood. *See* Little Red Riding Hood.
Red roses of nectar. Olcott. Wonder garden.
Red shoes. I. Andersen. Fairy tales (Lucas tr.).
Andersen. Fairy tales (Paull tr.).
Andersen. Wonder stories (Author's ed.).
Chisholm. Enchanted land.
Scudder. Children's book.
(play). Stevenson. Plays for the home.
Red shoes. II. Bakewell. True fairy stories.
Red skeleton. Bayliss. Treasury of Eskimo tales.
Red slipper. Landa. Aunt Naomi's Jewish fairy tales and legends.
Red Swan. Compton. American Indian fairy tales.
Pyle. Where the wind blows.
Schoolcraft. Indian fairy book.
Red, the black, the yellow. Gate. Broom fairies.
Red thread of courage. Bryant. How to tell stories to children.
Sly. World stories retold. (Wrists bound with the red thread.)
Red troll. Brown. Mermaid's gift.
Redbreast and the sparrow. Æsop. Fables (Burt ed.).
Redeeming power of the Ganges. Bradley-Birt. Bengal fairy tales.
Redemption from fairy land. Douglas. Scottish fairy tales.
Reed that was a maiden. *See* Pan.
Reeds and the oak. *See* Oak and the reed.
Reeds that told a secret. *See* Midas. II.
Reflected glory. Rouse. Talking thrush.
Reflections. Hearn. Japanese fairy tales.
James. Green willow.
See also Mirror of Matsuyama; Mirror that made trouble.
Reformed pirate. Stockton. Floating prince.
Regulus. Baldwin. Fifty famous stories.
Reign of King Oberon. Jerrold. Reign of King Oberon.
Reign of the twelve kings. Brooksbank. Legends of ancient Egypt.
Reinecke's revenge on Isegrim. Houghton. Russian grandmother's wonder tales.

Reinecke's revenge on Isegrim—*continued.*
*Van Sickle and Seegmiller. Riverside readers. 2d reader. (Fox and the colt.)
Remaking of real people. *See* Creation of mankind (Indian.)
Remarkable rocket. Wilde. Fairy tales.
Renaud of Montauban. Wilmot-Buxton. Stories from old French romance. (Story of the Castle of Montauban.)
See also Sons of Aymon.
Renowned hero, Bova Korolevich and the Princess Drushneva. Steele. Russian garland of fairy tales.
Rent-day. Yeats. Irish fairy and folk tales.
Repentant peacock. Pearson. Laughing lion and other stories.
Rescue of the Princess Winsome (play). Johnson. Little Colonel's hero.
Rescue from the elves. *See* Smith and the fairies.
Rescued knight. Guerber. Legends of the Rhine.
Resurrection of St. Maternus. Guerber. Legends of the Rhine.
Retribution. Martens. Chinese fairy book.
Retrospection. Linderman. Indian why stories.
Rerir, King. Guerber. Myths of northern lands. (*In* Frigga.)
Return of Glooscap. Partridge. Glooscap the great chief.
See also Glooskap and the giant's frolic; Glooskap and the tortoise.
Return of the dead wife. Lang. Strange story book.
Revenge of Horus. Jewett. Egyptian tales of magic.
Revenge of the fawns. Lummis. Pueblo Indian folk stories.
Revenge of the fireflies. Walker. Sandman's goodnight stories.
Revenge of the gnomes. Walker. Sandman's goodnight stories.
Revengeful ghost. Guerber. Legends of the Rhine.
Revere, Paul. Baldwin. Fifty famous people. (Midnight ride.)
Reward of industry. Bourhill and Drake. Fairy tales from South Africa.
Reward of kindness. Fillmore. Mighty Mikko.
Reward of the world. Bosschère. Folk tales of Flanders.
See also Camel driver and the adder; Ingratitude; Snake's thanks; Way of the world; Well done, ill paid.
Reynard and Bruin. Jacobs. Europa's fairy book.
Reynard and Chanticleer. *See* Cock and the fox. III.
Reynard and his adventures. *See* Why the bear has a stumpy tail.
Reynard and the cock. *See* Cock and the fox. III.
Reynard and the fox-hunter. Jacobs. More Celtic fairy tales. (*In* Russet dog.)
Johnson. Book of fairy-tale foxes.

Reynard and the fox-hunter—*continued.*
Spaulding and Bryce. Aldine readers. Book 3. (*In* Russet dog.)
Reynard and the little birds. *See* Bird, the fox, and the dog.
Reynard tastes horseflesh. *See* Reynard wants to taste horseflesh.
Reynard the fox. Bosschère. Folk tales of Flanders. (Trial of Reynard the fox.)
This contains: How Chanticleer the cock made complaint against Reynard; How Bruin the bear was sent to bring Reynard to court; King's messenger and how he fared; How the badger brought Reynard to court; How Reynard told the king of a hidden treasure.
Darton. Wonder book of beasts.
Guerber. Legends of the middle ages.
Hodgkins. Atlantic treasury of childhood stories. (How Bruin fared with Reynard the fox.)
Reynard wants to taste horse-flesh. Asbjörnsen. Fairy tales from the far north.
Asbjörnsen. Tales from the fjeld.
Dasent. Norse fairy tales. (Reynard tastes horseflesh.)
Johnson. Book of fairy-tale foxes. (Reynard's ride.)
Patten. Junior classics. v. 1. (Bear and the fox.)
Wiggin and Smith. Tales of laughter.
Reynard's ride. *See* Reynard wants to taste horse-flesh.
Rhine gold. *See* Ring: Rhine gold.
Rhodanthe. *See* Rose-tree queen.
Rhodopis and her little gilded sandals. My Bookhouse. v. 3.
Rhœcus. Beckwith. In mythland. v. 2.
*Benson. Really truly fairy stories.
Coe. Second book of stories.
Firth. Stories of old Greece.
Olcott. Good stories for great holidays. (Dryad of the old oak.)
Storytellers' magazine. June 1914, p. 609. (Story of Rhoecus.)
See also Comatos and the bees; Love of the dryad.
Rhys and Llywelyn. Thomas. Welsh fairy book.
Rice measure. *See* Measure of rice.
Rich brother and the poor brother. Lang. Lilac fairy book.
Rich dog and poor dog. Nordau. Dwarf's spectacles.
Rich farmer's wife. *See* Squire's bride.
Rich goose. Bailey and Lewis. For the children's hour.
(play). Elson and Runkel. Elson readers. Book 2. (Foolish goose.)
Rich Klaus. Froelicher. Swiss stories.
Rich man and the bundle of wood. Bidpai. Tortoise and the geese.
Rich man's guest. Bryce. Fables from afar.
(play). Lansing. Quaint old stories.

Rich man's prayer. Success library. v. 3.
Rich Peter the huckster. *See* Rich Peter the pedlar.
Rich Peter the pedlar. Dasent. Popular tales from the Norse.
Dasent. Norse fairy tales.
Thorpe. Yule-tide stories. (Rich Peter the huckster.)
See also Giant with the golden hair.
Rich woman and the poor woman. Bosschère. Christmas tales of Flanders.
Richard Cœur de Leon. Baldwin. Thirty more famous stories. (King Richard and Blondel.)
Blaisdell. English history story book.
Evans. Old time tales. (Adventures of Richard the lion heart.)
Evans. Old time tales. (Meeting of King Richard and Saladin.)
Guerber. Legends of the Rhine. (Faithful minstrel.)
Johonnot. Stories of the olden time. (King Richard Cœur de Leon in the Holy Land.)
Herbertson. Heroic legends. (How the minstrel saved the king.)
Mabie. Heroes and fairies. (Richard the Lion-hearted.)
Mabie. Heroes every child should know. (Richard the Lion-hearted.)
Morris. Historical tales: English.
Wilmot-Buxton. Stories of early England. (Story of Richard Lion-Heart.)
Richest man. Thomas. Welsh fairy book.
Richman, Fairman and Humility. Winnington. Outlook fairy book.
Ricky of the tuft. *See* Riquet with the tuft.
Riddle. I. Grimm. Fairy tales (Paull tr.).
Grimm. Household tales (Burt ed.).
Lang. Green fairy book.
Lang. Three dwarfs and other stories.
See also Ridere of riddles.
Riddle. II. *See* Œdipus.
Riddle of the Sphinx. *See* Œdipus.
Ride on the wooden horse. *See* Enchanted horse.
Ridere of riddles. Jacobs. More Celtic fairy tales.
See also Riddle I.
Rieggi and the white chamois. Froelicher. Swiss stories.
See also White Chamois.
Riger. *See* Heimdall.
Right answer. Storytellers' magazine. Sept. 1917, p. 352.
Right time to laugh. My Bookhouse. v. 2.
"Rikki-tikki-tavi." Kipling. Jungle book.
Rinaldo and Bayard. *See* Sons of Aymon.
Rinaldo and his wonderful horse Bayard. *See* Sons of Aymon.
Rinda. *See* Odin and Rinda.
Ring. Baring. Blue rose fairy book.

Ring: Rhine gold. Barber. Wagner opera stories.
McSpadden. Stories from great operas. (Ring of the curse; Rhinegold.)
McSpadden. Stories from Wagner. (Ring of the curse: Rhine-gold.)
Wheelock. Stories of Wagner operas.
See also Andvare's golden ring.
Ring: Siegfried. Barber. Wagner opera stories.
Bryant. Treasury of hero tales. (Siegfried the fearless. Abridged.)
McSpadden. Stories from great operas. (Ring of the curse: Siegfried the fearless.)
McSpadden. Stories from Wagner. (Ring of the curse: Siegfried the fearless.)
Maud. Wagner's heroines. (Brunhilda.)
Stewart. Tell me a hero story. (Sigurd and the dragon; The golden hoard. Adapted.)
Wheelock. Stories of Wagner operas.
See also Horse who rode though fire; Nibelungenlied; Siegfried with the horny skin; Sigurd the Volsung.
Ring: Twilight of the gods. Barber. Wagner opera stories. (Götterdämmerung.)
McSpadden. Stories from great operas. (Ring of the curse: Downfall of the gods.)
McSpadden. Stories from Wagner. (Ring of the curse: Downfall of the gods.)
Maud. Wagner's heroines. (Brunhilda.)
Wheelock. Stories of Wagner operas. (Dusk of the gods.)
See also Nibelungenlied; Sigurd the Volsung.
Ring: War maidens. Barber. Wagner opera stories. (Walküre; or, Story of Brunhilde.)
McSpadden. Stories from great operas. (Ring of the curse: War maidens.)
McSpadden. Stories from Wagner. (Ring of the curse: War maidens.)
Maud. Wagner's heroines. (Brunhilda.)
Wheelock. Stories of Wagner operas. (Walkyries.)
See also Nibelungenlied; Sigurd the Volsung.
Ring and the veil. Byrne. Modern Greek fairy tales.
Ring of Polycrates. Brooksbank. Legends of ancient Egypt. (*In* Shadow of the end.)
Francillon. Gods and heroes. (*In* The kingdom.)
Shaw. Stories of the ancient Greeks. (Ring of Polycrates.)
Storr. Half a hundred hero tales.
Ring of the curse. *See* Ring: Rhine-gold.
Ring with twelve screws. Curtin. Wonder-tales from Russia.
See also Enchanted ring.
Ringfinger. Underhill. Dwarfs' tailor and other fairy tales.
Ringtail's journey. Bigham. Merry animal tales.
See also Rat and the oyster.

Rip Van Winkle. I. Almost true tales.
Arnold and Gilbert. Stepping stones to literature. v. 6.
Baker and Carpenter. Language readers. 6th year.
Blaisdell. Child life. 5th reader.
Lang. Strange story book.
Mabie. Legends every child should know.
Norton. Heart of oak books. v. 5.
Patten. Junior classics. v. 2.
Stone. Children's stories that never grow old.
Tappan. Modern stories.
Van Sickle and Seegmiller. Riverside readers. 8th reader.
Welsh. Stories children love.
See also Fairy huntsmen; Feast of lanterns; Karl Katz; Sleep of one hundred years; Vision of Tsunu; Woodman and the mountain fairies.
Rip Van Winkle. II. *See* Miser of Takhoma.
Rip Van Winkle. III. *See* Vision of Tsunu.
Rip Van Winkle, Jewish. *See* Sleep of one hundred years.
Ripple, the water sprite. Alcott. Flower fables.
Alcott. Lulu's library. v. 2.
Riquet of the tuft. *See* Riquet with the tuft.
Riquet with the tuft. Douglas. Favourite French fairy tales.
Jerrold. Reign of King Oberon.
Lansing. Fairy tales. v. 2.
Mulock. Fairy book.
Perrault. Fairy tales. (Riquet of the tuft.)
Perrault. Old-time stories. (Ricky of the tuft.)
Perrault. Tales of Mother Goose.
Perrault. Tales of passed times.
Scudder. Children's book.
Valentine. Old, old fairy tales (Warne ed.).
Welsh. Fairy tales children love.
Wiggin and Smith. Fairy ring.
Rising in the north (poem). Lanier. Boy's Percy.
Riul doamnei. *See* River of the princess.
Rival roosters. Stafford. Animal fables.
River dragon's bride. Fisher. River dragon's bride.
River-fish and the money. Shedlock. Eastern stories and legends.
River-fish and the sea-fish. Æsop. Fables (Black ed.).
Æsop. Fables (Burt ed.).
River of gold. *See* King of the Golden River.
River of the princess. Sylva and Strettell. Legends from river and mountain. (Riul doamnei, river of the princess.)
Road. Richards. Golden windows.
Road and the light. Sologub. Sweet-scented name.
Road to fortune. Wiggin and Smith. Fairy ring.
Road to the castle. Bailey. Stories for Sunday telling.
Road up the hill. Bailey. Stories for Sunday telling.

Roaring bull o' Bagbury. Hartland. English folk and fairy tales.
Roast pig, Origin of. Olcott and Pendleton. Jolly book. (Dissertation upon roast pig.)
Tappan. Book of humor. (Dissertation upon roast pig.)
Thomas. Young folk's book of mirth.
Robber bridegroom. Grimm. Fairy tales (Lucas tr.).
Grimm. Fairy tales (Paull tr.).
Grimm. Household stories (Crane tr.).
Grimm. Household tales (Burt ed.).
Grimm. Household tales (Everyman's ed.).
See also Mr. Fox; Sweetheart in the wood.
Robber fox and the little red hen. *See* Little red hen. II.
Robber kitten (poem). O'Grady and Throop. Teachers' storyteller's book.
Robber knight. Guerber. Legends of the Rhine.
Robber rat and the kitten. Carter. Cat stories.
Pyle. Careless Jane.
Robbers. *See* Bremen town musicians.
Robe of feathers. Nixon-Roulet. Japanese folk stories and fairy tales. (Angel's robe. Adapted.)
Olcott. Wonder garden.
Storytellers' magazine. Nov. 1915, p. 424.
Robe of Kemush. Judson. Myths and legends of the Pacific Northwest.
See also Raven's dancing blanket.
Robert of Sicily. *See* King Robert of Sicily.
Robert Scott and the gnomes. Johnson. Birch-tree fairy book.
Robert the evil. Baring-Gould. Old English fairy tales.
Robin. I. *See* How the robin came.
Robin. II. *See* Why the robin has a red breast. II.
Robin. III. Young Plantation bird legends.
Robin and the raven. Dyer and Brady. Merrill readers. 2d reader.
Robin and the salmon berry. Chandler. In the reign of coyote.
Robin and the turtle. Ketchum and Jorgensen. Kindergarten gems.
Robin and the violet. Field. Little book of profitable tales.
Robin Goodfellow. Hodgkins. Atlantic treasury of childhood stories. (Merry pranks of Robin Goodfellow.)
(poem). Jerrold. Reign of King Oberon. (Pranks of Robin Goodfellow.)
Lansing. Tales of old England.
Olcott. Book of elves and fairies. (Adventures of Robin Goodfellow.)
Rhys. Fairy gold.
(poem). Rolfe. Fairy tales in prose and verse. (Merry pranks of Robin Goodfellow.)
Skinner. Turquoise story book.

Robin Hood. Baldwin. Fifty famous stories. (A story of Robin Hood.)
Blaisdell. English history story book. (Robin Hood's last shot.)
Bryant. Treasury of hero tales. (How Robin Hood met Little John.)
Cowles. Art of story telling. (Robin Hood and Sir Richard-at-the-Lee.)
Crommelin. Famous legends.
Haaren. Ballads and tales. (Robin Hood and Little John.)
Hartwell. Story hour readings. 5th year. (Greenwood hunter.)
Hartwell. Story hour readings. 6th year. (Archery contest.)
Herbertson. Heroic legends. (With bow and arrow.)
Lang. Book of romance.
Lang. Tales of romance.
(poem). Lanier. Boy's Percy. (Robin Hood and Guy of Gisborne.)
Mabie. Heroes and fairies.
Mabie. Heroes every child should know.
Macleod. Book of ballad stories. (Robin Hood and his merry men.)
Morris. Historical tales: English. (Robin Hood and the knight of the rueful countenance.)
My Bookhouse. v. 5. (Merry doings of Robin Hood.)
Murray. Story book treasures. (Robin Hood and the golden arrow.
Patten. Junior classics. v. 4.
(poem). Scudder. Children's book. (Robin Hood and Allin a Dale; Robin Hood and the Bishop of Hereford.)
Stebbins. 3d reader.
Stewart. Tell me a hero story. (*In* Forest of Sherwood.)
Tappan. Old ballads in prose.
Tappan. Stories of legendary heroes. (Robin Hood and the butcher; Robin Hood and the sorrowful knight.)
Wickes. Happy holidays. (A-maying.)

Robin Redbreast. I. *See* How the robin came.

Robin Redbreast. II. *See* Why the robin has a red breast. V and VII.

Robin Red-breast and the red rose. Faulkner. Story lady's book.

Robin that would not go south (play). Field third reader.

Robin, the crow, and the fox. *See* Fox and the crow. II.

Robin's Christmas. *See* Robin's Christmas song.

Robin's Christmas song. *Bailey. Stories children need.
Bailey. Once upon a time animal stories.
*Baldwin. Second fairy reader. (Wee Robin Redbreast.)
Cowles. Art of story telling. (Robin's Christmas.)
Curry. Little classics. (Marriage of Cock Robin and Jenny Wren.)

Robin's Christmas song—*continued.*
(play). Doheny. Play awhile. (Wedding of Robin Redbreast and Jenny Wren.)
Douglas. Scottish fairy tales. (Marriage of Robin Redbreast and the wren.)
Grierson. Scottish fairy book. (Wedding of Robin Redbreast and Jenny Wren.)
Johnson. Birch-tree fairy book.
Lansing. Rhymes and stories. (Robin's Yule song.)
My Bookhouse. v. 1. (Wee robin's Christmas song.)
O'Grady and Throop. Teachers' story teller's book. (Wee Robin's Christmas day.)
Wiggin and Smith. Tales of laughter. (Wee Robin's Yule-song.)
See also Cock Robin.

Robin's return. Thomas. Welsh fairy book.

Robin's summer in town. Donahey. Tales to be told to children.

Robinsen. Gregory. Kiltartan wonder book.

Robinson Crusoe. Baker and Carpenter. Language readers. 5th year.
Baldwin. Fifty famous people. (Story of a great story.)

Rock. *See* Rolling rock.

Rock elephant. Scudder. Seven little people.

Rock of the measuring worm. Bouvé. Lamplight fairy tales. (Legend of the measuring worm.)
Brooks. Stories of the red children. (How the patient worm saved the children.)
Cowles. Indian nature myths.
Harper. Story-hour favorites. (Legend of the tutokanula.)
Judson. Old Crow and his friends. (More sky-land adventures.)
Pratt. Legends of the red children. (Mount Tutokanula.)

Rocks removed. Darton. Tales of the Canterbury pilgrims. (Franklin's tale: The rocks removed.)
McSpadden. Stories from Chaucer. (Franklin's tale: Dorigen.)
Storr and Turner. Canterbury chimes. (Franklin's tale: Dorigen.)

Roebuck hunt. Cary. French fairy tales.

Roedeer princess. Grundtvig. Danish fairy tales.

Rogue and the herdsman. Lang. Crimson fairy book.
Lang. Little Wildrose.

Rogue and the simpleton. Tappan. Folk stories and fables.

Rogue's holiday. *See* Vagabonds.

Roland. I. Grimm. Fairy tales (Lucas tr. Sweetheart Roland.)
Grimm. Household stories (Crane tr.).
Grimm. Household tales (Burt ed. Shepherd's flower.)

Roland. II. Baker and Carpenter. Language readers. 5th year. (Roland and his horn.)

Roland. II.—*continued.*
Baldwin. Hero tales told in school. (What happened at Roncesvaux.)
Crommelin. Famous legends.
Evans. Old time tales. (Roland becomes a knight; Death of Roland.)
Guerber. Legends of the Rhine. (Roland's first adventure.)
Haaren. Ballads and tales. (Death of Roland.)
Herbertson. Heroic legends. (Keeping of the passes.)
Johonnot. Stories of thè olden time. (Roland for an Oliver.)
Lang. Book of romance.
Lansing. Page, esquire and knight. (Roland, a knight of France.)
Mabie. Heroes and fairies.
Mabie. Heroes every child should know.
My Bookhouse. v. 5. (Story of Roland, a song of deeds.)
Patten. Junior classics. v. 4. (Roland for an Oliver; Treason of Ganelon; Battle of Roncesvalles.)
Stewart. Tell me a hero story. (Boyhood of Roland; Song of Roland.)
Storytellers' magazine. Sept. 1914, p. 655.
Wilmot-Buxton. Stories from old French romance. (Roland and Oliver; Death of Roland.)
Roland at Drachenfels. Guerber. Legends of the Rhine. (Story of Roland.)
Roland for an Oliver. *See* Roland. II.
Roleyboley and his comrades. English. Fairy stories and wonder tales.
Rolf of Örkanäs. Nyblom. Jolly Calle.
Roll-call of the reef. Smith. More mystery tales.
Tyler. Twenty-four unusual stories.
Rolling rock. Grinnell. Blackfoot lodge tales. (Rock.)
Olcott. Red Indian fairy book.
See also Coyote and rolling rock; Coyote steals a blanket; Why the nighthawk's wings are beautiful; Wolverine and the rock.
Rollo. Evans. Old time tales. (How Normandy came by its name.)
Haaren and Poland. Famous men of the middle ages.
Johonnot. Stories of the olden time. (Rolf the ganger.)
Rollright stones, Legend of the. Hartland. English folk and fairy tales.
Roman father. *See* Virginius and his daughter.
Romeo and Juliet. Pleasanton. Fairyland of opera.
Romulus and Remus. Baldwin. Thirty more famous stories. (How Rome was founded.)
*Burchill. Progressive road to reading. Book 3.
Guerber. Myths of Greece and Rome. (*In* Mars.)
Guerber. Story of the Romans. (Wolf and the twins.)
Haaren and Poland. Famous men of Rome. (Romulus.)
Laing. Seven kings of the seven hills.

Romulus and Remus—*continued.*
Patten. Junior classics. v. 3. (Story of Romulus and of Numa.)
Storr. Half a hundred hero tales.
Rondel. Fyleman. Rainbow cat.
Roof of sausages. Tappan. Golden goose.
See also Hansel and Grethel.
Rooster telephone. Cocke. Bypaths in Dixie.
Rooster, the cat, and the reap-hook. *See* Fortune seekers. I.
Rooster, the handmill and the swarm of hornets. Stroebe and Martens. Swedish fairy book.
Roots. Richards. Silver crown.
Rope dance. *See* Rope dancer and his pupil.
Rope dancer and his pupil. Æsop. Fables (Burt ed. Rope dance.)
(poem). Wiggin and Smith. Talking beasts.
Rope of hair. Guerber. Legends of the Rhine.
Rory Macgillivray. Gibbon. Reign of King Cole.
Rory the robber. MacManus. In chimney corners.
Rosamond the swift of foot. Coussens. Jade story book.
See also Atalanta's race.
Rosanella. Lang. Green fairy book.
Lang. Magician's gifts.
Wiggin and Smith. Magic casements.
Rose and the ring. Jenks. Tales of fantasy.
Patten. Junior classics. v. 9.
Rose-beauty. Chodzko. Fairy tales of the Slav. (Tears of pearl.)
Kunos. Forty-four Turkish fairy tales.
Kunos. Turkish fairy tales.
Stebbins. 3d reader. (Tears of pearl.)
Rose-elf. *See* Elf of the rose.
Rose from Homer's grave. Andersen. Best fairy tales (Henderson tr. Rose from the grave of Homer.)
Andersen. Fairy tales (Lucas tr.).
Andersen. Fairy tales (Paull tr.).
Storytellers' magazine, July 1913, p. 77.
Rose from the grave of Homer. *See* Rose from Homer's grave.
Rose garden of Persia. Gate. Fortunate days.
Rose of Evening. Martens. Chinese fairy book.
Rose-leaf. Bay. Danish fairy and folk tales.
Rose-princess. Hume. Chronicles of fairyland.
Rose-tree. Jacobs. English fairy tales.
See also Juniper tree.
Rose-tree queen. Olcott. Wonder garden.
Rosebloom and Thornbloom. Brown. One-footed fairy.
Rosebud. *See* Sleeping beauty.
Rosebud princess. Faulkner. Story lady's book.
Roselinda. Storytellers' magazine. Jan. 1915, p. 13.
Roses and the sparrows. *See* Neighboring families.

Rosstrappe. Dasent. Popular tales from the Norse.
Thorpe. Yule-tide stories.
Roswal and Lillian. Harrison. Old-fashioned fairy book.
Rosy's journey. Alcott. Lulu's library. v. 1.
Rosy's stay-at-home parties. Harrison. Old-fashioned fairy book.
Round Table, Founding of. Clay. Stories from Le Morte d'Arthur. (Round Table.)
Cutler. Stories of King Arthur and his knights. (Noble order of the Round Table.)
Lang. Tales of the Round Table. (How the Round Table began.)
Lansing. Page, esquire and knight.
Patten. Junior classics. v. 4. (Round Table.)
See also King Arthur.
Rover of the plain. Lang. Orange fairy book.
Rowan tree. *See* Fairy tree of Dooros; Mountain ash; Rondel.
Royal engine. Stocking. Golden goblet.
See also Little engine that could.
Royal Oak Day. Blaisdell. English history story book. (Royal oak.)
Morris. Historical tales: English. (*In* Adventures of a royal fugitive.)
Rubezahl. Lang. Brown fairy book.
Lang. Three dwarfs, and other stories.
Rubies, Origin of. Mabie. Folk tales every child should know.
Ruby prince. Steel. Tales of the Punjab.
Ruby ring. Pyle. Counterpane fairy.
Rule of the king. Storytellers' magazine. Nov. 1917, p. 454.
Ruler. Richards. Silver crown.
Rummage sales. *See* Why there are white elephants; Mrs. Mouse's rummage sale.
Rumpelstiltskin. Bailey and Lewis. For the children's hour.
Bates. Once upon a time.
*Benson. Really truly fairy tales.
Chisholm. In fairyland.
Coussens. Child's book of stories. (Rumpelstiltskin; or, The miller's daughter.)
Forty famous fairy tales. (Rumpelstiltzkin.)
Grimm. Fairy tales (Lucas tr.).
*Grimm. Fairy tales (Wiltse. Rumpelstiltsken.) v. 1.
Grimm. Household stories (Crane tr.).
Grimm. Household tales (Burt ed. Gold-spinner.)
Grimm. Household tales (Everyman's ed. Rumpelstiltsken.)
Jerrold. Big book of fairy tales.
Jerrold. Reign of King Oberon. (Rumpelstiltsken.)
Lang. Blue fairy book.
Lang. Cinderella and other fairy tales. (Rumpelstiltzkin.)

Rumpelstiltskin—*continued.*
Lansing. Fairy tales. v. 1.
Mulock. Fairy book.
Norton. Heart of oak books. v. 3. (Rumpelstiltzkin.)
Nursery tales.
Perkins. Twenty best fairy tales. (Rumpelstiltzchen.)
Pyle. Mother's nursery tales. (Brittle legs.)
Scudder. Children's book. (Rumpelsteltzkin.)
Singleton. Wild flower fairy book.
Success library. v. 3. (Rumpelstiltzkin.)
Welsh. Fairy tales children love.
Wiggin and Smith. Fairy ring.
See also Forest elemental; Girl who could spin gold from clay and long straw; Kinkach Martinko; Tom Tit Tot; Trillevip; Whippity-Stourie.
Rumpty-Dudget's tower. St. Nicholas. Jan.–Mr. 1879, p. 198.
Runaway beavers. Donaldson. Little papoose listens.
Runaway cats. *See* Cat's elopement.
Runaway cave. Bailey. Friendly tales.
Runaway clothes. Storytellers' magazine. March 1917, v. 5.
Runaway pancake. *See* Pancake.
Runaway watch. Aspinwall. Short stories for short people.
Runaways. Eastman. Wigwam evenings.
Storytellers' magazine. April 1917, p. 220.
Running stick. Riggs. Animal stories from Eskimo land.
Runphast. English. Fairy stories and wonder tales.
Ruse of the princess. Brown, Mermaid's gift.
Rushen Coatie. *See* Rashin-Coatie. II.
Rushy-coat. *See* Rashin-Coatie I.
Russet dog. Jacobs. More Celtic fairy tales.
Spaulding and Bryce. Aldine readers. Book 3.
Rustem and Sohrab. *See* Sohrab and Rustem.
Rustic and the nightingale. Bidpai. Tortoise and the geese.
Rusty key. Hauff. Caravan tales.
Ruth's resolutions. Faulkner. Story lady's book.

S

Saaoud and his steed; or, Whittington in Arabia. Goddard. Fairy tales in other lands.
Sabot of little Wolff. Alderman. Classics old and new. 3d reader. (Little Carl's Christmas.)
Blaisdell. Child life. 5th reader.
Curtiss. Christmas stories and legends. (Little Jean.)
Dickinson and Skinner. Children's book of Christmas stories. (Little Wolff's wooden shoes.)
Hartwell. Story hour readings. 5th year. (Little Wolff and his wooden shoe.)

Sabot of little Wolff—*continued.*
Olcott. Good stories for great holidays. (Wooden shoes of Little Wolff.)
Storytellers' magazine. Dec. 1915, p. 469. (Little Wolff's wooden shoe.)
Sacred flame. Lagerlöf. Christ legends.
Sacred milk of Koumongoe. Lang. Brown fairy book.
Lang. Twelve huntsmen and other stories.
Sacrifice to Kompira. *See* Prince Yamato's adventures.
Sacrilegious painter. Guerber. Legends of the Rhine.
Sad experience of poor Pomposity. Aspinwall. Short stories for short people.
Sad fate of Mr. Fox. Harris. Uncle Remus, his songs and his sayings.
Sad story of Pyramus and Thisbe. *See* Pyramus and Thisbe.
Saddle to rags. Macleod. Book of ballad stories.
Tappan. Old ballads in prose.
Saddler's son and the dragon. Pearson. Laughing lion and other stories.
Sagacious monkey and the boar. Ozaki. Japanese fairy book.
Sagacious snake. Wiggin and Smith. Talking beasts.
Sage damsel. Polevoi. Russian fairy tales.
See also Peasant's clever daughter.
Said, Adventures of. Hauff. Caravan tales. (Golden whistle.)
Hauff. Fairy tales.
Sailor man. Bryant. How to tell stories to children.
Richards. Golden windows.
Sailor's star. Van Sickle and Seegmiller. Riverside readers. 4th reader.
St. Ailbe. *See* Wolf-mother of St. Ailbe.
Saint and the tyrant. *See* St. Martin.
St. Anthony of Italy. Macdonnell. Italian fairy book.
St. Athracta's stags (poem). Brown. Book of saints and friendly beasts.
St. Benedetto. Noyes. Saints of Italy.
St. Berach. Brown. Book of saints and friendly beasts. (Wonders of Saint Berach.)
St. Beuno and the curlew. Thomas. Welsh fairy book.
St. Blaise and his beasts. Brown. Book of saints and friendly beasts.
St. Brandan. Crommelin. Famous legends. (Unknown island.)
Higginson. Tales of the enchanted islands of the Atlantic. (Voyage of St. Brandan.)
St. Bridget. Sawyer. This way to Christmas.
St. Bridget and the King's wolf. Brown. Book of saints and friendly beasts.
St. Cecilie. Darton. Tales of the Canterbury pilgrims. (Second nun's tale: St. Cecilie.)

St. Christopher, Legend of (poem). Arnold and Gilbert. Stepping stones to literature.
Bailey and Lewis. For the children's hour.
Cabot. Ethics for children.
Cross and Statler. Story-telling. (Story of St. Christopher.) (poem). Curry. Little classics.
Fuller. Book of friendly giants. (Giant who became a saint.)
Gask. Folk tales from many lands.
Guerber. Legends of the Rhine.
Herbertson. Heroic legends. (Quest of Offero.)
Olcott. Good stories for great holidays. (St. Christopher.)
Patten. Junior classics. vol. 2.
Proudfoot. Child's Christ tales. (St. Christopher and the Christ child.)
Scudder. Book of legends.
Shedlock. Art of the storyteller.
Sly. World stories retold.
Storytellers' magazine. July 1913, p. 85. (Story of St. Christopher.)
Storytellers' magazine. Dec. 1916, p. 641.
Wiltse. Kindergarten stories.
St. Collen and the King of Faery. Thomas. Welsh fairy book.
St. Comgall and the mice. Brown. Book of saints and friendly beasts.
St. Cuthbert's eagle. Olcott. Good stories for great holidays.
St. Cuthbert's peace. Brown. Book of saints and friendly beasts.
St. Denis. Crommelin. Famous legends.
St. Domenica's swallow. Pitré. Swallow book. (Why the swallow lives in warm climates.)
St. Elizabeth and the roses. Storytellers' magazine. March 1916, p. 184.
Wiltse. Kindergarten stories.
St. Elizabeth and the sick child. Wiltse. Kindergarten stories.
St. Felix, Ballad of. Brown. Book of saints and friendly beasts.
St. Francis and the Soldan. Peers. Saints in story.
St. Francis of Assisi. Baldwin. Fifty famous people. (Little brothers of the air.)
Brown. Book of saints and friendly beasts.
Cabot. Ethics for children. (St. Francis of Assisi and the wolf.)
Keyes. Five senses. (What the birds heard from Francis.)
Peers. Saints in story. (St. Francis preaches to the birds and tames the wolf of Gubbio.)
Pitrè. Swallow book. (St. Francis and the birds.)
St. Fridolin. Guerber. Legends of the Rhine.

St. Fronto's camels. Brown. Book of saints and friendly beasts.
St. Galgano. Noyes. Saints of Italy. (Marvelous sword.)
St. Geneviève, Legend of. Guerber. Legends of the Rhine.
St. George and the dragon. Bailey and Lewis. For the children's hour.
Herbertson. Heroic legends.
Lansing. Page, esquire and knight. (Order of St. George.)
Mabie. Heroes and fairies. (St. George.)
Peers. Saints in story.
Scudder. Book of legends.
Sly. World stories retold.
Tweed. Fairy tales everyone should know.
St. George and the dragon, Belgian. *See* Golden dragon of the Boringue.
St. Gerasimus and the lion. Brown. Book of saints and friendly beasts.
St. Gertrude. Guerber. Legends of the Rhine.
St. Giles and the deer, Ballad of. Brown. Book of saints and friendly beasts.
St. Goar. Guerber. Legends of the Rhine. (Miracles and shrine of Goar.)
St. Gothard, the petrified Alp. Storytellers' magazine. Jan. 1915, p. 18.
St. Guthlac and the swallows. Pitrè. Swallow book.
St. Hervé. Brown. Book of saints and friendly beasts. (Blind singer, Saint Hervé.)
St. James of Galicia and the swallows. Pitrè. Swallow book.
St. Jerome and the lion. Evans. Old time tales. (Jerome and the lion.)
Peers. Saints in story.
St. John's eve. Williams. Fairy tales from folklore.
St. Kenelm, Story of. Hartland. English folk and fairy tales.
St. Keneth of the gulls. Brown. Book of saints and friendly beasts.
St. Kentigern and the robin. Brown. Book of saints and friendly beasts.
St. Launomar's cow. Brown. Book of saints and friendly beasts.
St Leonard. Olcott. Wonder garden. (Dragon Sin.)
St. Louis. Mabie. Heroes every child should know.
St. Margaret and the dragon. Peers. Saints in story.
St. Martin. Noyes. Saints of Italy. (Journey of San Martino; Saint and the tyrant; Soldier of God.)
St. Nicholas. Butterworth. Zigzag journeys in the Orient. (*In* Ch. 13.)
This includes: St. Nicholas and the nobleman's son; St. Nicholas and the purses.
Cross and Statler. Story-telling.
Griffis. Dutch fairy tales. (Santa Klaas and black Pete.)

St. Nicholas—*continued.*
Magnus. Russian folk tales. (Elijah the prophet and St. Nicholas.)
Magnus. Russian folk-tales. (Story of St. Nicholas.)
Noyes. Saints of Italy. (Good bishop; Three princes.)
Storytellers' magazine. Dec. 1915, p. 457.
See also Three purses.
St. Nicholas and the children. Macmillan. Canadian fairy tales.
Noyes. Saints of Italy. (Famine.)
St. Nicholas and the nobleman's son. Cross and Statler. Story-telling.
St. Nothburga. Skinner. Topaz story book. (Sickle moon.)
Saint of the white robe. *See* St. Romnaldo
St. Patrick. Faulkner. Story lady's book.
St. Patrick and the snakes. Olcott. Wonder garden. (Why there are no snakes in Ireland.)
Sly. World stories retold.
St. Patrick's day. *See* Emerald; Last of the serpents.
St. Peter and St. George. Guerber. Legends of the Rhine.
St. Peter and the two women. Djurklo. Fairy tales from the Swedish.
St. Peter's thirst. Guerber. Legends of the Rhine.
St. Prisca, the child martyr. Brown. Books of saints and friendly beasts.
St. Rigobert's dinner. Brown. Book of saints and friendly beasts.
St. Ritza. Guerber. Legends of the Rhine.
St. Romnaldo. Noyes. Saints of Italy. (Saint of the white robe.)
St. Rufino. Noyes. Saints of Italy.
St. Simeon Stylites. Evans. Old time tales. (Saint who stood on a pillar.)
St. Theonest. Guerber. Legends of the Rhine.
St. Ursula and the eleven thousand virgins. Guerber. Legends of the Rhine. (Eleven thousand virgins.)
St. Valentine. Faulkner. Story lady's book.
St. Valentine's day. *See* Bishop's valentine; *Cooky valentine; *Crane and the heron; Cupid and Psyche; Elaine's valentines; *Fairy queen and the carrier doves; Housekeeper; *Molly Anne's valentine; †Two cakes that loved each other in silence; Where Valentine hid; Why Venus liked doves.
St. Veronica's handkerchief. Lagerlöf. Christ legends.
St. Werburgh and her goose. Brown. Book of saints and friendly beasts.
See also Greedy geese.
Saint who stood on a pillar. *See* St. Simeon Stylites.
St. Winifred's well. Thomas. Welsh fairy book.
Salad. *See* Donkey cabbage.
Sallie Hick's forefinger. Walker. Sandman's goodnight stories.

Sally Migrundy. Gruelle. Friendly fairies.
Salt. Chisholm and Steedman. Staircase of stories.
Salt fish and the eel. Johnson. Oak-tree fairy book.
Salt of life. Pyle. Twilight land.
Samba the coward. Lang. Olive fairy book.
Lang. Little King Loc.
Sambo and Jerry. Messer. Next time stories.
Sammy's snow-man. Faulkner. Story lady's book.
Samodiva. Byrne. Modern Greek fairy tales.
Samovar's story. Harrison. Bric-a-brac stories.
Sampo Lappelil. Hodgkins. Atlantic treasury of children's stories. (Sampo, the little Lapp.)
Poulsson. Top of the world stories.
Samson and Delilah. Pleasanton. Fairyland of opera.
Sanartia. Wardrop. Georgian fairy tales.
Sand-hills, Story from the. Andersen. Fairy tales (Paull tr.)
Andersen. Stories and tales (Author's ed.)
Sandal-wood necklace. *See* Chundun Rajah.
Sandman. *See* Ole Luk Oie.
Sandpiper and the sea. *Dyer and Brady. Merrill readers. 2d reader.
See also Canute, King.
Sandy road. Babbitt. Jataka tales.
My Bookhouse. v. 2.
See also Wise and the foolish merchant.
Sanntraigh. Douglas. Scottish fairy tales.
Santa Claus. Field. Christmas tales. (Symbol and the saint.)
See also Animals' Christmas tree. II. Boy's visit to Santa Claus.
Santa Claus and Black Pete. *See* St. Nicholas.
Santa Claus and the fairy shoemaker. Faulkner. Story lady's book.
Santa Claus and the toys that came to life (play). Field. Field third reader.
Santa Claus at home. Bouvé. Lamp-light tales.
Santa Claus at Patch Hill. Bailey. Friendly tales.
Santa Claus's helpers. *Dillingham and Emerson. Tell it again stories.
Santa Claus's parents. *See* Saint and the symbol.
Sapient ass. *See* Old man and his ass.
Sapphira and the flying pig. Edey. Six giants and a griffin.
Satin surgeon. Lang. Olive fairy book.
Lang. Satin surgeon and other stories.
Satni and the Magic Book of Thoth. Jewett. Egyptian tales of magic.
Saturn. Francillon. Gods and heroes.
Satyr and the traveller. Æsop. Fables (Black ed.).
Æsop. Fables (Burt ed.)
Æsop. Fables (Jacobs. Man and Satyr.)
Æsop. Fables (Stickney).

Satyr and the traveller—*continued.*
Bosschère. Folk tales of Flanders. (Peasant and the satyr.)
Bryce. Fables from afar. (Man and the satyr.)
Wiggin and Smith. Talking beasts.
Saucy Jesper. Bay. Danish fairy and folk tales.
See also Golden goose; Hans who made the princess laugh; Magic swan.
Saudan Og and the daughter of the king of Spain; Young Conal and the yellow king's daughter. Curtin. Hero tales from Ireland.
Sausage, The. *See* Three wishes.
Saved. Aspinwall. Short stories for short people.
Saved by a rose. Aunt Naomi. Jewish fairy tales and fables.
Saving brother. Bailey. Friendly tales.
Saving snowball. Donahey. Tales to be told to children.
Saving the birds. *See* Lincoln and the little birds.
Savitri—The faithful wife. Maud. Heroines of poetry.
Stewart. Tell me a hero story. (Stronger than death.)
Saying of Socrates. *See* Socrates and his house.
Scandal (play). Lansing. Quaint old stories.
Scandinavian Jack the giant killer. Goddard. Fairy tales in other lands.
Scar. Richards. Golden windows.
Scar Face. I. *See* Little Scar Face.
Scar Face. II. Partridge. Glooscap the great chief. (Oochigeopsch the scarred young brave.)
See also Girl who rejected her cousin.
Scar Face. III. Cornyn. Around the wigwam fire. (Son of the morning star.)
Grinnell. Punishment of the stingy. (First medicine lodge.)
Olcott. Red Indian fairy book.
Scar Face. IV. Grinnell. Blackfoot lodge tales.
Nixon-Roulet. Indian folk tales. (Trail of the far-off lodge.)
Washburn. Indian legends.
Scarecrow. Keyes. Stories and story-telling.
Scarf of the Lady. Skinner. Topaz story book.
Scarface. *See* Scar Face.
Scarlet blanket. *See* Pedlar's pack.
Scarlet tanager. *Bryant. New stories to tell to children.
Scat. Bacon. True philosopher.
Scheherazade. *See* King Schahriar and Scheherazade.
Schippeitaro. Lang. Violet fairy book.
Nixon-Roulet. Japanese folk stories and fairy tales. (Phantom cats.)
Olcott. Good stories for great holidays. (Shippeitaro.)
Pyle. Fairy tales from far and near.
Wickes. Happy holidays.
Wiggin and Smith. Tales of wonder.
Williston. Japanese fairy tales. (Shippeitaro.)

Schmat-Razum. Wheeler. Russian wonder tales.
Scholar's tale. *See* Little cripple; Merry clown.
School of black art. Grundtvig. Danish fairy tales.
Scissors. Jacobs. Europa's fairy book.
See also Goody 'Gainst-the-Stream.
Scorpion and the tortoise. Bidpai. Tortoise and the geese.
Scotch hunting horn's story. Harrison. Bric-a-brac stories. stories.
Scotch maid's tale. *See* Olaf of the golden harp.
Scotch princesses and the swallows. Pitrè. Swallow book.
Scourge of God. *See* Attila.
Scrap-book fairy. Patterson. Enchanted bird.
Scrapefoot. Esenwein and Stockard. Children's stories.
Jacobs. More English fairy tales.
Wiggin and Smith. Tales of laughter.
See also Three bears.
Scratch Tom. Campbell. Beyond the border.
Scullion who became a sculptor. *See* Canova, Antonio.
Sculptor and the image. *See* Pygmalion and Galatea.
Scylla and Charybdis. Carpenter. Long ago in Greece. (Sirens.)
Evans. Heroes of Troy.
Guerber. Myths of Greece and Rome. (Charybdis and Scylla.)
Kupfer. Stories of long ago. (Sea god and a wicked enchantress.)
Pratt. Myths of old Greece. v. 2. (Glaucus and Scylla.)
See also Heroes of Troy.
Scylla, daughter of Nisus. Kupfer. Stories of long ago. (Lock of purple hair. and what came of it.)
Storr. Half a hundred hero tales.
Sea and the rivers. Æsop. Fables (Burt ed.).
Sea god and a wicked enchantress. *See* Scylla and Charybdis.
Sea god and the magic tide jewels. *See* Ambitious hunter and skilful fisher.
Sea king's gift. Lang. Lilac fairy book.
Lang. White doe.
See also Fisherman and his wife.
Sea-maiden. Douglas. Scottish fairy tales.
Jacobs. Celtic fairy tales.
Wiggin and Smith. Tales of wonder.
Sea, the fox, and the wolf. Patten. Junior classics. v. 1.
Tappan. Folk stories and fables.
Sea Tsar and Vasilisa the wise. Magnus. Russian folk tales.
See also Vasilisa the cunning and the Tsar of the sea.
Seal catcher. *See* Seal catcher and the merman.
Seal catcher and the merman. Douglas. Scottish fairy tales. (Seal catcher's adventure.)
Grierson. Scottish fairy book.
Johnson. Elm-tree fairy book. (Seal catcher.)

Seal catcher's adventure. *See* Seal catcher and the merman.
Search for a friend. Ortoli. Evening tales.
Search for a good child. Lindsay. Mother stories.
Search for Norumbega. Higginson. Tales of the enchanted islands of the Atlantic.
Search for the golden fruit. *See* Hercules and his labors.
Search for the seven cities. Cather. Educating by story telling.
Search for wisdom. *See* Odin's search for wisdom.
Search that Ma-ui's brother made for his sister Hina-of-the-sea. Colum. At the gateways of the day.
Seashore story. Faulkner. Story lady's book.
Second Calendar. Arabian nights (Lang. Story of the second Calender, son of a king.)
Arabian nights (Olcott. Story of the second royal mendicant.)
Arabian nights (Townsend. History of the second Calender.)
Second old man and the two black dogs. Arabian nights (Dodge ed.).
Arabian nights (Lang. Story of the second old man and the two black dogs.)
Arabian nights (Townsend. Story of the second old man and the two black dogs.)
Jenks. Tales of fantasy.
Scudder. Children's book. (History of the second old man and the two black dogs).
Second royal mendicant, Story of the. *See* Second Calender.
Second sight. Welsh. Stories children love.
Secret church. Stroebe and Martens. Norwegian fairy book.
Secret Empire. Nordau. Dwarf's spectacles.
Secret marriage. Guerber. Legends of the Rhine.
Secret name of Ra. *See* Ra and Isis.
Secret of fire. Colum. At the gateways of the day. (How Ma-ui won fire for men.)
Cooke. Nature myths and stories.
Farmer. Nature myths.
Pope. Hawaii the beautiful. (Island hero: Maui gets fire.)
Thrum. Hawaiian folk tales. (Exploits of Maui: Origin of fire.)
See also How coyote put fire in sticks; How fire was brought to the Indians. I.
Secret of Labra. Rolleston. High deeds of Finn.
See also Midas. II.
Secret of the Khan's barber. Jewett. Wonder tales from Tibet.
See also Midas. II.
Secret of the little dwarf. Froelicher. Swiss stories.
Secret of the violet. Donaldson. Moons of long ago.
See also Old Winter Man and the Spring.

Seed, Legend of the. *See* Proserpina.
Seed, Story of a. Bailey. Stories for Sunday telling. (Seed)
Seeds of love. Chisholm and Steedman. Staircase of stories. (Magic candles.)
Nichols and DeMorgan. Princess Girlikin and other fairy stories.
Seeing the world (play). Lansing. Quaint old stories.
Seekers after gold. Sylva and Strettell. Legends from river and mountain.
Selene's steeds. Stories of classic myths. (*In* Some mythological horses.)
Self-burning fire. Eastman. Indian legends retold.
Self-convicted. Fielde. Chinese fairy tales.
Self did it. Stroebe and Martens. Norwegian fairy book.
See also My own self.
Self-made kitten. Bacon. True philosopher.
Selfish chief. Pope. Hawaii.
Selfish giant. Bailey. For the story-teller.
Cross and Statler. Story-telling.
Harper. Story-hour favorites.
Hartwell. Story hour readings. 5th year.
My Bookhouse. v. 2.
Skinner. Emerald story book.
Storytellers' magazine. June 1917, p. 278.
Wickes. Happy holidays.
Wilde. Fairy tales.
Selfish sea-gull. Faulkner. Story lady's book.
Selfish sparrow and the houseless crows. Coussens. Child's book of stories.
Frere. Old Deccan days.
Wiggin and Smith. Tales of laughter.
See also Woodpecker who was selfish.
Selfish tamarack tree. Donaldson. Little papoose listens.
See also Why the evergreen trees keep their leaves all winter. I.
Selkirk, Alexander. *See* Robinson Crusoe.
Seller of dreams. Hodgkins. Atlantic treasury of childhood stories.
Beston. Firelight fairy book.
Semai-mai. Bourhill and Drake. Fairy tales from South Africa.
Sennin the hermit. Coe and Christie. Story hour readers. 3d book.
Senosoris, the wonder child. Jewett. Egyptian tales of magic.
Sense of the weasel. Stafford. Animal fables.
Sensible ass. Æsop. Fables (Black ed.)
Æsop. Fables (Burt ed.)
Senta. Maud. Wagner's heroines.
Seppy, Story of. Bosschère. Christmas tales of Flanders.
See also Man who was going to mind the house.
Septimus. Valentine. Old, old fairy tales.
Sermon. Richards. Silver crown.

Serpent. Richards. Silver crown.
Serpent and the file. Æsop. Fables (Black ed. Viper and the file.)
Æsop. Fables (Burt. ed. Viper and the file.)
Æsop. Fables (Jacobs).
(poem). Success library. v. 3. (Viper and the file.)
Serpent and the kettle. *See* Thor: Thor's fishing.
Serpent and the man. Æsop. Fables (Black ed.).
Æsop. Fables (Burt ed.).
Serpent and the peasant. Wardrop. Georgian folk tales.
Serpent-czarevitch and his two wives. Bain. Cossack fairy tales.
Serpent-isle. Sylva and Strettell. Legends from river and mountain.
Serpent king. Wilmot-Buxton. Stories of Persian heroes.
Serpent-peri and the magic mirror. Kunos. Forty-four Turish fairy tales. (Snake-peri and the magic mirror.)
Kunos. Turkish fairy tales.
Serpent-wife. Bain. Cossack fairy tales.
Serpent woman. Maud. Heroines of poetry.
Serpent's bride. Bourhill and Drake. Fairy tales from South Africa.
Serpent's gift. *See* Melampus.
Serra. Rhys. Fairy gold.
Sesshiu, painter of Japan. Chandler. Pan the piper. (*In* China, the land of many dragons.)
Setuli; or, King of the birds. Bourhill and Drake. Fairy tales from South Africa.
Seven against Thebes. *See* Thebes.
Seven at one blow. *See* Brave little tailor.
Seven boys and the monster. Wiggin and Smith. Tales of laughter.
Seven brothers Simeon. *See* Seven Simons.
Seven brothers who were turned into Champa trees. Bradley-Birt. Bengal fairy tales.
Seven corn maidens. Olcott. Wonder garden.
See also Spirit of the corn.
Seven crows. *See* Seven ravens.
Seven doves. Macdonell. Italian fairy book.
Seven dwarfs. *See* Snowdrop.
Seven families of the Lake Pipple-Popple. Wiggin and Smith. Tales of laughter.
Seven fathers in the house. *See* Father of the family.
Seven fishers. Gregory. Kiltartan wonder book.
Seven foals. Dasent. Popular tales from the Norse.
Dasent. Norse fairy tales.
Lang. Red fairy book.
Lang. White doe.
Underhill. Dwarfs' tailor and other fairy tales. (Seven reindeer.)
Seven giants. Grayl. Fairy tales from foreign lands.
See also Twelve dancing princesses.

Seven golden peahens. Pyle. Fairy tales from many lands.
See also Nine peahens and the golden apples.
Seven goslings. *See* Wolf and the seven little goslings.
Seven great deeds of Ma-ui. Colum. At the gateways of the day.
This includes: How Ma-ui won a place for himself in the house; How Ma-ui lifted up the sky; How Ma-ui fished up the great island; How Ma-ui snared the sun and made him go more slowly across the heavens; How Ma-ui won fire for men; How Ma-ui overcame Kuna Loa the long eel; Search that Ma-ui's brother made for his sister Hina-of-the-sea; How Ma-ui strove to win immortality for men.
Seven-headed serpent. Lang. Three dwarfs and other stories.
Lang. Yellow fairy book.
Success library. v. 3.
Seven Inches. *See* Three crowns.
Seven kingdoms and the hidden spring. Alden. Boy who found the king.
Seven-league boots. *See* Hop o' my Thumb.
Seven little goats. *See* Wolf and the seven little kids.
Seven little travellers. Bigham. Merry animal tales.
See also Rats and their son-in-law.
Seven ravens. *Benson. Really truly fairy tales.
Dasent. Popular tales from the Norse.
Grimm. Fairy tales (Lucas tr.).
Grimm. Fairy tales (Paull tr.).
*Grimm. Fairy tales (Wiltse. Seven crows.) v. 2.
Grimm. Household tales (Burt ed.).
Grimm. Household tales (Everyman's ed.).
Storytellers' magazine. Sept. 1914, p. 651.
Thorpe. Yule-tide stories.
Winnington. Outlook fairy book.
Seven reindeer. *See* Seven foals.
Seven sheepfolds. Armfield. Wonder tales of the world.
Seven Simeons. *See* Seven Simons.
Seven Simons, Story of the. Blumenthal. Folk tales from the Russian. (Seven Simeons.)
Curtin. Wonder-tales from Russia. (Seven Simeons, full brothers.)
Lang. Crimson fairy book.
Lang. Snow-queen and other stories.
Steele. Russian garland of fairy tales. (Seven brothers Simeon.)
Seven sisters. I. *See* Pleiades. I.
Seven sisters. II. Guerber. Legends of the Rhine.
Seven sleepers of Ephesus. Mabie. Legends every child should know.
Scudder. Book of legends.
Seven stars. *See* Pleiades.
Seven stars of Pleiades. *See* Pleiades.

Seven Swabians. *Grimm. Fairy tales (Wiltse). v. 2.
Wiggin and Smith. Tales of laughter.
Seven swans. *See* Wild swans.
Seven voyages of Sinbad the sailor. *See* Sinbad the sailor, Story of.
Shadow. I. Andersen. Fairy tales (Paull tr.).
Andersen. Wonder stories (Author's ed.).
Shadow. II. Aspinwall. Short stories for short people.
Shadow. III. Richards. Golden windows.
Shadow canoe. Judd. Wigwam stories.
Shadow posy. Bailey. Stories for Sunday telling.
Shadow wife. Eastman. Indian legends retold.
Shadowland. Hume. Chronicles of fairyland.
Shadows. Macdonald. Light princess, and other fairy tales.
Shah Jussuf. Kunos. Forty-four Turkish fairy tales.
Shah Meram and Sultan Sade. Kunos. Forty-four Turkish fairy tales.
Shaking-head. Curtin. Myths and folk-lore of Ireland.
Sham prince. Hauff. Caravan tales. (False prince.)
Lang. Crimson fairy book. (Story of the sham prince; or, The ambitious tailor.)
Lang. Little Wildrose. (Story of the sham prince; or, The ambitious tailor.)
Shan Ban and Ned Flynn. MacManus. In chimney corners.
Shankha, the garland of shells. Bradley-Birt. Bengal fairy tales.
Sharazad. *See* King Schahriar and Scheherazade.
Sharing love and sorrow. Grimm. Fairy tales (Paull tr.).
Sharp eyes plays caddy. Bailey. Friendly tales.
Sharp lesson. Storytellers' magazine. Sept. 1917, p. 349.
Sharpshooter. McSpadden. Stories from great operas.
Shas and the demons. Wilmot-Buxton. Stories of Persian heroes.
Shaun "of the leaf." Leamy. Fairy minstrel of Glenmalure.
Shawano, who killed the Uktena. Bayliss. Treasury of Indian tales.
Shawneen. Gregory. Kiltartan wonder book.
She was good for nothing. Andersen. Fairy tales (Paull tr.).
Andersen. Stories and tales (Author's ed. "Good for nothing.")
She who wore a crown. Sologub. Sweet-scented name.
Shee an Gannon and the Gruagach Gaire. Curtin. Myths and folklore of Ireland.
Jacobs. Celtic fairy tales.
Sheem, the forsaken boy. Schoolcraft. Indian fairy book.
See also Boy and the wolves; Mishosha.
Sheep and the bramble. Æsop. Fables (Burt ed.).
Sheep and the dog. Æsop. Fables (Burt ed.).
Sheep and the pig. *See* Ram and the pig.

Sheep and the pig that built the house. *See* Ram and the pig.
Sheep and the pig that made a home. *See* Ram and the pig.
Sheep and the pig who set up house. *See* Ram and the pig.
Sheep and the pig who set up housekeeping. *See* Ram and the pig.
Sheep-biter. Æsop. Fables (Black ed.).
Æsop. Fables (Burt ed.).
Sheep in the pasture. Olcott. Wonder garden.
Sheep, the pig, the cow and the goose. *See* Ram and the pig.
Sheet and Basanta. Bradley-Birt.. Bengal fairy tales.
Sheik Chilli. Lansing. Quaint old stories.
Sheltering wings. *Dillingham and Emerson. Tell it again stories.
Skinner. Pearl story book.
Shemyák the judge. Magnus. Russian folk tales.
Shepherd and his dog (poem). Wiggin and Smith. Talking beasts.
Shepherd and the child of fortune. Wardrop. Georgian folk tales.
Shepherd and the dragon. Gask. Folk tales from many lands.
Gask. Treasury of folk tales.
Shepherd and the lion (poem). Wiggin and Smith. Talking beasts.
Shepherd and the nightingale. Success library. v. 3.
Shepherd and the spirit. Froelicher. Swiss stories.
Shepherd and the young wolf. Æsop. Fables (Burt ed.).
Shepherd boy and the king. Grimm. Fairy tales (Paull tr.).
Spaulding and Bryce. Aldine readers. Book 3. (Wise shepherd boy.)
Storytellers' magazine. Nov. 1914, p. 740.
Wiggin and Smith. Tales of laughter. (Little shepherd boy.)
See also King John and the Abbot of Canterbury.
Shepherd boy and the wolf. *See* Boy who cried "Wolf."
Shepherd-boy painter. *See* Giotto.
Shepherd Hynek. Baudiš. Czech folk tales.
Shepherd judge. Wardrop. Georgian folk tales.
Shepherd maiden's gift. Skinner. Pearl story book.
Shepherd of clouds. Beston. Firelight fairy book.
Shepherd pacha. *See* Shepherd pashaw.
Shepherd pashaw. Laboulaye. Fairy tales.
Laboulaye. Last fairy tales. (Shepherd pacha.)
Shepherd of Myddvai. Jacobs. Celtic fairy tales.
Shepherd Paul. Lang. Crimson fairy book.
Lang. Little Wildrose.
See also Strong Jack.
Shepherd prince. Stewart. Tell me a hero story.
Shepherd turned merchant. Æsop. Fables (Black ed.).
Æsop. Fables (Burt ed.).

Shepherd who didn't go. Curtiss. Christmas stories and legends.
Stocking. City that never was reached.
Shepherd who forgot. Froelicher. Swiss stories.
Shepherd who turned back. Cather. Educating by story telling.
Shepherd who won the king's daughter by a single word. Cary. French fairy tales.
See also Jack and the king who was a gentleman.
Shepherdess and the chimney-sweep. Andersen. Fairy tales (Paul tr.)
Andersen. Stories and tales (Author's ed.).
Scudder. Children's book.
Shepherd's boy. *See* Boy who cried "Wolf."
Shepherd's daughter. *See* Sweet Pea and Sweet William.
Shepherd's death. Guerber. Legends of the Rhine.
Shepherd's dog and the wolf (poem). Wiggin and Smith. Talking beasts.
Shepherd's flower. *See* Roland. I.
Shepherd's gift. Lagerlöf. Christ legends. (Holy night.)
Storytellers' magazine. Dec. 1916, p. 468.
Shepherd's nosegay. Fillmore. Shoemaker's apron.
Shepherds of Salisbury Plain. Baring-Gould. Old English fairy tales.
Macleod. Book of ballad stories. (Strange lives of two young princes.)
Shepherd's son and the ogre. Douglas. Scottish fairy and folk tales. (Two shepherds.)
Johnson. Elm-tree fairy book.
Shepherd's story of the bond of friendship. Andersen. Fairy tales (Paull tr.)
Shet-up posy. Skinner. Topaz story book.
Slosson. Story-tell Lib.
Storytellers' magazine. Oct. 1916, p. 515. (Shut-up posy. Adapted.)
Shield Quiver's wife. Grinnell. Punishment of the stingy.
Shifty lad, the widow's son. Douglas. Scottish fairy tales.
Lang. Lilac fairy book.
Lang. Magic book.
See also Jack the cunning thief.
Shinansha; or, The south pointing carriage. Ozaki. Japanese fairy book.
Shingebiss. *See* North wind and the duck.
Shining child and the wicked Mouche. Olcott. Book of elves and fairies.
Shining princess, Story of. Bourhill and Drake. Fairy tales from South Africa.
Ship and the sailors. Æsop. Fables (Burt ed.).
Ship that could sail over land and sea. Silver fairy book.
See also Ashiepattle and his goodly crew.
Shippeitaro. *See* Schippeitaro.
Shipwrecked man and the sea. Æsop. Fables (Burt ed.).

Shirt-collar. Andersen. Fairy tales (Paull tr.).
Andersen. Wonder stories (Author's ed. False collar.)
Lang. Golden mermaid and other stories.
Lang. Pink fairy book.
Shoe. *See* Man's boot.
Shoemaker and his servant Prituitshkin, Story of. Steele. Russian garland of fairy tales.
Shoemaker and the elves. *See* Elves and the shoemaker.
Shoemaker and the fairies. *See* Elves and the shoemaker.
Shoemaker's apprentice. Grundtvig. Fairy tales from afar.
Shoemaker's apron. Fillmore. Shoemaker's apron.
See also Smith and the devil. III.
Shoemaker's secret. Eggleston. Queer stories for boys and girls.
Shoes for hats. Griffis. Korean fairy tales.
Shoo Fly. Cocke. Bypaths in Dixie.
Shooting of the Red Eagle. Zitkala-Ŝa. Old Indian legends.
Shopboy and his cheese. Asbjörnsen. Tales from the fjeld.
Shortshanks. Dasent. Popular tales from the Norse.
Dasent. Norse fairy tales.
Lang. Blue parrot. (Minnikin.)
Lang. Red fairy book. (Minnikin.)
Thorpe. Yule-tide stories. (Lillekort.)
Short story. Houghton. Russian grandmother's wonder tales.
See also Box with something pretty in it; Tail.
Shower of gold. *See* Star dollars.
Shreds. *See* Flax leavings.
Shroud. *See* Child's grave.
Shut-up posy. *See* Shet-up posy.
Shy deer. Donaldson. Little papoose listens.
Sibyl. Guerber. Story of the Romans. (Mysterious books.)
Haaren and Poland. Famous men of Rome. (The Tarquins.)
Laing. Seven kings of the seven hills. (*In* Tarquinius Superbus.)
Judd. Classic myths. (Lesson of the leaves.)
Morris. Historical tales: Roman. (Books of the sibyl.)
Sick-bed elves. Olcott. Book of elves and fairies.
See also Little hunting dog.
Sick child. Richards. Silver crown.
Sick kite. Æsop. Fables (Black ed.).
Æsop. Fables (Burt ed.).
Sick lion. I. Æsop. Fables (Black ed. Old lion.)
Æsop. Fables (Burt ed.).
Æsop. Fables (Jacobs).
Sick lion. II. Houghton. Russian grandmother's wonder tales.
Sick princess. Harrison. Prince Silverwings.
Sick stag. Æsop. Fables (Burt ed.).
Æsop. Fables (Stickney).
(poem). Wiggin and Smith. Talking beasts.

Sickle moon. *See* Saint Nothburga.
Sickness and medicine, Origin of. *See* Disease, Origin of; Medicine, Origin of.
Sidi-Nouman. Arabian nights (Dodge ed. Syed Nouman.)
Arabian nights (Lang).
Arabian nights (Townsend).
Ketcham. Oriental fairy tales.
Scudder. Children's book.
Sidney, Philip. *See* Sir Philip Sidney and the cup of water.
Siege of Calais. Blaisdell. English history story book. (Brave men of Calais.)
Morris. Historical tales: English.
Siegfrid and Handa. Nichols and DeMorgan. Princess Girlikin and other fairy tales.
Siegfried. *See* Nibelungenlied; Ring: Siegfried; Siegfried with the horny skin; Sigurd the Volsung.
Siegfried with the horny skin. Klingensmith. Old Norse wonder tales.
Tappan. Stories of legendary heroes. (Siegfried; The dragonstone.)
See also Nibelungenlied; Ring: Siegfried; Sigurd the Volsung.
Siegmund. *See* Nibelungenlied; Ring: War maidens; Sigurd the Volsung.
Sif's hair. *See* Dwarf's gifts.
Sighing pine tree. Bryce. That's why stories.
Sigmund. I. *See* Nibelungenlied; Ring: War maidens; Sigurd the Volsung.
Sigmund. II. *See* Horse who rode through fire.
Sigurd the Volsung. I. Baker and Carpenter. Language readers. 5th year. (Siegfried the Volsung.)
Forty famous fairy tales. (Story of Sigurd.)
Guerber. Myths of northern lands. (Sigurd saga.)
Hall. Icelandic fairy tales. (Sigurd.)
Klingensmith. Old Norse wonder tales.
Lang. Red fairy book. (Story of Sigurd.)
Stewart. Tell me a hero story. (Sigurd and the dragon; Golden hoard. Adapted.)
Wilmot-Buxton. Stories of Norse heroes.
This includes: Story of the magic sword; How Sigmund fought his last battle; Story of the magic gold; How Sigurd slew the dragon; How Sigurd won the hand of Brunhild; How the curse of the gold is fulfilled.
See also Andvare's golden ring; Horse who rode through fire; Nibelungenlied; Ring: Siegfried; Ring: Twilight of the gods; Ring: War maidens; Siegfried with the horny skin.
Sigurd the Volsung. II. Crommelin. Famous legends. (Sigurd.)
Guerber. Myths of northern lands. (Sigurd saga.)
See also Aslaug and Ragnar.
Sikku and the trolls. Poulsson. Top of the world stories.

Sila Tsarevich and Ivanshka with the white smock. Steele. Russian garland of fairy tales.
Silence. *See* Dwarfs' tailor.
Silent princess. Kunos. Forty-four Turkish fairy tales.
Lang. Olive fairy book.
Lang. Satin surgeon.
Sili go Dwt. Griffis. Welsh fairy tales. (Red bandits of Montgomery.)
Thomas. Welsh fairy book.
Silkworm. Jenkins. Interesting neighbors. (A queen discovers the silk worm.)
Silkworm and the spider. I. Æsop. Fables (Burt ed.). (poem). Success library. v. 3.
Silkworm and the spider. II. Æsop. Fables. (Burt ed. Spider and the silkworm.)
Silkworm goddess. *See* Girl with the horse's head.
Silly jelly fish. *See* Monkey and the jelly-fish.
Silly Jura. Baudis. Czech folk tales.
Silly kid. *See* Kid and wolf. II.
Silly little brook. Bailey. Stories children need.
My Bookhouse. v. 2. (Brooklet's story.)
Silly Matt. Asbjörnsen. Tales from the fjeld.
See also Epaminondas and his auntie; Lazy Jack; Prudent Hans.
Silly men and cunning wives. Asbjörnsen. Folk and fairy tales. (Foolish men and scolding wives.)
Asbjörnsen. Tales from the fjeld.
Gade. Norwegian fairy tales. (Stupid fellows with jades for wives.)
Silly Mutton. Campbell. Beyond the border.
Douglas. Scottish fairy tales (Burt ed.)
Silly old man (poem). Lansing. Quaint old stories.
Silly sand piper. Faulkner. Story lady's book.
Silly snake and his money. Young. Behind the dark pines.
Silly son. Partridge. Glooscap the great chief.
Silver bell. Stebbins. Sunken city.
Silver bridge. Guerber. Legends of the Rhine.
Silver brooches. Olcott. Red Indian fairy book.
Silver cones. Cather. Educating by story telling.
Silver cross (poem). Alexander. Hidden servants.
Silver crown. Richards. Silver crown and other stories.
Silver florin, Story of the. Hauff. Fairy tales.
Silver hen. Wilkins. Pot of gold.
Storytellers' magazine. Jan. 1916. p. 25. (Little silver hen.)
Silver Locks. *See* Three bears.
Silver mountain. Baring. Blue rose fairy book.
Silver nail. Sylva and Strettell. Legends from river and mountain.
Silver party. Alcott. Lulu's library. v. 3.
Silver penny. Jokai and others. Golden fairy book.
Wiggin and Smith. Magic casements.

Silver porringer, Story of the. Bailey. In the animal world.
Harrison. Bric-a-brac stories.
Silver saucer and the crystal apple. Magnus. Russian folk-tales. (Tale of the silver saucer and the crystal apple.)
Patten. Junior classics. v. 1. (Story of Little Simpleton.)
Silver shilling. Andersen. Fairy tales (Paull tr.).
Andersen. Wonder stories (Author's ed.).
Field. Famous fairy tales.
Silver ship. Hartwell. Story hour readings, 6th year.
Silver shoes. Potter. Pinafore pocket story book.
Silver shower. Miller. Philippine folklore stories.
Silver tracks. Fillmore. Laughing prince.
Silvercap, king of the frost fairies. Bailey and Lewis. For the children's hour.
Silverwhite and Lillwacker. Stroebe and Martens. Swedish fairy book.
Sim Chung. *See* Dutiful daughter.
Simeli-Mountain. Grimm. Fairy tales (Paull tr.).
See also Ali Baba and the forty thieves.
Similar diseases. Fielde. Chinese fairy tales.
See also How one went out to woo.
Simon and the black-gum tree. Skinner. Nursery tales from many lands.
Simon and the Garuly. Eggleston. Queer stories for boys and girls.
Simple John. Bosschère. Christmas tales of Flanders.
See also Hans in luck.
Simple-minded giant. Tappan. Golden goose.
See also Jack the giant killer.
Simpleton. I. Lang. Grey fairy book.
Lang. Snake prince.
See also How six travelled through the world.
Simpleton. II. *See* Cinder youth.
Simpleton and his little black hen. Pyle. Wonder clock.
Sinbad of the Talmud. Landa. Aunt Naomi's Jewish fairy tales and legends.
Sinbad the sailor, Story of. Arabian nights (Colum. Voyages of Es-Sindibad of the sea.)
Arabian nights (Dodge ed.).
Arabian nights (Lang. Seven voyages of Sinbad the sailor.)
Arabian nights (Olcott. Story of the seven voyages of Sinbad the sailor.)
Arabian nights (Townsend).
Arabian nights (Wiggin and Smith. Story of Sinbad the voyager.)
Baker and Carpenter. Language readers. 5th year. (Second and fifth voyages.)
Blaisdell. Child life. 5th reader. (First, sixth and seventh voyages.)
Favorite fairy tales. (Second voyage of Sinbad the sailor.)

Sinbad the sailor, Story of—*continued.*
Jenks. Tales of fantasy. (Sinbad the sailor and the rocs.)
Jerrold. Big book of fairy tales. (Sinbad the sailor and the rocs.)
Ketcham. Oriental fairy tales.
Mabie. Fairy tales every child should know. (Second voyage of Sinbad the sailor.)
Mabie. Heroes and fairies. (Second voyage of Sinbad the sailor.)
Norton. Heart of oak books. v. 4.
Scudder. Children's book. (First, second and fifth voyages.)
Tappan. Stories from seven old favorites.
Welsh. Stories children love. (Two stories of Sinbad the sailor. First and second voyages.)
Unless otherwise specified, each reference contains the seven voyages of Sinbad the sailor.
See also Thousand-and-second tale of Scheherazade.
Since when Mister Blackbird wears red epaulets. Young Behind the dark pines.
Sing Li's fortune. Pitman. Chinese fairy stories.
Sing-song of Old Man Kangaroo. Kipling. Just so stories.
Singer mother. Field. Second book of tales.
Singers. *See* Bremen town musicians.
Singer's lesson. Ketchum and Jorgensen. Kindergarten gems.
Singh Rajah and the cunning little jackals. *See* Little jackals and the lion.
Singing bird of heaven. James. Green willow.
Singing birds, Origin of. Grinnell. Birds of song and story.
See also How the birds came; Voices of nature.
Singing bone. Grimm. Household tales (Burt ed.).
See also Binnorie; Blue lily; King and his three sons; Three brothers; Three griffin's feathers.
Singing insects. Murray. Story book treasures.
Singing leaves (poem). Alderman. Classics old and new. 4th reader.
Singing maidens. *See* Pleiades. VI.
Singing-match. Harris. Little Mr. Thimblefinger.
Singing of the dwarfs. Froelicher. Swiss stories.
Singing plant. Donaldson. Little papoose listens.
Singing prisoner. Fielde. Chinese fairy tales.
Singing sack. Caballero. Spanish fairy tales.
Singing tree and the speaking bird. Magnus. Russian folk-tales.
See also Three sisters. I.
Single lantern of Iroka. Wickes. Happy holidays.
Single lantern of Yamato. Nixon-Roulet. Japanese folk stories and fairy tales.
Sir Accalon. Cutler. Stories of King Arthur and his knights. (Stag-hunt and what came of it.)

Sir Andrew Barton (poem). Lanier. Boy's Percy.
Sir Balin. Church. Heroes of chivalry and romance.
Clay. Stories from Le Morte d' Arthur. (Balin and Balan.)
Cutler. Stories of King Arthur and his knights. (Dolorous stroke.)
Lang. Book of romance.
Lang. Tales of the Round Table.
Storytellers' magazine. March 1914, p. 483. (Dolorous stroke.)
Sir Beaumains, the kitchen knight. *See* Sir Gareth.
Sir Bevis. Lang. Red romance book. (Sir Bevis the strong.)
Wilmot-Buxton. Stories of early England. (Sir Bevis of Hampton.)
Baldwin. Horse fair. (Arundel the swallow.)
Sir Bors and Sir Lionel. Clay. Stories from Le Morte d'Arthur. (Adventures of Sir Bors.)
Cutler. Stories of King Arthur and his knights. (Victory of Sir Bors over himself.)
Tappan. Stories of legendary heroes.
Sir Bumble. *See* Sir Buzz.
Sir Buzz. Johnson. Elm-tree fairy book.
Lansing. Quaint old stories. (Sir Bumble.)
Steel. Tales of the Punjab.
Sir Cauline (poem). Lanier. Boy's Percy.
Macleod. Book of ballad stories.
Sir Cleges and the Christmas cherries. *See* Sir Cleges, Tale of.
Sir Cleges, Tale of. Storytellers' magazine. Dec. 1915, p. 518. (Sir Cleges and the Christmas cherries.)
Wilmot-Buxton. Stories of early England.
Sir Eglamour. Harrison. Old-fashioned fairy book. (Sir Eglamour and Crystabel.)
Wilmot-Buxton. Stories of early England.
Sir Galahad. Alderman. Classics old and new. 3d reader.
Bryant. Treasury of hero tales. (Coming of Sir Galahad.)
Clay. Stories from Le Morte d'Arthur. (Holy Grail.)
Cutler. Stories of King Arthur and his knights.
Field third reader. (How Sir Galahad found his sword and shield.)
Mabie. Heroes and fairies.
Mabie. Heroes every child should know.
MacGregor. Stories of King Arthur's knights. (Sir Galahad and the sacred cup.)
Patten. Junior classics. v. 4.
Storytellers' magazine. April 1914, p. 525. (Coming of Galahad.)
See also Holy Grail.
Sir Gamelyn. Darton. Tales of the Canterbury pilgrims. (Cook's tale: Sir Gamelyn.)
McSpadden. Stories from Chaucer. (Chaucer's tale: Gamelyn.)

Sir Gamelyn—*continued.*
Storr and Turner. Canterbury chimes. (Chaucer's tale: Gamelyn.)
Sir Gammer Vans. Jacobs. More English fairy tales.
Johnson. Oak-tree fairy book. (Fate of a little old woman.)
Wiggin and Smith. Tales of laughter.
Sir Gareth. Baker and Carpenter. Language readers. 5th year. (Adventure of Sir Gareth.)
Baldwin. Stories of the King. (Fellow fresh from the fields; Disdainful maiden.)
Chisholm and Steedman. Staircase of stories. (Gareth and Lynette.)
Church. Heroes of chivalry and romance.
Clay. Stories from Le Morte d'Arthur.
Cutler. Stories of King Arthur and his knights. (How a kitchen page came to honor.)
Greene. King Arthur and his court. (Gareth and Lynette.)
Herbertson. Heroic legends. (Beaumains, the knight of the kitchen.)
Lang. Book of romance. (What Beaumains asked of the king.)
Lang. Tales of the Round Table. (What Beaumains asked of the king.)
My Bookhouse. v. 5. (Sir Beaumains, the kitchen knight.)
Patten. Junior classics. v. 4.
Storytellers' magazine. Nov. 1913, p. 279. (Adventures of Gareth the kitchen knave.)
See also Fair unknown.
Sir Gawain and the green knight. Brooks. Wonder stories from the Mabinogion.
Lansing. Page, esquire and knight.
Rhys. Fairy gold. (Green knight.)
Wilmot-Buxton. Stories of early England. (Sir Gawayne and the green knight.)
Sir Gawain and the lady. Clay. Stories from Le Morte d'Arthur.
See also Sir Gawain's marriage. II.
Sir Gawain's marriage. I. Baldwin. Stories of the king. (Hideous lady.)
(poem). Lanier. Boy's Percy.
Macleod. Book of ballad stories.
Pyle. Where the wind blows.
Sir Gawain's marriage. II. Darton. Tales of the Canterbury pilgrims. (Wife of Bath's tale: Old woman and the knight.)
McSpadden. Stories from Chaucer. (Wife of Bath's tale: Woman's wish.)
Patten. Junior classics. v. 4. (Old woman and the knight.)

Sir Gawain's marriage. II.—*continued.*
Storytellers' magazine. Oct. 1914, p. 693. (Sir Gawain's quest.)
Sir Gawain's quest. *See* Sir Gawain's marriage. II.
Sir Geraint. Brooks. Wonder stories from the Mabinogion. (Geraint and Enid.)
Clay. Stories from Le Morte d'Arthur.
Clay. Stories of King Arthur and the Round Table.
Lanier. Knightly legends of Wales. (Geraint the son of Erbin.)
Storytellers' magazine. Dec. 1913, p. 337. (Adventures of Geraint with the Sparrow Hawk.)
Sir Geynleyn. *See* Fair unknown.
Sir Godfrey Macculloch. Douglas. Scottish fairy tales.
Sir Greenhat. Grundtvig. Fairy tales from afar.
Sir Grey, Sir Graham, and Sir Greyskin. Baring-Gould. Old English fairy tales.
Sir Isaac Newton and the apple. Baldwin. Thirty more famous stories.
Sir Isumbras. Harrison. Old-fashioned fairy book. (Trials of Sir Isumbras.)
Wilmot-Buxton. Stories of early England. (Story of Sir Isumbras.)
Sir James Ramsay of Bamff, Tale of. Douglas. Scottish fairy tales.
Sir Lancelot. Church. Heroes of chivalry and romance.
Clay. Stories from Le Morte d'Arthur. (Sir Launcelot.)
Clay. Stories of King Arthur and the Round Table. (Sir Launcelot.)
Cutler. Stories of King Arthur and his knights.
Higginson. Tales of the enchanted islands of the Atlantic. (Sir Launcelot of the lake.)
Lang. Book of romance. (Lancelot and Guenevere.)
Patten. Junior classics. v. 4.
See also Knight, the lady and the falcon.
Sir Lancelot and Elaine. Almost true tales. (Tournament at Winchester; Lady of Shalott.)
Baldwin. Stories of the king. (Crimson sleeve; Lily maid of Astolat.)
Clay. Stories from Le Morte d'Arthur. (Fair maid of Astolat.)
Cutler. Stories of King Arthur and his knights. (Sir Launcelot's repentance.)
Greene. King Arthur and his court. (Launcelot and Elaine.)
Lang. Book of romance. (Fair maid of Astolat.)
Lang. Tales of the Round Table. (Fair maid of Astolat.)
MacGregor. Stories of King Arthur's knights.
Maud. Heroines of poetry. (Fair maid of Astolat.)
Patten. Junior classics. v. 4. (Fair maid of Astolat.)

Sir Lancelot and Elaine—*continued.*
Storytellers' magazine. Feb. 1914, p. 429. (Adventures of Lancelot and the Lily Maid of Astolat.)
Tappan. Stories of legendary heroes.
Sir Launcelot. *See* Sir Lancelot.
Sir One Long Body and Madame Thousand Feet. Griffis. Unmannerly tiger, and other Korean tales.
Griffis. Korean fairy tales.
Sir Owain and the lady of the fountain. Brooks. Wonder stories from the Mabinogion. (Lady and the fountain.)
Clay. Stories from Le Morte d'Arthur. (Lady of the fountain.)
Clay. Stories of King Arthur and the Round Table. (Lady of the fountain.)
Lang. Lilac fairy book. (Lady of the fountain.)
Lanier. Knightly legends of Wales. (Lady of the fountain.)
Patten. Junior classics. v. 4.
Tappan. Stories of legendary heroes. (Owain and the lady of the fountain.)
Wilmot-Buxton. Stories of early England.
Sir Owen and the dragons. Johnson. Elm-tree fairy book.
Sir Patrick Spens. Greenwood. Stories from famous ballads.
Grierson. Children's tales from Scottish ballads.
(poem). Lansing. Tales of old England.
(poem). Scudder. Children's book.
Sir Pellinore. Baldwin. Stories of the king. (Sir Griflet and Pellinore; In the Forest Perilous.)
Sir Percival. Baldwin. Stories of the king. (Making of a knight.)
Barber. Wagner opera stories (Parsifal.)
Clay. Stories from Le Morte d'Arthur. (Adventures of Sir Percivale.)
Cutler. Stories of King Arthur and his knights.
Lansing. Page, esquire and knight.
McSpadden. Stories from great operas. (Parsifal.)
Maud. Wagner's heroes. (Parsifal.)
Patten. Junior classics. v. 4.
Pleasanton. Fairyland of opera. (Parsifal.)
(poem). Storytellers' magazine. Dec. 1914, p. 765. (Parsifal's childhood.)
Wheelock. Stories of Wagner operas. (Parsifal.)
Sir Peredur. Baldwin. Fifty famous rides. (How Peredur became a knight.)
Brooks. Wonder stories from the Mabinogion. (Peredur, the son of Evrawc.)
Clay. Stories from Le Morte d'Arthur.
Clay. Stories of King Arthur and the Round Table. (Adventures of Sir Peredur.)
Higginson. Tales of the enchanted islands of the Atlantic. (Castle of the active door.)

Sir Peredur—*continued.*
Lanier. Knightly legends of Wales. (Peredur, the son of Evrawc.)
Sir Philip Sidney and the cup of water. Baldwin. Fifty famous stories. (Sir Philip Sidney.)
Blaisdell. English history story book.
Sly. World stories retold. (Sir Philip Sidney.)
Sir Richard Lee. *See* Robin Hood.
Sir Richard Whittington and his cat. *See* Dick Whittington and his cat.
Sir Ronan and the princess. Johnson. Elm-tree fairy book.
Sir Skip-and-a-jump. Fairy tales from Brentano.
Sir Turquine. Cutler. Stories of King Arthur and his knights.
(How Sir Turquine was slain and his prisoners delivered.)
Sir Tristram. Clay. Stories of King Arthur and the Round Table.
Clay. Stories from Le Morte d'Arthur.
Cutler. Stories of King Arthur and his knights.
Chapin. Wonder stories from Wagner. (Tristan and Iseult.)
Guerber. Legends of the middle ages. (Tristan and Iseult.)
Maud. Wagner's heroines. (Isolda.)
Storytellers' magazine. Jan. 1914, p. 385. (Adventures of Tristram, the forest knight.)
Wheelock. Stories of Wagner operas. (Tristan and Isolde.)
Sir Walter Raleigh. *See* Raleigh's cloak.
Siren of La Fresnaye. Cary. French fairy tales.
Siren of the Rhine. *See* Lorelei.
Sirens. Carpenter. Long ago in Greece.
Sis' Dove. Young. Plantation bird legends.
Sister and brother. *See* Stag prince.
Sister and half-sister. Cary. French fairy tales.
See also Mother Holle.
Sister of the sun.
Lang. Brown fairy book.
Lang. Magician's gifts.
See also Sun's sisters.
Sister with the yellow hair. Gate. Broom fairies.
Sisyphus. Cooke. Nature myths and stories.
Sisyphus and Autolycus. Baldwin. Story of the golden age. (*In* King of cattle thieves.)
Six and four are ten. Thomas. Welsh fairy book.
Six companions. *See* How six men travelled through the wide world.
Six comrades. *See* How six men travelled through the wide world.
Six giants and a griffin. Edey. Six giants and a griffin.
Six hungry beasts. *See* Fox and his five hungry comrades.
Six-in-one. *See* Beautiful bride. II.

Six little glow worms. Nordau. Dwarf's spectacles.
Six sillies. Lang. Red fairy book.
Lang. White doe.
See also Three sillies.
Six soldiers of fortune. *See* How six traveled through the world.
Six swans. Forty famous fairy tales.
Grimm. Fairy tales (Paull tr.).
*Grimm. Fairy tales (Wiltse.) v. 1.
Grimm. Household stories (Crane tr.).
Lang. Magic ring and other stories.
Lang. Yellow fairy book.
Mulock. Fairy book.
My Bookhouse. v. 3.
Patten. Junior classics. v. 1.
Scudder. Children's book.
Tappan. Folk stories and fables.
See also Twelve brothers; Twelve wild ducks; Wild swans.
Sixty minutes make an hour. St. Nicholas. Jan. 1879, p. 207.
Skadi. *See* How Skadi chose her husband.
Skalunda giant. Stroebe and Martens. Swedish fairy book.
Skilful huntsman. Pyle. Pepper and salt.
Skilful John. Cary. French fairy tales.
Skilful thief. Cary. French fairy tales.
See also Treasure chamber of Rhampsinitus.
Skillywidden. Olcott. Book of elves and fairies.
Skipper and Old Nick. Asbjörnsen. Tales from the fjeld.
Gade. Norwegian fairy tales.
Skipper and Sir Urian. Stroebe and Martens. Norwegian fairy book.
Skipping shoes. Alcott. Lulu's library. v. 1.
Skirnir. *See* Wooing of Gerd.
Skrymir. *See* Thor and his journey to Jötunheim.
Skrymsli. Guerber. Myths of northern lands. (*In* Loki.)
Sky bridge of birds. Griffis. Unmannerly tiger, and other Korean tales.
Griffis. Korean fairy tales.
Headland. Chinese boy and girl. (Heavenly river with the people who dwell thereon.)
James. Green willow. (Star lovers.)
Tappan. Myths from many lands. (Star-lovers.)
See also Trials of two heavenly lovers. pt. 1.
Sky country. Judson. Myths and legends of Alaska.
Sky elk. Olcott. Red Indian fairy book.
Sky is falling. Burchill. Progressive road to reading. Book 1. (Sky is falling; Brown hen.)
See also Chicken-Little.
Sky O'Dawn. Martens. Chinese fairy book.
Slave who became a king. Aunt Naomi. Jewish fairy tales and fables.
Slave's fortune. Landa. Aunt Naomi's Jewish fairy tales and legends.

Slayer of the spotted calf. *See* Dun horse.
Slayers of innocent babes. Sologub. Sweet-scented name.
Slaying of Hallgerda's husbands. Lang. Red romance book.
Slaying of the Tanuki. Lang. Pink fairy book.
Sleep house. Judson. Myths and legends of Alaska.
Sleep of one hundred years. Landa. Aunt Naomi's Jewish fairy tales and legends.
See also Rip Van Winkle. I.
Sleeper awakened. *See* Abou Hassan.
Sleeping apple. *Elson and Runkel. Elson readers. Book 1.
Sleeping beauty. I. Aunt Louisa's book of fairy tales.
*Baldwin. Fairy reader. (Briar Rose.)
Baker and Carpenter. Language readers. 3d year.
Bates. Once upon a time. (Briar Rose.)
Boy's and girl's fairy book. (Story of the sleeping beauty.)
Burt. Story of the German Iliad. (Sleeping beauty in the wood.)
Canton. Reign of King Herla. (Briar Rose.)
Cather. Educating by story telling. (Briar Rose.)
Chisholm. In fairyland.
Coe and Christie. Story hour readers. 3d book. (Thorn Rose.)
Coussens. Child's book of stories.
(play). Doheny. Play awhile. (Sleeping beauty; Briar Rosebud.)
Douglas. Favourite French fairy tales.
*Dyer and Brady. Merrill readers. 2d reader.
Favorite fairy tales. (Sleeping beauty in the wood.)
Forty famous fairy tales. (Sleeping beauty in the wood.)
Grimm. Fairy tales (Lucas tr. Briar Rose.)
Grimm. Fairy tales (Paull tr. Briar Rose.)
Grimm. Fairy tales (Wiltse. Briar Rose.) v. 1.
Grimm. Household stories (Crane tr.).
Grimm. Household fairy tales (Burt ed. May Blossom.)
Grimm. Household tales (Everymans' ed. Briar Rose.)
Harris. Favorites from fairyland. (Sleeping beauty in the woods.)
Hodgkins. Atlantic treasury of childhood stories. (Briar rose.)
Howard. Dick Whittington and other stories.
Hoxie. Kindergarten story book. (Briar Rose.)
Jerrold. Big book of fairy tales. (Briar Rose.)
Johnson. Fir-tree fairy book.
Lang. Blue fairy book.
Lang. Sleeping beauty in the wood and other stories.
Lansing. Fairy tales. v. 2.
Larned. Fairy tales from France. (Sleeping beauty in the wood.)
Mabie. Fairy tales every child should know.
Mabie. Heroes and fairies. (Sleeping beauty in the wood.)
Marshall. Fairy tales of all nations. (Rosebud.)

Sleeping beauty—*continued.*
Mother Goose rhymes, jingles and fairy tales (Altemus ed.).
Mulock. Fairy book.
My Bookhouse. v. 3.
Norton. Heart of oak books. v. 2. (Sleeping beauty in the wood.)
Nursery tales.
Olcott. Book of elves and fairies. (Sleeping beauty in the wood.)
Patten. Junior classics. v. 1. Fairy and wonder tales.
Perkins. Twenty best fairy tales.
Perrault. Fairy tales.
Perrault. Old-time stories. (Sleeping beauty in the wood.)
Perrault. Tales of Mother Goose. (Sleeping beauty in the wood.)
Perrault. Tales of passed times.
Pyle. Mother's nursery tales.
Quiller-Couch. The sleeping beauty.
Rhys. Fairy gold.
Rolfe. Fairy tales in prose and verse. (Sleeping beauty in the wood.)
(poem). Rolfe. Fairy tales in prose and verse.
Scudder. Book of folk stories. (Sleeping beauty in the wood.)
Scudder. Children's book. (Sleeping beauty in the wood.)
Scudder. Fables and folk stories.
Singleton. Wild flower fairy book.
Skinner. Emerald story book. (Brier Rose.)
Sly. World stories retold.
Stone. Children's stories that never grow old.
Success library. v. 3.
Tappan. Folk stories and fables. (Sleeping beauty in the wood.)
Tweed. Fairy tales everyone should know.
·Valentine. Old, old fairy tales (Warne ed. Sleeping beauty in the wood.)
Van Sickle and Seegmiller. Riverside readers. 3d reader. (Sleeping princess.)
Washburn. Old-fashioned tales.
Welsh. Fairy tales children love.
Wiggin and Smith. Fairy ring. (Briar Rose.)
Winnington. Outlook fairy book.

Lang and Valentine versions give a second part of the story which the others omit. Briar Rose is a simpler version of the same story, and is therefore included here.

See also Ocean sleeping beauty.
Sleeping beauty. II. Mendes. Fairy spinning wheel.
Sleeping beauty in the wood. *See* Sleeping beauty.
Sleeping fox and the boy with a stone. *See* Lad and the fox.
Sleeping king. Storytellers' magazine. Sept. 1915, p. 304.
See also Emperor's sleep.

Sleeping princess. *See* Sleeping beauty.
Sleepy Hollow, Legend of. Almost true tales.
Arnold and Gilbert. Stepping stones to literature. v. 7.
Baker and Carpenter. Language readers, 6th year. (Headless horseman.)
Hartwell. Story hour readings. 7th year. (Schoolmaster's ride.)
Mabie. Legends every child should know.
Norton. Heart of oak books. v. 5.
Patten. Children's classics. v. 2.
Scudder. Book of legends.
Sleepy John. Baudis. Czech folk tales.
Sleepy story. Stebbins. 3d reader.
See also Endless tale; Story without an end.
Slice of tongue. Gask. Folk tales from many lands.
Slip pine-root, grip fox-foot. *See* Slip root, catch Reynard's foot.
Slip root, catch Reynard's foot. Asbjörnsen. Fairy tales from the far north. (Slip pine-root, grip fox-foot.)
Asbjörnsen. Tales from the fjeld.
Jacobs. Europa's fairy book. (*In* Reynard and Bruin.)
Johnson. Book of fairy-tale bears. (Bruin outwitted.)
Patten. Junior classics. v. 1. (Bear and the fox.)
Wiggin and Smith. Tales of laughter. (How Reynard outwitted Bruin.)
Slippers of Abou-Karem. Jokai and others. Golden fairy book.
Slippers of the king. Griswold. Hindu fairy tales.
Sluggard. Chodzko. Fairy tales of the Slav.
Sly fox and sly fish. Aunt Naomi. Jewish fairy tales and fables.
Small green caterpillar and the beautiful white butterfly, Story of. Harrison. In story land.
See also Lesson of faith.
Smallhead and the king's sons. Jacobs. More Celtic fairy tales.
Yeats. Irish fairy and folk tales.
See also Molly Whuppie.
Smart young tiger. Partridge. Story telling in home and school.
Smile fairy. Bailey. Friendly tales.
Smith and the devil. I. Asbjörnsen. Folk and fairy tales.
Dasent. Popular tales from the Norse. (Master smith.)
Gade. Norwegian fairy tales. (Smith who could not get into hell.)
See also Impty-umpty and the blacksmith; Little blacksmith Verholen; Three wishes. IV.
Smith and the devil. II. Magnus. Russian folk-tales.
Smith and the devil. III. Wenig. Beyond the giant mountains. (About the devil and the blacksmith.)
See also Shoemaker's apron.
Smith and the fairies. Douglas. Scottish fairy tales.

Smith and the fairies—*continued.*
Grierson. Children's book of Celtic stories.
Johnson. Elm-tree fairy book. (Rescue from the elves.)
Olcott. Book of elves and fairies.
Wiggin and Smith. Tales of wonder.
Smith who could not get into hell. *See* Smith and the devil. I.
Smithy. Children's story garden. (Adapted.)
Olcott. Good stories for great holidays.
Smolicheck. Fillmore. Shoemaker's apron. (Smolicheck, the little boy who opened the door.)
Snail and the beaver. Pratt. Legends of the red children.
Wade. Indian fairy tales.
Snail and the bees. Davis. Chow-Leung. Chinese fables and folk stories.
Snail and the rose-tree. Andersen. Wonder stories (Author's ed.).
Keyes. Five senses.
Snail and the statue. Æsop. Fables (Burt ed.).
Snake. Stroebe and Martens. Danish fairy book.
Snake and the hedgehog. Bryce. Fables from afar.
See also Arab and his camel.
Snake and the sparrows. *See* Sparrows and the snake.
Snake brother. Grinnell. Pawnee hero stories.
Snake-charm. Burlingame. Grateful elephant.
Snake lady. Guerber. Legends of the Rhine.
Snake-ogre. Cornyn. Around the wigwam fire.
Snake-peri and the magic mirror. *See* Serpent-peri and the magic mirror.
Snake prince. Lang. Olive fairy book.
Lang. Snake prince and other tales.
Snake princess. Magnus. Russian folk-tales.
Snake-woman. Cornyn. Around the wigwam fire.
Snake-woman and King Ali Mardan. Steel. Tales of the Punjab.
Snake's thanks. Friedlander. Jewish fairy book.
See also Way of the world.
Snap-dragons. Patten. Junior classics. v. 6.
Snapping turtle. *See* Talkative tortoise.
Sneezing Colossus. Griffis. Unmannerly tiger, and other Korean tales.
Griffis. Korean fairy tales.
Snegourka. *See* Snowflake. I.
Snip, Snap, Snorium. Stanley. Animal folk tales.
See also Three dogs. I.
Snow-Blanche. *See* Snowflake. I.
Snow-child. Chisholm and Steedman. Staircase of stories.
Snow-daughter and the Fire-son. Lang. Three dwarfs, and other stories.
Lang. Yellow fairy book.
Snow-Drop and the seven dwarfs. *See* Snow-White and the seven dwarfs.

Snow fairy. Patterson. Enchanted bird.
Snow-image. Blaisdell. Child life. 4th reader.
Hawthorne. Little Daffydowndilly.
Judson and Bender. Graded literature readers. v. 4.
Mabie. Famous stories every child should know.
Skinner. Pearl story book.
See also Snowflake. I.
Snow maiden. *See* Snowflake. I.
Snow makers. Seton. Woodland tales. (Snowstorm.)
Snow man. I. Andersen. Fairy tales (Paull tr.).
Andersen. Fairy tales (Turpin).
Andersen. Wonder stories (Author's ed.).
Bailey and Lewis. For the children's hour.
Lang. Golden mermaid and other stories.
Lang. Pink fairy book.
Skinner. Pearl story book.
Snow man. II. Lindsay. Story garden.
Snow man. III. *See* Ice king.
Snow-man's bride. Kennedy. New world fairy book.
Snow queen. Andersen. Fairy tales (Paull tr.).
Andersen. Fairy tales and stories (Toksvig.)
Andersen. Stories (Riverside ed.).
Andersen. Wonder stories (Author's ed.).
Bailey. In the animal world. (Of the snow queen's palace. Adapted.)
Chisholm. Enchanted land
Field. Famous fairy tales.
Lang. Pink fairy book.
Lang. Snow-queen and other stories.
My Bookhouse. v. 3.
Skinner. Garnet story book. (Abridged.)
Success library. v. 3.
Tales for bedtime.
Snow queen and the magic bees. Stewart. Once upon a time.
Snow shovels for two. Bailey. Stories for Sunday telling.
Snow, the crow and the blood. MacManus. Donegal fairy stories.
Snow-White. *See* Snowflake I.
Snow-White and Rose-Red. Alllison and Perdue. Story in primary instruction.
Blaisdell. Child life. 2d reader.
Chisholm. In fairyland.
Chisholm and Steedman. Staircase of stories.
Coussens. Child's book of stories.
Favorite fairy tales.
*Grimm. Fairy tales (Wiltse). v. 1.
Johnson. Book of fairy-tale bears. (Snow-White and Rose-Red and the big black bear.)
Lang. Blue fairy book.
Lang. Little Red Riding-Hood, and other stories.
Lang. Snake prince.

Snow-White and Rose-Red—*continued.*
Mulock. Fairy book.
My Bookhouse. v. 2.
O'Grady and Throop. Teachers' story teller's book.
Patten. Junior classics. v. 1.
Perkins. Twenty best fairy tales.
Singleton. Goldenrod fairy book.
Storytellers' magazine. Feb. 1914, p. 447.
Success library. v. 3.
Welsh. Fairy tales children love.
Wiggin and Smith. Fairy ring.
Snow-White and the seven dwarfs. Aunt Louisa's book of fairy tales. (Little Snowdrop.)
Bailey. Stories children need.
Baldwin. Second fairy reader. (Snowdrop.)
Canton. Reign of King Herla. (Little Snow-White.)
Chisholm. In fairyland. (Snow-Drop and the seven dwarfs.)
Coussens. Child's book of stories. (Snowdrop.)
Favorite fairy tales. (Little Snowdrop.)
Forty famous fairy tales. (Snowdrop.)
Grimm. Fairy tales (Lucas tr. Snowdrop.)
Grimm. Household stories (Crane tr. Little Snow-White.)
Grimm. Household tales (Burt ed. Magic mirror.)
Grimm. Household tales (Everyman's ed. Snowdrop.)
Harris. Favorites from fairyland. (Little Snowdrop.)
Heller and Bates. Little Golden Hood. (Snowdrop.)
Hodgkins. Atlantic treasury of childhood stories. (Little Snow White.)
Jacobs. Europa's fairy book. (Snowwhite.)
Jerrold. Big book of fairy tales. (Snowdrop.)
Lang. Red fairy book. (Snowdrop.)
Lansing. Fairy tales. v. 2. (Snowdrop.)
Mabie. Fairy tales every child should know. (Magic mirror.)
Mabie. Heroes and fairies. (Magic mirror.)
Mulock. Fairy book. (Little Snowdrop.)
Pyle. Where the wind blows. (Magic mirror.)
Tappan. Folk stories and fables.
Valentine. Old, old fairy tales. (Snow-drop.)
See also Gold-tree and silver tree; Little sister of the giants.
Snow-white bull. *See* Europa.
Snowball hares. *See* First rabbits.
Snowball that didn't melt. Skinner. Pearl story book.
Stocking. Golden goblet.
Snowball's Christmas eve. Esenwein and Stockard. Children's stories.
Snowbird and the water tiger. Compton. American Indian fairy tales.
Nixon-Roulet. Indian folk tales. (Wicked mother-in-law.)
Snowbirds. *Coe and Christie, Story hour readers. Book I.

Snowdrop. I. *Bailey. Folk stories and fables.
Bailey and Lewis. For the children's hour.
Olcott. Good stories for great holidays.
Skinner. Emerald story book.
Storytellers' magazine. Jan. 1915, p. 12.
See also Awakening.
Snowdrop. II. *See* Snow-White and the seven dwarfs.
Snowdrop. III. Pratt. Fairyland of flowers. (Legend of the snowdrop.)
See also First snowdrops. I and II.
Snowdrop fairy. Olcott. Wonder garden.
Snowflake. I. *Carrick. Picture tales from the Russian.
Gask. Folk tales from many lands. (Snow-White.)
Lang. Golden mermaid and other stories.
Lang. Pink fairy book.
Marshall. Fairy tales of all nations. (Little girl of snow.)
My Bookhouse. v. 2. (Little snow maiden.)
O'Grady and Throop. Teachers' story teller's book. (Snyegurka.)
Olcott. Wonder garden. (Snow-Blanche.)
Shedlock. Art of the storyteller. (Snegourka.)
Skinner. Pearl fairy book. (Snow maiden.)
Storytellers' magazine. Feb. 1916, p. 88. (Snow maiden.)
See also Snow image.
Snowflake. II. Ingelow. Stories told to a child. v. 2.
Snowflake. III. Bigham. Merry animal tales.
See also Wolf, the she-goat and the kid.
Snowheart. Mendes. Fairy spinning wheel.
Snowwhite. *See* Snow-White and the seven dwarfs.
Snuff-box. Lang. Green fairy book.
Lang. Pretty Goldilocks, and other stories.
Patten. Junior classics. v. 1.
So arose a misunderstanding. Sologub. Sweet-scented name.
Snyegurka. *See* Snowflake. I.
So born, so die. Houghton. Russian grandmother's wonder tales.
See also Rats and their son-in-law.
So-So. *See* Just as well.
Soaring lark. Canton. Reign of King Herla.
Grimm. Fairy tales (Lucas tr. Lady and the lion.)
Grimm. Houshold tales (Everyman's ed. Lily and the lion.)
Sobbing pine. Lummis. Pueblo Indian folk stories.
Society to make fairy tales come true. Griffis. Belgian fairy tales.
Socrates and his friends. Æsop. Fables (Burt ed.).
Socrates and his house. Baldwin. Fifty famous stories.
(poem). Success library, v. 3. (Saying of Socrates.)
Sodewa Bai. Frere. Old Deccan days.
Sohrab and Rustem. Baldwin. Fifty famous rides. (How Rustem rode to Mazinderan.)
Baldwin. Horse fair. (Rakush.)

Sohrab and Rustem—*continued.*
Chandler. Pan the piper. (Magic carpet of old Persia.)
Mabie. Legends every child should know.
Maud. Heroines of poetry. (A hero's mother.)
My Bookhouse. v. 5. (Story of Rustem, hero of Persia.)
Scudder. Book of legends.
Tappan. Stories of legendary heroes.
Wilmot-Buxton. Stories of Persian heroes.
Soldier and death. Magnus. Russian folk-tales.
Soldier and his horses. Æsop. Fables (Burt ed.).
Soldier and the devil. Baudis. Czech folk tales.
Soldier and the dragon. Johnson. Fir-tree fairy book.
Soldier and the Tsar in the forest. Magnus. Russian folk-tales.
See also King and the miller of Mansfield.
Soldier of God. *See* St. Martin.
Soldier who lived in the drum. Bailey. Stories for Sunday telling.
Sole. Farmer. Nature myths.
Grimm. Fairy tales (Paull tr.).
Wiggin and Smith. Tales of laughter. (Sole's mouth.)
Wiltse. Folklore stories and proverbs.
Sole's mouth. *See* Sole.
Solomon. *See* King Solomon.
Somebody. Pyle. Prose and verse for children.
"Something." Andersen. Fairy tales (Paull tr.).
Andersen. Stories and tales (Author's ed.).
Son-in-law. Eastman. Wigwam evenings.
Son of Adam. Jacobs. More English fairy tales.
Wiggin and Smith. Tales of laughter.
Son of seven mothers. *See* Son of seven queens.
Son of seven queens. Jacobs. Indian fairy tales.
Steel. Tales of the Punjab. (Son of seven mothers.)
Tappan. Folk stories and fables.
Wiggin and Smith. Magic casements.
Son of the bright morning. *See* Perseus.
Son of the fairy queen. Rhys. Fairy gold.
Son of the King of Erin, and the giant of Loch Lein. *See* Yellow Lily.
Son of the King of Ireland, and the daughter of the King of the Redcap, Tale of the. Grierson. Book of Celtic stories.
Son of the morning star. *See* Scar-Face. III.
Son of the soap seller. James. Cat and the mouse.
Son of the strong man of the wood. Grierson. Book of Celtic stories.
Son of the Thunder-god. *See* Child of the thunder.
Son of the wolf-chief. Lang. Strange story book.
Song-bird and the healing water. *See* Hidden waters.
Song in the heart (play). Stevenson. Plays in the home.
Song of a fairy. Winnington. Outlook fairy book.
Song of Roland. *See* Roland.

Song of the fairy queen. Rhys. Fairy gold.
Song of the ghost (poem). Yeats. Irish fairy and folk tales.
Song of the winds. *See* Indian story of the winds. III.
Song sparrow, Story of the. Stewart. Once upon a time.
Song that travèled. Lindsay. Story-teller.
Sons of Aymon. Bryant. Treasury of hero tales. (Rinaldo and Bayard.)
Baldwin. Horse fair. (Bayard.)
Griffis. Belgian fairy tales. (Rinaldo and his wonderful horse Bayard.)
Guerber. Legends of the middle ages.
Patten. Junior classics. v. 4. (Rinaldo and Bayard.)
Wilmot-Buxton. Stories of old French romance. (Castle of Montauban.)
Sons of Feridoun. Hartwell. Story hour readings. 6th year.
Wilmot-Buxton. Stories of Persian heroes. (Three brothers.)
Sons of the caliph. Baldwin. Fifty famous people.
Sons of the Conqueror. *See* William the Conqueror.
Soothsayer. Kunos. Forty-four Turkish fairy tales.
Soothsayer's son. Jacobs. Indian fairy tales.
Sophie's secret. Alcott. Lulu's library. v. 3.
Sorcerer of the White Lotus Lodge. Martens. Chinese fairy book.
Sorceress. Æsop. Fables (Burt ed.).
Soria Moria castle. Asbjörnsen. Fairy tales from the far North. (Soria Moria's castle.)
Dasent. Norse fairy tales.
Dasent. Popular tales from the Norse (Soria Maria's castle).
Gade. Norwegian fairy book.
Lang. Red fairy book.
Stroebe and Martens. Norwegian fairy book.
Wiggin and Smith. Magic casements.
Soria Maria's castle. *See* Soria Moria castle.
Sorrow. Magnus. Russian folk-tales.
See also Woe Bogotar.
Sorrow-singing. Hume. Chronicles of fairyland.
Sorry drunkard. Magnus. Russian folk-tales.
Soul cages. Yeats. Irish fairy tales.
Soul of the licentiate. Olcott and Pendleton. Jolly book.
Soul of the Samurai. Nixon-Roulet. Japanese folk stories and fairy tales.
Soup from a sausage skewer. Andersen. Fairy tales (Paull tr.).
Andersen. Wonder stories. (Soup made of a sausage stick.)
Darton. Wonder book of beasts. (Soup on a sausage peg.)
Soup made of a sausage stick. *See* Soup from a sausage skewer.

Soup on a sausage peg. *See* Soup from a sausage skewer.
Sour and Civil. Browne. Granny's wonderful chair.
"Sour grapes." See Fox and the grapes.
South pointing carriage. *See* Shinansha.
South Wind and the dandelion. *See* Prairie dandelion.
South Wind, Legend of. *See* Prairie dandelion.
Southernwood. Baring-Gould. Old English fairy tales.
Sovereign of the mineral kingdom. Chodzko. Fairy tales of the Slav.
Sow and the bitch. Æsop. Fables (Black ed.).
Sow and the cat. Æsop. Fables (Burt ed.).
Sow and the wolf. Æsop. Fables (Black ed.).
Æsop. Fables (Burt ed.).
Spaniel and the mastiff. Æsop. Fables (Burt ed.).
Spanish cavalier. Æsop. Fables (Burt ed.).
Spanish tale. Fairy stories retold from the St. Nicholas
Spare minutes. Wickes. Happy holidays.
Sparrow and his four children. Grimm. Fairy tales (Paull tr.).
Storytellers' magazine. Jan. 1915, p. 2. (Sparrow and his young ones.)
Sparrow and his young ones. *See* Sparrow and his four children.
Sparrow and the bush. Bain. Cossack fairy tales.
Wiggin and Smith. Fairy ring.
See also Cat and the mouse; Grain of corn; How the mouse got into his hole; Little Tuppen; Munachar and Manachar; Nanny who wouldn't go home to supper; Old woman and her pig.
Sparrow and the crow. *Field first reader.
Johnson. Birch-tree fairy book.
(play). Lansing. Quaint old stories.
Steel. Tales of the Punjab.
Sparrow and the hare. Æsop. Fables (Black ed.).
Æsop. Fables (Burt ed.).
Sparrow in the swallow's nest. Pitrè. Swallow book.
Sparrow with the slit tongue. *See* Tongue-cut sparrow.
Sparrows and the falcon. Wiggin and Smith. Talking beasts.
Sparrows and the snake. Bidpai. Tortoise and the geese.
Wiggin and Smith. Talking beasts. (Snake and the sparrow.)
Sparrow's revenge. Rouse. Talking thrush.
Sparrow's search for the rain. Macmillan. Canadian fairy tales.
Speaking a piece. Baldwin. Fifty famous people.
Speaking cave. Dyer and Brady. Merrill readers. 2d reader.
See also Heyo, house; Jackal and the crocodile.
Speaking statue. Olcott. Good stories for great holidays.
Spectacles. Æsop. Fables (Burt ed.).
Wiggin and Smith. Talking beasts.

Specter bride of Falkenberg. Guerber. Legends of the Rhine.
Specter in Fjelkinge. Stroebe and Martens. Swedish fairy book.
Specter wedding. Guerber. Legends of the Rhine.
Spectral foot. *See* Knight who married a water nymph.
Spectral ship. Smith. Mystery tales.
Spectre dogs. Hartland. English folk and fairy tales.
Speedwell, Legend of the. Pratt. Fairyland of flowers.
Spell of the laughing raven. Judson. Myths and legends of the Pacific Northwest.
Spendthrift and the swallow. Æsop. Fables (Burt ed.).
Æsop. Fables (Stickney).
Scudder. Children's book.
Scudder. Fables and folk stories.
See also Young man and the swallow.
Spendthrift merchant's son. *See* Golden mountain.
Sphinx. *See* Œdipus.
Spice bird. *See* Phœnix.
Spider and the bee. Wiggin and Smith. Talking beasts.
Young and Field. Literary readers. Book 2.
Spider and the crows. Macnair. Animal tales from Africa.
Spider and the flea. *Burchill. Progressive road to reading. Book 1. (Lady Bird and Little Fly.)
Grimm. Household tales. (Burt ed. Lady-bird and the fly.)
Lansing. Rhymes and stories. (Ladybird and the fly.)
Storytellers' magazine. April 1915, p. 125. (Lady-bird and the fly.)
Wiggin and Smith. Tales of laughter.
See also Death and burial of poor hen-sparrow; Death of Chanticleer; Master Chanticleer and Dame Hen; Titty-mouse and Tatty-mouse.
Spider and the fly (poem). Norton. Heart of oak books. v. 2.
(poem). Scudder. Children's book.
(poem). Tappan. Old-fashioned stories and poems.
Spider and the lion. Macnair. Animal tales from Africa.
Spider and the silk-worm. *See* Silkworm and the spider. II.
Spider-man. *See* Anansi the spider-man; Spider and the lion; Spider and the crows; Spider, the hippopotamus and the elephant; Why spiders live in dark corners.
Spider, the hippopotamus and the elephant. Macnair. Animal tales from Africa.
Storytellers' magazine. Oct. 1916, p. 532.
Spider woman's mistake. Nixon-Roulet. Indian folk tales.
Spindle, shuttle and needle. Bailey and Lewis. For the children's hour.
Forty famous fairy tales.
Grimm. Fairy tales (Paull tr.).
*Grimm. Fairy tales (Wiltse). v. 2.
Lang. Green fairy-book.

Spindle, shuttle and needle—*continued.*
Lang. Three dwarfs, and other stories.
Storytellers' magazine. Dec. 1914, p. 762. (Spindle, the needle and the shuttle.)
Wiggin and Smith. Fairy ring.
Spindle, the needle and the shuttle. *See* Spindle, shuttle, and needle.
Spinners. *See* Habetrot and Scantlie Mab.
Spinning fairies. *See* Three spinning fairies.
Spinning queen. Baldwin. Second fairy reader.
Laboulaye. Fairy tales. (Idle maiden. *In* Captain John's travels.)
Laboulaye. Last fairy tales.
See also Three spinning fairies; Three little crones each with something big; Habetrot and Scantlie Mab.
Spinning wheel of stars. Farmer. Nature myths.
Spirit. Richards. Silver crown.
Spirit and life. Skinner. Emerald story book.
Spirit boy. Nixon-Roulet. Indian folk tales.
Spirit of Snow. Judson. Myths and legends of the Pacific Northwest.
Spirit of the corn. Olcott. Good stories for great holidays.
Skinner. Topaz story book. (O-na-tah, the spirit of the corn fields.)
Tanner. Legends from the red man's forest. (Things of the garden.)
See also Seven corn maidens.
Spirit of the singing house. Bayliss. Treasury of Eskimo tales.
Spirit of the steppes. Chodzko. Fairy tales of the Slav.
Polevoi. Russian fairy tales.
Spirit of the Wu Lian Mountain. Martens. Chinese fairy book.
Spirit that lived in a tree. Shedlock. Eastern stories and legends.
Spirit voices. Cornyn. Around the wigwam fire.
Spirits of spring. Stocking. Golden goblet.
Spirits of the Yellow River. Martens. Chinese fairy book.
Spirits, seen and unseen. Harris. Nights with Uncle Remus.
Spokane Falls, Origin of. Judson. Myths and legends of the Pacific Northwest.
Sportsman and the spaniel. Æsop. Fables (Burt ed.).
Spotty and Gosling. Darton. Wonder book of beasts.
Spousken and the giant. Bosschère. Folk tales of Flanders.
Sprig of holly. St. Nicholas. Jan. 1880, p. 255.
Stockton. Floating prince.
Sprig of rosemary. Lang. Aladdin, and other stories.
Lang. Pink fairy book.
Sprightly tailor. Jacobs. Celtic fairy tales.
Spring and her helpers. Poulsson. In the child's world.
Spring beauty. *See* Old Winter Man and the Spring. I.

Spring girl. Storytellers' magazine. Apr. 1915, p. 105.
Spring lover and autumn lover. *See* Autumn and spring.
Spring maiden and the frost giants. *See* Iduna's apples.
Spring running. Kipling. Second jungle book.
Spring song. Bakewell. True fairy stories.
Spring wakes. Eliot. House on the edge of things.
Storytellers' magazine. Mar. 1916, p. 159.
Spring water. *See* Magic well.
Springtime. I. *See* Proserpina.
Springtime. II. Field. Little book of profitable tales.
Skinner. Emerald story book.
Springtime. III. Judson. Flower fairies.
Sprite of the mill-pond. *See* Nix in the pond.
Spry Mouse and Mr. Frog. *Coe and Christie. Story hour readers. Book 2.
Squeaky and the scare box. Ladies' Home Journal. Dec. 1915. (*In* Christmas bedtime stories.)
Squire Peter. *See* Lord Peter.
Squire's bride. Asbjörnsen. Fairy tales from the far north.
Gade. Norwegian fairy tales. (Rich farmer's wife.)
My Bookhouse. v. 4.
Olcott and Pendleton. Jolly book.
Patten. Junior classics. v. 1.
Thorne-Thomsen. East o' the sun and west o' the moon.
Squire's lady's tale. *See* Three sons.
Squire's tale. *See* Cambuscan bold, Story of; Wonder horse.
Squirrel and the horse (poem). Wiggin and Smith. Talking beasts.
Squirrel and the kingship. Stafford. Animal fables.
Squirrel and the leopard. Bryce. Fables from afar.
Squirrel in service. Æsop. Fables (Stickney. Supplement).
Squirrel's devotion. Cabot. Ethics for children.
See also Chipmunk's stripes. I.
Squirrel's dream. Darton. Wonder book of beasts.
Squirrel's secret. Stewart. Once upon a time.
Squirrel's sweetheart. Tales for bedtime.
Squirrel's tea party. Bouvé. Lamp light fairy tales.
Sswanda the piper, Story of. Laboulaye. Fairy tales.
Staff. Richards. Golden windows.
Staff and fiddle. Pyle. Wonder clock.
Stag. *See* Stag at the lake.
Stag and the fawn. Æsop. Fables (Black ed.).
Æsop. Fables (Burt ed.).
Stag and the hedgehog. Houghton. Russian grandmother's wonder tales.
Stag and the lion. *See* Stag at the lake.
Stag and the vine. Æsop. Fables (Black ed. Hart and the vine.)
Wiggin and Smith. Talking beasts.
Stag at the lake. Æsop. Fables (Black ed. Stag looking into the water.)
Æsop. Fables (Burt ed. Stag looking into the pool.)

Stag at the lake—*continued.*
Æsop. Fables (Burt ed. Hart and the hunter.)
Æsop. Fables (Jacobs. Hart and the hunter.)
Æsop. Fables (Stickney).
Arnold and Gilbert. Stepping stones to literature. v. 2.
Baldwin. Fairy tales and fables. (Deer.)
Scudder. Children's book. (Stag and the lion.)
Scudder. Fables and folk stories. (Stag and the lion.)
Stanley. Animal folk tales. (Deer's horns.)
Storytellers' magazine. Oct. 1914, p. 705. (Vain stag.)
Wiggin and Smith. Talking beasts. (Deer and the lion.)
Stag hunt and what came of it. *See* Sir Accalon.
Stag in the ox-stall. Æsop. Fables (Black ed.).
Æsop. Fables (Burt ed.).
Æsop. Fables (Jacobs. Hart in the ox-stall.)
Stag looking into the pool. *See* Stag at the lake.
Stag looking into the water. *See* Stag at the lake.
Stag-prince. Kunos. Forty-four Turkish fairy tales. (Sister and brother.)
Kunos. Turkish fairy tales.
Stag, the crow, and the jackal. Rouse. Talking thrush.
Stag's valley. Sylva and Strettell Legends from river and mountain.
Stain of sin. Guerber. Legends of the Rhine.
Stan Bolovan. Lang. Violet fairy book.
Lang. Marvellous musician.
Underhill. Dwarfs' tailor and other fairy tales. (Steven Bolovan and the dragon.)
Star. Curtiss. Christmas stories and legends.
Star and the lily. *See* Star maiden.
Star beautiful. Pratt. Legends of the red children.
Star boy. I. Grinnell. Punishment of the stingy.
Star boy. II. Curtis. Indian days of the long ago. (Strange trail.)
See also Star wives.
Star bride. *See* Maid who married the morning star.
Star child. I. Storytellers' magazine. Dec. 1916, p. 651.
Wilde. Fairy tales.
Star child. II. Landa. Jewish fairy tales and legends.
Star dipper. *See* Dipper.
Star dollars. Allison and Perdue. Story in primary instruction.
Bryant. How to tell stories to children.
Grimm. Fairy tales (Paull tr.).
*Grimm. Fairy tales (Wiltse). ✝ I.
Ketchum and Jorgensen. Kindergarten gems. (Shower of gold.)
Pyle. Mother's nursery tales. (Star jewels.)
Whittier. Child life in prose.
Star-eyed Deirdre. *See* Deirdre.
Star fairies. Harrison. Star fairies.
Star gazer. Scudder. Fables and folk stories.

Star jewels. I. Brown. Star jewels and other wonders.
Star jewels. II. *See* Star dollars.
Star-lovers. *See* Sky bridge of birds.
Star maiden. I. *Boston collection of kindergarten stories. (Star and the lily.)
Brooks. Stories of the red children. (Star that became a lily.)
Coe and Christie. Story hour readers. 3d book. (Water lilies.)
Compton. American Indian fairy tales.
Danielson. Story telling time. (Indian legend of the water-lily.)
*Donaldson. Moons of long ago. (Legend of the water lily.)
Farmer. Nature myths. (Water-lily.)
Judd. Wigwam stories. (How the water lily came.)
Mabie. Myths every child should know. (Star and the lily.)
McFee. Treasury of flower stories. (Water lily.)
My Bookhouse. v. 2. (Legend of the water lily.)
Olcott. Red Indian fairy book. (Star and the water lilies.)
Pratt. Legends of the red children. (Lily-star.)
Skinner. Turquoise story book. (Legend of the water lily.)
Storytellers' magazine. May 1916, p. 278. (*In* Nature legends—Story of the water-lily.)
Tanner. Legends of the red man's forest. (Water-lily.)
Wade. Indian fairy tales. (Star and the lily.)
Wilson. Nature study reader. (Star and the lily.)
Young and Field. Literary reader. Book 2. (Water lily.)
Star maiden. II. *See* Pleiades. VI.
Star that became a lily. *See* Star maiden.
Star that never moves. Judd. Wigwam stories.
Star tree. Storytellers' magazine. Dec. 1915, p. 467.
Star wife. *Cowles. Indian nature myths. (White Hawk.)
Esenwein and Stockard. Children's stories.
Grayl. Fairy tales from foreign lands. (Daughter of the stars.)
Kennedy. New world fairy book.
Nixon-Roulet. Indian folk tales.
Schoolcraft. Indian fairy book. (Celestial sisters.)
Success library. v. 3. (Celestial sisters.)
Tanner. Legends from the red man's forest. (Waupee, the white hawk.)
Wade. Indian fairy tales. (Daughter of the stars.)
See also Sun Princess.
Star wives. Cornyn. Around the wigwam fire. (Tall One and the Short One.)
Nixon-Roulet. Indian folk tales. (Story of the two weasels.)
Partridge. Glooscap the great chief. (Badger and the star wives.)
Partridge. Glooscap the great chief. (Star wives.)
See also Quo-too-quat; Star-boy.

Starch. Griffis. Dutch fairy tales. (Elves and their antics.)
Starkad and Bale. Stroebe and Martens. Swedish fairy book.
Starlein and Silverling. Pyle. Counterpane fairy.
Stars. I. Murray. Story book treasures.
Richards. Golden windows.
Stars. II. Eliot. House on the edge of things.
Stars and the pine. *See* Pleiades. II.
Stars in the sky. Bailey. Firelight stories. (Little girl who wanted the stars.)
Grover. Folk-lore readers. v. 1.
Jacobs. More English fairy tales.
O'Grady and Throop. Teachers' story teller's book.
Spaulding and Bryce. Aldine readers. Book 3.
Wiggin and Smith. Magic casements.
Stars, Stories of. *See* Alaka's eyes; Aurora, the white arch and the Great Bear; Callisto and Arcas; Child's dream of a star; Dipper; Enchanted youth; Girl who married the star; Maid who married the morning star; Morning star, Legend of; Pleiades; Pole star; Sailor's star; Sky bridge of birds; Twin stars; Wandering star; also titles beginning with the word star.
Stars that dance. *See* Pleiades. II.
Stars with wings. Donaldson. Moons of long ago.
See also Wandering star.
Starving of Mrs Leghorn. *See* Mr. and Mrs. Leghorn.
Statue. *See* Critics silenced.
Statue and the birds. Aspinwall. Short stories for short people.
Stavesacre fairies. Rhys. Fairy gold.
Steadfast tin-soldier. *See* Brave tin soldier.
Stealing of Iduna. *See* Iduna's apples.
Steam. Griffis. Dutch fairy tales. (Ice king and his wonderful grandson.)
Steamboat and the locomotive. My Bookhouse. v. 4.
Steel cane. Lang. Olive fairy book.
Steelpacha. Houghton. Russian grandmother's wonder tales.
Wiggin and Smith. Tales of wonder.
Stellante. Chisholm and Steedman. Staircase of stories.
Step-mother. Pyle. Wonder clock.
Stephan of Servia. *See* Price of a life.
Stephen and friendly fairy. Eliot. House on the edge of things.
Storytellers' magazine. Nov. 1915, p. 401.
Steps. Richards. Silver crown.
Steven Bolovan and the dragon. *See* Stan Bolovan.
Steward's shroud. Guerber. Legends of the Rhine.
Stick of gold and a stick of silver. Bradley-Birt. Bengal fairy tales.
Stock im eisen. Mendel. Our little Austrian cousin.
Stolen charm. Williston. Japanese fairy tales. 1st series.
Stolen child. Noyes. Twilight stories.

Stolen corn. Bailey and Lewis. For the children's hour.
*Haaren. Songs and stories. 2d reader.
Stolen garlic. Fielde. Chinese fairy tales.
Stolen plow. Babbitt. More Jataka tales.
Stolen princess. Tappan. Golden goose.
Stolen sacrament. Guerber Legends of the Rhine.
Stolen wine. *See* Odin and the mead.
Stompe Pilt. Stroebe and Martens. Swedish fairy book.
Stone and worm. Æsop. Fables (Stickney. Supplement).
Young and Field. Literary readers. Book 2.
Stone baby. *Bailey. Folk stories and fables.
Bailey and Lewis. For the children's hour.
See also Bambino.
Stone blocks. Richards. Silver crown.
Stone breaker. *See* Stone cutter.
Stone broth. Æsop. Fable (Stickney).
Olcott and Pendleton. Jolly book. (Limestone broth.)
See also Old woman and the tramp; Soup from a sausage skewer.
Stone canoe. *See* In the land of souls.
Stone-cold heart. Field. Famous fairy tales.
Hauff. Fairy tales.
Sylva and Strettell. Legends from river and mountain. (Little Glass-man.)
Stone cutter. Alderman. Classics old and new. 4th reader.
Bailey and Lewis. For the children's hour.
Bone. Children's stories. (Huffi the stone-breaker.)
Dyer and Brady. Merrill readers. 3rd reader.
Lang. Crimson fairy book.
Lang. Snow-queen and other stories.
Lyman. Story telling.
Olcott. Good stories for great holidays. (Hofus the stone-cutter.)
Shedlock. Art of the storyteller. (Hafiz the stone cutter.)
Silver fairy book. (Stone-breaker.)
Storytellers' magazine. April 1914, p. 516.
Van Sickle and Seegmiller. Riverside readers. 2d reader.
See also Peter the stone cutter; Unhappy blacksmith.
Stone in the cock's head. Wiggin and Smith. Tales of laughter.
See also Magic ring.
Stone in the road. I. Arnold and Gilbert. Stepping stones to literature. v. 3.
Bailey and Lewis. For the children's hour.
Stone in the road. II. Dyer and Brady. Merrill readers. 3d reader.
Stone lion. Partridge. Story telling in home and school.
Skinner. Merry tales.
Storytellers' magazine. June 1913, p. 26.
Stone-moving song. Lummis. Pueblo Indian folk stories.
Stone of gratitude. *See* Bell of justice. I.
Stone of the wise men. *See* Philosopher's stone.

Stone-patience and knife-patience. Kunos. Forty-four Turkish fairy tales. (Patience-stone and patience-knife.)
Kunos. Turkish fairy tales.
See also King who slept.
Stone-Shirt and the One-Two. Compton. American Indian fairy tales.
Stone statue. Djurklo. Fairy tales from the Swedish.
Stone that shed tears. *See* Niobe.
Stones of five colours and the Empress Jokwa. Ozaki. Japanese fairy book.
Stones of Plouhinec. *See* Thirst of the standing stones. I.
Stones of Plouvinec. *See* Thirst of the standing stones. I.
Stonish giants. Kennedy. New world fairy book.
Stony head. Slosson. Story-tell Lib.
Stool of fortune. Pyle. Twilight land.
Stoorworm. *See* Ashiepattle and the stoorworm.
Storehouse key in the distaff. Asbjörnsen. Fairy tales from the far north.
See also Suitor.
Stories about snakes. Grimm. Fairy tales (Paull tr.).
Stork and the toad. Wiggin and Smith. Talking beasts.
Storks. Andersen. Fairy tales (Lucas tr.).
Andersen. Fairy tales (Paull tr.).
Andersen. Wonder stories (Author's ed.).
Blaisdell. Child life. 3d reader.
Chisholm. In fairyland.
Chisholm and Steedman. Staircase of stories.
Field. Famous fairy tales.
Forty famous fairy tales.
Johnson. Elm-tree fairy book.
Ketchum and Jorgensen. Kindergarten gems.
Storks and the night owl. *See* Caliph Stork.
Storm fiend. *See* Wind-demon.
Storm magic. Asbjörnsen. Folk and fairy tales. (Mackerel trolling.)
Stroebe and Martens. Norwegian fairy book.
Storm moves the sign-boards. Andersen. Stories and tales (Author's ed.).
Storm swallows. Stewart. Once upon a time.
Stormy fool. *See* Paup-Puk-Keewis.
Story. Andersen. Fairy tales (Paull tr.).
Story of, etc. *See* the first important word of the title.
Story-teller. *See* Endless tale. III.
Story-teller at fault. Jacobs. Celtic fairy tales.
Tappan. Folk stories and fables.
Story-teller himself. *See* Iagoo, the great story-teller.
Story that Eskimos tell their children. *See* Bank swallows, Origin of.
Story that had no end. *See* Endless tale. I. and II.
Story that never ends. *See* Endless tale. IV.
Story that the buttercups told. Olcott. Wonder garden.
Story the shell told. Bouvé. Lamp light fairy tales.

Story without an end. I. *See* Water-drop.
Story without an end. II. *See* Endless tale. I.
Strange adventures of little Maia. *See* Thumbelina.
Strange adventure of Schalu's wife. Jewett. Wonder tales from Tibet.
Strange bird. Guerber. Legends of the Rhine.
Strange deeds of Kutoyis. *See* Kutoyis, the avenger.
Strange friends in time of need. Bradley-Birt. Bengal fairy tales.
See also Ito and his friends.
Strange godfather. Canton. Reign of King Herla.
In some editions not indexed here, this story has the title Godfather Death.
Strange little man from Venice. Froelicher. Swiss stories.
Strange lives of two young princes. *See* Shepherds of Salisbury Plain.
Strange otter. Welsh fairy book.
Strange tale of Doctor Dog. Pitman. Chinese wonder book.
Strange visitor. Bailey. Firelight stories. (Queer company.)
*Burchill. Progressive road to reading. Book 2. (Old woman and her company.)
Douglas. Scottish fairy tales.
Jacobs. English fairy tales.
Olcott. Good stories for great holidays.
Wickes. Happy holidays. (Queer company.)
Stranger. Richards. Golden windows.
Stranger child. *See* Christmas tree. I.
Strassburg clock. Evans. Old time tales. (Legend of the Strassburg clock.)
Guerber. Legends of the Rhine. (*In* Strassburg Cathedral legends.)
Straw ox. Bain. Cossack fairy tales.
Hodgkins. Atlantic treasury of childhood stories.
O'Grady and Throop. Teachers' story teller's book.
Skinner. Nursery tales from many lands.
Spaulding and Bryce. Aldine readers. Book 3.
Wiggin and Smith. Tales of laughter.
Straw, the coal and the bean. Allison and Perdue. Story in primary instruction.
Bailey and Lewis. For the children's hour. (Why the bean wears a stripe down its back.)
Baker and Carpenter. Language readers. 3d year.
Blaisdell. Child life. 3d reader.
Coe. First book of stories.
Coussens. Child's book of stories.
Field. Famous fairy tales.
Grimm. Fairy tales (Lucas tr.).
Grimm. Fairy tales (Paull tr.).
*Grimm. Fairy tales (Wiltse). v. 2.
Grimm. Household stories (Crane tr.).
Grimm. Household tales (Burt ed.).

Straw, the coal and the bean—*continued.*
*Haaren. Songs and stories. 2d reader.
Judson and Bender. Graded literature readers. v. 4.
Keyes. Stories and story-telling.
Pyle. Mother's nursery tales.
*Spaulding and Bryce. Aldine readers. 2d reader. (How the bean got its black seam.)
Strong. All the year round. v. 3. Spring.
Welsh. Stories children love.
See also Tailor and the pea.
Strawberry-girl. Harris. Little Mr. Thimblefinger.
Strawberry thief. Underhill. Dwarfs' tailor, and other fairy tales.
Stray cow. Thomas. Welsh fairy book.
Stream that ran away. Austin. Basket woman.
Olcott. Good stories for great holidays.
Street musicians. *See* Bremen town musicians.
Street sweeper. Guerber. Legends of the Rhine.
Strikes-and-kills. Linderman. Indian Old-man stories.
Striking a corpse candle. Thomas. Welsh fairy book.
String of carts. Æsop. Fables (Stickney. Supplement).
String of pearls. Andersen. Stories and tales (Author's ed.).
Stripe on the chipmunk's back. *See* Chipmunk's stripes. II.
Strong boy. *See* Chib, Adventures of.
Strong Boy snares the sun. *See* Why sun follows his trail. III.
Strong child. Richards. Golden windows.
Strong Desire and the red sorcerer. *See* White Hawk, the lazy.
Strong Frank. Thorpe. Yule-tide stories.
Strong Jack. Stroebe and Martens. Danish fairy book.
See also Shepherd Paul.
Strong Jura. Winnington. Outlook fairy book.
Strong man. Froelicher. Swiss stories.
Strong man and the dwarf. Wardrop. Georgian folk tales.
Strong prince. Lang. Crimson fairy book.
Lang. Little Wildrose.
Strongarm. English. Fairy stories and wonder tales.
Stronger than death. *See* Savitri—the faithful wife.
Strongest—who? or which? Harris. Little Mr. Thimblefinger.
Stupid monkeys. *See* Monkey gardeners.
Stupid fellows with jades for wives. *See* Silly men and cunning wives.
Stupid princess. Olcott. Whirling king.
Stupid's cries. Hartland. English folk and fairy tales. (Stupid's mistaken cries.)
Jacobs. More English fairy tales.
See also Walk to the mill.
Stupid's mistaken cries. *See* Stupid's cries.

Stylish Misses Woge. Bouvé. Lamplight fairy tales.
Subjugation of the thunderbird. Chandler. In the reign of coyote.
Such is the world's reward. *See* Way of the world. I.
Such women are. *See* All women are alike.
Sugar candy house. Bosschère. Folk tales of Flanders.
Sugar pine. Austin. Basket woman.
Sugar plum princess. Potter. Pinafore pocket story book.
Suitor. Bay. Danish fairy and folk tales.
See also Storehouse key in the distaff.
Sultan Misnar and the four enchanters, History of. Olcott. Tales of the Persian genii.
Sultan of Casgar's purveyor. *See* Sultan's steward's story.
Sultana of the flowers. Olcott. Wonder garden.
Sultan's steward's story. Arabian nights. (Townsend. Story told by the Sultan of Casgar's purveyor.)
Arabian nights, More tales (Olcott. Story told by the Sultan's steward: The chest of the Lady Zobeide.)
Summer. *See* How summer came to earth. II.
Summer birds. *See* How summer came to the earth. I.
Summer fairies. *See* How summer came to the earth. II.
Summer-gowk. Andersen. Wonder stories (Author's ed.).
Summer maker. *See* How summer came to the earth. I.
Summer night in a Norwegian forest. Asbjörnsen. Folk and fairy tales.
Summer princess. Skinner. Turquoise story book.
Summer snow. Skinner. Turquoise story book.
Summer yellowbird, Legend of the. Grinnell. Birds of song and story.
Summoner and the fiend. Darton. Tales of the Canterbury pilgrims. (Friar's tale: The summoner and the fiend.)
McSpadden. Stories from Chaucer. (Friar's tale: Wicked summoner.)
Sun. I. *See* Giant with the golden hair. II.
Sun. II. Bryne. Modern Greek fairy tales.
Sun a prisoner. I. Bailey. Firelight stories. (Why the field mouse is little.)
Bailey. Once upon a time animal stories. (Why the field mouse is little. Adapted.)
Blaisdell. Child life. 3d reader. (Why the mole is blind.)
Brooks. Stories of the red children. (Brave little mole.)
Farmer. Nature myths. (Blind mole.)
Judson. Old Crow stories. (When the sun was caught in a snare.)
Patten. Junior classics. v. 2. (Boy who set a snare for the sun.)
Pratt. Legends of the red children.
Schoolcraft. Indian fairy book. (Boy who set a snare for the sun.)
Skinner. Turquoise story book. (How the sun was caught and freed.)
See also Trapping in the Happy Hunting Grounds.

Sun a prisoner. II. Austin. Basket woman. (Little Tavwots, and how he caught the sun in a snare.)
Bryant. Best stories to tell to children. (Story of Little Tavwots.)
Bryant. How to tell stories to children. (Story of Little Tavwots.)
Dyer and Brady. Merrill readers. 3d reader. (Why the rabbit has a yellow spot.)
*Field second reader. (What Mr. Rabbit caught in his trap.)
Olcott. Wonder garden. (Why rabbits have yellow hairs.)
Wilson. Myths of the red children. (How the little rabbit snared the sun.)
Sun a prisoner. III. Cooke. Nature myths. (Indian story of the mole.)
Nixon-Roulet. Indian folk tales. (Hunter who trapped the sun.)
Stanley. Animal folk tales. (Mole and the sun.)
Tanner. Legends from the red man's forest. (Why the mole is blind.)
Sun a prisoner. IV. Chandler. In the reign of coyote. (Why the sun travels regularly.)
Coe and Christie. Story hour readers. Book 3. (Gray mole and the Indian. Adapted.)
Compton. American Indian fairy tales. (Fighting hare.)
See also Why sun follows his trail.
Sun a prisoner. V. Colum. At the gateways of the day. (How Ma-ui snared the sun.)
Farmer. Nature myths. (Why the sun travels slowly.)
My Bookhouse. v. 3. (Fisherman who caught the sun.)
Pope. Hawaii the beautiful. (Island hero: Maui makes the sun go slowly.)
Thrum. Hawaiian folk tales. (Exploits of Maui: Snaring the sun.)
Sun and how it was made by divine will. Magnus. Russian folk-tales.
Sun and the little plant. Bryce. Fables from afar.
Sun and the moon. I. Judd. Wigwam stories.
Sun and the Moon. II. Pyle. Fairy tales from many lands.
Sun and the north wind. *See* Wind and the sun.
Sun and the wind. *See* Wind and the sun.
Sun-boy. Bayliss. Treasury of Indian tales. (*In* Sun-bright heroes.)
Sun children kill the great monsters. Young. Algonquin. Indian tales. (*In* Ch. 16.)
Sun-flower. *See* Clytie.
Sun-goddess. *See* Mirror of the sun goddess.
Sun-heroes. Bayliss. Treasury of Indian tales. (Sun-bright heroes.)
This includes: Kulooshap; Manabozho; Napi, the Old Man; Olelbis; Santa Clara Sun-boy.

Sun is shining. *Burchill. Progressive road to reading. Book 1. (Sun is shining; Lark, the fox, the cat and the snake.)
Sun lady. *See* Little Surya Bai.
Sun man and the moon (poem). Wilson. Myths of the red children.
Sun, Moon and Morning Star. Eells. Tales of enchantment from Spain.
Sun, moon and stars. I. Farmer. Nature myths.
Sun, moon and stars. II. Skinner. Turquoise story book.
Sun, moon and stars. III. Storytellers' magazine. May 1915, p. 145. (Story of the moon and stars.)
Sun, moon and stars. IV. Bouvé. Lamplight fairy tales. (How the sun and moon came.)
See also Why the moon waxes and wanes.
Sun, moon and stars. V. Judson. Old Crow and his friends. (First moon; Real moon.)
Sun, moon and stars. VI. Byrne. Modern Greek fairy tales. (Sun.)
Sun, moon and wind. *See* Why all men love the moon.
Sun, moon, and wind go out to dinner. *See* Why all men love the moon.
Sun princess. Cornyn. Around the wigwam fire.
See also Daughter of Tiogaughwa; Star wife.
Sun, Stories of. *See* Daylight, Origin of; How sun became so bright; Mother Moon; Why sun follows his trail; also titles beginning with the word sun.
Sun, the moon and Crow Crowson. Magnus. Russian folk-tales.
Sun, the moon and the star giant. *See* Orion.
Sun, the moon, and the wind. *See* Why all men love the moon.
Sunbeam and the captive. Andersen. Fairy tales (Lucas tr. Picture from the ramparts.)
Andersen. Fary tales (Paull tr.).
Andersen. Stories and tales (Author's ed. Picture from the castle ramparts).
Sunbeams. Boston collection of kindergarten stories.
Sunchild. Laboulaye. Last fairy tales. (Sun's daughter.)
Lang. Grey fairy book.
Lang. Invisible prince, and other stories.
Sunflower and the cat-tail. Storytellers' magazine. Sept. 1917, p. 371.
Sunken castle. Guerber. Legends of the Rhine.
Sunken city. Cather. Educating by story telling. (Lady of Stavoren.)
Griffis. Dutch fairy tales. (When the wheat worked woe.)
Guerber. Legends of the Rhine.
Stebbins. 3d reader.
Van Sickle and Seegmiller. Riverside readers. 3d reader.
Sunling. Wiggin and Smith. Talking beasts.
Sun's daughter. *See* Sunchild.

Sun's sisters. Bailey and Lewis. For the children's hour.
St. Nicholas. March 1889, p. 331.
See also Sister of the sun.
Sunshine. *See* Little Sunshine. II.
Sunshine and her brothers and sisters. Alcott. Lulu's library. v. 2.
Sunshine and Moonshine. Jewett. Wonder tales from Tibet.
Sunshine fairies. Storytellers' magazine. Nov. 1913, p. 263.
Sunshine flowers. Judson. Flower fairies.
Sunshine stories. Andersen. Wonder stories (Author's ed.).
Keyes. Five senses. (Fortune's feather.)
Suora Marianna (poem). Alexander. Hidden servants.
Surly guest. Baldwin. Fifty famous people.
Surprise in the freight car. Bailey. Friendly tales.
Surya Bai. *See* Little Surya Bai.
Susa, the impetuous. James. Green willow.
See also Mirror of the sun-goddess; Sword of the assembled clouds of heaven.
Susan Walker, what a talker. *See* How a fish swam in the air and a hare in the water.
Susie and the squirrels. Faulkner. Story lady's book.
Susy's dream. Ketchum and Jorgensen. Kindergarten gems.
Svend's exploits. Thorpe. Yule-tide stories.
Swallow. *See* Why the swallow's tail is forked.
Swallow and other birds. *See* Swallow and the other birds.
Swallow and the birds. *See* Swallow and the other birds.
Swallow and the cook. Pitrè. Swallow book.
Swallow and the crow. Æsop. Fables (Burt ed.).
Æsop. Fables (Jacobs).
Æsop. Fables (Stickney).
Swallow and the little birds (poem). Æsop. Fables (Stickney. Supplement).
Swallow and the monkey. Pitrè. Swallow book.
Swallow and the other birds. Æsop. Fables (Stickney).
Æsop. Fables (Black ed. Swallow and other birds.)
Æsop. Fables (Burt ed. Swallow and other birds.)
Bryce. Fables from afar.
Patten. Junior classics. v. 1. (Swallow and the birds.)
Pitrè. Swallow book. (Swallows and the flax.)
Wiggin and Smith. Talking beasts.
Swallow and the raven. Pitrè. Swallow book.
Swallow king's rewards. Allen. Korean tales. (Hyung Bo and Nahl Bo; or, The swallow king's rewards.)
Griffis. Korean fairy tales. (King of the sparrows.)
Griffis. Unmannerly tiger, and other Korean tales. (King of the sparrows.)
Wickes. Happy holidays. (Little friend sparrow.)
See also Two melons.
Swallowed court. Thomas. Welsh fairy book.
Swallow's nest. Boston collection of kindergarten stories.
See also Sparrow in the swallow's nest.

Swallows, Origin of. I. Farmer. Nature myths.
Pitrè. Swallow book.
Swallows, Origin of. II. Young. Algonquin Indian tales. (*In* Ch. 5. Legend of the swallows.)
Swallows, Origin of. III. Donaldson. Little papoose listens.
Swallows, Origin of. IV. *See* Procne and Philomela.
Swamp robin. Young. Plantation bird legends.
Swan and the cook (poem). Wiggin and Smith. Talking beasts.
Swan and the crow. Rouse. Talking thrush.
Swan and the linnet (poem). Wiggin and Smith. Talking beasts.
Swan and the paddy-bird. Rouse. Talking thrush.
Swan-children of Lir. *See* Fate of the children of Lir.
Swan fairy's present. Patterson. Enchanted bird.
Swan maiden. Pyle. Wonder clock.
Swan maidens. Cooke. Nature myths.
Jacobs. Europa's fairy book.
Swan maidens and the silver knight. *See* Lohengrin.
Swan's nest. Andersen. Stories and tales (Author's ed.).
Swan's song. Bakewell. True fairy stories.
Sweep and Little Sweep. Brady. Green forest fairy book.
Sweet and low. Storytellers' magazine. March 1917, p. 187. (Memory gem.)
Sweet-One-Darling and the dream-fairies. Field. Second book of tales.
Sweet-One-Darling and the moon-garden. Field. Second book of tales.
Sweet Pea and Sweet William. Baring-Gould. Old English fairy tales. (Shepherd's daughter.)
Williams. Fairy tales from folklore.
Sweet porridge. *See* Wonderful porridge pot.
Sweet rice porridge. *See* Wonderful porridge pot.
Sweet-scented name. Sologub. Sweet-scented name, and other stories.
Sweet soup. *See* Wonderful porridge pot.
Sweet Water. Allen. Indian fairy tales.
Sweet wild rose. *See* Why roses have thorns. V.
Sweetheart in the wood. Asbjörnsen. Tales from the fjeld.
See also Mr. Fox; Robber bridegroom.
Sweetheart Roland. *See* Roland I.
Swift runner. *See* Deer and the rabbit.
Swiftest runners. Andersen. Fairy tales (Paull tr. Racers.)
Andersen. Wonder stories (Author's ed.).
Swineherd. Andersen. Fairy tales (Lucas tr.).
Andersen. Fairy tales (Paull tr.).
Andersen. Fairy tales and stories (Toksvig).
Chisholm. Enchanted land.
(play). Chisholm and Steedman. Staircase of stories. (Princess and the swineherd.)
Lang. Twelve huntsmen, and other stories.

Swineherd,—*continued.*
Lang. Yellow fairy book.
My Bookhouse. v. 4.
Olcott and Pendleton. Jolly book.
Scudder. Children's book.
Shedlock. Art of the storyteller.
Swiss clock's story. Alderman. Classics old and new. 3d reader.
Harrison. Bric-a-brac stories.
Swiss patriot and the spears. *See* Winkelried, Arnold.
Sword-blade. Wiggin and Smith. Talking beasts.
Sword Excalibur. *See* King Arthur's sword.
Sword in the stone. *See* King Arthur's coming.
Sword of Avalon. *See* King Arthur's sword.
Sword of Damocles. Baldwin. Fifty famous stories.
Sword of honour. Gate. Fortunate days.
Sword of might. Macdonell. Italian fairy tales.
Sword of the assembled clouds of heaven. Ballard. Fairy tales from far Japan.
Nixon-Roulet. Japanese folk stories and fairy tales. (Sword of the clustering clouds of heaven.)
See also Mirror of the sun-goddess; Prince Yamato's adventures; Susa, the impetuous.
Sword of the clustering clouds of heaven. *See* Sword of the assembled clouds of heaven.
Sword of the Lady Isobel. Meigs. Kingdom of the winding road.
Sword that mowed the grass. *See* Prince Yamato's adventures.
Sword, the golden fowl, the golden lantern, and the golden harp. Thorpe. Yule-tide stories.
Sworded falcon. Nixon-Roulet. Japanese folk stories and fairy tales.
Sybilla, Myrtillo, and Furiosa. Harrison. Old-fashioned fairy book.
Syed Nouman. *See* Sidi-Nouman.
Syfaddon Lake. Thomas. Welsh fairy book.
Sylvian and Jocosa. Field. Famous fairy tales.
Lang. Green fairy book.
Lang. Magician's gifts.
Welsh. Fairy tales children love.
Wiggin and Smith. Magic casements.
Symbol and the saint. Field. Christmas tales.
Field. Little book of profitable tales.
Syrinx. *See* Pan.

T

Tabby and the mice. Cowles. Art of story-telling.
Jones. 2d reader.
Skinner. Very little child's book of stories.
See also Three little pigs.

Table, the ass and the stick. Field. Famous fairy tales. (Tailor's three sons.)
Grimm. Fairy tales (Paull tr. Wishing table, the gold ass and the cudgel.)
Grimm. Household stories (Crane tr.).
Grimm. Household tales (Burt ed.. Tailor's three sons.)
Grimm. Household tales (Everyman's ed. Wishing table, the gold ass and the cudgel.)
Jacobs. English fairy tales. (Ass, the table and the stick.)
Johnson. Oak-tree fairy book. (Donkey, the table and the stick.)
Marshall. Fairy tales of all nations.
Wiggin and Smith. Fairy ring.
Winnington. Outlook fairy book. (Table, the donkey and the stick.)
See also Bottle hill; Father Grumbler; Juan, Adventures of; Jump in my sack; Ogre. II; Tailor and the hurricane.
Table, the donkey and the stick. *See* Table, the ass and the stick.)
Tail. Jacobs. More Celtic fairy tales.
Wiggin and Smith. Tales of laughter.
See also Box with something pretty in it; Short story.
Tail of a mouse. Aspinwall. Short stories for short people.
Tail of the Baron's war-horse. Richards. Joyous story of Toto.
Tail of the serpent. Æsop. Fables (Burt ed.).
Wiggin and Smith. Talking beasts.
Taileypo. *See* Taily-po. I.
Tailless dog. Guerber. Legends of the Rhine.
Tailor. Arabian Nights (Townsend. Story told by the tailor.)
Olcott and Pendleton. Jolly book. (Story told by the tailor: Young man and the barber.)
Arabian nights, More tales (Olcott. Story told by the tailor: The young man and the barber.)
See also Little hunchback.
Tailor and the giant. Griffis. Swiss fairy tales.
See also Brave little tailor.
Tailor and the hurricane. Cary. French fairy tales.
See also Table, the ass, and the stick.
Tailor and the pea. Ketchum and Jorgensen. Kindergarten gems.
See also Straw, the coal and the bean.
Tailor and the three beasts. Bryant. Stories to tell to children.
Tailor and the witch. Asbjörnsen. Folk and fairy tales. (Legend of the mill.)
Gade. Norwegian fairy tales.
Tailor's daughter. Laboulaye. Fairy tales. (Tailor's story. *In* Captain John's travels.)
Laboulaye. Last fairy tales.

Tailor's story. *See* Tailor's daughter.
Tailor's three sons. *See* Table, the ass and the stick.
Taily-po. I. Storytellers' magazine. June 1913, p. 10. (Taileypo.)
Taily-po. II. Harris. Uncle Remus returns.
Taken at his word. Guerber. Legends of the Rhine.
Taking away the sun. Bayliss. Treasury of Eskimo tales.
Tale of, etc. See the first important word of the title.
Tale that cost a dollar. Finger. Tales of silver lands.
Tales of Hoffman. Pleasanton. Fairyland of opera.
Taliesen. Brooks. Wonder stories from the Mabinogion.
Higginson. Tales of the enchanted islands of the Atlantic. (Taliessin of the radiant brow.)
Lanier. Knightly legends of Wales.
Wilmot-Buxton. Stories of early England.
Taliessin of the radiant brow. *See* Taliesen.
Talisman. Field. Second book of tales.
Talisman of Solomon. Pyle. Twilight land.
Talkative sparrow. *See* Tongue-cut sparrow.
Talkative tortoise. Babbitt. Jataka tales. (Turtle who couldn't stop talking.)
Baker and Carpenter. Language readers. 3d year.
Bidpai. Tortoise and the geese.
Bowen. Second story reader. (Tortoise that would talk.)
Bryant. Stories to tell to children.
Jacobs. Indian fairy tales.
Lang. Olive fairy book. (Fate of the turtle.)
My Bookhouse. v. 1. (Turtle who could not stop talking.)
Peck. Stories for good children. (Snapping turtle.)
Storytellers' magazine. Nov. 1914, p. 728. (Turtle who couldn't stop talking.)
Wiggin and Smith. Talking beasts. (Geese and the tortoise.)
See also Kerchunk.
Talking bells. Storytellers' magazine. Sept. 1914, p. 673.
Talking bird, Story of. *See* Three sisters. I.
Talking bird, the singing tree, and the golden water. *See* Three sisters. I.
Talking eggs. Johnson. Oak-tree fairy book.
Pyle. Tales of folks and fairies.
Talking fish. Pitman. Chinese wonder book.
Talking grass. Bailey. Once upon a time animal stories.
Talking head of Donn-Bo. Graves. Irish fairy book.
Talking-saddle. Harris. Little Mr. Thimblefinger.
Talking silver foxes. Martens. Chinese fairy book.
Talking stones. Tales for bedtime.
Talking thrush. Johnson. Fir-tree fairy book. (Ambitious thrush.)
Rouse. Talking thrush.
Talking tree. Macdonell. Italian fairy book.
Talking tree, the singing bird and the golden water. *See* Three sisters. I.

Talking turtle. I. James. Enchanted castle.
Talking turtle. II. James. Magic bed.
Tall One and the Short One. *See* Star wives.
Tallapus and the cedar. Judson. Myths and legends of the Pacific Northwest.
Tam o' Shanter. Tyler. Twenty-four unusual stories.
See also Witches at the cross.
Tamamo. *See* Fox maiden.
Tame lion. Nordau. Dwarf's spectacles.
Tamerlane. Baldwin. Fifty famous people. (Try, try again.)
Haaren and Poland. Famous men of the middle ages.
Taming of Pegasus. *See* Pegasus.
Taming the shrew. I. *See* Princess whom nobody could silence.
Taming the shrew. II. *See* Most obedient wife.
Tamlane. Jacobs. More English fairy tales.
Macleod. Book of ballad stories. (Young Tamlane.)
Pyle. Wonder tales retold.
Richards. Little master.
Success library. v. 3.
See also Wild Robin.
Tangled skein. Murray. Story book treasures.
Richards. Silver crown.
Tannhauser. Dasent. Popular tales from the Norse. (Legends of Tannhauser.)
Chapin. Wonder stories from Wagner.
Guerber. Legends of the Rhine.
Maud. Wagner's heroes.
McSpadden. Stories from great operas.
Wheelock. Stories of Wagner operas.
Tantalizing fruits. *See* Tantalus.
Tantalus. Hutchinson. Golden porch. (Favorite of the gods.)
Olcott. Wonder garden. (Tantalizing fruits.)
Taper Tom. *See* Hans, who made the princess laugh.
Tapestry prince. Gate. Punch and Robinetta.
See also Three robes; Asmund and Signy.
Tar-baby. I. (poem). Harris. Tar-baby and other rhymes. (Brer Rabbit and the tar-baby.)
Harris. Uncle Remus, his songs and his sayings. (Wonderful tar-baby story.)
My Bookhouse. v. 3. (How Brer Rabbit met Brer Tar Baby.)
Tar-baby. II. Klingensmith. Just stories. (Brother Rabbit and Brother Goat.)
Ortoli. Evening tales. (French tar baby.)
Spaulding and Bryce. Aldine readers. Book 3.
Tar-baby. III. Stafford. Animal fables. (Rabbit and his ears.)
Tar-baby stories. For other versions see: Demon with the matted hair; How Rabbit deceived fox: Masoy and the

Tar-baby stories—*continued.*
ape; Rabbit and tar-wolf; Raccoon and the man of tar; Why spiders live in dark corners; Why the banana belongs to the monkey.
Taradiddles, Tale of. Caballero. Spanish fairy tales.
Taro and the turtle. *See* Uraschimataro and the turtle.
Tarpeia. Bryant. Best stories to tell to children.
Bryant. How to tell stories to children.
Guerber. Story of the Romans. (Maidens carried off.)
Haaren. Famous men of Rome. (*In* Romulus.)
Laing. Seven kings of the seven hills. (*In* Romulus.)
Tarquin and the eagle. Guerber. Story of the Romans.
Laing. Seven kings of the seven hills. (*In* Ancus Marcius.)
Tarquin and the sibyl. *See* Sibyl.
Tattercoats. Duncan-Jones. English folk-lore stories.
Jacobs. More English fairy tales.
Wiggin and Smith. Fairy ring.
See also Cinderella.
Tatterhood. *See* Goat girl.
Tau Kesuk. Allen. Indian fairy tales.
Tea and the sage (poem). Success library. v. 3.
Wiggin and Smith. Talking beasts.
Tea kettle. *See* Accomplished and lucky teakettle.
Tea pot. Andersen. Stories (Riverside ed.).
Andersen. Stories and tales (Author's ed.).
Tears of pearl. *See* Rose-beauty.
Tears of repentance (poem). Alexander. Hidden servants.
Tease and what happened to him. Storytellers' magazine. Sept. 1917, p. 346.
Teasing ogre, Story of. Donahey. Tales to be told to children.
Teddy Bear and the Ha Ha bird. Storytellers' magazine. Sept 1917, p. 335.
Teddy Bear and the mud-pie mask. *Bryant. New stories to tell to children.
Teddy-Bear mystery. Bailey. Friendly tales.
Teddy bears. *See* Black tower.
Teddy's tree planting. *See* Boy who hated trees.
Teenchy Duck. Coe. Second book of stories.
Harris. Uncle Remus and the little boy. (Teenchy-tiny duck.)
*Klingensmith. Just stories. (Little Wee Duck.)
Ortoli. Evening tales.
See also Cock's wife; Drakesbill and his friends.
Teenchy-Tiny Duck. *See* Teenchy Duck.
Teeny-Tiny. I. Coussens. Child's book of stories.
Jacobs. English fairy tales.
Johnson. Oak-tree fairy book.
Mother Goose's nursery rhymes, tales and jingles (Warne ed.).
Quiller-Couch. Fairy tales far and near.
Welsh. Stories children love. (Story of Teeny-Tiny.)

Teeny-Tiny. II. My Bookhouse. v. 1.
Teeny-Tiny. III. Grayl. Fairy tales from foreign lands.
See also Little red hen. II.
Teeny, tiny lady. Bailey. Firelight stories.
See also Teeny-Tiny. II.
Teeny, tiny woman. *See* Wee, wee woman.
Teeth and no-teeth. Wardrop. Georgian folk tales.
Teig O'Kane and the corpse. Yeats. Irish fairy tales.
See also Andrew Coffey.
Tell, William. Baldwin. Fifty famous stories. (Story of William Tell.)
Crommelin. Famous legends.
Dyer and Brady. Merrill readers. 3d reader.
Evans. Old time tales. (William Tell, the Swiss patriot.)
Haaren. Ballads and tales.
Herbertson. Heroic legends. (Archer of Schwitz.)
Mabie. Heroes and fairies.
Mabie. Heroes every child should know.
My Bookhouse. v. 5. (Legend of William Tell.)
Noyes. Twilight stories.
Scudder. Book of legends.
Tell-tale goblin. Walker. Sandman's goodnight stories.
Tempest. *See* Prospero and Miranda.
Templar's home. Guerber. Legends of the Rhine.
Temptations. Dasent. Popular tales from the Norse.
Thorpe. Yule-tide stories.
Tempted lady. Douglas. Scottish fairy tales.
Ten at a stroke. *See* Valiant Vicky, the brave weaver.
Ten blowers. Brown. Flower princess.
Ten fairies. Bryant. Stories to tell to children.
See also Charlotte and the ten dwarfs; Elsa and the ten elves.
Ten little dwarfs. *See* Charlotte and the ten dwarfs.
Ten little Indians. Kennedy. New world fairy book.
Ten princes. Eastman. Indian legends retold.
Ten sources. Gask. Folk tales from many lands.
Ten trails. Seton. Woodmyth and fable.
Ten virgins. Eastman. Wigwam evenings.
Ten workmen of Mother Watergreen. *See* Charlotte and the ten dwarfs.
Tender mother. Guerber. Legends of the Rhine.
See also Dead mother.
Terrible bull, Story of the. Success library. v. 3.
Terrible cyclone. Henderson. Sea yarns for boys.
Terrible head. *See* Perseus.
Terrible Olli. Fillmore. Mighty Mikko.
See also Esben and the witch.
Testing of the two knights. Poulsson. Top of the world stories.
Thanksgiving. *See* Dobbin's Thanksgiving; Ears of wheat; First corn; Good Thanksgiving; Good time; Grandmother's Thanksgiving present; Horn of plenty; Lame squirrel's

Thanksgiving—*continued.*
Thanksgiving; Little leaf's Thanksgiving; Master of the harvest; Monkey that brought Thanksgiving; Mooly's Thanksgiving; Old Man Rabbit's Thanksgiving; Queer little baker man; St. Cuthbert's eagle; Spirit of the corn.
Thanksgiving cake. Bailey. Stories for Sunday telling.
Thanksgiving dinners. Potter. Pinafore pocket story book.
Thanksgiving for the peanut roaster. Bailey. Friendly tales.
Thanksgiving in the henhouse. *See* Making the best of it.
Thanksgiving turkey. Faulkner. Story lady's book.
That horrid rain. *Dillingham and Emerson. Tell it again stories.
That is nothing to me. Welsh. Stories children love.
Thebes, Founding of. *See* Cadmus and the dragon's teeth.
Thebes, Destruction of. Darton. Tales of the Canterbury pilgrims. (John Lydgate's tale: Destruction of Thebes.)
Their best club. Bailey. Friendly tales.
Their block party. Bailey. Friendly tales.
Theft of the king's treasure. *See* Treasure-chamber of Rhampsinitus.
Theft from the sun. *See* Fire-leggings.
Theology. Richards. Golden windows.
There are better things than gold. *See* Midas. I.
There is no fear for those with whom all women are in love. *See* Best wish.
"There's a difference." *See* Conceited apple branch.
Thermopylae. *See* Brave three hundred.
Theseus. Adams. Myths of old Greece.
*Bailey. Wonder stories. (Where the labyrinth led.)
Bailey and Lewis. For the children's hour. (Story of Theseus.)
Baldwin. Old Greek stories. (Adventures of Theseus; Cruel tribute.)
Beckwith. In mythland. v. 1. (Theseus the brave.)
Burt and Ragozin. Herakles, and other heroes.
Carpenter. Long ago in Greece. (Theseus and the ring.)
Church. Greek story and song. (Story of Theseus.)
Cole. Heroes of the olden time.
Francillon. Gods and heroes. (Champion of Athens.)
Guerber. Myths of Greece and Rome.
Haaren and Poland. Famous men of Greece.
Hawthorne. Tanglewood tales. (Minotaur.)
Hyde. Favorite Greek myths.
Kingsley. Heroes (Everyman's ed.).
Kupfer. Stories of long ago. (Cruel king; Thread that saved many lives.)
Partridge. Story telling in home and school.
Patten. Junior classics. v. 3. (How Theseus slays the Minotaur.)
Pratt. Myths of old Greece. v. 3.

Theseus—*continued.*
Shaw. Stories of the ancient Greeks. (Black sails or white.)
Storr. Half a hundred hero tales.
Tappan. Myths from many lands. (Minotaur.)
Thetis. *See* Peleus and the sea-king's daughter.
Thiassi carries off Loki. *See* Iduna's apples.
Thief and his master. Grimm. Fairy tales (Paull tr.).
Thief and the boy. Æsop. Fables (Black ed.).
Æsop. Fables (Burt ed.).
Thief and the dog. Æsop. Fables (Black ed.).
Æsop. Fables (Burt ed.).
Thief and the elephant. Davis and Chow-Leung. Chinese fables and folk stories.
Thief and the fox. Patten. Junior classics. v. 1.
See also Judgment of the jackal.
Thief and the innkeeper. Æsop. Fables (Burt ed.).
Thief and the travelers (poem). Success library. v. 3.
Thief in heaven. Guerber. Legends of the Rhine.
Thieves and the cock. Æsop. Fables (Black ed.).
Æsop. Fables (Burt ed.).
Thing of most worth. Bailey. Stories for Sunday telling.
Things of the water. *See* Glooskap and the bull frog.
"Think I can." *See* Little steam engine.
Thinking only of myself. *Alderman. Classics old and new. 3d reader.
Third Calender. Arabian nights (Lang. Story of the third Calender, son of a king.)
Arabian nights (Olcott. Story of the third royal mendicant.)
Arabian nights (Townsend. History of the third Calender.)
Third fiddler's tale. Gibbon. Reign of King Cole.
Thirst of the standing stones. I. Lang. Lilac fairy book. (Stones of Plouhinec.)
Pyle. Wonder tales retold. (Stones of Plouvinec.)
See also Lost fiddle; Thirst of the standing stones. II.
Thirst of the standing stones. II. Canton. Reign of King Herla.
Field third reader. (Thirsty stones.)
Thirsty pigeon. Æsop. Fables (Burt ed.).
Æsop. Fables (Stickney).
Thirsty stones. *See* Thirst of the standing stones. II.
Thirteen jewelled letters. Tales for bedtime.
Thirteenth son of the king of Erin. Curtin. Myths and folklore of Ireland.
This is the lad who sold the pig. Asbjörnsen. Tales from the fjeld.
Thistle, Story of the. I. Wilson. Nature study reader.
Thistle, Story of the. II. (poem). Storytellers' magazine, Sept. 1917, p. 319. (Legend of the thistle.)
See also What happened to the thistle.
Thom and Willie. Douglas. Scottish fairy tales.

Thomas a Becket. *See* English merchant and the Saracen lady.

Thomas Berennikov. Polevoi. Russian fairy tales.

Thomas the rhymer. Douglas. Scottish fairy tales.
Grierson. Children's tales from Scottish ballads.
Grierson. Scottish fairy book.
Macleod. Book of ballad stories.

Thor. Arnold and Gilbert. Stepping stones to literature. v. 5.
Edmison. Stories from Norseland. (Thor outwits the dwarf Alvis.)
Judd. Classic myths. (Thunder-god and his brother.)
See also Geirrod and Thor; Dwarf's gifts.

Thor and his journey to Jötunheim. Baker and Carpenter. Language readers. 5th year. (How Thor went to the land of giants.)
Bradish. Old Norse stories. (Thor and Skrymir.)
Brown. In the days of giants. (Thor's visit to the giants.)
Edmison. Stories from the Norseland. (Giants fool Thor.)
Foster and Cummings. Asgard stories. (Thor's wonderful journey.)
Fuller. Book of friendly giants. (How the giants got the best of Thor.)
Guerber. Myths of northern lands. (*In* Thor.)
Hartwell. Story hour readings. 6th year. (Thor's journey.)
Hodgkins. Atlantic treasury of childhood stories. (Feats of the giants.)
Johonnot. Stories of the olden time. (Thor's visit to Jötunheim.)
Keary. Heroes of Asgard. (How Thor went to Jotunheim.)
Klingensmith. Old Norse wonder tales. (Thor.)
Litchfield. Nine worlds. (Thor and Skrymir.)
Mabie. Norse stories. (Thor's wonderful journey.)
McFee. Treasury of myths. (Thor's visit to Jötunheim.)
My Bookhouse. v. 4. (Thor's journey to Jötunheim.)
Patten. Junior classics. v. 2. (How Thor went to Jötunheim.)
Pratt. Legends of Norseland. (Thor and Skrymir; Thor and the Utgard-King.)
Pyle. Where the wind blows. (Thor at Jötunheim.)
Tappan. Myths from many lands. (Thor's adventures among the Jötuns.)
Wickes. Beyond the rainbow bridge. (Thor's visit to Jötunheim.)
Wilmot-Buxton. Stories of Norse heroes. (How the pride of Thor was brought low.)

Thor and the frost giants. *See* Thor and his journey to Jötunheim.

Thor: Quest of the hammer. Bradish. Old Norse stories. (Thrym.)
Brown. In the days of giants. (Quest of the hammer.)

Thor: Quest of the hammer—*continued.*
Edmison. Stories from Norseland. (How Thor got his hammer back.)
Foster and Cummings. Asgard stories. (How Thor lost his hammer.)
Guerber. Myths of northern lands. (*In* Thor.)
Klingensmith. Old Norse wonder tales. (Thor and Thrym.)
Litchfield. Nine worlds. (Thor and Thrym.)
Mabie. Myths every child should know. (Quest of the hammer.)
Mabie. Norse stories. (How Thor found his hammer.)
McFee. Treasury of myths. (Thor and his wonderful hammer.)
Patten. Junior classics. v. 2. (How Thor's hammer was lost and found.)
Pratt. Legends of Norseland. (Finding of the hammer.)
Tappan. Myths from many lands. (Quest of the hammer.)
Wickes. Beyond the rainbow bridge. (Forging of the hammer; How Thor humbled his pride.)
Wilmot-Buxton. Stories of Norse heroes. (How Thor's hammer was lost and found.)

Thor: Thor and Hrungnir. Bradish. Old Norse stories. (Thor's duel with Hrungnir.)
Brown. In the days of giants. (Thor's duel.)
Edmison. Stories from Norseland. (Thor and Hrungnir fight a duel.)
Guerber. Myths of northern lands. (*In* Thor.)
Klingensmith. Old Norse wonder tales. (Thor's fight with Hrungner.)
Mabie. Norse stories. (How Thor fought the giant Hrungner.)
Wickes. Beyond the rainbow bridge. (Coward heart.)

Thor: Thor's fishing. Bradish. Old Norse stories (Ægir's feast.)
Brown, A. F. In the days of giants. (Thor's fishing.)
*Burchill. Progressive road to reading. Book 3. (Great kettle.)
Edmison. Stories from Norseland. (Thor fishes for the Midgard serpent.)
Foster and Cummings. Asgard stories. (Ægir's feast.)
Guerber. Myths of northern lands. (*In* Ægir.)
Hodgkins. Atlantic treasury of childhood stories. (Mighty fisherman.)
Judd. Classic myths. (Thunder-god and his brother.)
Keary. Heroes of Asgard. (Serpent and the kettle.)
Klingensmith. Old Norse wonder tales. (Thor and Hymer.)
Litchfield. Nine worlds. (Thor's journey to get the kettle for Ægir.)
Mabie. Norse stories. (Thor goes a-fishing.)
Pratt. Legends of Norseland. (Thor and the Midgard serpent.)

Thor: Thor's fishing—*continued.*
Wickes. Beyond the rainbow bridge. (Story of the iron kettle.)
Thorn. Richards. Silver crown.
Thorn of Glastonbury. Olcott. Good stories for great holidays. (Christmas thorn of Glastonbury.)
Olcott. Wonder garden. (Christmas thorn of Glastonbury.)
Thorn Rose. *See* Sleeping beauty.
Thorny path of honor. Andersen. Stories and tales (Author's ed.).
Thor's duel. *See* Thor: Thor and Hrungnir.
Thor's hammer. *See* Dwarf's gifts.
Thor's wonderful journey. *See* Thor and his journey to Jötunheim.
Thorstein. Hall. Icelandic fairy tales.
Thoughtless word. Magnus. Russian folk-tales.
Thousand-and-second tale of Scheherazade. Olcott and Pendleton. Jolly book.
Thousand-faced jewel. Griffis. Japanese fairy tales.
Three aunts. *See* Three little crones each with something big. I.
Three bears. I. Adams. Folk-story and verse.
Arnold and Gilbert. Stepping stones to literature. v. 2.
Aunt Louisa's book of fairy tales.
Bailey. Firelight stories.
Bailey and Lewis. For the children's hour.
Baldwin. Fairy stories and fables.
Blaisdell. Child life. 2d reader. (Silver Locks.)
Boston collection of kindergarten stories.
*Bowen. Second story reader. (Little Golden Hair.)
Bryant. Best stories to tell to children. (Story of the three bears.)
Bryant. How to tell stories to children.
Burke. Fairy tales.
Chisholm. In fairy land.
Coe. First book of stories.
*Coe and Christie. Story hour readers. Book 2.
Coussens. Child's book of stories. (Goldilocks; or, The three bears.)
Darton. Wonder book of beasts.
Dyer. What-happened-then stories.
Faulkner. Old English nursery tales.
Favorite fairy tales.
Forty famous fairy tales.
Golden goose, and the three bears.
*Grover. Folk-lore readers. v. 1.
*Howard. Banbury cross stories.
Jacobs. English fairy tales.
Jerrold. Big book of fairy tales.
Johnson. Book of fairy-tale bears.
Johnson. Oak-tree fairy book.
Ketchum and Jorgensen. Kindergarten gems.

Three bears—*continued.*
Klingensmith. Household stories.
Lang. Forty thieves, and other stories.
Lang. Green fairy book. (Story of the three bears.)
Lansing. Rhymes and stories.
Mabie. Fairy tales every child should know.
May. Little Prudy's fairy book. (Goldilocks.)
My Bookhouse. v. 1. (Goldilocks and the three bears.)
Norton. Heart of oak books. v. 2.
Nursery tales.
O'Grady and Throop. Teachers' story teller's book. (Story of the three bears; Goldenhair and the three bears.)
O'Shea. Six nursery classics. (Story of the three bears.)
*Old, old tales retold.
Pyle. Mother's nursery tales. (Goldilocks and the three bears.)
Rhys. Fairy gold.
Scudder. Book of folk stories.
Scudder. Children's book.
*Skinner. Very little child's book of stories.
Sly. World stories retold. (Goldilocks and the three bears.)
Success library. v. 3.
Tappan. Folk stories and fables.
Tweed. Fairy tales everyone should know.
Valentine. Old, old fairy tales.
Welsh. Stories children love. (Story of the three bears.)
Wiltse. Folk lore stories.
Wiltse. Kindergarten stories.
See also Scrapefoot.

Three bears. II. *Bailey. Folk stories and fables.
*Burchill. Progressive road to reading. Book 1.
Jacobs. English fairy tales.
Lang. Forty thieves and other stories.
Lang. Green fairy book.
Patten. Junior classics. v. 1. (Story of the three bears.)

Three bears
In English fairy tales and the Green fairy book Southey's text is followed exactly. In the other versions a little girl has been substituted for the old woman, and there are minor variations. In Old old fairy tales the story has been greatly changed and lengthened.

Three Billy-goats Bruse. *See* Three billy goats gruff.

Three billy goats gruff. Asbjörnsen. Folk and fairy tales. (Three billy goats who went up into the hills to get fat.)
Bailey. Firelight stories.
Bailey. Once upon a time animal stories.
Baldwin. Fairy stories and fables. (Three goats named Bruse.)
Coe. First book of stories.
Coussens. Child's book of stories.
Dasent. Norse fairy tales.
Dasent. Popular tales from the Norse.

Three billy goats gruff—*continued.*
Dyer. What-happened-then stories.
*Elson and Runkel. Elson readers. Book 1.
Esenwein and Stockard. Children's stories. (Billy goats gruff.)
Haaren. Fairy life. (Three goats and the troll.)
Hodgkins. Atlantic treasury of childhood stories. (Three Billy-goats Bruse.)
Klingensmith. Household stories. (Three goats.)
Lansing. Rhymes and stories.
O'Grady and Throop. Teachers' story teller's book.
*Skinner. Very little child's book of stories.
Thorne-Thomsen. East o' the sun and west o' the moon.
Thorpe. Yule-tide stories. (Three goats named Bruse that went to the mountain-pasture to fatten.)
*Treadwell. Reading literature: primer. (Billy goats gruff.)
Van Sickle and Seegmiller. Riverside readers. 2d reader.
Wiggin and Smith. Tales of laughter. (Three goats.)
See also Giant Giro; Three piggy-wigs.
Three black princesses. Grimm. Fairy tales (Paull tr.).
Three brother beasts. Jokai and others. Golden fairy book.
Singleton. Wild flower fairy book.
Three brother pigs. *See* Three little pigs. I.
Three brothers. I. Grimm. Fairy tales (Lucas tr.).
*Haaren. Songs and stories.
Lang. Pink fairy book.
Lang. Snow-queen. and other stories.
Storytellers' magazine. June 1914, p. 614.
Wiggin and Smith. Tales of laughter.
Three brothers. II. Lang. Beauty and the beast, and other stories.
Lang. Yellow fairy book.
Patten. Junior classics. v. 1.
Three brothers. III. Cary. French fairy tales. (Three brothers; or, The cat, the cock and the ladder.)
See also Fortune seekers. I.
Three brothers. IV. Bain. Cossack fairy tales.
See also Singing bone.
Three brothers. V. *See* Sons of Feridoun.
Three brothers and the giant. Cary. French fairy tales.
Three brothers and three sisters. Byrne. Modern Greek fairy tales.
Three bugs (poem). Arnold and Gilbert. Stepping stones to literature. v. 2.
Cary. Poems.
Three cakes. Bailey. For the story teller.
Three Calendars, sons of kings and five ladies of Bagdad.
Arabian nights (Lang. Story of the three Calendars.)
Arabian nights (Olcott. Story of the porter and the ladies of Bagdad and the three royal mendicants.)
Arabian nights (Townsend).

Three chests. Fillmore. Mighty Mikko.
Three children of fortune. *See* Fortune seekers. I.
Three citrons. I. Laboulaye. Fairy book.
Three citrons. II. Fillmore. Czechoslovak fairy tales.
Three cows. I. Jacobs. More English fairy tales.
Three cows. II. *See* Bee, the harp, the mouse and the bum-clock.
Three crowns. Graves. Irish fairy book.
Lang. King of the waterfalls.
Lang. Lilac fairy book.
Three crows. Grimm. Household tales (Everyman's ed.).
*Grimm. Fairy tales (Wiltse.) v. 1.
See also Grateful beasts. I.; True and Untrue.
Three daughters of King O'Hara. Curtin. Myths and folk-lore of Ireland.
Three daughters of the King of the East, and the son of a king in Erin. Curtin. Myths and folklore of Ireland.
Three dogs. I. Lang. Beauty and the beast.
Lang. Green fairy book.
See also Snip, Snap, Snorium.
Three dogs. II. Dasent. Popular tales from the Norse.
Stroebe and Martens. Swedish fairy book.
Thorpe. Yule-tide stories.
Underhill. Dwarfs' tailor, and other fairy tales.
Wiggin and Smith. Magic casements.
Three doves. Baudis. Czech folk tales.
Pyle. Tales of wonder and magic.
Three dwarfs. *See* Three little men in the wood.
Three eels. Houghton. Russian grandmother's wonder tales.
Three eggs. Cary. French fairy tales.
Three evils. Martens. Chinese fairy book.
Three farmers, Adventures of. Thomas. Welsh fairy book.
Three feathers. I. Grimm. Fairy tales (Paull tr.).
Ketchum and Jorgensen. Kindergarten gems. (Dummling and the toad.)
Wiggin and Smith. Fairy ring.
See also Betrothal gifts; Cherry the frog bride; Doll in the grass; Forest bride; Frog princess I and II; King's three sons. I.; Mother Roundabout's daughter.
Three feathers. II. Jacobs. More English fairy tales.
Johnson. Birch-tree fairy book.
Three fish. I. Æsop. Fables (Burt ed. Fish and the fishermen.)
Bidpai. Tortoise and the geese.
Van Sickle and Seegmiller. Riverside readers. 2d reader.
Three fish. II. Babbitt. More Jataka tales. (Three fishes.)
Three fishes, Story of the. Bellamy. Wonder children.
Three foolish bears. Storytellers' magazine. Oct. 1916, p. 548.
See also Three sillies.
Three friends. Skinner. Nursery tales from many lands.
See also Mouse and the sausage; Spider and the flea.

Three frogs. Alcott. Lulu's library. v. 1.
Three gallant outlaws (poem). Lanier. Boy's Percy. (Adam Bell, Clym of the Clough and William of Cloudesly.)
Macleod. Book of ballad stories.
Three giants. Welsh. Stories children love.
Three gifts. I. Singleton. Goldenrod fairy book.
See also Diamonds and toads.
Three gifts. II. English. Fairy stories and wonder tales.
Three gifts. III. Thorpe. Yule-tide stories.
Three gifts. IV. Storytellers' magazine. Jan. 1915, p. 3.
Three girls who went to a boy's school. Davis and Chow-Leung. Chinese fables and folk stories.
Three goats. I. *See* Three billy goats gruff.
Three goats. II. *See* Goats in the turnip field.
Three goats and the troll. *See* Three billy goats gruff.
Three goats named Bruse. *See* Three billy goats gruff.
Three goats named Bruse, that went to the mountain pasture to fatten. *See* Three billy goats gruff.
Three gold fishes. Boston collection of kindergarten stories.
Three golden apples. *See* Hercules and his labors.
Three golden hairs. *See* Giant with the golden hair. I.
Three golden hairs of the old man Vsévède. *See* Giant with the golden hair. II.
Three green men of Glen Nevis. Campbell. Beyond the border.
Douglas. Scottish fairy tales (Burt ed.).
Three griffin's feathers. Macdonell. Italian fairy book.
See also Singing bone.
Three happy tailors. Bay. Danish fairy and folk tales.
Three heads. *See* Bushy bride.
Three heads of the well. Duncan-Jones. English folk-lore stories.
Jacobs. English fairy tales.
Mother Goose's nursery rhymes, tales and jingles (Warne ed.).
Three ivory bobbins. *See* Bewitched huntsman.
Three jumpers. *See* Leaping match.
Three kingdoms. Curtin. Wonder-tales from Russia.
Three kingdoms,—the copper the silver and the golden. Curtin. Wonder-tales from Russia.
Three kings of Cologne (poem). Field. Christmas tales.
Olcott. Good stories for great holidays.
Three kittens see the world. Potter. Pinafore pocket story book.
Three knocks on the door. Potter. Pinafore pocket story book.
Three languages. Grimm. Fairy tales (Lucas tr.).
*Grimm. Fairy tales (Wiltse). v. 2.
Grimm. Household tales (Burt ed.).
See also Language of the birds.

Three lemons. I. Asbjörnsen. Tales from the fjeld.
Gade. Norwegian fairy tales.
Pyle. Tales of folks and fairies. (Three silver citrons.)
Stroebe and Martens. Norwegian fairy book.
See also Three lemons. II.
Three lemons. II. Gask. Folk tales from many lands
Gask. Treasury of folk tales.
Jokai and others. Golden fairy book.
Laboulaye. Fairy tales.
Patten. Junior classics. v. 2.
Singleton. Goldenrod fairy book.
See also Three lemons. I.
Three little butterflies. Olcott. Good stories for great holidays. (Three little butterfly brothers.)
Skinner. Turquoise story book.
Three little Christmas trees that grew on the hill. O'Grady and Throop. Teachers' story teller's book.
Three little crones each with something big. I. Dasent. Popular tales from the Norse. (Three aunts.)
Dasent. Norse fairy tales. (Three aunts.)
Gade. Norwegian fairy tales. (Three aunts.)
Thorpe. Yule-tide stories. (Three aunts.)
Three little crones each with something big. II. Jerrold. Reign of King Oberon.
Thorpe. Yule-tide stories.
Three little crones each with something big. III. MacManus. In the chimney corner. (Widow's daughter.)
Wiggin and Smith. Fairy ring. (Widow's daughter.)
Yeats. Irish fairy and folk tales. (Lazy beauty and her aunts.)
Three little crones each with something big. I, II and III.
See also Habetrot and Scantlie Mab; Luck fairies; Spinning queen; Three spinning fairies.
Three little eggs. Bourhill and Drake. Fairy tales from South Africa.
Three little gnomes. Gruelle. Friendly fairies.
Three little kittens who lost their mittens. *Burchill. Progressive road to reading: Story steps. (Three little kittens.)
*Coe and Christie. Story hour readers. Book 1.
(poem). Klingensmith. Just stories.
(poem). Lansing. Rhymes and stories.
Three little men in the wood. Forty famous fairy tales. (Three dwarfs.)
Grimm. Household stories (Crane tr).
Grimm. Household tales (Burt ed.).
Lang. King of the waterfalls. (Three dwarfs.)
Lang. Red fairy book. (Three dwarfs.)
Lang. Three dwarfs, and other stories. (Three dwarfs.)
Nursery tales. (Three dwarfs.)
Singleton. Wildflower fairy book.

Three little pigs. I. Aunt Louisa's book of fairy tales.
*Bailey. Folk stories and fables.
Bailey and Lewis. For the children's hour.
*Bowen. Second story reader.
Bryant. Best stories to tell to children. (Story of the three little pigs.)
Bryant. How to tell stories to children.
*Burchill. Progressive road to reading. Book I. (Three brother pigs.)
Chisholm. In fairy land.
*Coe and Christie. Story hour readers. Book 1. (Three pigs.)
Coussens. Child's book of stories.
Darton. Wonder book of beasts.
Dyer. What-happened-then stories.
*Elson and Runkel. Elson readers. Book 2. (Three pigs.)
Faulkner. Old English nursery tales.
Forty famous fairy tales.
*Grover. Folk-lore readers. v. 1.
Jacobs. English fairy tales.
Johnson. Oak-tree fairy book.
Lansing. Rhymes and stories.
Mother Goose's nursery rhymes, tales and jingles (Warne ed.).
O'Grady and Throop. Teachers' story teller's book. (Story of the three little pigs.)
Pyle. Mother's nursery tales.
Skinner. Nursery tales from many lands.
*Skinner. Very little child's book of stories.
Three little pigs and Tom Thumb.
Wiggin and Smith. Tales of laughter.
See also Farmer Broom, Farmer Leaves and Farmer Iron; Tabby and the mice.
Three little pigs. II. Baldwin. Fairy stories and fables. (Three pigs.)
Klingensmith. Household stories. (Three pigs.)
Lang. Green fairy book.
Lang. Pretty Goldilocks, and other stories.
Wiggin and Smith. Tales of laughter. (Three ways to build a house.)
Three little pigs. III. O'Grady and Throop. Teachers' story teller's book.
*Old, old tales retold.
Three little pigs and the ogre. Pyle. Wonder clock.
Skinner. Very little child's book of stories.
Three low masses. Smith. More mystery tales.
Three luck children. *See* Fortune-seekers. I.
Three miners. Guerber. Legends of the Rhine.
Three minstrels. Curry. Little classics.
Three monkeys. Bosschère. Folk tales of Flanders.
Three musicians. Lang. Beauty and the beast, and other stories.

Three musicians—*continued.*
Lang. Green fairy book.
Wiggin and Smith. Magic casements.
Three orange peris. Kunos. Forty-four Turkish fairy tales.
Kunos. Turkish fairy tales.
Three peasant maidens. Hall. Icelandic fairy tales.
Three pennies. Bay. Danish fairy and folk tales.
See also Traveling companion.
Three phoebes of Windygoul. Seton. Woodmyth and fable.
Three piggy-wigs. Burchill. Progressive road to reading. Book 2.
See also Three billy goats gruff.
Three pigs. *See* Three little pigs. II.
Three pink candles. Storytellers' magazine. June 1915, p. 208.
Three powers. Bailey. Little man with one shoe.
Three precepts. Wardrop. Georgian folk tales.
Three princes. *See* St. Nicholas.
Three princes and their beasts. Lang. Violet fairy book.
Three princesses in the blue mountain. Asbjörnsen. Fairy tales from the far north.
Three princesses of Whiteland. Dasent. Popular tales from the Norse.
Dasent. Norse fairy tales.
Lang. Red fairy book.
Stroebe and Martens. Norwegian fairy book. (Three princesses in Whiteland.)
Three princesses with glass hearts. Jokai and others. Golden fairy book. (Three sisters and their glass hearts.)
Underhill. Dwarfs' tailor. and other fairy tales.
Three purses. Olcott. Good stories for great holidays.
See also St. Nicholas.
Three questions. I. Cabot. Ethics for children.
Tolstoi. Twenty-three tales.
Three questions. II. Mother Goose's nursery rhymes, tales and jingles (Warne ed.).
Welsh. Stories children love.
See also Hans Clodhopper.
Three rabbits. Bailey. Stories and rhymes for a child.
Three red piggies. Grundtvig. Danish fairy tales.
Three remarks. Richards. Toto's merry winter.
Tappan. Book of humor.
Three revellers and death. Darton. Tales of the Canterbury pilgrims. (Pardoner's tale: Three revellers and death.)
McSpadden. Stories from Chaucer. (Pardoner's tale: Three rioters.)
Patten. Junior classics. v. 4. (Death and the three revellers.)
See also King's ankus.
Three rhymsters. Martens. Chinese fairy book.
Three rioters. *See* Three revellers and death.
Three robes. Lang. Crimson fairy book.

Three robes—*continued.*
Lang. Golden mermaid, and other stories.
See also Asmund and Signy.
Three robes of wonder. *See* Three wonderful dresses.
Three roses. Baudis. Czech folk tales.
See also Beauty and the beast.
Three ruling gods. Martens. Chinese fairy book.
Three sillies. Forty famous fairy tales.
Hartland. English folk and fairy tales.
Jacobs. English fairy tales.
Johnson. Elm-tree fairy book.
My Bookhouse. v. 4.
Tappan. Folk stories and fables.
Wiggin and Smith. Tales of laughter.
See also Believing husbands; Clever Alice; Six sillies; Three foolish bears.
Three silver bells, Legend of. Peck. Stories for good children.
See also Silver bell; Why the chimes rang.
Three silver citrons. See Three lemons. I.
Three silver feathers. Harrison. Bric-a-brac stories.
Three singing leaves. *See* Prince Hatt under the earth.
Three sisters. I. Arabian nights (Lang. Story of two sisters who were jealous of their younger sister).
Arabian nights (Townsend).
Arabian nights, More tales (Olcott. Story of the Princess Periezade and the speaking bird, the singing tree, and the golden water.)
Arabian nights (Wiggin and Smith. Talking tree, the singing bird and the golden water.)
Cary. French fairy tales. (Baker's three daughters.)
Jacobs. Europa's fairy book. (Dancing water, the singing apple, and the speaking bird.)
Marshall. Fairy tales of all nations. (Dancing water, singing stone, and talking bird.)
My Bookhouse. v. 4. (Talking bird. Abridged.)
See also Bird of truth; Fountain of Giant Land; Kirunmala, wreath of light; Singing tree and the speaking bird.
Three sisters. II. *See* Three sisters and their stepmother.
Three sisters and their glass hearts. *See* Three princesses with glass hearts.
Three sisters and their stepmother. Pyle. Tales of wonder and magic. (Three sisters.)
Wardrop. Georgian folk tales.
Three sisters trapped in a mountain. Dasent. Norse fairy tales. (Old dame and her hen.)
Dasent. Popular tales from the Norse. (Old dame and her hen.)
Thorpe. Yule-tide stories. (Three sisters who were entrapped into a mountain.)
See also Featherbird.

Three sisters who were entrapped into a mountain. *See* Three sisters trapped in a mountain.
Three sleepy young men. Guerber. Legends of the Rhine. (Three sleepers.)
Noyes. Twilight stories.
Three sluggards. Grimm. Fairy tales (Lucas tr.).
Grimm. Fairy tales (Paull tr.).
*Grimm. Fairy tales (Wiltse). v. 2.
Grimm. Household tales (Everyman's ed.).
Wiggin and Smith. Tales of laughter.
Three snake leaves. Grimm. Household tales (Burt ed. Two white snakes.)
Lang. Green fairy book.
Lang. Three dwarfs, and other stories.
Three sneezes. Jerrold. Reign of King Oberon.
Three soldiers. Jacobs. Europa's fairy book.
Jerrold. Big book of fairy tales.
See also Little soldier; Nose-tree; Princess Longnose.
Three soldiers and the dwarf. *See* Nose-tree.
Three sons. I. Gregory. Kiltartan wonder book.
Patten. Junior classics. v. 1.
Three sons. II. Lindsay and Poulsson. Joyous travelers. (Tale told by the squire's lady.)
Three sons of Hali, Story of the. Lang. Grey fairy book.
Lang. Marvellous musician.
Three sowers. Mendes. Fairy spinning wheel.
Three spinners. *See* Three spinning fairies.
Three spinning fairies. Coussens. Child's book of stories. (Three spinners.)
Grimm. Fairy tales (Paull tr.).
Grimm. Household stories (Crane tr. Three spinsters.)
Grimm. Household tales (Burt ed. Spinning fairies.)
Grimm. Household tales (Everyman's ed.).
Pyle. Mother's nursery tales. (Three spinners.)
(play). Stevenson. Plays in the home. (Three spinners.)
Storytellers' magazine. Nov. 1914, p. 718.
See also Habetrot and Scantlie Mab; Three little crones each with something big; Spinning queen.
Three spinsters. *See* Three spinning fairies.
Three suitors. Marshall. Fairy tales of all nations.
Three swords. Marshall. Fairy tales of all nations.
Three sworn brothers. Fielde. Chinese fairy tales.
Three tails, Tale of. Finger. Tales from silver lands.
Three talismans. Fielde. Chinese fairy tales.
See also Little soldier.
Three tasks. Baldwin. Another fairy reader.
See also Morning dew; True and Untrue; Vilas' spring.
Three tradesmen. Æsop. Fables (Stickney).
Three treasures of the giants. Lang. Faery nurse.
Lang. Orange fairy book.
Three vases. Æsop. Fables (Burt ed.)

Three ways to build a house. *See* Three little pigs. II.
Three weavers. Johnston. Little Colonel at boarding school.
Three white mice (play). Storytellers' magazine Oct. 1916, p. 517.
Three wishes. I. Alderman. Classics old and new. 3d reader.
*Burchill. Progressive road to reading. Book 2.
Forty famous fairy tales.
Hartland. English folk and fairy tales.
Jacobs. More English fairy tales.
Johnson. Fir-tree fairy book.
Pyle. Mother's nursery tales.
Success library. v. 3.
Welsh. Fairy tales children love.
See also Health and hygiene.
Three wishes. II. Butterworth. Zigzag journeys in the Orient. (*In* Ch. 12. Wish three times.)
Caballero. Spanish fairy tales.
Larned. Fairy tales from France.
My Bookhouse. v. 3.
Spaulding and Bryce. Aldine readers. Book 3. (Black pudding.)
Wiggin and Smith. Tales of laughter.
Three wishes. III. Djurklo. Swedish fairy tales. (Sausage.)
Skinner. Merry tales.
Three wishes. IV. Yeats. Irish fairy and folk tales.
See also Smith and the devil.
Three wishes. V. *See* Glooscap and the magic gifts. VI.
Three wishes. VI. Scudder. Seven little people.
Three wishes. VII. Marshall. Fairy tales of all nations.
Three wishes. VIII. Laboulaye. Last fairy tales.
Three wishes. IX. Bellamy. Wonder children. (Story of the three wishes.)
Three wishes. X. *See* Poor man and the rich man.
Three wishes. XI. Donahey. Tales to be told to children.
See also Tired of being a little girl; Wishing spring.
Three wonderful beggars, Story of. Lang. Violet fairy book.
Polevoi. Russian fairy tales. (Marko the rich and Vasily the luckless.)
Wheeler. Russian wonder tales. (Wassily the unlucky.)
See also Giant with the golden hair. I and II.
Three wonderful dresses. Byrne. Modern Greek fairy tales.
Quiller-Couch. Fairy tales far and near. (Three robes of wonder.)
Three wonders of the world. Laboulaye. Last fairy tales.
Three years without wages. Asbjörnsen. Tales from the fjeld.
Dasent. Norse fairy tales.
Stroebe and Martens. Norwegian fairy book. (Youth who was to serve three years without pay.)

Three years without wages—*continued.*
See also Enchanted ring. II; Wonderful ring.
Thresher and the ear of corn. Æsop. Fables (Burt ed.).
Thriftless wife. Fielde. Chinese fairy tales.
Thring, Eoth Apf, and old Castor Fiber. Taylor. Thrings of the dark mountain.
Thring, the borough president, and the butcher's boy. Taylor. Thrings of the dark mountain.
Thring, the curator's son, and the upstairs dungeon. Taylor. Thrings of the dark mountain.
Thring, the robber baron, and the lacuna. Taylor. Thrings of the dark mountain.
Thring, the Swedish interpreter and the library of Dr. Elif Rozar. Taylor. Thrings of the dark mountain.
Through the fire. Nichols and DeMorgan. Princess Girlikin and other fairy tales.
Through the mouse hole. My Bookhouse. v. 3.
Thrush and the swallow. Æsop. Fables (Burt ed.).
Thrym. *See* Thor: Quest of the hammer.
Thumbelina. Andersen. Fairy tales (Lucas tr.).
Andersen. Fairy tales (Paull tr. Little Tiny.)
Andersen. Fairy tales and stories (Toksvig. Tommelisa.)
Andersen. Wonder stories. (Thumbling.)
Bailey. Stories children need.
*Baldwin. Fairy reader.
Boston collection of kindergarten stories. (Little Thumb.)
Coussens. Child's book of stories. (Little Totty.)
Esenwein and Stockard. Children's stories. (Adapted.)
Field. Famous fairy tales.
Haaren. Fairy life. (Thumblina.)
Jerrold. Big book of fairy tales.
Jerrold. Reign of King Oberon. (Thumbeline.)
Ketchum and Jorgensen. Kindergarten gems. (Thumbling.)
Keyes. Stories and story-telling.
Lang. Little King Loc. (Strange adventures of Little Maia.)
Lang. Olive fairy book. (Strange adventure of little Maia.)
Lang. Twelve huntsmen, and other stories.
Lang. Yellow fairy book.
Lansing. Fairy tales. v. 2.
My Bookhouse. v. 2. (Thumbelisa.)
Olcott. Book of elves and fairies. (Little Tiny.)
Singleton. Goldenrod fairy book. (Little Tiny.)
Welsh. Fairy tales children love.
Thumbeline. *See* Thumbelina.
Thumbelisa. *See* Thumbelina.
Thumbietot and the bears. *See* Nils and the bear.
Thumbikin. Dasent. Popular tales from the Norse.
Dasent. Norse fairy tales.
Thumbkin. I. *See* Boots and his brothers.
Thumbkin. II. *See* Thumbling. I.
Thumblina. *See* Thumbelina.

Thumbling. I. Grimm. Fairy tales (Lucas tr. Tom Thumb).
Grimm. Household stories (Crane tr. Tom Thumb; Tom Thumb's travels.)
Grimm. Household tales (Burt ed. Little Thumb.)
Grimm. Household tales (Everyman's ed. Tom Thumb.)
Jacobs. Europa's fairy book. (Thumbkin.)
Patten. Junior classics. v. 1.
Scudder. Book of folk stories. (Tom Thumb.)
Scudder. Children's book. (Tom Thumb.)
Scudder. Fables and folk stories. (Tom Thumb.)
Tappan. Folk stories and fables.
Van Sickle and Seegmiller. Riverside readers. 4th reader. (Little Thumb.)
See also Man who was only a finger and a half in stature.
Thumbling. II. *See* Thumbelina.
Thumbling the dwarf and Thumbling the giant. *See* Young giant.
Thumbling the dwarf who became a giant. *See* Young giant.
Thunder-bird. I. Judson. Myths and legends of the Pacific Northwest. (Origin of the Thunder-bird.)
Thunder bird. II. Farmer. Nature myths.
Thunder bird of Puget Sound. Bayliss. Treasury of Indian tales.
Thunder-bird of the Dakotas. Judd. Wigwam stories.
Thunder-god and his brother. *See* Thor: Thor's fishing.
Thunder maker and cold maker. Grinnell. Punishment of the stingy.
Thunder oak. Olcott. Good stories for great holidays.
See also Christmas tree. VI.
Thunder people. Cowles. Indian nature myths.
Thunder sends the great flood upon the earth. Sexton. Gray wolf stories.
Thunderbolt. Guerber. Legends of the Rhine.
Thunderers. Eastman. Indian legends retold.
Kennedy. New world fairy book.
Pratt. Legends of the red children.
Ti-ke-wa-kush, the man who called the buffalo. Grinnell. Pawnee hero stories.
Ti-tiriti-ti. Macdonell. Italian fairy book.
Tide-jewels. I. Griffis. Japanese fairy tales.
Williams. Fairy tales from folk lore.
Tide-jewels. II. *See* Ambitious hunter and skilful fisher.
Tides. *See* Cause of tides; Crab that played with the sea; Crab and the moon.
Tiger and the giraffe. Wiggin and Smith. Talking beasts.
Tiger and the man, Story of. Olcott. Wonder garden.
Tiger and the shadow. Baker and Carpenter. Language readers. 3d year.
Wiggin and Smith. Talking beasts.
Tiger gets his deserts. Wiggin and Smith. Talking beasts.

Tiger lily, snap-dragon and elephant ear, Origin of. Bigham. Overheard in fairy land.
Tiger on the Hudson. Aspinwall. Short stories for short people.
Tiger, the Brahmin and the jackal. *See* Brahmin, the tiger and the jackal.
Tiger, the fox, and the hunters. Patten. Junior classics. v. 1.
Tappan. Folk stories and fables.
Wiggin and Smith. Talking beasts.
Tiger! Tiger! Kipling. Jungle book.
Tiger's decoy. Martens. Chinese fairy book.
Tiidu, the piper. Lang. Crimson fairy book.
Lang. Little Wildrose.
Tilly's Christmas. Judson and Bender. Graded literature readers. 4th reader.
Tim Tim Tamytam. Gruelle. Friendly fairies.
Timbertop and Betsian. English. Fairy stories and wonder tales.
Time and the kings of the elements. Chodzko. Fairy tales of the Slav.
Time that will come again. Keyes. Stories and storytelling.
Timid Agnes. Harrison. Old-fashioned fairy book.
Timid hare. Babbitt. Jataka tales. (Foolish, timid rabbit.)
Bailey. Once upon a time animal stories. (Rabbit who was afraid.)
Bailey. Stories children need. (Rabbit who was afraid.)
Burlingame. Grateful elephant. (Buddhist Henny-Penny.)
Curry. Little classics. (Timid hare that frightened the beasts.)
Harper. Story-hour favorites. (Folly of panic.)
Hodgkins. Atlantic treasury of childhood stories. (Flight of the beasts.)
My Bookhouse. v. 2. (Foolish, timid, little hare.)
Patten. Junior classics. v. 2. (Hare who thought the world had come to an end.)
Peck. Stories for good children. (Hare and the elephant.)
Shedlock. Art of the storyteller. (Folly of panic.)
Shedlock. Eastern stories and legends. (Hare that ran away.)
Young and Field. Literary readers. Book 2. (Timid hares.)
See also Chicken-Little.
Timmy's mixed-up moving. Bailey. Friendly tales.
Timothy Tuttle and the little imps. Olcott. Book of elves and fairies.
Tin rooster. Bowen. Second story reader.
Tinder box. *Andersen. Best fairy tales (Henderson tr.).
Andersen. Fairy tales (Lucas tr.).
Andersen. Fairy tales (Paull tr.).

Tinder box—*continued.*
Andersen. Fairy tales and stories (Toksvig.)
Andersen. Wonder stories (Author's ed.).
Forty famous fairy tales.
Gibbon. Reign of King Cole.
Lang. Yellow fairy book.
Patten. Junior classics. v. 1.
Welsh. Fairy tales children love.
Winnington. Outlook fairy book.
See also Blue light.
Ting-a-ling. Stockton. Ting-a-ling tales.
Ting-a-ling and the five magicians. Stockton. Ting-a-ling tales.
Ting-a-ling's visit to Tur-i-li-ra. Stockton. Ting-a-ling tales.
Tiniest star. Storytellers' magazine. Dec. 1917, p. 520.
Tinkey. Fairy stories from St. Nicholas.
Tinklebell. Messer. Next night stories.
Tinkling laugh. Segovia. Spanish fairy book.
Tinkling, singing music box. Bailey. Stories for Sunday telling.
Tinsel and lightning. Wiggin and Smith. Talking beasts.
Tintelle's mother. Kennedy. New world fairy book.
Tiny Tim. Skinner. Very little child's book of stories.
Tiny Tim's Christmas dinner. *See* Cratchit's Christmas dinner.
Tip of a tail. Storytellers' magazine. Feb. 1917, p. 90. (Tale of a tip of a tail.)
See also Monkey's bargains.
Tip-top, History of. Arnold and Gilbert. Stepping stones to literature. v. 4.
Cowles. Art of story-telling.
Ketchum and Jorgensen. Kindergarten gems. (Story of Tip Top.)
Tippy Toes, Adventures of. Bailey. Stories and rhymes for a child.
Tired of being a little girl. Coussens. Child's book of stories
Sly. World stories retold.
See also Three wishes. XI; Wishing spring.
Tit for tat. Bryant. Stories to tell to children. (Little jackal and the camel.)
*Burchill. Progressive road to reading. Book 2. (Camel and the jackal.)
Coussens. Child's book of stories.
Frere. Old Deccan days.
O'Grady and Throop. Teachers' story teller's book.
Stanley. Animal folk tales.
Tappan. Folk stories and fables.
Wiggin and Smith. Fairy ring.
Young and Field. Literary readers. Book 2. (Camel and the jackal.)

Titans. Bailey. Wonder tales. (What became of the giants.)
Francillon. Gods and heroes. (Gods and the giants; Saturn.)
Guerber. Myths of Greece and Rome. (*In* Beginning of all things.)
Hutchinson. Orpheus with his lute. (Coming of Zeus.)
See also Prometheus.
Tithonus. *See* Aurora and Tithonus.
Titty Mouse and Tatty Mouse. Coussens. Child's book of stories.
Forty famous fairy tales.
*Haaren. Songs and stories. 2d reader.
Hodgkins. Atlantic treasury of childhood stories.
Howard. Banbury cross stories.
Jacobs. English fairy tales.
Johnson. Oak-tree fairy book.
*Klingensmith. Just stories.
Mother Goose's nursery rhymes and jingles (Warne ed.).
O'Grady and Throop. Teachers' story teller's book.
Welsh. Stories children love. (Story of Titty Mouse and Tatty Mouse.)
Wiggin and Smith. Tales of laughter.
See also Death and burial of poor hen-sparrow; Death of Chanticleer; Spider and the flea.
Titurel and the Holy Grail. Guerber. Legends of the middle ages.
To-day or to-morrow? Hartwell. Story hour readings. 5th year.
To the devil with the money! I know what I know. *See* I know what I have learned.
To your good health! Harper. Story-hour favorites.
Lang. Crimson fairy book.
Lang. Magic ring, and other stories.
Shedlock. Art of the storyteller.
Toad. I. Andersen. Stories (Riverside ed.).
Andersen. Wonder stories (Author's ed.).
Bailey. Stories children need. (Adapted).
Toad. II. Aspinwall. Short stories for short people.
Toad and the boy. Zitkala-Ša. Old Indian legends.
Toad and the may-fly. Æsop. Fables (Burt ed.).
Toad-boy. Aspinwall. Short stories for short people.
Toad-woman. Schoolcraft. Indian fairy book.
Toads and diamonds. *See* Diamonds and toads.
Toad's jewel. Pyle. Prose and verse for children.
Toadstool and the acorn. Sly. World stories retold.
Toadstool stairway. Donaldson. Little papoose listens.
Toadstools, Origin of. Bigham. Overheard in fairy land.
Tobacco boy. Gade. Norwegian fairy tales.
Tobacco fairy from the Blue Hills. Macmillan. Canadian fairy tales.
Tobacco of Harisaboqued. Miller. Philippine folklore stories.

Toinette and the elves. Coolidge. Round dozen.
Dickinson and Skinner. Children's book of Christmas stories.
Tokgabi and his pranks. Griffis. Unmannerly tiger, and other Korean tales.
Griffis. Korean fairy tales.
Tokgabi's menagerie, cats and dogs. *See* Why the dog and cat are enemies. II.
Toller's neighbors. Dasent. Popular tales from the Norse.
Thorpe. Yule-tide stories.
Tolstoy's daughter and the peasant boy. Sly. World stories retold.
Tom and the knockers. Olcott. Book of elves and fairies.
Tom Connor's cat. Olcott and Pendleton. Jolly book. (Ye marvellous legend of Tom Connor's cat.)
Tom goes down to sea. *See* Tom, the water baby.
Tom Hickathrift. Duncan-Jones. English folk-lore stories.
Gibbon. Reign of King Cole.
Jacobs. More English fairy tales.
Johnson. Elm-tree fairy book.
Mother Goose's nursery rhymes, tales and jingles (Warne ed.).
Rhys. Fairy gold.
Tom of the goatskin. Armfield. Wonder tales.
Tom, the chimney sweep. *See* Tom, the water baby.
Tom, the water baby. Arnold and Gilbert. Stepping stones to literature. v. 4. (Water babies.)
Bailey and Lewis. For the children's hour.
Blaisdell. Child life. 4th reader.
Cabot. Ethics for children. (Tom, the chimney sweep.)
Field. Famous fairy tales. (Water baby.)
Judson and Bender. Graded literature readers. v. 4. (Tom goes down to sea.)
Sly. World stories retold.
Wiltse. Kindergarten stories.
Tom Thumb. I. Adams. Folk-story and verse.
Aunt Louisa's book of fairy tales.
Baldwin. Fairy stories and fables.
Bates. Once upon a time.
*Blaisdell. Child life. 2d reader.
Chisholm. In fairy land.
Chisholm and Steedman. Staircase of stories.
Coe. First book of stories.
Coussens. Child's book of stories.
Esenwein and Stockard. Children's stories.
Forty famous fairy tales. (History of Tom Thumb.)
Hartland. English folk and fairy tales. (History of Tom Thumb.)
Jacobs. English fairy tales. (History of Tom Thumb.)
Johnson. Birch-tree fairy book.
Keyes. Stories and story-telling.
Lansing. Tales of old England.

Tom Thumb. I.—*continued.*
Mabie. Fairy tales every child should know.
Mabie. Heroes and fairies.
Mother Goose's nursery rhymes, tales and jingles (Warne ed.).
Mother Goose rhymes, jingles and fairy tales (Altemus ed. History of Tom Thumb.)
Mulock. Fairy tales.
My Bookhouse. v. 2. (Story of Tom Thumb.)
Norton. Heart of oak books. v. 2. (History of Tom Thumb.)
O'Shea. Old world wonder stories.
Patten. Junior classics. v. 1.
Perkins. Twenty best fairy tales.
Rhys. Fairy gold.
Rolfe. Fairy tales in prose and verse.
Singleton. Wild flower fairy book.
Tappan. Folk stories and fables.
Three little pigs and Tom Thumb.
Tweed. Fairy tales everyone should know.
Valentine. Old, old fairy tales (Warne ed.).
Welsh. Fairy tales children love.
Wiggin and Smith. Fairy ring. (History of Tom Thumb.)
Wiltse. Hero folk of ancient Britain.
See also Hop-o'-my-Thumb. II.
Tom Thumb. II. *See* Thumbling.
Tom Thumb. III. *See* Hop-o'-my-Thumb.
Tom Tim Tot. *See* Tom Tit Tot.
Tom-tit and the bear. *See* Wren and the bear.
Tom Tit Tot. Baldwin. Fairy tales.
*Bowen. Second story reader. (Black thing.)
Chisholm and Steedman. Staircase of stories.
Coussens. Child's book of stories.
Hartland. English folk and fairy tales.
Jacobs. English fairy tales.
Johnson. Oak-tree fairy book.
Lansing. Quaint old stories.
Mabie. Folk tales every child should know. (Tom Tim Tot.)
Partridge. Story telling in home and school. (Nimmy Nimmy Not.)
Rhys. Fairy gold.
Storytellers' magazine. June 1913, p. 1. (Nimmy Nimmy Not.)
Wiggin and Smith. Tales of laughter.
*Young and Field. Literary readers. Book 2.
See also Habetrot and Scantlie Mab; Rumpelstiltskin.
Tom Totherhouse. Dasent. Popular tales from the Norse.
Tommelisa. *See* Thumbelina.
Tommy Tart. *Coe and Christie. Story hour readers. Book 1.
Tommy's grumbles. Bailey. Friendly tales.

Tomorrow. Richards. Golden windows.
Tomts. Olcott. Book of elves and fairies.
Tongue-cut sparrow. Armfield. Wonder tales. (Talkative sparrow.)
Bailey and Lewis. For the children's hour.
Chisholm and Steedman. Staircase of stories.
Griffis. Japanese fairy tales.
Hearn. Japanese fairy tales.
Lang. Elf maiden. (Sparrow with the slit tongue.)
Lang. Pink fairy book. (Sparrow with the slit tongue.)
Lyman. Story-telling.
My Bookhouse. v. 2.
Olcott. Good stories for great holidays.
Ozaki. Japanese fairy tales.
Tappan. Folk stories and fables.
Wiggin and Smith. Tales of laughter.
Williston. Japanese fairy tales.
Tongues. Æsop. Fables (Burt ed.).
Tontlawald, Tale of the. Lang. Violet fairy book.
Tony Bear at the peacock house. Danielson. Story telling time.
Too dear. Tolstoi. Twenty-three tales.
Too many to marry. *See* Brazen brogues.
Too much gold. *See* Midas. I.
Toomai of the elephants. Kipling. Jungle book.
Tooth for a tooth. Bacon. True philosopher.
Top and ball. Andersen. Fairy tales (Paull tr.).
Andersen. Stories (Riverside ed. Lovers.)
Andersen. Wonder stories (Author's ed. Lovers.)
*Bailey. Folk stories and fables.
Bailey and Lewis. For the children's hour.
Scudder. Children's book. (Lovers.)
Top Off—Half Off—All Gone. *See* Cat and the mouse in partnership.
Topaz. Murphy. Necklace of jewels.
Topknots and crockery hats. Griffis. Unmannerly tiger, and other Korean tales.
Griffis. Korean fairy tales.
Torch-bearer. Richards. Silver crown.
Toreador's sword, Story of the. Harrison. Bric-a-brac stories.
Tornit. Bayliss. Treasury of Eskimo tales.
Torpedo that was lost. Hendersen. Sea yarns for boys.
Torre Jeppe. Stroebe and Martens. Swedish fairy book.
Tortoise and a mischievous monkey, Tale of. Lang. Brown fairy book.
Lang. Magician's gifts.
See also How the elephant and the whale were tricked.
Tortoise and the birds. *See* Foolish tortoise.
Tortoise and the eagle. *See* Foolish tortoise.
Tortoise and the elephant. *See* How the elephant and the whale were tricked.

Tortoise and the geese. *See* Talkative tortoise.
Tortoise and the hare. *See* Hare and the tortoise.
Tortoise that would talk. *See* Talkative tortoise.
Totem of the son of Yelth. Nixon-Roulet. Indian folk tales.
Touch of clay. *See* Bride from the red lake.
Touch of iron. Griffis. Welsh fairy tales.
Thomas. Welsh fairy book. (Fairy wife.)
Tournament at Winchester. *See* Sir Lancelot and Elaine.
Tower of the birds. Alden. Boy who found the king.
Town mouse and the country mouse. *See* Country mouse and the town mouse.
Town-mouse and the fell-mouse. *See* Country mouse and the town mouse.
Town musicians. *See* Bremen town musicians.
Town of the snake girls. Lummis. Pueblo Indian folk stories.
Toy of the giant child. *Benson. Really truly fairy tales. (Toy of the giant's child.)
Griffis. Swiss fairy tales. (*In* Mountain giants.)
Guerber. Legends of the Rhine. (Giantess' playthings.)
Stebbins. Sunken city. (Giant maiden.)
Toy princess. Chisholm. Enchanted land.
Chisholm and Steedman. Staircase of stories.
Nichols and DeMorgan. Princess Girlikin and other fairy tales.
Tprru. Butterworth. Zigzag journeys in the Orient. (*In* Ch. 11.)
Trading babies. *Cöe and Christie. Story hour readers. Book 1.
See also Lark and the child.
Trail of the far-off-lodge. See Scar Face. IV.
Trailing arbutus, Legend of. *See* Old Winter Man and the Spring. I.
Tramp and the old woman. *See* Old woman and the tramp.
Trapping in the Happy Hunting Grounds. Judd. Wigwam stories.
See also Sun a prisoner. I.
Traveler. Æsop. Fables (Burt ed.).
Traveler and his dog. Æsop. Fables (Burt ed.).
Traveler and the tiger. Wiggin and Smith. Talking beasts.
Traveler and the viper. Scudder. Children's book.
Scudder. Fables and folk stories.
Traveler, the cook and the little old man. Richards. Joyous story of Toto.
Travelers. Æsop. Fables (Black ed.).
Travelers and the axe. Æsop. Fables (Burt ed. Two travelers).
Æsop. Fables (Stickney. Two travelers.)
Dyer and Brady. Merrill readers. 3d reader. (I and we.)
Lansing. Quaint old stories. (Travelers and the hatchet.)
Scudder. Fables and folk stories.

Travelers and the axe—*continued.*
(play). Stevenson. Plays for the home. (Travelers and the hatchet.)
Welsh. Stories children love. (Two travelers.)
Wiggin and Smith. Talking beasts. (Two travelers.)
Travelers and the bear. Æsop. Fables (Black ed.).
Æsop. Fables (Burt ed.).
Æsop. Fables (Burt ed. Bear in the woods.)
Æsop. Fables (Jacobs. Two fellows and the bear.)
Æsop. Fables (Stickney. Bear and the two travelers.)
Bryce. Fables from afar.
Scudder. Fables and folk stories.
Wiggin and Smith. Talking beasts.
See also Bear and the two huntsmen.
Travelers and the crow. Æsop. Fables (Black ed.).
Æsop. Fables (Burt ed.).
Travelers and the hatchet. *See* Travelers and the axe.
Travelers by the seaside. Æsop. Fables (Burt ed.).
Traveling companion. Andersen. Fairy tales (Lūcas tr.).
Andersen. Fairy tales (Paull tr.).
Andersen. Fairy tales and stories (Toksvig.)
Andersen. Wonder stories (Author's ed.).
Marshall. Fairy tales of all nations.
Singleton. Wild flower fairy book.
See also Companion.
Traveling musicians. *See* Bremen town musicians.
Travels of a fox. Bailey. For the story teller.
*Bailey. Folk stories and fables.
Bailey and Lewis. For the children's hour.
Johnson. Oak-tree fairy book.
Skinner. Nursery tales from many lands.
See also Boy who was called Thick-head; Rat's wedding.
Travels of Baron Munchausen. Olcott and Pendleton. Jolly book. (Baron Munchausen goes a-hunting.)
Scudder. Children's book.
Tappan. Stories from seven old favorites.
Welsh. Stories children love. (Tales from the travels of Baron Munchausen.)
See also Embellishment; True history.
Travels of the two frogs. *See* Frog travellers.
Tray of glass. *See* Barber's fifth brother.
Treacherous crow and his cousin, the mink. Riggs. Animal stories from Eskimo land.
Treasure at the end of the rainbow. St. Nicholas. July 1898, p. 719.
Treasure castle. Beston. Firelight fairy book.
Treasure chamber of Rhampsinitus. Brooksbank. Legends of ancient Egypt.
Jewett. Egyptian tales of magic. (Theft of the king's treasure.)
See also Skilful thief.
Treasure seeker. Lang. Crimson fairy book.

Treasure seeker—*continued.*
Lang. Snow-queen, and other stories.
Treasure seeking. Thomas. Welsh fairy book.
Treasure stone of the fairies. Griffis. Welsh fairy tales.
Tree and the reeds. *See* Oak and the reed.
Tree-bound. Zitkala-Ša. Old Indian legends.
Tree in the city. Richards. Golden windows.
Tree in the dark wood. Sholl. Faery tales of Weir.
Tree of health. Stroebe and Martens. Danish fairy book.
Trees. Brown. Star jewels.
Tremsin, the bird zhar, and Nastasia, the lovely maid of the sea. *See* Feather of the zhar bird.
Trevina, Story of. Nicholas and DeMorgan. Princess Girlikin and other fairy tales. (*In* Hair tree.)
Trial. Bay. Danish fairy and folk tales.
Trial of brides. Grimm. Fairy tales (Paull tr.).
Trials of two heavenly lovers. Allen. Korean tales. (Ching Yuh and Kyain Oo; or, The Trials of two heavenly lovers.)
See also Sky bridge of birds.
Tribes, Origin of the. Judson. Myths and legends of the Pacific Northwest.
Tribulations of a cobbler. Caballero. Spanish fairy tales.
Trick of old Aicha. *See* Aicha's stratagem.
Tricks of the fox. Judson. Myths and legends of Alaska.
See also Fox and the crow. II; Fox and the dove; Jackal and the heron.
Tricky wolf and the rats. Babbitt. More Jataka tales.
Trillevip. Stroebe and Martens. Danish fairy book.
See also Rumpelstiltskin.
Triple crown. Smith. Good old stories.
Triptolemos. Beckwith. In mythland. v. 2. (Story of Ceres.)
Burt and Ragozin. Herakles and other heroes.
Guerber. Myths of Greece and Rome. (*In* Ceres and Proserpina.)
Guerber. Myths of Greece and Rome. (Ceres and Triptolemus.)
Hutchinson. Orpheus with his lute. (*In* Mother and the maid.)
Trishka's caftan. Æsop. Fables (Stickney. Supplement).
Wiggin and Smith. Talking beasts.
Tristram. *See* Sir Tristram.
Tristan. *See* Sir Tristram.
Tritill, Litill, and the birds. Lang. Crimson fairy book.
Lang. Little Wildrose.
Triumph of truth. Pyle. Tales of folks and fairies.
Trojan war. Adams. Myths of old Greece. (Fall of Troy.)
Arnold and Gilbert. Stepping stones to literature. v. 4.
*Bailey. Wonder stories. (How a golden apple caused a war; How a wooden horse won a war.)
Baldwin. Story of the golden age.

Trojan war—*continued.*
Baldwin. Thirty more famous stories. (Fall of Troy.)
*Burchill. Progressive road to reading. Book 3. (Fall of Troy.)
Church. Greek story and song. (Story of Troy; Strange story of the false Helen.)
Evans. Heroes of Troy.
Guerber. Myths of Greece and Rome. (Trojan war.)
Haaren and Poland. Famous men of Greece. (Agamemnon.)
Hutchinson. Golden porch (Builders of Troy.)
Patten. Junior classics. v. 3. (Tales of the Trojan war from Homer.)
Peabody. Old Greek folk stories. (House of Agamemnon.)
Shaw. Stories of the ancient Greeks. (Trojan war.)
Storr. Half a hundred hero tales. (Sack of Troy.)
Tappan. Stories from the classics.
See also Apple of discord; Helen of Troy; Paris; Wooden horse.

Troll wedding. Stroebe and Martens. Norwegian fairy book.

Troll-wife. Stroebe and Martens. Norwegian fairy book.

Trolls. Stroebe and Martens. Swedish fairy book. (Tales of the trolls.)

Troll's daughter. Lang. Aladdin, and other stories.
Lang. Pink fairy book.

Troll's hammer. Haaren. Fairy life.
Jerrold. Reign of King Oberon.
Thorpe. Yule-tide stories.
Wiggin and Smith. Fairy ring.

Trolls in Hedale wood. Asbjörnsen. Folk and fairy tales. (Lads who met the trolls in the Hedale wood.)
Asbjörnsen. Tales from the fjeld.
Gade. Norwegian fairy tales. (Boys who met the trolls in Hedal woods.)

Trooper and his horse. Æsop. Fables (Burt ed.).

Troubadour. *See* Trovatore.

Trouble and care. Stroebe and Martens. Norwegian fairy book.

Troublesome old witch. Storytellers' magazine. April 1917, p. 229.

Troublesome visitors. *See* Herr Korbes.

Trovatore. McSpadden. Stories from great operas. (Troubadour.)
Pleasanton. Fairyland of opera. (Il Trovatore.)

Trudel's siege. Alcott. Lulu's library. v. 3.
St. Nicholas. April 1888, p. 421.

True and false prince. Haaren. Ballads and tales.

True and Untrue. Dasent. Popular tales from the Norse.
Dasent. Norse fairy tales.
Gade. Norwegian fairy tales. (Faithful and Faithless.)

True and Untrue—*continued.*
See also Morning dew; Three tasks; Two soldiers; Vilas' spring.
True bride. I. Grimm. Fairy tales (Paull tr.).
Lang. Green fairy book.
True bride. II. Fillmore. Mighty Mikko.
See also Princess Rosette. I.
True cross. Guerber. Legends of the Rhine.
True friend. Bradley-Birt. Bengal fairy tales.
True friendship. I. Skinner. Merry tales.
True friendship. II. Babbitt. More Jataka tales. (Woodpecker, turtle and deer.)
Burlingame. Grateful elephant. (Antelope, woodpecker, tortoise and hunter.)
Coussens. Jade story book. (Four friends.)
Noyes. Twilight stories.
True history. Carpenter. Long ago in Greece.
True philosopher and his cat. Bacon. True philospher.
True spirit of a festival day. See Hare in the moon. II.
Trumpeter of Säkingen. Guerber. Legends of the Rhine.
Trumpeter taken prisoner. Æsop. Fables (Black ed.).
Æsop. Fables (Burt ed.).
Æsop. Fables (Jacobs).
Trus' or intrus'. Young. Behind the dark pines.
Trusty John. *See* Faithful John.
Truth, Story of. Bakewell. True fairy stories.
Truthful little Persian. *See* Little Persian.
Truth's triumph. Frere. Old Deccan days.
Wiggin and Smith. Tales of wonder.
"Try, try again." Baldwin. Fifty people.
See also Bruce and the spider.
Tsar and the angel. Bain. Cossack fairy tales.
See also King Robert of Sicily.
Tsar Angéy and how he suffered for pride, Story of. Magnus. Russian folk-tales.
See also King Robert of Sicily.
Tsar Saltan. Wheeler. Russian wonder tales. (Tzar Saltan.)
Tsarévich and Dyad'ka. Magnus. Russian folk-tales.
Tsarevich Ivan and the harp that harped without a harper. My Bookhouse. v. 4. (Little man as big as your thumb with mustaches seven miles long. Adapted.)
Polevoi. Russian fairy tales.
Tsarevich Ivan, the glowing bird and the gray wolf. *See* Ivan and the gray wolf.
Tsarevich Petr and the wizard. Wheeler. Russian wonder tales. (Tzarevich Petr and the wizard.)
Tsarevna frog. *See* Frog queen.
Tsarevna Loveliness-Inexhaustible. Curtin. Wonder tales from Russia. (Koschei without death.)
Polevoi. Russian fairy tales.

Tsaritsa harpist. Magnus. Russian folk-tales.
Tudur ap Einion. My Bookhouse. v. 3.
Thomas. Welsh fairy book.
Tufte-people on Sandflaesen. *See* Lucky Andrew.
Tula Oolah. Aspinwall. Short stories for short people.
Tulchuherris. Washburn. Indian legends.
Tulip bed. I. Duncan-Jones. English folk-lore stories. (Tulips.)
Hartland. English folk and fairy tales.
Olcott. Good stories for great holidays. (Fairy tulips.)
Tulip bed. II. Keyes. Five senses. (Fragrant tulip bed.)
Keyes. Stories and story telling. (Pixies' thanks.)
McFee. Treasury of flower stories. (Pixies and tulips.)
Tulips. *See* Tulip bed. I.
Tulips, Origin of. *See* Little nymph who loved bright colors; Turk, turban, tulip and dragon.
Tulman. Douglas. Scottish fairy tales.
Tune that makes the tiger drowsy. Tappan. Folk stories and fables.
Wiggin and Smith. Talking beasts.
Tunny and the dolphin. Æsop. Fables (Black ed.).
Æsop. Fables (Burt ed.).
Turandina. Sologub. Sweet-scented name.
Turk, turban, tulip, and dragon. Griffis. Belgian fairy tales.
Turkey factor. Baring-Gould. Old English fairy tales.
Turkey-given corn. Olcott. Wonder garden.
Turkey maiden. Olcott. Red Indian fairy book. (Poor turkey girl.)
Skinner. Merry tales. (Poor little turkey girl.)
Wilson. Myths of the red children.
Turkey queen. *See* Blondina.
Turkeys turning the tables. Howells. Christmas every day.
Turned loaf. English. Fairy stories and wonder tales.
Turning everything into gold. *See* Midas. I.
Turnip. Grimm. Fairy tales (Lucas tr.).
Grimm. Fairy tales (Paull tr.).
Grimm. Household tales (Everyman's ed. Man in the bag.)
Turtle and his bride. Lang. Brown fairy book.
Lang. Elf maiden.
Turtle-Dove, Sage-Cock and the witch. Compton. American Indian fairy tales.
Turtle, the wolf, and the hyena. *See* Why turtles stay near the water.
Turtle who could not stop talking. *See* Talkative tortoise.
Turtle who couldn't stop talking. *See* Talkative tortoise.
Turtle's shell. Patten. Junior classics. v. 2. (How the turtle got his shell.)
Stanley. Animal folk fables.
See also Helpful turtles.
Tutokanula, Legend of. See Rock of the measuring worm.
Twelve brothers. Forty famous fairy tales.

Twelve brothers—*continued.*
Grimm. Fairy tales (Paull tr.).
Grimm. Household stories (Crane tr.).
Grimm. Household tales (Burt ed.).
Grimm. Household tales (Everyman's ed.).
Lang. Forty thieves and other stories.
Lang. Red fairy book.
Mabie. Fairy tales every child should know.
Mabie. Heroes and fairies.
Welsh. Fairy tales children love.
See also Six swans; Twelve wild ducks; Wild swans.
Twelve children in the sky. *See* Pleiades. II.
Twelve by the mail. *See* Mail-coach passengers.
Twelve dancing princesses. Bates. Once upon a time. (Dancing shoes.)
Chisholm. Enchanted land.
Grimm. Fairy tales (Lucas tr.).
Grimm. Household tales (Everyman's ed. Dancing shoes.)
Lang. Red fairy book.
My Bookhouse. v. 2.
Singleton. Goldenrod fairy book. (Dancing shoes.)
Wiggin and Smith. Magic casements.
See also Midnight dance; Princess with the twelve pair of golden shoes.
Twelve hunters. *See* Twelve huntsmen.
Twelve huntsmen. Chisholm. Enchanted land.
Chisholm and Steedman. Staircase of stories.
Grimm. Fairy tales (Lucas tr.).
*Grimm. Fairy tales (Wiltse. Twelve hunters.) v. 2.
Grimm. Household tales (Burt ed. Bride's venture.)
Lang. Green fairy book.
Lang. Twelve huntsmen, and other stories.
Tales for bedtime.
Twelve idlers. Grimm. Fairy tales (Paull tr.).
Twelve months. I. Bailey. Stories children need. (Months.)
*Baldwin. Second fairy reader.
Baudis. Czech folk tales.
Chodzko. Fairy tales of the Slav.
*Elson and Runkel. Elson readers. Book 2. (Adapted.)
Farmer. Nature myths.
Fillmore. Shoemaker's apron.
Gask. Folk tales from many lands. (Four seasons.)
*Gask. Treasury of folk tales. (Four seasons.)
Johnson. Elm-tree fairy book.
Laboulaye. Fairy book.
My Bookhouse. v. 3.
Olcott. Good stories for great holidays.
Patten. Junior classics. v. 2. (Four seasons.)
Pyle. Tales of wonder and magic.
Storytellers' magazine. June 1913, p. 13.
Storytellers' magazine. June 1916, p. 370.

Twelve months. I.—*continued.*
Van Sickle and Seegmiller. Riverside readers. 2d reader.
Welsh. Stories children love.
Wiggin and Smith. Fairy ring.
See also Months I and II; Old woman who met the months; Two brothers II.
Twelve months. II. Canton. Reign of King Herla. (Little Snow-flake.)
Twelve silly sisters that the Pooka carried away. Colum. Peep-show man.
Twelve white peacocks. Dasent. Popular tales from the Norse.
Twelve wild ducks. Asbjörnsen. Fairy tales from the far north.
Dasent. Norse fairy tales.
Dasent. Popular tales from the Norse.
Gade. Norwegian fairy tales.
Hodgkins. Atlantic treasury of childhood stories.
Thorne-Thomsen. East o' the sun and west o' the moon.
See also Six swans; Twelve brothers; Wild swans.
Twelve wild geese. Yeats. Irish fairy and folk tales.
Twigmuntus, Cowbelliantus, Perchnosius. Djurklo. Fairy tales from the Swedish.
Wiggin and Smith. Fairy ring.
Twilight of the gods. I. Foster and Cummings. Asgard stories.
Guerber. Myths of northern lands.
Wickes. Beyond the rainbow bridge. (Tale of the end.)
Wilmot-Buxton. Stories of Norse heroes. (End of all things.)
Twilight of the gods. II. *See* Ring: Twilight of the gods.
Twin brothers. I. Grundtvig. Fairy tales from afar.
Twin brothers. II. Lang. Grey fairy book.
Lang. Invisible prince, and other stories.
Twin brothers. III. *See* Two brothers. III.
Twin children of the sorcerer. Pope. Hawaii.
Twin lambs. My Bookhouse. v. 1.
Twin sisters. Gruelle. Friendly fairies.
Twin stars. Holbrook. Book of nature myths.
James. Magic jaw bone.
Twist-mouth family. Johnson. Oak-tree fairy book.
Twm of the fair lies. Thomas. Welsh fairy book.
Two bad bargains. My Bookhouse. v. 3.
Two baker boys. Stebbins. 3d reader.
Two bells. Guerber. Legends of the Rhine.
Two bottles. *See* Bottle hill.
Two brass kettles. Blaisdell. Child life. 3d reader.
Pumphrey. Stories of the pilgrims.
Two brothers. I. Andersen. Stories and tales (Author's ed.).
Two brothers. II. Chodzko. Fairy tales of the Slav.
Marshall. Fairy tales of all nations. (Brothers.)
See also Month of March.

Two brothers. III. Grimm. Household tales (Burt ed. Twin brothers.)
*Grimm. Fairy tales (Wiltse). v. 1.
Grimm. Household tales (Everyman's ed.).
See also Hare, the bear and the fox.
Two brothers. IV. Baudis. Czech folk tales. (Twin brothers.)
Lang. Golden mermaid, and other stories.
Lang. Pink fairy book.
Two brothers. V. Steel. Tales of the Punjab.
Two brothers. VI. Keyes. Stories and story-telling.
Wardrop. Georgian folk tales.
See also True and Untrue.
Two brothers. VII. Gask. Folk tales from many lands.
Gask. Treasury of folk tales.
Storytellers' magazine. Nov. 1915, p. 420.
Two brothers. VIII. Nixon-Roulet. Japanese folk stories and fairy tales.
Two brothers. IX. Johnson. Birch-tree fairy book.
Two brothers. X. *See* Valentine and Orson.
Two brothers. XI. *Lindsay. Story-teller.
See also Nail.
Two brothers. XII. *See* Ambitious hunter and skilful fisher.
Two brothers. XIII. *See* Bata, the Egyptian boy.
Two brothers and the old witch. *See* Old hag's long leather bag.
Two cakes that loved each other in silence. Andersen. Stories and tales. (Under the willow tree.)
Keyes. Stories and story-telling.
Two caravan-leaders. *See* Wise and foolish merchant.
Two caskets. *See* Man's daughter and the woman's daughter.
Two cat witches. *See* Cat witches.
Two charms (poem). Rhys. Fairy gold.
Two chests. St. Nicholas. Jan. 1916, p. 228.
Two chickens; or, Two ears. Bosschère. Christmas tales of Flanders.
See also Clever Grethel.
Two companions. Lindsay and Poulson. Joyous travelers. (Tale told by the aunt.)
Two countrymen (play). Stevenson. Plays for the home.
Two crabs. *See* Crab and his mother.
Two daisies. Mendes. Fairy spinning wheel.
Two daughters. Welsh. Stories children love.
Two deer. Field second reader.
Two dicers. Burlingame. Grateful elephant.
Two discreet statues, Legend of. Smith. More mystery tales.
Irving. Alhambra.
Two dogs. Æsop. Fables (Stickney. Supplement).
Two ears. *See* Two chickens.
Two fellows and the bear. *See* Travelers and the bear.
Two flags. *Dillingham and Emerson. Tell it again stories.

Two foolish birds. Baldwin. Fairy stories and fables.
See also Blackbird and the doves; Jay and the peacock; Vain jackdaw.
Two foxes. I. Æsop. Fables (Burt ed.).
Storytellers' magazine. Dec. 1914, p. 775.
Two foxes. II. Douglas. Scottish fairy tales.
Two foxes and the hot rolls. Johnson. Book of fairy-tale foxes.
See also Hare and the fox; Two foxes. II.
Two friends. Macé. Home fairy tales.
Two friends and the barrel of grease. Bosschère. Folk tales of Flanders.
See also Cat and the mouse in partnership; Fox as partner; Wolf's butter.
Two frogs. I. Æsop. Fables (Stickney).
Two frogs. II. Æsop. Fables (Black ed.).
Æsop. Fables (Burt ed.).
Grover. Folk-lore readers. v. 1.
Two frogs. III. *See* Frog travelers.
Two frugal men. Fielde. Chinese fairy tales.
Two genies. Silver fairy book.
Wiggin and Smith. Tales of wonder.
Two gifts. Gask. Folk tales from many lands.
Patten. Junior classics. v. 6.
Two goats. Æsop. Fables (Stickney).
See also Fleetfoot and Billy.
Two great painters. Baldwin. Fifty famous people.
Two in a sack. Lang. Violet fairy book.
Two jewels. Friedlander. Jewish fairy book.
Two jugglers. Pitman. Chinese wonder book.
Two king's children. Grimm. Fairy tales (Paull tr.).
Two little birds and a great man. *See* Lincoln and the little birds.
Two little boys that were supposed to have become two little bears. Butterworth. Zigzag journeys in the Orient. (*In* Ch. 4.)
Two little cooks. Bailey and Lewis. For the children's hour.
Two little fir trees. *Storytellers' magazine. Jan. 1917, p. 45.
Two little seeds, Story of. Skinner. Emerald story book.
Two little wooden shoes. Dyer and Brady. Merrill readers. 2d reader.
Two lizards. Æsop. Fables (Burt ed.).
Bryce. Fables from afar.
Patten. Junior classics. v. 1.
Two losses. Wardrop. Georgian folk tales.
Two maidens. Andersen. Stories and tales (Author's ed.).
Two maidens, the gawo-tree, and the lizard. Macnair. Animal tales from Africa.
Two melons. Fielde. Chinese fairy tales.
Wiggin and Smith. Tales of wonder.

Two melons—*continued.*
See also King of the sparrows; Swallow king's rewards.
Two merchants, Tale of. Coussens. Jade story book.
Two millers. Underhill. Dwarfs' tailor, and other fairy tales.
Two monkeys. Bryce. Fables from afar.
Two Moqui heroes. Wiggin and Smith. Tales of wonder.
Williams. Fairy tales from folklore.
Two mothers and a child. Davis and Chow-Leung. Chinese fables and folk stories.
Two mountains. Davis and Chow-Leung. Chinese fables and folk stories.
Two mules (poem). Wiggin and Smith. Talking beasts.
Two old men. *See* Two pilgrims.
Two old soldiers. Blaisdell. Child life. 5th reader.
Two old women and the lake. Storytellers' magazine. Oct. 1915, p. 364.
See also Lake that walked.
Two out of the knapsack. Polevoi. Russian fairy tales.
Two packs. Scudder. Children's book.
Scudder. Fables and folk stories.
Two paths. Lindsay. More mother stories.
Two pilgrims. My Bookhouse. v. 5.
Tolstoi. Russian proprietor and other stories. (Two old men.)
Tolstoi. Twenty-three tales. (Two old men.)
Two poor seamstresses. Gate. Punch and Robinetta.
Two pots. *See* Earthen pot and the pot of brass.
Two princes. Bain. Cossack fairy tales.
Two rabbits. Æsop. Fables (Burt ed.).
Two raccoon cubs and two man cubs, Story of. Quiroga. South American jungle tales.
Two rats. I. Æsop. Fables (Burt ed.).
Two rats. II. *See* Rats and their son-in-law.
Two rats, the fox and the egg. *See* Blackie's egg; Rats, the fox and the egg.
Two scholars. Martens. Chinese fairy book.
Two scythes. Æsop. Fables (Burt ed.).
Two serving damsels. *See* Pixies' vengeance. II.
Two shepherds. *See* Shepherd's son and the ogre.
Two sides to every question. Hartwell. Story hour readings. 7th year.
See also Blind men and the elephant; Red-bud tree.
Two sisters. I. *See* Rakshas' palace.
Two sisters. II. *See* Mother Holle.
Two sisters. III. *See* Man's daughter and woman's daughter.
Two sisters. IV. Chisholm and Steedman. Staircase of stories.
Two sisters who were jealous of their younger sister. *See* Three sisters. I.
Two soldiers. Cary. French fairy tales.
See also True and Untrue.

Two soldiers and the robber. Æsop. Fables (Burt ed.).
Two sons of Ivan the soldier. Polevoi. Russian fairy tales.
Two springs. Æsop. Fables (Burt ed.).
Two step-sisters. *See* Man's daughter and woman's daughter.
Two tails. Skinner. Turquoise story book. (Tale of two tails.)
Two thieves. Wardrop. Georgian folk tales.
Two thieves and the bear. Æsop. Fables (Burt ed.).
Two travelers. I. *See* Travelers and the axe.
Two travelers. II. Bidpai. Tortoise and the geese.
Cabot. Ethics for children.
Two travelers and the oyster. Æsop. Fables (Burt ed.).
Wiggin and Smith. Talking beasts.
Two travelers of differing humors. Æsop. Fables (Burt ed.).
Two wanderers. Grimm. Fairy tales (Paull tr.).
Two ways. Richards. Golden windows.
Two ways of telling a story. Ingelow. Stories told to a child. v. 1.
Two weasels, Story of. *See* Star wives.
Two white snakes. *See* Three snake leaves.
Two wild creatures at meals. Keyes. Five senses.
Two windows. Bailey. Stories for Sunday telling.
Two wishes. Coolidge. Round dozen.
St. Nicholas. March 1877, p. 319.
Two wishes and a half. Campbell. Beyond the border.
Two wives. Field. Second book of tales.
Two young lions. Storytellers' magazine. March 1914, p. 478.
Two young men and the restaurant keeper. Success library. v. 3.
Two young ploughmen. Douglas. Scottish fairy tales.
Twopenny town. Meigs. Kingdom of the winding road.
Twrch Trwyth. *See* Kilwch and Olwen.
Typhon. *See* Isis and Osiris, Story of.
Tyr and the wolf *See* Binding of the Fenris wolf.
Tyrant who became a just ruler. Bidpai. Tortoise and the geese.
See also How a bad king became a good one.
Tyrone, Legend of (poem). Yeats. Irish fairy and folk tales.
Tyr's sword. Guerber. Myths of northern lands. (Tyr.)
Tzar. *See* Tsar.

U

Udea and her seven brothers. Lang. Grey fairy book.
Lang. Marvellous musician.
Ugly duckling. *Andersen. Best fairy tales (Henderson tr.).
Andersen. Fairy tales (Lucas tr.).

Ugly duckling—*continued.*
Andersen. Fairy tales (Paull tr.).
Andersen. Fairy tales and stories (Toksvig).
Andersen. Fairy tales (Turpin ed.).
Andersen. Stories (Riverside ed.).
Andersen. Wonder stories (Author's ed.).
Arnold and Gilbert. Stepping stones to literature. v. 3.
Baker and Carpenter. Language reader. 3d year.
Bailey and Lewis. For the children's hour.
*Baldwin. Fairy reader.
Blaisdell. Child life. 2d reader.
Boston collection of kindergarten stories.
*Bowen. Second story reader.
*Burchill. Progressive road to reading. Book 2.
Coe. First book of stories.
Coussens. Child's book of stories.
*Dyer and Brady. Merrill readers. 2d reader.
Esenwein and Stockard. Children's stories. (Adapted.)
Favorite fairy tales.
Field. Famous fairy tales.
Gibbon. Reign of King Cole.
Harris. Favorites from fairyland.
Jerrold. Big book of fairy tales.
Johnson. Birch-tree fairy book.
Klingensmith. Household stories.
Lang. Orange fairy book.
Mabie. Fairy tales every child should know.
Mabie. Heroes and fairies.
Norton. Heart of oak books. v. 3.
Patten. Junior classics. v. 1.
Perkins. Twenty best fairy tales.
Scudder. Children's book.
Sly. World stories retold. (Adapted.)
(play). Stevenson. Plays for the home.
Stone. Children's stories that never grow old.
Strong. All the year round. v. 4. Summer.
Tappan. Folk stories and fables.
Tweed. Fairy tales everyone should know.
Whittier. Child life in prose.
Wiltse. Kindergarten stories.
Ugly wild boy. Olcott. Red Indian fairy book.
Ulysses. Adams. Myths of old Greece. (Wanderings of Ulysses; Homecoming of Ulysses.)
Baldwin. Story of the golden age.
Carpenter. Long ago in Greece. (Odysseus and Leucothea.)
Church. Greek story and song.
Evans. Heroes of Troy.
Guerber. Myths of Greece and Rome. (Adventures of Ulysses.)
Haaren and Poland. Famous men of Greece. (Adventures of Ulysses.)
My Bookhouse. v. 5. (Homecoming of Ulysses.)

Ulysses—*continued.*
Norton. Heart of oak books. v. 3. (Adventures of Ulysses.)
Patten. Junior classics. v. 3. (Homeward voyage of the Greek hero, Ulysses.)
Peabody. Old Greek folk stories. (Adventures of Odysseus.)
Pratt. Myths of Old Greece. v. 3.
Shaw. Stories of the ancient Greeks.
Storr. Half a hundred hero tales.
Tappan. Stories from the classics.
See also Eumaeus.

Ulysses and Penelope. Baldwin. Stories of the golden age. (*In* Race for a wife.)

Ulysses and Polyphemus. *Bailey. Wonder stories (Cyclops).
Baker and Carpenter. Language readers. 5th year. (Ulysses and the Cyclops.)
Evans. Heroes of Troy. (Cave of the Cyclops.)
Guerber. Myths of Greece and Rome. (*In* Adventures of Ulysses.)
Johonnot. Stories of the olden time. (Polyphemus.)
Mabie. Myths every child should know. (Cyclops.)
Patten. Junior classics. v. 3. (Ulysses and the Cyclops.)
Peabody. Old Greek folk stories. (Curse of Polyphemus.)
Pratt. Myths of old Greece. v. 3. (Polyphemus.)
Scudder. Children's book. (Cyclops.)
Shaw. Stories of the ancient Greeks. (Giant's cave.)

Ulysses and the bag of winds. *Burchill. Progressive road to reading. Book 3. (Bag of winds.)
Coe and Christie. Story hour readers. Book 3. (Bag of winds.)
Dyer and Brady. Merrill readers. 3d reader. (Bag of winds.)
Evans. Heroes of Troy. (Bag of the winds.)
Hyde. Favorite Greek myths. (Bag of winds.)
Judd. Classic myths. (Bag of winds.)
Olcott. Wonder garden. (Bag of the winds.)
Poulsson. In the child's world. (Odysseus and the bag of winds.)
Van Sickle and Seegmiller. Riverside readers. 2d reader.
Wilson. Nature study reader. (Bag of winds.)

Ulysses and the sirens. Patten. Junior classics. v. 3.

Ulysses at Circe's palace. Almost true tales. (Circe's palace.)
Baker and Carpenter. Language readers. 5th year. (Ulysses and Circe.)
Evans. Heroes of Troy. (Circe the beautiful enchantress.)
Guerber. Myths of Greece and Rome. (*In* Adventures of Ulysses.)
Hawthorne. Tanglewood tales. (Circe's palace.)
Hyde. Favorite Greek myths.
Olcott. Wonder garden. (Enchanted swine.)

Ulysses at Circe's palace—*continued.*
Patten. Junior classics. v. 3. (Circe's palace.)
Pratt. Myths of old Greece. v. 3. (Circe's palace.)
Shaw. Stories of the ancient Greeks. (Enchanted island.)
Ulysses's return. Dyer and Brady. Merrill readers. 3d reader. (Faithful Argus.)
Johonnot. Stories of the olden time.
Umbrellas, Origin of. *See* Elf and the dormouse.
Una and the Red Cross Knight. Lang. Red romance book. (How the Red Cross Knight slew the dragon; Una and the lion.)
My Bookhouse. v. 5.
Unambitious queen. Brown. One-footed fairy.
Unanana and the elephant. Gibbon. Reign of King Cole.
Uncle Curro and his cudgel. Caballero. Spanish fairy tales.
Uncle David's nonsensical story. Patten. Junior classics. v. 6.
Smith. Good old stories.
Uncle Jack's story. Patten. Junior classics. v. 6.
Uncle Lion. James. Man elephant.
Uncle Rain and Brother Drouth. Van Sickle and Seegmiller. Riverside readers. 3d reader.
Under the willow-tree. Andersen. Fairy tales (Paull tr.).
Andersen. Stories and tales (Author's ed.).
Underground workers. Lang. Violet fairy book.
Lang. Satin surgeon.
Undertakers. Kipling. Second jungle book.
Underworld, Story of the. Bellamy. Wonder children.
Undine. I. Mabie. Famous stories every child should know.
Undine. II. Skinner. Turquoise story book.
Undutiful daughter. Baring-Gould. Old English fairy tales.
Unexpected Prince and the King of the Underground. Storytellers' magazine. Sept. 1913, p. 138.
Unfruitful tree. Olcott. Good stories for great holidays.
Ungrateful children and the old father who went to school again. Bain. Cossack fairy tales.
Ungrateful guest. Baldwin. Fifty famous stories.
Ungrateful soldier. Baldwin. Fifty famous stories.
Unhappy blacksmith.* Field first reader.
See also Stone cutter.
Unhappy grass stalk. *See* Discontented grass plant. I.
Unhappy son. Brown. Tale of the red children.
Unhappy tadpole. Donaldson. Little papoose listens.
Unhappy twins. Guerber. Legends of the Rhine.
Unicorn. Silver fairy book.
Wiggin and Smith. Tales of wonder.
Union gives strength. *See* Bundle of sticks.
Unknown island. *See* St. Brandan.
Unknown knight. Guerber. Legends of the Rhine.
Unktomee and his bundle of songs. Eastman. Wigwam evenings.

Unktomee and his bundle of songs—*continued.*
See also Iktomi and the ducks.
Unktomee and the elk. Eastman. Wigwam evenings.
Unlooked-for prince. Lang. Grey fairy book.
Unlucky Daniel. Bain. Cossack fairy tales.
Unlucky John. Lang. All sorts of stories book.
Unmannerly tiger. Griffis. Unmannerly tiger, and other Korean tales.
Griffis. Korean fairy tales.
Unnatural mother. Bourhill and Drake. Fairy tales from South Africa.
Unpalatable advice. Caballero. Spanish fairy tales.
Unpoetical chancellor. Birch. Green-faced toad.
Unseen bridegroom. Jacobs. Europa's fairy book.
Unseen giant. Coussens. Child's book of stories.
Unselfish moon. Farmer. Nature myths.
Unsinkable pilot boat. Henderson. Sea yarns for boys.
Up to the top of the sky and down to the bottom of the sea. Bayliss. Treasury of Eskimo tales.
Upon a peak in Darien. Baldwin. Thirty more famous stories.
Ups and downs. Bosschère. Folk tales of Flanders.
See also Old Mr. Rabbit he's a good fisherman.
Upsidedownians. Aspinwall. Short stories for short people.
Uraschima Taro, the fisher lad. *See* Uraschimataro and the turtle.
Uraschimataro and the turtle. Baker and Carpenter. Language readers. 3d year. (Fisher boy Urashima.)
*Elson and Runkel. Elson readers. Book 2. (Taro and the turtle.)
Finnemore. Peeps at many lands: Japan.
Hearn. Japanese fairy tales. (Urashima.)
James. Green willow. (Urashima.)
Johnson. Birch-tree fairy book. (Fisher-boy.)
Lang. Pink fairy book.
Lang. Snow-queen. and other stories.
Marshall. Fairy tales of all nations. (Japanese fisherman.)
Nixon-Roulet. Japanese folk stories and fairy tales. (Princess of the sea.)
Norton. Heart of oak books. v. 3. (Fisher-boy Urashima.)
Olcott. Wonder garden. (Fisher boy Urashima.)
Ozaki. Japanese fairy book. (Urashima Taro, the fisher lad.)
Pyle. Where the wind blows. (Urashima.)
Singleton. Wild flower fairy book. (Urashima. the fisherboy.)
Success library. v. 3.
Williston. Japanese fairy tales. 1st series. (Urashima.)
Urashima, the fisher-boy. *See* Urashimataro and the turtle.
Useful cannon. Bailey. Friendly tales.

Useful coal. Richards. Toto's merry winter.
Useful little worm. Bailey. Stories and rhymes for a child.
Usheen in the island of youth. *See* Last of the Feni.
Ut-Röst cormorants. *See* Cormorants of Udröst.
Utgard-king. *See* Thor and his journey to Jötunheim.

V

Vagabond. Baring. Blue rose fairy book.
Vagabonds. Allison and Perdue. Story in primary instruction. (Cock and the hen.)
Coussens. Child's book of stories. (Ragamuffins.)
Grimm. Fairy tales. (Paull tr. Pack of vagabonds.)
Grimm. Household stories (Crane tr.).
Grimm. Household tales (Burt ed. Rogue's holiday.)
Pyle. Mother's nursery tales. (Pack of ragamuffins.)
See also Chanticleer and Partlett, Adventures of; Cock and the hen in the nutwood; Herr Korbes.
Vain jackdaw. Æsop. Fables (Black ed.).
Æsop. Fables (Burt ed.).
Æsop. Fables (Stickney).
Wiggin and Smith. Talking beasts. (Jackdaw with borrowed plumes.)
See also Jay and the peacock; Two foolish birds.
Vain Lamorna, Story of. Nichols and De Morgan. Princess Girlikin and other stories.
Vain stag. *See* Stag at the lake.
Valentine. *See* St. Valentine.
Valentine and Orson. Herbertson. Heroic legends. (Two brothers.)
Jerrold. Big book of fairy tales.
Macleod. Book of ballad stories.
Richards. Little master.
Scudder. Children's book. (History of Valentine and Orson.)
Valentine and Orson in Arabia. Goddard. Fairy tales in other lands.
Vali. *See* Odin and Rinda.
Valiant blackbird. Canton. Reign of King Herla.
Rouse. Talking thrush.
See also Drakesbill and his friends.
Valiant chanticleer. Djurklo. Fairy tales from the Swedish.
Valiant chattee-maker. Frere. Old Deccan days.
Wiggin and Smith. Fairy ring.
Valiant tailor. *See* Brave little tailor.
Valiant Vicky, the brave weaver. Peck. Stories for good children. (Ten at a stroke.)
Steel. Tales of the Punjab.
See also Brave little tailor.
Valkyr. *See* Nibelungenlied; Ring: War maidens; Sigurd the Volsung.

Value of silence. *See* Dwarfs' tailor.
Vampire and St. Michael. Bain. Cossack fairy tales.
Vanderdecken. *See* Flying Dutchman.
Vanished island. Jewett. Egyptian tales of magic.
Vanemuine, god of song. *See* Voices of nature.
Vardiello. Macdonell. Italian fairy book.
Vasilísa Popóvna. Magnus. Russian folk-tales.
Vasilisa the beauty. Butterworth. Zigzag journeys in the Orient, (*In* Ch. 14. Doll that spoke.)
Chisholm. Staircase of stories. (Baba Yaga and the little girl with the kind heart.)
Dole. White duckling, and other stories.
Magnus. Russian folk tales. (Vasilisa the fair.)
Pyle. Where the wind blows. (Vasilissa the fair.)
Wheeler. Russian wonder tales. (Wassilissa the beautiful.)
Vasilisa with the golden tress and Ivan the Pea. Curtin. Wonder tales from Russia. (Vassilissa golden tress, bareheaded beauty.)
Singleton. Goldenrod fairy book. (Story of Vasilisa with the golden tress.)
Vassilissa golden tress, bareheaded beauty. *See* Vasilisa with the golden tress and Ivan the Pea.
Vassilissa the cunning, and the tsar of the sea. Curtin. Wonder tales from Russia.
Vasilissa the fair. *See* Vasilisa the beauty.
Vazúza and Vólga. Magnus. Russian folk-tales.
Vedabbha and the thieves. Burlingame. Grateful elephant.
Vehm-gericht. Guerber. Legends of the Rhine.
Veiled lady. Harrison. Prince Silverwings.
Vengeance of Apollo. Patten. Junior classics. v. 2.
Vengeance of Mesgedra. Rolleston. High deeds of Finn.
Vengeance of the pixies. *See* Pixies' vengeance. II.
Venus and the cat. Æsop. Fables (Jacobs. Cat-maiden.)
Æsop. Fables (Black ed. Young man and his cat.)
Æsop. Fables (Burt ed. Young man and his cat.)
Carrick. Kitty cat tales.
Venus's looking glass. Olcott. Wonder garden.
Verified predictions. Fielde. Chinese fairy tales.
Verlioka. Polevoi. Russian fairy tales.
Vertumnus. *See* Little nymph who loved bright colors; Pomona.
Very bad boy, Story of a. Lang. Lilac fairy book.
Lang. King of the waterfalls.
Very hot contest. Henderson. Sea yarns for boys.
Vesper star. May. Little Prudy's fairy book.
Vice and fortune. Æsop. Fables (Burt ed.).
Viggo and Allarm. Hodgkins. Atlantic treasury of childhood stories.
Vila in the golden castle. Houghton. Russian grandmother's wonder tales.

Vila of Muhlenburg. Houghton. Russian grandmother's wonder tales.
Vilas' spring. Fillmore. Laughing prince.
See also Morning dew; Three tasks; True and Untrue.
Village quack. Æsop. Fables (Burt ed.).
Vine dryad, Story of. Storytellers magazine. Nov. 1914, p. 721.
Violet. Cowles. Indian nature myths. (Origin of the violet.)
Olcott. Red Indian fairy book. (Legend of the violet.)
Violin that sang to a king. Storytellers' magazine. Dec. 1915, p. 473.
Viper and the file. *See* Serpent and the file.
Virful cu Dor. Sylva and Strettell. Legends from river and mountain.
Virgilius the sorcerer. Lang. Beauty and the beast.
Lang. Violet fairy book.
Virg'n Mary as godmother. *See* Lassie and her godmother.
Virginia. Darton. Tales of the Canterbury pilgrims. (Physician's tale: Virginia.)
Guerber. Story of the Romans. (New laws; Death of Virginia.)
Johonnot. Stories of the olden time. (Roman father.)
Virgin's victory. Guerber. Legends of the Rhine.
Virtue its own reward. *See* Way of the world. I.
Vision of Anton. Cross and Statler. Story-telling.
Storytellers' magazine. Feb. 1916, p. 71.
Vision of Dante. Harrison. In story land.
Vision of MacConglinney. Jacobs. More Celtic fairy tales.
Vision of the last day. Andersen. Stories and tales (Author's ed.).
Vision of Tosonu. *See* Vision of Tsunu.
Vision of Tsunu. Griffis. Unmannerly tiger, and other Korean tales. (Woodman and the mountain fairies.)
Griffis. Korean fairy tales. (Woodman and the mountain fairies.)
Headland. Chinese boy and girl. (Rip Van Winkle: or, Wang Chih.)
Johnson. Elm-tree fairy book. (Vision of Tosonu.)
Tappan. Myths from many lands.
See also Rip Van Winkle.
Visit from an elf. Keyes. Stories and story-telling.
Visit of the wishing man. Stocking. City that never was reached.
Visit to Santa Claus land. Esenwein and Stockard. Children's stories.
Visit to the moon. *See* Daniel O'Rourke.
Visiting ghost. Judson. Myths and legends of the Pacific Northwest.
Visitor from paradise. Jacobs. Europa's fairy book.
See also All women are alike.
Vitazko the victorious. Baudis. Czech folk tales. (Vitazko.)

Vitazko the victorious—*continued.*
Fillmore. Shoemaker's apron.
See also Forest lad and the wicked giant.
Vive la France. Stewart. Tell me a hero story.
Vivionn the giantess. Rolleston. High deeds of Finn.
Vizier and the fly. Silver fairy book.
Vizier that was punished. *See* Vizier who was punished.
Vizier, the monkey, the lion and the serpent. Ortoli. Evening tales.
Vizier who was punished. Arabian nights (Dodge ed. Vizier that was punished.)
Arabian nights (Lang. Story of the vizier who was punished.)
Arabian nights (Townsend. History of the vizier who was punished.)
Welsh. Fairy tales children love. (Vizier that was punished.)
Voice of death. Lang. Red fairy book.
Voice of the bell. Griffis. Unmannerly tiger, and other Korean tales.
Griffis. Korean fairy tales.
Voice of the pine trees. Skinner. Pearl story book.
See also Wind in the pine.
Voices at the window. Bain. Cossack fairy tales.
Voices of nature. Judd. Classic myths.
Volcanoes, Origin of. Bailey. Wonder stories. (What became of the giants.)
Volund's revenge. Edmison. Stories from Norseland.
Vow of obedience. Guerber. Legends of the Rhine.
Vox Angelica and Lieblich Gedacht, Story of. Baring. Blue rose fairy book.
Voyage of Maelduin (poem). Graves. Irish fairy book. (Voyage of Maeldune.)
Higginson. Tales of the enchanted islands of the Atlantic. (Maelduin's voyage.)
Jacobs. Book of wonder voyages.
Joyce. Old Celtic romances. (Voyage of Maildun.)
Voyage of Ohthere. Wilmot-Buxton. Stories of early England.
Voyage of the bottle doll. Bailey. Friendly tales.
Voyage of the sons of O'Corra. Joyce. Old Celtic romances.
Voyage of the wee red cap. Dickinson and Skinner. Children's book of Christmas stories.
Sawyer. This way to Christmas. (Wee red cap.)
Tyler. Twenty-four unusual stories.
Yeats. Irish fairy and folk tales. (Witches' excursion.)
Voyage to Lilliput. *See* Gulliver's travels: Lilliput land.
Voyages of Es-Sindibad of the sea. *See* Sinbad the sailor, Story of.
Vulcan. Bailey. Wonder tales. (How Vulcan made the best of things.)
Francillon. Gods and heroes. (God of fire.)

Vulcan—*continued.*
Guerber. Myths of Greece and Rome.
*Poulsson. In the child's world.

W

Wackemhard and his five sons. Fairy tales from Brentano (Lovell ed.).
Wagtail and the jackal. Wiggin and Smith. Talking beasts.
Wait and see. Poulsson. In the child's world.
Wait till Martin comes. Wickes. Happy holidays.
Waits of Bremen. *See* Bremen town musicians.
"Wake up" story. My Bookhouse. v. 1.
O'Grady and Throop. Teachers' storyteller's book.
Poulsson. In the child's world.
See also Go-to-sleep story.
Wakeful star baby, Story of. Donahey. Tales to be told to children.
Wakontas and the two maidens. Young. Algonquin Indian tales. (*In* Ch. 4.)
Wali Dad the simple-hearted. Lang. Brown fairy book.
Walk to the mill. Stróebe and Martens. Danish fairy book.
See also Stupid's cries.
Walküre. *See* Ring: War maidens.
Walkyr. *See* Nibelungenlied; Ring: War maidens; Sigurd the Volsung.
Wall flower and the thyme. Bryce. Fables from afar.
Walled garden. Richards. Golden windows.
Walls of Sparta. Brown. Stories of childhood and nature.
Walnut tree that wanted to bear tulips. Wiltse. Kindergarten stories. (Walnut tree that bore tulips.)
Walpurgis Night, Legend of. Sylva and Strettell. Legends from river and mountain.
Walrus tooth's story. Harrison. Bric-a-brac stories.
Walter's new pony. *Dillingham and Emerson. Tell it again stories.
Wampum-bird and the boy, Legend of the. Judd. Wigwam stories.
Wandering Jew. Baring-Gould. Curious myths of the middle ages.
Mabie. Legends every child should know.
Scudder. Book of legends.
Wandering star. Brooks. Stories of the red children. (Will-o'-the-Wisp.)
Brown. Tales of the red children.
Pratt. Legends of the red children. (Will-o'-the-wisp.)
See also Stars with wings.
Wandering Willie's tale. Smith. More mystery tales.
Wanderings of Arasmon. Chisholm. In fairyland.
Wanderings of Vicram Maharajah. Frere. Old Deccan days.

Wanderings of Vicram Maharajah—*continued.*
Pyle. Where the wind blows.
Wang Chih, Story of. *See* Vision of Tsunu.
Wanton calf. Æsop. Fables (Black ed.).
Æsop. Fables (Burt ed.).
War between animals and sky people. Sexton. Gray wolf stories.
War dance of the mice. Lummis. Pueblo Indian folk tales.
War horse and ass. *See* Horse and ass.
War of the wolf and the fox. Baldwin. Fairy stories and fables. (Battle of the beasts.)
Johnson. Book of fairy tale foxes. (Fox and the old cat and dog.)
Klingensmith. Household stories.
Lang. Beauty and the beast, and other stories.
Lang. Green fairy book.
Spaulding and Bryce. Aldine readers. Book 3. (Battle of the beasts.)
See also Fox and the cat IV and V; Old Sultan; Whiteling's war with Isegrim; Why the test did not come off.
War with the wind people. Judson. Old Crow and his friends.
Warlike seven. Zitkala-Ša. Old Indian legends.
Warlock o' Oakwood. Grierson. Children's tales from Scottish ballads.
See also Michael Scott.
War party. Eastman. Wigwam evenings.
Wars of Wa-Kee-Yan and Unk-Tay-Hee. Eastman. Wigwam evenings.
Was it the Field Fairy? Walker. Sandman's goodnight stories.
Was it the first turtle? Holbrook. Book of nature myths.
Van Sickle and Seegmiller. Riverside readers. 2d reader.
Washington and the cherry tree. Baldwin. Fifty famous stories. (George Washington and his hatchet.)
Esenwein and Stockard. Children's stories. (George Washington and the cherry tree.)
Ketchum and Jorgensen. Kindergarten gems.
Olcott. Good stories for great holidays. (*In* Three old tales.)
Storytellers' magazine. Feb. 1916, p. 75. (*In* Anecdotes of George Washington.)
Washington and the colt. Esenwein and Stockard. Children's stories. (George Washington and the colt.)
Faulkner. Story lady's book. (George Washington and his mother.)
Ketchum and Jorgensen. Kindergarten gems. (Mrs. Washington's horses.)
Van Sickle and Seegmiller. Riverside readers. 3d reader. (Story of Washington's boyhood.)
Washington does not go to sea. Baldwin. Fifty famous stories. (Going to sea.)

Washington's birthday. *See* Coach in the forest; George Washington boy; Raising the flag.
Wassilissa the beautiful. *See* Vasilisa the beauty.
Wassily the unlucky. *See* Three wonderful beggars.
Waste not, want not. Edgeworth. Waste not. want not, and other stories.
Scudder. Children's book.
Wasted oak leaf. Children's story garden.
Watch that told animal time. Potter. Pinafore pocket story book.
Watch-tower between earth and heaven. Houghton. Russian grandmother's wonder tales.
Wiggin and Smith. Tales of wonder.
Watchman with a hundred eyes. *See* Io.
Water-babe. Landa. Aunt Naomi's Jewish fairy tales and legends.
Water babies. *See* Tom, the water baby.
Water baby. I. *See* Aqua; or, The water baby.
Water baby. II. *See* Tom, the water baby.
Water dolly. Tales for bedtime.
Van Sickle and Seegmiller. Riverside readers. 2d reader. (Abridged.)
Water-drop. I. Olcott. Good stories for great holidays.
Skinner. Emerald story book. (Story without an end: In the green meadow; Story of a drop of water.)
Whittier. Child life in prose. (Story without an end.)
Wickes. Happy holidays. (Endless story.)
Water drop. II. Dyer and Brady. Merrill readers. 3d reader. (Story of the water drops.)
See also Cloud.
Water fairy. *See* Nix in the pond.
Water kelpie. May. Little Prudy's fairy book.
Water lilies. *See* Star maiden.
Water-lily. I. *See* Gold-spinners.
Water-lily. II. *See* Star maiden.
Water-lily. III. Ingelow. Stories told to a child. v. 2.
Water nix. Haaren. Fairy life.
Water nixie. Harper. Story-hour favorites.
Shedlock. Art of the storyteller.
Water nymphs. Guerber. Legends of the Rhine.
Water of forgetfulness. Baumbach. Tales from Wonderland.
Water of life. I. Aunt Louisa's book of fairy tales.
Grimm. Fairy tales (Lucas tr.).
*Grimm. Fairy tales (Wiltse). v. 2.
Grimm. Household tales (Everyman's ed.).
Jerrold. Reign of King Oberon.
Wiggin and Smith. Magic casements.
Water of life. II. Lang. Golden mermaid, and other stories.
Lang. Pink fairy book.
Water of life. III. Pyle. Wonder clock.

Water of light. Baring-Gould. Crock o' gold.
Olcott. Wonder garden. (Drop of the water of light. Adapted.)
Water of Wearie's well. Tappan. Old ballads in prose.
Water of youth. Chisholm and Steedman. Staircase of stories.
Noyes. Twilight stories.
See also Wonderful mill.
Water of youth, water of life, and water of death. Curtin. Wonder tales from Russia.
Water-snake. Sylva and Strettell. Legends from river and mountain.
Water sprite. Grimm. Fairy tales (Paull tr.).
Pyle. Mother's nursery tales.
Water sprites. Guerber. Legends of the Rhine.
Water-witch. Hume. Chronicles of fairyland.
Water witch of Zancopinca. Storytellers' magazine. Oct. 1917, p. 412.
Water wolves. Kennedy. New world fairy book.
Waterfall which flowed saké. Nixon-Roulet. Japanese folk stories and fairy tales.
Pyle. Tales of wonder and magic. (Enchanted waterfall.)
Wiggin and Smith. Tales of wonder. (Enchanted waterfall.)
Williston. Japanese fairy tales. 1st series. (Woodcutter's saké.)
Waternick. Baudis. Czech folk tales.
Watogo who saved his tribe from the Thunderbird. *See* Indian who saved his tribe from the Thunderbird.)
Watt and the teakettle. Baldwin. Thirty more famous stories. (James Watt and the teakettle.)
Blaisdell. English history story book. (James Watt and the steam engine.)
Dyer and Brady. Merrill readers. 3d reader. (Boy who studied the tea-kettle.)
My Bookhouse. v. 2. (Jamie Watt and his grandmother's tea kettle.)
Waubenoo, Story of. Young. Algonquin Indian tales. (*In* Ch. 13 and 14.)
Waukewa's eagle. Tyler. Twenty-four unusual stories.
Waupee, the white hawk. *See* Star wife.
Wavilocks and the crab. Brown. Star jewels.
Wax and the tallow candle (The). *See* Candles.
Wax house. Bigham. Merry animal tales.
See also Hornets and the bees.
Way of the world. I. Asbjörnsen. Fairy tales from the far north. (World's reward.)
Asbjörnsen. Tales from the fjeld.
Gade. Norwegian fairy tales. (Such is the world's reward.)
Grundtvig. Danish fairy tales. (Virtue its own reward.)
Jacobs. Europa's fairy book. (Inside again.)

Way of the world. I.—*continued.*
Spaulding and Bryce. Aldine readers. Book 3. (World's reward.)
See also Brahmin, the tiger and the jackal; Camel driver and the adder: Ingratitude; Man and the snake; Reward of kindness; Reward of the world; Shepherd and the dragon; Snake's thanks; Well done, ill paid.
Way of the world. II. *See* Brahmin, the tiger and the jackal.
Wayland, the smith. Guerber. Myths of northern lands. (*In* Valkyrs.)
Lang. Book of romance.
Lang. Tales of romance.
See also Boy and the blacksmith; Weland's sword.
Ways of giving advice. Curry. Little classics.
Wealthy suitor. Underhill. Dwarfs' tailor, and other fairy tales.
Weasel and her husband. *See* Dame Weasel and her husband.
Weasel girl, the war maiden. Bayliss. Treasury of Indian tales.
Weasel girls. *See* Star wives.
Weasel in the granary (poem). Wiggin and Smith. Talking beasts.
Weather maiden. Molesworth. Fairies afield.
Weather vane. Guerber. Legends of the Rhine.
Weaver's lass. Bailey. Seven peas in the pod.
Weaver's son and the giant of the White Hill. Curtin. Myths and folklore of Ireland.
Web and a spider. *See* Arachne.
Webster and the woodchuck. Baldwin. Thirty more famous stories.
Wedding guests. Richards. Golden windows.
Wedding of Mrs. Fox. Grimm. Fairy tales (Lucas tr. Marriage of Mrs. Reynard.)
Grimm. Household stories (Crane tr. How Mrs. Fox married again.)
Grimm. Household tales (Burt ed. Wedding of Widow Fox.)
Grimm. Household tales (Everyman's ed. Mrs. Fox.)
Johnson. Book of fairy-tale foxes. (How Mrs. Fox married again.)
Wedding of Robin Redbreast and Jenny Wren. *See* Robin's Christmas song.
Wedding of Widow Fox. *See* Wedding of Mrs. Fox.
Wee bannock. Douglas. Scottish fairy tales. (Wee bunnock.)
Grierson. Scottish fairy book.
Jacobs. More English fairy tales.
Johnson. Elm-tree fairy book.
Pyle. Fairy tales from far and near. (Oat cake.)
Skinner. Nursery tales from many lands.
See also Gingerbread man: Johnny cake; Pancake.

Wee birdies. Bigham. Merry animal tales.
See also Lark and her young ones.
Wee birdies' neighbors. Bigham. Merry animal tales.
Wee bunnock. *See* Wee bannock.
Wee red cap. *See* Voyage of the wee red cap.
Wee robin redbreast. *See* Robin's Christmas song.
Wee robin's Christmas day. See Robin's Christmas song.
Wee robin's Yule song. *See* Robin's Christmas song.
Wee, wee man. I. *See* Little boy and big cow.
Wee, wee man. II. (poem). Rhys. Fairy gold.
(poem). Winnington. Outlook fairy book.
Wee, wee mannie. *See* Little boy and big cow.
Wee, wee woman. Skinner. Nursery tales from many lands. (Teeny, tiny woman.)
Van Sickle and Seegmiller. Riverside readers. 2d reader.
Weeds. Skinner. Topaz story book.
Weendigoes and the bone-dwarf. Schoolcraft. Indian fairy book.
Weeng, the spirit of sleep. *See* Weenk the sleep-bringer and his warriors.
Weenk the sleep-bringer and his warriors. Judd. Wigwam stories.
Tanner. Legends from the red man's forest. (Weeng, the spirit of sleep.)
Weeping waters. Olcott. Wonder garden.
Weighing an elephant. Dyer and Brady. Merrill readers. 3d reader.
See also Eureka.
Weland's sword. Kipling. Puck of Pook's Hill.
See also Wayland, the smith.
Well done, ill paid. Asbjörnsen. Fairy tales from the far north.
Dasent. Norse fairy tales. (Well done and ill paid.)
Dasent. Popular tales from the Norse.
Wiggin and Smith. Tales of laughter.
See also Fox, the bear and the poor farmer.
Well of St. Ludgvan. Hartland. English folk and fairy tales.
Well of the world's end. Grierson. Scottish fairy book.
Jacobs. English fairy tales.
Tyler. Twenty-four unusual stories.
See also Frog prince; Maiden and the frog.
Well-trained elephant. Shedlock. Eastern stories and legends.
Welsh rabbits and hunted hares. *See* Melangell's lambs.
Welshery and the Normans. *See* Ancients of the world.
Were-wolf. *See* Werewolf. II.
Werewolf. I. Marshall. Fairy tales of all nations.
Stroebe and Martens. Swedish fairy book.
Thorpe. Yule-tide stories. (Werwolf.)
Underhill. Dwarfs' tailor, and other fairy tales. (Wolf.)

Werewolf. II. Macdonell. Italian fairy book. (Werewolf.)
Werewolf. III. *See* William of Palermo and the werwolf.
Werewolf. IV. Field. Second book of tales.
Werwolf. *See* Werewolf. I.
West, Benjamin. Baldwin. Fifty famous people. (Our first great painter.)
Westminster Abbey, Legends of. Peer. Saints in story.
Whang the miller. Curry. Little classics.
What a lame boy did for his country. Field first reader.
What a spider and a fly did. *Jones. 2d reader.
What ailed the king. Bailey. Little man with one shoe.
What Beaumains asked of the king. *See* Sir Gareth.
What became of the giants. *See* Titans.
What came of picking flowers. Lang. Grey fairy book.
Lang. Trusty John, and other stories.
Success library. v. 3.
What else the moon saw. *See* What the moon saw: 31st evening.
What employment our Lord gave to insects. Wiggin and Smith. Talking beasts.
What frightened Peter Rabbit. Skinner. Very little child's book of stories.
What happened in the bee's cannery. Bailey. Friendly tales.
What happened to the lone woman of St. Michael. *See* First woman. I.
What happened to the thistle. Andersen. Stories and tales (Author's ed.).
What is a man? Rouse. Talking thrush.
What Marget Rolant saw. Thomas. Welsh fairy book.
What men live by. Tolstoi. Twenty-three tales.
What Mr. Rabbit caught in his trap. *See* Sun a prisoner. II.
What mother says is always right (play). Doheny. Play awhile.
What one can invent. Andersen. Stories and tales (Author's ed.).
What puss did. *Dillingham and Emerson. Tell it again stories.
What Robin saw. Boston collection of kindergarten stories.
What shall baby's name be? Djurklo. Fairy tales from the Swedish.
See also Three sillies.
What the birds heard from Francis. *See* St. Francis of Assisi.
What the bird said. Fielde. Chinese fairy tales.
Spaulding and Bryce. Aldine readers. Book 3. (Little bird told me.)
Wiggin and Smith. Tales of wonder.
What the chairs said. Arnold and Gilbert. Stepping stones to literature. v. 3.

What the children see in the moon. Hall and Gilman. Storyland. 2d reader.
What the Christmas star sees. Bay. Danish fairy and folk tales.
What the flowers told Martha. Walker. Sandman's good-night stories.
What the goodman does is always right. *See* "What the goodman does is sure to be right!"
"What the goodman does is sure to be right!" Andersen. Fairy tales (Paull tr. What the old man does is always right.)
Andersen. Fairy tales (Turpin. What the old man does is always right.)
Andersen. Stories and tales (Author's ed.).
(play). Lansing. Quaint old stories. (What the good man does is always right.)
Scudder. Children's book.
(play). Stevenson. Plays for the home. (What the good-man does is always right.)
Tyler. Twenty-four unusual tales.
See also Dame Gudbrand.
What the lily needed. Bailey. Stories for Sunday telling.
What the man in the moon did. *See* Man in the moon and the orphan boy.
What the moon saw. *Andersen. Best fairy tales (Henderson tr.).
Andersen. Fairy tales (Lucas tr.).
Andersen. Fairy tales (Paull tr.).
Andersen. Fairy tales (Turpin. Abridged.)
Ketchum and Jorgensen. Kindergarten gems. (Moon and the boy. Abridged.)
My Bookhouse. v. 1. (16th evening. Adapted.)
What the moon saw: 31st evening. Andersen. Stories (Riverside ed. Bear that played at soldiers.)
Baldwin. Fairy reader. (Moon's story.)
Blaisdell. Child life. 2d reader. (Bear that played at soldiers.)
*Elson and Runkel. Elson readers. Book 2. (Bear who played soldier.)
My Bookhouse. v. 1. (What else the moon saw.)
Van Sickle and Seegmiller. Riverside readers. 4th reader. (Bear that played at soldiers.)
What the old man does is always right. *See* "What the goodman does is sure to be right!"
What the rose did to the cypress. Lang. Aladdin, and other stories.
Lang. Brown fairy book.
What the snow man did. Dodge. Land of pluck.
What the squirrel did for Richard. Aspinwall. Short stories for short people.
What the stars foretold. Macdonell. Italian fairy book.

What the tea-kettle said. Eggleston. Queer stories for boys and girls.
What the whole family said. Andersen. Stories and tales (Author's ed.).
What the Yen Tzi taught the hunter. Davis and Chow-Leung. Chinese fables and folk stories.
What was her name? Lyman. Story telling.
What was it? Bryce. Fables from afar.
Wheat-field. Richards. Golden windows.
When Apollo was herdsman. *See* Admetus and Alcestis.
When Bob White won his name. Burgess. Mother West wind "when" stories.
When Brer Wolf have his corn shucking. Patten. Junior classics. v. 2.
When Brother Rabbit was king. Harris. Told by Uncle Remus.
When coyote was blue. *See* Bluebird and coyote.
When coyote was hard to please. *See* Manabozho caught.
When Glooskap smokes his pipe. *See* How summer came to the earth. II; Indian summer.
When Great-Grandfather Swift first used a chimney. Burgess. Mother West Wind "when" stories.
When Isis sought her lord. *See* Quest of Isis.
When Jack Frost was young. Walker. Sandman's good-night stories.
When Mink went to sun's house. Judson. Old Crow stories.
See also Phaeton.
When Mr. Bluebird won his beautiful coat. Burgess. Mother West Wind "when" stories.
See also Bluebird. III; How the bluebird got its color.
When Mr. Hummingbird got his long bill. Burgess. Mother West Wind "when" stories.
When Mr. Kingfisher took to the ground. Burgess. Mother West Wind "when" stories.
When Mr. Moose lost his horns. Burgess. Mother West Wind "when" stories.
When Mr. Wood Mouse learned from the birds. Burgess. Mother West Wind "when" stories.
When Mud Village moved. Bailey. Friendly tales.
When Neil a-Mughan was tuk. MacManus. In chimney corners.
When Old Mr. Badger learned to stay at home. Burgess. Mother West Wind "when" stories.
When Old Mr. Bat got his wings. Burgess. Mother West Wind "when" stories.
See also Birds' ball game.
When Old Mr. Gopher first got pockets. Burgess. Mother West Wind "when" stories.
When Old Mr. Grouse got his snowshoes. Burgess. Mother West Wind "when" stories.

When Old Mr. Hare became a turn coat. Burgess. Mother West Wind "when" stories.
See also White rabbit. I and II.
When Old Mr. Panther lost his honor. Burgess. Mother West Wind "when" stories.
When Old Mr. Rat became an outcast. Burgess. Mother West wind "when" stories.
When Peter Rabbit first met Bluffer the Adder. Burgess. Mother West Wind "when" stories.
When real people were baked. *See* Creation of man (Indian).
When Teeny-Weeny became grateful. Burgess. Mother West Wind "when" stories.
When the balloon boy blew up. Bailey. Friendly tales.
When the lamb was a hero. Bailey. In the animal world.
See also How the elephant and the whale were tricked.
When the lilies return. Miller. Philippine folklore stories.
When the man in the moon met the little star babies. Donahey. Tales to be told to children.
When the real people stole sun. *See* Daylight, Origin of. II.
When the sky began to fall. *See* Chicken-Little.
When the sun was caught in a snare. *See* Sun a prisoner I.
When the wheat worked woe. *See* Sunken city.
When Toby ran away. Bailey. Friendly tales.
When tomato was a love apple. Storytellers' magazine. Nov. 1917, p. 476.
Where love is, God is. *See* Where love is, there God is also.
Where love is, there God is also. Bailey. Stories children need.
Cabot. Ethics for children. **(Where love is, God is.)**
Cross and Statler. Story-telling.
Lyman. Story telling.
My Bookhouse. v. 4.
Peck. Stories for good children. **(Aydevich.)**
Skinner. Pearl story book.
Sly. World stories retold. **(Where love is, God is.)**
Tolstoi. Tales.
Tolstoi. Twenty-three tales. **(Where love is, God is.)**
Where Mister Snake's cunning failed him. Young. Behind the dark pines.
Where stories came from. Borland. Rocky mountain tipi tales.
Where the frogs came from. *See* Latona and the frogs.
Where the labyrinth led. *See* Theseus.
Where the harrycane comes from. Harris. Uncle Remus and his friends.
Where the morning star came from. *See* Morning star.
Where to lay the blame. Pyle. Twilight land.
Tyler. Twenty-four unusual stories.
Where Valentine hid. Storytellers' magazine. Feb. 1916, p. 67.
Wickes. Happy holidays.

Which is best? Pyle. Wonder clock.
Which was the foolishest? Lang. Brown fairy book.
Which was the happiest? Andersen. Stories and tales (Author's ed.)
Which was the king. Baldwin. Fifty famous people.
Which was the stronger, the tortoise, the tapir or the whale? *See* How the elephant and the whale were tricked.
Whimsical avalanche. Griffis. Swiss fairy tales.
Whippity-Stourie. Grierson. Scottish fairy book.
See also Rumpelstiltskin.
Whirling king. Olcott. Whirling king.
Whirlwind. Glinski. Polish fairy tales.
Whiskey Jack, Legend of. *See* Waubenoo, Story of.
Whisperers. Baldwin. Fifty famous people.
Whispering sea shell. Chisholm and Steedman. Staircase of stories.
Whistle. Baker and Carpenter. Language reader. 5th year.
Baldwin. Fifty famous people.
Norton. Heart of oak books. v. 4.
Welsh. Stories children love.
White and the black bride. Grimm. Fairy tales (Paull tr.).
White as snow, red as blood and black as a raven's wing. Pyle. Tales of wonder and magic.
White Aster. My Bookhouse. v. 5.
White-barked pine. Austin. Basket woman.
White bear. *See* Callisto and Arcas.
White bear's Christmas. *See* Bear and skrattel.
White bird. Pyle. Wonder clock.
White bird's wife. Jewett. Wonder tales from Tibet.
White blackbird. Colum. Peep-show man.
White cat. Aulnoy. Fairy tales.
*Bailey. In the animal world (Adapted.)
Burke. Fairy tales.
Carrick. Kitty cat tales.
Chisholm. In fairy land.
*Coe and Christie. Story hour readers. Book 2. (Prince Roland.)
Coussens. Child's book of stories.
Douglas. Favourite French fairy tales.
Klingensmith. Just stories.
Lang. Blue fairy book.
Lang. Prince Darling, and other fairy stories.
Lansing. Fairy tales. v. 2.
Mabie. Fairy tales every child should know.
Mabie. Heroes and fairies.
Mulock. Fairy book.
Nursery tales.
Perkins. Twenty best fairy tales.
Pyle. Mother's nursery tales.
Scudder. Book of folk stories.
Scudder. Children's book.

White cat,—*continued.*
Scudder. Fables and folk stories.
Singleton. Goldenrod fairy book.
Storytellers' magazine. Nov. 1916, p. 604.
Tappan. Folk stories and fables.
Valentine. Old, old fairy tales (Warne ed.).
Welsh. Fairy tales children love.
Wiggin and Smith. Fairy ring.
See also Peter Humbug and the white cat; Miller's boy and his cat.
White chamois. Griffis. Swiss fairy tales.
See also Rieggi and the white chamois.
White Cloud's visit to the Sun-prince. Compton. American Indian fairy tales.
See also Glooskap and the magic gifts. III.
White clover and Honey-bee. Hubbard. Chats with Colorkin.
White doe. *See* Hind in the forest.
White dogs of Arran. Tyler. Twenty-four unusual stories.
White dove. I. Grundtvig. Fairy tales from afar.
Lang. Aladdin. and other stories.
Lang. Pink fairy book.
Wiggin and Smith. Magic casements.
White dove. II. Bourhill and Drake. Fairy tales from South Africa.
White dove. III. Lindsay. More mother stories.
White dove of the city of the swinging gate. Eells. Tales of enchantment from Spain.
White duck. Dole. White duckling, and other stories. (White duckling.)
Lang. Magic ring, and other stories.
Lang. Yellow fairy book.
Polevoi. Russian fairy tales.
White duckling. *See* White duck.
White elephant. I. *See* Elephant and the ungrateful forester.
White elephant. II. *See* Why there are white elephants.
White elephant. III. *See* Grateful elephant.
White Feather and the six giants. Compton. American Indian fairy tales. (Magic feather.)
Cornyn. Around the wigwam fire. (Chacopee, the giant killer; Chacopee and the grandfather giant.)
Schoolcraft. Indian fairy book.
Wade. Indian fairy tales.
White fire. Richards. Silver crown.
White flowering almond. Olcott. Wonder garden.
White gifts, Legend of the. Curtiss. Christmas stories and legends.
White hands. Bailey. Seven peas in the pod.
White hare and the crocodiles. *See* Eighty-one brothers.
White hares. *See* First rabbits.
White Hawk. *See* Star wife.

White Hawk, the lazy. Compton. American Indian fairy tales.
Pyle. Fairy tales from far and near. (Story of Harka.)
Schoolcraft. Indian fairy book. (Strong Desire and the red sorcerer.)
See also Boy afraid of dark.
White-headed Zal. Baldwin. Thirty more famous stories.
Bryant. Treasury of hero tales.
Wilmot-Buxton. Stories of Persian heroes.
White-horned, Tale of the. *See* Cattle raide of Cooley.
White lady. Johnson. Elm-tree fairy book.
White lady of Blenkinsopp. Hartland. English folk and fairy tales.
White lily. Stocking. Golden goblet.
White mouse. Silver fairy book.
White palace. Harrison. Star fairies.
White parrot. Eells. Tales of enchantment from Spain.
See also Three sisters. I.
White pebble. Children's story garden.
White pet. Baldwin. Second fairy reader. (Pet lamb.)
Darton. Wonder book of beasts.
Douglas. Scottish fairy tales.
See also Bremen town musicians; How Jack went to seek his fortune.
White pigeon. Meigs. Kingdom of the winding road.
White rabbit. I. Coe and Christie. Story hour readers. Book 3. (Brother Rabbit.)
Stanley. Animal folk tales.
White rabbit. II. Skinner. Pearl story book. (Why the wild rabbits are white in winter.)
Young. Algonquin Indian tales. (*In* Ch. 19. Why the wild rabbits are white in winter.)
See also When Mr. Hare became a turncoat.
White rabbit. III. Bryce. That's why stories.
White rabbit and the Christmas tree. Faulkner. Story lady's book.
White rabbit and the marten. Stanley. Animal folk tales.
White sea gull. Donaldson. Little papoose listens.
White seal. Alderman. Classics old and new. 3d reader.
Kipling. Jungle book.
White ship. Baldwin. Fifty famous stories.
Blaisdell. English history story book. (Henry I. and the White Ship.)
Hartwell. Story hour readings. 5th year.
Morris. Historical tales: English. (How the White Ship sailed.)
White slipper. Lang. Orange fairy book.
Lang. Satin surgeon.
White snake. Grimm. Fairy tales (Lucas tr.).
*Grimm. Fairy tales (Wiltse). v. 1.
Grimm. Household stories (Crane tr.).
Lang. Green fairy book.

White snake—*continued.*
Lang. Three dwarfs, and other stories.
See also Golden hair; Language of beasts.
White spot of the kingfisher. *See* How the kingfisher got his ring and his ruffle.
White stone canoe. *See* In the land of souls.
White trout. Graves. Irish fairy book.
Johnson. Fir-tree fairy book.
Yeats. Irish fairy tales.
White wolf. Lang. Grey fairy book.
Lang. Marvellous musician.
Whiteling's war with Isegrim. Houghton. Russian grandmother's wonder stories.
See also Fox and the cat IV and V; Old Sultan; War of the wolf and the fox.
Whittington and his cat. *See* Dick Whittington and his cat.
Whittington in Arabia. *See* Saaoud and his steed.
Who art thou? Sologub. Sweet-scented name.
Who is strongest? *Spaulding and Bryce. Aldine readers. Book 2.
See also Little ant that was going to Jerusalem.
Who killed Cock Robin? *See* Cock Robin.
Who killed the otter's babies? Bryant. Best stories to tell to children.
Bryant. Stories to tell to children.
Tappan. Folk stories and fables.
Who married the princess? Macdonell. Italian fairy book.
Who stole the bird's nest? (poem). *Coe and Christie. Story hour readers. Book 2.
Who was the mightier? *See* Why the baby says "goo."
Who was the sinner? Martens. Chinese fairy book.
Who will bell the cat? *See* Belling the cat.
Who's thankful? Bailey. Stories for Sunday telling.
Why? Coussens. Child's book of stories.
Welsh. Stories children love.
Why all men love the moon. Blaisdell. Child life. 2d reader. (Sun, the moon and the wind.)
Coe, Second book of stories. (How the sun, the moon and the wind went out to dinner.)
Frere. Old Deccan days. (How the sun, the moon and the wind went out to dinner.)
Holbrook. Book of nature myths.
Jacobs. Indian fairy tales. (Sun, moon and the wind go out to dinner.)
Patten. Junior classics. v. 1. (Sun, moon and wind.)
Wiggin and Smith. Tales of laughter. (How the sun, the moon and the wind went out to dinner.)
See also Mother moon.
Why and how geese call each other. Young. Plantation bird legends.
Why animals cannot speak. Storytellers' magazine. Oct. 1915, p. 341.

Why animals do not talk. Cornyn. When the camp fire burns.
Why apples have stars within. Bigham. Overheard in fairyland.
Why bears are afraid of men. Farmer. Nature myths.
Why bears sleep all winter. *See* Why the bear sleeps all winter.
Why Blackfeet never kill mice. Linderman. Indian why stories.
Why Bobby Coon has rings on his tail. Burgess. Mother West Wind "why" stories.
Why Brer Buzzard likes the old way best. Young. Behind the dark pines.
Why Brer Dog barks. Young. Behind the dark pines.
Why Brer Fox did not get the goobers. Young. Behind the dark pines.
Why Brer Possum and Brer Pig parted company. Young. Behind the dark pines.
Why Brer Possum's tail is bare. *See* Why the possum's tail is bare. II.
Why Brer Rabbit wears a round-about. Young. Behind the dark pines.
Why Brother Bear has no tail. Harris. Nights with Uncle Remus.
Mabie. Folk tales every child should know.
Tappan. Folk stories and fables.
See also Why the bear has a stumpy tail.
Why Brother Bear wears a stumpy tail. *See* Why the bear has a stumpy tail.
Why Brother Bull growls and grumbles. Harris. Uncle Remus and his friends.
See also Jean Malin and the bull man.
Why Brother Fox's legs are black. Harris. Uncle Remus and his friends.
Why Brother Wolf didn't eat the little rabbits. Harris. Uncle Remus and his friends.
See also Little rabbits.
Why bruin has a stumpy tail. *See* Why the bear has a stumpy tail.
Why Buster Bear appears to have no tail. Burgess. Mother West Wind "why" stories.
Why cats always wash after eating. Bosschère. Folk tales of Flanders.
See also Why the cat washes after eating.
Why cats eat mice. *See* Country cat.
Why cats hate rats. Farmer. Nature myths.
Why Chestnuts are in prison. Bigham. Overheard in fairyland.
Why children lose their teeth. Linderman. Indian Old-man stories.
Why crocus holds up his golden cup. Olcott. Wonder garden.

Why crows caw. *See* Crow children.
Why dandelions have wings. Bigham. Overheard in fairyland.
Why Deunant has the front door in the back. Griffis. Welsh fairy tales. (Why the back door was front.)
Thomas. Welsh fairy book.
Why dog and cat are enemies. *See* Why the dog and cat are enemies.
Why dogs have long tongues. Olcott. Wonder garden.
Why dogs wag their tails. Coussens. Jade story book.
Stanley. Animal folk tales. (Dog, the cat, and the magic ring.)
Why Flitter the Bat flies at night. Burgess. Mother West Wind "why" stories.
Why flowers have bright colors. Bigham. Overheard in fairyland.
Why fox became red. I. Judson. Old Crow and his friends.
Why fox became red. II. Judson. Myths and legends of Alaska. (How the fox became red.)
See also Why Reddy Fox wears red.
Why Gran'daddy Long-Legs knows about cows. Young. Behind the dark pines.
Why grizzly bear goes on all fours. Bailey. Once upon a time animal stories. (How the first bears came.)
Cather. Educating by story telling.
Judson. Myths and legends of the Pacific Northwest. (Old Man Above and the grizzlies.)
Why Hassan became chief steward. Stebbins. 3d reader.
Why he carried the turkey. Baldwin. Fifty famous people.
Why heartleaves have pitchers. Bigham. Overheard in fairyland.
Why Indians whip the buffalo-berries from the bushes. Linderman. Indian why stories.
Why Jerry Muskrat builds his house in the water. Burgess. Mother West Wind "why" stories.
Why Jimmy Skunk never hurries. Burgess. Mother West Wind "why" stories.
Why leaves turn red and yellow. *See* Why the autumn leaves are red. II.
Why Miner the Mole lives under ground. Burgess. Mother West Wind "why" stories.
Why Miss Rabbit never got married. Young. Behind the dark pines.
Why Mr. Billy-goat's tail is short. Harris. Little Mr. Thimblefinger.
Why Mr. Cricket has elbows on his legs. Harris. Told by Uncle Remus.
Why Mr. Dog is tame. Harris. Told by Uncle Remus.
Thomas. Young folks' book of mirth.
See also Why the dog sits by the fire.
Why Mr. Dog runs Brother Rabbit. Harris. Nights with Uncle Remus.

Why Mister Frog is still a bachelor. Young. Behind the dark pines.

Why Mr. Possum has no hair on his tail. *See* Why the possum's tail is bare. III.

Why Mr. Possum loves peace. Harris. Uncle Remus, his songs and his sayings.

Why Mr. Snake cannot wink. Burgess. Mother West Wind "why" stories.

Why nasturtiums have lines. Bigham. Overheard in fairy-land.

Why old king walrus went away from the mountaineer's country. Roberts. Flying plover.

Why Old Man Coyote has many voices. Burgess. Mother West Wind "why" stories.

Why one woodpecker has a red head. Powers. Around an Iroquois story fire.

See also Why the woodpecker's head is red.

Why our sight fails with age. Linderman. Indian Old-man stories.

See also Wonderful bird.

Why Paddy the Beaver has a broad tail. Burgess. Mother West Wind "why" stories.

Why Peter Rabbit cannot fold his hands. Burgess. Mother West Wind "why" stories.

Why petunias are sticky. Bigham. Overheard in fairy-land.

Why pigs have curly tails. Fyleman. Rainbow cat.

Why pine trees have needles. Bigham. Overheard in fairy-land.

Why poppies make you sleep. Bigham. Overheard in fairy-land.

Why possum has a large mouth. Eastman. Indian legends retold.

Why rabbits have yellow hairs. *See* Sun a prisoner. II.

Why ravens croak. *Spaulding and Bryce. Aldine readers. 2d reader.

Why Reddy Fox wears red. Burgess. Mother West Wind "why" stories.

See also Why fox became red.

Why rivers have golden sands. *See* Midas. I.

Why roses have thorns. I. Bigham. Overheard in fairy-land.

See also Angel of the flowers. II.

Why roses have thorns. II. Field third reader. (How the wild roses got their thorns.)

Olcott. Red Indian fairy book. (Why wild roses have thorns.)

Skinner. Turquoise story book.

Young. Algonquin Indian tales. (*In* Ch. 19.)

Why roses have thorns. III. Storytellers' magazine. Sept. 1916, p. 484.

Why roses have thorns. IV. Olcott. Wonder garden.

Why roses have thorns. V. Donaldson. Moons of long ago. (Sweet wild rose.)
Why roses have thorns. VI. Nordau. Dwarf's spectacles. (Why the rose bush has thorns.)
Why roses have thorns. VII. Walker. Sandman's good-night stories. (What the flowers told Martha.)
Why Sammy Jay has a fine coat. Burgess. Mother West Wind "why" stories.
Why some clover is red. Hubbard. Chats with Color-kin.
Why some hawthorns are pink. Fyleman. Rainbow cat. (Second adventure of the rainbow cat.)
Why some willows are red. Young. Algonquin Indian tales. (*In* Ch. 21.)
Why spiders live in dark corners. Olcott. Wonder garden.
Why spiders live under stones. Olcott. Wonder garden.
Why Spotty the Turtle carries his house with him. Burgess. Mother West Wind "why" stories.
Why Striped Chipmunk is proud of his stripes. Burgess. Mother West Wind "why" stories.
See also Chipmunk's stripes. I.
Why sun follows his trail. I. Judson. Old Crow stories.
See also Sun. II.
Why sun follows his trail. II. Powers. Around an Iroquois story fire. (Why the sun travels from East to West.)
Why sun follows his trail. III. Borland. Rocky Mountain tipi tales. (Strong Boy snares the sun.)
See also Sun a prisoner. II and IV.
Why sunshine follows rain. Powers. Around an Iroquois story fire.
See also Woman in the moon. I.
Why swallows build their nests in windows. Pitrè. Swallow book.
Why the alligator's back is rough. Harris. Nights with Uncle Remus.
Why the animals no longer fear the sheep. *See* Brother Tiger and Daddy Sheep.
Why the aspen leaves are never still. *See* Why the aspen leaves tremble. III.
Why the aspen leaves tremble. I. Holbrook. Book of nature myths.
Why the aspen leaves temble. II. Olcott. Good stories for great holidays. (Why the aspen quivers.)
Why the aspen leaves tremble. III. *Cowles. Indian nature myths. (Why the aspen leaves are never still.)
Young. Algonquin Indian tales. (*In* Ch. 4. Love story of Wakontis.)
Why the aspen leaves tremble. IV. Storytellers' magazine. Feb. 1917, p. 101. (Legend of the quaking aspen.)
Why the aspen quivers. *See* Why the aspen leaves tremble. II.
Why the autumn leaves are red. I. Macmillan. Canadian fairy tales. (Rainbow and the autumn leaves.)

Why the autumn leaves are red. I.—*continued.*
Skinner. Topaz story book.
Why the autumn leaves are red. II. Judd. Wigwam stories. (Great bear in the sky.)
Powers. Around an Iroquois story fire. (Why leaves turn red and yellow.)
Tanner. Legends from the red man's forest. (Great bear.)
Why the baby robin has a spotted breast. Meyer. Little green door.
Why the baby says "goo." Coe. Second book of stories. (Who was the mightier?)
*Cowles. Indian nature myths.
Leland. Algonquin legends. (How the lord of beasts and men strove with the mighty Wasis.)
Partridge. Glooscap the great chief. (How Glooscap was conquered by Wasis.)
Wilson. Myths of the red children.
See also Manabozho and his toe.
Why the back door was front. *See* Why Deunant has the front door in the back.
Why the banana belongs to the monkey. Storytellers' magazine. April 1917, p. 220.
Why the bat is blind. Chandler. In the reign of coyote.
Why the bean wears a stripe down its back. *See* Straw, the coal and the bean.
Why the bear has a stumpy tail. Bailey. Firelight stories.
Bailey. Once upon a time animal stories.
Bosschère. Folk tales of Flanders. (Why the bear is stumpy-tailed.)
Coussens. Child's book of stories. (Why the bear is stumpy-tailed.)
Cowles. Indian nature myths. (Why Brother Bear wears a stumpy tail.)
Dasent. Norse fairy tales.
Dasent. Popular tales from the Norse. (Why the bear is stumpy-tailed.)
Farmer. Nature myths. (Bear's short tail.)
Gade. Norwegian fairy tales. (Bear and the fox.)
Holbrook. Book of nature myths.
Jacobs. Europa's fairy book. (*In* Reynard and Bruin.)
Johnson. Book of fairy-tale bears. (Reynard and his adventures.)
Judd. Wigwam stories. (How the bear lost his tail.)
Patten. Junior classics. v. 1. (Why the bear is stumpy-tailed.)
Skinner. Pearl fairy book. (Why bruin has a stumpy tail.)
Sly. World stories retold.
Storytellers' magazine. Sept. 1915, p. 311. (Fox and the bear.)
Thorne-Thomsen. East o' the sun and west o' the moon. (Why the bear is stumpy-tailed.)
Thorpe. Yule-tide stories. (Why the bear has a stump tail.)

Why the bear has a stumpy tail—*continued.*
Wiggin and Smith. Tales of laughter.
See also Why Brother Bear has no tail.
Why the bear is stumpy-tailed. *See* Why the bear has a stumpy tail.
Why the bear sleeps all winter. Bailey. Firelight stories.
Bailey. Once upon a time animal stories.
Cowles. Art of story telling.
Farmer. Nature myths. (Why bears sleep all winter.)
Van Sickle and Seegmiller. Riverside readers. 2d reader.
Why the bee buzzes. Farmer. Nature myths.
See also Why the swallow's tail is forked.
Why the birch tree bark is scarred. I. Young. Algonquin Indian tales. (*In* Ch. 1.)
Why the birch tree bark is scarred. II. Linderman. Indian why stories. (Why the birch tree wears the slashes in its bark.)
Why the birch tree bark is scarred. III. Grinnell. Blackfoot lodge tales. (Old Man and the lynx.)
Why the birch-tree wears the slashes in its bark. *See* Why the birch tree bark is scarred. II.
Why the bittersweet climbs. Meyer. Little green door.
Why the buzzard's head is bald. *See* Why the turkey-buzzard is bald-headed.
Why the cat always falls upon her feet. Holbrook. Book of nature myths.
Tappan. Folk stories and fables.
Why the cat came to man's house. Stafford. Animal fables.
Why the cat catches mice. *See* Why the dog and cat are enemies. III.
Why the cat dislikes wet feet. Bailey. In the animal world.
Why the cat scratches. Bailey. In the animal world.
See also Colony of cats; House in the wood.
Why the cat spits at the dog. Storytellers' magazine. Nov. 1913, p. 278.
Why the cat washes after eating. Bryce. That's why stories.
See also Why cats always wash after eating.
Why the chicadee goes crazy twice a year. Seton. Woodland tales.
Why the chimes rang. Alden. Why the chimes rang.
Dickinson and Skinner. Children's book of Christmas stories.
Harper. Story-hour favorites.
Storytellers' magazine. Dec. 1914. p. 755. (Christmas bells. Adapted.)
See also Silver bell; Three silver bells, Legend of the.
Why the chipmunk's back is striped. *See* Chipmunk's black stripes. II.
Why the cock cannot fly. Farmer. Nature myths.
Why the cock crows at dawn. Farmer. Nature myths.

Why the coyote is so cunning. Chandler. In the reign of coyote.

Why the crocodile has a wide mouth. Holbrook. Book of nature myths.

Why the crow has a hoarse voice. Meyer. Little green door.

Why the crow is black. I. Baldwin. Old Greek stories. (*In* Lord of the silver bow.)

Darton. Tales of the Canterbury pilgrims. (Manciple's tale: How crows became black.)

McFee. Treasury of myths. (Apollo and the crow.)

*Wilson. Nature study reader.

Why the crow is black. II. Farmer. Nature myths. (Owl and the raven.)

Riggs. Animal stories from Eskimo land. (Crow and the owl.)

Why the crow is black. III. Storytellers' magazine. Oct. 1914, p. 708. (Crane and the crow.)

Why the crow is black. I, II and III.

See also Why the raven's feather's are black. I, II and III.

Why the curlew's bill is long and crooked. Linderman. Indian why stories.

Why the dead do not come back. Chandler. In the reign of coyote.

Why the deer has no gall. *See* Fast runners.

Why the deer have antlers. *See* Deer's horns.

Why the deer's teeth are blunt. Eastman. Indian legends retold.

Why the diver duck has so few tail feathers. *See* How the duck came to have a flat back.

Why the dog and cat are enemies. I. Johnson. Elm-tree fairy book.

Pitman. Chinese wonder book. (Golden beetle; or, Why the dog hates the cat.)

Why the dog and cat are enemies. II. Allen. Korean tales. (Enchanted wine jug.)

*Burchill. Progressive road to reading. Book 3. (Lost charm.)

Griffis. Korean fairy tales. (Tokgabi's menagerie.)

Griffis. Unmannerly tiger, and other Korean tales. (Tokgabi's menagerie, cats and dogs.)

Pyle. Wonder tales retold. (Magic rice kettle.)

Why the dog and cat are enemies. III. Bailey. In the animal world. (Why the cat catches mice.)

Cowles. Art of story telling. (Why the dog cannot endure the cat, nor the cat the mouse.)

Houghton. Russian grandmother's wonder tales. (Why the dog cannot endure the cat, nor the cat the mouse.)

Why the dog and cat are enemies. IV. Bailey. In the animal world. (Quarrel of the dog and cat.)

Landa. Aunt Naomi's Jewish fairy tales and legends. (Quarrel of the cat and dog.)

Why the dog and cat are enemies. V. Martens. Chinese fairy book. (Why dog and cat are enemies.)
Why the dog cannot endure the cat, nor the cat the mouse. *See* Why the dog and cat are enemies. III.
Why the dog hangs out his tongue. Powers. Around an Iroquois story fire.
Why the dog hates the cat. *See* Why the dog and cat are enemies. I.
Why the dog sits by the fire. Bailey. In the animal world.
See also Why Mr. Dog is tame.
Why the dogs howl at night. Linderman. Indian Old-man stories.
Why the dove is timid. Holbrook. Book of nature myths.
Why the eagle has no song. Donaldson. Moons of long ago.
Why the elephant has small eyes. Patten. Junior classics. v. 2.
Why the evergreen trees keep their leaves in winter. I. Bryant. How to tell stories to children.
Coe and Christie. Story hour readers. Book 2. (Cedar tree's reward.)
Holbrook. Book of nature myths. (Why the evergreen trees never lose their leaves.)
Olcott. Good stories for great holidays. (Why the evergreen trees never lose their leaves.)
Tappan. Folk stories and fables. (Why the evergreen trees never lose their leaves.)
Van Sickle and Seegmiller. Riverside readers. 2d reader. (Why the evergreen trees keep their leaves.)
See also Selfish tamarack tree.
Why the evergreen trees keep their leaves in winter. II. Borland. Rocky Mountain tipi tales. (Pine trees keep their leaves.)
Why the evergreen trees never lose their leaves. *See* Why the evergreen trees keep their leaves in winter. I.
Why the executioner is called assessor. Djurklo. Fairy tales from the Swedish.
Why the face of the moon is white. *See* Bride of the wind.
Why the ferns stand guard. Donaldson. Moons of long ago.
Why the field mouse is little. *See* Sun a prisoner. I.
Why the fish laughed. Jacobs. Indian fairy tales.
Patten. Junior classics. v. 1.
Wiggin and Smith. Tales of laughter.
Why the flowers bloom only half the year. *See* Proserpina.
Why the frog has no tail (poem). Harris. Tar-baby, and other rhymes.
Why the frogs call the buttercups. Olcott. Wonder garden.
Why the frogs croak. *See* Glooskap and the bullfrog.
Why the goat left the jungle. Stafford. Animal fables.
Why the guinea-fowls are speckled. Harris. Nights with Uncle Remus.

Why the hawk catches chickens. Harris. Uncle Remus and his friends.
Stanley. Animal fables. (Hawk and the rooster.)
Why the hippopotamus lives in the water. Patten. Junior classics. v. 2.
Why the honeysuckle came out at night. Keyes. Five senses.
Why the hoofs of the deer are split. Holbrook. Book of nature myths.
Why the hyacinth has bells. Bigham. Overheard in fairyland.
Why the iris wears rainbow colors. *See* Iris. II.
Why the ivy is always green. Bigham. Overheard in fairyland.
Skinner. Emerald story book.
Why the Jack-Spaniard's waist is small. Dasent. Popular tales from the Norse.
Why the Japanese love the stork. *See* Man who did not wish to die. II.
Why the juniper has berries. Holbrook. Book of nature myths.
Why the kingfisher always wears a war-bonnet. Linderman. Indian why stories.
Why the kingfisher wears a white collar. *See* How the kingfisher got his ring and his ruffle.
Why the lady-bug is said to be beloved of God. Skinner. Turquoise story book.
Storytellers' magazine. Oct. 1917, p. 408.
Why the leaves shake. Bigham. Overheard in fairyland.
Why the lion has a long tail. *See* Why the mountain lion is long and lean.
Why the little bird that brags cries cuckoo! Olcott. Wonder garden.
Why the magpie's nest is not well built. *See* Magpie's nest. II.
Why the maple wears a beaded dress. Powers. Around an Iroquois story fire.
Why the mole is blind. *See* Sun a prisoner. III.
Why the moon follows the sun. Farmer. Nature myths.
See also Why the moon waxes and wanes. I.; Why the moon's face is smutty.
Why the moon waxes and wanes. I. Bayliss. Treasury of Eskimo tales.
Judson. Myths and legends of Alaska. (Boy in the moon. Eskimo.)
Why the moon waxes and wanes. II. Fyleman. Rainbow cat. (Moon.)
Why the moon waxes and wanes. III. Pratt. Legends of the red children. (Aurora, the white arch, and the great bear.)
Why the moon waxes and wanes. IV. Skinner. Turquoise story book. (Legend of the sun, moon and stars.)

Why the moon's face is smutty. I. Harris. Uncle Remus and his friends.
Why the moon's face is smutty. II. Macmillan. Canadian fairy tales. (Rabbit and the moon-man.)
Why the morning glory climbs. Bryant. How to tell stories to children.
Why the mosquito hates smoke. Chandler. In the reign of coyote.
See also How mosquitoes came.
Why the mountain lion is long and lean. Bailey. In the animal world. (Why the lion has a long tail.)
Linderman. Indian why stories.
See also Coyote pushes in mountain lion's face; Old Man and the lynx.
Why the mulberry's berry is purple. *See* Pyramus and Thisbe.
Why the narcissus grows by the water. *See* Echo and Narcissus.
Why the negro is black. Harris. Uncle Remus, his songs and his sayings.
Why the night-hawk's wings are beautiful. Linderman. Indian why stories.
Why the Owl cries hoot! hoot! Olcott. Wonder garden.
See also Conjure wives; Why the owl says "who."
Why the owl eats only small creatures. Chandler. In the reign of coyote.
Why the owl flies by night. I. Donaldson. Moons of long ago.
See also Why the owl says "who."
Why the owl flies by night. II. Meyer. Little green door. (Why the owls fly at night.)
Why the owl is not king of the birds. Babbitt. Jataka tales.
Why the owl says "who." Bryce. That's why stories.
Why the owls fly at night. *See* Why the owl flies by night. II.
Why the parrot repeats the words of men. Holbrook. Book of nature myths.
Why the partridge flies low. *See* Why the partridge stays near the ground.
Why the partridge stays near the ground. Baldwin. Old Greek stories. (Perdix.)
Farmer. Nature myths. (Why the partridge flies low.)
Judd. Classic myths.
See also Daedalus and Icarus.
Why the peacock's tail has a hundred eyes. *See* Io.
Why the peetweet cries for rain. Holbrook. Book of nature myths.
Wickes. Happy holidays.
Why the peewee looks for brother. Olcott. Wonder garden.

Why the persimmon tree has its fruit in three colors. Bigham. Overheard in fairyland.
Murray. Story book treasures. (Persimmon tree.)
Why the pomegranite wears a crown and royal robes. Olcott. Wonder garden.
Why the Possum's tail is bare. I. Eastman. Indian legends retold.
Stanley. Animal folk tales. (Opossum's tail.)
Why the possum's tail is bare. II. Young. Behind the dark pines. (Why Brer Possum's tail is bare.)
Why the possum's tail is bare. III. Harris. Uncle Remus, his songs and sayings. (Why Mr. Possum has no hair on his tail.)
Why the rabbit has a yellow spot. *See* Sun a prisoner. II.
Why the rabbit is timid. Holbrook. Book of nature myths.
Why the raccoon has rings on his tail. Young. Algonquin Indian tales. (*In* Ch. 1.).
See also Why Bobby Coon has rings on his tail.
Why the raven's feathers are black. I. Holbrook. Book of nature myths.
Why the raven's feathers are black. II. Farmer. Nature myths. (Owl and the raven.)
Judson. Myths and legends of the Pacific Northwest. (Owl and Raven.)
See also Daylight, Origin of; Why the crow is black. II.
Why the raven's feathers are black. III. Judson. Myths and legends of Alaska. (Raven and coot.)
Why the red dragon is the emblem of Wales. Griffis. Welsh fairy tales. (Great red dragon of Wales.)
Thomas. Welsh fairy book.
Why the robin has a red breast. I. Bailey and Lewis. For the children's hour. (How the robin's breast became red.)
Cooke. Nature myths. (How the robin's breast became red.)
Farmer. Nature myths.
Faulkner. Story lady's book. (How robin's breast became red.)
Lyman. Story telling. (How the robin's breast became red.)
Sly. World stories retold. (Why the robin's breast is red.)
Strong. All the year round. v. 3. Spring. (How the robin got its red breast.)
Why the robin has a red breast. II. (poem). Olcott. Wonder garden. (Robin.)
Thomas. Welsh fairy book. (Why the robin's breast is red.)
Why the robin has a red breast. III. Stebbins. 3d reader.
Why the robin has a red breast. IV. Donaldson. Little papoose listens. (Bird-with-breast-of-fire.)

Why the robin has a red breast V. Lagerlöf. Christ legends. (Robin redbreast.)
Skinner. Emerald story book. (Robin redbreast.)
Why the robin has a red breast. VI. *See* How the birds got their colors. I.
Why the robin has a red breast. VII. Young. Plantation bird legends. (Robin red breast.)
Why the robin says, "cheer up." Bryce. That's why stories.
Storytellers' magazine. May 1914, p. 555.
Why the robin's breast is red. *See* Why the robin has a red breast. I and II.
Why the rose bush has thorns. *See* Why roses have thorns. VI.
Why the sea is salt. I. Edmison. Stories from the Norseland. (How the sea became salt.)
Farmer. Nature myths.
Grierson. Scottish fairy book. (Magic quern.)
Guerber. Myths of northern lands. (*In* Frey.)
Holbrook. Book of nature myths.
Patten. Junior classics. v. 2. (Wonderful quern stones.)
Tappan. Myths from many lands. (Wonderful quern stones.)
Why the sea is salt. II. Asbjörnsen. Fairy tales from the far north. (Quern at the bottom of the sea.)
Bailey. Stories children need.
Coe and Christie. Story hour readers. 3d book.
Coussens. Child's book of stories.
Dasent. Norse fairy tales.
Dasent. Popular tales from the Norse.
Field. Famous fairy tales. (Quern at the bottom of the sea.)
Lang. Blue fairy book.
Lang. Cinderella, and other fairy tales.
Mabie. Folk tales every child should know.
My Bookhouse. v. 3.
Stebbins. 3d reader.
Storytellers' magazine. Jan. 1915, p. 9. (Adapted.)
Stroebe and Martens. Danish fairy book. (Mill at the bottom of the sea.)
Tappan. Folk stories and fables.
Thorne-Thomsen. East o' the sun and west o' the moon.
Welsh. Stories children love.
Wiggin and Smith. Tales of laughter.
Why the sea is salt. III. Bay. Danish fairy and folk tales. (Coffee-mill which grinds salt.)
Chambers. Miscellany of useful and entertaining tracts. v. 18.
Why the sea is salt. IV. Bryant. How to tell stories to children.
Esenwein and Stockard. Children's stories. (Adapted.)
Why the serpent sheds his skin. Holbrook. Book of nature myths.

Why the snakes change their skins. Chandler. In the reign of coyote.
Why the snow is white. Olcott. Wonder garden.
Why the squirrel barks. Coe and Christie. Story hour readers. Book 3. (Manitou and the squirrels.)
Cowles. Indian nature myths. (Why the squirrel coughs.)
Schoolcraft. Indian fairy book. (*In* Manabozho the mischief maker.)
Tanner. Legends from the red man's forest.
Wade. Indian fairy tales. (Manabozho and the squirrels.)
Why the squirrel coughs. *See* Why the squirrel barks.
Why the squirrel gave up farming. Bailey. In the animal world.
Why the stork loves Holland. Griffis. Dutch fairy tales.
Why the sun travels from East to West. *See* Why sun follows his trail. II.
Why the sun travels regularly. *See* Sun a prisoner. IV.
Why the sun travels slowly. *See* Sun a prisoner. V.
Why the sunflowers hang their heads. Bigham. Overheard in fairyland.
Why the swallow does not sing. Pitre. Swallow book.
Why the swallow lives in warm climates. Pitrè. Swallow book.
Why the swallows are not molested. Pitrè. Swallow book.
Why the swallow's tail is forked. I. Byrne. Modern Greek fairy tales. (Swallow.)
Holbrook. Book of nature myths.
Pitrè. Swallow book.
See also Why the bee buzzes.
Why the swallow's tail is forked. II. Pitrè. Swallow book. (Why the swallow's tail is forked. Siberian version.)
Why the swallow's tail is forked. III. Pitrè. Swallow book. (Why the swallow has a forked tail and a red breast.)
Why the sweet laburnum comes first in the spring. Bigham. Overheard in fairyland.
Why the tail of the fox has a white tip. I. *See* Fox as herdsboy.
Why the tail of the fox has a white tip. II. Johnson. Book of fairy-tale foxes. (Fox and his five hungry comrades.)
Why the tail of the fox has a white tip. III. *See* Reynard wants to taste horseflesh.
Why the test did not come off. Powers. Around an Iroquois story fire.
See also War of the wolf and the fox.
Why the tick is now small. Chandler. In the reign of coyote.
Why the tide runs out. Storytellers' magazine. Sept. 1915, p. 296.

Why the tide runs out—*continued.*
See also Cause of tides.

Why the tiger and the stag do not like each other. Field third reader.

Why the turkey-buzzard is bald-headed (poem). Harris. Tar-baby, and other rhymes. (Why the buzzard's head is bald.)
Harris. Told by Uncle Reums.

Why the turkey buzzard is bald-headed. II. Young. Algonquin Indian tales. (*In* Ch. 22.)

Why the turkey gobbles. Judson. Old Crow and his friends.
Olcott. Red Indian fairy book.

Why the water in rivers is never still. Holbrook. Book of nature myths.

Why the weasel is white. Linderman. Indian Old-man stories.

Why the white bear lives alone. Brown. Tales of the red children.

Why the white hares have black ears. *See* First rabbits.

Why the wild rabbits are white in winter. *See* White rabbit. II.

Why the wind wails. *See* Bride of the wind.

Why the woodchuck comes out in midwinter. I. Powers. Around an Iroquois story fire.

Why the woodchuck comes out in midwinter. II. Seton. Woodland tales. (Woodchuck Day.)

Why the woodpecker has red head feathers. *See* Why the woodpecker's head is red. II.

Why the woodpecker's head is red. I. Asbjörnsen. Fairy tales from the far north. (Woodpecker.)
Bailey and Lewis. For the children's hour. (Legend of the woodpecker.)
Cary, Phoebe. Poems. (Legend of the Northland.)
Cooke. Nature myths and stories. (Red-headed woodpecker.)
Dasent. Popular tales from the Norse. (Gertrude's bird.)
*Elson and Runkel. Elson readers. Book 2. (Old woman who wanted all the cakes.)
Farmer. Nature myths. (Woodpecker.)
Gade. Norwegian fairy tales. (Gertrude bird.)
Hall and Gilman. Storyland. 2d reader. (Origin of the woodpecker.)
Holbrook. Book of nature myths. (Story of the first woodpecker.)
(poem). Klingensmith. Household stories. (Legend of the Northland.)
Lyman. Story telling. (Woodpecker.)
Olcott. Good stories for great holidays. (Old woman who became a woodpecker.)
(poem). Smith. Good old stories. (Legend of the Northland.)

Why the woodpecker's head is red—*continued.*
Stebbins. 3d reader. (Why the woodpecker wears a red cap.)
Storytellers' magazine. Feb. 1915, p. 55. (Woodpecker.)
Strong. All the year round. v. 3. Spring. (Origin of the woodpecker.)
Why the woodpecker's head is red. II. Holbrook. Book of nature myths.
Judd. Wigwam stories. (*In* Manabozho swallowed by a large fish.)
Patten. Junior classics. v. 1. (Why the woodpecker has red head feathers.)
*Tanner. Legends of the red man's forest. (Woodpecker's red crown.)
See also How Drummer the Woodpecker came by his red cap; Why one woodpecker has a red head; Woodpecker Gray.
Why the wren flies close to the earth. Holbrook. Book of nature myths.
See also King Wren.
Why there are no snakes in Ireland. *See* St. Patrick and the snakes.
Why there are no snakes in Takhoma. Judson. Myths and legends of the Pacific Northwest.
Why there are old maids. Nixon-Roulet. Indian folk tales. (Spider woman's mistake.)
Why there are tailless cats. Bailey. In the animal world.
Why there are white elephants. Storytellers' magazine. Sept. 1917, p. 328.
Why there is a black head in the buzzard family. Burgess. Mother West Wind "why" stories.
Why there is a hare in the moon. *See* Hare in the moon. I.
Why there is a man in the moon. *See* Man in the moon.
Why there is but one moon. Brown. Tales of the red children.
Why there is only one southwest wind. Chandler. In the reign of coyote.
Why they have summer on St. Lawrence island. Riggs. Animal stories from Eskimo land.
Why turkeys have red eyes. Wilson. Myths of the red children.
Why turtles stay near the water. *Bryce. That's why stories.
Stafford. Animal fables. (Turtle, the wolf and the hyena.)
See also How the turtle saved his own life; Mr. Fox tackles Old Man Tarrypin.
Why Unc' Billy Possum plays dead. Burgess. Mother West Wind "why" stories.
See also Why Mr. Possum loves peace.
Why unlucky iron kills. *See* Wicked hornet.
Why Venus liked doves. Olcott. Wonder garden.
Why violets have golden hearts. Bigham. Overheard in fairyland.
Murray. Story book treasures.

Why waters laugh and shout when winds blow. Powers. Around an Iroquois story fire.
Why wild roses have thorns. *See* Why roses have thorns. II.
Wicked daughters-in-law. Laboulaye. Last fairy tales.
Wicked fairies. Olcott. Wonder garden.
See also Midas. I.
Wicked half-brothers, Story of. *See* Codadad and his brothers, History of.
Wicked hoptoad and the little yellow dragon. *See* Butter and eggs.
Wicked hornet. Baldwin. Sampo. (*In* Ch. 4.)
Hartwell. Story hour readings. 7th year. (Story of iron.)
Olcott. Wonder garden. (Why unlucky iron kills.)
Wicked king and his bride. Friedlander. Jewish fairy book.
Wicked mother-in-law. *See* Snowbird and the water tiger.
Wicked prince. Andersen. Wonder stories (Author's ed.).
Wicked summoner. *See* Summoner and the fiend.
Wicked wolverine. *See* Wolverine and the rock.
Widow and her friend. Success library. v. 3.
Widow and her little maids. *See* Old woman and her maids.
Widow and her son. Davis and Chow-Leung. Chinese fables and folk stories.
Widow and the sagacious magistrate. Fielde. Chinese fairy tales.
Widow Wiggins' wonderful cat. Eggleston. Queer stories for boys and girls.
Widows and the strangers. Ewing. Old fashioned fairy tales.
Widow's daughter. *See* Three little crones each with something big. III.
Widow's son. I. Asbjörnsen. Folk and fairy tales.
Dasent. Norse fairy tales.
Dasent. Popular tales from the Norse.
Gade. Norwegian fairy tales.
Pyle. Tales of folks and fairies.
Thorpe. Yule-tide stories.
Widow's son. II. Coussens. Jade story book.
Widow's two daughters. *See* Mother Holle.
Wife of Auchtermuchty. Macleod. Book of ballad stories.
See also Man who was going to mind the house.
Wife of Bath's tale. *See* Sir Gawain's marriage. II.
Wife with two husbands. Fielde. Chinese fairy tales.
Wife's vengeance. Fielde. Chinese fairy tales.
Wigwam giants. *See* Good giants.
Wild and tame geese. Æsop. Fables (Burt ed.).
Wild boar and the fox. Bryce. Fables from afar.
Wild ducks and the goose. Johnson. Birch-tree fairy book.
Wild Edric. Duncan-Jones. English folk-lore stories.
Hartland. English folk and fairy tales.
Wild hunt. Guerber. Legends of the Rhine.
Wild man of the marsh. Grundtvig. Fairy tales from afar.

Wild Robin. May. Little Prudy's fairy book.
Patten. Junior classics. v. 6.
See also Tamlane.
Wild swans. Andersen. Fairy tales (Lucas tr.).
Andersen. Fairy tales (Paull tr.).
Andersen. Fairy tales and stories (Toksvig).
Andersen. Wonder stories (Author's ed.).
Chisholm. In fairyland.
Favorite fairy tales.
Jerrold. Reign of King Oberon.
(play). Stevenson. Plays for the home.
Wiggin and Smith. Fairy ring.
See also Eagles; Princess who was dumb; Six swans; Twelve brothers; Twelve wild ducks.
Wild trailer. Bailey. Friendly tales.
Wild woodsman. Harrison. Old-fashioned fairy book.
Will. Thorpe. Yule-tide stories.
Will-o'-the-wisp. I. *See* Wandering star.
Will-o'-the-wisp. II. Guerber. Legends of the Rhine.
Will-o'-the-wisp. III. Noyes. Twilight stories.
"Will-o'-the-wisp is in the town." Andersen. Stories and tales (Author's ed.).
William and the werwolf. *See* William of Palermo and the werwolf.
Wliam of Palermo and the werwolf. Lang. Red romance book. (How William of Palermo was carried off by the werwolf.)
Wilmot-Buxton. Stories from old French romance. (Story of William and the werwolf.)
William Short Nose, Adventures of. Lang. Book of romance.
Lang. Tales of romance.
William the Conqueror. Baldwin. Fifty famous stories. (Sons of William the Conqueror.)
Hartland. English folk and fairy tales. (Legend of the sons of the Conqueror.)
Willie Wallace. Tappan. Old ballads in prose.
Willow man (poem). Skinner. Pearl story book.
Willow plate, Legend of. *See* Willow ware, Story of.
Willow tree. *See* Willow ware, Story of.
Willow tree, Legend of the. Skinner. Topaz story book.
Willow trees. Storytellers' magazine. March 1916, p. 163.
See also Poplar tree. I.
Willow ware, Story of. James. Jeweled sea. (Willow tree.).
(poem). Pyle. Pepper and salt. (Ye story of a blue china plate.)
Skinner. Myths and legends of flowers and trees. (Willow tree.)
Werner's recitations. No. 3. (Legend of the willow plate.)
Willow wren. *See* King Wren.
Willy Faith. Grundtvig. Danish fairy tales.

Wily Brahmin. Bradley-Birt. Bengal fairy tales.
Wily tortoise. Rouse. Talking thrush.
Wind, an' wave, an' wandherin' flame. Tyler. Twenty-four unusual stories.
Wind and the clouds. *See* Hermes and Apollo.
Wind and the moon (poem). Burchill. Progressive road to reading. Book 3.
Wind and the sun. Æsop. Fables (Black ed.).
Æsop. Fables (Burt ed.).
Æsop. Fables (Jacobs).
Æsop. Fables (Stickney).
Arnold and Gilbert. Stepping stones to literature. v. 2.
Bailey. Folk stories and fables.
Bailey and Lewis. For the children's hour.
Baldwin. Fairy stories and fables.
Boston collection of kindergarten stories. (North wind and the sun.)
Bryant. Stories to tell to children. (Sun and the wind.)
Coussens. Child's book of stories. (Sun and the wind.)
*Jones. First reader.
Ketchum and Jorgensen. Kindergarten gems.
My Bookhouse. v. 1.
Norton. Heart of oak books. v. 2. (Sun and the north wind.)
Poulsson. In the child's world.
Scudder. Children's book. (Sun and the wind.)
Scudder. Fables and folk stories.
Sly. World stories retold.
Tappan. Folk stories and fables. (Sun and the wind.)
Welsh. Stories children love.
(poem). Wiggin and Smith. Talking beasts. (Phoebus and Boreas.)
Wiltse. Kindergarten stories.
Young and Field. Literary readers. Book 2.
Wind bird. Farmer. Nature myths.
Wind blower. *See* Wuchowson the wind blower.
Wind-demon. Kunos. Forty-four Turkish fairy tales. (Storm fiend.)
Kunos. Turkish fairy tales.
Wind flower. *See* Adonis.
Wind-flower's story. Walker. Sandman's goodnight stories.
Wind in the pine. James. Green willow. (Wind in the pine tree.)
Olcott. Wonder garden.
See also Voice of the pine trees.
Wind people. *See* Raid on the wind people.
Wind, Story of the. I. Cossack fairy tales. (Story of the wind.)
Wind, Story of the. II. *See* Wind's tale.
Wind, Story of the. III. *See* Unseen giant.
Wind, the clouds and the snow. Davis and Chow-Leung. Chinese fables and folk stories.

Winding road. Meigs. Kingdom of the winding road.
Winding up time. Bailey. Stories children need.
Windmill. Andersen. Stories and tales (Author's ed.).
Windmills, Adventures with. *See* Don Quixote.
Windows. Richards. Golden windows.
Winds, Legends of the. *See* Indian story of the winds.
Winds, Origin of. I. Judson. Myths and legends of Alaska. (Athapascan version.)
Winds, Origin of. II. Judson. Myths and legends of Alaska (Tlingit version.)
Winds, Origin of. III. Judson. Old Crow and his friends. (Raven and the winds.)
This includes both I and II.
Winds, Origin of. IV. Bayliss. Treasury of Eskimo tales.
Judson. Myths and legends of Alaska. (Eskimo version.)
Wind's tale. Andersen. Fairy tales (Lucas tr.).
Andersen. Fairy tales (Paull tr. Story of the wind.)
Andersen. Stories and tales (Author's ed.).
Winds, the birds and the telegraph wires. Stocking. City that never was reached.
Tyler. Twenty-four unusual stories.
Wine-crust, the Bluebeard of Flanders. Griffis. Belgian fairy tales.
Winged horse. *See* Pegasus.
Winged hunter. *See* Hunter who could fly.
Wings. Sologub. Sweet-scented name.
Tyler. Twenty-four unusual stories.
Winkelried, Arnold. Baldwin. Fifty famous stories.
Evans. Old time tales. (Sacrifice of Arnold Winkelried.)
Froelicher. Swiss stories. (Arnold von Winkelried and the Battle of Sempach.)
Sly. World stories retold. (Swiss patriot and the spears.)
Winnedumah and Tinnemaha. Austin. Basket woman.
Winner of Talking-Bird. *See* Dun horse.
Winning of Atalanta. *See* Atalanta's race.
Winning of Olwen. *See* Kilwch and Olwen.
Winning of Swallow. Baldwin. Fifty famous rides.
Winning of the golden fleece. *See* Argonauts.
Winter and Spring. *See* Old Winter Man and the Spring. I.
Winter clothes. *Bryant. New stories to tell to children.
Winter spirit and his visitor. See Old Winter man and the Spring. II.
Wisakaha slays the cloud Manitous. *See* Indians' flood. III.
Wisdom's wages and folly's pay. Pyle. Twilight land.
Wise and the foolish merchant. Babbitt. Jataka tales.
Burlingame. Grateful elephant. (Two caravan leaders.)
Peck. Stories for good children.
Storytellers' magazine. April 1914, p. 509.
See also Sandy road.
Wise bird and the foolish bird. Harris. Nights with Uncle Remus.

Wise cockscomb. Darton. Wonder book of beasts.
Wise crow. *See* Crow and the pitcher.
Wise fairy (poem). Arnold and Gilbert. Stepping stones to literature. v. 3.
Wise fools of Gotham. *See* Wise men of Gotham.
Wise girl. *See* Maiden who was wiser than an emperor.
Wise goat. Baldwin. Fairy tales and fables.
Wise goat and the wolf. Babbitt. More Jataka tales.
Wise jackal. I. James. Enchanted castle.
Wise jackal. II. James. Magic bed.
Wise judge. Storytellers' magazine. Nov. 1914, p. 737.
Wise king and the bee. *See* King Solomon's answer.
Wise man and the hyena. Macnair. Animal tales from Africa.
Wise men of Gotham. Baldwin. Fifty famous stories. (Three men of Gotham; Other wise men of Gotham.)
Forty famous fairy tales.
Hartland. English folk and fairy tales. (Wise fools of Gotham.)
Jacobs. More English fairy tales.
Johnson. Oak-tree fairy book.
(play). Lansing. Quaint old stories.
My Bookhouse. v. 3.
Wiggin and Smith. Tales of laughter.
See also Cheeses that ran away; Crane in the wheatfield; Diccon the foot-boy; Gotham men and the cuckoo; Hare that was sent to York; Hiding of the church bell; Kettle that would not walk; Little horse and its kind master; Lost legs; Men of Gotham and the cheeses; Men of Gotham and the watch; Missing man found; Salt fish and the eel.
Wise men's well. Lagerlöf. Christ legends.
Wise merchant. Friedlander. Jewish fairy book.
Wise mouse. Grover. Folk-lore readers. v. 1.
Wise old shepherd. Canton. Reign of King Herla.
Rouse. Talking thrush.
Shedlock. Art of the storyteller.
Wise physician. Shedlock. Eastern stories and legends.
Wise princess. Baring. Blue rose fairy book.
Wise queen. Grundtvig. Danish fairy tales.
See also Maiden who was wiser than an emperor; Peasant's clever daughter; Sage damsel.
Wise rightly, Wisest wrongly. Children's story garden.
Wise shepherd boy. *See* Shepherd boy and the king.
Wise snake. Bryce. Fables from afar.
Wish ring. *See* Wishing ring.
Wish three times. *See* Three wishes. II.
Wishbone. Gruelle. Friendly fairies.
Wishes. *See* Glooscap and the magic gifts. III.
Wishing-box. Grundtvig. Fairy tales from afar.
Grundtvig. Danish fairy tales.

Wishing ring. Cowles. Art of story telling. (Plowman who found content.)
Fairy stories from St. Nicholas. (Wish ring.)
Noyes. Twilight stories.
See also Bar of gold.
Wishing-spring. Stein. When fairies were friendly.
Wishing star. Pyle. Prose and verse for children.
Wishing-table, the gold ass, and the cudgel. *See* Table, the ass and the stick.
Wishing well. Lindsay. Joyous travelers. (Tale told by the nurse.)
Wishing wishes. Lindsay. More mother stories.
Witch. I. Asbjörnsen. Folk and fairy tales.
Witch. II. Lang. Twelve hunstmen, and other stories.
Lang. Yellow fairy book.
Witch and hare. *See* Witch hare.
Witch and her servants. Lang. Yellow fairy book.
Lang. Blue parrot.
Witch and the horseshoes. Baudis. Czech folk tales.
See also Blacksmith's wife of Yarrowfoot.
Witch and the sister of the sun. Magnus. Russian folk-tales.
Witch and the toad. Hartland. English folk and fairy tales.
Witch and the wind man. Cornyn. Around the wigwam fire.
Witch bluebird. Young. Behind the dark pines.
Witch cat. Olcott. Wonder garden.
See also Witch of Laggan.
Witch hare. Hartland. English folk and fairy tales. (Witch and hare.)
Yeats. Irish fairy and folk tales.
Witch in the stone boat. Hall. Icelandic fairy tales. (Giantess and the granite boat.)
Lang. Twelve huntsmen. and other stories.
Lang. Yellow fairy book.
Patten. Junior classics. v. 1.
Success library. v. 3.
Witch of Fife. Grierson. Scottish fairy book.
Witch of Laggan. Douglas. Scottish fairy and folk tales.
See also Witch cat.
Witch of the well. Harris. Little Mr. Thimblefinger.
Witch princess. Byrne. Modern Greek fairy tales.
Witches at the cross. Baudis. Czech folk tales.
See also Tam o' Shanter.
Witches' cellar. Bosschère. Christmas tales of Flanders.
Witches' excursion. *See* Voyage of the wee red cap.
Witches' horn. Thorpe. Yule-tide stories.
Witches' wards. Taylor. Thrings of the dark mountain.
Witching stone. Baumbach. Tales from wonderland.
Witch's cat. Bosschère. Folk tales of Flanders

Witch's stronghold. Sylva and Strettell. Legends from river and mountain.
Witch's waste basket. *Potter. Pinafore pocket story book.
With bow and arrow. *See* Robin Hood.
Witty answer. Wardrop. Georgian folk tales.
Wives of Weinsberg. Evans. Old time tales.
Wizard and his pupil. Kunos. Forty-four Turkish fairy tales.
See also Farmer Weatherbeard; Fisherman's son and the Gruagach of tricks; Magician's pupil; Master and pupil; Oh.
Wizard and the beggar. Johnson. Birch-tree fairy book.
Wizard-dervish. Kunos. Forty-four Turkish fairy tales.
Wizard Didi and the child. Jewett. Egyptian tales of magic.
Wizard king. Lang. Invisible prince, and other stories.
Lang. Yellow fairy book.
Wizard of Roccanera. Macdonell. Italian fairy tales.
Wodin. *See* Odin.
Woe Bogotir. *See* Gore-gorinskoe.
Wolf. I. *See* Werewolf. I.
Wolf. II. Stroebe and Martens. Danish fairy book.
See also Cat and the parrot; Kuratko the terrible; Greedy cat.
Wolf and Godfather Fox. Grimm. Fairy tales (Paull tr.).
Wolf and his bridge. *Bowen. Second story reader.
Wolf and his cub. Wiggin and Smith. Talking beasts.
Wolf and his two dinners. Stafford. Animal fables.
Wolf and the ass. Æsop. Fables (Burt ed.).
Wolf and the cat. Æsop. Fables (Stickney. Supplement).
Wiggin and Smith. Talking beasts.
Wolf and the crane. Æsop. Fables (Black ed.).
Æsop. Fables (Burt ed.).
Æsop. Fables (Jacobs).
Æsop. Fables (Stickney).
Arnold and Gilbert. Stepping stones to literature. v. 2.
Scudder. Children's book.
Scudder. Fables and folk stories.
*Spaulding and Bryce. Aldine readers. 2d reader. (Wolf and the stork.)
Wiggin and Smith. Talking beasts.
*Young and Field. Literary readers. Book 2.
Wolf and the dog. *See* Dog and the wolf.
Wolf and the five little goats. *See* Wolf and the seven little kids.
Wolf and the fox. I. Allison and Perdue. Story in primary instruction.
*Field second reader.
Grimm. Fairy tales (Paull tr.).
Wiggin and Smith. Tales of laughter.
Wolf and the fox. II. Æsop. Fables (Burt ed.).

Wolf and the fox. II.—*continued.*
(poem). Wiggin and Smith. Talking beasts.
Wolf and the goat. I. Æsop. Fables (Stickney).
Scudder. Children's book.
Scudder. Fables and folk stories.
Wolf and the goat. II. Laboulaye. Last fairy tales.
Wolf and the house-dog. *See* Dog and the wolf.
Wolf and the kid. I. *See* Kid and the wolf. II.
Wolf and the kid. II. Æsop. Fables (Burt ed.).
Coe and Christie. Story hour readers. Book I. (Billy Goat and the wolf.)
*Spaulding and Bryce. Aldine readers. 2d reader.
Wolf and the kid. III. Æsop. Fables (Burt ed.).
Wolf and the kid. IV. Æsop. Fables (Black ed.).
Wolf and the lamb. I. Æsop. Fables (Black ed.).
Æsop. Fables (Burt ed.).
Æsop. Fables (Jacobs).
Æsop. Fables (Stickney).
Baldwin. Fairy tales and fables.
Norton. Heart of oak books. v. 2.
Patten. Junior classics. v. 1.
Scudder. Children's book.
Scudder. Fables and folk stories.
Wiggin and Smith. Talking beasts.
Wolf and the lamb. II. Æsop. Fables (Burt ed.).
Wiggin and Smith. Talking beasts.
Wolf and the lean dog (poem). Wiggin and Smith. Talking beasts.
Wolf and the lion. Æsop. Fables (Burt ed.).
Wolf and the man. *Baldwin. Fairy reader.
Grimm. Fairy tales (Lucas tr.).
Grimm. Fairy tales (Paull tr.).
*Grimm. Fairy tales (Wiltse). v. 2.
Grimm. Household tales (Burt ed. Boasting wolf.)
Wolf and the mastiff. *See* Dog and the wolf.
Wolf and the seven goslings. *See* Wolf and the seven little goslings.
Wolf and the seven kids. *See* Wolf and the seven little kids.
Wolf and the seven little goats. *See* Wolf and the seven little kids.
Wolf and the seven little goslings.
Blaisdell. Child life. 2d reader. (Wolf and the seven goslings.
Coussens. Child's book of stories. (Wolf and the seven young goslings.)
Darton. Wonder book of beasts. (Wolf and the seven goslings.)
Johnson. Oak-tree fairy book. (Wolf and the seven little goslings.)
*Klingensmith. Just stories. (Seven goslings.)
Mulock. Fairy book. (Wolf and the seven goslings.)

Wolf and the seven little goslings—*continued.*
Perkins. Twenty best fairy tales. (Wolf and the seven young goslings.)
Wolf and the seven little kids. Allison and Perdue. Story in primary instruction. (Seven little goats.)
Aunt Louisa's book of fairy tales.
Grimm. Fairy tales (Lucas tr. Wolf and the seven kids.)
Grimm. Fairy tales (Paull tr. Wolf and the seven young kids.)
Grimm. Household stories (Crane tr. Wolf and the seven little goats.)
Grimm. Household tales (Burt ed. Wolf and the seven young kids.)
Pyle. Mother's nursery tales. (Wolf and the five little goats.)
Wiggin and Smith. Tales of laughter. (Wolf and the seven kids.)
See also Carlanco; Hill-nanny and her kids; Wolf and the three little cats.
Wolf and the seven young goslings. *See* Wolf and the seven little goslings.
Wolf and the seven young kids. *See* Wolf and the seven little kids.
Wolf and the sheep. Æsop. Fables (Burt ed.).
Wiggin and Smith. Talking beasts.
Wolf and the shepherd. Æsop. Fables (Stickney).
Scudder. Fables and folk stories.
Wolf and the shepherds. Æsop. Fables (Burt ed.).
Æsop. Fables (Stickney).
Wolf and the stork. *See* Wolf and the crane.
Wolf and the tailor. Magnus. Russian folk-tales.
Wolf and the three little cats. Burchill. Progressive road to reading. Book 1.
See also Wolf and the seven little kids.
Wolf and the twins. *See* Romulus and Remus.
Wolf as a Roman. Houghton. Russian grandmother's wonder tales.
Wolf boy. *See* Boy and the wolves. II.
Wolf in disguise. Æsop. Fables (Burt ed.).
(poem). Æsop. Fables (Stickney. Supplement. Wolf turned shepherd.)
(poem). Wiggin and Smith. Talking beasts. (Wolf turned shepherd.)
Wolf in sheep's clothing. Æsop. Fables (Black ed.).
Æsop. Fables (Burt ed.).
Æsop. Fables (Jacobs).
Æsop. Fables (Stickney).
Scudder. Children's book.
Scudder. Fables and folk stories.
Wiggin and Smith. Talking beasts.
Wolf man. Grinnell. Blackfoot lodge tales.

Wolf-mother of Saint Ailbe. Brown. Book of saints and friendly beasts.
Coe. Second book of stories.
Wolf on his deathbed. Success library. v. 3.
Wolf sings. Fillmore. Mighty Mikko.
Wolf, the fox and the ape. Æsop. Fables (Black ed.).
Æsop. Fables (Burt ed.).
Æsop. Fables (Stickney).
Wolf, the goat and the kid. *See* Wolf, the she-goat and the kid.
Wolf, the she-goat and the kid. Æsop. Fables (Burt ed.).
(poem). Wiggin and Smith. Talking beasts. (Wolf, the goat and the kid.)
See also Snowflake; Wolf and the seven little kids.
Wolf turned shepherd. *See* Wolf in disguise.
Wolf! Wolf! *See* Shepherd's boy and the wolf.
Wolf's butter. Stafford. Animal fables.
See also Cat and the mouse in partnership.
Wolverine and the rock. Judson. Old Crow and his friends. (Wolverine gets into trouble.)
Lang. Brown fairy book. (Wicked wolverine.)
Lang. Magician's gifts. (Wicked wolverine.)
Storytellers' magazine. Nov. 1916, p. 597. (How the wolverine's legs were shortened.)
Young. Algonquin Indian tales. (*In* Ch. 15.)
See also Coyote and rolling rock; Rolling rock; Why the night-hawk's wings are beautiful.
Wolves and the deer. Coe and Christie. Story reader. Book 3.
Curtis. Indian days of long ago.
Judson. Myths and legends of Alaska.
See also Brother Tiger and Daddy Sheep.
Wolves and the sheep. Æsop. Fables (Black ed.).
Æsop. Fables (Burt ed.).
Baldwin. Fairy stories and fables. (Wolves, the dogs and the sheep.)
Scudder. Children's book.
Scudder. Fables and folk stories.
Wolves and the sick ass. Æsop. Fables (Black ed.).
Æsop. Fables (Burt ed.).
Wolves, the dogs and the sheep. *See* Wolves and the sheep.
Woman accuser. *See* How a fish swam in the air and a hare in the water.
Woman and her hen. *See* Woman and the fat hen.
Woman and her kid. Boston collection of kindergarten stories.
See also Old woman and her pig.
Woman and her maids. *See* Old woman and her maids.
Woman and the fat hen. Æsop. Fables (Burt ed.).
Æsop. Fables (Stickney. Woman and her hen).

Woman from Lalo-hana, the country under the sea. Colum. At the gateways of the day.
Woman in the moon. I. Judd. Wigwam stories.
See also Why sunshine follows rain.
Woman in the moon. II. Borland. Rocky mountain tipi tales.
Woman in the moon. III. Pope. Hawaii.
Woman in the moon. I, II and III.
For other versions *See* Frog in the moon; Hina, the woman in the moon; Lady in the moon; Maiden in the moon.
Woman magician. Bayliss. Treasury of Eskimo tales.
Woman that was a great fool. Gregory. Kiltartan wonder book.
Woman who became a beaver. Eastman. Indian legends retold.
Woman who forgot her cat. Potter. Pinafore pocket story book.
See also Cat's house under the hill.
Woman who married a buffalo. Borland. Rocky Mountain tipi tales. (Woman who married a buffalo; Men learn the buffalo dance.)
Grinnell. Blackfoot lodge tales. (Origin of the I-kun-uh-kah-tsi.)
See also King of the buffaloes.
Woman with three hundred and sixty-six children. Griffis. Dutch fairy tales.
See also Beggar's curse.
Woman's wish. *See* Old woman and the knight.
Woman's wit. Pyle. Twilight land
Women's words part flesh and blood. Martens. Chinese fairy book.
Wonder. Skinner. Emerald story book.
Stone and Fickett. Trees in prose and poetry. (Parable.)
Wonder bridge. Guerber. Legends of the Rhine.
Wonder child. *See* Longnose the dwarf.
Wonder egg. Bailey. Stories for Sunday telling.
Wonder garden. Brown. Kisington town.
Wonder gift. Bailey. Stories for Sunday telling.
Wonder horse. Lindsay and Poulsson. Joyous travelers. (Tale told by the squire.)
Wonder tree. Olcott. Good stories for great holidays.
Wonderful Alpine horn. *See* How the Swiss came to use the Alpine horn.
Wonderful artisan. *See* Daedalus and Icarus.
Wonderful attraction. Mendes. Fairy spinning wheel.
Wonderful basket. Lang. Strange story book.
Wonderful birch. Lang. Red fairy book.
Lang. Snake prince.
Wonderful bird. Grinnell. Blackfoot lodge tales.
See also Why our sight fails with age.
Wonderful box. *See* Pandora.
Wonderful cake. Graves. Irish fairy book.

Wonderful cake—*continued.*
See also Johnny cake; Little red hen. I.
Wonderful cap that mother made. *See* Anders' new cap.
Wonderful cow. Curtin. Hero tales of Ireland. (Elin Gow, the swordsmith from Erin, and the cow Glas Gainach.)
*Field third reader.
Wonderful doors. Bailey. Friendly tales.
Wonderful exploits of Grasshopper. *See* Paup-Puk-Keewis.
Wonderful fiddler. *See* Wonderful musician.
Wonderful fish. Bosschère. Christmas tales of Flanders.
See also Fisherman and his wife.
Wonderful flower. Thorpe. Yule-tide stories.
Wonderful glass. Grimm. Household tales (Burt ed.).
Some editions of Grimm not indexed here use the title "Godfather" for this story.
Wonderful hair. Fillmore. Laughing prince.
Mabie. Folk tales every child should know.
Patten. Junior classics. v. 1.
Wonderful lamp. *See* Aladdin.
Wonderful mallet. Wiggin and Smith. Tales of laughter.
Wonderful mill. Noyes. Twilight stories.
See also Water of youth.
Wonderful mirror. I. *See* Mirror of Matsuyama.
Wonderful mirror. II. Finger. Tales from silver lands.
Wonderful musician. Grimm. Fairy tales (Paull tr.).
Grimm. Household stories (Crane tr.).
Grimm. Household tales (Burt ed. Wonderful fiddler.)
Grimm. Household tales (Everyman's ed.).
Lang. Marvellous musician and other stories. (Marvellous musician.)
Lang. Red fairy book. (Marvellous musician.)
Wonderful plough. Gibbon. Reign of King Cole.
Haaren. Fairy life.
Wonderful porridge pot. Allison and Perdue. Story in primary instruction. (Sweet rice porridge.)
Bailey and Lewis. For the children's hour.
Elson and Runkel. Elson readers. Book 1. (Sweet porridge.)
Johnson. Fir-tree fairy book. (Sweet porridge.)
Wiggin and Smith. Tales of laughter. (Sweet soup.)
Wonderful pot. Bailey. Firelight stories.
Bay. Danish fairy and folk tales.
Hodgkins. Atlantic treasury of childhood stories. (Magic pot.)
My Bookhouse. v. 3. (Marvelous pot.)
Murray. Story book treasures. (Old iron kettle.)
Peck. Stories for good children. (Magic iron pot.)
Pyle. Mother's nursery tales. (Sweet porridge.)
Storytellers' magazine. Nov. 1913, p. 271. (Old iron pot.)
Wonderful quern stones. *See* Why the sea is salt. I.
Wonderful ring. Pyle. Tales of wonder and magic.
Steel. Tales of the Punjab.

Wonderful ring—*continued.*
See also Charmed ring; Enchanted ring. II.
Wonderful sculptor. *See* Pygmalion and Galatea.
Wonderful sea god. *See* Proteus.
Wonderful sheep. *See* Ram.
Wonderful ship. Keyes. Stories and story-telling.
Wonderful slave. *See* Magic palace.
Wonderful story. Houghton. Russian grandmother's wonder tales.
Wonderful tapestry. Brown. One-footed fairy.
Wonderful tar-baby story. *See* Tar baby.
Wonderful teakettle. *See* Accomplished and lucky teakettle.
Wonderful traveler. *See* Poor man and the rich man.
Wonderful tree in Ditmarschen. Thorpe. Yule-tide stories.
Wonderful turnip. Johnson. Fir-tree fairy book.
Wonderful weaver. *See* Arachne.
Wondering Jack. *See* Boots and his brothers.
Wondering Tom. Dodge. Land of pluck.
Fairy stories from St. Nicholas.
St. Nicholas. Jan. 1879, p. 184.
Wonderous change. *See* Lesson of faith.
Wonderous story of Ivan Golic and the serpents. Bain. Cossack fairy tales.
Wonogquos. Allen. Indian fairy tales.
Woo Sing and the mirror. Davis and Chow-Leung. Chinese fables and folk stories.
Wood and the clown. Æsop. Fables (Black ed.).
Æsop. Fables (Burt ed.).
Wood-chopper. *See* Honest woodman.
Wood-chopper and berry picker. Eastman. Wigwam evenings.
Wood-chopper's children. Eggleston. Queer stories for boys and girls.
Wood fairy. *See* Wood maiden.
Wood-folk. *See* Pan.
Wood lady. *See* Wood maiden.
Wood maiden. Fillmore. Czechoslovak fairy tales.
Noyes. Twilight tales. (Wood fairy.)
Olcott. Book of elves and fairies. (Wood lady.)
Wood mouse. Donaldson. Little papoose listens.
Wood sprite. Magnus. Russian folk-tales.
Wood-violet that was a maiden. Olcott. Wonder garden.
Woodchopper. *See* Wood-chopper.
Woodchuck Day. *See* Candlemas; Why the woodchuck comes out in midwinter. II.
Woodcock and the mallard. Æsop. Fables (Burt ed.).
Woodcutter and the fairy. *See* Honest woodman.
Woodcutter's child. *See* Fairy Tell-True.
Woodcutter's daughter. Mulock. Fairy book.
Wiggin and Smith. Magic casements.
Woodcutter's saké. *See* Waterfall which flowed saké.

Woodcutter's son and the two turtles. Eells. Tales of enchantment from Spain.
Wooden bowl. *See* Maiden with the wooden helmet.
Wooden-headed clothes pins, Tale of. Storytellers' magazine. Jan. 1915, p. 28.
Wooden horse. I. Arnold and Gilbert. Stepping stones to literature. v. 4.
*Bailey. Wonder stories. (How a wooden horse won a war.)
Baldwin. Horse fair.
Baldwin. Thirty more famous stories.
Evans. Heroes of Troy.
Patten. Junior classics. v. 3. (*In* Trojan war.)
Peabody. Old Greek folk stories.
Scudder. Children's book. (Horse of wood.)
Storr. Half a hundred hero tales.
Tappan. Stories from the classics.
Wooden horse. II. *See* Enchanted horse.
Wooden shoe. Griffis. Dutch fairy tales. (Legend of the wooden shoe.)
Wooden shoes of Little Wolff. *See* Sabot of Little Wolff.
Wooden tablet. Pitman. Chinese wonder book.
Wooden wife. Eastman. Indian legends retold.
See also Indian who lost his wife.
Woodman and Mercury. *See* Honest woodman.
Woodman and the deer. Dyer and Brady. Merrill readers. 2d reader.
Woodman and the goblins. Esenwein and Stockard. Children's stories.
Woodman and the mountain fairies. *See* Vision of Tsunu.
Woodman and the serpent. *See* Countryman and the snake.
Woodman and the trees. Æsop. Fables (Jacobs. Man and the wood.)
Æsop. Fables (Stickney).
(poem). Wiggin and Smith. Talking beasts. (Woods and the woodman.)
Woodpecker. *See* Why the woodpecker's head is red. I.
Woodpecker and the lion. Babbitt. More Jataka tales.
Woodpecker girls. *See* Rabbit and the woodpecker girls.
Woodpecker Gray. Olcott. Red Indian fairy book.
Skinner. Turquoise story book. (How woodpecker changed his colors.)
See also Why the woodpecker's head is red. II.
Woodpecker, turtle and deer. *See* True friendship. II.
Woodpecker who was selfish. Bailey. For the story teller.
See also Selfish sparrow and the houseless crows.
Woodpecker's joke. Farmer. Nature myths.
Woodpecker's red crown. *See* Why the woodpecker has a red head. II.
Woodrat and rabbits. Judson. Myths and legends of the Pacific Northwest.

Woods and the woodman. *See* Woodman and the trees.
Wooing. Keyes. Stories and story-telling.
Wooing of Gerd. Bradish. Old Norse stories. (Frey.)
Brown. In the days of giants. (Giantess who would not.)
Edmison. Stories from the Norseland. (Frey and Gerd.)
Guerber. Myths of northern lands. (*In* Frey.)
Keary. Heroes of Asgard. (Frey.)
Klingensmith. Old Norse wonder tales. (Gerd.)
Litchfield. Nine worlds. (Frey climbs into Odin's high seat; Frey's love for Gerd; Skirnir's journey to win Gerd for Frey.)
Mabie. Norse stories.
Wickes. Beyond the rainbow bridge. (Wooing of Gerda.)
Wooing of Olwen *See* Kilwch and Olwen.
Wooing of Pomona. *See* Pomona.
Wooing of the daughter of the King of Ireland. Patten. Junior classics. v. 2.
Worcestershire fairies. Hartland. English folk and fairy tales.
Work and play. Blaisdell. Child life. 2d reader.
Work basket egg. Potter. Pinafore pocket story book.
Worker in sandal-wood. Cross and Statler. Story-telling.
Curtiss. Christmas stories and legends.
Storytellers' magazine. Dec. 1915, p. 445.
Wickes. Happy holidays.
Workman king. *See* Peter the Great.
World within the wall. Coolidge. Mischief's Thanksgiving.
World's birthday (poem). Potter. Pinafore pocket story book.
World's most beauteous damsel. Kunos. Turkish fairy tales.
World's reward. *See* Way of the world. I.
Worm pipe. *See* Ghost wife. III.
Worme of Linton. Douglas. Scottish fairy tales.
Grierson. Scottish fairy book.
Wormwood. Richards. Silver crown.
Wound. Richards. Silver crown.
Wound and the scar. Rouse. Talking thrush.
Wounded eagle. *See* Eagle and the arrow.
Wounded lion. Lang. Pink fairy book.
Wreath. Thorpe. Yule-tide stories.
Wreaths of Nava-Ratna. Griswold. Hindu fairy tales.
Wrekin. Duncan-Jones. English folk-lore stories. (Building of the Wrekin.)
Farmer. Nature myths. (How a giant made a mountain.)
Hartland. English folk and fairy tales. (Origin of the Wrekin.)
Wren. I. Wiggin and Smith. Talking beasts.
Wren. II. (poem). Wilson. Myths of the red children.
Wren and the bear. Darton. Wonder book of beasts. (Tomtit and the bear.)

Wren and the bear—*continued.*
Grimm. Fairy tales (Lucas tr.).
Grimm. Household tales (Everyman's ed. Tom-tit and the bear.)
Johnson. Book of fairy-tale bears. (Bear and the wrens.)
Wiggin and Smith. Tales of laughter.
Wren and the eagle. *See* King Wren.
Wrestlers. Steel. Tales of the Punjab.
Wrists bound with the red thread. *See* Red thread of courage.
Writing a composition. Baldwin. Fifty famous people.
Wuchowson the wind-blower. Cornyn. When the camp fire burns. (Wuchosen the wind-blower.)
Olcott. Red Indian fairy book. (Wind-blower.)
Partridge. Story telling in home and school. (Glooscap and the great wind bird.)
Storytellers' magazine. Jan. 1916, p. 21. (Glooscap and the great wind bird.)
Wilson. Myths of the red children.
Wulfstan, Bishop of Worcester, Legend of. Peer. Saints in story.
Wunzh, the father of Indian corn. *See* First corn. III.
Wylie, Story of. Bryant. How to tell stories to children.

X–Y

Xanthippe, Story of. Field. Second book of tales.
Xerxes. Wiltse. Kindergarten stories. (Man who wanted to chain the sea.)

Yallery Brown. Jacobs. More English fairy tales.
Yanechek and the water demon. Singleton. Goldenrod fairy book.
Yang Gui Fe. Martens. Chinese fairy book.
Yang Oerlang. Martens. Chinese fairy book.
Yara, Story of the. Lang. Brown fairy book.
Lang. Elf maiden.
Yard that grew. Bailey. Friendly tales.
Year, Story of the. Andersen. Fairy tales (Paull tr.).
Andersen. Stories and tales (Author's ed.).
Olcott. Wonder garden. (New Year.)
Storytellers' magazine. May 1916, p. 305.
Wickes. Happy holidays.
Yehl and the beaming maiden. *See* Daylight, Origin of. V.
Yelina the wise. Curtin. Wonder tales from Russia.
Yellow daisy. Storytellers' magazine. Oct. 1917, p. 393.
Yellow dwarf. Aulnoy. Fairy tales.
Aulnoy. Children's fairy tales.
Coussens. Child's book of stories.
Lang. Blue fairy book.
Lang. Prince Darling, and other fairy stories.

Yellow dwarf—*continued.*
Mulock. Fairy book.
Nursery tales.
Valentine. Old, old fairy tales (Warne ed.).
Wiggin and Smith. Fairy ring.
Yellow fox. Grinnell. Pawnee hero stories
Yellow Lily. Curtin. Myths and folklore of Ireland. (Son of the King of Erin, and the giant of Loch Lein.)
Williams. Fairy tales from folklore.
Yew. Skinner. Pearl story book.
You must not work on Sunday. Cary. French fairy tales.
See also Knockgrafton, Legend of.
You-To's first lesson. Pitman. Chinese fairy stories.
Young Bekie. Grierson. Children's tales from Scottish ballads.
Young-boy-chief. Olcott. Red Indian fairy book.
Young cupbearer. *See* Cyrus and his grandfather.
Young fellow and the devil. *See* Lad and the devil.
Young giant. Grimm. Household tales (Everyman's ed. Thumbling the dwarf and Thumbling the giant).
Grimm. Fairy tales (Wiltse. Thumbling, the dwarf who became a giant.) v. 1.
Wiggin and Smith. Tales of laughter.
Young head of the family. Fielde. Chinese fairy tales.
Pitman. Chinese fairy tales. (Little Jewel.)
Wiggin and Smith. Tales of laughter.
See also Lantern and the fan.
Young hunters and the bears. Johnson. Book of fairy-tale bears.
Young king. Storytellers' magazine. July 1917, p. 317.
Wilde. Fairy tales.
Young king of the Black Isles, History of. Arabian nights (Dodge ed.).
Arabian nights (Colum. Story of the young king of the Black Isles.)
Arabian nights (Housman. Story of the King of the Ebony Isles.)
Arabian nights (Lang. Story of the young king of the Black Isles.)
Arabian Nights. (Olcott. Story of the young king of the Black Isles.)
Arabian nights (Townsend).
Arabian nights (Wiggin and Smith).
Welsh. Fairy tales children love. (Young king of the Black Isles.)
Young laird of Lorntie. Douglas. Scottish fairy tales.
Young lord's servant's tale. *See* Master fox.
Young lord's tale. *See* Queen's tree.
Young man and his cat. *See* Venus and the cat.
Young man and the barber. *See* Tailor's story.
Young man and the cook. *See* Young men and the cook.
Young man and the lion. Æsop. Fables (Black ed.).

Young man and the lion—*continued.*
Æsop. Fables (Burt ed.).
Young man and the swallow. Æsop. Fables (Black ed.), *See also* Spendthrift and the swallow.
Young man who would have his eyes opened. Lang. Violet fairy book.
Young men and the cook. Æsop. Fables (Black ed. Young man and the cook.)
Æsop. Fables (Burt ed.).
Young mouse. Grover. Folk-lore readers. v. 1.
Young mouse, the cock and the cat. *See* Mouse, the cat and the cock.
"Young Neverfull." Houghton. Russian grandmother's wonder tales.
Wiggin and Smith. Tales of laughter.
Young piper. Jerrold. Reign of King Oberon.
Young scout. Baldwin. Fifty famous people.
Young sister's tale. *See* Lucy on May morning.
Young soap-boiler. Eggleston. Queer stories for boys and girls.
Young swallow. Success library. v. 3.
Young Tamlane. *See* Tamlane.
Young thief and his mother. Æsop. Fables (Burt ed.).
Young tiger. Wiggin and Smith. Talking beasts.
Young Waters (poem). Lanier. Boy's Percy.
Younger son of the jackal. *See* Jackal's younger son.
Youth and the dog-dance. Macmillan. Canadian fairy tales. *See also* Boy who was sacrificed.
Youth and the Vila. Houghton. Russian grandmother's wonder tales.
Youth and Wild Thyme. Storytellers' magazine. May 1915, p. 130.
Youth, the hawk, and the raven. Bidpai. Tortoise and the geese.
Youth who could not lie. Hartwell. Story hour readings. 6th year.
Youth who could not shiver and shake. Grimm. Fairy tales (Lucas tr.).
Grimm. Household tales (Burt ed.).
Johnson Fir-tree fairy book.
Lang. Blue fairy book. (Tale of a youth who set out to learn what fear was.)
Lang. Princess on the glass hill, and other stories. (Tale of a youth who set out to learn what fear was.)
Patten. Junior classics. v. 1. (He who knew not fear.)
Some editions of Grimm not indexed here use the title "One who traveled to learn what shivering meant" for this story.
Youth who set out to learn what fear was, Tale of a. *See* Youth who could not shiver and shake.
Youth who wanted to win the daughter of the mother in the corner. *See* Mother Roundabout's daughter.

Youth who was to serve three years without pay. *See* Three years without wages.
Youth who went to the North wind and demanded his flour again. *See* Lad who went to the North wind.
Youth who would not tell his dream. Storytellers' magazine. Jan. 1914, p. 375.
See also How six traveled through the world.
Youth without age, and life without death. Kunos. Turkish fairy tales.
Yow Tow's first lesson. Pitman. Chinese fairy tales.
Yu-Kong and the demon. Pitman. Chinese fairy stories.
Yucca plant, Legend of. Cross and Statler. Story-telling.
Storytellers' magazine. July 1914, p. 624.
Yuletide specters. Stroebe and Martens. Swedish fairy book.
Yussuf's three punishments. Aunt Naomi. Jewish fairy tales and fables.
Yvon and Finette. Gask. Folk tales from many lands.
Laboulaye. Fairy book.
Storytellers' magazine. Nov. 1915, p. 383.
Wiggin and Smith. Fairy ring.
See also Battle of the birds; Master maid. I.

Z

Zadig. *See* Perplexity of Zadig.
Zerbin the woodcutter. Jokai and others. Golden fairy book.
Laboulaye. Fairy tales. (Zerbino, the bear.)
Laboulaye. Last fairy tales. (Zerbino, the savage.)
Zerbino, the bear. *See* Zerbin, the woodcutter.
Zerbino, the savage. *See* Zerbin, the woodcutter.
Zeus. *See* Jupiter.
Zeuxis and Parrhasius. Baldwin. Fifty famous people. (Two great painters.)
Haaren and Poland. Famous men of Greece. (*In* Socrates.)
Zirac. Wiggin and Smith. Tales of laughter.
Zirbel. Noyes. Twilight stories.
Zlatovlaska the golden haired. *See* Golden Hair.
Zobeide, Story of. Arabian nights (Townsend).
Zoulvisia, Story of. Lang. Olive fairy book.
Lang. Fairy nurse.

LIST OF BOOKS ANALYZED IN THE INDEX

The titles of books, a part only of whose contents has been indexed in the foregoing list, have been indicated by the addition of a dagger (†). The asterisk (*) after the price indicates that no later edition and price has been located.

Prices are given for aid in estimating approximate cost; but, on account of the rapidly changing price conditions in the book market, it will be necessary to verify all prices with current catalogs.

Adams, William, *ed.*
Folk story and verse. 1899. Amer. Book Co., $.60.
†Myths of old Greece in story and song. 1900. Amer. Book Co., $.64.

Aesop.
Fables. Illus. by Charles Folkard. 1912. Black, 6s.*
Fables. Ed. 3. n.d. Burt, $1.00.
Fables. Joseph Jacobs, ed. c1894. Macm., $1.75.
Fables, with supplement. J. H. Stickney, ed. n.d. Ginn, $.72.

Afanasev, A. N.
See Magnus, L. A., tr.

Alcott, L. M.
Lulu's Library. 3 v. Little, $1.50 each.
Flower fables. n.d. Altemus, $.75.

Alden, R. M.
Boy who found the king. c1922. Bobbs, $1.75.
Why the chimes rang. c1908. Bobbs, $1.00 to $2.50.

Alderman, E. A.
Classics old and new: a series of school readers. 1906. Amer. Book Co. 1st reader, $.48; 2d reader, $.52; 3d reader, $.60; 4th reader, $.64.

Aldine readers.
See Spaulding, F. E., and Bryce, C. T., ed.

Alexander, Francesca.
Hidden servants. 1912. Little, $2.50.

Allen, H. N.
Korean tales. c1889. Putnam, $1.25.*

Allen, Lewis.
Indian fairy tales. 1912. Luce, $1.00.*

Allison, S. B. and Perdue, H. A.
Story in primary instruction. c1902. Flanagan, $.60.*

Almost true tales. n.d. Putnam, $1.75.

Andersen, H. C.
*Best fairy tales. A. C. Henderson, tr. 1911. Rand., $.75. For primary grades.
Fairy tales. Mrs. E. M. Lucas, tr. n.d. Dutton, $2.50.*
Fairy tales. E. H. L. Turpin, ed. 1904. Merrill, $.40. For primary grades.
Fairy tales. Mrs. H. B. Paull, tr. n.d. Warne, $1.50.
Fairy tales and stories. Signe Toksvig, ed. Illus. by Erie Pape. 1921. Macm., $1.75.

Andersen, H. C.—*continued.*
Stories. c1891. Houghton, $.56. (Riverside literature series.)
Stories and tales. c1870. Houghton, $2.00. (Author's ed.)
Wond stories. n.d. Houghton, $2.00. (Author's ed.)
Andrews, M. R. S.
Enchanted forest and other stories. c1909. Dutton, $2.00.
Annals of fairyland.
See True annals of fairyland.
Arabian night's entertainment; 130 illus. n.d. Dodge, $1.50.*
The same; Andrew Lang, ed. 1907. Longmans, $2.00, $1.75.
The same; F. J. Olcott, ed. 1913. Holt, $2.00.
The same; Padraic Colum, ed. Illus. by Eric Pape. 1923. Macm., $1.75.
The same; G. T. Townsend, ed. n.d. Warne, $1.50.*
The same; K. D. Wiggin and N. A. Smith, ed. Illus. by Maxfield Parrish. 1909. Scribner, $2.50.*
More tales from the Arabian nights; F. J. Olcott, ed. Illus. by Willy Pogany. 1915. Holt, $2.00.
Stories from the Arabian nights; retold by Laurence Housman. Illus. by Edmond Dulac. c1911–1916. Hodder & Stoughton. Several eds. with prices varying from 20s to 7s. 6d.
Armfield, C. S.
Wonder tales of the world. 1920. Harcourt, $2.50.
Armfield, C. S. and Maxwell.
Armfields' animal-book. 1923. Holt, $2.25.
Arnold, S. L. and Gilbert, C. B.
†Stepping stones to literature. v. 2–7. Silver, v. 2, $.80; v. 3, $.84; v. 4, $.92; v. 5, $.96; v. 6, $1.00; v. 7, $1.04.
Asbjörnsen, P. C.
Fairy tales from the far north. n.d. Burt, $1.00.
Folk and fairy tales; tr. by H. L. Braekstad. 6th ed. 1884. N. Y. Armstrong.
Tales from the fjeld. 1896. London. Gibbings, 6s.* Same. New ed., tr. by G. W. Dasent. Putnam, $2.50.
See also Gade, H. & J.
Aspinwall, Alicia.
Short stories for short people. 1896. Dutton, $2.00.
Aulnoy, M. C. J. de B., Comtesse de.
Children's fairy-land; trans. and adapted. c1919. Holt, $1.75.
Fairy tales. 1895. Scribner; Same. McKay, $3.50.
Aunt Louisa's book of fairy tales. n.d. Warne, $.75.
Aunt Naomi.
See Landa, Gertrude.
Austin, Mary.
Basket woman. c1904. Houghton, $2.00; school ed. $1.00.
Babbitt, E. C.
Jataka tales. c1912. Century, $1.25; school ed. $.60.
More Jataka tales. 1922. Century, $1.25; school ed. $.60.
Bacon, Peggy.
True philosopher and other cat tales. c1919. Four Seas Co., $1.25.
Bailey, C. S.
Firelight stories. 1907. Bradley, $1.50.
Folk stories and fables. 1919. Bradley, $.85.
For the story teller. 1913. Bradley, $1.75.
Friendly tales. c1923. Bradley, $1.75.
In the animal world. 1924. Bradley, $1.75.
Once upon a time animal stories. 1920. Bradley, $1.00.

Bailey, C. S.—*continued.*
†Stories and rhymes for a child. 1913. Bradley, $1.25.
Stories children need. 1923. Bradley, $1.75.
†Stories for Sunday telling. c1916. Pilgrim Press, $1.25.
Wonder stories. 1920. Bradley, $2.00.
Bailey, C. S. and Lewis, C. M.
†For the children's hour. 5th ed. 1909. Bradley, $1.00.
Bailey, Margery.
Little man with one shoe. 1921. Little, $2.25.
Seven peas in the pod. c1919. Little, $2.25.
Bain, R. N., tr.
Cossack fairy tales. 1899. Burt, $1.00.
Russian fairy tales. *See* Polevoi, P. N.
Turkish fairy tales. *See* Kunos, Ignacz.
See also Tolstoi, L. N.
Baker, F. T., Carpenter, G. R., and Kirchway, M. F., *ed.*
Language readers. c1906–1916. Macm. 3d. year, $.88. 4th year, $.96; 6th year, $.96.
Bakewell, M. E.
True fairy stories. 1902. Amer. Book Co., $.52.
Baldwin, James.
Another fairy reader. 1907. Amer. Book Co., $.52.
Fairy reader. c1905. Amer. Book Co., $.52.
Adapted from Grimm and Andersen.
Fairy stories and fables. n.d. Amer. Book Co., $.56.
†Fifty famous rides and riders. 1900. Amer. Book Co., $.72.
Fifty famous people. c1912. Amer. Book Co., $.52.
†Fifty famous stories retold. 1896. Amer. Book Co., $.56.
†Golden fleece. c1905. Amer. Book Co., $.72.
Hero tales told in school. 1909. Scribner, $.80.
†Horse fair. Century, $2.00.
Old Greek stories. 1895. Amer. Book Co., $.60.
†Sampo. 1912. Scribner, $2.00.
Second fairy reader. 1907. Amer. Book Co., $.52.
†Stories of the king. 1910. Amer. Book Co., $.72.
†Stories of the golden age. 1923. c1887–1915. Scribner, $2.00.
†Thirty more famous stories. 1905. Amer. Book Co., $.72.
Ballard, Susan.
Fairy tales from far Japan. 1909. Revell, $1.00.*
Barber, G. E.
Wagner opera stories. 1919. Public School.
Baring, Maurice.
Blue rose fairy book. 1911. Dodd, $2.00.*
Baring-Gould, Sabine.
Crock of gold. 1899. Page.*
Curious myths of the Middle Ages. Longmans, $1.25.*
Old English fairy tales. n.d. Burt, $1.00.
Bassett, Wilbur.
Wander ships. 1917. Open Court, $1.50.
Bateman, G. W.
Zanzibar tales told by natives of the east coast of Africa. 1904. Saalfield, $1.00.*
Bates, K. L., *ed.*
Once upon a time: a book of old time fairy tales. Illus. by M. E. Price. 1921. Rand, $2.00.
Bates, Lois.
See Heller, T. E.

Baudis, Josef, *comp.* and *tr.*
Czech folk tales. 1917. London. Allen and Unwin; 1918; N. Y. Macmillan, $1.25.
Baumbach, Rudolph.
*Tales from wonderland; tr. by H. S. Dole. Adapted for American children by W. S. Silber. 1915. c1903. Simmons, $.52.
Bay, J. C., *tr.* and *comp.*
Danish fairy and folk tales. A collection of popular stories and fairy tales from the Danish of Svend Grundtvig; E. T. Kristensen; Ingvor Bondeson; and L. Budde. 1899. Harper, $1.75.
Bayliss, C. K.
Treasury of Eskimo tales. 1922. Crowell, $.75.
Treasury of Indian tales. 1921. Crowell, $.75.
Beckwith, M. H.
In mythland. 2 v. Educ. Pub. Co., $.60.
Bell, J. M.
See Brown, A. F.
Bellamy, C. J.
Wonder children: their quests and curious adventures. c.1906. Macm., $.75.*
Bender, I. C.
See Judson, H. P.
Benson, A. B.
Really truly fairy tales. 1923. Flanagan, $.60.
Beston, H. B.
Firelight fairy book. c1919. Atlantic, $3.00.
Bidpai.
Tortoise and the geese and other fables of Bidpai; retold by M. B. Dutton. Illus. by E. Boyd Smith. 1908. Houghton, $1.50.
Bigham, M. A.
Merry animal tales. 1923. c1906. Little, $1.50.
Overheard in fairyland. c1909. Little, $1.50.
Biggs, M. A., *tr.*
See Glinski, A. J.
Birch, V. B.
Green-faced toad. 1923. Stokes, $2.00.
Blaidsell, A. F. and Ball, F. K.
†American history story book. c1912. Little, $.80.
†English history story book. c1912. Little, $1.20.
Pub. by Ginn in 1897 with title Short stories from English history.
Blaisdell, E. A. and M. F.
†Child life. 1906. Macm, $.64.
†Child life in tale and fable. (2d reader.) 1906. Macm., $.72.
†Child life in many lands. (3d reader.) 1906. Macm., $.72.
†Child life in literature. (4th reader.) 1904. Macm., $.80.
†Child life fifth reader. 1904. Macm., $.45.
Blumenthal, V. X. K.
Folk tales from Russia. c1903. Rand, $.75.
Bondesen, Ingvor.
See Bay, J. C., *tr.*
Bone, W. A.
Children's stories and how to tell them. c1924. Harcourt, $1.50.
Booth, M. L., *tr.*
See Macé, Jean.

Borland, H. G.
Rocky Mountain tipi tales. 1924. Doubleday, $1.75.
Bosschère, Jean de.
Christmas tales of Flanders. Collected and illus. by J. de Bosschère, tr. by M. C. O. Morris. 1917. London Heinemann, 12s.6d.; N. Y. Dodd, $4.00.
Folk tales of Flanders. Collected and illus. by J. de Bosschère. 1918. London. Heinemann, 12s. 6d.; Dodd, $3.50.
Boston collection of Kindergarten stories. 1898. Hammet, $.60*
Bourhill, Mrs. E. J. and Drake, Mrs. J. B.
Fairy tales from South Africa. 1910. c1908. Macm., $1.50.*
Bouvé, P. C.
†Lamp-light tales. 1923. Grosset, $1.00.
†Lamp-light fairy tales. 1923. Grosset, $1.00.
Bowen, J. A.
†Story reader for the second year at school. 1907. Globe School Book Co., $.40.*
Boys' and girls' fairy stories. n. d. Dutton, $.60.*
Bradish, S. P.
Old Norse stories. 1900. Amer. Book Co., $.60.
Bradley-Birt, F. B.
Bengal fairy tales. Illus. by Abanindranath Tagore. 1920. London. Lane, 15.s.
Brady, M. J.
See Dyer, F. B., jt. author.
Brady, L. E.
Green forest fairy book. 1920. Little, $2.00.
Braekstad, H. L.
See Asbjörnsen, P. C.; Djurklo, N. G.
Brentano, Clemens.
Fairy tales from Brentano; told in English by K. F. Kroeker. 1884. N. Y. Lovell; 1925. Stokes, $2.50.
Brooke, L. L.
See Golden goose; Three little pigs.
Brooks, Dorothy.
Stories of the red children. 1908. Educ. Pub. Co., $.40.
Brooks, Edward.
Wonder stories from the Mabinogion. 1909. Penn, $1.75.
Brooksbank, F. H.
†Legends of ancient Egypt. 1924. Crowell, $2.00.
Brown, A. F.
Book of saints and friendly beasts. 1900. Houghton, $1.50.
Flower princess. c1904. Houghton, $1.50; $1.00
In the days of the giants. c1902. Houghton, $1.50.
Kisington town. 1915. Houghton, $1.90.
Star jewels and other wonders. 1905. Houghton, $1.50.
Brown, A. F. and Bell, J. M.
Tales of the red children. 1901. Appleton, $1.75.
Brown, Alice.
One-footed fairy and other stories. c1911. Houghton, $2.00.
Brown, E. V.
†Stories of childhood and nature. 1913. World Book Co., $1.00.
†Stories of woods and fields. 1913. World Book Co., $1.00.
†When the world was young. 1913. World Book Co., $.80.
Brown, Julia.
Mermaid's gift and other stories. 1912. Rand, $1.25.*
Browne, Frances.
Granny's wonderful chair. c1900.
There are various editions of this, ranging in price from one

Browne, Frances—*continued.*
by Dutton, at $3.00, to Doubleday's at $1.50, or the Everyman's at $.85.
Browning, Robert.
†Poems. (Cambridge ed.) 1895. Houghton. $3.00.
Bryant, A. C.
Treasury of hero tales. c1920. Crowell, $.75.
Bryant, S. C.
Best stories to tell to children. 1912. Houghton, $2.50.
†How to tell stories to children. 1905. Houghton, $2.00.
New stories to tell to children. 1923. Houghton, $1.75.
†Stories to tell to children. 1907. Houghton, $2.00.
Bryce, C. T.
Fables from afar. c1910. Newson, $.76. (Aldine supplementary readers).
That's why stories. c1910. Newson, $.76. (Aldine supplementary readers).
Bryce, C. T.
See also Spaulding, F. E., jt. author.
Bryce, C. T. and Spaulding, F. E.
†Aldine language series. 1924. Newson.
Buckley, E. F.
†Children of the dawn. 1909. Stokes, $2.50. Same. London, Wells. 7s. 6d.
Budde, L.
See Bay, J. C., *tr.*
Burchill, Georgine and others.
Progressive road to reading. 4v. c1909–1917. Silver, Story steps, $.60; Book 1, $.72; Book 2, $.76; Book 3, $.76.
Burgess, T. W.
Mother West Wind "how" stories. 1924. c1916. Little, $1.00.
Mother West Wind "when" stories. 1924. c1915. Little, $1.00.
Mother West Wind "why" stories. 1923. c1915. Little, $1.00.
Burke, S. J.
Fairy tales for little readers. c1894. Ainsworth; 1924. Parker-Simmons, $.64.
Burlingame, E. W.
Grateful elephant, and other stories; tr. from the Pali. 1923 Yale Univ. Press, $3.00.
Burt, M. E.
†Story of the German Iliad. 1895. Merrill, $.50.*
Burt, M. E. and Ragozin, Z. A.
Herakles, the hero of Thebes and other heroes of myth. 1900. Scribner. $.72.
Butterworth, Hezekiah.
†Zigzag journeys in the Orient. 1882. Estes and Lauriat.
Buxton, E. M. Wilmot-.
See Wilmot-Buxton, E. M.
Byrne, J. A., ***comp.***
Modern Greek fairy tales. c1906. Flanagan, $.40.*
Caballero, Fernan.
Spanish fairy tales. n.d. Burt, $1.00.
Cabot, E. L.
†Ethics for children. c1910. Houghton, $2.00.
Campbell, W. D.
Beyond the border. c1898. N. Y. R. H. Russell.
Same. 4th ed. 1902. London. Constable, 6s.*

Canton, William.
In the reign of King Herla. n.d. Dutton, $2.50. (True annals of fairy land.) Also in Everyman's library, $.80.
Carpenter, E. J.
Long ago in Greece. 1906. Little, $1.50.*
Carpenter, G. R.
See Baker, F. T., jt. author.
Carrick, A. V. L.
Kitty-cat tales. c1907. Lothrop, $1.35.
Carrick, Vallery.
Picture tales from the Russian; tr. by Neville Forbes. n.d. Stokes, $1.25
Carter, M. H., *ed.*
Cat stories retold from St. Nicholas. Century, $1.25.
Cary, Alice and Phoebe.
†Poetical works. c1882. Houghton. (Household ed.), $2.25.
Cary, Mrs. M., *tr.*
French fairy tales. c1887–1903. Crowell, $1.60.
A new edition of "Fairy legends of the French provinces."
Cather, K. D.
Educating by story-telling. 1920. World Book Co., $2.20.
Chadwick, M. L. Pratt-.
See Pratt, M. L.
Chambers, William, *ed.*
Chambers' miscellany of useful and entertaining tracts. n.d. Edinburgh, Wm. and Robert Chambers.
Chandler, A. C.
Pan the piper and other marvellous tales. 1923. Harper, $3.00.
Chandler, Katherine.
In the reign of coyote. 1905. Ginn, $.64. (Once upon a time series.)
Chapin, A. A.
Wonder stories from Wagner. c1898. Harper.
Chaplin, Alethea.
Treasury of fairy tales. n.d. Crowell, $.75.
Children's story garden; collected by a committee of the Philadelphia yearly meeting of the Society of Friends. 1920. Lippincott, $1.50.
Chisholm, Louey.
Enchanted land. 1906. Putnam, $3.00: 1924. Nelson, $2.00.
In fairyland. 1904. Putnam, $2.50.
Chisholm, Louey and Steedman, Amy.
Staircase of stories. 1920. Putman, $3.75.
Cnodzks, A. E. B., *comp.*
Fairy tales of the Slav peasants and herdsmen; tr. by E. J. Harding. 1896. Dodd.
Same, with title Slav fairy tales. 1905. Burt, $1.00.
Chow Leung.
See Davis, M. H.
Christie, A. J.
See Coe, Ida.
Church, A. J.
†Greek story and song. c1903. Macm., $1.75.*
Heroes of chivalry and romance. c1898. Macm., $1.75.*
Clay, Beatrice.
Stories from Le Morte d'Arthur and the Mabinogion. n.d. Dutton, $.60. (King's treasuries of literature series.)
†Stories of King Arthur and the Round Table. 1905. Dutton, $3.00.

Cocke, S. J.
Bypaths in Dixie; folk tales of the South. 1911. Dutton, $2.00.
Coe, F. E.
†First book of stories. 1910. Houghton, $2.00; school ed. $1.40.
†Second book of stories for the story-teller. 1913. Houghton, $2.00; school ed., $1.40.
Coe, Ida and Christie, A. J.
†Story hour readers. Amer. Book Co., 1st. $.60; 2d, $.72; 3d. $.76.
Cole, P. McA.
Heroes of the olden time. 1904. Macm., $.40.
Colum, Padraic.
At the gateways of the day. 1924. Yale Univ. Press, $2.50. (Tales and legends of Hawaii. v. 1).
†Boy in Eirinn. 1913. Dutton, $2.00. (Little schoolmate series.)
Island of the mighty; being the hero stories of Celtic Britain retold from the Mabinogion. 1924. Macm., $2.50.
Peep-show man. 1924. Macm., $1.00.
See also Arabian Nights.
Compton, Margaret, *pseud.* **(Mrs. A. M. Harrison.)**
American Indian fairy tales. c1895. 1910. Dodd, $1.75. New ed. of Snowbird and the water tiger.
Cooke, F. J.
Nature myths and stories for little children. 1895. Rev. ed. 1919. Flanagan, $.50.
Coolidge, Susan.
†Mischief's Thanksgiving. 1909. Little, $1.75.
†New Year's bargain. 1901. Little, $1.75.
†Round dozen. 1906. Little, $1.75.
Cornyn, J. H.
Around the wigwam fire. 1921. Little, $1.50.
When the camp fire burns. 1923. Little, $1.50.
Couch, A. T. Quiller-
See Quiller-Couch, A. T.
Coussens, P. W.
†Child's book of stories. Illus. by Jessie Wilcox Smith. 1911. Duffield, $3.50.
Jade story book: stories from the Orient. 1922. Duffield, $2.00.
Cowles, J. D.
†Art of story telling. 1914. McClurg, $1.00.*
†Indian nature myths. 1920. c1918. Flanagan, $.60.
Cox, J. W.
Tales of ancient Greece. 1905. McClurg, $2.00.
Craik, D. M.
See Mulock, D. M. C.
Crane, Lucy.
See Grimm, J. L. C.
Crane, Walter.
Red Riding Hood's picture book; containing Little Red Riding Hood, Jack and the beanstalk, The forty thieves. n.d. Lane, $1.25.
Crommelin, E. G.
Famous legends adapted for children. 1910. Century, $.85.
Cross, Allen and Statler, N. M.
Story-telling for upper grade teachers. c1918. Row, $1.25.

Cruikshank, George.
Fairy book. 1910. Putnam, $2.00.
Cummings, M. H.
See Foster, M. H., jt. author.
Curry, S. S.
†Little classics for oral English. 1912. Expression Co., $1.25.
Curtin, Jeremiah.
Hero tales from Ireland. 1921. Little, $2.00.
Myths and folk lore of Ireland. n.d. Little, $2.00.
Wonder tales from Russia. c1890–1921. Little, $2.00.
Curtis, E. S.
†Indian days of the long ago. 1921. World Book Co., $1.60.
Curtiss, Phoebe A., *comp.*
†Christmas stories and legends. 1916. Meigs.
Cutler, U. W.
Stories of King Arthur and his knights. Rev. ed. c1904–1924. Crowell, $2.50.
Danielson, F. W.
†Story telling time. c1912. Pilgrim Press, $1.25.
Darton, F. J. H.
Tales of the Canterbury pilgrims, retold from Chaucer and others. n.d. Stokes, $2.50; London. Wells, 7s 6d.
Wonder book of beasts. 1909. Stokes, $2.50; London. Wells. 7s 6d.
Dasent, G. W., *tr.*
Norse fairy tales; selected and adapted from the trans. of G. W. Dasent by F. J. Simmons. London. Routledge; Phila. Lippincott, $2.00.
This contains stories selected from his "Popular Norse Tales" and "Tales from the Fjeld."
Popular tales from the Norse. 1904. Putnam, $2.50*; Dutton, $1.00.*
Davis, M. H. and Chow-Leung.
Chinese fables and stories. 1908. Amer. Book Co., $.52.
DeMorgan, Mary.
On a Pincushion and other fairy tales. 1924. Duffield, $1.75.
See also Nichols, I. P. jt. author.
Dickinson, A. D., and Skinner, A. M.
†Children's book of Christmas stories. 1913. Doubleday, $1.75.
Dillingham, E. T. and Emerson, A. P.
Tell it again stories. c1911. Ginn, $.72.
Djurklo, N. G.
Fairy tales from the Swedish; tr. by H. L. Braekstad. c1901. Stokes, $2.00.
Dodge, M. M.
†Land of pluck. 1907. Century, $1.75.
Doheny, M. A.
Play awhile; a dramatic reader for the 3d school year. 1923. c1916. Little, $.75.
Dole, N. H. *comp.* and *tr.*
White duckling and other stories. 1913. Crowell, $1.50.
A new edition of the "Russian fairy book."
See also Baumbach, Rudolph.
Donahey, M. D.
Tales to be told to children. 1915. Howell, $.75.
Donaldson, E. M.
*Little papoose listens. 1924. Bradley, $1.00.
*Moons of long ago. 1922. Bradley, $1.00.

Douglas, Barbara.
Favorite French fairy tales; retold from the French of Perrault, Mme d'Aulnoy, and Mme. deBeaumont. n.d. N. Y. Dodd.
Douglas, George, *ed.*
†Scottish fairy and folk tales. n.d. Scribner, imported, $1.50. Also pub. by Burt, $1.00.
Duncan-Jones, C. M.
English folklore stories. n.d. London. Soc. for promoting Christian knowledge; N. Y. Macm., $.80.
Dutton, M. B., *tr.*
See Bidpai.
Dyer, F. B. and Brady, M. J.
Merrill readers. c1915. Merrill, 2d, $.72; 3d, $.76.
Dyer, R. O.
What-happened-then stories. 1918. Lothrop, $1.50.
Eastman, C. A. and E. G.
Wigwam evenings; Sioux folk tales retold. 1909. Little, $1.75.
Eastman, E. G.
Indian legends retold. 1924. c1919. Little, $1.60.
Edey, B. O.
Six giants and a griffin. 1903. Harper, $1.25.*
Edgeworth, Maria.
†Waste not, want not and other stories. 1901. Heath, $.60. Also Amer. Book Co., $.68.
Edmison, J. P.
Stories from the Norseland. 1909. Penn, $1.75.
Eells, E. S.
Tales of enchantment from Spain; old Spanish folk lore kept alive in S. America. 1920. Harcourt, $2.00.
Tales of giants from Brazil. 1918. Dodd, $1.50.
Eggleston, Edward.
Queer stories for boys and girls. 1896. Scribner, $1.00.*
Eliot, E. C.
†House on the edge of things. 1923. Beacon Press, $2.00.
Elson, W. H. and Runkel, L. E.
†Elson readers. 1920. Scott, Foresman Co., Book I, $.32; Book 2, $.40.
Emerson, A. P.
See Dillingham, E. T., jt. author.
English, T. D.
Fairy stories and wonder tales. c1897. Hurst, $.35.*
Esenwein, J. B. and Stockard, Marietta.
†Children's stories and how to tell them. 1917. Home Corres. School, $1.50. (Writers' Library.)
Evans, L. B.
†Heroes of Troy. 1924. Bradley, $2.00.
Old time tales. 1922. Bradley, $2.00.
Ewing, J. H.
†Old fashioned fairy tales; Brothers of pity and other tales of beasts and men. n.d. Little, $1.00.*
Fairy stories retold from St. Nicholas. 1906. Century $1.25.
Fairy tales from Brentano; told in English by K. F. Kroeker, c1884. N. Y. Lovell; New ed. 1925. Stokes, $2.50.
Farmer, F. V., *ed.*
Nature myths of many lands. c1910. Amer. Book Co., $.60.
Faulkner, Georgene.
Old English nursery tales. 1920. Daughaday, $1.00.
Story lady's book. c1921. Small, $1.75.

Favorite fairy tales; illus. by Peter Newell. c1907. Harper, $1.75.

Fee, M. H., and others.
†First year book. 1907. World Book Co., $.42.*

Fickett, M. G.
See Stone, G. L., jt. author.

Field, Eugene.
Christmas tales and Christmas verse. Illus- by F. Storer. 1919. c1912. Scribner, $2.50.
†Little book of profitable tales. 1892. Scribner, $1.75.
†Second book of tales. c1896. Scribner, $1.75.

Field, R. M.
Famous fairy tales. c1902. (v. 3 of Young Folks Library, ed. by T. B. Aldrich.)

Field, W. T.
Field first reader. Illus. by M. W. Enright. 1921. Ginn, $.64.
Field second reader. 1922. Ginn, $.64.
Field third reader. 1924. Ginn, $.72.
Quest of the four-leaved clover; adapted from Laboulaye's Abdallah. 1910. Ginn, $.45.
See also Young, E. F., jt. author.

Fielde, A. M.
Chinese fairy tales. c1893. Putnam, $1.75.

Fillmore, Parker H.
Czechoslovak fairy tales. 1919. Harcourt, $2.25.
Laughing prince: a book of Jugoslav fairy and folk tales. 1921. Harcourt, $2.50.
Mighty Mikko; a book of Finnish fairy tales. Illus. by Jan Van Everen. 1922. Harcourt, $2.25.
Shoemaker's apron. 1920. Harcourt, $2.50.

Finger, C. J.
Tales from silver lands. 1924. Doubleday, $1.35.

Finnemore, John.
†Peeps at many lands: Japan. 1907. Macm., $.55.

Firth, E. M.
Stories of old Greece. c1894. Heath, $.75.

Fisher, L. L.
†River dragon's bride. 1922. Abingdon Press, $1.25.

Forbes Neville, *tr.*
See Carrick, Vallery.

Forbush, Wm. B.
†Young folk's book of ideals. 1916. Lothrop, $2.50.

Forty famous fairy tales. 1912. Putnam, $.75.

Foster, M. H. and Cummings, M. H.
Asgard stories; tales from Norse mythology. c1901. Silver, $.72.

Francillon, R. E.
†Gods and heroes; or, The kingdom of Jupiter. 1895. Ginn, $.65.

Frary, M. H.
See Stebbins, C. M., jt. author.

Free, Margaret.
See Treadwell, H. T., jt. author.

Freeman, Mrs. M. E.
See Wilkins, M. E.

Frere, M. E. I.
Old Deccan days; or, Hindoo fairy legends current in Southern India. c1868. Lippincott.
Same. 1924. London. Murray. 7s. 6d.

Friedlander, Gerald, *tr.*
Jewish fairy tales. 1924. London. Scott; N. Y. Bloch.
Jewish fairy book. Illus. by G. W. Hood. c1920. Stokes.
Froelicher, F. M.
Swiss stories and legends. 1917. Macm., $.40. (Everychild series).
Frost, W. H.
Fairies and folk of Ireland. 1900. Scribner. imp.
Fuller, Eunice.
Book of friendly giants. 1914. Century, $3.00.
Fyleman, Rose.
Rainbow cat. 1923. Doran, $2.00.
Gade, Helen and John, *tr.*
Norwegian fairy tales, from the collection of Abjörnsen and Moe. 1924. American Scandinavian Foundation. $2.00.
Gallichan, Mrs. C. G.
See Hartley, C. G.
Gask, Lilian.
Folk tales from many lands. n.d. Crowell. $1.50.*
Treasury of folk tales. 1917. Crowell, $.75.
Gate, E. M.
Broom fairies and other stories. Illus. by Maud and Miska Petersham. 1922. c1917. Yale Univ. Press, $1.00.
Fortunate days. 1922. Yale Univ. Press, $1.00; $2.00,
Punch and Robinetta. 1923. Yale Univ. Press, $2.00.
Gatty, Mrs. Margaret (Scott).
Parables from nature. 1910. Bell; 1912. Macm., $1.00. Also in Everyman's Library, $.80.
Gibbon, J. M.
In the reign of King Cole. n.d. Dutton, $1.50. (True annals of fairyland.) Also in Everyman's Library, $.80.
Gilbert, C. B.
See Arnold, S. L., jt. author.
Glinski, A. J.
Polish fairy tales; tr. by M. A. Biggs. Illus. by Cecile Walton. 1920. Lane, $5.00.
Goddard, Julia.
Fairy tales in other lands. c1892. Hurst. $.50.*
Golden fairy book.
See Jokai and others.
Golden goose, and The three bears. Illus. by L. Leslie Brooke. n.d. Warne, $2.00.
Gould, S. Baring-.
See Baring-Gould, Sabine.
Graham, Stephen, *ed.*
See Sologub, Fedor.
Graves, A. P., *comp.*
Irish fairy book. n.d. Stokes, $1.50.
Grayl, Druid, *pseud.*
Fairy tales from foreign lands. 1918. Oxford. B. H. Blackwell.
Greene, F. N.
Legends of King Arthur and his court. c1901. Ginn, $.60.
Greenwood, Grace. (Mrs. S. J. Lippincott.)
Stories from famous ballads. 1906. Ginn, $.50.
Gregory, A. P., Lady.
Kiltartan wonder book. 1911. Dutton, $1.50

Grierson, E. W.
Children's book of Celtic stories. 1908. Macm., $2.25.
Children's tales from Scottish ballads. 1906. Macm., $2.00.
Scottish fairy book. 1910. Stokes, $1.50.

Griffis, W. E.
†Belgian fairy tales. 1919. Crowell, $1.60.
†Dutch fairy tales. 1918. Crowell, $1.60.
Japanese fairy tales. c1908–1923. Crowell, $1.60.
New ed. of Firefly's lovers and other fairy tales.
Korean fairy tales. 1922. Crowell, $1.60.
†Swiss fairy tales. c1920. Crowell, $1.60.
Unmannerly tiger and other Korean tales. 1911. Crowell, $1.00.
Welsh fairy tales. 1921. Crowell, $1.60.

Grimm, J. L. C. and W. C.
Fairy tales; tr. by Mrs. Edgar Lucas. Illus. by Arthur Rackham. n.d. Lippincott, $2.00.
Fairy tales and household stories; tr. by Mrs. H. B. Paull and L. A. Wheatley. n.d. Warne. $1.50.*
Fairy tales; ed. by Sara E. Wiltse. 2v. 1923. c1895–1896. Ginn, $.76 ea.
Household fairy tales. n.d. Burt, $1.00.
Household stories; tr. from German by Lucy Crane and done into pictures by Walter Crane. 1899. Macm., $1.75.
Household tales. Illus. by R. A. Bell. n.d. Dutton, $.85. (Everyman's library.)
There are several new eds. suitable for library use, published by Harper, McKay, Penn and Rand.

Grinnell, Elizabeth and Joseph.
†Birds of song and story. 1901. Mumford, $1.00.*

Grinnell, G. B.
†Blackfoot lodge tales. c1892. Scribner, $2.50.
†Pawnee hero stories and folk tales. 1904. Scribner, $3.00.
Punishment of the stingy and other Indian stories. c1901. Harper, $1.15.

Griswold Florence.
Hindu fairy tales retold for children. c1918. Lothrop, $1.50.

Grover, E. O.
†Folk lore readers. 1905. Atkinson, Book 1, $.68; Book 2, $.76; Book 3, $.85.

Gruelle, Johnny.
*Friendly fairies. 1919. Volland, $1.25. (Happy children books.)

Grundtvig, Svend.
Danish fairy tales; tr. by Gustave Hein. London. Harrap. c1914. Also Crowell, $2.50.
Fairy tales from afar; tr. from the Danish by Jane Mulley. 1910. Wessels, $1.25.*
See also Bay, J. C., tr.

Guerber, H. A.
†Legends of the Rhine. c1895. 1924. Laidlaw.
†Myths of Greece and Rome. c1893–1921. Amer. Book Co., $2.00.
†Myths of northern lands. c1895. Amer. Book Co., $2.00.
†Legends of the Middle Ages. c1896. Amer. Book Co., $2.00.
†Story of the Romans. c1896. Amer. Book Co., $.72.

Haaren, J. H., *comp.*
Ballads and tales: a 4th reader. c1905. Univ. Pub. Co.; 1924. Newson, $.44. (Golden rod books).
Fairy life: a 3d reader. c1896. Univ. Pub. Co.; 1924. Newson, $.44. (Golden rod books.)
Songs and stories: a 2d reader. (1896.) Univ. Pub. Co; 1924. Newson, $.44. (Golden rod books.)
Haaren, J. H. and Poland, A. B.
†Famous men of Greece. c1904. Amer. Book Co., $.72.
†Famous men of Rome. c1904. Amer. Book Co., $.72.
† Famous men of the middle ages. c1904. Amer. Book Co., $.72.
Hackländer, F. W.
Enchanting and the enchanted. 1900. Lippincott, $.75.*
Hall, Mrs. A. W., *tr.*
Icelandic fairy tales. n.d. Warne, $1.50.* Also a Burt ed., $1.00.
Hall, M. F. and Gilman, M. L.
†Story land: a 2d reader. c1901. Globe Book Co., $.36.*
Harding, Emily J., *tr.*
See Chodzko, A. E. B.
Harper, Wilhelmina.
Story-hour favorites. 1919. Century, $1.75.
Harris, A. V. S.
Favorites from fairyland. 1911. Harper, $.75.
Harris, J. C.
†Little Mr. Thimblefinger and his queer country. 1895. Houghton, $1.50.
Nights with Uncle Remus. c1883. Houghton, $2.25.
†Plantation pageants. 1899. Houghton, $2.00.
†Tar-baby and other rhymes. 1905. Appleton, $2.00.
Told by Uncle Remus. n.d. Doubleday, $2.00.
†Uncle Remus and his friends. c1892–1920. Houghton, $2.25.
Uncle Remus and the little boy. c1910. Small, $1.75.
Uncle Remus, his songs and his sayings. 1908. Appleton, $2.00.
†Uncle Remus returns. c1918. Houghton, $2.00.
See also Ortoli, Frederic.
Harrison, Mrs. A. M.
See Compton, Margaret, *pseud.*
Harrison, C. C. (Mrs. Burton Harrison.)
†Bric-a-brac stories. c1885. Scribner, $1.50.*
Old fashioned fairy book. 1910. Scribner, $1.25.*
Harrison, E. O.
Moon princess. 1905. McClurg, $1.25.*
Prince Silverwings. 1903. McClurg, $1.25.*
Star fairies. 1903. McClurg, $1.25.*
Harrison, Elizabeth.
In story land. n.d. Central Pub. Co., $1.25.*
Hartland, E. S.
English fairy and folk tales. Scribner, imported, $1.50.*
Hartley, C. G. *pseud.* **(Mrs. C. G. Gallichan.)**
Stories from the Greek legends. n.d. Lippincott, $1.25.*
Hartwell, E. C.
Story hour readings. 1921. Amer. Book Co., 5th year, $.88; 6th year, $.88; 7th year, $.92.
Hauff, Wilhelm.
Caravan tales and some others; retol by J. G. Hornstein. 1914. Stokes, $1.35; London. Wells. 7s 6d.
Fairy tales; tr. by P. S. Pinkerton. n.d. McKay, $.75.*

Hawthorne, Nathaniel.
Little Daffydowndilly. n.d. Houghton; $.44, (Riverside literature series).
Tanglewood tales. n.d. Houghton, $1.25; also in Riverside
Wonder book. n.d. Houghton, $1.25; also in Riverside litera-
literature series; also Rand. (Windermere ed.,) $1.75.
ture series; also Rand. (Windermere ed.,) $1.75; and Jacobs.
(Washington Sq. Classics,) $1.50.

Headland, I. T.
†Chinese boy and girl. 1901. Revell, $1.75.

Hearn, Lafacadio, and others.
Japanese fairy tales. c1918–1924. Boni, $1.20 and $1.50.

Hein, Gustave, *tr.*
See Grundtvig, S. H.

Heller, Mrs. T. E. and Bates, Lois.
Little Golden-Hood, and other fairy stories. 1919. c1903. Longmans, $.56.

Henderson, W. J.
Sea yarns for boys. 1907. Harper, $.60.

Herbertson, A. G.
Heroic legends. 1908. Caldwell, $2.00.*

Higginson, T. W.
Tales of the enchanted islands of the Atlantic. 1898. Macm., $2.00.

History of little Goody Two-Shoes. 1904. Heath, $.56.

Hodgkins, Mrs. M. D. H., *ed.* and *comp.*
Atlantic treasury of childhood stories. c1924. Atlantic Mo. Press, $3.50.

Hofer, Andrea.
See Proudfoot, A. F. H.

Holbrook, Florence.
Book of nature myths. c1902. Houghton, $1.25.
Northland heroes. c1905. Houghton, $.56.
Round the year in myth and song. c1897. Amer. Book Co., $.76.

Hornstein, J. G. *tr.*
See Hauff, Whilhelm.

Houghton, L. S.
Russian grandmother's wonder tales. 1906. Scribner, $1.75.

Housman Laurence, *ed.*
See Arabian Nights.

Howard, F. W. *ed.*
Banbury Cross stories. c1909. Merrill, $.60.
Dick Whittington and other stories. 1909. Merrill, $.64.

Howard, V. S., *tr.*
See Lagerlöf, Selma.

Howells, W. D.
Christmas every day and other stories, 1908. Harper, $1.75.

Hoxie, J. L.
Kindergarten story book. 1906. Bradley, $.50.*

Hubbard, W. L.
Chats with Color-kin. Illus. by Donn P. Crane. c1909. [Chicago. Carrol Groff & Co. Press.]; 2d ed. 1919. Theosophical pub. house.

Hull, Eleanor.
Cuchulain. n.d. Crowell, $2.00.

Hume, Fergus.
Chronicles of fairyland. 1911. Lippincott, $1.50.* (Stories all children love series.)

Hutchinson, W. M. L.
Golden porch; a book of Greek fairy tales. 1925. c1967. Longmans, $2.00.
Orpheus with his lute. 1909. Longmans, $1.40.*
Hyde, L. S.
Favorite Greek myths. 1904. Heath, $1.00.
Ingelow, Jean.
†Stories told to a child. 2 v. 1881. Little, $2.50.*
Three fairy tales. 1901. Heath, $.20.*
Island stories retold from St. Nicholas. 1907. Century, $1.25.
Irving, Washington.
†Alhambra. Putnam.
†Spanish papers. Putnam.
Jacobs, Joseph, *ed.*
Book of wonder voyages. 1896. Nutt. 5s; Macm., $1.50.*
Celtic fairy tales. n.d. Putnam, $1.75; Burt, $1.00.
English fairy tales. c1904. Putnam, $1.75; Burt, $1.00.
Europa's fairy book. 1915. Putnam, $1.75.
Indian fairy tales. n.d. Putnam, $1.75; Burt, $1.00.
More Celtic fairy tales. n.d. Putnam, $1.75.
More English fairy tales. 1911. Putnam, $1.75.
James, Grace.
Green willow and other Japanese fairy tales. 1923. Macm., $2.50.
James, Hartwell, *ed.*
Cat and the mouse; a book of Persian fairy tales. c1906. Altemus, $.40.*
Enchanted castle: a book of fairy tales from flower land. Altemus, $.40.*
Jewelled sea: a book of Chinese fairy tales. c1906. Altemus, $.40.*
Magic bed: a book of East Indian fairy tales. 1906. Altemus, $.40.*
Magic jaw bone: a book of fairy tales from the South Sea Islands. 1906. Altemus, $.40.*
Man elephant: a book of African fairy tales. 1906. Altemus $.40.*
Jenkins, O. P.
†Interesting neighbors. 1922. Blakiston, $1.50.
Jenks, Tudor.
Tales of fantasy. c1902. (v. 4 of Young folk's library, ed. by T. B. Aldrich.)
Jerrold, W. C., *ed.*
Big book of fairy tales. 1911. Caldwell, $2.50.*
†Big book of nursery rhymes. c1903. Dutton, $3.00.*
In the reign of King Oberon. n.d. Dutton, $1.50. (True annals of fairyland.) Also in Everyman's Library, $.85.
Jewett, E. M.
Egyptian tales of magic. 1924. Little, $2.00.
Wonder tales from Tibet. c1922. Little, $2.00.
Johnson, A. E., *tr.*
See Perrault. Charles.
Johnson, Clifton, *ed.*
Birch-tree fairy book. 1906. Little, $2.00.
Book of fairy-tale bears. 1913. Houghton, $1.50; school ed., $.90.
Book of fairy-tale foxes. 1914. Houghton, $1.50; school ed., $.90.
Elm-tree fairy book. 1909. Little, $2.00.

Johnson, Clifton—*continued.*
Fir-tree fairy book. 1912. Little, $2.00.
Oak-tree fairy book. 1905. Little, $2.00.
Johnston, A. F.
†Giant scissors. n.d. Page, $1.25; $.50.
In the desert of waiting. Page, $.75. (Jewel series.)
Jester's sword. Page, $.75. (Jewel series.)
Keeping tryst. Page, $.75. (Jewel series.)
Legend of the bleeding heart. Page, $.75. (Jewel series.)
†Little Colonel at boarding school. 1903. Page, $1.50.
†Little Colonel in Arizona. 1904. Page, $1.50.
†Little Colonel's Christmas vacation. 1905. Page, $1.50.
†Little Colonel's hero. 1902. Page, $1.50.
†Little Colonel's house party. 1900. Page, $1.50.
†Mary Ware, the little Colonel's chum. 1906. Page, $1.50.
Rescue of the Princess Winsome. Page, $.75. (Jewel series.)
Three weavers. Page, $.75. (Jewel series.)
Johonnot, James.
†Grandfather's stories. n.d. Amer. Book Co., $.52.
†Stories of heroic deeds for boys and girls. n.d. Amer. Book Co., $.52.
†Stories of the olden time. n.d. Amer. Book Co., $.68.
Jokai, Maurus and others.
Golden fairy book. n.d. Burt, $1.00.
Jones, L. H.
†Jones readers by grades. c1903. 1st and 2d readers. Ginn, $.60 each.
Jorgensen, I. M.
See Ketchum, A. T., jt. author.
Joyce, P. W.
Old Celtic romances, tr. from the Gaelic. 3d ed. 1920. Longmans, $1.80.
Judd, M. C.
†Classic myths. c1894. Rand, $.60.
†Wigwam stories, told by North American Indians. 1906. Ginn, $.92.
Judson, C. I.
Flower fairies. c1915. Rand, $1.25.
Judson, H. P. and Bender, I. C.
†Graded literature readers: 4th, 6th, 7th. c1900. Merrill, $.80 each.
Judson, K. B.
Myths and legends of Alaska. 1911. McClurg, $1.50.*
†Myths and legends of the Pacific Northwest. 1910. McClurg, $1.50.*
Old Crow and his friends; animal adventures based upon Indian myths. Illus. by C. L. Bull. 1921. c1918. Little, $1.75.
Old Crow stories. Illus. by C. L. Bull. 1921. c1917. Little, $1.75.
Keary, Annie and Eliza.
Heroes of Asgard. n.d. Macm., $.50.*
Kennedy, H. A.
New world fairy book. 1922. c1904. Dutton, $2.00.
Ketcham, Henry, *ed.*
Oriental fairy tales. c1905. Burt, $1.00.
Ketchum, A. T., and Jorgensen, I. M.
†Kindergarten gems. c1890. Christian Pub. Co., $1.00.*

Keyes, A. M.
†Five senses; illus. by Jessie Willcox Smith. 1911. Moffat. $1.00.*
Stories and story-telling. 1916. c1911. Appleton, $2.00.

Kipling Rudyard.
Jungle book. Century, $1.50; Doubleday, $1.90.
Just so stories. 1902. Doubleday, $1.90.
†Puck of Pook's Hill. 1906. Doubleday, $1.90.
†Rewards and fairies. 1910. Doubleday, $1.90.
Second jungle book. 1903. Century, $1.50; Doubleday, $1.90.

Kingsley, Charles.
Heroes. Dutton, $.85. (Everyman's library.)

Klingensmith, Annie.
†Household stories for little readers. 1901. Flanagan, $.35.*
†Just stories. 1920. c1917. Flanagan, $.40.
Old Norse wonder tales. 1923. Flanagan, $.60.

Knowles, R. L. and H. G.
See Dasent, G. W.

Kristensen, E. T.
See Bay, J. C.

Kroeker, K. F., *tr.*
See Brentano, Clemens.

Kunos, Ignacz, *comp.*
Forty-four Turkish fairy tales. Illus. by Willy Pogany. 1914. Crowell, $3.00.*
Turkish fairy tales and folk tales; tr. from the Hungarian version by R. N. Bain. 1901. Bullen. Also Burt, $1.00.

Kupfer, G. H.
†Stories of long ago. 1911. Heath, $.75.*

Laboulaye, E. R. L.
Fairy book. c1866. Harper, $1.75.
Fairy tales. n.d. Dutton, $2.50.
Last fairy tales. 1904. c1884. Harper, $2.50.
See also Field, W. T.

Lagerlöf, Selma.
Christ legends; tr. from the Swedish by V. S. Howard. 1908. Holt, $1.50.

Laing, Mrs. C. H. B.
Seven kings of the seven hills. c1872. Winston.*

Landa, Gertrude.
Aunt Naomi. Jewish fairy tales and fables. 1908. Bloch, $1.00.
Jewish fairy tales and legends. 1921. c1919. Bloch, $1.50.

Lang, Andrew.
Aladdin and the wonderful lamp and other stories. 1912. Longmans, $1.25.
Beauty and the beast and other stories. 1910. Longmans, $1.25.
Blue fairy book. 1905. Longmans, $1.75; $1.00; Burt, $1.00.
Blue parrot and other stories. 1923. Longmans, $1.25.
Book of romance. 1902. Longmans, $1.75; $1.00.
Brown fairy book. 1904. Longmans, $1.75; $1.00.
Cinderella, and other stories. 1900. Longmans, $.56.
Crimson fairy book. 1903. Longmans, $1.75; $1.00.
Dick Whittington and other stories. Longmans, $.68.
Elf maiden and other stories. 1910. Longmans, $1.00.
Fairy nurse and other stories. 1923. Longmans, $1.00.
Forty thieves and other stories. 1910. Longmans, $.60.

Lang, Andrew—*continued.*
Golden mermaid and other stories. 1906. Longmans, $.60.
Green fairy book. n.d. Longmans, $1.75; $1.00; Burt, $1.00.
Grey fairy book. 1900. Longmans, $1.75; $1.00.
History of Jack the giant-killer and other stories. 1908. Longmans, $.68.
Invisible prince and other stories. 1912. Longmans, $.60.
King of the waterfalls and other stories. 1923. Longmans, $1.25.
Lilac fairy book. 1910. Longmans, $1.75; $1.00.
Little King Loc and other stories. 1923. Longmans, $1.25.
Little Red Riding-Hood and other stories. 1899. Longmans, $.68.
Little Wildrose and other stories. 1924. Longmans, $1.25.
Magic book and other stories. 1923. Longmans, $1.00.
Magic ring and other stories. 1911. Longmans, $1.00.
Magician's gifts and other stories. 1909. Longmans, $1.25.
Marvellous musician and other stories. 1909. Longmans, $1.25.
My own fairy book. n.d. Longmans, $2.00.
†Nursery rhyme book. 1907. Warne, $2.50.
Olive fairy book. 1907. Longmans, $1.75; $1.00.
Orange fairy book. 1906. Longmans, $1.75; $1.00.
Pink fairy book. 1910. Longmans, $1.75; $1.00.
Pretty Goldilocks and other stories. 1911. Longmans, $.60.
Prince Darling and other fairy stories. 1908. Longmans, $.76.
Princess on the glass hill, and other stories. 1899. Longmans, $.68.
†Red book of animal stories. c1899. 1916. Longmans, $1.75.
Red fairy book. 1904. Longmans, $2.00; $1.00; Burt, $1.00.
Red romance book. 1905. Longmans, $1.75; $1.00.
Satin surgeon and other stories. 1923. Longmans, $1.00.
Sleeping beauty in the wood and other stories. 1899. Longmans, $.68.
Snake prince and other stories. 1923. Longmans, $1.00.
Snow-queen and other stories. 1911. Longmans, $1.25.
Tales of romance. 1911. Longmans, $1.00.
Tales of the Round table. 1923. Longmans, $1.00.
Three dwarfs and other stories. 1910. Longmans, $1.00.
Trusty John and other stories. 1912. Longmans, $1.25.
Twelve huntsmen and other stories. 1910. Longmans, $1.00.
Violet fairy book. 1901. Longmans, $1.75; $1.00.
White doe and other stories. 1923. Longmans, $1.25.
Yellow fairy book. 1906. Longmans, $1.75; $1.00; Burt, $1.00.

Lang, Mrs. L. B.
†All sorts of stories book. 1911. Longmans, $1.75.
†Strange story book. 1913. Longmans, $1.75.

Language readers.
See Baker, F. T. ed.

Lanier, Sidney, *ed.*
Boy's Percy. 1923. c1909. Scribner, $2.25.
Knightly legends of Wales; or, The boy's Maginogion. 1923. c1910. Scribner, $2.25.

Lansing, M. F.
Dramatic readings for schools. 1922. c1914. Macm., $1.00.
Fairy tales. 2v. 1907. Ginn, $.64 ea.
†Page, esquire and knight. c1910. Ginn, $.64.
†Quaint old stories to read and act. c1912. Ginn, $.64.

Lansing, M. F.—*continued.*
†Rhymes and stories. 1907. Ginn, $.64.
†Tales of old England in prose and verse. 1908. Ginn, $.64.
Larned, W. T.
Fairy tales from France. c1920. Volland, $1.35. (Happy children books.)
Leamy, Edmund.
Fairy minstrel of Glenmalure. 1913. Warne, $1.00.
Golden spears and other fairy tales. 1911. Warne, $1.50.
LeFevre, Felicite.
Cock, the mouse and the little red hen. Altemus, $.50; Jacobs, $1.00.
Leland, C. G.
†Algonquin legends of New England. c1884. Houghton, $3.00.
Lewis, C. M.
See Bailey, C. S., jt. author.
Linderman, F. B.
Indian why stories; tales told by the Blackfeet, Chippewa and Cree tribes. 1915. Scribner, $2.50; school ed., $.72.
Indian Old-man stories. 1920. Scribner, $2.50.
Lindsay, Maud.
†More mother stories. 1905. Bradley, $1.50.
†Mother stories. 1907. Bradley, $1.50.
†Story garden for little children. 1913. Lothrop, $1.25.
†Story-teller. 1915. Lothrop, $1.25.
Lindsay, Maud and Poulsson, Emilie.
Joyous travelers. 1919. Lothrop, $2.00.
Lippincott, S. J.
See Greenwood, Grace, pseud.
Litchfield, M. E.
Nine worlds stories from Norse mythology. 1895. Ginn, $.50.*
Lowell, D. O. S.
Jason's quest. 1904. Lothrop, $1.00.*
Lucas, E. M., *tr.*
See Andersen, H. C.; Grimm, J L. C.
†Lütkenhaus, A. M. *ed.*
Plays for school children. c1915. Century, $1.75.
Lummis, C. F.
Pueblo Indian folk stories. 1910. Century, $1.75.
Published in 1894 under the title "Man who married the moon and other Pueblo Indian folk stories."
Lyman, Edna, (Mrs. E. L. Scott.)
Story-telling; what to tell and how to tell it. 1910. McClurg, $1.25.
Mabie, H. W.
Fairy tales every child should know. 1905. Doubleday, $1.75; Also Grossett, $1.00.
†Famous stories every child should know. 1907. Doubleday, $.90. Also Grossett, $1.00.
†Folk tales every child should know. 1910. Doubleday, $.90. Also Grossett, $1.00.
†Heroes and fairies. c1907. Christian Herald, $1.50.
†Heroes every child should know. 1906. Doubleday, $.90. Also Grossett, $1.00.
†Heroines every child should know. 1908. Doubleday, $1.50. Also Grossett, $1.00.
†Legends every child should know. 1906. Doubleday, $.90. Also Grossett, $1.00.

Myths every child should know. 1905. Doubleday, $1.75. Also Grossett, $1.00.
Norse stories retold from the Eddas. 1904. Dodd, $1.25.

MacDonald, George.
Dealings with fairies. London. Routledge.
Light princess and other fairy tales. n.d. Putnam, $1.50.

Macdonell, Anne.
Italian fairy book. 1914. Stokes, $1.50.

Macé, Jean.
Home fairy tales; tr. by Mary L. Booth. 1904. c1867. Harper, $1.50.*

McFee, I. N.
Treasury of flower stories. c1921. Crowell, $.75.
Treasury of myths. c1921. Crowell, $.75.

MacGregor, Mary.
†Stories of King Arthur's knights told to the children. n.d. Dutton, $.50.*

Macleod, Mary.
Book of ballad stories. 1906. Stokes, $1.50. Also Wells. 7s. 6d.

MacManus, Seumas.
Donegal fairy stories. c1900. Doubleday, $2.00.
In chimney corners, 1899. Doubleday, $1.75.

Macmillan, Cyrus.
Canadian fairy tales. 1922. Dodd, $5.00.

MacNair, J. H.
Animal tales from Africa, adapted from Hausa folk lore. Illus. by Harry Rountree. n.d. Wells, 2s, 6d.

McSpadden, J. W.
Stories from Chaucer. n.d. Crowell, $1.75.
Stories from great operas. c1923. Crowell, $2.50.
Stories from Wagner. c1905–1914. Crowell, $2.00.

Magnus, L. A., *tr.*
Russian folk-tales; tr. from Russian of Afanasev. 1916. Dutton, $3.00.

Marden, O. S., *ed.*
Success library. v. 3. c1901. Success Co.

Marshall, Logan, *tr.*
Fairy tales of all nations. 1910. Winston, $2.00.

Martens, F. H., *tr.*
Chinese fairy book; ed. by R. Wilhelm; tr. after original sources by F. H. Martens. c1921. Stokes, $2.50.
See also Stroebe, Clara, *ed.*

Maud, C. E.
Heroines of poetry. 1903. Lane, 5s.*
Wagner's heroes. n.d. Longmans, $1.75.*
Wagner's heroines. n.d. Longmans, $1.75.*

May, Sophie.
Little Prudy's fairy book. Lothrop.

Meigs, Cornelia.
Kingdom of the winding road. 1922. Macm., $1.75.

Mendel, F. E.
†Our little Austrian cousin. 1913. Page, $.60.*

Mendes, Catulle.
Fairy spinning wheel and the tales it spun; tr. from the French by T. J. Vivian. 1919. Four Seas Co., $2.00.
This is an English version of Les contes de Roust.

Messer, C. J.
Next night stories. 1912. Lothrop, $1.00.*

Meyer, Zoe.
Little green door. c1921. Little, $1.00.
Miller, J. M.
†Philippine folklore stories. 1904. Ginn.
Miller, O. B., *ed.*
See My Bookhouse.
Mokrejs, L. P., *tr.*
See Wenig, Adolf.
Molesworth, Mrs. M. L.
†Fairies afield, 1911. Macm., $1.80.*
Morris, Chas.
†Historical tales: Roman. Lippincott.
†Historical tales: English. Lippincott.
The Historical tales were published in 15 v. as a sub. book.
Morris, M. C. D., *tr.*
See Bosschère, Jean de.
Mother Goose rhymes, jingles and fairy tales. n.d. Altemus, $1.00; $.40.
Mother Goose's nursery rhymes, tales and jingles. n.d. Warne. $2.00; $.60.
Mulock, D. M.
Fairy book. n.d. Harper, $1.00; Nelson, $1.60.
Murphy, Marguerite.
Necklace of jewels. c1918. Page, $1.35.
Murray, Clara.
†Story book treasures. c1913. Little, $1.25.
My Bookhouse. 6v. Ed. by Olive Beaupré Miller. c1920. Bookhouse for Children, $30.00.
Newman, D. S. *See* Riggs, R. C.
Nichols, I. P., and DeMorgan, Mary.
Princess Girlikin; or, The magic thimble, and other fairy tales. 1892. Dutton.
With the exception of the title-story, this is the same as DeMorgan's "On a pincushion." 1922. Duffield.
Nixon-Roulet, M. F.
Indian folk tales. c1911. Amer. Book Co. $.56.
Japanese folk stories and fairy tales. 1908. Amer. Book Co., $.56.
Nordau, M. S.
Dwarf's spectacles, and other fairy tales; tr. by M. J. Safford. 1905. Macm., $.75.*
Noyes, Ella.
Saints of Italy. 1901. London, Dent; N. Y., Dutton.
Noyes, M. B.
Twilight stories. c1917. Simmons-Peckham, $.88.
Nursery tales. 1900. McKibbin.
Norton, C. E., *ed.*
†Heart of oak books. v. 1–7. 1899. Heath. v. 1, $.25; v. 2, $.35; v. 3, $.40; v. 4, $.45; v. 5, $.50; v. 6; $.55; v. 7, $.60.
Nyblom, Helena.
Jolly Calle and other Swedish fairy tales. 1912. Dutton, $2.50.
O'Grady, Alice, and Throop, Francis.
†Teachers' story teller's book. 1912. Rand, $1.25.
Olcott, F. J.
Book of elves and fairies. Illus. by Milo Winter. c1918. Houghton, $3.00.
†Good stories for great holidays. 1914. Houghton, $3.00.
Red Indian fairy book. c1917. Houghton, $3.00.

Olcott, F. J.—*continued.*
Tales of the Persian genii. Illus. by Willy Pogany. 1917. Houghton, $3.00.
Wonder garden. c1919. Houghton, $3.00.
See also Arabian nights.
Olcott, F. J. and Pendleton, Amena.
†Jolly book for boys and girls. c1915. Houghton, $3.00.
Olcott, H. M.
Whirling king and other French fairy tales. 1920. Holt, $1.50.
***Old,** old tales retold. c1923. Volland.
Orcutt, W. D.
Princess Kallisto and other tales of the fairies. 1911. Harper, $1.50.*
Ortoli, Frederic.
Evening tales; tr. by Joel Chandler Harris. 1911. Scribner, $1.00.*
O'Shea, M. V., *ed.*
Old world wonder stories. c1901. Heath, $.60.
Six nursery classics. 1904. Heath, $.56.
Ozaki, Y. T.
Japanese fairy book. 1904. Dutton, $2.00; Burt, $1.00.
Partridge, E. N.
Glooscap, the great chief, and other stories of the Micmacs. c1913. Macm., $1.25.
Partridge, E. N. and G. E.
†Story-telling in home and school. 1914. Sturgis & Walton.
Patten, Wm., *ed.*
†Junior classics. 10 v. 1912. Collier.
Patterson, A. deC.
Enchanted bird. 1922. c1917. Penn, $.50.
Paull, H. B., *tr.*
See Andersen, H. E. and Grimm, J. L. C.
Peabody, J. P.
Old Greek folk stories. n.d. Houghton, $.48. (Riverside literature series.)
Pearson, Adelaide.
Laughing lion and other stories. c1921. Dutton, $2.00.
Peck, L. B.
Stories for good children. c1920. Little, $1.50.
Peers, Mrs. C. R.
Saints in story. 1910. Macm., $1.50.*
Perdue, H. A. and Allison, S. B.
Story in primary instruction. c1902. Flanagan.
[**Perkins, Mrs. L. F.,** *ed.*]
Twenty best fairy tales of Hans Andersen, Grimm and Miss Mulock. c1907. Stokes, $1.50.
Perrault, Charles.
Fairy tales. n.d. Estes, $1.50.* Also Small.
Old-time stories; tr. from the French by A. E. Johnson. Illus. by W. Heath Robinson. 1921. Dodd, $5.00.
Tales of Mother Goose as first collected in 1696. A new tr. by Charles Welsh. 1902. Heath, $.20.*
Tales of passed times. n.d. Dutton, $.45.*
Pinkerton, P. S., *tr.*
See Hauff, Wilhelm.
Pitman, N. H.
Chinese fairy stories. 1910. Crowell, $1.00.*
Chinese fairy tales. c1903. Crowell, $1.60.

Pitman, N. H.—*continued.*
Chinese wonder book. Illus. by Li Chu-T'ang. 1919. Dutton, $3.00.
Pitré, Giuseppe.
Swallow book; tr. by Ada W. Camehl. c1913. Amer. Book Co., $.52.
Pleasanton, L. M.
Fairyland of opera. 1923. Penn, $2.00.
Poland, A. B.
See Haaren, J. H., jt. author.
Polevoi, N. A.
Russian fairy tales; tr. by R. N. Bain. n.d. Burt, $1.00.
Pope, Katharine.
†Hawaii the rainbow land. 1924. Crowell, $3.00.
Potter, M. C.
Pinafore pocket story book. 1922. Dutton, $2.00.
Poulsson, Emilie, *comp.*
†In the child's world. 1906. Bradley, $2.00, and $2.50.
See also Lindsay, Maud.
Poulsson, Emilie and Laura E., *tr.*
Top of the world stories for boys and girls; tr. from the Scandinavian languages. 1916. Lothrop, $1.50.
Powers, Mabel.
Around an Iroquois story fire. 1923. Stokes, $1.00.
Pratt, M. L.
†Fairyland of flowers. n.d. Educ. Pub. Co.
Myths of Old Greece. 3 v. n.d. Educ. Pub. Co., v. 1, $.40; v. 2, $.60; v. 3, $.60.
Legends of Norseland. c1894. Educ. Pub. Co., $.60.*
Legends of the red children. c1897. Amer. Book Co., $.30.*
Proudfoot, A. H. F., *tr.*
Child's Christ tales. 1922. Flanagan.
Pumphrey, M. B.
†Stories of the pilgrims. c1912. Rand, $1.25.
Pyle, Howard.
†Pepper and salt. c1885. Harper, $.200.
Twilight land. 1895. Harper, $1.75.
Wonder clock. c1887. Harper, $2.00.
Pyle, Katharine.
Counterpane fairy. 1898. Dutton, $1.50.
Fairy tales from far and near. 1922. Little, $2.00.
Fairy tales from many lands. 1911. Dutton, $2.00.
Mother's nursery tales. 1918. Dutton, $2.50.
†Prose and verse for children. c1899. Amer. Book Co., $.60.
Tales of folk and fairies. c1919. Little, $2.00.
Tales of wonder and magic. c1920. Little, $2.00.
Where the wind blows. c1902. Dutton, $2.00.
Wonder tales retold. 1916. Little, $2.00.
Quiler-Couch, A. T.
Fairy tales far and near, retold by Q. c1895 Stokes. Same, 1904. Cassell.
Sleeping beauty and other fairy tales from the old French. retold. Illus. by Dulac. 1910. Doran, $5.00.
Quinn, E. V., *tr.*
See Segovia, Gertrude.
Quiroga, Horacio.
South American jungle tales. 1922. Duffield, $1.75.
Rabelais, Francois.
Three good giants.

Ragozin, Z. A.
See Burt, M. E.
Rhys, Ernest, *comp.*
Fairy gold. 1906. Dutton, $2.50.* Everyman's Library, $.85.
Richards, L. E.
Golden windows. n.d. Little, $1.65.
†Joyous story of Toto. 1900. Little, $1.75.
†Little master. c1913. Estes.
Published in 1922 by Page with title "Our little feudal cousin."
Silver crown. 1921. c1906. Little, $.65.
†Toto's merry winter. 1900. Little, $1.75.
Riggs, R. C.
Animal stories from Eskimo land; adapted from collection of D. S. Newman. 1923. Stokes, $1.00.
Roberts, G. E. T.
†Flying plover. 1909. Page, $1.00.*
Rolfe, W. J., *ed.*
†Fairy tales in prose and verse. c1889. Harper. Also Amer. Book Co., $.72.
Rolleston, T. W.
High deeds of Finn. Crowell, $1.75.
Roulet, M. F. Nixon-
See Nixon-Roulet, M. F.
Rouse, W. H. D.
Talking thrush and other tales from India, 1898, Dutton, $1.50.*
Runkel, L. E.
See Elson, W. H., jt. author.
Ruskin, John.
King of the Golden River and other wonder stories. Houghton. (Riverside literature series); Lippincott, $.75.
Safford, M. J., *tr.*
See Nordau, M. S.
Saint Nicholas Magazine. N. Y. Century Co.
See also Fairy stories retold; Carter. Cat stories retold; Island stories retold; Stories of classic myths retold.
Sawyer, Ruth.
This way to Christmas. c1916. Harper, $3.00.
Schoolcraft, H. R.
Indian fairy book. c1916. Stokes, $2.50.
Scott, Mrs. E. L.
See Lyman, Edna.
Scudder, H. E.
†Bodley's telling stories. 1881. c1877. Houghton, $3.00.
Book of folk stories. c1887. Houghton, $1.00.
Book of legends. c1899. Houghton, $1.00. (Riverside literature series)
†Children's book. c1881. Houghton, $5.00.
†Doings of the Bodley family in town and country. 1895. Houghton, $3.00.
Dream children. n.d. Houghton, $.65.
Fables and folk stories. c1906–1910. Illus. ed. Houghton. 2.00 & $.85.
Title page of this ed. reads "Book of fables and folk stories."
Seven little people and their friends. c1862. Houghton, $.65.
Seegmiller, W.
See Van Sickle, J. H., jt. author.
Segovia, Gertrudis.
Spanish fairy book, tr. by E. V. Quinn. 1918. Stokes, $1.50.

Segur, Sophie, Comtesse de.
French fairy tales. n.d. Winston, $.50.*
Old French fairy tales. c1920. Penn, $5.00.
Seton, E. T.
†Woodland tales. 1921. Doubleday, $2.00.
†Woodland myth and fable. 1905. Century, $1.75.
Sexton, Bernard.
Gray wolf stories. c1921. Macm., $1.50.
Shaw, C. D.
†Stories of the ancient Greeks. c1903. Ginn, $.80.
Shedlock, M. L.
Art of the storyteller. 1915. Appleton, $2.25.
Eastern stories and legends. c1920. Dutton, $2.00.
Sholt, A. M.
Faery tales of Weir. Illus. by K. Pyle. c1918. Dutton, $2.00.
Silber, W. S. ***comp.***
See Baumbach, Rudolph.
Silver fairy book, 1895. Putnam, also Burt, $1.00.
Simmons, F. J. ***comp.***
See Dasent, G. W.
Singleton, Esther, ***ed.***
Goldenrod fairy book. 1913. Dodd. $2.00.*
Wild flower fairy book. 1910. Dodd, $1.25.
Skinner, Ada and Eleanor, ***comp. and ed.***
†Emerald story book. 1921. c1915. Duffield.
†Garnet story book. c1920. Duffield, $2.00.
†Topaz story book. 1921. Duffield. $2.00.
†Turquoise story book. 1918. Duffield, $2.00.
†Pearl story book. 1921. Duffield, $2.00.
†Very little child's book of stories. 1923. Duffield, $3.50.
Skinner, A. M.
See also Dickinson, A. D.
Skinner, C. M.
†Myths and legends of flowers, trees, fruits and plants. 1911. Lippincott, $3.00.
Skinner, E. L. and A. M.
Merry tales. c1915. Amer. Book Co., $.52.
Nursery tales from many lands. Illus. by B. F. Wright. c1917. Scribner, $.72 and $.90.
Slosson, A. T.
†Story-tell Lib. 1922. c1900. Scribner, $.60.
Sly, W. J.
†World stories retold, with practical suggestions for telling. 1922. c1914. Amer. Baptist Pub. Soc., $1.50.
Smith, E. S., ***ed.***
Good old stories for boys and girls. 1919. Lothrop, $2.00.
†More mystery tales for boys and girls. c1922. Lothrop, $2.00.
†Mystery tales for boys and girls. c1917. Lothrop, $2.00.
Smith, N. A.
See Wiggin, K. D., jt. author.
Sologub, Fedor.
Sweet scented name and other fairy tales, fables and stories; ed. by Stephen Graham. 1915. Putnam, $1.50.
Spaulding, F. E., and Bryce, C. T.
†Aldine readers: 2d reader. Newson, $.76.
See also Bryce, C. T.
Stafford, A. O.
Animal fables from the dark continent. c1906. Amer. Book Co., $.52.

Stanley, A. A.
Animal folk tales. c1916. Amer. Book Co., $.72.
Statler, N. M.
See Cross, Allen, jt. author.
Stebbins, C. M.
Sunken city and other stories; retold by M. H. Frary and C. M. Stebbins. 1919. Bradley.
Third reader. 1912. Amer. Book Co., $.76.
Steedman, Amy.
See Chrisholm, Louey, jt. author.
Steel, F. A.
Tales of the Punjab told by the people. 1894. Macm., $1.50.
Steele, Robert, *tr.* and *comp.*
Russian garland of fairy tales; being Russian folk legends, tr. from a collection of chap books in Moscow. 1916. McBride, $1.50.
Stein, Evaleen.
When fairies were friendly. c1922. Page, $1.65.
Stevenson, Augusta.
Plays for the home. 1913. Houghton, $1.25.*
This book was first published with the title Children's Classics in dramatic form: book 3.
Stewart, Mary.
Once upon a time. 1912. Revell, $1.75.
Tell me a hero story. c1916. Revell, $1.75.
Stockard, Marietta.
See Esenwein, J. B., jt. author.
Stocking, J. T.
†Golden goblet. 1914. Pilgrim Press, $1.25.
City that never was reached and other stories for children. c1911. Pilgrim Press, $1.25.
Stockton, F. R.
Bee-man of Orn and other fanciful tales. 1887. Scribner, $1.60.
†Fanciful tales. 1894. Scribner, $.50.*
Floating prince and other fairy tales. 1889. Scribner, $2.00.
†Queen's museum. 1906. Scribner, $3.50.
Ting-a-ling tales. 1869. Scribner, $1.00.
Stone, G. L. and Fickett, M. G.
†Trees in prose and poetry. 1902. Ginn.
Stone, Mary, *ed.*
†Children's stories that never grow old. c1908. Reilly & B. $1.00.*
Stories of classic myths; retold from St. Nicholas. 1909. Century, $1.25.
Storr, Francis.
†Half a hundred hero tales of Ulysses and the men of old. 1911. Holt, $1.35.*
Storr, Francis and Turner, Hawes.
Canterbury chimes; or, Chaucer tales retold for children. 1917. Little, $.75.
†Storytellers' magazine. June 1913–Dec. 1917. v. 1–5 (new series). N. Y. Storytellers' Pub. Co. [Ceased Publication.]
Strettell, Alma.
See Sylva, Carmen.
Stroebe, Clara, *ed.*
Danish fairy book; tr. by F. H. Martens. 1922. Stokes, $2.50.
Norwegian fairy book; tr. by F. H. Martens. c1922. Stokes, $2.50.

Stroebe, Clara, *ed.—continued.*
Swedish fairy book; tr. by F. H. Martens. 1921. Stokes, $2.50.
Strong, F. L.
†All the year round. 4 v. 1920. Ginn, ea. $.36.*
Sylva, Carmen and Strettell, Alma.
Legends from river and mountain. Illus. by L. H. Robinson, 1896. Allen.
Tales for bedtime. 1923. Putnam, $1.75.
Tanner, Dorothy.
Legends from the red man's forest. 1895. Flanagan, $.30.*
Tappan, E. M., *ed.*
†Adventures and achievements. n.d. Houghton. (Children's hour, v. 8.)
†Book of humor. (Children's hour. v. 13.) c1916. Houghton.
Folk stories and fables. n.d. Houghton, (Children's hour, v. 1.)
Golden goose. c1905. Houghton, $1.50.
†Modern stories. n.d. Houghton. (Children's hour, v. 10.)
Myths from many lands. n.d. Houghton. (Children's hour, v. 2.)
Old ballads in prose. 1901. Houghton, $1.10; Little, $2.25.
†Old fashioned stories and poems. n.d. Houghton. (Children's hour, v. 6.)
†Stories from seven old favorites. n.d. Houghton. (Children's hour, v. 5.)
Stories from the classics. n.d. Houghton. (Children's hour, v. 3.)
†Stories of legendary heroes. n.d. Houghton. (Chldren's hour, v. 4.)
Children's hour, of which eight of the preceding entries are a part, is published in 15 volumes by Houghton as a subscription book.
Taylor, Morgan.
Thrings of the dark mountain. Illus. by Irene M. Larson and Harold Sichel. 1924. c1922–24. Balch.
Thomas, M. R., *comp.*
†Young folk's book of mirth. 1924. Lothrop, $2.00.
Thomas, W. J.
Welsh fairy book. c1908. Stokes, $1.50.
Thorne-Thomsen, Gudrun.
†Birch and the star, and other stories. c1915. Row.
East o' the sun and west o' the moon, with other Norwegian folk tales. c1912. Row, $.60.*
Thorpe, Benjamin, *ed.*
Yule tide stories. 1892. Macm., $.80.*
Three little pigs and Tom Thumb. 1906. Warne, $.80. (Leslie Brooke's children's books.)
Throop, Francis.
See O'Grady, Alice, jt. author.
Thrum, T .G.
†Hawaiian folk tales. c1912. McClurg, $2.00.
Toksvig, Signe, *ea.*
Sec Andersen, H. C.
Tolstoi, L. N.
†More tales from Tolstoi; tr. by R. N. Bain. c1903. Brentano's, $.50.*
†Tales from Tolstoi; tr. by R. N. Bain. 1901. Page, $1.50.*

Tolstoi, L. N.—*continued.*
†Twenty-three tales, tr. by L. and A. Maud. 1907. Funk, $.75. Same 1900–1919. Oxford 2s. (World's Classics).
Townsend, G. T., *ed.*
See Arabian nights.
Treadwell, H. T. and Free, Margaret.
†Reading literature: the primer. 1910. Row, $.32.*
True Annals of fairyland. *See* Canton, William. In the reign of King Herla; Gibbon, J. M. In the reign of King Cole; Jerrold, W. C. In the reign of King Oberon.
Turner, Hawes.
See Storr, Frances.
Turpin, E. L. L., *ed.*
See Andersen, H. C.
Tweed, Anna, *ed.*
Fairy tales everyone should know. c1920. Bradley, $1.00.
Tyler, A. C.
Twenty-four unusual stories. 1921. Harcourt, $2.00.
Underhill, Z. D.
Dwarfs' tailor and other fairy tales. c1896. Harper, $1.75.
Valentine Laura, *ed.*
Old, old fairy tales. n.d. Warne, $1.50;* Burt, $1.00.
Van Dyke, Henry.
†Blue flower. 1916. c1902. Scribner, $1.25.
Van Sickle J. H. and Seegmiller, Wilhelmina.
Riverside readers. v.1–4. 1911–12. Houghton, 1, $.35; 2, $.40; 3, $.50; 4, $.55.
Vivian, C. J., *tr.*
See Mendes, Catulle.
Voltaire, M. A. de, and others.
See Silver fairy book.
Wade, M. H.
Indian fairy tales as told to the little children of the wigwam. 1906. Wilde, $1.00.*
Walker, A. P. ,
Sandman's goodnight stories. Illus. by R. C. Chase. c1921. Harper, $.60.
Wardrop, Majory, *tr.*
Georgian folk tales. 1894. London. Nutt.
Washburne, M. F.
Indian legends. c1915. Rand, $.45.*
Old fashioned fairy tales; retold from the poetic version of Tom Hood. c1909. Rand, $1.25.*
Welsh, Charles, *ed.*
Fairy tales children love. 1910. Dodge, $1.25.*
†Stories children love. c1909. Dodge, $1.25.*
Wenig, Adolf.
Beyond the giant mountains; tales from Bohemia, tr. by L. P. Mokrejs. c1923. Houghton, $2.00.
Werner, E. S., *comp.*
†Werner's recitations, no. 3. n.d. Werner, $.60.
Wheeler, Post.
Russian wonder tales. 1921. c1912. Century.
Wheelock, E. M.
Stories of Wagners operas for children. c1907–1910. Bobbs.
Whitney, A. D. T.
†Faith Gartney's girlhood. Boston. Houghton, $1.25.
Whittier, J. G., *ed.*
†Child life in rose. c1875. Osgood. Same. Houghton, $2.25.

Whittier, J. G.
†Poems. n.d. Houghton, $2.00. (Cambridge ed.)
Wickes, F. G.
Beyond the rainbow bridge. 1924. Bradley, $1.75.
Happy holidays. 1921. Rand, $.90.
Wiggin, K. D., and Smith, N. A.
Fairy ring. 1906. Doubleday, $1.50.
Magic casements. 1911. Doubleday, $1.75.
†Story hour. n.d. Houghton, $1.50.
Tales of laughter. 1908. Doubleday, $1.75.
Tales of wonder. 1909. Doubleday, $1.75.
Talking beasts. 1911. Doubleday, $1.50.
See also Arabian Nights.
Wilde, Oscar.
Fairy tales. 1913. Putnam, $1.25.
Wilhelm, R.
See Martens, F. H.
Wilkins, M. E. (Mrs. M. E. W. Freeman.)
†Pot of gold and other stories, Lothrop, $1.50.
†Young Lucretia and other stories. Harper, $1.75.
Williams Herschel.
Fairy tales from folklore. c1908. Moffat, $1.00.*
Williston, T. P.
Japanese fairy tales. Illus. by Sanchi O. Gawi. 2 v. 1904–11. Rand, Ser. 1, $.90; 2, $.90.
Wilmot-Buxton, E. M.
†Stories of early England. Crowell, $.50.*
Stories from old French romance. n.d. Stokes, $.75.*
Stories of Norse heroes from the Eddas and Sagas. n.d. Crowell, $2.00.
Stories of Persian heroes. Crowell, $1.75.
Wilson, G. L.
Myths of the red children. 1907. Ginn, $.76.
Wilson, Mrs. L. L. W.
†Nature study in elementary schools: Reader. 1898. Macm., $.35.*
Wiltse, S. E., *ed.*
†Folklore stories and proverbs. 1900. Ginn, $.60.
Hero folk of ancient Britain. c1911. Ginn, $.45.*
†Kindergarten stories and morning talks. 1896. Ginn, $1.00.
See also Grimm, S. L. C.
Winnington, Laura.
Outlook fairy book. 1903. Macm., $1.25.
Yeats. W. B., *ed.*
Irish fairy and folk tales. 1910. Scribner, $1.50;* Burt, $1.00.
Yonge, C. M.
Book of golden deeds, Dutton, $.85. (Everyman's Library.)
Young, E. R.
Algonquin Indian tales. 1915. c1903. Abingdon, $1.50.
Young, E. F. and Field, W. T.
Literary readers. Bk. 2. 1916. Ginn.
Young, Martha.
Behind the dark pines. 1912. Appleton, $1.50.*
Plantation bird legends. 1916. c1902. Appleton.
Young folks library; ed. by T. B. Aldrich. 1902. Boston., Hall and Locke.
This was published in 20 v. as a subscription book.
Zitkala-Sa.
Old Indian legends. 1901. Ginn, $.60.

LISTS FOR STORY TELLERS

Geographical and Racial

Africa
Bateman, G. W. Zanzibar tales. 1904.
Bourhill, E. J., and Drake, J. B. Fairy stories from South Africa. 1910.
‡Fleming, R. M. Round the world in folk tales. 1925.
James, Hartwell. Man elephant. 1906.
Macnair, J. H. Animal tales from Africa.
‡ Patten, William. Junior classics. v. 2. 1912.
Stafford, A. O. Animal fables from the dark continent. 1906.
‡Wiggin, K. D. and Smith, N. A. Magic casements. 1911.
See also Negro stories.

Alaska
See Eskimo; Indians of North America.

America
See Canada; Eskimo; Indians of North America; Mexico; Negroes; South America; United States.

Arabia
Arabian nights' entertainments.
Field, W. T. Quest of the four-leaved clover. 1910.
See also Orient.

Australia
‡Fleming, R. M. Round the world in folk tales. 1925.
‡ Patten, William. Junior classics. v. 1. 1912.

Azores Islands
Eells, E. S. Islands of magic. 1922.

Belgium
Bosschère, Jean de. Christmas tales of Flanders. 1917.
Bosschère, Jean de. Folk tales of Flanders. 1918.
Griffis, W. E. Belgian fairy tales. 1919.

Bohemia
Lee, James and Carey, J. T. Silesian folk tales.
Wenig, Adolf. Beyond the giant mountains. 1923.
See also Czechoslovakia.

Canada
Macmillan, Cyrus. Canadian fairy tales. 1922.
Macmillan, Cyrus. Canadian wonder tales.
‡Skinner, C. M. Myths and legends beyond our borders. 1899.

China
Davis, M. H. and Chow-Leung. Chinese fables and folk stories. 1908.
Fielde, A. M. Chinese nights entertainment. 1893.
Fisher, L. L. River dragon's bride. 1922.
‡Fleming, R. M. Round the world in folk tales. 1925.
Headland, A. T. Chinese boy and girl. 1901.
James, Hartwell. Jewelled sea. 1906.
Martens, F. W. Chinese fairy book. 1921.
Olcott, F. J. Wonder tales from China seas. 1925.

China—*continued.*
‡Patten, William. Junior classics. v. 1. 1912.
‡Pearson, Adelaide. Laughing lion. 1921.
Pitman, N. H. Chinese fairy tales. 1903.
Pitman, N. H. Chinese fairy stories. 1910.
Pitman, N. H. Chinese wonder book. 1919.
‡Wiggin, K. D. and Smith, N. A. Tales of laughter. 1908.
‡Wiggin, K. D. and Smith, N. A. Tales of wonder. 1908.
See also Korea.

Cossack
Bain, R. N. Cossack fairy tales. 1899.
‡Wiggin, K. D. and Smith, N. A. Tales of laughter. 1908.
See also Russia.

Croatia
Ballic-Mazuranic, I. Croatian tales of long ago. 1925.

Czechoslovakia
Baudis, Josef. Czech folk tales. 1917.
Fillmore, P. H. Czechoslovak fairy tales. 1919.
Fillmore, P. H. Shoemaker's apron. 1920.
‡Pyle, Katherine. Tales of wonder and magic. 1920.
See also Bohemia.

Dalmatia
‡Martens, F. H. Wonder tales from far away. 1925.
‡Wiggin, K. D. and Smith, N. A. Tales of wonder. 1909.

Denmark
Andersen, H. C. Stories and tales.
Bay, J. C. Danish fairy and folk tales. 1899.
Grundtvig, S. H. Danish fairy tales. 1914.
Patten, William. Junior classics. v. 1. 1912.
‡Perkins, L. F. Twenty best fairy tales. 1907.
Stroebe, Clara and Martens, F. H. Danish fairy book. 1922.
‡Tappan, E. M. Folk stories and fables.

Dutch
See Holland.

East India
Babbitt, E. C. Jataka tales. 1912.
Babbitt, E. C. More Jataka tales. 1922.
Bidpai. Tortoise and the geese and other fables. 1908.
Bradley-Birt, F. B. Bengal fairy tales. 1920.
Burlingame, E. W. Grateful elephant and other stories. 1923.
‡Fleming, R. M. Round the world in folk tales. 1925.
Frere, M. E. I. Old Deccan days. c1868.
Griswold, Florence. Hindu fairy tales. 1918.
Jacobs, Joseph. Indian fairy tales.
Jacobs, Joseph. More Indian fairy tales.
James, Hartwell. Magic bed. 1906.
Kipling, Rudyard. Jungle book.
Kipling, Rudyard. Just so stories. 1902.
Kipling, Rudyard. Second jungle book. 1903.
‡Patten, William. Junior classics. v. 1–2. 1912.
‡Pyle, Katherine. Tales of wonder and magic. 1920.
Rouse, W. H. D. Talking thrush and other tales from India. 1899.
Shedlock, M. L. Eastern stories and legends. 1920.
‡Skinner, E. L. Merry tales. 1915.
Steel, F. A. Tales of the Punjab. 1894.
‡Tappan, E. M. Folk stories and fables. 1907.
‡Tappan, E. M. Myths from many lands. 1907.

East China—*continued.*

‡Wiggin, K. D. and Smith, N. A. Magic casements. 1911.
‡Wiggin, K. D. and Smith, N. A. Talking beasts. 1911.
‡Wiggin, K. D. and Smith, N. A. Tales of laughter. 1908.
‡Wiggin, K. D. and Smith, N. A. Tales of wonder. 1909.
Williston, T. P. Hindu fairy tales. 1923.
Wilson, Richard. Indian story book. 1914.

Egypt

Brooksbank, F. H. Legends of ancient Egypt. 1924.
Jewett, E. M. Egyptian tales of magic. 1922.

England

Baring-Gould, Sabine. Old English fairy tales.
‡Church, A. J. Heroes of chivalry and romance.
Clay, Beatrice. Stories of King Arthur and the Round Table. 1905.
Cutler, U. W. Stories of King Arthur. 1924.
Duncan-Jones, C. M. English folklore stories.
Ebbutt, M. T. Hero myths and legends of the British race.
Faulkner, Georgene. Old English nursery tales. 1920.
Greenwood, Grace (*pseud.*). Merrie England.
Hartland, E. S. English folk and fairy tales.
Jacobs, Joseph. English fairy tales. 1904.
Jacobs, Joseph. More English fairy tales. 1911.
Kipling, Rudyard. Puck of Pook's Hill. 1906.
Kipling, Rudyard. Rewards and fairies.
Lang, Andrew. Tales of the Round Table. 1923.
Lanier, Sidney. Boy's Percy. 1909.
Lansing, M. F. Tales of old England.
Pyle, Howard. Merry Adventures of Robin Hood.
Rhys, Ernest. English fairy book.
Rhys, Ernest. Fairy gold.
Steel, Mrs. F. A. English fairy tales. 1918.
Tregarthen, Enys. North Cornwall fairies and legends. n.d.
‡Wiggin, K. D. and Smith, N. A. Tales of laughter. 1908.
‡Wiggin, K. D. and Smith, N. A. Talking beasts. 1911.
Wilmot-Buxton, E. M. Stories of early England.
Wiltse, S. E. Hero folk of ancient Britain. 1911.

Eskimo

Bayliss, C. K. Treasury of Eskimo tales. 1922.
Judson, K. B. Myths and legends of Alaska. 1911.
Riggs, R. C. Animal stories from Eskimo land. 1923.

Finland

Baldwin, James. Sampo. 1912.
Fillmore, P. H. Mighty Mikko. 1922.
Fillmore, P. H. Wizard of the north. 1923.
Poulsson, Emilie and L. E. Top of the world stories. 1916.
Thorne-Thomsen, Gudrun. Birch and the star. 1915.

Flanders

See Belgium.

France

Aulnoy M. C. J. Children's fairy-land. 1919.
Aulnoy, M. C. J. Fairy tales. 1919.
Cary, Mrs. M. French fairy tales. c1887–1908.
Douglas, Barbara. Favourite French fairy tales. 1921.
Duncan-Jones, C. M. Stories from France. 1921.
Laboulaye, E. R. L. Fairy book.
Larned, W. T. Fairy tales from France. 1920.

France—*continued.*

Macé, Jean. Home fairy tales. c1867.
Mendes, Catulle. Fairy spinning wheel. 1919.
Olcott, H. M. Whirling king and other French fairy tales. 1920.
‡Ortoli, Frederic. Evening tales. 1911.
‡Patten, William. Junior classics. v. 1. 1912.
Perrault, Charles. Fairy tales.
Perrault, Charles. Old-time stories. 1921.
Perrault, Charles. Tales of Mother Goose. 1902.
Quiller-Couch, A. T. Sleeping beauty and other fairy tales. 1910.
Segur, Sophie. Old French fairy tales. 1920.
Spurr, H. A. Dumas fairy tale book. 1924.
‡Wiggin, K. D. and Smith, N. A. Magic casements. 1911.
‡Wiggin, K. D. and Smith, N. A. Tales of laughter.
‡Wiggin, K. D. and Smith, N. A. Talking beasts. 1911.
Wilmot-Buxton, E. M. Stories from old French romance.

German

Barber, G. E. Wagner opera stories. 1916.
Baumbach, Rudolph. Tales from wonderland. c1903.
Brentano, Clemens. Fairy tales. 1925.
Burt, M. E. Story of the German Iliad. c1895.
Grimm, J. L. C. and Grimm, W. C. Fairy tales.
Guerber, H. A. Legends of the Rhine. c1895.
Hackländer, F. W. Enchanting and the enchanted. c1900.
Hauff, Wilhelm. Fairy tales. n.d.
Keller, Gottfried. Fat of the cat. 1925.
Nordau, M. S. Dwarf's spectacles. 1905.
‡Patten, William. Junior classics. v. 1–2. 1912.
‡Perkins, L. F. Twenty best tales. 1907.
‡Underhill, Z. D. Dwarf's tailor. c1896.
‡Wiggin, K. D. and Smith, N. A. Magic casements. 1911.
‡Wiggin, K. D. and Smith, N. A. Tales of laughter. 1908.

Great Britain

See Australia; England; Ireland; Scotland; Wales.

Greece, Ancient

Adams, William. Myths of old Greece. c1897.
Bailey, C. S. Wonder stories. 1920.
Baldwin, James. Golden fleece. c1905.
Baldwin, James. Old Greek stories. c1895
Beckwith, M. H. In mythland. n.d.
Buckley, E. L. Children of the dawn. c1909.
Burt, M. E. and Ragozin, Z. A. Herakles. c1900.
Carpenter, E. J. Long ago in Greece. c1906.
Church, A. J. Greek story and song. c1903.
Church, A. J. Stories of the old world. 1916.
Cox, G. W. Tales of ancient Greece. c1905.
Evans, L. B. Heroes of Troy. 1924.
Farrar, F. A. Old Greek nature stories. n.d.
Firth, E. M. Stories of old Greece. c1894.
Francillon, R. E. Gods and heroes. c1895.
Gayley, C. M. Classic myths.
Guerber, H. A. Myths of Greece and Rome. c1893–1921.
Haaren, J. A. and Poland, A. B. Famous men of Greece. c1904.
Hartley, C. G. Stories from Greek legends. n.d.
Hawthorne, Nathaniel. Tanglewood tales. n.d.

Greece, Ancient—*continued.*
Hawthorne, Nathaniel. Wonder book.
Hutchinson, W. M. L. Golden porch. c1907-25.
Hutchinson, W. M. L. Orpheus with his lute. c1909.
Hyde, L. S. Favorite Greek myths. c1904.
Judd, M. C. Classic myths. c1894.
Kingsley, Charles. Heroes. n.d.
Kupfer, G. H. Stories of long ago. 1911.
Lowell, D. O. S. Jason's quest. 1904.
Peabody, J. P. Old Greek folk stories. n.d.
Pratt, M. L. Myths of old Greece. n.d.
Shaw, C. D. Stories of the ancient Greeks. c1903.
Stories of classic myths retold from St. Nicholas. 1909.
Storr, Frances. Half a hundred hero tales. 1917.
Tappan, E. M. Stories from the classics. n.d.
Greece, Modern
Byrne, J. A. Modern Greek fairy tales. c1905.
Hawaii
Colum, Padraic. At the gateways of the day. 1924.
Colum, Padraic. Bright Islands. 1925.
Pope, Katherine. Hawaii the rainbow land. 1924.
‡Skinner, C. M. Myths and legends of our new possessions. 1902.
Thrum, T. G. Hawaiian folk tales. c1912.
Hebrews
See Jews.
Holland
Griffis, W. E. Dutch fairy tales. 1918.
Hungary
‡Fleming, R. M. Round the world in folk tales. 1925.
Pogany, Willy. Hungarian fairy book. 1913.
‡Wiggin, K. D. and Smith, N. A. Magic casements. 1911.
Iceland
‡Fleming, R. M. Round the world in folk tales. 1925.
Hall, A. W. Icelandic fairy tales. n.d.
India
See East India.
Indians of North America
Allen, Lewis. Indian fairy tales. 1912.
Austin, Mary. Basket woman. 1904.
Bayliss, C. K. Treasury of Indian tales. c1921.
Borland, H. G. Rocky Mountain tipi tales. 1924.
Brooks, Dorothy. Stories of the red children. 1908.
Brown, A. F. and Bell, J. M. Tales of the red children. 1901.
Chandler, Katherine. In the reign of coyote. 1905.
Compton, Margaret. American Indian fairy tales. 1910.
Cornyn, J. H. Around the wigwam fire. c1921.
Cornyn, J. H. When the camp fire burns. 1923.
Cowles, J. D. Indian nature myths. c1918.
Curtin, Jeremiah. Myths of the Modocs. 1912.
Curtis, E. S. Indian days of long ago. 1921.
DeHuff, E. W. Taytay's memories. c1924.
DeHuff, E. W. Taytay's tales. 1922.
Donaldson, E. M. Little papoose listens. c1924.
Donaldson, E. M. Moons of long ago. c1922.
Eastman, C. A. and Eastman, E. G. Wigwam evenings. 1909.
Eastman, E. G. Indian legends retold. 1919.
Grinnell, G. B. Blackfoot lodge tales. c1892.

Indians of North America—*continued.*
Grinnell, G. B. Pawnee hero stories. 1904.
Grinnell, G. B. Punishment of the stingy. c1901.
Judd, M. C. Wigwam stories. 1906.
Judson, K. B. Myths and legends of the Pacific Northwest. 1910.
Judson, K. B. Old Crow and his friends. c1918.
Judson, K. B. Old Crow stories. c1917.
Kennedy, H. A. New world fairy book. c1904.
Leland, C. G. Algonquin legends. c1884.
Linderman, F. B. Indian Old-man stories. 1920.
Linderman, F. B. Indian why stories. 1915.
Lummis, C. F. Pueblo Indian folk stories. 1910.
Nixon-Roulet, M. F. Indian folk tales. 1911.
Olcott, F. J. Red Indian fairy book. c1917.
Partridge, E. N. Glooscap the great chief. 1913.
Partridge, E. N. Joyful Star. 1915.
Powers, Mabel. Around an Iroquois story fire. 1923.
Pratt, M. L. Legends of the red children.
Roberts, G. E. T. Flying prover. 1909.
Roberts, G. E. T. Red feather.
Schoolcraft, H. R. Indian fairy book. c1916.
Sexton, Bernard. Gray wolf stories. c1921.
Tanner, Dorothy. Legends from the red man's forest. 1895.
Wade, M. H. Indian fairy tales. 1906.
Washburn, M. F. Indian legends. c1915.
Wilson, G. L. Myths of the red children.
Young, E. R. Algonquin Indian tales. c1903.
Zitkala Sä. Old Indian legends.
See also Canada.

Ireland
Campbell, W. D. Beyond the border.
Colum, Padraic. Boy of Eirinn. 1913.
Curtin, Jeremiah. Hero tales from Ireland. 1921.
Curtin, Jeremiah. Myths and folklore of Ireland.
Frost, W. H. Fairies and folk of Ireland. 1900.
Graves, A. P. Irish fairy book.
Gregory, I. A. P. Book of saints and wonders. 1907.
Grierson, E. W. Children's book of Celtic stories. 1922.
Hull, Eleanor. Boy's Cuchulain. 1910.
Jacobs, Joseph. Celtic fairy tales.
Jacobs, Joseph. More Celtic fairy tales.
Joyce, P. W. Old Celtic romances. 1920.
Leamy, Edmund. Fairy minstrel of Glenmalure. 1913.
Leamy, Edmund. Golden spears and other fairy tales. c1911.
MacManus, Seumas. Donegal fairy stories. 1900.
MacManus, Seumas. In chimney corners. 1899.
MacManus, Seumas. Lo, and behold ye!
‡Olcott, F. J. Book of elves and fairies. 1918.
‡Pyle, Katherine. Tales of wonder and magic.
Rolleston, J. W. High deeds of Finn.
Stephens, James. Crock of gold.
Stephens, James. Irish fairy tales. 1921.
‡Tappan, E. M. Folk stories. n.d.
‡Wiggin, K. D. and Smith, N. A. Tales of laughter. 1908.
‡Wiggin, K. D. and Smith, N. A. Tales of wonder. 1909.
Yeats, W. B. Irish fairy and folk tales. 1910.

Island stories
‡Fleming, R. M. Round the world in folk tales. 1925.
Higginson, T. W. Tales of the enchanted islands of the Atlantic. c1898.
Island stories retold from St. Nicholas. 1907.
James, Hartwell. Magic jawbone. 1906.
‡My Bookhouse.
‡Skinner, C. M. Myths and legends of our new possessions. 1902.
See also Australia; Azores; Hawaii; Jamaica; Java; New Guinea; New Zealand; Philippines.

Italy
Faulkner, Georgene. Italian fairy tales.
Macdonell, Anne. Italian fairy book. 1914.
Noyes, Ella. Saints of Italy. 1901.
Steedman, Amy. Legends and stories of Italy. 1914.
‡Wiggin, K. D. and Smith, N. A. Tales of laughter. 1908.
See also Rome.

Japan
Ballard, Susan. Fairy tales from far Japan. 1909.
Champney, E. W. Romance of old Japan. c1917.
Finnemore, John. Peeps at many lands: Japan. 1907.
‡Fleming, R. M. Round the world in folk tales. 1925.
Griffis, W. E. Japanese fairy tales. c1908–23.
Hearn, Lafcadio and others. Japanese fairy tales. c1918–24.
Henderson, Bernard, and Calvert, C. Wonder tales of old Japan. n.d.
James, Grace. Green Willow and other Japanese fairy tales. 1923.
James, Hartwell. Enchanted castle. 1906.
Mitford, E. B. Tales of old Japan. 1918.
Nixon-Roulet, M. F. Japanese folk stories and fairy tales. 1908.
Ozaki, Y. T. Japanese fairy book. 1904.
‡Patten, William. Junior classics. v. 1. 1912.
‡Tappan, E. M. Folk stories.
‡Tappan, E. M. Myths from many lands.
Whitehorn, A. L. Wonder tales of old Japan. c1912.
‡Wiggin, K. D. and Smith, N. A. Magic casements. 1911.
‡Wiggin, K. D. and Smith, N. A. Tales of laughter. 1908.
‡Wiggin, K. D. and Smith, N. A. Tales of wonder. 1909.
Williston, T. P. Japanese fairy tales. 1st and 2d series.

Jews
Friedlander, Gerald. Jewish fairy book. c1920.
Friedlander, Gerald. Jewish fairy tales. 1924.
Isaacs, A. S. Stories from the rabbis. 1898.
Landa, Gertrude. (Aunt Naomi) Jewish fairy tales. 1908.
Landa, Gertrude. (Aunt Naomi) Jewish fairy tales and legends. c1919.
Steinberg, Jehudah. Breakfast of the birds and other stories.

Jugoslavia
Fillmore, P. H. Laughing prince. 1921.

Korea
Allen, H. N. Korean tales. c1889.
Griffis, W. E. Korean fairy tales. 1922.
Griffis, W. E. Unmannerly tiger and other tales. 1911.
Hulbert, H. B. Omjee, the wizard: Korean folk tales. 1925.
See also China.

Mexico
‡ Skinner, C. M. Myths and legends beyond our borders. 1899.
Negro
Cocke, S. J. By paths in Dixie. 1911.
Fortier, Alcée. Louisiana folk-tales. c1895.
Harris, J. C. Nights with Uncle Remus. c1883.
Harris, J. C. Told by Uncle Remus. n.d.
Harris, J. C. Uncle Remus and his friends. c1892–1920.
Harris, J. C. Uncle Remus and the little boy. c1910.
Harris, J. C. Uncle Remus, his songs and sayings. 1908.
Harris, J. C. Uncle Remus returns. c1918.
Messer, C. J. Next night stories. 1912.
Young, Martha. Behind the dark pines. 1912.
Young, Martha. Plantation bird legends. c1902.
See also Africa.
Netherlands
See Holland.
New Guinea
‡My Bookhouse. v. 2.
‡Patten, William. Junior classics. v. 1.
New Zealand
‡Armfield, C. S. Wonder stories of the world.
‡Fleming, R. M. Round the world in folk tales.
Norway
Asbjörnsen, P. C. Fairy tales from the far north.
Asbjörnsen, P. C. Tales from the fjeld.
Brown, A. F. In the days of giants. c1902.
Dasent, G. W. East o' the sun and west o' the moon.
Dasent, G. W. Norse fairy tales.
Edmison, J. P. Stories from the Norseland.
Foster, M. H. and Cummings, M. H. Asgard stories.
Gade, Helen and John. Norwegian fairy tales.
Guerber, H. A. Myths of northern lands. c1895.
Holbrook, Florence. Northland heroes. c1905.
Klingensmith, Annie. Old Norse wonder tales. 1923.
Litchfield, M. E. Nine worlds. 1895.
Mabie, H. W. Norse stories retold from the Eddas. 1904.
Pratt, M. L. Legends of Norseland. c1894.
Stroebe, Clara. Norwegian fairy book. c1922.
Thorne-Thomsen, Gudrun. East o' the sun and west o' the moon.
Thorpe, Benjamin. Yule tide stories.
Wilmot-Buxton, E. M. Stories of Norse heroes from the Eddas and sagas.
Orient
Arabian nights' entertainments.
Cluoston, W. A. Eastern romances. c1889.
Coussens, P. W. Jade story book. 1922
Hauff, Wilhelm. Caravan tales. 1914.
Ketcham Henry. Oriental fairy tales. c1905.
Martens, F. H. Fairy tales from the Orient.. 1923.
Shedlock, M. L. Eastern stories and legends. 1920.
See also Arabia; China; East India; Korea; Turkey.
Persia
‡Armfield, C. S. Wonder tales of the world. 1920.
‡Coussens, P. H. Jade story book. 1922.
‡Church, A. J. Stories of the magicians.

Persia—*continued.*
James, Hartwell. Cat and the mouse. 1906.
Olcott, F. J. Tales of the Persian genii. 1917.
Renninger, E. D. Story of Rustem and other Persian hero tales from Firdusi. 1909.
‡Wiggin, K. D. and Smith, N. A. Tales of wonder. 1909.
Wilmot-Buxton, E. M. Stories of Persian heroes retold.

Philippine Islands
Cole, M. C. Philippine folklore tales. McClurg.
‡Coussens, P. W. Jade story book. 1922.
‡Farmer, F. V. Nature myths.
Miller, J. M. Philippine folklore stories. 1904. Ginn.

Poland
Glinski, A. J. Polish fairy book. 1920. Lane.
‡Patten, William. Junior classics. v. 1.

Portugal
‡My Bookhouse.
‡Wiggin, K. D. and Smith, N. A. Tales of wonder. 1909.

Rome, Ancient
‡Farmer, F. V. Nature myths.
Guerber, H. A. Story of the Romans.
Haaren, J. H. and Poland, A. B. Famous men of Rome.
Laing, Mrs. C. H. B. Seven kings of the seven hills. c1872.
‡Patten, William. Junior classics. v. 2.
‡Tappan, E. M. Myths from many lands.

Rome, Modern
See Italy.

Roumania
Elizabeth, queen of Roumania. Legends from river and mountain.
—— Real queen's story book.
Marie, queen of Roumania. Peeping pansy.
‡Wiggin, K. D. and Smith, N. A. Magic casements.

Russia (incl. Slavic.)
Bailey, C. S. In the animal world. 1924.
—— Russian fairy tales from Polevoi.
Bain, R. N. Cossack fairy tales. c1899.
Blumenthal, V. X. X. Folk tales from the Russian. c1903.
Carrick, Vallery. Picture tales from the Russian.
Chodzko, A. E. B. Slav fairy tales.
Curtin, Jeremiah. Wonder-tales from Russia. c1921.
Dole, N. H. White duckling.
Faulkner, Georgene. Old Russian fairy tales.
Houghton, L. S. Russian grandmother's wonder tales. c1906.
Kriloff, I. A. Fables (In Æsop Fables. Stickney, ed.)
Magnus, L. A. Russian folk-tales. 1916.
Mamin, D. N. Verotchka's tales; tr. by R. Davidson. n.d.
Ransome, Arthur. Old Peter's Russian tales. 1917.
Sologub, Fedor. Sweet scented name and other stories. 1915.
Steele, Robert. Russian garland of fairy tales. 1916.
Tolstoi, Leon. Tales.
Wheeler, Post. Russian wonder tales. 1921.
Wilson, Richard. Russian story book. 1916.
Wiggin, K. D. and Smith, N. A. Tales of laughter.
—— Talking beasts.

Scandinavia
See Denmark; Iceland; Norway; Sweden.

Scotland
Douglas, George. Scottish fairy and folk tales.
Greenwood, Grace. Bonnie Scotland.
Gregory, A. P. Kiltartan wonder book.
Grierson, E. W. Children's tales from Scottish ballads.
—— Scottish fairy book.
Mackenzie, D. A. Wonder tales from Scottish myth and legend. 1918.

Servia
Petrovic, V. M. Hero tales and legends of the Serbians.

Silesia
See Bohemia.

Slavic
See Croatia; Czechoslovakia; Jugoslovakia; Russia, Roumania.

South America
Eells, E. S. Tales of enchantment from Spain.
Eells, E. S. Tales of giants from Brazil. 1918.
Finger, C. J. Tales from silver lands. 1924.
Quiroga, Horacio. South American jungle stories. 1922.

South seas
See Australia; Island stories.

Spain
Caballero, Fernan. Spanish fairy tales.
Eells, E. S. Tales of enchantment from Spain. 1920. Harcourt.
Irving, Washington. Tales from the Alhambra; adapted by J. Brower.
Plummer, M. W. Stories from the Chronicles of the Cid. n.d. Holt.
Segovia, Gertrudis. Spanish fairy book. 1918.

Sweden
Djurkio, N. J. Fairy tales from the Swedish. 1901.
Lagerlof, S. O. L. Wonderful adventures of Nils.
Nyblom, Helen. Jolly Calle. 1912.
Patterson, A. deC. Old Swedish fairy tales. 1925.
Poulsson, E. and L. E. Top of the world stories. 1916.
Stroebe, Clara. Swedish fairy book. 1921.

Switzerland
Froelicher, F. M. Swiss stories and legends. 1917.
Griffis, W. E. Swiss fairy tales. c. 1920.
Guerber, H. A. Legends of Switzerland. c. 1899–1914.
Keller, Gustave. Fat of the cat. 1925.

Thuringia
Baumbach, Rudolph. Tales from wonderland. 1915.
‡Cather, K. D. Educating by story-telling. 1920.
‡My Bookhouse.

Thibet
Jewett, E. M. Wonder tales from Tibet. c. 1922.
Shelton, A. L. Tibetan folk tales. 1925.

Turkey
Garnett, L. M. Ottoman wonder tales. 1915.
Kunos, Ignacz. Forty-four Turkish fairy tales. 1914.
Kunos, Ignacz. Turkish fairy tales. 1901.
Martens, F. H. Wonder tales from far away. 1925.
See also Orient.

United States
Hawthorne, Nathaniel. Twice told tales.

United States—*continued.*

Irving, Washington. Stories and legends. n.d. Putnam.
Morris, Charles. Historical tales: America.
Pumphrey, M. B. Stories of the pilgrims.
Sandburg, Carl. Rootabaga stories.
Skinner, C. M. Myths and legends of our own land.

Wales

Brooks, Edward. Wonder stories from the Mabinogion. 1909.
Clay, Beatrice. Stories from Le Morte d'Arthur and the Mabinogion.
Duncan-Jones, C. M. Stories from Wales. 1921.
Farmer, F. V. Nature myths.
Griffis, W. E. Welsh fairy tales. c1921.
Henderson, Bernard and Jones, Stephen. Wonder tales of ancient Wales. Small.
Lanier, Sidney. Knightly legends of Wales; or, The boy's Mabinogion.
Thomas, W. J. Welsh fairy book. c1908.

FOR FURTHER REFERENCES THE FOLLOWING BOOKS MAY BE CONSULTED; ALSO THE EXCELLENT GEOGRAPHICAL INDEX IN MY BOOKHOUSE V. 6.

Armfield, C. S. Wonder tales of the world. 1920.
Bailey, C. S. Folk stories and fables. 1919.
—— In the animal world. 1924.
Bigham, M. A. Merry animal tales. 1923.
Bryce, C. T. Fables from afar. c1910.
Cooke, F. J. Nature myths. 1919.
Coussens, P. W. Jade story book. 1922.
Farmer, F. V. Nature myths of many lands. c1910.
Fleming, R. M. Ancient tales from many lands. 1922.
Gask, Lilian. Treasury of folk tales. 1917.
Grayl, Druid. Fairy tales from foreign lands.
Jacobs, Joseph. Europa's fairy book. c1915.
Mabie, H. W. Folk tales every child should know.
—— Legends every child should know.
—— Myths every child should know.
McFee, I. N. Treasury of myths. c1921.
Marshall, Logan. Fairy tales of all nations.
Martens, F. H. Wonder tales from far away. 1925.
Olcott, F. J. Book of elves and fairies.
—— Wonder garden.
Patten, Wm. Junior classics. v. 1–2.
Pyle, Katharine. Fairy tales from far and near.
—— Tales of folk and fairies.
—— Tales of wonder and magic.
—— Where the wind blows.
—— Wonder tales retold.
Scudder, H. E. Book of fables and folk stories.
Skinner, E. L. and A. M. Happy tales for story time. c1918.
—— Nursery tales from many lands. c1917.
Stanley, A. A. Animal folk tales. c1916.
Tappan, E. M. Folk stories and fables.
—— Myths from many lands.
Underhill, Z. D. Dwarfs' tailor. c1896.

Wiggin, K. D. and Smith, N. A. Magic casements. 1911.
—— Tales of laughter. 1908.
—— Talking beasts. 1911.
—— Tales of wonder. 1909.
Williams, Herschel. Fairy tales from folklore. c1906.

HELPS FOR STORY TELLERS

Atlanta (Ga.) Carnegie library. Bulletin, Jl.–Sept., 1913.
Story hour number. Contains: Local history outline; and short lists on spring, birds, flowers.
Bone, W. A. Children's stories and how to tell them. c1924. Harcourt.
Brotherton, N. C. Fairy tales to tell and suggestions for the story teller. 1915. Wilson. Cleveland public library reprint.)
Bryant, S. C. How to tell stories to children. c1905. Houghton.
—— Stories to tell to children. c1907. Houghton.
Cabot, E. L. Ethics for children. c1910.
Cabot, E. L. and others. Course in citizenship and patriotism. rev. ed. 1918. Houghton.
Cather, K. D. Education by story telling. 1920. World Book Co.
Children's reading list on animals. 1899. Boston Bk. Co.
Children's story garden. 1920. Lippincott.
Cross, Allen and Statler, N. M. Story-telling for upper grade teachers. 1918. Row.
D'Ooge, B. L. Helps to the study of classical mythology for the lower grades and secondary schools. c1899.
Esenwein, J. B. and Stockard, Marietta. Children's stories and how to tell them. 1917. Home corres, school.
Forbush, W. B. Manual of stories. c1915. Jacobs.
—— Young folks' book of ideals. 1916. Lothrop.
Gilbert, G. B. and Harris, A. vanS. Graded list of poems and stories for use in schools. c1901. Silver.
Hassler, H. E. and Scott, C. E. Graded list of stories to tell or read aloud. 4th ed. rev. 1923. A. L. A. pub. bd.
Keyes, A. M. Stories and story telling. 1916. Appleton.
Kready, L. F. Study of fairy tales. 1916. Houghton.
Lyman, Edna. Story-telling; what to tell and how to tell it. 1910. McClurg.
Marzials, A. M. Stories for the story hour from January to December. 1916. Dodd.
My Bookhouse. v. 6. c1920. Bookhouse for children.
Power, E. L. Lists of stories and programs for story hours. 2d ed. rev. 1921. Wilson.
Pittsburgh (Pa.) Carnegie library. Stories to tell to children. 3d ed. 1921. Pittsburgh Carnegie library.
—— Story telling to children from Norse mythology and the Nibelungenlied. 1903.
—— Lists of good stories to tell to children under twelve years of age. 1906.
—— Story-hour cycle 1911–1912: Stories from the Greek myths, the Iliad, and the Odyssey. 1912.
St. Louis Public Library. Monthly bulletin, August, 1914.
Contains: Stories for very little children from three to six; Stories for special days for little children; Cycle stories, hero stories, ballad stories.

Salisbury, C. E. and Beckwith, M. E. Index to short stories. c1907. Row.
Shedlock, M. L. Art of the storyteller. 1915. Appleton.
Sly, W. G. World stories retold. 1922. c1914. Am. Bapt.
(With practical suggestions for telling and an ethical index.)
U. S. Bureau of education. Library division. Stories for young children. 1919. (Library leaflet 6.)
For Kindergarten, and First and Second grades.
Whiteman, E. L., *comp.* One hundred stories for the amateur storyteller; compiled for Cleveland Public Library. 1923. Wilson.
Contents: For little children; For children over nine years of age; Myths, Animal stories, Humorous stories.
—— Stories to tell to children. 2d ed. 1918. Pittsburgh. Carnegie library.
Contents: A selected list by ages; Stories and poems for holiday programs; A classified list—humorous, legend, cumulative.

ETHICAL STORIES (AND LISTS)

Bailey, C. S. Stories for Sunday telling. c1916.
Cabot, E. L. Ethics for children.
—— Course in citizenship and patriotism.
Cather, K. D. Educating by story telling.
Children's story garden.
Coe, F. E. Second and third book of stories for the story-teller.
Cross and Statler. Story-telling for upper grade teachers.
Eggleston, M. W. Stories for special days in the church school. c1922. Doran.
Forbush, W. B. Manual of stories.
—— Young folks' book of ideals.
Gatty, M. S. Parables from nature.
My Bookhouse. See Ethical index in v. 6.
Richards, L. E. Golden windows.
—— Silver crown.
Salisbury and Beckwith. Index to short stories.
Slosson, A. S. Story-tell Lib.
Sly, W. J. World stories retold.
Steedman, Amy. In God's garden. 1906.
Stories for talks to boys.
See also Children's catalog. 3d ed.

LISTS OF STORIES BY SUBJECTS MAY BE FOUND IN THE FOLLOWING BOOKS

Cabot. Course in citizenship.
—— Ethics for children.
Cather. Educating by story telling.
Children's catalog. 3d ed.
Cross and Statler. Story telling for upper grades.
D'Ooge, B. L. Helps to the study of classical mythology.
Forbush. Manual of stories.
—— Young folks' book of ideals.
Lyman. Story-telling.
My Bookhouse. v. 6—subject index.
Olcott. Book of elves and fairies.
—— Wonder garden.
Shedlock. Art of the story-teller.

ART AND MUSIC

Anecdotes of the early painters. (In Chambers. Miscellany v. 18.)
Brower, Harriette. Story lives of the great musicians. 1922.
Chandler, A. C. Magic pictures of the long ago. c1918.
Scobey, K. L. and Horne, O. B. Stories of great musicians, c1905.
Steedman, Amy. Knights of art. 1907.

DIRECTORY OF PUBLISHERS

Abingdon. Abingdon Press, 150 Fifth Avenue, N. Y. City.
Ainsworth & Co., 623–633 S. Wabash Ave., Chicago, Ill.
Allen & Unwin, 40 Museum St., London, W. C. 1, England.
Altemus. Henry Altemus Co., 1326 Vine St., Philadelphia, Pa.
American Baptist Pub. Soc. (The Judson Press), 1701 Chestnut St., Philadelphia, Pa.
Amer. Book. American Book Co., 100 Washington Sq., New York City.
American Scandinavian Foundation, 25 W. 45th St., New York City.
American Unitarian Association. See Beacon Press.
Appleton. D. Appleton & Co., 29–35 W. 32d St., New York City.
Armstrong. A. C. Armstrong & Son, New York City. Succeeded by G. H. Doran Co.
Atkinson. Atkinson, Mentzer & Co., Chicago. See Mentzer.
Atlantic. Atlantic Monthly Press, Inc., 8 Arlington St., Boston. Books distributed by Little, Brown & Co.
Balch. Minton, Balch & Co., 11–17 E. 45th St., New York City.
Barnes. A. S. Barnes & Co., 7 W. 45th St., New York City, See also Laidlaw.
Beacon Press. American Unitarian Association, 25 Beacon St., Boston.
Bell. Geo. Bell & Sons, York House, Portugal St., London, W. C. 2, England.
Black. A. & C. Black, 4 Soho Square, London, W. I.
Blackiston. P. Blackiston's Sons & Co., 1012 Walnut St., Philadelphia.
Blackwell. Basil H. Blackwell, 50–51 Broad St., Oxford, England.
Bloch. Bloch Publishing Co., 26 E. 22nd St., New York City.
Bobbs. Bobbs-Merrill Co., 18 University Sq., Indianapolis, Ind.
Boni & Liveright, 61 W. 48th St., New York City.
Bookhouse for Children, 608 S. Dearborn St., Chicago.
Bradley. Milton Bradley Co., 74 Park St., Springfield, Mass.
Brentano. Brentano's, 5th Ave. & 27th St., New York City.
Bullen. A. H. Bullen, 47 Great Russell St., London. (1908)
Burt. A. L. Burt Co., 114–120 E. 23rd St., New York City.
Cassell & Co., Amer. Branch, 354 4th Avenue, New York City.
Caldwell. H. M. Caldwell Co., New York & Boston.
Central Publishing Co., Chicago, Ill.
Century. Century Co., 353 Fourth Ave., New York City.
Christian Pub. Co., 2712 Pine St., St. Louis, Mo.
Collier. P. F. Collier & Co., 416–430 W. 30th St., New York City.
Crowell. T. Y. Crowell Co., 387–393 Fourth Ave., New York City.
Daughaday & Co., 168 Michigan Ave., Chicago, Ill.
Dent. J. M. Dent & Sons, Toronto and London. See also Duttor

Dodd. Dodd, Mead & Co., Fourth Ave. and 30th St., New York City.
Have acquired publications of the John Lane Co. and Moffat, Yard & Co.
Dodge. Dodge Pub. Co., 148–153 W. 23d St., New York City.
Doran. George H. Doran Co., 244 Madison Ave., New York City.
Doubleday. Doubleday, Page & Co., Garden City, New York.
Duffield. Duffield & Co., 211 E. 19th St., New York City.
Dutton. E. P. Dutton & Co., 681 Fifth Ave., New York City.
American representatives of Dent & Sons.
Eaton. Eaton & Mains. New York City.
Succeeded by Abingdon Press.
Educational Pub. Co., 221 Fourth Ave., N. Y. City.
Estes and Lauriat. Succeeded by Page and Co.
Expression Co., 12 Hunt Ave., Boston, Mass.
Flanagan. A. Flanagan Co., 521 South Laflin St., Chicago, Ill.
Four Seas Co., 454 Stuart St., Boston, Mass.
Funk. Funk & Wagnalls Co., 354–360 Fourth Ave., New York City.
Gardner. See Wells, Gardner, Darton & Co.
Gibbings & Co., Ltd., 18 Bury St., London, W. C. (1910)
Ginn. Ginn & Co., 15 Ashburton Pl., Boston.
Globe School Book Co., New York City.
Sold to World Book Co.
Grosset. Grosset & Dunlap, 1140 Broadway, New York City.
Hall and Locke Co., Boston, Mass. (1902)
Hammett. T. L. Hammett Co., Kendall Sq., Cambridge, Mass.
Harcourt. Harcourt, Brace & Co., 383 Madison Ave., New York City.
Harper. Harper & Brothers, 49 E. 33d St., New York City.
Harrap. Geo. G. Harrap & Co., 39–41 Parker St., Kingsway, London, W. C. 2.
Heath. D. C. Heath & Co., 50 Beacon St., Boston.
Heineman. Wm. Heineman, 21 Bedford St., London, W. C. 2, England.
Hodder and Stoughton. St. Paul's House, Warwick Sq., London, E. C. 4.
Holt. Henry Holt & Co., 19 W. 44th Street, New York City.
Home Correspondence School, 17 Worthington St., Springfield, Mass.
Houghton. Houghton, Mifflin Co., 2 Park St., Boston.
Howell. Howell Publishing Co., 536 S. Clark St., Chicago.
Hurst & Co., New York City. (1897) See Platt and Munk.
Jacobs, Geo. W. Jacobs & Co., Philadelphia. Sold out to Macrae-Smith Co.
Laidlaw Bros., 118 E. 25th St., New York City.
Have taken over some of A. S. Barnes Co. publications.
Lane. John Lane Co., American Branch, Fourth Ave. & 30th St., New York City.
See also Dodd.
Lippincott. J. B. Lippincott Co., E. Washington Sq., Philadelphia.
Little. Little, Brown & Co., 34 Beacon St., Boston.
Longmans. Longmans, Green & Co., 55 Fifth Ave., New York City.
Lothrop. Lothrop, Lee & Shepard Co., 275 Congress St., Boston, Mass.
Lovell, John W. Succeeded by P. P. Simmons Co.
Luce. John W. Luce & Co., 212 Summer St., Boston.

McBride. Robert M. McBride, 7 W. 16th St., New York City.
McClurg. A. C. McClurg & Co., 330–352 E. Ohio St., Chicago.
McKay. David McKay, 604–608 S. Washington Sq., Philadelphia.
McKibben. Gilbert H. McKibben. 474 Broadway, New York City. (1905).
Macmillan. The Macmillan Co., 66 Fifth Ave., New York City. Acquired business of Sturgis & Walton.
Macrae-Smith Co., 1712–1714 Ludlow St., Philadelphia. Successors to Geo. W. Jacobs & Co.
Meigs Publishing Co., 41 W. Washington Street, Indianapolis, Ind.
Mentzer, Bush & Co., 31–33 E. 10th St., New York City. Formerly Atkinson, Mentzer & Co.
Merrill. Charles E. Merrill Co., 440 Fourth Ave., New York City. Successors to Maynard, Merrill & Co.
Moffat. Moffat, Yard and Co., 30 Union Square, New York City. See also Dodd.
Mumford. A. W. Mumford Co., Chicago, Ill. (1901)
Murray. John Murray, Albermarle St., London, W. 1.
Nelson. Thos. Nelson & Sons., 381 Fourth Ave., New York City.
Newson. Newson & Co., 73 Fifth Ave., New York City. Acquired publications of Universal Pub. Co.
Nutt. David A. Nutt. 212 Shaftsbury Ave., London, W. C. 2. Succeeded by Simpkins, Marshall, Hamilton, Kent & Co.
Open Court Publishing Co., 122 S. Michigan Ave., Chicago.
Oxford. Oxford University Press (American branch), 35 W. 32d St., New York City.
Page. L. C. Page & Co., 53 Beacon St., Boston.
Penn. Penn Publishing Co., 925 Filbert St., Philadelphia.
Pilgrim Press, 14 Beacon St., Boston and 19 S. LaSalle St., Chicago.
Platt & Munk Co., Inc., 118–120 E. 25th St., N. Y. City. Have acquired publications of Hurst & Co.
Public School. Public School Publishing Co., Bloomington, Ill.
Putnam. G. P. Putnam's Sons, Putnam Bldg., 2 W. 45th St., New York City.
Rand. Rand-McNally & Co., 538 S. Clark St., Chicago, Ill.
Reilly & Lee Co., 536 Lake Shore Drive, Chicago. Formerly Reilly & Britton Co.
Revell. Fleming H. Revell & Co., 158 Fifth Ave., New York City.
Row. Row, Peterson & Co., 623 S. Wabash Ave., Chicago.
Routledge. George Routledge & Sons, Broadway House, 68–74 Carter Lane, London, London E. C. 4.
Russell, R. H., New York. Merged with Harper Co. in 1903.
Saalfield Publishing Co., Akron, Ohio.
Scott. Robert Scott, Roxburgh House, Paternoster Row, London, E. C. 4.
Scott, Foresman. Scott, Foresman & Co., 633 S Wabash Ave., Chicago, Ill.
Scribner. Charles Scribner's Sons, 597 Fifth Ave., New York City.
Silver. Silver, Burdett & Co., 41 Union Sq. W., New York City.
Simmons. Simmons-Peckham Co., 112 E. 19th St., New York City. Formerly Parker P. Simmons Co.
Simpkin, Marshall, Hamilton, Kent and Co., Ltd., Stationers Hall, London, E. C. 4, England.

Small. Small, Maynard & Co., 41 Mt. Vernon Pl., Boston, Mass.
Society for promoting Christian knowledge, Northumberland Ave., London, W. C. 2.
Stokes. F. A. Stokes Co., 443–449 Fourth Ave., New York City.
Sturgis & Walton. See Macmillan.
Success Company. Success Magazine Corp., 251 Fourth Ave., New York City. (1901)
Theosophical Publishing House, Los Angeles, Cal., and Chicago. (1918)
Univ. Pub. Co. Universal Publishing Co., Normal, Ill.
Publications taken over by Newson & Co.
Volland. P. F. Volland & Co., 58 E. Washington St., Chicago, Ill.
Warne. Frederick Warne & Co., American Branch, 26 E. 22nd St., New York City.
Wells, Gardner, Darton Co., 3–4 Paternoster Buildings, London, E. C. 4.
Werner. E. S. Werner & Co., 11 E. 14th St. New York City.
Wessels. Wessels & Bissell Co., 225 Fifth Ave., New York (1912)
Wilde. W. A. Wilde, 131 Clarendon St., Boston, Mass. (1906)
Winston. John C. Winston Co., 1006–1016 Arch St., Philadelphia, Pa.
World Book Co., Park Hill, Yonkers-on Hudson, N. Y.
Yale University Press, 143 Elm St., New Haven, Conn.